D1594878

A HISTORY OF WORLD FURNITURE

LUIS FEDUCHI

EDITORIAL BLUME MILANESADO, 21-23 BARCELONA-17

749.2
F319h
1977

PACKARD LIBRARY

MAY 30 1978

OF THE COLUMBUS COLLEGE OF ART AND DESIGN

New Image Collection
Originally published by Editorial Blume under the title *Historia del Mueble*

© 1975, Editorial Blume, Barcelona

ISBN 84-7031-031-3

First English edition, 1977
Printed in Spain
Depósito legal: B. 13552-1977
Printed by Imprenta Juvenil. Maracaibo, 11. Barcelona

All rights reserved. No part of this book may be reproduced in any form or by any means, electronic or mechanical, including photocoping, reading, or by any information storage and retrieval system, without permission in writing from the publisher.

CONTENTS

ILLUSTRATIONS

FOREWORD

According to the tradition recorded by Diodorus of Sicily, Menes, a Pharoah of the First Dynasty, was the first ruler to seek to beautify household objects of everyday use.

Furniture is one of the best such examples of the combination of technology and art. Furniture making is an industrial art. It combines utility and beauty to make an object of wood into an expression of the soul.

All furniture derives from four basic types known and used since the earliest civilizations. They are the chair, the table, the ark, and the bed. The development of these four types from Antiquity down through the succeeding ages is the subject of our study.

Furniture is very closely related to other industrial arts such as metal working, weaving, etc. But the arts that have most strongly influenced furniture making are architecture and sculpture. They have provided an infinity of forms and shapes to be copied by furniture makers over the years. There is an undeniable parallel between architecture and furniture throughout history, though furniture styles tend to be shorter lived because they are constantly being up-dated. We shall also see that there has always been a greater diversity of local and national substyles.

In 1946 we published The History of Furniture *with a prologue by the Marquis of Lozoya. It contained 200 pages, 1000 photographs, and a few synoptic illustrations of the different styles. It sold out almost immediately.*

In 1966 we printed a new edition. The text was thoroughly revised and more photos were included. Also, the synoptic illustration were redone with clearer and more modern graphic techniques. We added a list of terms commonly used in furniture making. Most of them were Spanish, but we included some French and English words. They were accompanied by photos and drawings for non-specialized readers. We have followed the same order in each chapter in the third edition just as we did in the first two. We chose this order to make it easier for the reader to use the book as a reference work.

The third edition has been up-dated and the text corrected once again. Some of the illustrations have been enlarged and changed and the vocabulary has been revised.

Madrid, July 1975

EGYPT

It was in Egypt, that ancient civilization on the banks of the Nile, that the history of furniture began. Over the centuries this great Stone Age people discovered or invented many things, from the first diplomatic formulas to some of the earliest discoveries in geometry. Along with the development of trade routes protected by vast imperial armies, an architecture of gigantic pyramids and temples arose. In their shadow a host of sculptors, decorators, and artisans practiced and perfected their arts. It was in this context that the first embryonic furniture structures were brought to life. It is interesting to note that in the 19th century, at a time of imperialist idealism, these same forms reappear in furniture styles inspired by the ancient civilization beside the river.

In contrast to the objects obtained from other ancient civilizations around the Mediterranean, those from Egypt are in amazingly good condition. This includes even the first centuries of the Christian Era, from which so few examples remain. It can be easily explained. The royal tombs were hermetically sealed and the atmosphere was so dry that not only the structures, but even the materials themselves, have remained in perfect condition. To the amazement of explorers, the entire household furnishings of the royal residence have been found in the tombs of some of the ancient kings. These included furniture, jewelry, and clothing along with figures representing other persons and even food on the table!

Besides all this, the abundance of reliefs, sculptures, and paintings covering the walls of temples and tombs provide us with ample illustrations of the use and variety of furniture in that ancient society.

There are many examples of objects from the royal tombs not only in Egypt but also in museums all over Europe. Most of these are from the tombs of Abydos, Amenophis III, and especially Tutankhamen, whose tomb was discovered with all its riches in 1924. There are more than 6000 objects classified and preserved in the Cairo Museum. There are more than 1700 from the tomb of Tutankhamen alone, and among them furniture items are of great importance. A detailed study has been made of them, since they can be studied first hand. The furniture of other civilizations has been examined almost entirely in paintings, engravings, and bas-reliefs, making it much more difficult.

Egyptian furniture in general, like architecture, conforms to certain tectonic laws. These were developed during the earliest dynasties and reflect a vigorous creativity and a highly varied ornamentation. These prototypes evolved over the years, though always obeying the same laws and conventional formulas. One example is the frontal law in statuary. Many illustrations of this are found in the engravings on the backs of chairs.

MATERIALS

Wood is practically the only material suitable for the construction of furniture. But Egypt is a country in which only palm trees and a few others like the sycamore, tamarind, and willow grow. These are of little use because of their small size. The only solution was to import wood from other countries. Ebony was brought from Sudan and olive, fig, cedar, and pine were imported mainly from Syria and Phoenicia. This wood was used naturally in popular furniture for normal use. The splendid furnishings for the court were covered with richer materials such as silver and gold, bone and ivory. Other more delicate materials such as fabric, leather, embroidery, and feather cushions (some have been preserved in spite of their delicacy) were used mostly in beds and chairs. Here too, woven rushes and other fibers were frequently employed.

DECORATION

In the buildings we discover the sort of ornamentation and colors used in decoration. They are geometrical designs repeated in pure, bright colors such as white, red, and yellow without intermediate shades.

Other objects were completely covered with tiny carvings and bas-reliefs which even included stylized plants, especially the lotus and papyrus. They even carved beautiful figures of animals like the lion, scarob, falcon, and duck. In these luxury items the use of ceramic, glass, enamel, and gold and ivory inlays was common. Other parts of furniture were often carved, especially the legs, backs, and arms of chairs. As we pointed out in the introduction, there was a tradition of embellishing objects of everyday use. It is a tradition which has been preserved through the centuries; it should not surprise us that furniture was constructed with utmost care and with the aim of achieving a real work of art.

STRUCTURES

We must remember that we are dealing with the oldest furniture that mankind has produced. It displays a simplicity of form and structure and a very minimum of complications. Thus the structural elements are clearly seen, especially the vertical parts created in a context of utmost simplicity. The object is completely cubical and smooth with only a few simple moldings.

Joints appeared to connect different pieces. They were rudimentary and reinforced with pins or nails. The large surfaces on the fronts and sides of chests were made of panels. At first they were placed side by side in the same direction as the frame, later perpendicular to it and held in place with bars inside the chest to keep them from bowing. In other cases the panels were fastened to a rigid frame with lathes and pins, but they were never grooved. For this reason a small box from the XII dynasty at Thebes is an interesting finding. The front of the box is connected to the sides with a dovetail joint. This example and other boxes and chests in the Cairo Museum indicate a considerable advance in the art of furniture making (fig. 13).

Technique was brought to perfection in this period, although the lathe and plane were unknown. Pumis was used to smooth and finish furniture. Inlays were fastened with tiny wooden nails and panels were fixed with a glue made of fish viscera. Wood was even curved with heat to make wheels out of two semicircles, like those found in the royal tombs of Amenophis III (1400 B.C.).

Simple wooden table in natural finish

Scissor chair

In the III dynasty they began to make plywood of six crisscrossed leaves.

Curious little models of artisan shops have been found in some of the tombs. We are especially interested in a little model carpenter's shop. The men can be seen at work with their tiny tools and even their techniques can be observed. They are busy cutting, sawing, gluing, carving, nailing, and painting.

Chairs of all kinds are the most richly decorated. The most common type of vertical supports were made to look like the legs of animals, especially felines. There are also square, cylindrical, and turned legs, smooth or with carved circles.

Carved legs, which were the most luxurious, were covered with gold or other materials or inlaid. They usually had a heel of some hard material on the bottom to protect them from the friction of the floor. These chair or bench legs were always connected to each other with various cross pieces which were likewise fastned to the seat with vertical or diagonal braces.

An interesting structural element is the angle braces made of wood or metal that were used to connect the back to the seat. They can be seen in figures 8, 4, 2, and 12. Notice also the vertical pieces that support and unite the rear part of the back of the chair to the seat. We shall refer to them later in speaking about particular items of furniture.

KINDS OF FURNITURE

Chairs

As a consequence of the high level of civilization, furniture achieved a similarly high degree of development. Many kinds of furniture were used during this period: chairs, tables, beds both for resting (real *chaises longues*) and for burial, coffers, and other variants. Naturally, most of those which have been preserved in the tombs are of greaty beauty. There are many different kinds of chairs. The simplest and most primitive is probably the X-shaped folding chair called the scissor chair. It has continued to be used right down to our own day, each period decorating it in its own style. In Egypt the legs were simply round or ended in the shape of ducks' heads with the cross piece between the two legs held in their bills. They are similar to the *uol*, or head rest at the head of a bed. The seat was concave, made of woven plant fibers or leather, either in one piece or in woven strips. Three- or four-legged stools were of less importance (fig. 7). They were used for getting into the beds, which were of great height. The simplest had round legs without decoration. Others were intricately carved with imaginary figures. Though the chairs were all more or less alike, different prototypes can be distinguished. One of the most original and beautiful is the throne used by Tutankhamen when acting as high priest. It is a scissor chair with duck heads on the legs. It has a rich back covered with beautiful ornamental materials. The angle braces connecting the back and seat can be observed.

Other types have four legs (figs. 3, 4). The finest example is that found in the Louvre (fig. 2) with feline legs. The front legs are rigid and straight, the back legs are bent in a more natural position.

The seats are concave, doubtless to keep cushions from falling off and also for greater comfort (fig. 5). The back was perfectly straight in the old empire, slanted backward in the middle period, and both sloping and concave for greater comfort in the new empire. In the latter periods there was a brace from the seat to the top of the back providing greater strength. Much later this same sort of support to hold up a light, sloping back is found in the Windsor chair of the 18th century. (Figs. 4-8)

The last type of chair is the armchair. It is like the other types but much richer. The sides as well as the back were covered with carvings, paintings, metal appliqués, and inlays. Like the other chairs, the legs were connected with a number of cross pieces which, while they strengthened them, also destroyed their visual harmony.

In some cases, however, more care was used

in design. The result was a combination of simple lines and great elegance, a work of real aesthetic purity.

Beds

The most important object after the chair was the bed. It was made of a simple rectangular frame with interwoven strips of material supporting a mattress. Some of them, especially funeral beds and beds for repose, were so high that they required a bench or a stool to get into them. The legs were either round or shaped like the legs of feline animals. These forms were imitated later on in the Empire period. (Figs. 18, 19, 20)

Beds usually had a foot board richly decorated like the backs of chairs to keep cushions and bedclothes from falling off onto the floor. The frame had the same concave shape as the chairs. Beds for repose were higher and shorter, sloping and with a thicker mattress. Queen Hetepheres' reposing bed was made with very simple and beautiful lines and covered with gold. The head is higher than the foot, which includes ceramic decoration (fig. 19).

These beds should not be confused with funeral beds in which the bodies of kings and other important figures were laid. Those found in the tomb of Tutankhamen have feline profiles covered with gold, silver, and enamels. They are very high and very short. The silhouettes of the animals are beautiful. These beds take on an animal shape not only in the legs but also in the headpiece and foot where the head and tail of the animal are represented. The mattress was most often made to look like the body of a lion, jackel, ox, or sphinx (fig. 17). One of the most interesting discoveries in the tomb of Tutankhamen was a folding bed. The hinges of this bed reveal the amazingly high degree of technology achieved by the Egyptian artisans (figs. 15, 16).

The portable headrests called *uols* are another very interesting detail. They served as pillows and the simplest were just a half moon. They were made of high quality materials such as precious woods, ivory, and metals and were used to keep the head raised for good breathing and to protect complicated hairdoes. These headrests or moveable cushions were used in Japan and are still used today in some parts of central Africa (figs. 20, 21).

Tables

The tables were composed of the same structural elements and the same decoration as the chairs, that is, carvings, paintings, inlays, etc. The legs, also often shaped like the legs of animals, do not have so many cross pieces as the chairs and beds. This is because they were used to support inert weight and not the constant movement of the human body. This detail reveals something of the observation and sensitivity of those early artisans.

Other furniture

Coffers and other similar objects were generally quite alike. Their form was simple and cubic (fig. 13) with the occasional addition of a molding. If they had doors, they swung on a post or pivot like modern cabinet doors. Chests and coffers were often painted with geometric designs or covered with inlays and leaves of precious metals. In some coffers the vertical parts of the framework extended to the floor like legs (fig. 14). The tops were square, curved, or shaped like a roof tile, which was also characteristic of Egyptian furniture. Some small coffers were finished with carvings of papyrus as if woven like a basket. In others from the Greco-Roman and Ptolemaic periods, the Greco-Roman influence is seen.

In the history of art the Middle Eastern civilizations such as the Assyrians, Sumerians, and Persians are usually studied after the Egyptians. Since practically nothing remains of the furniture of these peoples we shall pass directly

Small coffer with ogee

to Greece. However, we should point out that their influence, observable in the sculptures and bas-reliefs of chairs, thrones, and benches, can be seen in the art of furniture-making throughout the eastern Mediterranean world.

Examples can be found in the pictures of thrones, chairs, and tables in all of Asia Minor and in the detailed descriptions of thrones, tables, and arks in the books of the Old Testament: Exodus, chapters 30 and 38; I Kings 10, verses 18 to 20; II Chronicles 4; and II Chronicles 9, verses 17 and 18.

GREECE

Drawing of a *klismos*

There is little that can be said about classical Greek furniture. Hardly anything has been preserved for us from that period. The little that we know is derived from literary descriptions, sketches, engravings, bas-reliefs, burial steles, pottery, and fragments found in tombs. Homer describes some objects in the *Odyssey* and the *Iliad*, items such as chairs, tables, and beds. In Pausianas we find the description of a famous coffer attributed to the artist Eumelos.

G. M. A. Richter's work on Greek, Etruscan, and Roman furniture is an extremely valuable source of information on the subject.

On the basis of our scant information the only clear conclusion we can draw is that of a definite Oriental and Egyptian influence. Mycenaean furniture and furniture from the Cyclades should be considered the earliest examples of Greek furniture. Much later, in the Golden Age under Pericles, at the height of classical art, furniture reached its greatest perfection. At this time new forms arose which, like all of the art of that period, produced works of great personality though only known today in the paintings on pottery.

MATERIALS

Mostly native wood was used: cedar, pine, cypress, and a few others. But wood was not the only material used in Greece. Public life and even private life was carried on in the open air. This meant that more weather resistent materials than wood were needed. Stone, marble, and bronze were used, a few examples of which can still be found today. Just as in Egypt and in the eastern countries, wood was covered and inlaid with more costly materials such as precious metals, ivory, and exotic woods. Furniture was painted with geometric motifs like architecture.

DECORATION

We discover almost all of the elements and motifs that were used in decorating furniture in architecture: perfectly proportioned profiles, rich ornamentation—ovals, dentils, stria, rosettes—and lively combination of pure colors—red, blue, yellow, and green. Both the frame and the panels were decorated with inlays of exotic wood or covered with precious metals. Bronze furniture was hammered and engraved and identical patterns were chiseled in stone and marble. Large tables were decorated with bas-reliefs and paintings. Beds, couches, and other furniture for sitting were covered with rich oriental fabrics.

STRUCTURES

Just as in Egypt, frames were very simple and jointing was still unknown. Pieces were held together with pegs and panels were held in place with bars on the under side. Here, too, the process of curving wood with heat was practiced. All four legs of the so-called *klismos* chair were curved outward. Poulsen, in his book *Decorative Arts in Antiquity* points out that they were made in this way so they would not stick into the ground, since these chairs were often used out of doors. The vertical parts of Greek furniture, round or carved, were more elegant than Egyptian furniture besides being lighter and more rational and natural (fig. 31).

KINDS OF FURNITURE

Chairs

An interesting model is found in a very old and beautiful statuette from the Cyclades, a small alabaster figure of a seated harpist (fig. 25). The legs of the chair are curved, the top of the back is semi-circular, and the other parts are also circular. The whole chair is composed of curved shapes similar to a Thonet chair of curved wood. Different types of tables and arks are preserved in little clay models. They date from an indefinite period sometime between 3000 and 1400 B.C.

Although objects made of stone do not really belong to our study because of their immobility, we should mention a few stone armchairs. The first is the so-called King Minos' throne in the Knossos Palace in Crete. It is very simple in design, with a certain elegance about it, especially in the original shape of the back. Another later example is the famous seats in the Dyonisos theater in Athens at the foot of the Acropolis. The form of the back and legs of the *klismos* chair is carved into the back of these stone seats. The so-called Ludovisi and Boston thrones of the early Greek period are also made of stone and are similar in shape. They are made of two blocks of marble with beautifully carved U shapes in the back and sides. The Ludovisi throne is 1.6 meters wide, though the seat, which was probably made of wood, is missing. There are niches in either side to hold the wooden seat (figs. 23, 24).

Also dating from a very early period is a series of tiny models of clay thrones. They were found in a tomb called the Kamilari tomb and were part of a religious scene in which the gods were seated on the thrones. They are of such curious shape that they remind us of contemporary art objects. (Figs. 26, 27).

In this period as in all others the chair is man's most personal furniture item owing to its proportions and use. In Greek art there are two kinds of chairs, one without a back, called *diophros* (fig. 28), and one with one, called *klismos* (figs. 32, 33). Among the earliest we find scissor chairs and chairs with perfectly straight legs and backs. The most original and interesting was developed later on. Its legs curved out to create a broader base of support. The back was concave and sloped backward affording a much better adaptation to the body (fig. 32).

Although we have no actual examples of Greek chairs, we have a splendid collection of illustrations in the reliefs on burial steles. The Museum of the Pottery Cemetery of Athens provides us with some excellent examples. With these we can continue our study of different types of chairs.

Each of these types gave rise to the Roman models later on. But the most original and the most imitated was the last, the chair with curved legs. Innumerable variations have been produced ever since the return to classicism in the 18th century. They can be found in Neo-Classicism, Empire, the Romanticism of the 30's, and even in the stylized Empire furniture of today. The Greek chair, often with a cushion on the seat, achieved a perfection of design that offered practical and comfortable use and also great artistic value.

Tables

Tables were generally portable and conformed to the same principles of construction as the

Triclinium in a mosaic

chairs. Light, three-legged tables were used near the couches to serve drinks. Like the chairs, we have practically no actual models that have survived the years; we depend entirely on the bas-reliefs and paintings. There is a bronze table with engravings in the Metropolitan Museum of New York (fig. 35). There are also several models of different pieces of furniture in bronze in the National Museum of Athens. The rest of the examples are found in Hellenic paintings found in Rome and other parts of Italy.

Arks

The arks were prismatic in shape, some perfectly flat, others with rounded tops. They were usually made of wood and often decorated with paintings and carvings.

We are fortunate in that good examples have been found in the Cimmerian Bosphorus—some in the Museum of Leningrad—which go back as far as the 4th century B.C. Their decoration consists of inlays and paintings of mythological subjects, foliage, palms, eggs, etc. in greens, reds, and browns. The sarcophagi of Clazomene in Asia Minor and Herakleion in Crete are shaped like the arks. The latter is quite like those from the north of Spain, with thick feet holding it up from the floor to protect the coffer from dampness. To give a better idea of what these arks were like in style and composition, we could compare them with the famous sarcophagus of Alexander, though of course the arks were much simpler and more stylized. Other good examples are the Egyptian chests from the Ptolemaic and Hellenic period, preserved in the Cairo Museum. The tops of the sarcophagi were usually slanted in two directions like a roof and completely polychromed. Some curious little clay models of arks and coffers are preserved in Athens.

Beds

There is little we can say about Greek beds, but we can get some idea of what they were like from the many sketches and paintings such as the so-called "Wedding of Aldobrandini" (fig. 40). The legs were either round like the chair legs of the earlier periods or flat with stylized carvings of grooved columns like those found in Greek and Roman dining couches. The Greek beds, called *kline*, were very simple. They consisted of a simple rectangular frame on high legs which were either round or wide and flat with carvings of classical scenes, grooved palmetas, eggs, or other designs (fig. 41). Many were so high that a stool was needed to get into them.

One derivation of the bed was the triclinium. The triclinium was a large couch or *kline* in a U shape, for three persons (whence its name), used for dining. Diners usually gathered around small individual tables with a larger one in the center for serving. The Greeks lay on one side, propped up on the left elbow, leaving the right hand free to eat with. Eating was an important activity for them and they did it with great solemnity. The use of the triclinium did not end with the Romanization of Greece nor with the fall of the empire. It continued well into the Byzantine period. This can be seen in the many mosaics from that period.

In summary we should say that except for the remains of a few sarcophagi, practically nothing has been preserved for us of ancient Greek furniture. We owe our knowledge to the paintings on Greek pottery and the carvings on burial steles. Thanks to them we now know much more about classical Greece than just their mythology and fables.

ROME

Many pieces of bronze and stone furniture have been found in the Etruscan necropolises of Caere, Cerveteri, Tarquinia, Herculaneum, and other places in Italy. Some wooden objects, though reduced to charcoal, have also been found in excavations at Pompeii and more especially at Herculaneum. These are of incalculable worth in studying classical furniture. It is exciting to contemplate dwellings in Herculaneum, some of two stories, belonging to a way of life that came to an end nearly twenty centuries ago.

Remains of wooden furniture have been found in almost all the houses destroyed by the earthquake and eruption of 79 A.D. The daily life of the city can be reconstructed with the help of beds, tables, cupboards, and other objects of everyday use found there (figs. 66, 67, 68). These are so important that one of the houses is called the "house of furniture". In others a single object such as a door, a piece of furniture, a fireplace, reveals the high level of technical skill that those ancient artisans had achieved. There is even a folding door in one house that reminds us of those used in store fronts today.

These findings, plus literary references and paintings, especially paintings found in houses in Pompeii, give us a good source of information for our study. Pliny wrote about some furniture objects, particularly about certain tables made of exotic woods.

Chest in the Bardo Museum, Tunis

The Greek influence was so strong that some types are repeated exactly. But the use of bronze gave rise to new techniques producing original elements and decorations. Stone furniture was also widely used.

MATERIALS

Wood of great variety and high quality was used. It was imported from the far-flung colonies and provinces of the empire.

Most luxury items were made of bronze. Wood was used where it was absolutely necessary, in cupboards, tables, lerariums, etc. Like the Greeks, the Romans made furniture of stone and marble mainly for public use. They display a perfection of technique and finish. They were sometimes covered with fabric and other materials for greater elegance. A rather unusual material which can be observed in some bas-reliefs in the Museum of Treves was wicker. It was used to create solid shapes like bronze or stone. (Fig. 44)

DECORATION

We find the same ornamental designs and

stylized animal and vegetable motifs as in the architecture inspired by the Greeks.

Bronze furniture was sometimes engraved, sometimes overlaid with silver and other precious metals. Bronze was hammered and engraved by a special technique. The areas to be decorated were covered with a pitch-like substance. Lines were sketched in the pitch and then acid was applied to the whole area. The pitch protected the bronze from the acid except where it had been scratched away. The acid traced the same pattern in the bronze as that made in the pitch with a stylus. This technique is called nielloing. The vertical parts of the chairs and beds were usually round with exagerated profiles. These shapes were borrowed from other older cultures, usually eastern colonies belonging to the empire.

Roman furniture was the same in the big cities and in the most distant provinces. Interesting fragments of engraved bronze pieces by Boethos of Chalcedon from the 2nd century B.C. have been found in the remains of the shipwrecked galley Madhia off the coast of Tunisia. They are similar to those found on the peninsula, which we shall describe later on. Wooden arks from Punic tombs in Byzacene dating from the 2nd century B.C. and also preserved in the Museum of Tunis are similar to Greek arks from Clazomene.

In the wooden furniture preserved beneath the ashes of Herculaneum the moldings and carvings can be clearly seen in the charred wood. Even some of the paintings can still be seen on stone objects. Decoration was very architectural. Sturdy bas-reliefs of animals are found on the thick feet of the tables called trapezophrums. They look like those seen in the friezes on the ceilings (fig. 64). Fabrics and tapestries of varying quality were also used as decoration even in the most remote villages throughout the vast empire.

The oldest furniture was very rigid. At first an oriental influence can be seen and there was always a strong Greek influence. These reached Etruria first and later Rome. But soon the frames evolved into more curving and natural shapes, more appropriate to their use. This can be seen in the backs of the chairs, heads of beds, and table legs. In every case the outlines became more complex with the addition of decorative elements. Bronze and stone furniture quite naturally developed into different shapes from wooden objects. The techniques involved required the use of big blocks either founded or carved. Wooden pieces, on the other hand, were composed of many small pieces joined and fitted as caissons, panels, pediments, and columns, all in an architectural type of composition. It is interesting to see how all these forms were later repeated in the Italian Renaissance deriving its inspiration from classical antiquity.

KINDS OF FURNITURE

Chairs

We can study beautiful examples of Etruscan and Roman furniture in the museums of Villa Julia, Rome, Orvieto, Pompeii, Herculaneum, and Tunis.

The same four basic types continued to be built with minor variations but now new models were invented to meet the needs of new ways of life.

One of the oldest examples in our possession today is an Etruscan bronze chair found in the tomb of Praeneste (fig. 45). The back is curved and connected to the seat. The seat rests on a cylindrical support instead of legs like some stone and wicker types. It is very finely hammered and engraved.

Another model, also made of bronze, in the Vatican Museum has a high, fancy back (fig. 46).

The oldest stone chairs are those found in the Etruscan tombs, such as the one at Cervetari. The chair is monolithic in shape, yet elegant and graceful in spite of its size (fig. 52).

After the Etruscans were absorbed into the Roman world we find the scissor chair like those made by the Egyptians and Greeks being used. There were also simple stools (fig. 47), some made in two pieces and called bisellium. They appear to have been folding and were used with a small footstool (fig. 55). They were

Lectus

usually made of bronze. The legs or pedestals were cylindrical with typical lense-shaped disks. The bisellium had a horizontal part corresponding to an armrest or the head of a bed. One of these horizontal parts bearing the head of an ox or an ass was found in the excavations at Azaila (Teruel). It may be the oldest piece of Spanish furniture in existence.

These bronze chairs were beautifully engraved in spite of the fact that they were used with cushions. They were uncomfortable, however, since they had no back. Stone chairs were made with backs and were technically so well constructed that they were very comfortable in constructed that they were very comfor spite of the hardness of their material. Some of the examples of these chairs preserved today give the impression of lightness and thinness (fig. 53). The chair used by the Roman citizens was none other than the elegant Greek *klismos* with its curved legs (fig. 58).

The most typical and representative kind of chair was called the *curule*. It was a simple stool like a scissor chair without a back. Some had double curving legs, richly carved, and rings to pick them up and move them about with. They were used exclusively for important persons and dignitaries.

Bronze or stone benches called *scamnum* were used in public places. It is curious that many of these bronze objects were made to imitate wooden pieces in spite of the difficulty in reproducing them in these materials.

Tables

Tables—mensa—occupied a very important place in the Roman household. We still have pedestals made of bronze or stone belonging to these tables, though the tops, usually made of exotic woods, have long since disappeared. In some cases the legs were long and grooved and sometimes ended in talons.

Marble *cartibulum* tables were typical. They were composed of a long slab resting on two sturdy legs at either end called trapezophrum. They were carved with lions, scrolls, and leaves. An interesting example is found in the house of Cornelius Rufus in Pompeii (fig. 64). Other remains of these marble legs are preserved in the Archeological Museums of Madrid and Tarragona. The same ideas are portrayed in a lighter fashion in the bronze tables. The legs were thinner and the lions' heads were replaced with smaller figures of mythical animals (figs. 61, 63). In some cases three legs were used instead of four (figs. 60, 63) and in other cases just one. These were called *monopodium*. In all of them the decorative motifs were of unquestionably Greek and Oriental influence, especially the carved legs and mythical animals.

Cupboards

There are other types of furniture that have been preserved beneath the ashes of Pompeii and Herculaneum since the eruption of 79 A.D. Though reduced to carbon they still retain their shape and even carved decorations. Cupboards have been found in almost perfect condition. The *lararium* (fig. 67) was a little closet or cupboard in the atrium of the Roman house where the protecting hearth was worshipped. Some of these are found today in the same houses in Herculaneum, others have been restored and placed in the Naples Museum.

Arks were of a similar type to the Greek and Egyptian arks, prismatic with thick feet holding them up off the floor. The Punic sarcophagi in the Museum of Tunis serve as an example of this prototype that we shall see repeated with the same features right down to the Renaissance.

Beds

There is a great difference between Etruscan beds of the first centuries and those used by the Romans. The Etruscan beds had broad, flat legs carved with scrolls and palmettes like Greek beds. At the top there were carvings of Greek and Lybian origin. These beds can be observed in paintings in Etruscan tombs and more especially in the tombs excavated at Cerveteri. Here full sized beds were reproduced in baked clay, showing a clear Hellenistic influence in the ornamentation (fig. 69). Similar remains have been found in the tombs at Caere, including fragments of polychrome.

Bronze beds with round legs and lenticular ornamentation have been found at Pompeii. The head is made in the shape of a gently curving S, like the arm rests of a modern sofa. This *lectus* of the Roman "cubicle" was practically identical to the tricliniums in the banquet halls. The frame was made of bronze or wood. The head and foot were made of wood with a double curvature that was the inspiration for a lot of Neo-Classical furniture in the 18th century. Both the *lectus* and the triclinium were covered with rich fabrics, pillows, and cushions which took on increasing importance in the decoration of the home (figs. 71, 72, 73).

Other furniture

There were many other types of furniture of lesser importance: floor lamps, *brucia-profumi*, pedestal tables, brassiers, ovens, etc. They were usually made of bronze. They are all very interesting in shape and decoration which was highly refined and stylized. We can imagine and reconstruct a Roman household almost exactly as it really was.

PALEOCHRISTIAN AND BYZANTINE

With the coming of Christianity, the greatest revolution of all times, every aspect of human life was transformed. Even in the area of art new ideas, problems, and necessities were born. These came to their culmination much later, in the Middle Ages, in the Gothic style, arising from new problems of construction as well as from the spiritual impulses of the people. And both of these derived from the impact of the Christian way of life.

Logically, Christian civilization did not influence only the fine arts but also the industrial arts, including furniture making.

The earliest centuries of Christianity is a rather obscure period as regards furniture. There are few objects remaining from this period and the few that we have are not of great importance. It was a long period of initiation and uncertainty. All the arts reflected an excessive imitation of the eastern world.

When the Roman and Eastern Empires converted to the new faith a new art gradually and at first timidly began to make its appearance. It sought expression in the context of classical art and was obviously derived from Rome, Byzantium, or Asia Minor. But soon there were recognizable common features throughout.

In these centuries of adaptation and change various styles or schools can be observed. They did not last any great length of time, but they do reflect the influence of two great forms—Latin and Byzantine. They bore the seeds of the first great Christian style of the West, the Romanesque. In these early years furniture was still conceived as a purely utilitarian object devoid of artistic interest. We should not forget that Christianity first developed among the lower classes. Most often objects were composed of simple frames covered with fabric of varying quality. They were modest and of little artistic worth. There are only a few examples to be found in Ravenna, Italy corresponding to the western Byzantine Empire.

Chair by Bernini

MATERIALS

As elsewhere wood was the most important material in furniture making. So naturally very few objects have endured until the present. We are acquainted with early Christian art chiefly through models made of more lasting materials, paintings, mosaics, and other graphic and literary records. Fortunately these are quite numerous.

Ivory was the material most used in important objects in Byzantium. Ivory leaf was widely used in the east. Many pieces of furniture in both the east and west were completely covered with metal or decorated with metal inlays and then further covered with tapestries.

With the great advance in silk production in the 6th century, furniture in general became softer and more comfortable as this material was used more and more in upholstery.

DECORATION AND STRUCTURE

Byzantine industrial arts achieved great splendor as a result of contact with the neighboring eastern cultures. Likewise art objects such as paintings and sculptures from the classical period served as inspiration to the new art forms. The miniatures of the codices and the marvelous reliefs on boxes and cryptics afford us good examples of the rich ornamentation of those centuries.

Luxury furniture, especially items covered with ivory leaf, was carved in great profusion. Another one of the principal elements used for decoration was exquisite fabrics. Many of these still serve as inspiration to modern decorators because of their original patterns and colors. Sasanide and Coptic textiles should be example enough.

All kinds of chairs, tables, and beds were covered with cloth and fabrics. An important structural element was the turned pieces, both vertical and horizontal, in which sperical shapes often appeared. Large surfaces were covered with carvings and reliefs.

Sometimes furniture was covered with leaves of precious metals, sometimes it was decorated and painted. As usual, the primary source of composition was found in architecture. Arcades of semi-circular arches, striated and carved wooden columns, and enamel, gold, and silver appliqués are found. In some cases—like some buildings—the front and sides were covered with mosaics.

In the West, on the other hand, luxury items were practically non-existent and furniture holds little interest for us. Structure was simple and there was no interest in solving problems of composition or in offering new ideas. Furniture followed the slow evolution of the Roman world.

KINDS OF FURNITURE

Chairs

The earliest western furniture differed very little from that of the Romans. There were furniture factories of real worth in the Christian communities around the Mediterranean, especially at Antioch and Alexandria. But we have very few examples in existence today. In a frieze in the catacombs of San Callisto we can observe a tripod that is essentially the same as the Roman type (fig. 80). The same could be said about the chair of the Virgin and Child in a small painting from the 2nd–3rd century in the catacomb of Saint Priscilla in Rome (fig. 84). Generally the chairs, or *cathedras,* were rigid, adorned with a profusion of carvings and architectural compositions of arcades and carved panels. The most typical example, aside from its historical interest, is the so-called chair or cathedra of Saint Peter (though far from being contemporary with the Apostle). The most recent and likely hypothesis attributes the throne to the emperor Charles the Bald (875) and was a gift to the priest who was to crown him (fig. 77). It is cubic in structure; the back is made of an arcade topped with a pediment and it has rings on the sides like the old Roman *curuliis* to carry it. The front of the throne is covered with 18 little marble squares with carvings of pagan themes. They are very significant and typical of the period of Constantine. One hypothesis suggests that these marble plaques originally belonged to the throne of the emperor Constantine and that he donated it to the high priest Saint Melchiades (314) or Saint Sylvester (336).

Thus the present work belongs to both of these periods, though it is clearly pre-Romanesque. It is completely hidden by the chair designed and constructed by Bernini in 1656 for St. Peter's Basilica.

Many items of furniture are represented on the earliest *pixis* or little boxes for relics or other uses in the religious meetings of the first centuries. There are scissor chairs, thrones, reposing beds, etc. such as those seen on the box preserved in Brescia (figs. 74, 76). The same can be said for the furniture carved in marble in Alexandria. The most interesting example from this period is the chair or portable cathedra of the Bishop of Ravenna (figs. 75, 79). It is an outstanding piece, cubic in shape, with a concave back similar to Roman chairs we have mentioned. The frame is made of wood completely covered with delicately carved leaves of ivory held together with pins made of the same material. The scenes represented are like those of other chairs of the period. They contain details typical of both Antioch and Alexandria making it impossible to identify the exact place where it was built. It can be dated in the 6th century, however, because of the monogram on the front of the chair identifying it with the Bishop Maximian from the time of Justinian. It is truly an outstanding item and one of the most prized objects in the Cathedral of Ravenna. In the old codices a great many scissor chairs or cube-shaped chairs are found. They often have exagerated legs in the shape of talons or turned elements and spheres. But these kinds of decorations are employed without the distinction and elegance of the classical types from which they drew their inspiration.

We find representations of massive armchairs like the old type in the reliefs on the magnificent Antioch chalice of the 4th century (fig. 78).

In the mosaics on the ceiling of the baptistry of the Cathedral of Ravenna, there is a series of armchairs with concave backs and curious curved legs ending in talons that look like English chairs from the 18th century.

Tables

Tables consisted of a simple board on a pair of trestles covered with a cloth. They continued in use until the Renaissance (fig. 81).

Little else can be said about other Byzantine pieces. They are known to us only in graphic representations.

Cupboards

Closed furniture objects including cupboards, arks, and desks are seen with relative frequency in paintings and mosaics. Cupboards and other pieces can be studied among those preserved in the Bardo Museum obtained from Tabarka. Among them is a table which can be closed up like an ark similar to the ones used in Rome at an earlier time. It could be used by a writer, serving as a sort of primitive desk or writing table. These *scriptorium* were the precursers of the tables used by the monks in the monasteries. A cupboard of architectural shape with a typical crown pediment can be seen in the mosaic in the mausoleum of Gala Placidia (fig. 86).

Coffers were similar to small arks, of which some beautiful marble examples have been preserved. Beds in this period were only used for resting. Since they were not used for eating or for reclining during the day, the heads were high and decorative.

Beds

Beds were covered with fabric and curtains. The vertical parts holding up the head and foot were turned and connected horizontally with cords to hold the mattress (fig. 87).

We do not have sufficient examples to establish an orderly classification of types. It is not until after the 10th century that different types of furniture repeat the same characteristics and details for us to classify them in what we might call the Pre-Romanesque period.

PRE-ROMANESQUE

The coffer of the Cathedral of Terracina (fig. 98) could be considered an example of Pre-Romanesque. It was made in Lombardy in the 7th and 8th centuries. The whole front of it is covered with very flat chiseled carvings. We have included other Pre-Romanesque pieces seen in various miniatures and images in the graphic section (fig. 88). Another example from this rather ill-defined period is a tree trunk converted into a chair with a rude sort of back. The only decorative detail is a star inscribed in a circle, a popular theme among all the Romanized peoples of Europe (fig. 92). Other examples such as Scandinavian trunks are repeated as late as the 16th century. As we have seen, the examples are very scarce, but on the other hand they are very suggestive and decorative. They show us, better than any other language, that furniture as yet had not found any enduring types and that the influences exerted were so far relative and often merely circumstantial.

ROMANESQUE

During the first centuries of our era furniture in both the northern and southern countries developed only very slowly as it sought to meet the most basic needs of the period. Although it showed increasing signs of sensitivity, it responded to practical necessities and was limited by the still crude methods of construction. Furniture was built with a simple utilitarian aim in view.

Like those of the earlier period, furniture objects from the Romanesque are better known through paintings and miniatures than through the few examples still available to us today. What we have are heavy, strong, massive pieces with stylized decoration based on flora and fauna and fantastic figures.

Later, in the 12th century, they were decorated with paintings and sculptural forms taken from architecture and with iron and ivory appliqués. This offered new possibilities to furniture, opening the door to real creativity. From this point on decoration was to fulfill the double role of beautifying the object and providing form, paralleling the fine arts. Other themes were always subordinated to architectural forms, especially in early religious furniture. Most of the objects which have endured to the present belong to this category. We have been able to reconstruct some objects on the basis of paintings in codices and manuscripts. We know, for instance, that because of the nomadic impulse of the period (conquests, invasions, etc.) many objects were collapsible for easy transportation. Often the horizontal parts of the frame passed through the vertical parts and were fastened with pins permiting them to be taken apart quickly and easily. Likewise the draperies and cushions on beds and chairs were not fastened; they could be removed and stored in coffers.

In the 12th and 13th centuries near the end of this period some of the crudeness of the earlier years disappeared. Architectural and sculptural motifs had a greater tendency toward luxury and beauty. This was due no doubt to the eastern influences brought west by the crusades.

In the midst of the Reconquest in Spain a very important Moorish influence made itself felt. It was to become very firmly rooted in this country in the succeeding years.

MATERIALS

As usual, wood was the most important material in furniture making. Along with pine and other inferior woods, walnut, oak, and chestnut were used. Oak was used principally in the northern countries, linden and soft Alpine woods in central Europe, and oak, walnut, and chestnut in Spain.

Both the use of marquetry, in Spanish Mudejar furniture for example, and iron and ivory appliqués were common. Some models made of forged iron have been preserved, especially thrones and episcopal chairs. Iron, however, was used most often as reinforcements in the still embryonic art of cabinet making, though as we pointed out it did on occasion serve as the basic material for some objects.

DECORATION

Furniture was mostly decorated with paintings or carvings. Paintings were no longer limited to copying purely ornamental elements such as geometric or plant forms, but now included even the human body and whole scenes. They were usually religious or symbolic. The carvings were more vigorous than in the Pre-Romanesque period, being made on thick panels permiting a deeper relief. Stylized forms of flora and fauna were common motifs. They were derived from earlier styles including Byzantine and Roman and from Romanesque schools such as the Lombard, Celtic, and Nordic schools. There was an increasingly national character about them.

Simple, sturdy turned elements abounded including alternating disks and spheres in the vertical supports like those which we have seen in the Byzantine and Pre-Romanesque styles. Marquetry was always in the form of geometric designs and star shaped polygons found in furniture of Oriental or Moorish influence. Cloth and tapestries were widely used to decorate and enrich rough objects of iron or wood; they were usually of eastern origin.

The use of iron parts was by no means only for decorative purposes. They were necessary to reinforce structures which were generally badly jointed. Near the end of the period these reinforcements came to be the principal decorative element with the scroll in many different forms being almost the only decorative motif.

FORMS AND STRUCTURES

Technique in furniture making developed very slowly throughout Europe. Butt joints and mortise and tenon joints were used with big nails and iron reinforcements which, as we have already mentioned, were employed artistically. As furniture making improved in the 13th century mortise-and-tenon and dovetail joints began to be used. Iron reinforcements were used less and less until they practically disappeared in the Gothic period. This was not the case with the iron trimmings and appliqués which can still be found on many objects of the latter period. The use of richer woods and higher quality materials such as bronze, copper, mother-of-pearl, and ivory gradually made its appearance. They were used as decorative material superimposed on the objects themselves. The objects made of iron were usually made with metal-working techniques but imitating the forms of wooden objects. Generally they were used for sitting and were covered with thick tapestries.

The forms were rectangular and massive. They were very simple and the supporting structures were nearly always vertical. The scissor chair with its crossed legs, however, was still used. Arks and chests were not topped with a simple flat panel but had a top like a roof. This was the case in many examples from central Europe.

As we have already pointed out, many pieces of furniture were made with long pieces that passed through the frame to make them easier to take apart.

Spanish and Sycilian Mudejar furniture offers excellent examples of fine craftsmanship. The surfaces are made of innumerable pieces forming complicated geometric designs. They were miter-jointed or simply flush-jointed for mere decorative value. They were reinforced inside with other pieces that served as the real framework.

Scandinavian furniture displayed some very original forms and carvings, although they achieved no great influence other than in popular carvings found in some pieces in central Europe, England, and Brittany. One

Detail from the bench of the presbitery. Church of Tahull

of the most typical elements was the runic loop inspired in their ancient writings. It was used in very fine carvings completely covering the surface areas no matter how small they might be.

KINDS OF FURNITURE

Chairs

Furniture was still relatively scarce at this time —we must keep in mind the nomadic spirit of the age. There were very few chairs and these were mostly used for seats of honor for civil and ecclesiastical dignitaries. They were most often in the form of scissor chairs. There are some interesting examples that have been preserved such as the magnificent chair in the Cathedral of Roda (fig. 105), with highly original and strange carvings. They remind us of Scandinavian or Oriental types or of the Salzburg chair (fig. 120) inlaid with ivory. Another similar example is the bronze chair by Dagobert restored in the 13th century by the Abbey Seger, who added a back to strengthen and preserve it (fig. 97).

Aside from these main types there were some typical chairs with a triangular seat and curious turned rungs which were very popular in Germany, England, and the Basque Country (fig. 96).

In commoner chairs the turned parts and vertical staves were connected with sturdy arcades of semi-circular arches in the back, sides, and beneath the seat. Sometimes these parts were carved and polychromed. We know them well because were still being built as late as the 18th century. The majority of the chairs that have been preserved from the Romanesque period are of this type (figs. 98, 99, 108). The seats and benches in the churches of this period were forerunners of the excellent works achieved in the Gothic period throughout Europe. We must not neglect to mention here some choir stalls of great artistic merit and singular characteristics. These are the three stalls remaining from the convent of Gradefes (Leon). Though dating from the 13th and 14th centuries, they belong to the late Romanesque style with strong Mudejar influence. Only three stalls from the lower choir have been preserved, separated by little columns topped with typical Roman capitals with very fine Mudejar decoration.

There are popular Moorish stalactite arches on the sides of the stalls. The vertical supporting parts are decorated with foliage carved with a chisel. The seats were made of pine and walnut. The lower parts of the three stalls are identical to those of the four stalls from the choir of Santa Clara de Astudillo (in Palencia), which are in bad condition because of dampness and neglect. The bottom ends of the legs, which were probably connected with cross pieces, are missing.

We will speak of these stalls in the convent of Astudillo and Santa Clara de Moguer in the next chapter on Gothic furniture. These three examples are unique and of enormous importance in the study of church furniture. In the presbitery of the Romanesque church in Tahull (Catalonia) there was a bench with Romanesque decoration including horseshoe arches of Mudejar origin very rare in Catalonia. This exceptional item is preserved in the Museum of Barcelona. The bench has three seats and is covered with a high dais. The front is decorated with Romanesque arcade on top of slender columns like those in the previous two examples. There are also remains of polychrome (fig. 107).

The famous bench of Alpirsbach (Black Forest) is six yards long and has an interesting arrangement of turned pieces that cover the whole back resembling a stuffed or quilted upholstery (fig. 116). There are other benches with this sort of decoration in Germany. They continued to be popular until the 18th century.

Tables

The tables appearing in paintings and codices are shown to be simple boards on a pair of trestles. They were crude and rough and were always covered with a cloth when in use (figs. 103, 111). There were others of octogonal or circular shape supported by a central leg or column imitating architectural forms. The most important Romanesque piece was the chest which could be found in homes both rich and poor, in palaces and in church sacristies. Arks also served as benches, tables, and wardrobes. More than thirty could sometimes be found in the house of a single family. Their construction began with a simple hollowed out log (fig. 135) and quickly evolved into more complex forms often finding inspiration in the old Greek and Roman sarcophagi. At first they were very rough but were gradually brought to greater perfection.

Cupboards

The most common form of ark was a long box with iron trimmings. They were found in Germany, Spain, France, and England. The top was almost always flat, though sometimes it was in the shape of a roof or tile. The wood was carved or covered with cloth or leather and reinforced with nails and iron fittings. The French and German arks are the best examples of this type (figs. 122, 127). Often the vertical parts of the frame were of one piece with the feet resting on the floor like the Greek and Roman models. There were marked differences between the Greek arks from the north and south of the country. This was due to the use of different kinds of wood and the resulting variations in decoration. In the south where fir and linden were used there was abundant ornamentation because these types of wood are quite soft. The use of oak in the north limited decoration because of its hardness.

In Spain the famous Astorga chest covered with a polychromed "roof" is a unique and beautiful specimen. Other interesting Hispano-Arabian arks have been preserved. They belong to the Arabic school with geometric decoration of lace and stars. The legendary ark named after El Cid probably dates from this period. It has a typical tile-shaped top (figs. 109, 110).

At this time cupboards of a similar construction to that of the arks began to appear. They were tall and narrow with a single door. They had many iron reinforcments. The top was usually flat or roof-shaped with a steep pitch. The doors were made of jointed or mortised panels with iron reinforcements (fig. 25). The most important examples are the French cupboard in Obazine (figs. 101, 102) built into a stone wall, and a German one in the museum of Nuremburg with carvings of stars of Barbarian origin and paintings on the doors. A few English models with iron parts can be considered in transition from Romanesque to Gothic (fig. 133). The typical cupboards from southern Germany are well known for their openwork carvings and iron braces.

Beds

The beds had turned legs and very high headboards. These were sometimes slightly curved. They were always covered with curtains and tapestries covering the blankets, skins, and bags of straw which served as primitive mattresses. In miniatures from this period we observe that people slept in these beds entirely naked. The beds from the early Middle Ages had such high sides that a space had to be left in one side to make it easier to get in and out of bed (fig. 95). The many beds included in the illustrations in the Cantigas of Alphonso the Wise show an obvious sturdy Romanesque structure. Not only the turned elements can be observed, but even the pegs and pins to disassemble them (fig. 112).

The most commonly found items were the ark and the bench, which might be just a box covered with cloth. The primary interest in Romanesque is its function as a historic link in the chain. There are few examples and the few types that existed were copied with little variation. Forms were simple, rough, and sturdy like the architecture in which they were inspired. But we should emphasize that they were quite different in conception and structure from the pseudo-Romanesque objects built in the second half of the 19th century in an attempt to romanticize the styles of the Middle Ages.

GOTHIC

Art history and art theory describe for us the origins, causes, and essence of Gothic art and architecture. Here we need only point out its unquestionably German background and its gradual progress towards its high point in France at the time of Saint Louis. For three hundred years it spread across Europe taking on varying characteristics in each individual country. Gothic furniture was always closely related to architecture.

French Gothic was the purest and most harmonious. It achieved its greatest splendor under the patronage of J. DuBerry and Philippe Hardy during the reign of Charles IV.

In Spain the Gothic style was coarser and more vigorous. It was never entirely free from Moorish influences since Mudejar art and architecture was developing throughout the same period. We must not forget that the two cultures, Spanish and Arabic, coexisted on the Iberian Peninsular until after the Renaissance was under way.

English Gothic was simple and without refinement. It had a very national character about it which at the end of the period in the 16th century led into the so-called Tudor style or perpendicular style. It was so called after the rhythmic repetition of vertical elements, especially ogives.

Gothic art was very important in Flanders, almost as pure and sober as in France. It was here that the folds of cloth were painted to excess along with pilasters and statuettes. On the other hand, new advances in the art of furniture-making were made here. The use of frames and panels constituted a revolution in this craft.

Germany developed two types of Gothic art simultaneously in the north and south. The softer wood obtained in the great conifer forests was used in the south. Linden, pine, savin, and fir were carved and decorated with vines and leaves and geometric shapes. Strangely enough it was the frames and rails that were profusely carved and not the panels, which would seem more logical to us. Oak was used in the north. It was harder than the wood used in the south with the result that furniture was simpler in structure and decoration.

Last of all, Italian ogival art developed very differently from other countries. It was not so subject to norms and rules, probably because the tradition of classical art was still strongly felt. Thus furniture continued to be strong and heavy like that of the preceding period with influences deriving from the ancient traditions. When the rest of Europe was fully immersed in the Gothic style, a certain pre-Renaissance movement can be detected in Italian art and furniture. The best examples would be the *cassoni*, the front of which were covered with a peculiar ornamentation called *certosina* composed of plaster and stucco.

Gothic art was essentially religious. Church and monastery furniture was the first to be developed. When furniture used in civil functions still bore only carvings or metal appliqués, religious objects had become greatly developed offering examples of great artistic interest. The stalls in the cathedral choir lofts typified some of the greatest works of the period. We shall not study them here, however, since because of their architectural and fixed nature they do not correspond to the history of furniture.

Generally speaking, Gothic art developed in the same three stages all across the continent and especially in France. They were the formative or primitive period, maturity and height of style, and the Baroque or flamboyant period. These stages correspond roughly to the 13th century, the 14th and early 15th centuries, and middle and late 15th century. Of course these dates are very inexact.

The stages can be defined more precisely in England. They would be: formative, 13th century; height, 14th century; perpendicular (equivalent to flamboyant), end of the 14th and 15th centuries; and Tudor, 16th century to 1560. In Spain late Gothic persisted well into the 16th century and while there are many Romanesque works dating from the 13th century.

STRUCTURES

Solid and prismatic shapes inherited from the Romanesque period continued to be used. The stiffness and vertical tendency in furniture were accentuated especially in the later stages. Later on we shall see how this vertical tendency was disrupted in the Renaissance. Perhaps it was due to the resurgence of pagan forms as opposed to the religious fervor of the Middle Ages.

Furniture of simple frames and straight lines acquired more character as a result of greater decoration. This was mainly carving and sculpture.

Chairs were always square in shape with perfectly straight backs. The frames of arks and cupboards went clear to the floor and were connected with socles which were covered with carvings. Sometimes these objects had short legs which were independent pieces attached to the bottom. The legs of the beds were prolonged to hold up the canopy. These parts were also carved in the typical style of the period with laces, bunches of columns, thistle leaves, and stylized plants with nervures and spirals, etc. The same applies to chair legs which were sometimes turned like Romanesque chairs, but usually rectangular. Sometimes they were decorated and beveled to make them appear lighter. The columns and moldings in the carvings were copied from architecture. Lastly there were objects made of metal, especially scissor chairs of forged iron with bronze appliqués. They were used as faldstools or seats of honor (fig. 137).

As the Middle Ages advanced, progress in technology also advanced. New types of joints such as the dovetail and miter joints were used. Different pieces were fitted together more perfectly. From 1320 on the hydraulic saw came into use making it possible to saw boards instead of having to split logs with axe and adz.

Sometimes geometric designs were carved in an openwork silhouette and superimposed on a flat background to make decoration easier. This was the case with many arcades on the fronts of chests. They were laid over a painted background. But the real change came in the 15th century near the end of the Gothic period. This change came in the form of a transformation of technique in creating broad surfaces. The wide boards held in place with bars or joints were replaced with rectangular frames of stringers and rails holding inserted panels. This type of construction was perfectly suited to any kind of furniture. It was even employed on the interior walls of the finer houses throughout northern Europe—England, the Low Countries, Germany, etc. This use of a "filler" finds a parallel in Gothic architecture as well. The nervatures of the vaults and pillars were, like the frames of furniture, completely independent from the lateral vaults or walls. The walls themselves had stained glass windows for "fillers". This new step in construction coincided with the beginning of the Renaissance, represented in the paintings of Jan Van Eyck (fig. 135).

All of these advances were aided by the old European sculptors' and furniture-makers' guilds. With the development of civic life and government, laws and rules were made to apply to the exercise of these functions, freeing them from feudal and ecclesiastical power which had dominated Europe throughout most of the Middle Ages.

DECORATION

In the 13th century features of the new architectural style began to appear in the rather rough furniture of that period. These included arcades along the fronts of arks, bunches of columns and pillars on the frames, and crests and gables on top.

The old sculptural motifs like the Romanesque mythical animals gave way to more naturalistic carvings, stylizations of flora and fauna, thistles, vines, domestic animals, and geometric designs. As Worringer says in *The Essence of Gothic*, it was "real geometry brought to life. While it may seem overdone when applied to architecture and furniture, it is also solemn and majestic."

Abstract loop and geometric designs from northern Europe became popular all over the continent. A new decorative motif was also born at this time, the parchment or folded cloth. It came as the result of improved techniques with the plane and gouge. This theme was used in decoration all over Europe until well into the Renaissance. In the regions of central Europe where soft wood was widely used another kind of ornamentation was common. It was called hollow carving and consisted of open filigree work laid over a flat background. Both parts were painted, usually red and green. This type of decoration also lasted until well into the Renaissance. Carving was the most usual kind of decoration in the Gothic period. It consisted basically of four types: high relief, parchment, low relief, and openwork.

The first type was very thick, and the highest part of the figure was even with the frame of the object. The second type, made to look like rippled or folded cloth, was derived from the new techniques mentioned above, especially the use of curved gouges. The third was flatter, more like an engraving. The fourth type was laid over a flat background. It usually involved geometric and architectural patterns.

It is interesting that the first two types were usually applied to panels and flat surfaces, whereas the second two were usually employed on the frames. The actual carvings were most often of vines and thistles. Overlaid traceries generally involved geometric themes. In both cases the background was frequently painted or gilt.

Towards the end of the period, at the end of the 15th century and the beginning of the 16th, certain Renaissance forms can be seen superimposed on basically Gothic structures. Arabesque and grotesque figures very typical of this period were applied to objects still very much a product of the earlier period.

In much of the furniture from Spain there are Mudejar figures, polygonal traceries, and star shapes mixed with the usual cubic motifs and structures belonging to the Gothic style. The combination is not hybrid, however, but perfectly balanced in composition. It comprises a very interesting and unique style characterizing a particular nation and period.

These inlays were made of tiny incrustations of ivory in the shape of rhomboids and diverse geometric patterns of oriental origin. They were undoubtedly the origin of the Italian *certosina* introduced mainly by the Carthusian monks and Sicilian artisans.

Naturally all of these forms went through a process of evolution as the period progressed. For example the pointed arch became flatter at the end of the 15th century and eventually evolved into the ogee arch. Decoration increased and became more florid leading into the Baroque. Vertical elements were repeated in series producing flamboyant arcades.

We should not forget that other materials were also used in decoration. Iron was used especially in hinges and locks. They were of great beauty, especially flat pieces with openwork silhouettes. Gold leaf was also widely used to cover furniture panels and sometimes the ornamentation itself.

MATERIALS

Just as in the Romanesque period, wood was used almost exclusively in furniture making. Varying characteristics gave rise to a variety of decoration.

Oak was used on the whole continent, especially in the southern countries. Walnut was used to a lesser extent in France, Spain, and Italy, softer woods in central Europe as far as the Black Sea.

There were still some objects, mostly for seating, made of metal and completely covered with cushions and fabric. Iron was most often used in locks, trimmings, reinforcements, and hinges. These parts were hammered and often made of openwork.

Marquetry disappeared almost completely except for Mudejar furniture and a few other isolated cases. Practically the only decoration was gilding, carving, and painting. The use of tapestries, fabric, and cushions was as usual reserved for objects of higher quality.

KINDS OF FURNITURE

As we pointed out at the beginning of this chapter, the most important furniture from this period was religious furniture. The most important of all, for their artistic interest, were the benches in the choir lofts. However, because of their construction they really belong to the study of architecture and not to this book. The episcopal chairs are part of the same arrangement and will not be described in this book except for a few isolated examples.

FRANCE

We shall begin with France, the real center of the Gothic style, where furniture was purist in composition and decoration.

Chairs

The typical chair of this period was the scissor chair and variations. It was usually made of wood or metal and can be observed in innumerable graphic representation. Viollet le Duc has made a detailed study of these chairs. They were often covered with rich tapestries.

The seats of metal chairs were usually made of little iron chains covered with cushions. The episcopal chair of Bayeux is a beautiful example of the scissor chair (fig. 137). One variation was the chair made of a row of crossed wooden sticks deriving from the Italian Proto-Renaissance. The most typical chair from this period was the armchair with a high rectangular back topped with a cresting. It had carvings or tracery on the back. The seat opened like a box and had the same sort of decoration on the front and sides (figs. 138, 140).

Another common sort of seat was the three-legged stool. The legs were turned like the Romanesque type and it was used with a footstool. There were also benches and chests with arms and backs like the earlier types.

There was an interesting sort of bench for use in the middle of the room. The back was in the middle and people could sit on both sides facing in opposite directions. In other cases the back was moveable; the bench could be made to face the fireplace or away from it (figs. 151, 152).

Small chest in the Cluny Museum

Tables

Like in the Romanesque period, tables were covered with cloths and rested on a pair of trestles. There were other smaller either round or polygonal tables that rested on one central leg usually shaped like a pillar.

Cupboards

The chest continued to be the main means of storage. There were different models and variations such as *dressoirs* already well known in ancient Rome.

There were arks and coffers of many shapes and sizes from large pieces with grooved boards and iron reinforcements to those from the end of the period with frames and carved panels. In some cases the sides were made of one solid piece like the Romanesque chests, but were then subdivided in false sections. An example of this can be seen in a small chest in the Museum of Cluny dating from the 14th century. It clearly demonstrates the transition from the earlier chests with iron reinforcements to the later types with individual panels and delicate carvings. In the first the decoration extends across the whole front in one composition. In the latter the subdivisions of panels makes it possible to separate the ornamentation into different groupings.

The front of the chests were covered with Gothic tracery as well as iron trimmings. Near the end of the period they were covered with the typical carved folded parchment. Others were painted with floral and animal motifs or covered with leather (figs. 144, 147).

Guilds were becoming well organized at this time. Thanks to E. Boileau's book *Masters of Paris* we know the names of several *huchiers* who built and carved the *huches* or coffers. Some of the earliest companies dated from the middle of the 13th century.

Cupboards were still not as widely used as chests. In old manuscripts we can observe many arks and chests for storing clothing and other effects without once seeing a cupboard or wardrobe. The French examples were mainly for religious use. One example is from Noyons. It has paintings on the doors and a roof-shaped top complete with gables and fronds on the arrises. The one from Bayeux, from the 13th century has iron reinforcements and remains of the paintings on the doors with organ pipe joints. The one from the treasury of Saint Germain de Auvernois is a bench with an openwork cresting. It is framed and has parchment carvings on the panels and hammered openwork iron parts on the doors. It dates from the 15th century.

The *dressoir* or buffet was developed in Burgundy during this period. Burgundy was an important furniture making district. The *dressoir* was a kind of ark on high legs with a series of steps on top leading up to a sort of dais. The number of steps corresponded to the particular social class. A baron had only two steps, his immediate superior one more, and so on up to the royal *dressoir*. The one presented to Henry VIII of England on the arrival of the French ambassadors at Greenwich had twelve steps. There were few of these buffets and they were mainly found in the Rhine, Flanders, and Burgundy, which were the cultural centers of the age. The credenza was similar to the ark but higher and without steps. It was simply a chest on legs like columns resting on a base below. The main part had two or three doors sometimes chamfered to the sides. It is not surprising to find, at the end of the period—late 15th century and early 16th—grotesque and Arabesque ornamentation inspired by Raphael, especially in French and Spanish models.

Viollet le Duc in his *Dictionaire du Meuble au Moyen-Age* has done and excellent study of that period.

Beds

The upper class dwellings of the age consisted of a single room serving all the family needs. It served as bedroom, dining room, and living room. The table and stools were arranged around the large fireplace. In one corner of the room a huge bed was found. It had high columns holding up a canopy and drapes. These were necessary to divide off the bed at night into a small isolated chamber. At this time just as during the early Middle Ages, people slept completely naked. This can be confirmed from many pictures and engravings dating from this period. A rare French miniature from the 14th century shows the interior of a wayside inn with the travelers making their way to their beds completely naked (fig. 232).

Other beds show evidence of high quality furniture making with a high dais supported by wooden columns. Sometimes the dais itself was made of wood, sometimes of cloth of varying quality. Those that lay against the wall usually had panelling at the head and along the wall to an appreciable height to protect against the damp. One of these beds from near the end of the period was completely covered with parchment decoration on the lower panels and geometric patterns on the higher ones.

SPAIN

Chairs

In Spain we can appreciate normal developments of the Gothic style on the one hand in such examples as the bench from Cuenca (fig. 163), the Enríquez armchair (fig. 162), or the priory chair of Valldemosa (fig. 160). The first is very classical in structure with splendid carvings on the back. The second is of the so-called drawer type. The back of the third has beautiful inlays. We simply mention here two fragments of stalls from Gothic choir lofts, one from Rueda and the other from Palencia. Both have gables over the backs, which with their fine traceries are similar to those in the rest of Europe. We also possess two unique examples of rare Mudejar style. These are the chairs from Santa Clara de Moguer, restored in 1940, and those from Santa Clara de Astudillo. They are quite similar but while the first are preserved intact in three sides of the choir loft in the convent of Santa Clara in Andalusia, there are only four of the latter preserved in the Archeological Museum of Madrid. They are from Astudillo in Palencia and are of exceptional interest, being the only such stalls of Mudejar style. There are four high stalls with octagonal columns holding up a canopy. The columns are topped with balls and three-lobed arches between them. They are in quite good condition though the lower parts have been lost probably due to the damp. There are remains of the original Moorish polychrome. They are carved in pine and date from the 14th century. It was at this time that Doña María Padilla, whose shield appears in the dais, assisted the Monastery of Santa Clara (fig. 182, 183).

Remains of the choir stalls from the Cathedral of Salamanca have also been preserved. One of the armchairs is cube-shaped, like the one in the Valencia de Don Juan Museum. The decoration is clearly from the end of the period, flamboyant and very vertical.

There are armchairs with metal frames such as the one from Belmonte or the metal chair of Don Martin in Barcelona (fig. 156). It has excellent silver work. In some of these a French influence can be seen. This is true in caisson chairs and arks. A southern German influence can be perceived in the cupboard in the Archives of Tarragona in the geometric carvings on the stringers. Italian influence appears in chests decorated with paintings and sgraffito. These are found mostly along the east coast which had more direct contact with Italy.

Cupboards

There were chests with traceries and carvings on the front. Others were covered with leather and had openwork iron reinforcements.

All of the chests with sgraffito, leather, paintings, and metal appliqués are very interesting. One of the most famous of these is the Ark of Saint Isidro. The top is tile shaped and painted, though the paintings have practically disappeared. The paintings were typical of the Catalan region and arranged in classical composition with clear Italian Renaissance

Ark of Saint Isidro

influence (figs. 168, 171, 172). It is impossible to emphasize too much the importance of Mudejar furniture in Spain. It was built by the Arabs who were under the domination of the Christian kingdoms. There are few copies left but those that have been preserved illustrate clearly the simple, cubic structures of the period. They were decorated with polygonal shapes in the railings and Moorish type star traceries. They were of great artistic interest and unique in all of Europe. Even in Italy where Sicilian influence was appreciable there were only isolated cases.

This influence was seen in all the industrial arts in Spain, most especially in architecture, in the floor plans and roofs.

Mudejar caissoned ceilings were quite common. They were very beautiful with different star shapes and original types of vaults. The most important piece of Mudejar furniture from the Gothic period is the famous relic closet from the Monasterio de Piedra. The panels of the closet are covered with beautiful paintings. Only the frame is covered with inlays. Another closet named after Saint Ursula and preserved in the Archeological Museum of Madrid has doors made of starred pieces with paintings on the inside (fig. 196). There are two other examples exactly like this one, one in the San Juan Museum in Valencia and the other in the Museum of Decorative Arts. The cupboard in the Diocesan Museum of León (figs. 190, 191, 192) is a "true monument and renowned example of the Moorish furniture of the 13th century" according to Gómez Moreno. There is a small cupboard on double uprights with traceries on the outside and paintings on the inside in Barcelona. There are a number of boxes, tables, and chairs in the same kind of work. Among them we should point out the folding hip chairs of Gothic structure. The seats were covered with leather or cloth. They were embroidered or carved and decorated with delicate Mudejar marquetry (fig. 185).

Chests also were completely covered with geometric inlays. In some cases the front was collapsible and a second front appeared in the form of a set of drawers. These were undoubtedly the antecedents of the secretaries of later periods.

The oriental art forms did not disappear with the arrival of the Renaissance in the 16th century. We can observe objects of obvious Renaissance form and decoration in Spain that still retain Mudejar influences.

There were two types of Mudejar furniture, the first type with superimposed starred traceries and the second with inlays. There is one exceptional example in the form of a secretary with folding top, handles on the sides, and a cover that can be lifted over a drawer. The whole thing is covered with inlays that are smaller than the so-called Renaissance "wheat grain". It is perfectly flat in appearance both inside and out. It is a warm leather color with tiny inlays of boxwood, ivory, bone, and a few green colored appliqués. All of the figures are geometric. There are some very original stylized castles and interlaceries.

ITALY

In Italy Gothic art developed completely differently from the rest of Europe. Many objects have similar characteristics to those from France, Tyrol, and the Alpes but they often bear decorative motifs peculiarly Italian, such as *certosina*, stucco, engravings, and sgraffito. These elements and techniques were unmistakeable forerunners of the Renaissance (figs. 205, 206, 210, 211, 212).

The most interesting examples are found in the armchairs, cupboards, etc., and especially a series of arks from Adigio in northern Italy decorated with stucco.

ENGLAND

Gothic furniture was coarser and stronger in England than on the continent. Among the objects that most closely imitate the motifs found on the continent is the famous Westminster Coronation Chair. It has the traditional and legendary Coronation Stone under the seat (fig. 217). It is topped with a gable bordered with crockets. The "monk" benches with a back that folds down to form a table are similar to the French ones.

The cupboards used for storing wine and food were even more interesting. They had openwork and holes most likely for ventilation. They were shaped like trilobal figures, arcades, or, in the 16th century, like balustrades (figs. 227, 228).

Boxes with Norman carvings, chairs, benches with high backs, and beds like those on the continent can still be found. The use of folded parchment decoration is common just as in Europe (fig. 221). Beds were shaped like arks with a roof and fronds carved on the arrises along with other details. There are numerous beds, credenzas, *dressoirs*, and wall tables. The beds were mostly of the same sort with ample curtains drawn up during the day as can be seen in the drawings and carvings from this period. But if the furniture that has been preserved is interesting, much more so are the paintings dating from the same time. Memling, Van Eyck, and Flemalle painted beautiful interiors of credenzas, beds, benches, tables, and seats of all kinds. In the carvings on the Flemish Altarpiece of the Saviour in Valladolid there are an armchair, a triangular seat of Romanesque type, and a scissor chair from the beginning of the Renaissance (figs. 229, 245, 250).

Besides all these objects which were usually decorated with folded parchment, we should not neglect to mention the famous Santa Ursula box. The backgrounds were painted by Memling, though the box itself is mostly of gold (fig. 237). It is shaped like an ark with a sloping roof. There are fronds, arcades and other Gothic decorations on the eaves. It is similar to many other boxes made of wood.

CENTRAL EUROPE

The groups of furniture from Germany are very interesting. Those from the north were made of oak with clear influences from the Low Countries and Burgundy. Those from the south were made of softer wood showing the more southerly Lombard influences (figs. 265, 270).

Many of the items from the central regions, Tyrol, and Austria, are of popular style. They have typical flat or openwork carvings on the frames and traceries and other decorative motifs in which Nordic and Romanesque traditions can be clearly seen. There are metal appliqués in the middle of the panels and iron hinges and reinforcements.

In central Europe there were two types of cupboards derived from the ark. One type was created by placing one ark with two doors on top of another, thus forming a cupboard with four doors. These were most often from southern Germany. One variation had a post in the middle and drawers on either side. The other type had just two doors that opened down. They were mostly from northern Germany, Flanders, and Burgundy (figs. 270, 271, 274).

The tops were usually flat with moldings, but it was not uncommon to find ones with roof-shaped tops. These had battlements or pinions and gables across the front, decorated with thistle leaves and crockets like the famous Brandenburg cupboard (fig. 275).

The same different types of decoration were found in the credenzas, benches, chairs, and beds. The popular types of tables had two legs at either end with openwork decoration and connected with thick boards or pegged crosspieces. Sometimes they had panels that connected the legs in the middle in the form of an "H". They were decorated with low carvings and traceries.

They were all very rugged with drawers along the sides. Perhaps the most interesting were those from Tyrol. Polygonal or circular shaped tables rested on crossed legs of stylized silhouette or on a single pillar (figs. 253, 254, 557).

Mudejar carving on the front of a cupboard in the Cathedral of Leon

Drawing of figure 217

Also in Tyrol there were very interesting and graceful beds. The wooden dais reached to the middle of the bed.

Furniture was still rough and heavy well into the Middle Ages. They were simple objects embellished with carvings, paintings, and appliqués. The carpenter built them to meet particular needs; it was the work of the sculptor, ironsmith, or goldsmith to beautify it. Even in Scandinavian furniture from the 16th and 17th centuries we can observe the same features from central European medieval furniture.

It is still hard to find unity in interior composition. Individual items were very interesting but there was no overall pattern. This was because furniture was still not considered very important. It would not be so until the height of the Renaissance in the 18th century.

The Gothic style corresponds to a period of sharp contrasts. It was a period of spirituality and feudalism into which the new ideal of nationality penetrated. For this reason there can be no miraculous resurrections. The materialists and democrats of the 19th century sought to copy the Gothic style but were utterly incapable of capturing its essential universalistic spirit.

RENAISSANCE

It is very difficult to set a date for the beginning of the Renaissance. The historian, sociologist, and art critic all have different points of view and come to different conclusions about periods of history.

For Vasari the Renaissance was the period following Gothic embracing the second half of the 15th century to the end of the 16th. For Hauser, in his *Social History of Literature and Art*, the Renaissance began in the second half of the Middle Ages, about the end of the 12th century "when the money economy was revitalized, new cities were born, and the bourgeoisie acquired their own character".

From our standpoint in dealing with the history of furniture, a minor art dependent of architecture and social setting, the Renaissance was the period of powerful nation states and new discoveries. It was the time of humanism and the study of classical art, the power of Popes and the Reformation, and the growth of bourgeois cities in Italy.

It was at this time that palaces replaced castles. The *comuni* and *podesta* organized society and gave a great impulse to art, industry, and commerce.

A new kind of house gave rise to a whole new set of needs, including entrances, drawing rooms, dining rooms, bedrooms, and servants' quarters. All the rooms became better proportioned, more balanced in size in relation to their use, and more human.

A fresh interest in art, philosophy, and science was revived. Without the printing press progress would have been much slower. But with its invention the humanist culture and new discoveries in science and exploration were quickly spread. Some historians such as Voltaire affirm an essentially irreligious nature of the Renaissance. This is not altogether true. There was a sincere religious background to this period. It was a time when the clergy came under attack, but not the Church itself. Budack also qualifies the idea that the Renaissance was a return to Paganism, and Neumann affirms that it actually originated from a vigorous Christian education.

We could say that the Renaissance of the arts was evidence of the triumph of Christianity. Christianity at this point incorporated the beauty associated with the now extinct Paganism into the fold of Catholicism, just as Pagan philosophy had already been incorporated. Menéndez Pelayo says that Saint Thomas sought to Christianize Aristotle. Chesterton says in his book about this saint that he "baptized" him.

The Renaissance was essentially an Italian

phenomenon. Not only economic and social causes bore upon it, but also the enormous impulse and personality of the cities. As we already pointed out, Gothic art and architecture was not as fully assimilated in Italy as on the rest of the continent. At the same time she never lost her Classical tradition.

Another cause was the deep crisis which the Gothic style experienced once the circle from Romanesque to the superficial and exagerated Gothic of the mid-15th century was complete.

These characteristics can be reduced to a simpler formula when dealing with furniture, keeping in mind of course the dangers of simple formulas. We could say that in the Renaissance the naturalism and personality which had appeared in the Gothic period came to the forefront. Previously, furniture had been vertical, perhaps reflecting the spirituality of the times. Now it was horizontal, expressing Classical serenity.

Geometric and symbolic decoration gave way to more natural and Pagan carvings.

Gothic furniture was mostly religious—choir stalls, abbot's chairs, faldstools, church cupboards and benches. Civic furniture was born with the Renaissance and its importance increased rapidly. The study of models and prototypes previous to the 15th century was very difficult because of the scarcity of examples. But from the 15th century on there are abundant examples of great beauty and in excellent condition. In fact we have whole interiors still intact which permit us to study objects in their own environment. We shall begin our study then, with Italy, the cradle of the Renaissance. The models which would later be imitated all over Europe were first found here.

ITALY

The tradition of Classical art was never altogether lost in Italy. Nor was the Gothic spirit as fully assimilated in Italy as in the rest of Europe.

Archeological findings generated a great admiration for ancient Greece and Rome. At the same time the interest in improving cultural, scientific, and civil life furthered the humanistic and philosophic movement which had begun in the 12th century. This "resurrection" began in Tuscany long before the rest of Europe. The best example of Proto-Renaissance is the pulpit of the baptistry of Pisa. It is the work of Nicholas Pisano (1260) and bears clear classical forms.

Florence was the first of the Renaissance cities. It was a center of tremendous artistic and cultural importance. It is amazing the number of artists who worked there during the 14th, 15th, and 16th centuries. Naturally the same forces and tendencies bearing upon the major arts also influenced furniture making, a minor art dependent on the major arts. Just as in the other arts, furniture retained some of the characteristics of decadent Gothic in this period of transition.

Around Florence these same ideas were developing in other cities like Mantua, Ferrara, and Urbino. Venice was a city with her own particular personality. Her location on the coast and her long time sea traffic with the east helps to explain something of her peculiar types of decoration. But Venetian furniture was especially noted for one characteristic, sobriety. Around 1500 the center of artistic interest moved from Florence to Rome due to the enormous influence of the Papal court. Sixtus IV (1471–84) and Julius II (1503–13) were very influential, but it was the Papacy of Leon X (1513–21) that marked the high point.

The carvers were the only artisans of the Gothic period. Now they were aided by other artists in decorating furniture. Furniture objects were now embellished with many new techniques besides carving, which was practically the only decoration of the Middle Ages. Artists in the 14th and 15th centuries completely covered the front of *cassoni* and cupboards with their paintings. Choir stalls were decorated with geometric marquetry. Panels were covered with *certosini* in pictorial compositions of colored wood including stories and landscapes. Some examples are the views of cities in the choir loft of the Convent of Saint Helena in Venice, in the chapel of the Palace of Siena, and in the chairs of Monte Olivetti, etc.

From the middle of the 15th century on, new decorative motifs taken from Classical antiquity began to be used. They were done by real sculptors and painters who did not hesitate to undertake these lesser works of art.

This was a time of maturity in the arts. Artists were better prepared; architects were also painters or sculptors and sometimes both. All kinds of objects, including those for personal use were made by artists or at least inspired by them. It is not surprising then that Michaelangelo designed the shelves for the Laurentian Library in Florence (figs. 337, 338) with carvings of B. del Cinque and Ciapino, or that painters of the cuatrocento and cinqueciento collaborated with cabinet makers. The Botticelli panels in the Prado Museum were fronts of *cassoni*. Some works of art bore the artists' signature and today we know the names of many of them. This is especially true of the Carthusian *intarsiatori* such as Fra Giovanni of Verona, Fra Damiano of Bergamo, Pietro da Vallate, and Rafaello of Brescia whose works bear their signatures in the Carthusian monastary of Pavia, in San Miguel de Bosco, and in Monte Olivetti de Siena.

MATERIALS

The wood most used in the Renaissance was walnut. It replaced the coarse, strong oak used during the high Middle Ages. Walnut lent itself well to the delicate bas-reliefs of grotesque and Arabesque decoration because of its pleasant color and quality. Carvings were finished with oil-based mordant to preserve them. Walnut was not the only wood used; pine and cedar were employed when furniture was to be painted or stuccoed. Also oak, chestnut, and other inferior woods were used for ordinary furniture.

During the Renaissance furniture fronts began to be recovered with exotic woods of higher decorative quality. Ebony and holly were popular for their fine grain and, apart from their own beauty, they could be polished to produce a very brilliant surface.

In Italy a kind of marquetry called *intarsias* were used. Materials employed included finely worked metal appliqués, *pastiglia* or plaster and glue applied to gold leaf, and fabric including satin and brocade. Molded and garnished leather became increasingly more common on furniture for seating.

furniture and the first Renaissance works was that the former was purely the work of furniture makers while in the latter such architectural elements as moldings, columns, and arcades were superimposed. These, however, did not achieve real intrinsic value until the style came to maturity in the 16th century.

The profiles of the moldings were identical to those found in classical architecture. They were carefully imitated and herein lies the purity and personality of the furniture. It was always perfectly balanced in structure and decoration, naturally within the norms of the times and characteristics of the materials employed. The constant and careful study of antiquity made the Latin furniture superior to that of the rest of the continent. And Italian artists were in constant demand in all the courts of Europe.

STRUCTURES

Structures were obvious and could be seen from without as part of the overall decoration. Even when a different kind of wood was applied to the surface it was not merely superimposed, but fulfilled a real function. Just as in Gothic there was a parallel between the nervatures and plementaries in architecture and the frames and panels in furniture, so now we find the same similarity between the use of high quality wood overlaying wood of lesser quality in furniture and the use of stone and marble on building fronts over top of other materials. Usually in objects covered with cloth or leather the frame was not seen on the outside. In this case it served simply as skeleton over which the material was stretched.

Furniture was basically rectilinear and horizontal in silhouette though curves sometimes appeared in the tops of the *cassoni* and the backs of chairs. Perhaps this rectilinear aspect expressed the idea of emancipation from the vertical direction of Gothic and announced the new tendency towards the horizontal. But the real difference between the last of the Gothic

DECORATION

Some of the most important decorative motifs of the Renaissance included religious or civic scenes depicted on panels. Sometimes panels were covered with flowers, called *mille fiori*, like Botticelli's "Spring". There were paintings under glass, later called *églomisé*, stuccoes, *pastiglia* pastes, *tarsias*, *certosini*, hard stones, and mosaics. Carvings were done in both high and low relief and Damascene here called *azziminista* work.

As we mentioned earlier, all kinds of artists collaborated in the making of furniture. Painters like Ghirlandaio and Pinturichio, sculptors like Donatello, and architects like Girandolle, Michaelangelo, and others have left excellent examples of their works.

Carvings were real works of art; they were gilt and covered with plaster pastes. A 16th century painter invented a decoration for *cassoni* with white plaster over a gold leaf background. It was a stucco made of plaster and parchment glue. Guido del Conte from Capri used *scagliola*, a plaster paste that could be made into panels that were later carved out in certain places and refilled with other kinds of paste.

Geometric Gothic decoration was gradually replaced by Classical Greek and Roman forms, foliage, arabesque, figures of Hermes, caryatids and putti, meanders, ovals, palmettas, nature motifs, and mythological, historical, and pagan scenes such as weddings and civic processions.

Metal appliqués were made in the form of handles, knobs, and trim. They were hammered or carved and acquired great artistic value.

There was great variety in the shapes of the legs. There were columns and balusters with straight or spiral stria, all of great decorative interest.

Mosaic became an important ornamental element. It was composed of tiny pieces of hard stone and marble usually set in stucco. Florence was the real center of mosaic though it was employed all over Italy and spread to the rest of Europe from there. Mosaic in the form of pieces or sheets of wood was called *certosina* and *tarsia*. The former was probably of oriental origin, introduced into Italy by way of Sicily and Spain. It was usually geometric in design. Larger pieces of wood of different colors were inserted in hollowed out areas of the original material to form stars or other shapes. These *tarsias* made by the *intarsiatori* were real compositions in colored wood. They began in Siena with just black and white, but later the wood was stained in different colors. It was Guido of Verona who first began to shade and stain wood. There are innumerable examples of these *tarsias*.

Furniture was also enriched with inlays of ivory, mother-of-pearl and bone. Some examples can still be seen today. The decoration of musical instruments dating from this period can be admired in many museums in Europe, though this is not part of our study. The Florencian works in engraved steel and Damascene in oriental style are other examples.

The types of furniture used in this period include: the chair with many variations; the *cassapanca*, a precursor of the 18th century sofa; the *cassone*, the most typical item of the Proto-Renaissance and Renaissance; the credenza, writing table; cupboard; beds; and tables.

KINDS OF FURNITURE

Chairs

New types of chairs were developed about the end of the 15th century when Gothic influences disappeared. Generally speaking these new types were named after the poet, painter, politician, etc. who developed them. One example is the *sedia dantesca*, which was really the old Roman curul with the legs crossed like an X. The back and seat were made of brushed satin and richly carved wood inlayed with *certosina*. In Spain this model was known as the hip chair or saddle chair (fig. 302). Another similar type is the "Savonarola chair" (fig. 303) in the same X shape, the sides being made of a series of parallel bars. They usually had no back or just a simple crosspiece across the back. One example is found in Saint Mark's Convent in Florence, in Savonarola's own cubicle restored according to the painting by Fra. Bartolomeo (1498) (fig. 358). Another popular type was the scissor chair with cross braces and the back made as a continuation of one of the legs. They were usually made of pine and painted. Closed or box chairs were very common, deriving from Gothic. There was a kind with a semicircular or poligonal shaped seat and turned rungs rising from the seat to support an armrest. It is called the Andrea del Sarto chair. And there was a Dantesque armchair build on a box which could be used for storage.

Another interesting model was the *sgabello* with an octagonal or square seat. It could be found as early as the 15th century. It had two legs like slanted braces in front and back. It had a highly carved triangular back like the legs. It was similar to the tables with thick carved sides. This model was common in Switzerland, Austria, and southern Germany (figs. 291, 4).

The *pancheto* was like the *sgabello* though more popular and with Medieval overtones (fig. 295). The seat was small and triangular. It had three slanting legs and a triangular back with gouged carvings (figs. 292, 293, 295). Another type with Gothic influence is a folding chair from the Venetian region with strange loops. A few very original examples remain, such as the one in Petrarch's house (fig. 285) after whom it is named. There was an English model called Glawstonbury, though this type was never copied later on.

Chairs were numerous and in the 16th and 17th centuries they were made more and more comfortable. The backs were not so high as the Gothic chairs. They were made like arcades or carved. Sometimes both the back and seat were upholstered and there was an ornately carved crosspiece across the front. The legs were straight and square at first but in the 17th century they were turned. Some of these were like the Spanish *frailero* owing no doubt to the political influence Spain exerted over Italy in the 16th century. These types are especially interesting because they served as models for chairs all over Europe at this time.

Near the end of the period the number of upholstered chairs increased. Satin was decorated with gold braid fastened with nails. Isolated Baroque motifs appeared in the carvings on backs and crosspieces, but the structures remained the same, clear and straight.

There is one type which has no relationship to any of the other models. It is a chair in a painting on the interior of Carpaccio, of St. Jerome in his cell. A similar example is preserved in Milan collection (fig. 286). It has no known antecedents among the Classics.

After the chair came the *cassapanca*, precursor of the 18th century sofa and widely used in the 16th century. It was similar in structure to the cassone. It was an ark with wooden arms carved like acanthus leaves. Its horizontal lines were very classical. It was very luxurious and was often found on a platform and the back was divided into two panels. Without arms it was an arkbench, another derivative of the ark or *cassone* (figs. 296-299).

Tables

There were many different kinds of tables. Some were of a regional character like the ones from Tuscany and Umbria, severe and proportioned, others from Liguria, richer and more ornamental. There were rectangular, square and even octagonal tables. The so-called *bancone* were just a bench with a collapsible back such as we saw in the Gothic table-benches. There were still simple tables resting on X shaped trestles and covered with a cloth. These were gradually replaced by tables with decorated supports. In some of these latter, the supports were cut away and carved. They were connected with crosspieces that passed through them and were pinned like the old Roman stone tables (figs. 301, 306, 307, 308, 309, 311, 313).

Sometimes these lateral supports were separate, but even in this case it is easy to see their derivation from the classical Roman stone tables called *cartibulum.*

Round, hexagonal, and octagonal tables were the precursors of the center tables of the 17th century. They rested on a pedestal shaped like a pillar with feet decorated with corbels, talons and chimeras, caryatids, and atlantes, or on feet connected with volutes like the tables from Pompeii (figs. 305, 310).

Tables with turned legs began to appear later. They were connected with criss-crossed braces or crosspieces shaped like an H. They often had drawers (fig. 300), and sometimes pendants such as those in tables from Liguria (fig. 313). Other times the legs were square or rectangular shaped like balusters on talons (figs. 309, 312, 313).

Cassone

Florence and Siena were the most important centers for the construction of *cassone.* There were innumerable forms though all patterned after the ark. Ancient Roman sarcophagi made of stone were discovered at this time and the Romanesque types shaped like a trunk were also well known.

They were very simple in structure. The top and base were curved and the legs—if they had them—were usually extensions of the vertical parts of the frame. In other instances the base was a molding that was wider at the bottom. In the 16th century it was raised from the floor on talons (figs. 323, 324). The fronts were

Stipo

carved or gilt and finished with scagliola (fig. 317), or decorated with *tarsia* (fig. 322) and painted with typical scenes of the times, cities, saints, weddings, etc. (fig. 324). These were done by artists like Pinturichio, Ghirlandaio, and others of the Siena school of the *cuatrocento*. Others were completely covered with leather or satin or certosini like those made by the famous decorator of *cassone* Dello Delli. The Florentine *cassone* were more architectonic, sober, and elegant in composition. Those from Venice were more sumptuous, with more carvings, paintings, and rich ornamentation. There were even *cassone* in curved shapes with curved legs slanting inward. The fronts were made like the fronts of buildings and decorated with pillasters, frisos, caryatids, echini, naked children, shields, corbels, medallions, and moldings (figs. 318, 319).

Credenzas

At the height of the Renaissance a new piece of furniture appeared, the credenza. It was a low wardrobe with the drawers at the top made to look like the frieze of the top of a building. It was really something between a wardrobe and an ark. It was rectilinear in shape with architectonic ornamentation like pillasters, moldings, cornises, and baseboards (figs. 336, 339, 340, 341, 342). This type was born in the 15th century during the Gothic period. But now it took on a new structure and a new composition. The doors were separated by striated pillasters. The drawers formed a sort of frieze decorated with triglyphs and sometimes topped with a pediment or gallery at the back of the top.

Wardrobes and stipi

New furniture like desks and wardrobes came more and more into general use. Some examples found in Liguria show an unquestionably French influence. They reflect the same system of decoration and structure, but are of great size. Desks and writing tables showed little originality, being simply variations and adaptations of earlier models. Only at the end of the 16th century did secretaries in two parts with drawers in the upper part appear. The door folded down and there were drawers or other doors inside (figs. 341, 342). But these were really Baroque pieces.

We do not know exactly when boudoirs began to become popular. They were richly ornamented and called *stipi*. Some of them were very famous like one built in the time of Philip III of Naples. It should be considered Baroque, though it bore a view of the city it was built in and of various other European cities. Florence was one of the leading cities in *stipi* making and precious stones were used in decoration. This was more severe in Milan where carved and engraved ivory was more common. They were decorated with mother-of-pearl and painted glass in Venice while in Naples it was common to use mother-of-pearl on top of shell.

The first artist known to have built these pieces was P. Loccio at the end of the 16th century. Girandolle also made a wardrobe for Duke F. de Medici with agatha columns, hard stone appliqués, and miniatures of Florentine ladies.

These wardrobes were very architectonic in form. The fronts reproduced monumental building fronts with cupolas, doors, columns, etc. Later when the Renaissance invaded the rest of the continent while Italy embarked on the Baroque period, these forms were imitated all over Europe (figs. 339, 340).

Carved frame

Beds

Beds in general were simple in structure and covered with drapes and pillows. Some were raised on a platform. The head was composed of an architectural composition of frames and panels like the backs of the cassapanca. Usually they were all one piece and were profusely decorated with gold stucco and carvings (figs. 343, 344).

They were made in straight and horizontal lines like the rest of the furniture. Fancier beds had columns for legs. They had high balusters with gold or polychrome ornamentation holding up a cornise from which the drapes hung.

Some had high heads with arcades topped with a pendant. The hangings were beautiful additions to these structures. They were tapestries (figs. 344, 347, 348).

One of the most elegant examples can be seen in Sodoma's fresco *The Wedding of Alexander and Posanna* in the *Farnesina* of Rome (fig. 346).

Picture and mirror frames, musical instruments, etc. were always real works of art. They were of architectonic composition and were made of very rich materials.

In this chapter we should not fail to mention the engraved Damascene pieces. Their chief centers of production were Florence and Milan. They were oriental in origin and were very popular during the Renaissance. The artisans were sponsored by Francis I, Charles V, and other monarchs. According to Champeaux the most famous Damascene artist was Caprara. Among the best known works of this type are the geographic ark of Milan by the *azziminista* Paolo with drawers of Charles V's Escorial type (figs. 332, 333), and Philip II's secretary, now used as sacrarium in the Monastery of Guadalupe, made by Giovanni Glamin in 1561 (figs. 334, 335).

In the Renaissance the study of furniture becomes more complex and heterogeneous. Artistic construction became richer and more diverse with the new forms and materials. We know the names of the artists of many objects which have been preserved. One name we have not mentioned before is the Barili family who lived and worked in Florence and many of whose works have been preserved in the Vatican. The interiors dating from this period are innumerable; they are composed of furniture and paintings. One such interior is the hall of the College of Changes of Perusa by Dámaso Domenico Tasso and Bencivelli in 1490. Others include the rooms in the Palazzo Vecchio of Florence, the Laurentian Library by Michaelangelo, and a great many more. It would be impossible to even approximate the number of works and names of artist that are known to us. (Figs. 337, 338, 348, 352-358).

SPAIN

Spain achieved political unity under the Catholic Monarchs near the end of the 15th century. Three important events occurred at this time, precisely when the Renaissance was in full sway in Italy. The Moors were defeated and expelled from Granada, America was discovered, and Charles I, grandson of Ferdinand and Isabella received the imperial crown.

At the height of Spain's glory the courts, the Church, and the nobility all sent out appeals to artists from the rest of Europe. These were the men who produced so many of the great works of painting, sculpture, and architecture of the early 16th century. Guas, Siloe, Colonia, Torrigliano, Domenico Fancelli . . . Flemish, French, German, and above all Italians came under the patronage of the nobility. They brought with them all the new currents and ideas of their homelands. At the same time they learned in Spain what belonged to her own national heritage so that after a short time the Spanish Renaissance had characteristics all its own.

On the other hand, Spanish artists who came under the influence of the Renaissance that was spreading and developing all over the peninsular were stimulated to travel to Italy. There they learned Classical culture and came into contact with the great centers of the Renaissance.

Many local schools arose around the Spanish and foreign artists many of whom became nationalized. There was a school in Burgos under the shadow of Siloe, one in Granada under Machuca, and one in Toledo under Covarrubias, architect of the Alcázar, and Villalpando. Berruguete was a painter, architect, and sculptor who lived in the early days of the Spanish Renaissance (1480-1561). On his return from Italy where he worked close to Michaelangelo and was influenced by his teaching, he founded the Castillian school.

We should not forget that along with the now decaying Gothic and the beginnings of the Renaissance the purely national Mudejar art was very much in style at this time. It incorporated in its traceries and inlays decorative schemes belonging to both Gothic and Renaissance styles. The system of stays and panels belonging to the Gothic period, for example, was used by the Arabs who, as a matter of fact, took it as far away as Egypt. They subdivided the surfaces of Mudejar works into small areas with laces and railings. These later gave rise to the pure Spanish paneled furniture.

Another new style called Plateresque was inspired by the filigree work of the gold and silversmiths. We recommend the name of Arfe as an example. He employed a profuse decoration composed of grotesque and arabesque figures, conche shell niches, and columns with rings, strias, or carvings of mythical animals on the capitals all in a composition "a la Italiana". The original Plateresque was completely covered with ornamentation and carvings in imitation of silver filigree which gradually disappeared over the years to arrive at a simpler Greco–Roman architectonic style. During the Renaissance both the Mudejar and Plateresque were soon applied to the industrial arts. Thus there are many objects of furniture either Gothic or later Classical in structure whose decoration is Mudejar or Plateresque. The latter finally disappeared after reaching full maturity, but Mudejar has never completely died out and can still be appreciated today.

After the death of the first architect of El Escorial, Juan Bautista de Toledo, Juan de Herrera was named to continue the work in 1567. This was to have a decisive effect on the architecture during the reign of Philip II, the most important of the Spanish Renaissance monarchs.

Herrera's Humanist education and his close contact with the king played an important role in the development of architecture in general during the second half of the 16th century.

Herrera also designed some of the furniture in the monastery. The sacristy and the bookshelves of the library are made like a single unit. It is one of the most important compositions of this period (figs. 454, 455).

Herrera symbolizes the Spanish Renaissance. The same character that typified his architecture was also passed on to furniture. It was a style that was dramatically inflexible, yet it never lost its simple, strong, and serene beauty. Ortega y Gasset expressed it in the following way, "The curve is not to be conceived of in Castille." Even the furniture most directly influenced by Italy, Flanders, England, or France was sober and serene.

Technique was perfected during the Renaissance though not as well refined as in the rest of Europe. Guild laws controling furniture-making had a lot to do with the way furniture was finished. It changed in appearance from time to time according to the latest fashions. In some cases there was an exagerated imitation of Italian styles. Sometimes cabinets were made to look like little building fronts or architecture models. But in general Spanish furniture conserved a simple structure, covered with naturalistic Renaissance decoration or rudimentary architectural motifs.

The earliest evidences of Renaissance style appeared in the carvings and moldings of religious furniture. There are innumerable examples in choir seats. The one in Toledo done by Berruguete and Philip of Burgundy in 1543 is a masterpiece. Civic furniture, meanwhile did not develop in exactly the same ways all over the peninsula. Gothic forms persisted in the north throughout all of the 16th century. In the south the Moorish influence continued to be seen especially in the decoration of interiors. Caissoned ceilings, plaster decoration, and tiles on the lower part of the interior walls was common in the south, while in the north walls were often completely covered with panels. Likewise the cushions, tapestries, drapes, and cordovans of the southern regions were a reminder of seven centuries of Islamic domination.

Generally speaking the Spanish character fled from what was comfortable and superfluous. Divans and other unnecessary accessories were absent from the Spanish homes. Furniture like the French *dressoir* and the Italian *stipi* were scarce and even the commode did not make its appearance until the middle of the 18th century. That is to say, there were few types of furniture, but each type had many, many variations. Spanish furniture showed little inspiration in its shape and molding, but it possessed great vigor in structure and imagination in decoration. Like all Spanish art, it was dramatic and austere, even rigid, but it always maintained the essential characteristics of dignity and strength.

MATERIALS

The wood most widely used in this period was walnut. Near the end of the Renaissance mahogany reached Spain from the New World before the rest of Europe. Holly and other woods from America were also used as fillers, inlays, and overlays along with shell, ivory, and boxwood. Ebony was used a great deal in the 17th century producing a dark, somber furniture. It was characteristic of the period not only in Spain but also in Flanders and France from which the wood originated. Of course these were not the only woods used. There was an enormous variety of species in Spain. Oak and sometimes evergreen oak, chestnut, and pine were often employed on the east coast, either painted or natural.

Furniture was usually made of wood but just like in other countries there were a group of items made of iron. There were also metal appliqués and openwork iron trimmings laid over satin, found typically on secretaries.

Hard stone, imported from Italy, was not used very much. The few examples, mostly table tops, were the work of Italian artists. Satin and brocade were common. Brass or copper nails were used to hold tapestries in place. Embossed leather was also widely used. It was called "guadamecil" at first, after the town of Guadamés in Africa where it was produced. Later it was called cordovan after the city of Cordova. This became the most important center of its manufacture. Cordovan was used not only to cover chair seats, but also closets and secretaries and sometimes whole walls. It was sold all over Europe where it was used to cover French and Flemish furniture.

This sometimes makes it difficult to classify objects found in different countries.

STRUCTURES

In the 16th century furniture was still vertical and rectilinear with the same rigid Gothic lines. Parchment decoration also lasted until the 17th century in Spain as in the rest of Europe. Only the tops of a few arks were curved in the shape of a tile. Once the Renaissance was more advanced, structures were horizontal and very simple. Technique was perfected and on par with the rest of Europe. Construction was different from Gothic. Objects were more solid. Inferior wood less susceptible to atmospheric changes was covered with other richer, more decorative kinds. Sometimes they were inlaid, other times they were just sheets placed in geometric patterns. The use of finer wood signified an advance in technique because it kept the inferior wood from changing shape with changes of temperature and humidity. It also meant a more economic use of materials since just a thin sheet of the higher quality wood was used without losing any of its beauty. Objects were finished with a light coat of olive oil or wax to preserve them from humidity. The use of stringers and panels was brought to Spain from Flanders, though it had already been used by the Arabs. Some cases of inferior workmanship can be easily detected by the use of nails instead of the perfect joining found in other examples.

We do not find artists who formed shops or schools in Spain like in other countries. Nor did they publish books on design and decoration. Herrera sketched and corrected some of the furniture for El Escorial, but he was practically the only exception. Furniture making lacked direction and this can be seen at times in the roughness and poor technical skill. Only in the seating and drawers of choir lofts do we find real technical direction.

ORNAMENTATION

Spanish Renaissance decoration is tremendously varied. This is true in arabesque and naturalist types from Italy and Flanders, and in the Moorish and geometric of national origin.

The four main ornamental materials used in this period were turned elements, iron appliqués, inlays, and leather or cordovan. Turned elements were used in legs and supports. They included corolithic, striated, balustered, or annulated columns.

Openwork iron or bronze appliqués used in secretaries or beds were interesting and original. They were genuinely Spanish and Portuguese. Inlays were made of bone, conche, ivory, ebony, and bronze. Inlay was developed and used mostly in Andalusia, the region under Arab domination for the longest time. In Granada the "wheat grain" decoration was composed of tiny pieces of bone inlaid in walnut. It is easy to see the origin of Italian *certosini* here and sometimes to confuse the two. There was also work of a similar type in the coffers of Gerona using beech and walnut or boxwood and walnut. The use of bone over walnut was known as *pinyonet* in Catalonia and the Levant. When larger sheets of bone were used they were carved with Renaissance motifs. Generally speaking, inlays employed naturalistic, arabesque, or grotesque forms like the Italian *tarsias*.

As we mentioned earlier, embossed and painted leather was used not only to finish furniture, but also to cover whole interiors, including floors and walls.

KINDS OF FURNITURE

Chairs

There are innumerable examples of chairs and benches in existence today. Some have been preserved and are of great historic and artistic interest. Others can be seen in paintings.

The most expressive Spanish armchair is the so-called *frailero*. It was known in America as the "mission chair". There were French and Italian models contemporary with and perhaps deriving from the Spanish. There were a great many different variations of this chair in the period we are dealing with and in later periods.

In fact they are still being manufactured in the 20th century. We shall point out its chief characteristics and include various examples in the graphic section. (Figs. 359, 360, 368-372).

The legs were almost always square, not turned. Sometimes they were decorated very simply with bisque, uncut stones, or stria. Often the legs did not reach clear to the floor but rested on flat feet that connected on both sides like braces. The front legs were higher than the seat to hold up the arms. Near the end of the period the arm supports were independent from the legs and formed part of the seat itself. The hind legs were longer and served to hold the back of the chair. At first they were rigid and straight, but later they were slightly curved for greater comfort. And, lastly, the front legs were connected with a crosspiece that was usually decorated, sometimes in Mudejar style distinguishing it from the Italian and French models. (Figs. 368, 381).

The back and seat of these chairs was usually made of embossed leather, Satin brocade, or some similar material. They were held in place with large bronze nails made in many different shapes. They ranged from simple hemispherical and square shapes to cobras, shields, and eagles, etc. They often had ball or jug-shaped bronze appliqués on the tops of the back legs. A beautiful example can be seen in El Greco's portrait of San Ildefonso in the Illescas Hospital (fig. 398).

The arms of the simplest monachal types were broad and flat. Near the end of the period they were narrower and always ended in a volute as though the arm was rolled up at the end. Many *fraileros* were collapsible—perhaps we should say folding. They had small pins that connected the crosspieces with the sides (figs. 382, 383).

The classical Italian "Dantesque" armchairs still had a certain Gothic character especially in the cut of the legs. They soon became more natural in form and were covered with Granadine inlays. They were named after Charles V or called hip chairs. The seat and the back, which was very narrow, were made of leather and nailed to the legs. They had no frame so that the chair could be folded. The legs had a "block foot" that rested on the floor. Some of the English models were patterned after the *fraileros* taken to England by Philip II for his marriage to Mary Tudor.

Chairs varied a great deal from region to region. In Catalonia and Aragon, for example, it was common to see arcades in the backs of chairs, an obvious Italian influence (fig. 386). In the north and mountain regions the back was quadrangular with gouged carvings of popular motifs like circles and stars. A typical chair from Majorca had a high back, though this type might well be classified as Baroque. French models exerted very little influence over Spanish chairs. There are a few isolated examples of so-called *caqueteuse*. Between the end of Renaissance and beginning of Baroque the Portuguese chair appeared. It had a high embossed leather back, curved and stilted, turned legs, and S or C shaped crosspieces with early Baroque carvings. They were exported to France where they had an influence on the Louis XIII and Dutch styles. These models will be seen in the chapter on Spanish and Portuguese Baroque.

The most important benches were made for churches, town halls, and private palaces. Some of them were collapsible and the back folded down on the seat (fig. 384). Others had leather backs with cushions in the shape of conches, rhomboids, braids, etc. (fig. 387), carvings, or openwork metal appliqués. Other types still had arcades like the traditional Italian chairs. In almost every case the legs were similar to table legs, shaped like lyres and ending in volutes with metal braces (figs. 384, 390). There are so many interesting and beautiful examples of these different types of chairs and benches in Spain that it is very difficult to make a selection. We have picked out the most expressive of both chairs and benches. Among the first is the one named after the Archbishop Salassar (fig. 360) from the beginning of the 17th century. It is a typical "frailero" embellished with appliqués of painted glass imitating precious stones and marble inlaid in the legs. The upholstery is made of red velvet garnished with bronze nails. Another "frailero" was used by Philip II in his travels while the Monastery

Majorcan chair

was being built (figs. 362, 365). A scissor chair of the old curule type (fig. 361) with Renaissance carvings is said to have belonged to Charles V. For an example of benches we have included one named after the Medinacelli (fig. 391) built by Adrian Lombart in 1553. Its structure is massive and vertical with the lower part closed like a chest, all very typical of the Gothic period. But the carvings on the panels are beautiful examples of Plateresque art.

Tables

There are many kinds of tables but the most common was a long rectangular one called the "refectory" table because it was used in the convents. The top was a single thick plank which was completely smooth on the edges. (Tables that have carved edges may not be genuine according to observations by H. D. Eberlein and Ramsdel.) Below the top there were drawers that were inset somewhat and carved. The legs were thick, straight, and turned with many different profiles, connected with crosspieces forming an H or a square. Other times there were six or eight legs sometimes connected in pairs like the contemporary French type, the most typical of this style. Often the legs were oblique in relation to the top and connected in pairs with crosspieces that were also turned. The top was held secure by two S-shaped iron braces crossed like an X. There were three kinds of iron braces, simple (most common), double, and forked. The last two belong to the Baroque (figs. 393-404).

The table in the Cathedral of Gerona

Small tables (70 × 45 cm × 50 cm high) were typical of Toledo and Granada. They were decorated with inlays of fine wood, shell, ivory, bone, etc. These models were copied as late as the 19th century. The simplest of these tables, usually made of pine and somewhat smaller, was used as a salting board for salting and preparing meat.

There was the so-called "lyre Table" similar to the one with slanting legs. It also had braces and belonged to the end of the Renaissance period influenced by the Louis XIII style.

There is a famous table in the Cathedral of Gerona with legs like chair legs which show the beginning of the evolution toward Baroque.

Some of the tables with braces were collapsible. Once the braces were unscrewed the top and legs could be folded up. A well known example of this type of table belonged to the duke of the Infantado. It had an inlaid top on straight legs with bronze hinges etched or engraved. These portable tables were used for travel or in the country (fig. 397).

But these are not all the types of tables that existed. There were others with thick carved sides showing a marked Italian influence. Round and octagonal models were even more obviously Italian in origin. The last type we shall mention were the dressed tables. They were partly or completely covered with damask, velvet, or leather. Some of them are preserved in Philip II's rooms in El Escorial. They can often be seen in the paintings of the great artists of the period—Velázquez, El Greco (in the painting of San Ildefonso, in Illescas), and Titian's portraits of Charles V and Philip II.

Arks and secretaries

In Spain just as in Italy, arks and coffers were the most common furniture during the Renaissance. They were an indispensible item and they varied from region to region. The most popular and best known were from the north. In Asturias they were made with feet to keep them free from dampness. In the northwest they were often built on platforms or baseboards. They bore traditional carvings in geometric shapes made with a gouge. They were typical of traditional art all over Europe. Other interesting arks were from the Levant and Catalonia. The later were of better technical construction. The inside of the top was usually decorated with paintings and carvings and there was a second top so that the first could be left open to serve as decoration. The so-called "bride's chest" had a little compartment with a side door for jewelry. The technique, composition, and decoration of the arks from the eastern regions were similar to Italian models in moldings, paintings, inlays, and double arcades on the fronts (fig. 340).

Some were carved, some were sgrafittoed,

some were inlaid; some were made like trunks and others were covered with leather or fabric (figs. 405, 406). If they were covered with leather it was held in place with bronze nails in flowered or simple geometric patterns. Cloth covered arks had velvet or silk braid around the edges. The braid was usually held in place with hemispherical nails. We should also mention the Castillian arks, with wickets, painted Majorcan models, and the Andalusian types which were often leather covered.

Other types of furniture should be considered as derived from the ark and cupboard. They include sideboards, shelves, wardrobes, etc. It is a pity that so few genuine examples are left. Most of the ones we have are made of different parts of other furniture, and especially of the altar pieces of the many Spanish churches.

An authentic Spanish contribution to furniture was the *bargueño*, a kind of secretary. There are two versions of where the name came from, though it is not of great importance to us. One is that the *bargueño* was first made in Bargas, a town in the province of Toledo. The other is that it was first made by a cabinet maker in Toledo named Vargas. What we do know is that it is an object without architectonic antecedents and that it is of Moorish origin.

There are many variations, but they can be grouped into three main types, *frailero*, bridged legs, and table with braces. The *bargueño* was very easy to move about and may well have been invented to keep money and jewelry. Another characteristic is that it has no moldings on the outside; all the decoration is in the interior. There is a clear parallel here with the Arab houses. There were utterly plain on the outside but richly decorated on the inside. Another evidence of the extent that the Arab decorative spirit had penetrated Spain.

In spite of the later Baroque and Neoclassical reactions, the *bargueño* is still being made today. It may adopt modern decorative modes, but its basic shape has not changed. In other cases it is constructed exactly as it was built in the 16th and 17th centuries.

The upper part, or coffer, had the following characteristics: box-shaped, with one side that folded down and rested on two arms that could be pulled out of the lower part. It thus formed a table that would be used not so much as a desk as place to put the things that were taken out of the "box". The interior was composed of a whole series of pigeon holes, drawers, and doors. Sometimes they were secret or disguised. They were decorated with a tremendous variety of drawings, carvings, and polychrome. The most common were divided into doors and drawers with little columns made of carved bone. There were Renaissance moldings and split pendants ending in volutes. The subdivisions looked like little doors. They bore tiny corolithic and striated columns. The overall effect of the decoration reveals an unquestionable Moorish background (figs. 429, 436, 438, 444).

This was the most common sort of decoration in the interior of the *bargueño*, but there were others that were carved in Renaissance motifs or covered with Mudejar inlays or Italian *tarsias*. Even less common were paneled fronts, vermicular carvings, Gothic–Mudejar geometric openwork carvings over wood or velvet, and embossed leather. The variations, of course, were innumerable. They often had no cover and rested on little onion-shaped legs. These were called either *bargueños* or *contadores*.

As time passed and partly due to Italian influence, the fronts took on a more architectonic composition. Columns, moldings, panels, galleries, etc. were made of richer materials like engraved ivory and ebony, shell, and bronze. These particular characteristics serve to classify these objects in the Baroque period. Once the top was removed, we can see a similarity to the French *cabinet* or the Italian *stipo*, which were very highly developed in the Baroque period.

The most classical outer cover of the *bargueño* was made of walnut, flat, stuccoed, and decorated with iron trim. Some of the iron parts were purely decorative, for example the nails around the frame of the cover (remember that the cover fit into the frame and did not cover it). Other parts were more functional, including locks, angle braces, and handles for carrying. Often the outer cover was decorated in the same style as the interiors we have

Philip II by Titian

already described. We mentioned earlier that there were three types of lower part of the *bargueño*. The first, known as *frailero*, was like a chest or low credenza with four drawers or doors. They had simple, geometric carvings either chiseled or openwork, similar to the decoration of the interior. They were either gilt or polychromed (fig. 436).

The second type, called bridged legs, consisted of a stand or table with six vertical elements. The outer ones had a balustrade, Plateresque, or striated column profile. The inner ones were like cololithic columns which were connected with an arcade. The whole arrangement formed an H shape or a bridge from which the name was derived (fig. 429, 431).

The third type was a table with slanting legs and crossed iron braces (fig. 430) in classic Spanish style. All the doors and drawers had iron or bone handles in different shapes or sometimes leather straps. The *bargueño* named after Charles V reveals the transition of this model into the cabinet, with clear Italian and Burgundy influence. The top was flat and collapsible. It had iron trimming and the frame was decorated with classic moldings superimposed figures of warriors and other important people in rough carvings called *bambocci* (dolls). The interior was decorated with naturalistic Renaissance carvings. It was made entirely of walnut without polychrome (figs. 427, 430).

This is a brief description of the *bargueño*. It had many more variations, some of which are shown in other monographs and articles. Some really striking examples belong to private collections. We have tried to give a good selection of examples in the graphic section.

Credenzas

It is easy to see that the wardrobe or cupboard was derived from the chest. In Spain there are some in which it is even more obvious than in the *bargueño*. The *frailero* closet usually had a third part on top. It often had openwork doors with balusters—an obvious Moorish influence—and was topped with a pendant. The composition is quite imperfect, but it is very interesting as a transition to what we would really call a wardrobe.

This type of closet with the openwork doors was usually used for a cupboard. They were chiseled with a gouge or had railings and wicker doors. The lower part had four large doors, and sometimes drawers in the middle part (fig. 428).

In some cases the transition from late Gothic can be seen in parchment folds in Plateresque panels. There are some later models with French and Flemish type Renaissance carvings but which still have parchments on some of the panels and almost always have balusters on the upper part (fig. 422). The Plateresque with carvings on the panels, half balusters on top of the frames, and even some with pendants are not very common. Chests of drawers and sacristy cupboards are more common, like those from Paredes de Nava, Huesca, Tuy, or the famous one from the sacristy of Toledo with carvings by Gregorio Pardo in 1540 (figs. 416, 435, 419).

Credenzas or *taquillones* were models derived from the cupboard and the ark. We have two examples in the Archeological Museum (fig. 428). Another model was the chest-wardrobe the most famous of which is the one from the chapel of the Condestable in Burgos (fig. 409). It has beautiful carvings from the Berruguete school. They are not only religious pieces, but we also have interesting examples of cupboards used in the Councils of cities like Huesca and Mérida.

The *taquillón*, the lower part of the *bargueño*, was a piece something like cupboard or credenza with drawers or doors with brackets or modillions on the frame (figs. 423, 424).

In conclusion we shall name just a few cupboard combinations which are especially interesting. One is the reliquary-cupboard in the Convent of the Incarnation, a beautiful work dating from the 17th century. It is made with very simple classical lines. Its only decoration consists of bronze nails shaped like stars. All of the panels are covered with lignum. It is perhaps one of the best works of the period though it is very little known because the convent is cloistered. Another earlier and more expressive combination belongs to the library of El Escorial. It was designed by Herrera himself and built by such eminent Italian and Spanish cabinet makers as J. Flecha and Gamboa. It consists of a set of shelves built into the walls forming "the most gallant and well treated piece that has been seen in this type of library" (P. Sigüenza, *Early History of the Monastery of El Escorial*). Besides walnut they used mahogany, acacia, ebony, cedar, orange wood, and tamarind. It is Greco–Roman style with sober, strong, serene lines.

Beds

Beds did not really become important until the Baroque in the 17th century. In the Renaissance the most luxurious ones were completely covered with brocade, embroidery, and rich hangings from a canopy like French and Italian beds. The more modest ones had neither canopy nor hangings but were covered with embroidered cushions. These were typical of the region around Toledo (fig. 446).

There were legs that rose above the mattress like columns or Plateresque posts (figs. 448, 449). In other cases the posts were just round. The most highly decorated boasted an architectonic headboard with pendant and arcades (fig. 446). Some of the Herrerian type ended in balls or pyramids like acroteria.

There are interesting examples of covered beds in El Escorial. Among them is one belonging to Philip II with rich tapestries, the Infanta Isabel Clara Eugenia's (known as the "bride of Europe"), and one kept in the Museum of Decorative Arts (fig. 457), perhaps of Italian origin. Near the end of the period when the heads were solid and painted, they were sometimes independent from the rest of the bed, built into the wall.

Other furniture

Interesting mirrors with thick ebony frames date from the end of the 17th century. They had ripply wavey moldings of Flemish origin with ivory, shell, and coral incrustations and fillets and metal interlaceries, though they were never as impressive as the Italian ones.

Thus far we have described furniture made of wood. But we must not leave out a large selection of iron furniture that was represented in Spain as well as in other countries. One example is the bed of Cau Ferrat in the Museum of Sitges with stylized posts, a pendant decorated with volutes at the head, and forged iron columns. This bed may have come from Italy (fig. 454).

There were tables with legs and crosspieces made of iron holding up marble or hard stone tops. Some had perfect, classical profiles.

And yet all these things were not sufficient to satisfy the appetite for luxury of the nobility. Much more furniture was imported from other countries. The number of cupboards and writing tables from Germany (Nuremberg being one of the largest centers of production) was so great that royal intervention was sought to protect the local industry. This was granted by Philip III in 1603.

As we have seen in this quick survey, Spanish furniture was vigorous and severe with little grace and delicacy of lines. Its dark color—whether the wood or the dark stain—gave it an air of sadness. Even in France the Louis XIII style under the influence of a Spanish queen bore this same melancholic note. But from it emanated great solemnity and dignity.

It is difficult to choose from among so many examples but we must not go beyond the limits of a chapter. The names of carvers, joiners, chair makers, etc. are known to us from the old archives. (See *Spanish Arts* by Riaño, giving names of artisans from the 16th and 17th centuries taken from the archives of the Academia de San Fernando; the *Dictionary of Sevillian Artists* by Gestoso; documents of the cathedrals of Toledo, Sedano, Zarco del Valle, Sigüenza, Valencia, Granada, etc.). Yet Spanish furniture was generally speaking impersonal and names appear only on the most important works. There is a painted cabinet, for example, in the Victoria and Albert Museum in London signed by Pinodo in the 12th century.

"Bargueño" cupboard with lattice doors, topped with a pendant

In ecclesiastical documents, on the other hand, not only the designers of the choir lofts are recorded, but even the inventors of drawers and cupboards in the sacristy. This is true of the Cathedral of Toledo, El Escorial by Juan de Herrera, and the sacristy of the Cathedral of Jaén made by the Valdevira in 1576.

At the turn of the 17th century the Renaissance did not die, but a reaction to its affectation began to set in. This spiritual restlessness had its outlet in all of the arts. With Calderón and Góngora, Velázquez and Ribera, Churriguera and Tomé, Gregorio Fernández and Salzillo a torrent of Baroque was let loose.

It is very difficult to find a Renaissance interior in its original state. Most of them in existence today are restorations done with a greater or lesser artistic sense, but all very subjectively.

The library of El Escorial is probably the only perfect example. Philip II's rooms in El Escorial, the Afuera Hospital of Toledo (figs. 450, 451, 452), the houses of Santillana del Mar, the Castillian and Andalusian houses and palaces, Lope de Vega's house in Madrid, and the rooms in the palaces of Segovia, etc. are all arranged on the false criteria of the Renaissance lived in the 20th century, if they are not the conventional restorations based on studies in the 19th century.

FRANCE

France was the first country to adopt the Italian Renaissance. The style began in France with the appearance of new ornamental themes in the Gaillon castle built for Cardenal Amboise in 1504. The first artists working under the Italian influence were Collin de Castille and Michelet Guesnon. The style began at the time of Charles VIII and Louis XII and lasted until Francis I and Henry II. The furniture corresponding to their reigns is named after them.

The French kings had a predilection for Italian artists and invited them to their courts. Rosso Rossi and Primaticcio were in charge of the decoration of Fontainebleau; they were joined by many other Italians. The architects Serlio, Cellini, and the famous Leonardo all lived and worked under the patronage of the French king Francis I.

The new Renaissance motifs were brought into France through Genoa and the northwestern Italian provinces. They gradually spread across the country forming small local schools. These can be generally divided into two large groups corresponding more or less to north and south. In spite of this strong influence from outside, however, the local traditions were preserved, in some cases for centuries. In Brittany, for example, furniture was still being built in the 17th century like it was in the 15th, and in the 19th century as in the 17th.

The first movements toward Renaissance under Francis I were copies of Italian art. By the time of Henry II it showed true national character. This reached its zenith under Henry IV and ended in the time of Louis XIII. This was the moment of transition to Baroque through Flemish influence.

It was in the Baroque period that furniture achieved its greatest importance. France was the leading center of furniture production until the 19th century. At this time furniture lost much of its artistic value because of industrialization.

We mentioned earlier that the French Renaissance was divided into two large groups, north and south. The first of these groups included the regions of Isle de France, Normandy, Touraine, Brittany, Picardy, Champagne, and Loraine. Here they followed the simple, classical inspiration of the architect and designer Ducerceau. He was a great early artist of the French Renaissance whose main characteristics were proportion, harmony, and sobriety.

The second group was made up of the schools of Burgundy, Lyon, Auvergne, Toulouse, and Midi. They followed the style of the architect Hugo Sambin from Dijon (Burgundy). It was characterized by an abundance of carvings, sculptures in high relief, trophies, warriors, caryatids, etc. It was bolder than the northern school. The famous Burgundy school sent many French artists to Spain. A predominance of Genoese *stipi* can be observed in this school along with a definite Spanish influence due to the constant intercourse between Italy, France, and Spain at this time. It was Ducerceau, however, whose influences reached across the north–south dividing line, mainly through the effect of his book on decorating motifs.

In summary, the northern school was characterized by tactfulness and sobriety while the southern school was known for its fantasy and profusion of carvings. The types of wood that were used had a lot to do with this. Walnut was used in the south; it is maleable and easy to carve. The oak used in the north was stronger and more difficult to work. On the other hand, the art introduced by the Italian artists brought to France by the kings did not affect the traditional structures and techniques at first. Only after much time had passed did they evolve into the new style.

Finally, after so many years of transition, architecture and the arts in general had renewed themselves in the same spirit as life and customs. All of the decorative and compositional elements preferred in Rome were now employed by those who sought to revive classical art. Thus a profound change developed in furniture. Bas-relief, ancient Pagan gods, chimeras, and trophies were revived and the

Carvings in Gaillon Castle

fronts of furniture were converted into miniature building fronts.

In the 15th century other artists besides Ducerceau and Sambin made their influence felt. Among them were Jean Goujon, a famous sculptor, author of the Diana of Poitiers; Philibert Delorme, architect and engraver; Delaune, architect and decorator, and J. Vizé, architect for the king of Navarre in 1570. He was partly responsible for the Castle of Pau and he exerted as much influence in Toulouse and the region of Midi as Sambin himself. But it was Ducerceau who was so familiar with the new decorative motifs of the period that practically all of them appeared in his book on the subject. It is hard to establish the particular style of an artist many times because there were so many of them and their frequent journeys brought them in contact with furniture in many different regions.

MATERIALS

Walnut was mostly used in the southern regions. In the north the main wood continued to be oak. The influence of the materials on the characteristics of the schools is unquestionable in terms of technique.

Near the end of the Renaissance the use of ebony became widespread. From it came the modern Spanish word for cabinetmaker, "ebanista". It was enriched with incrustations of other kinds of wood, ivory plaques and appliqués, metal, etc. Also tapestry was used with ever greater frequency just as in other countries.

STRUCTURES

The fronts of furniture were made to look like building fronts. Composition was very often truly architectonic. The fact that the initiators of the new movement were architects and some of them were also sculptors probably had a lot to do with it. Among these latter were Ducerceau, Delorme, and others. At first furniture continued to be straight and rigid, conserving Gothic forms, with the new ornamentation superimposed. The fronts were subdivided with moldings, columns, and pilasters. Structures were simple and strong. The stringers and uprights were columns, pilasters, and caryatids. The horizontal railings and cornices were decorated with classical panels. There was always a pendent and the whole was constructed in perfect symmetry. Also, the joints and angles which had always been flush were now mitered making them appear less rigid and more decorative.

It was at the end of the period in France that cabinetmaking was really born. This occured when oak was replaced by walnut and other richer and finer woods like ebony. At the same time other types of ornamentation came into vogue, such as marquetry and bronze. This was further encouraged by the patronage of the absolute monarchy.

ORNAMENTATION

Decoration in the first stages of the Renaissance under Francis I preserved much of Gothic ornamentation including folded parchment. But the new motifs used by the Italian artists at Fontainebleau were soon adopted by other national artists. They included columns, caryatids, corbels, classical moldings, arabesques, profiles of heads in dentiled medallions, rosaries, pearls, acanthus leaves, etc. As early as 1515 the niche with a conch shell at the top was in use. Every bit of flat surface on furniture was carved in Renaissance motifs. By the end of the period—1580—carving was bold and exuberant, though the forms were still clearly Renaissance, not Baroque, which is different in conception.

Generally speaking, marquetry was little used in the 16th century while gilding, on the other hand, was used in excess. Painting was only used to reinforce the relief of the carvings. Decoration was always symmetrical—acanthus, olive, and laurel leaves. These were copied from Roman monuments at first and later substituted with stylized local vegetation. Fauna was almost always of a fantastic nature, including caryatids, chimeras, griffins, naked children, horns of plenty, etc. The exagerated difference in scale among these different elements came to be one of the characteristics of the style.

KINDS OF FURNITURE

Just as the large rooms in the Gothic castles served as halls and general living quarters at the same time, so at the outset of the Renaissance the bedroom, dining room, and great hall were a single unit. This naturally influenced the creation of new types of furniture.

Chairs

Furniture for seating followed the lead of Italian and Flemish types, though not as elegant and fine as they. Carvings of medallions and arabesques were common on the backs of chairs (fig. 460). The so-called *caquetoire* was very expressive. It originated in Lyon and was imitated in England (figs. 464, 465, 467, 468, 469, 473) in the Shakespeare chair, in Italy, and in Spain, one of which is called Calvin's chair. Chairs began to be more comfortable in the 17th century because the arms, seat, and back were padded and upholstered with cloth or leather.

Another type was the *vertugadin* chair without arms or with very short ones. This was to make it easier to sit on. Women at this time wore wide skirts (*vertugadin* in French) and needed wide seats without obstructions (fig. 467). At the end of the 16th century the arms of the chairs were not horizontal but gently curving (fig. 470).

Tables

Tables were luxurious. They were typically long with four turned legs and crosspieces shaped like an H. There were other turned parts like pendants hanging from the edges. The legs were grooved like columns. Most tables were inspired in Ducerceau's model (figs. 480, 481, 483). On the other hand, another type with two *trapezophri* on talons resting on a flat base and connected with an arcade was more typical of Sambin (figs. 475, 478, 482). Ducerceau's sketches in books published during this period contributed to the diffusion of these models (fig. 484).

Cupboards

Other objects in transition were the arks, cupboards (figs. 485, 489, 492), buffets, and dressoirs (figs. 501, 503). The late Gothic types continued to be built incorporating a mixture of Gothic and Renaissance techniques and ornamentation.

Undoubtedly the most interesting and representative furniture of the period was the cupboard with two sections on four feet, subdivided with pilasters or caryatids and topped with a pendant. This was sometimes divided in two, sometimes it was a single piece. The cupboard was very large—especially those designed by Hugo Sambin. The upper part was usually set back somewhat. In the Henry IV period the panels were divided with moldings forming caissons in geometric combinations. They were usually richly carved and often revealed the influence of the sculptor Jean Goujon. He was the most representative French sculptor of the 16th century. French cupboards, many of them drawn by Ducerceau or Sambin, were very interesting because of their rich and varied ornamentation (figs. 490, 491, 493, 500).

Beds

Beds were very complicated. They had columns at both ends and were heavily laden with

Niche and conch shell decoration

drapes. The head was designed like the front of a cabinet. Other famous models besides those designed by Ducerceau were built by Catherine de Medici in the Chenonceaux Castle, one preserved in the Cluny Museum, and one named after Jeanne D'albret in the Castle of Pau (figs. 502, 504, 505).

The interiors of various castles dating from this period reveal rich decoration without the opulence of Flanders and Germany. They are pure and correct in composition with luxurious decoration like the Italian interiors, differing from the rigidity of the Spanish and rough simplicity of the English.

ENGLAND

When the Renaissance was well under way in France, in England Gothic forms and decoration still persisted, including parchment and Gothic traceries. Gradually the new style entered the country, mainly from Flanders. The first to introduce Renaissance forms was the architect Iñigo Jones (1573-1653). Holbein, one of the earliest artists of this period was invited to go to England by Henry VIII where he painted, designed houses, built furniture, and greatly influenced the spread of Renaissance art in general. There is a Tudor cabinet in the Victoria and Albert Museum which is attributed to him.

Modern ornamentation with medallions with floral wreaths and heads in the middle began under Henry VIII. These were alternated with the old Gothic carved parchments especially severe and crude in England. Renaissance art gained complete dominance under Queen Elizabeth (1558) and the last Gothic and Tudor forms disappeared.

This revolutionary artistic movement arrived at its fullness under James I and was called Jacobean. The Palace of Knole is practically a museum of this style. It achieved an even richer expression under Charles I. In spite of its abundant ornamentation at this time it should not be confused with Baroque because it still employed classical straight lines. With Cromwell's republic in 1649 there was a change back to simpler, more modest furniture something like Jacobean. After a few years the influence of Rubens and Van Dyck prepared the way for the Baroque during the reigns of James II and Charles II.

We can distinguish four periods in the English Renaissance: transition under Henry VIII until 1550; Elizabethan or early Renaissance to 1603; Jacobean lasting until the time of Charles I and Charles II with a brief return to simplicity under Cromwell; and the transition toward Baroque under James II in 1685.

Typical features of Elizabethan furniture were architectonic fronts that looked like little building fronts with half circle arches, flat carvings, and highly exagerated turned elements shaped like bulbs and mellons. In Jacobean the arabesques were flat and moldings were superimposed in crossed or X shapes. They demonstrated great purity and expression. The turned parts were very fine and sometimes they applied to furniture in semi-circular and hemispherical shapes.

Carvings were more abundant under Charles I and Charles II. An abrupt change occured in the shape of legs. They were made in S shapes or like two C's one on top of the other facing in opposite directions. They were connected with beautiful crosspieces and the chairs had high backs. Tables and cabinets had human and animal figures on the uprights reflecting a more European influence. The English Renaissance displayed a nascent national consciousness which left an indelible stamp on all its works. On the other hand, they lacked the universal quality found in the Latin countries.

MATERIALS

Oak was used almost exclusively in this period. Later, under Cromwell, (1650), walnut was imported from the south. It was better suited to carving and turning. Other materials, iron, tapestry, and leather, were similar to those used in the rest of Europe.

STRUCTURES

Just like in the Continental Renaissance, furniture frames were horizontal and straight, though rougher and simpler. Bourgeois furniture, which was strictly national, was very simple and found its greatest expression in the 18th century.

The furniture of the court was more luxurious. It was more universal and complex like furniture on the continent. It received its inspiration from there, though it preserved classical serenity.

The constructive elements in Elizabethan furniture were more architectonic, while they were more geometric in Jacobean. They also played a greater part in the general structure of the objects (fig. 514).

DECORATION

In the early Renaissance, in the period of Henry VIII, crowns and medallions alternating with parchment were used for decoration. These were inherited from the Gothic period. Other ornamentation included flat, squarish heads shaped like a nail or pyramid used not only on the fronts of furniture but also in chairs.

Flat carvings called vermicular arabesques were used in the Elizabethan period. Rows of pillars were almost always Ionic with arcades along the top. Fillets were in loops forming circles. Carvings were decorated with sgraffito, engravings were geometrical. Uprights and legs were often turned. The latter were very thick; sometimes they swelled to form a mellon or cup and were richly ornamented with echini, acanthus leaves, and other motifs. They were topped with Ionic capitals, sometimes exagerated like the Ware bed with its thick turned columns (figs. 524, 536, 541).

Jacobean art was more severe and restrained with sober, flat ornamentation and little relief in the carvings. The posts were strong and thick with cup shapes, but not to the same degree as Elizabethan. Turned parts were also carved. The bulbous characteristic so typical of the style probably originated in the Low Countries which had a long commercial relationship with England.

A lot of the roughness and exuberance disappeared in the Jacobean period and perfection was achieved in geometric ornamentation and carvings which were almost like engravings. Banisters were split lengthways and fastened to the posts. Panels bore geometric shapes in L, X, eight-sided, and semicircular patterns. The last were tangential with acanthus leaves in the middle. These four were the most typical patterns of the period (figs. 520, 522, 528).

Near the end of the period spiral shapes began to come into style. This was a result of a closer contact with Portugal. In 1661 queen Catherine of Braganza married Charles II and brought furniture with Solomonic elements with her to England.

KINDS OF FURNITURE

Chairs

Chairs were often imitations of Italian and European models. The scissor chair and the Glawstonbury chair were both copies of Italian types. There were other more national types with vertical elements and turned banisters and balls on the crossbars of the back and legs. They were rather rough and straight in shape. The Yorkshire chair had arcades across the back while the Derbyshire had crosspieces. Both had vigorous silhouettes and were richly carved (figs. 512, 513).

Another type of chair was the so-called "Shakespeare chair". It was the same thing as the French *caqueteuse* or armchair "for talking" (fig. 528).

The Elizabethan chair of the early Renaissance had a thick back with carvings like those on the continent. It had lateral pieces like ears and a fancy top. Armchairs with X legs of curule type came by direct influence from Italy and Spain. The so-called Tudor chairs in the Winchester Cathedral dating from the time of Philip II's wedding are of this type.

During the brief period corresponding to Cromwell's republic the luxuriousness of furniture was noticeably reduced. Chairs were very simple and rigid with turned legs reflecting a Dutch influence. Padded leather was sometimes used in the back and seat. At the end of the Renaissance, after the simplicity of the Cromwell period, the first signs of Baroque appeared in the reign of James II. Chairs were more refined. The high backs were made of lattice or vertical rungs. The crosspieces in front were like double S's or C's and finely carved. The backs were carved or turned.

Seats were made of wood, cane, straw, etc., and very seldom upholstered.

Tables

Tables were mostly long and rectangular with turned legs. The Gothic table on trestles were no longer to be found. When they were long and the legs were bulb- or mellon-shaped there was often one leg at each end or one at each corner.

In the Jacobean period the bulb shape was smoothed out into a normal turned element or at least brought into better proportion and balance. They were connected with long cross-pieces. There were other round folding tables on eight legs, four of them fixed and four that swung on hinges. They were called "gate-legs" and date from the 17th century (figs. 517, 519, 523).

There were tables with a double top that opened up. Others had a single bulb-shaped leg on a base shaped like a cross reflecting an obvious Dutch influence. The "monk's bench" could be found in England as well as on the continent. The back could be folded down to form a table. It was first used in the 15th century and remained in use until the 17th. The best-known and most interesting table from the end of the period was the Charles II table which we have already described. We can observe the influence that the Low Countries exerted on the English styles in the interiors drawn by the Dutch artist Vredeman de Vriese.

Cupboards

At the outset people continued to use the Gothic arks with openwork traceries and rough carvings. Later they were inlaid with architectonic patterns and arcades in the Elizabethan manner. Finally they arrived at the classical Jacobean decoration (figs. 524, 526, 527).

We shall only briefly mention the credenzas, sideboards, and buffets derived from the Dutch cupboard. Their features can be appreciated better in the photos.

At the end of the period wardrobes were built like two arks, one on top of the other. They were like commodes with four drawers or four doors. They were called "tall boys" and were very common in the time of Queen Anne. We shall have more to say about them in the chapter on Baroque. Cabinets were less refined than on the continent.

Other furniture from the same period such as boxes, pulpits for Bibles, and other kinds of cupboards were often simply one table on top of another.

The use of cupboards with incrustations and marquetry of Italian origin began under Charles I. After that the constant Dutch influence led to the creation of new models (figs. 530, 539). Flowered marquetry covered the whole front.

Beds were similar to those on the continent with a high canopy, four columns at the corners, spherical elements, and exagerated dimensions. Among the most famous are the Courtenay bed (1593) in the Victoria and Albert Museum and the Ware bed in Hertfordshire which is over three yards long. The head is like the front of an ark or a paneled wall with arcades and decorated panels. A historic object from this period is James I's cradle built in typical Elizabethan style but with an almost symbolic foreshadowing of the Jacobean style (figs. 537, 543).

The walls of the rooms were covered with paneling to protect from the damp in the same fashion as in the Netherlands. They were very simple with flat carvings, squares, pilasters in classical order, and echini on the cornices. It is interesting to notice that at this time there were no small, intimate rooms. They were forbidden because they tended to be used for frequent conspiracies (figs. 544, 545).

This was the time when English and Dutch expansion was reaching great proportions in North America. These models served as the base for American colonial furniture. These imitations of European styles were less pure in lines but they were simple and graceful with a personality all their own, constituting a genuine colonial style.

Chair with S-shaped cross-pieces

GERMANY

In Germany two main currents can be observed in the development of Renaissance art just as they could be observed during the Gothic period. In the south the Italian influence predominated, entering through the region of Lombardy. Flanders and Burgundy provided the stimulus for the northern Renaissance.

The spirit of the Renaissance, which took on a particular character wherever it was associated with the Reformation, was vitally linked to one man, Albert Durer, the great painter and engraver. His works display universal and objective values, but they never lose the mysterious Germanic character so evident in Gothic. Hundreds of his engravings reveal to us far better than any history book what the interiors of German houses during the Renaissance really looked like (figs. 549, 554).

The general prosperity of city life is reflected in the development of the houses and the luxury of their interiors. Furniture was most highly developed in the great centers in the south, Nuremberg and Augsburg. The architect Flötner introduced new details to this art after a trip to Italy in 1540. At this time he was the most important Renaissance artist in southern Germany. In ornamentation Wenderling probably exerted more influence than anyone else. German furniture is so richly carved that it is perhaps too rich and overladen. It reached its apogy in the regency of the Louises in the mid-18th century. At this time many German artists moved to the French court. The Louis XV style which was so European and so French was often the work of German artists.

MATERIALS

As usual, materials played an important part in the development of the character of furniture. In Germany this effect can be noted even more than elsewhere. In the south they used conifers, spruce, and Spanish fir with linden and ash as filler until walnut began to be used around 1600. Oak continued to dominate in the north until ebony came into use in the 17th century with conch shell and paintings. Damascene and tapestry were also introduced at the same time as in other countries. Other secondary materials included metal, coral, painted glass, and especially amber, along with large sheets of light colored woods and inlays. The use of such diverse materials produced a particularly characteristic furniture (figs. 558, 565).

STRUCTURES

Structures in the south were at first similar to the Gothic cupboards of the end of the 15th century. Flötner introduced not only new decoration—niches, classical columns, Roman moldings—but also the architectonic composition of furniture. The same thing can be seen in Switzerland where the H. S. Company built cupboards in rigid architectonic shapes which later evolved into rich, exuberant types. In the 17th century furniture had lost this architectural appearance. Corners were miter jointed and lines were fluid but continuous forming a unity. Objects were very beautiful and they were authentic works of cabinet making (figs. 557, 564).

Later, in the Baroque period, these forms persisted in some of the more out-of-the-way regions like Tyrol, just as we have seen in France, England, Spain, etc. Meanwhile in the north, Gothic forms like thick panels and lateral stringers were deeper rooted and longer lasting. Parchment took much longer to disappear in this region, doubtless because there was no artist like Flötner, though Cornelius Floris of Antwerp did exert an appreciable influence.

DECORATION

Inlays of light colored wood over a dark background were used in the south. They were introduced from Lombardy. Carvings of flora and fauna in the Italian style abounded. In the north the Renaissance wreaths were delicate, like the arabesques of Rafael, with medallions and profiles of heads alternating with Gothic motifs and later with caryatids and volutes. Around 1600 light colored inlays were popular in the Baltic region. One example is the work of Ever in Lübeck (figs. 565, 569).

The Renaissance had come to full maturity by the year 1600. All of the classic elements of this style were in use until 1630 when the first evidences of Baroque made their appearance. This was when metal and ivory incrustations were first used in furniture in the capitals and volutes. Also the plane began to replace the adz and other rough tools, paving the way for the Baroque. Schwanhard was the inventor of rippled moldings (1620) producing a beautiful decorative effect soon imitated in the Low Countries, France, Spain, and most of all in Portugal (fig. 569).

At the same time the decorative industry employing amber in the north was producing works of real artistic worth as well.

KINDS OF FURNITURE

Chairs

Aside from the faldstools and Roman type scissor chairs, the backs and seats of armchairs were now padded and the equivalent of the Spanish *frailero* was born. In Tyrol there were models similar to the *sgabello*. As an example of a damascene piece in Florentine style we include the curule type armchair of Rudolph II, signed by Thomas Rucker in 1574 (figs. 546, 547, 548, 550).

Tables

The same types of tables as in other countries were built in Germany but they were heavier, like the rest of German furniture. Many of them can be seen in old engravings. There is a group of tables originating in Tyrol (figs. 549, 554, 555).

The ark continued to be used especially in the north were people seemed to particularly value it. There its decoration also continued to be predominantly late Gothic. The best known were made by Ringelink and Gudewerth (fig. 563).

Cupboards

But the cupboard was the real representative of German furniture. Hamburg, Augsburg, and Nuremberg were the leading centers where they were built. In thse cities there were numerous shops where "de Alemaña" cupboards were made for export to Spain where many examples can still be found today. The cupboard with four doors was built like two arks one on top of the other, sometime with drawers between them. Cabinets of Italian origin began to be built in Augsburg. They imitated the Italian models in shape—like little buildings—and in decoration—inlays. Cabinets by Steinhart and Schieferstain were very decorative (fig. 564).

There was another type called the "corner cupboard" in two or three sections. The most famous were made by Walbaum and Hainofer of Augsburg. One was given to Gustavus Adolphus in 1632. Ringelink also built this type of cupboard as well as the famous arks and cupboards of Frensburg. Those by Gudewerth and Pergo are among the best known (fig. 556).

Beds

Beds had classical columns at the corners. The head and the part against the wall were finished with panels. The dais was like a board roof with heavy hangings (figs. 566, 573).

Generally speaking, popular furniture was more original and interesting than bourgeois and courtly types.

The German Renaissance did not have the universal, diaphanous, open character of the Latin Renaissance. It never lost its nation significance and Gothic spirit, nor its Puritanical streak.

Cupboard signed by H. S.

LOW COUNTRIES

Interior of the Neldorf-Holstein Museum

The importance of the Renaissance in Flanders is greater than it might appear at first glance. Her geographic location between Burgundy and Germany, her political ties with Spain, her commercial relations with England, and her vigorous colonial trade gave her a unique advantage in the development of the new style. This took place in three main centers, Antwerp, Bruges, and Liége.

The main protagonists of this vast movement were the Vriendt brothers, Francis and Cornelius, better known by the name of Floris. The first was a painter and the second a sculptor and architect. In all of their works a definite Italian influence can be seen just as on the rest of the continent. At first there was no marked national character.

Furniture, which achieved its greatest importance at the end of the 15th century, had Vredeman de Vriese as its best workman. Many of his works are still in existence today. He also published books on furniture-making that played an important role in his country. The change from Gothic to more architectonic forms was largely due to the impact of his writings.

At the same time national life encouraged the development of the industrial arts. It was a rich bourgeois country where a practical sense was mixed with an appreciation of real beauty well understood by the painters and artists of the period. They produced furniture that still adorns the world famous Flemish homes. They produced a familiar and hospitable atmosphere that can easily be detected in the paintings dating from so many years ago.

MATERIALS

Oak and later walnut were used with great delicacy in the Low Countries. At the height of the Renaissance ebony appeared. Its extraordinary hardness required a refinement of technique that really brought about the birth of what we would consider cabinet-making today.

Other exotic woods such as lignum, imported from the West Indies, were used to cover inferior woods. Other materials included cloth and leather commonly used in Europe, as well as shell, ivory, and engraved and gilt metal.

STRUCTURES

Structures were notably classical, due to the influence of Vriese. Ornamentation was arabesque and grotesque, but it was the lines, composition, and technique that gave the objects their personality.

DECORATION

The first signs of the Renaissance could be observed in details of ornamentation. They included grotesques, echinis, Hermes, etc. All these were imported by the Floris brothers from Italy. They were superficial adornments sometimes made of ebony. Carvings were very fine volutes, caissons, points of diamonds, and corbels. But above all it was the arrangements of the panels that marked the change from Gothic to the new Italian composition with pendants, cornices, columns, and socles, all very architectonic in character.

Other interesting features were the turned banisters alternating with square elements. Round parts were sometimes cup-shaped and the feet were typically carved in tiny leaves. These turned elements gave rise to the Jacobean style in England which went even further in this direction than in the original country. Paintings on doors and drawers and appliqués of other materials such as painted glass were used. They were made to imitate the Italian *églomisé* and *mille fiori*. At the end of the period, marking the approach of Baroque, rippled moldings appeared and were often found in painting and mirror frames.

Walls were often paneled with wood to keep

out the damp. The furniture arrangements around the great central fireplace offered great luxury and beauty. The most striking example is the Hall of Justice in Bruges with its huge fireplace carved by Lancelot Blondel at the end of the 15th century (fig. 591).

KINDS OF FURNITURE

The same types of furniture as in the rest of Europe were to be found in the Low Countries.

Chairs

We shall begin with chairs and arm-chairs covered with velvet or embossed leather fastened with nails. The legs were turned like Spanish chair legs and the back was usually carved with openwork, especially the top. These chairs were exported and imitated in France where they disappeared after the Louis XIII period (figs. 579, 584).

Tables

An interesting type of table was long and had legs and feet shaped like cups. This type was brought to perfection by the English. The Dutch exagerated all these shapes, making the moldings more protruding and the pilasters thicker and stronger (figs. 584, 588).

Cupboards

Buffets and cabinets with moldings and painted appliqués on the doors and drawers were influential in France, Italy, and Germany as well as in England (figs. 589, 591).

The most important piece nationally was the cupboard, both the cabinet type and the one with two doors.

In all the important collections we find various types, many of them signed by Vriese or other cabinet makers. They are garnished and embellished with Italian moldings, painted glass, ebony leaf, hard stone, etc. They have either two or four doors with sturdy columns on either side holding up the cornices and top (figs. 592, 593). They rest on enormous ball-shaped or onion-shaped feet.

Beds

The heads of beds were arranged in a composition similar to the fronts of the cupboards. They were heavy and architectonic with points of diamonds in the center panels. There were thick turned columns at the head and foot to hold up a heavy dais (figs. 594, 595).

The influence of the Flemish furniture was great not only in the bordering countries of Germany and France, but also in England and Spain. To find the origin of many models such as the Louis XIII armchair and cabinet, Jacobean elements, German cupboards, and the caissons and rippled moldings in Spanish and Portuguese furniture we must go to the Low Countries.

Not only were the great halls an expression of the Renaissance but also the small chambers covered with wooden panels and filled with furniture bearing exagerated moldings. They created a simple and pleasant atmosphere reflecting a quiet, happy life.

TRANSITION TO BAROQUE, LOUIS XIII

In the history of furniture, the passage from Renaissance to Baroque gave rise to a very clear transition. This transition, which began in Italy long before the rest of Europe, can be seen in the other countries in similar form, but it was in France where it took on a well defined uniqueness during the reign of Louis XIII.

When the Baroque style was well established, culminating in France with Louis XIV, its strongest influences began to spread out of the country. The Louis XIV style, with its highly national criteria, drew from the purest aspects of Italian and Flemish art and with them achieved a style of furniture design that would later be extended throughout Europe.

The transition in France corresponded to an era impregnated with a certain sadness. Louis XIII himself was a melancholy, tormented person, whose position in history was somewhat obscured by the figure of Cardinal Richelieu. At the end of the Renaissance early in the 17th century, furniture design was opulent and heavy, and gave the impression of being overpowered by mere practical utility. This was not a time of luxury or joyful expansion, and a feeling of austerity and sobriety was present in furniture due in part to the Spanish influence in the person of Anne of Austria, daughter of Philip III. The feeling of the period has been faithfully reflected in the famous etchings by Abraham Bosse (fig. 609) showing a variety of scenes of court and bourgeois life in the 17th century. Up to this time the large rooms of palaces and bourgeois homes were subdivided by curtains and folding screens. But the peculiarity of Madame Rambouillet, who received visitors seated on her bed, extended the custom of placing the beds in a room that came to be called a *ruelle* because of the narrow passageway between the bed and the walls of the room. In the engravings by A. Bosse, we can see clearly the diversity of uses of a single room and the monotony of the furnishings (figs. 609, 610, 612, 613).

Dutch cupboard

However, with Louis XIII the use of more varied pieces of furniture, many of them easier to move around, began and palaces took on new life.

MATERIALS

The woods most commonly used were oak and walnut. But at the end of the reign of Louis XIII ebony became popular and woodworking became a true art form (the word for woodworking or carpentry in French is *ébénisterie* and is derived from *ébène*, ebony; a similar semantic phenomenon occurs in other Romance languages). Marquetry in copper and tin also began at this time, and some examples of this work are still preserved. Fabrics also became important for upholstering furniture and as canopies and hangings on beds.

ORNAMENTATION

Rooms were lighter now than in previous eras because of a greater abundance of windows. Architectural design gave interiors a feeling of greater spaciousness, while in decoration walls were adorned and subdivided with moldings and other design features.

In general furniture was heavy. Pieces made of ebony were greatly sought after for their richness and austerity, to the extent that pieces made of other types of wood were painted to look like ebony. Chairs were also painted black and later gilded. Very typical of the reign of Louis XIII were the looped moldings of Flemish origin, used to adorn drawers and frames. Other chracteristic elements were twist-turned vertical supports and festooned carvings. The turned and tapered legs prepared the way for the monumentality of those of the Louis XIV style. Sharply protruding carvings were the most common form of ornamentation. Many French workers returned from abroad and contributed new techniques and decorative motifs, and the king himself put them to work in the cellar of the royal palace. Pierre Boulle—father of the famous Boulle of the reign of Louis XIV—was one of these, who used delicate tin and shell marquetry work in his pieces. It is now that we see the first curved and split pediments on cupboards, which were also found on Italian buildings at the end of the 16th century and the beginning of the 17th. Twist-turned columns also appear and in general, lines became very broken.

STRUCTURES

In chairs the vertical elements—carved, turned or twist-turned—were joined by similarly shaped and worked rungs. Chair backs were adapted better to the human body and their upholstered seats were more comfortable and softer. The capitoné appeared.

On cabinets we find the so-called French or tambour column, used originally by Philbert Delorme in the Tuilleries Palace.

Cupboards were lower and more practically designed. The tops were curved and the lower parts were widened in a bombé shape, but the structure was still solid and heavy.

Tables gradually became rounded and chairs took on a new elegance with fabric or Spanish leather upholstery. Colors were light and, although they were covered with dark woods like ebony, their Renaissance lines could still be seen.

In sum, in spite of these innovations, furniture design still preserved its unmistakable Renaissance characteristics. But ornamentation and moldings expressed a flexibility of the style toward its Baroque end, a slow and gradual change but at the same time continuous and perfectly recognizable.

KINDS OF FURNITURE

Chairs

With the Louis XIII style we see the beginning of modern, spacious armchairs with square backs, and chairs with festooned moldings that reached their height of elegance in the Louis XIV period. We can identify three types of chairs: those with high, square back and curved arms, called the Louis XIII chair; those with low back and inset arms; and finally, the armless chair, called the *vertugadin*, as in the Renaissance. But there were also other types of chairs with high, narrow cane backs, and others adorned with Cordoban leather, or the classical X-shaped curule chair. The seat widened in trapezoidal form, and the carvings on the front rung are very characteristic. All were upholstered with fabric, embroidered trim or leather with copper nails. The seats were sometimes stuffed with elastic materials for greater comfort (figs. 596, 597, 598, 599, 600, 601).

Tables

The easel table, characteristic of the Gothic and first Renaissance styles, had disappeared and was replaced by heavy, robust tables. The top was supported on columns with square blocks at intervals for mounting. The feet were balls or claws. Some tables had turned hanging pieces on the apron, and others were of octagonal shape with a single center leg. These pieces were usually not gilded; the wood was left in its natural color or painted in a dark color.

Cupboards

Chests had drawers on the front, and we now have the commode which achieves its greatest importance in the 18th century. There were also writing desks or bureaus, some of them very interesting, such as the one belonging to Marshal Crequi, attributed to Boulle's father, with copper and tin inlay. Typical of this period also was the ebony cabinet with silver and shell marquetry, a true specimen of the time, which can also be attributed to P. Boulle.

In the 16th century many cabinets were imported from Germany, and Henry IV of France himself sent Flemish woodworkers to

Bureau of Marshall Crequi

Italy to learn the techniques and rules of the art. The cabinet replaced the dresser and was adorned with the typical looped moldings of Flemish origin. This piece, doubtless the most characteristic of the style, was made up of a chest or cupboard with two doors supported on columns joined together by a shelf across the bottom resting on thick onion-shaped feet. It was entirely covered with rich carvings and looped moldings (figs. 602, 603).

Cupboards were no longer simple square pieces but heavy and ornate, topped with a large crest. The regional specimens were very suggestive, still made of oak with curved panels. Finally, the small bourgeois piece, easier to move around, began to appear (figs. 604, 605, 606, 607, 608).

Beds

Beds were not soft or comfortable as they would be in the 18th century because they had no springs. The most luxurious ones had high twist-turned columns or caryatids on the ends and were covered with rich hangings and plumes. They were very high and were impressive because of their sumptuous appearance (fig. 610).

In this brief overview we have attempted to point out the characteristics of this sad and sumptuous style that, nevertheless, had singular qualities and served as a true transition to the Louis XIV style, which culminated in the Baroque style.

BAROQUE

Rubens' house

This is not the most appropriate place for an in-depth study of the origins of the Baroque style, but we can say at least that the new style was not, like other great spiritual movements, exclusive to the arts but left its mark on all other aspects of life. The cradle of the Baroque style, in architecture as well as in furniture design, was Italy. Its first graphic expressions, at the end of the 16th century and the beginning of the 17th, were isolated decorative elements: rolls, brackets, split and curved pediments, scrolls, sharply turned pieces, etc. Nevertheless, they did not completely lose their Renaissance character.

It was more to the north, in the rolling green fields of the Netherlands, where the Baroque sensitivity of Rubens applied these new forms first to the decoration of his own house in Antwerp in 1613, and later to his other work, thus beginning the new style. First the Flemish and later the Dutch furniture makers captured and rapidly assimilated these original motifs and added them on to Renaissance forms, thinking they were only slight modifications of the familiar forms when, in reality, they were the beginning of a new interpretation of the artistic feeling of an era.

With the gradual transformation of life and the new customs of the bourgeoisie and the court, a new exuberance, richness and comfort was demanded in furniture. This gave rise, for example, to pieces with wide, fluffed and upholstered seats. On the other hand, the perfecting of the technique, the introduction of new materials—exotic wood like ebony, mahogany, lignum—and the creation of new pieces of furniture imposed the new style whose nature was still undecided in the minds of its creators. Little by little Baroque ornamentation, first used in isolation and superimposed somewhat timidly, infiltrated into structures until it became a new form, expressive and melodic, of the modern artistic current.

We can see, for example, that Renaissance furniture, in spite of being totally covered by carvings, does not have the true Baroque nature as compared to other pieces whose ornamentation is simpler but in whose flexible and moving line we can see already a subtle Baroque presence. Later the straight line becomes broken, continuity becomes discontinuous, static design grows dynamic and large flat surfaces curve, all within a harmonic unity that, for the first time, achieves a unitary sense of composition in the whole.

The Baroque style, in sum, is a natural step in the constant evolution of art toward perfection. In this case it resolves at the same time the new problems that free it from the mannerisms of the Renaissance style. Perhaps among its diverse features, referring strictly to furniture design, we should point out as most outstanding its aversion to the straight line, as opposed to the Renaissance style. Its dynamism is contrary to the static serenity of the 16th and 17th centuries. And finally it is highly picturesque, as evidenced by a preference to appearance over being.

Borromini and Bernini, the two great architects of the 17th century, are the true creators of the Baroque style, to the extent that it was called Borrominesque for some time because of its tremendous vivacity and dynamism.

Arabesque by Berain

FRANCE

LOUIS XIV

Louis XIV represents in France the fullness of the style after the brief transition period during the reign of Louis XIII. It is a solemn and meaningful moment; everything about it is rich, heavy, tumultuous, beautiful, inventive, that is to say, Baroque *par excellence*. It is a style we can call regal, characterized by the Sun King in that the Louis XIII style was presided over by a noble. The king's personal influence is evident in the industrial arts that spread outward from the country and were irrevocably imposed on all the continent.

It was in the time of Mazarino when furniture design achieved its greatest purity. This was when the Gobelin works were created, where a multitude of painters, sculptors, chisellers, carpenters, upholsterers and woodcarvers worked, some French and some foreign, especially Italian. Thus we have the bronzeworkers Cucci and Caffierei, or the cabinetmaker Pierre Gelle, brought by Mazarino himself. In this way a high degree of unity was achieved. The manufacturing works were directed by Charles Le Brun, "the king's first painter". It was a total artistic spirit, similar to that of the Renaissance, that exercised a true dictatorship over all the minor industrial arts and came to be for Louis XIV what David was for Napoleon later on.

Magot by Cressent

Only one man, A. C. Boulle, whom Henry IV brought from Switzerland, escaped this influence and was another man as representative of the style as Le Brun himself. A complete artist—architect, draughtsman, woodcarver, decorator and artist in marquetry—his pieces with shell and copper inlay known as "Boulle" were known universally and found in all the courts of Europe (he made two commodes for Philip IV in the Buen Retiro Palace). But we shall see how, in spite of his strong personality, Boulle followed, in many of his pieces, the designs and orientations of the Goebelin artists, all of them inspired by Le Brun. Among these artists the most representative were the engravers and stylists Berain and Lapoutre. The latter created highly beautiful and solid pieces, while the former, with greater delicacy and lightness, followed the arabesque motifs characteristic of the Renaissance school of Ducerceau in Fontainebleau and of the Pompeyan painters. Both of them, and especially Lapoutre, spread the style of the Sun King with their Baroque engravings and ornamentation that later, in the brief years of the Regency period and the Louis XV style, would overflow in an outburst of fancy in a complete break with symmetry and established order. In the meantime, the middle class imitated all these pieces in its modesty of plain wood and popular carved motifs.

REGENCY

From the Baroque Louis XIV style, majestic and imposing, we do not move brusquely to the light and graceful Rococo of Louis XV. The eight years of regency of the Duke of Orleans give the name to this brief transition period. Actually the pieces of this period do not correspond exactly to these eight years and this name is applied to it merely as a reference to facilitate its study. Neither did the Louis XV or Rococo style last until the king's death in 1775. In 1760 there was already a slight reaction toward a more rigid classical style, although the most characteristic pieces of the style were known by that name. This is not its only denomination; the pieces of the second half of the 18th century are also called Pompadour, since the king's favorite, from 1745 until her death in 1760, supported many artists and had numerous palaces furnished and decorated. Perhaps it was a misinterpretation to give her name to the Rococo or *rocaille* style since the reaction, around 1775, against the Baroque line and the return to classical purity was due to her. It is not strange that we find many pieces in these years described as "in the Greek style", with purer lines. Nor was the change brusque and in the more rigid structures toward the end of the century there were remnants of Louis XV ornamentation and vice versa. Thus, in full Neo-classical period, we see Boucher's son making highly ornate Baroque pieces.

But let us follow now the variations seen at the beginning of the 18th century. The angular decoration of Louis XIV continued its evolution, becoming more undulating and reflecting this era saturated with feminity, discretion and intimacy. Life took on a more refined sense and the predominance of women was extended universally. Decoration also changed; rooms became more intimate and smaller, although they were enlarged with ever bigger mirrors. The Louis XIV salon with its *lit de parade* in the background disappeared. On the contrary, a new room was created for each daily occupation: the library, the smoking room, the dining room, the intimate conversation room or *boudoir*, feminine and elegant, were lively expressions of the style of the era. Fireplaces were smaller, but had the same *trumeaux* with mirrors and paintings. Tapestries were less majestic and furnishings were smaller and more comfortable, reflecting the intimacy of the setting. In the Regency transition period (it cannot be considered a style) *rocaille* was born, inseparable afterward from the Louis XV style until 1770. It was Wateau, the gallant painter of palace feasts, inspirer of his *magot* and bizarre decorators, and two foreign draughtsmen, Meissonier and Oppenard, who added their names to the Regency period. They were the true creators of *rocaille*, whose name derived from the rustic structures decorated with stones, shells and cascades of water, like those that in the 16th century were stylized and rendered by Palissy in ceramic form. But the greatest Regency artist was Cressent, and he alone filled his brief transition years. His pieces, especially his commodes with their perfect, gently undulating lines, enriched by the bronze or *de moulu* work of the celebrated draughtsman Guillot, were even more important because of their composition and bronze-work than for their structural aspects. It was not until well into the Louis XV era that Cressent ceded his place to Oeben, the king's woodworker and disciple of Boulle, who also worked for Madame Pompadour. In collaboration with the Caffieri bronzeworkers and with his own marquetry, he made the best pieces of the style.

France, sharing with England the importance of this minor art, enjoyed a position of supremacy, especially in court furnishings, which in turn greatly influenced bourgeois furniture.

LOUIS XV

Furniture designs in the middle of the 18th century in all of Europe are known as Louis XV, even the German Rococo and the Spanish Charles III styles. In France it reached its height while in the center of Europe it was more ornate and in the south more coarse. As Wateau was the Regency painter, Boucher characterized the Rococo period.

We can see four essential characteristics in French 18th-century furniture. The first was the Baroque motifs spread throughout Italy by Borromini and Bernini. The second was the nationality of the main artists and woodworkers of the era: Italian, German and Dutch—Caffiere, Meissonier, Oeben and Oppenard. The third was the Oriental influence, with its porcelain, lacquer and *magot* and pagoda decoration that invaded interiors and were indispensable as a sign of good taste. And the fourth was represented by the appearance around 1700 of the curved leg in the form of an elongated S, called the cabriolet leg in France and England. It was introduced in all of Europe almost simultaneously by the Dutch who, through their Indies Company, were well connected with the Orient. Its use was a true revolution since its gently curved line varied the general rigidity in furniture design, and it became the most characteristic element of the style.

The Baroque style represented dynamism as opposed to tranquility, translated in its aversion to the straight line. We shall examine its

Clock by Caffieri and Passement

features further in decoration and structure. But between the Regency period, that retained the rigid lines of Louis XIV and began the illogical complications of the Louis XV style, and the Louis XV style itself, there was also an essential feature. This was the symmetry of the first style as opposed to the illogical zenith of the exuberant Rococo with its asymmetrical lines, though with admirable balance in its apparent disorder. Furniture design was clear and gay and its lines played with the social setting. The most characteristic pieces of the period were the luxurious furnishings of the court and the aristocracy. Bourgeois and provincial designs in France were inspired in them; they were simpler but possessed the peculiar charm of popular pieces.

MATERIALS

In the time of Louis XIV the wood used was walnut, nearly always gilded in court furnishings and natural in bourgeois pieces. These latter still used oak and beech for chairs and other types of seats. Boulle with his marquetry gave rise to the use of copper and shells in great profusion. Bronze appliqués were also used abundantly to reinforce angles and moldings that replaced carvings and even hid the wood. A piece of furniture became a true sculpture.

Tapestries also became extraordinarily important: Hungarian knits, Chinese silks, brocades, satins and the famous velvets and rugs of Utrecht (made by Huguenot refugees), damasks, repoussé leather, velvets from Genoa and, toward the end of the style, tapestries from Aubouson and Beauvais.

Already in the Regency and Louis XV periods, bronze, lacquers and tapestries were used together with wood. Porcelain appliqués, marble and cane were found also on some pieces. Although walnut was still the most important wood in the north and west, oak continued in use. On the other hand, in the southeast, whose center is Bordeaux, mahogany came into use while ebony disappeared almost completely. Beech, although an inferior wood, was also widely used, not only in provincial pieces but for court chairs and settees, either in its natural color or gilded. Woods of certain fruit trees, such as cherry and pearwood, were also used, as well as various exotic veneers for marquetry, such as amaranth, satinwood, violet, lignum, *bois de roi*, tulipwood and roots, some as extraordinary as elm root. The reign of tapestries continued; these fabrics closed off open spaces and covered walls and upholstered furniture. Velvets, like those from Utrecht and Genoa, silks and damasks were used. C. F. Oberkampf founded the *toile de Jouy* factory to imitate in France the so-called Indian printed or painted fabrics.

Bronze was a very important part of furniture. The pieces made by the Italian family of sculptors and bronzeworkers, the Caffieri, were true works of art. Some of them, like their famous clock in collaboration with A. Passement, were made entirely of metal. Large bronze appliqués, such as rams' heads, female busts (called *spagnolettes*) (fig. 665), *rocaille*, handles, locks, etc., were used continuously on all types of furniture, replacing the gilt carvings of Louis XIV and constituting true works of art.

Lacquers, very commonly used, are first original and later show Oriental influence, among them the type known as *coromandel* with its curious technique and original and beautiful decorative effect. Later they are replaced in Paris by other similar procedures such as the one employed by the Martin brothers with their varnished paintings of flowers, pastoral scenes and writers on gold backgrounds.

Marble tabletops, stone mosaics, Italian-style hard stone and stucco are not so common as in the last part of the 17th century. Toward the end of the century porcelain appliqués and gilded cane in chairs and settees begin to appear and assume greater importance.

DECORATION

In the first part of the Baroque period, with the Louis XIV style, ornamentation is harmonious, pompous and heavy. Rooms become more intimate and the fireplace, which represents the decorative center, is smaller than in the time of Louis XIII. It no longer reaches the ceiling but is in the form of a console, and the wall above it forms the *trumeau*, usually decorated with a mirror, as we still do today.

Ornamentation has a number of definite characteristics. The first is that of symmetry not only with respect to the vertical plane but to the horizontal as well. The second is the ornamental motifs such as heads, shells, claws, etc., that show greater disproportion among themselves since they follow no specific scale. And the third is the disappearance of carvings in the wood in favor of metal and gilt. We can distinguish three types of furniture: gilded pieces, those totally carved and those with bronze appliqués and marquetry, created by Boulle or at least carrying his name.

Following are the primary motifs used in ornamentation: many reflect ancient Rome such as the exuberant drawings of helmets, winged victories, suits of armor, trophies, classical moldings of eggs, rosaries and dentils, allegorical figures, Cupids and titans. There were also horns of plenty and garlands, all of them intertwined with the architecture and structure of the pieces. Cascades of acanthus and mantelets that are so characteristic of Berain were also used. The two most common themes found in the center of the various compositions were a head on a group of sunbeams and a shell, both in a circular design.

Very typical were the appliqués in the form of a lattice-work of rhombuses or squares with flowers in the center, pearls on grooved backgrounds, diamond tips in the angles of feet and a curve in the shape of a double C (basket handle). Vertical supports and legs were hardly ever turned, balusters were round, as well as square and tapering, and the feet of cupboards, commodes, etc., often rested on a flattened, turned block, either smooth or grooved (fig. 693).

The turned column was used only in reminiscence of Louis XIII and the Renaissance, but the grooves remained in columns and apron pieces.

Dutch influence also resulted in the appearance of flowers or bouquets in marquetry, or Oriental lacquers that were now in fashion. Varnishes were invented to replace or imitate them and the Liege chemist, Dagli, prepared a solid and brilliant varnish, an invention that won him entry into the Gobelin works.

With the Regency and especially the Louis XV styles, ornamentation exhibited an aversion to the straight line and was like a saraband of whimsical silhouetes of *magot*, grotesque figures, rounded lines and *chinoiseries*, reflected in the passion for Chinese and Japanese objects. The Regency style still retained the delirious fantasy of Rococo and its symmetrical composition became totally asymmetrical. With the Louis XV style all the ornamental elements inherited from the Louis XIV, like the shell, the *haricot*, acanthus leaf and the bracket, became exaggerated and twisted. The shell was changed until it lost its form in asymmetry. But the checkered rhombus pattern and the garlands, flowers and pomegranates, so characteristic of the Regency and Louis XIV styles, still remained.

Among the Louis XV elements we find twisted garlands, rolled and pleated ribbons, the serrated shell, foliage and bands that look like water. On the other hand, Cressent's simian decorative motif (figs. 681, 687) were typical of the Regency period.

Marquetry was used more than ever, because of the Dutch influence, in centers with flowers, fruit and pastoral scenes. Bronze frames were used, sometimes with matte finish and other times polished for contrast.

The most common veneers were sycamore, satinwood, violet, coral, jacaranda and tulipwood, sometimes in their natural colors and sometimes varnished and painted. They were used not only to make feathery designs by matching the grains, but also for motifs similar to those on Flemish and Dutch pieces. Animal decoration abounded, such as the rams' heads on the famous commodes by Gaudreaux (fig. 680), the hoof-shaped foot on curved legs and the so-called Jesuit or Indian turkey legs in the form of an S with feather carving and claw-and-ball feet, like their English counterparts, and other features such as angels, sphinxes, animals, etc. The turned leg had almost

"Haricot" (fig. 670)

Boulle marquetry

completely disappeared and was seen only on provincial pieces. "Martin varnish" was the richest finish and on top of its light, ochre and gold backgrounds were some of the best paintings of the period. The same technique was applied to more economical models using decals that imitate the painted engravings on the lacquered pieces.

The four Martin brothers did not merely imitate lacquer but invented a new procedure which they kept secret. Their work became the fashion of the day and they were praised as writers and poets. Their compositions of courtly or mythological scenes on gold-dusted backgrounds were used not only on furniture but also on carriages, handchairs, etc. There are numerous examples in the best palaces and collections of Europe (fig. 653). In the Louis XV period many pieces were decorated with Sévres porcelain from the factory established by Madame Pompadour. But this procedure achieved its maximum importance in the Louis XVI period at the end of the 18th century.

Gilded furniture, replaced by bronze, was seen less than in the Louis XIV period.

Finally, we should mention that the names of Oppenart and Meissonier, creators of many pieces of furniture and room decorations, were inseparably linked to the Rococo style and its ornamentation.

STRUCTURES

The most interesting aspect of furniture design is not the expression of all these ornamental details, but that the lines lost the rigidity of the classical styles and straight lines break into curves. The vertical elements in bracket form or S shape changed the structure and architectonic nature of furniture to make it more and more a work of carpenter's art.

Although the technique was perfect, in many cases the bronze reinforcements, that began with A. C. Boulle, allowed a lighter interior finish and the structural material that was hidden was of poorer quality, generally pine, beech, etc. During the reign of Louis XIV, rungs were still considered indispensable on chairs and tables. On tables they were usually in the form of an H, and on the chairs there could be an additional more decorative piece on the front rung. Later crossed rungs were seen, especially on slightly curved consoles, and their point of crossing was decorated with an urn or some other carved detail.

Turned pieces become twist-turned, and square plinths became pedestals tapering toward the bottom or in brackets ending in scrolls. The so-called Boulle-type marquetry was a new technique worth mentioning. It was made with two plaques of copper and shell, one following the line of the other and both on a panel in arabesque drawings. The panels were fretsawed following the line of the drawing and in this way, since the copper and the shell coincide perfectly, the drawings were repeated in both materials so that what in one is copper, in the other is shell. In this way there were panels for two pieces of furniture and one is the reverse of the other (*première partie*). The marquetry was not applied to the pieces to cover them totally with the drawings of one material and backgrounds of the other, but were alternated with no specific pattern (fig. 674). In 1700, at the end of the Louis XIV style, not only the legs changed, now becoming curved, but the ornamentation as well, which was simpler. On the other hand, it was no longer superimposed, but formed an intrinsic part of the structure that, with its bombé surfaces, gentle curves and perfect linking of its elements, formed a harmonious unit of woodwork.

With the Louis XV style we can see great innovations in technique but, on the other hand, the structures underwent an even more profound transformation. Previously the horizontal and vertical structural elements were visible on the outside, but now they were hidden. Rigid backs and seats became rounded, and firm and solid legs became arched and looked as if they were bent. The clearly defined structures were lost in a sea of undulations.

It was at this time, in 1740, when we see the true birth of the half century of dynamism, the curve and the obvious.

Even in the Regency period the straight line was maintained, and symmetry above all was considered highly important. Although S-shaped legs appeared with the curve known as the cross-bow form, crossed rungs still persisted (fig. 623).

In the Regency rocaille was predominant and decoration exuberant. Not only were seats and silhouettes in general curved, but the joints of the supports and the aprons formed a continuous line. Only in full Louis XV style was decoration (hardly ever the structure) absolutely asymmetrical. Rocaille became pure and stylized and the lines and silhouettes became rounded, dethroning the straight line and forming a whole, as if made of a single piece. We should note, however, the admirable balance between volume and ornamentation in this apparent disorder of asymmetrical lines (figs. 657, 658).

Legs appeared to be bent, the brackets of armchairs looked as though they might break and bombé pieces about to explode. Toward 1760 there was a regression to the straight, pure and classical line in some isolated works. With the Louis XVI style, in the last third of the century, this rigidity achieved its maximum development and again the structural elements became clearly distinguished from the decorative parts. It was a somewhat cold and academic protest against the illogical Rococo. A significant feature was that with the Louis XV style rungs disappear, doubtless for esthetic reasons, not to return either in the Neo-classical or Empire styles, since the shape of the leg allowed its construction in a continuous piece with the apron.

Bronze appliqués also responded to a unity or a whole and were often compound or combined in such a way that their true function was hidden. Examples are the handles of the commodes that formed a single decorative motif (figs. 685-88) on the drawers, which were smooth, and were hidden in the bronze and marquetry decoration, also forming a whole, with the divisions between drawers almost invisible to give an impression of continuity. Flower marquetry, which came from the Netherlands with an enormous variety of veneers dyed in different colors or burnt, had the same apparent function as bronze.

Fabrics covered walls and chairs completely. Often the structure of the chairs was visible, and these pieces were known as visible wood pieces (figs. 655, 664, 677).

These skeletons in search of curved and undulating lines were molded by hand. Since their widths were variable, the surfaces were interrupted with the change in direction of the curves, whether they were simple in the form of a C or an S, combined or in scrolls. These brusque changes and discontinuous pieces cut by small straight elements could not be made mechanically on large surfaces but had to be done by hand by woodcarvers, and in this way the piece became more personalized.

Thus doors and drawers were hidden with plaques and marquetry, and on chairs these moldings and small carvings hid the union of the vertical and horizontal elements in a continuous single line.

In summary, we can see how everything became rounded to soften the visual aspect of the lines, how commodes and similar pieces, chairs, bronze appliqués, legs and even the angles of rooms were rounded with corner pieces or with decorative elements that hid the edges. And then we see the appearance of a new material that we could call semi-structural and which at first sight seems insignificant: the spring in seats and backs, indispensable for comfort.

KINDS OF FURNITURE

With the Louis XIV style the four fundamental pieces of furniture were developed, and from them derived study tables, commodes, the first sofas and *chaise-longues*, and canopy beds, *queridon*, *chiffoniers*, etc., all of which were widely represented.

All these pieces spread throughout Europe in the Louis XV period, giving rise to prototypes and variations of great originality and artistic interest.

Small armchair in very pure Louis XV style

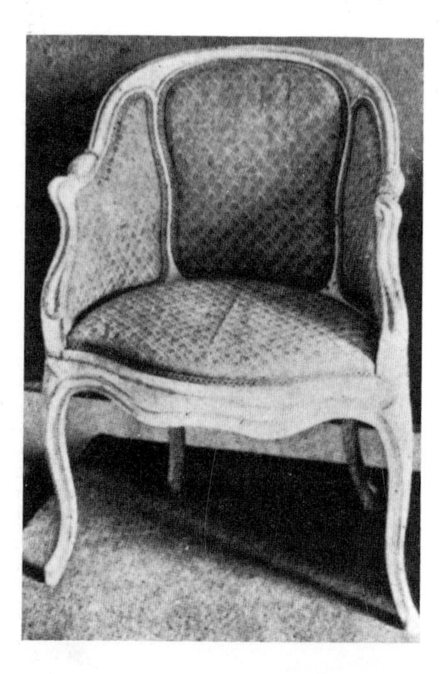

Chairs

The classical Louis XIV armchair was ample in size and line and had slightly curved arms and legs. It had rungs crossed in the form of an X or an H, also curved (fig. 614). It was easy to see its antecedent in the Louis XIII armchairs, with their turned legs, carved rungs and wide, high back. The type characteristic of the Louis XIV style had a higher back ending in a straight or slightly curved crest with a broadly sloping fall. The arms were wide and ended in scrolls (fig. 616). The brackets were carved in a large S shape; the legs were tapered and bracket-shaped (figs. 614, 615) and with a slight S shape that was the beginning of the cabriolet leg.

An interesting and simple type of chair had the arm, bracket and leg in a discontinuous line and the leg ending in a scroll. It was usually slightly carved with rounded edges. We see this model highly simplified in Spain, and it was authentically Louis XIV (figs. 616, 618).

It was during this period when the sofa and the *chaise-longue* were born. This was a chair with a long seat that was used for reposing somewhat like a reclining bed (fig. 636).

The legs of thse pieces were also tapered, profusely carved and with curved rungs. Many of them were completely gilded (fig. 642).

Chairs were of the same type as armchairs, but without arms. Stools were in the same style but lacking the back as well. The square stool and the X-shaped chair were luxurious court pieces with crossed, carved and gilded legs.

Other models of stools were similar to the lower parts of chairs, with legs in the form of a C or S, ending in scrolls (fig. 642).

Later we see Regency and Louis XV chairs with all their lines curved. In the former, however, the curves were gentle and contained, and the rocaille decoration was absolutely symmetrical (figs. 616, 617, 625). On the other hand, in the latter all the elements were curved and violent, but not overwhelming. In the middle of the century some examples unique in line, detail and proportion appeared, with delicate and frugal ornamentation.

The chair was a very feminine, slender, graceful, and elastic piece. Its Baroque movement was no longer an excess of decoration but eminently structural (figs. 636, 645).

Nearly all of them had cabriolet legs, turned, molded and ending in scrolls. Since the rungs had disappeared with the Regency style, they were lighter. The seats were also rounded and the backs, when they were somewhat pinched in the center, were called *violonnés*. The arms were usually joined to the back, and in this case they were known as gondola type, like many study chairs. Backs and seats were generally upholstered, but the wood on the outer edges was always visible. The origin of the chairs with cane seat and back was undoubtedly Dutch or Flemish; this feature was first seen in the so-called Louis XIII chairs at the end of the style. Now they were very common and varied (figs. 623, 624). The backs were frequently concave for greater comfort, in which case they were called cabriolet chairs (fig. 622).

The most important type of armchair was the *bergère*, an upholstered chair with a seat lower and wider than usual and with the sides of the arms closed and upholstered. Some had winged backs; this type, which had its origin in the Regency period, was called the confessional chair and was a totally upholstered chair with a loose seat cushion. It had the same details of line and decoration as the style in general, but its proportions were more careful and it was smaller in comparison with the monumental and majestic Louis XIV chairs, of which beautiful examples are still preserved. Many of the ones that today are natural color —usually beech—were gilded, a detail that can be noted by the sharper molding which was intended to be covered by plaster and gold dust. There was an abundance of popular straw chairs known as *capuchinas*, that began in the Louis XIV period. They had ladder backs with three or more horizontal rungs or with a vertical element in the center. Their silhouette was always gracefully curved. We will see examples of them later in the Louis XVI style at the end of the century.

There was a profusion of couches, sofas and ottomans with rolled arms. The types known whimsically as "Turkish" or "sultan" models were always made with similar characteristics (figs. 620-631). They were derivations of the *bergères*, like the so-called "duchess" couches, whose origin was also the *chaise-longue*. Sometimes this lengthened *bergère* had a small upright support at the foot of the seat. This was the true duchess couch, which could be made in a single piece, at that time called the *duquesa à bateau*, or in two or three pieces and known as the *duquesa briseé*.

Another variation of the duchesse was the so-called *veilleuse*, which was a divan or sofa with the arms of different heights, in the Empire style known as the *meridianne*.

The sofas and couches and their variations, with all types of details and always richly upholstered and with visible wood and careful and continuous lines, had small cabriolet legs ending in a scroll on a small ball.

Tables

The tables were very rich, carved, gilded and with the same type of legs as we have described. Many had marble tops, others had Boulle marquetry or marble mosaics made by Florentine and Dutch artists.

Dining tables sometimes had a broken and undulating or circular top like large *gueridon* and always had cabriolet legs.

Consoles, that replaced the Renaissance buffets, were simply tables placed against the wall with three visible sides and a highly decorated top. The legs and rungs were very large and the apron profusely carved and gilded (figs. 653, 654). In the Louis XV period they were even more unbalanced and exaggerated than in the Louis XIV.

There was an endless variety of "English" tables, that is with extending tops. These were even more common in the 19th century.

We also find small tables known as *gueridon* and *toilette* or *poudreuse* tables, and others like the *chiffonier* (a tall, narrow commode with drawers), *cabaret* tables to be placed beside the bed and, of these latter, the curious "flying" table that disappeared into the floor, returned and opened to reveal a complete table setting and meal. Dressing tables were simple frames with kidney-shaped tops covered with pleated curtains, used for make-up and hair styling and later called *toilettes* even though they did not have the same type of curtains.

The study table was a creation of this moment. With the Louis XIV style it was another piece with which Boulle triumphed. He made many of them with drawers on the sides and a single one in the center, on console or double-S legs. Many of these tables, always richly decorated, are still preserved (fig. 663).

Boulle in the Louis XIV style and Deben, Cressent, Riesener, etc., in the Louis XV successfully worked with all types of furniture, but the commode was still the most representative piece of the style. Boulle himself, whose most important works were the Delphin's rooms in Versailles, also made some commodes. The two preserved in the Mazarino gallery or library are the most important ones. Following a model by Le Brun, they are bombé and very Baroque, with sphinx heads. The body of the commode itself is supported on conical spiraled feet (fig. 674). The number of commodes and varying artistic details is extraordinary. Those drawn by Berain are worth mentioning (fig. 672), with their bronze chiselling by Cucci.

Boulle's *en tumba* commode was followed by another with a bombé front and one or two curves on the front and sides. The top is marble and its lines follow the bombé and curves of the commode itself.

With the Louis XV and Regency styles the commode was more lavishly and opulently decorated, with bronze appliqués that were true works of sculpture art, like those by Cressent (fig. 681) with their *spagnolettes* and other details. Many of them were done by the Caffieris or Gaudreaux, whose famous appliqués (fig. 680) were made for library medal commodes and were exceptional examples.

A certain type of simple commode was very common. Its curve was more gentle and its ornamentation less heavy, with cabriolet legs finished in bronze, loose and intertwined handles, corner pieces, etc. The marquetry or lacquers covering the front were particularly

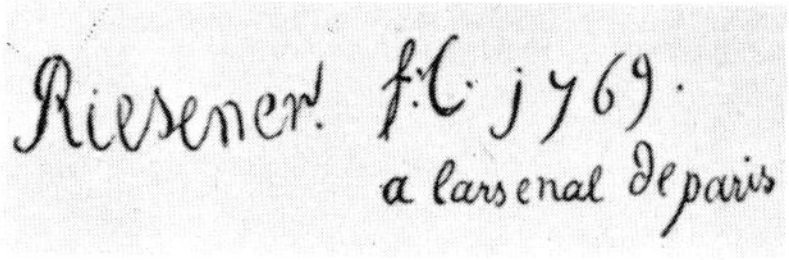

Riesener's stamp

interesting on these pieces, and there was an infinite variety of them (figs. 673, 687).

A derivation of the commode and the table was the bureau or secretary with inclined top (figs. 660, 661, 662) which when it was let down became a desk. These pieces often had another upper part with doors used for placing books or porcelain. We will see these in Germany and Italy.

The most famous bureau of the period was the one begun for Louis XV in 1760 by Oeben, the best woodworker of the time, which had all the characteristics of the style. It is known as a cylinder or roll-top desk; the top is a quarter cylinder and does not drop down but rolls into the body of the desk. Its creator died suddenly in 1766 and Riesener, his disciple, continued the work and finished it in 1769. His influence and the reaction of these years toward more classical styles can be noted in various details, such as the gallery on top (figs. 664, 665, 666). It is a work of exceptional artistic value, and its chiselled and gilded bronzes by Duplessis, Winant and Hervieux are true sculptures.

Cupboards

We have said earlier that a number of pieces with no specific use were created, such as small cupboards, bureaus, commodes, tables for various purposes and chairs and sofas. But these were not the most important pieces. Wardrobes were made in various regions with a certain provincial nature. In the west they were highly decorated, while in Lorraine the panels were in the shape of a four-leaf clover and the pieces from Normandy and the center of the country were more classical, with straight, bulky Renaissance cornices. The doors had rounded or broken angles and the panels were sometimes subdivided. These regional wardrobes, usually made of oak or walnut with beautiful ironwork on the hinges and locks, were very interesting. On the other hand the court wardrobes were simple carpentry works because they were placed in interior rooms. The regional types were made at the request of the wealthy French burgeoisie whose strong traditions are reflected in these pieces (figs. 694, 695).

With the Louis XV style these provincial wardrobes were still interesting with their curved cresting and angles rounded in a quarter circle with carvings and grooves along the sides (fig. 692). They can be distinguished from the Louis XIV models only by their profuse asymmetrical ornamentation. Those from the region of Bordeaux had two panels on each door with the lower one smaller. These panels had a broken, sinuous outline, like the crosspiece between them which was also slanted and carved. The decoration was completed by large iron fretwork plates around the keyholes and hinges. Finally, we see that they were sometimes made of mahogany since Bordeaux was the center of one of the most important regions in foreign trade (figs. 686, 688).

Also well known were the so-called Normandy wardrobes, usually made of oak or walnut. They had a very careful silhouette with two panels on each door and a wide crosspiece between them. On it, as in the center of the crest, were groups of carvings in the Louis XV style.

In the Louis XIV period the court wardrobe as such was a showcase or library. They were extraordinarily luxurious, Boulle type, with bronze appliqués and marquetry, like a cabinet after a drawing by Boulle and Lapoutre. The Boulle wardrobe in the Museum of Decorative Arts, another by Cressent and the one by Boulle himself in the Louvre (figs. 685, 690, 692, 693) are famous and well-known examples.

Alternating with these pieces was the smaller, lower wardrobe known as the *entredos* which was placed between two balconies or windows (thus its name, literally "between two") and had an average height of one meter. This piece was another precursor of the commode in which the doors became drawers.

The libraries, sideboards and corner cupboards, with the same carvings or marquetry and S-shaped legs, ending in scrolls resting on blocks (figs. 696, 697, 700) were derived from these.

Then came the buffets in two sections. The most pleasing models were the popular ones, like the wardrobe. Those of Provence, Normandy and the southwest (figs. 686, 688) with the upper section open were made with lively ceramic work in bright colors on polished white backgrounds.

Clocks

We now begin to see a new piece, the tall grandfather clock with the case widened in the shape of a guitar to allow for movement of the pendulum. It had the same general characteristics and ornamentation of the style (figs. 702, 704).

We have already mentioned the famous clock by Caffieri and Passement, preserved in the Versailles palace, made completely of bronze and of extraordinary interest.

Beds

One of the most important pieces of the period was the bed. With Louis XIV the bed was extraordinarily sumptuous and pompous, a truly monumental and regal piece of furniture. It was rectangular with high posts to hold the canopy and hangings. The curtains, which could be opened or closed, and the crowning of the dais with ostrich plumes completed the theatrical appearance. It was placed in the center of the room on a platform with the head against the wall and separated from the rest of the room by a balustrade or archway, as we can see in the engravings by Lapoutre, Berain and Marot.

In reality the bed, once the curtains were drawn, was a small room within the larger salon. Its use was indispensable, given the style of public life of the time. The bedroom was used for receiving audiences, expediting various and sundry matters, conversing, etc., and courtesans and servants passed through it continuously.

These beds, truly regal, were decorated with an enormous amount of fabric, including the canopy, curtains, hangings, etc. Even the bourgeois classes sacrificed other pieces of furniture to have their *lit de parade*, and they were so representative that in the court they were often given as gifts to ambassadors and illustrious personalities. There were various types of these reception beds: the "imperial" with a canopy in the form of a cupula, richly decorated and containing a large number of tapestries; the "duchess" (fig. 710) with the canopy hanging above the bed, which had no legs, and covering its entire length, with no curtains or hangings; the "Polish bed" with the canopy supported on four short columns; the "Turkish bed" with curtains that fell laterally over the head and foot of the same height (figs. 706, 708); the "tomb" with the foot lower than the head and the canopy at an angle, an esthetically unfortunate and inelegant shape; and many other types.

The fabrics used on these beds were, naturally, very rich, ranging from French and Genoese velvets to damask, satin, Chinese silks, etc.

The beds of the Regency and Louis XV styles were similar to those of the Louis XIV, but were generally smaller and less theatrical. Many had both headboard and footboard with a sinuous shape interrupted by small acanthus carvings and rocaille.

The duchess and Polish beds were still in use and there was a multitude of new types of drawings. Best known among them were those by Pineau, and the Turkish beds of the Rochecotte and Dampierre castles were also beautiful examples.

Imperial bed

Duchess bed

Fontainebleau, Versailles and the French castles give us innumerable examples of furnishings and decorative schemes.

The artists were also numerous. Boulle was perhaps the most representative of the Louis XV style. Others were Berain and Lapoutre, with their books of engravings on furniture and decoration (bedrooms, writing desks and arabesques); Cucci the Italian sculptor who comes to the court of the Sun King; the draughtsman Daniel Marot; and over all of them Le Brun. These artists spread the Sun King's style over all of Europe. It is a style that is far removed

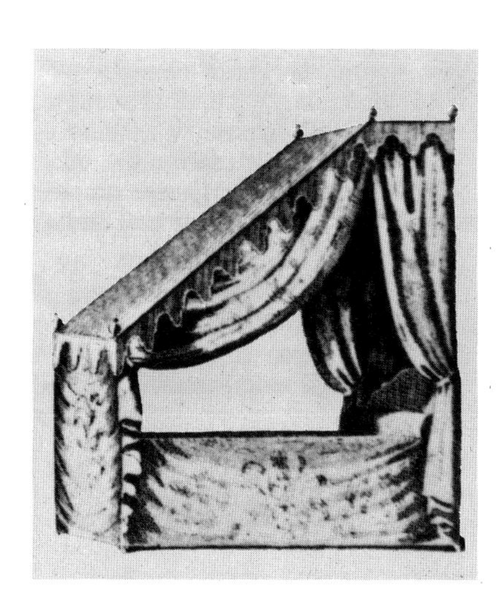

Bed in the shape of a tomb

from our own time in its heaviness and excess, without the softness and elegance of the Louis XV style, but representative of the importance of France on the continent at that time. Only some popular, regional or bourgeois models retain a certain interest today and are still copied.

With the Louis XV style decorating schemes multiply and the artists, many of them German or Italian, are even more numerous and well known. Thus Oeben, Riesener, the Cressents, Caffieri, Leleu, etc. stamp their names on their pieces, which are greatly sought after. With the Louis XV style the reign of Rococo is not ended. Even in the time of the Louis XVI style, in spite of its rigid lines and colder neo-classical decoration, it continues with a certain feminine feeling, light, intranscendent and unpreoccupied, like a reflection of the elegant parties in the Petit Trianon.

ITALY

Just as in the 15th century when a new art arose in Italy while the rest of Europe remained spiritually in the Middle Ages, now also in the 17th century the new style evolves and develops here before it spreads to the rest of the continent. All the rich ornamentation of Baroque furniture, that later will be interpreted and copied in Europe with frequent abuse, is created by Italian artists. But Italy, too attached to the Renaissance standards, does not allow more than the natural evolution of the old structures and produces few new types. This is in contrast to the other nations, like the French, because it is precisely France that sets the standards for Baroque furniture in Europe, although it is in Italy where we must look for its origin and the causes of the new structures and their ornamentation, that would bring about the birth and development of the exuberant Louis XIV style.

MATERIALS

Virtually the same materials were used as in the Renaissance. Although oak was largely replaced by walnut, the tapestries were richer and marquetry broadened its possibilities with the use of new exotic woods, but at the same time hard stone, painted glass and Renaissance chiselled copper and bronze appliqués persisted, but now with a new more decorative and picturesque feeling.

Ornamentation was more varied than in the preceding period. Gilt concentrated in various places was still in vogue. Carving, for which the softness of walnut was especially suited, with its rolls, scrolls, leaves, masks and human figures, was now finer, more detained, profuse and fluid—in a word fully Baroque. The most famous Italian woodcarver after the Renaissance was the Venetian A. Broustolón (1670-1732), whose works are reproduced here (fig. 713). Kingdoms and republics had schools with different decorative characteristics. The Tuscan and Roman were the most traditional and classical, while the Venetian was singled out for its exquisite taste, its pictorial ornamentation and its Oriental as well as locally made lacquers. The work of the Venetian woodworkers, the *marangoni*, was the most interesting contribution of Italian art to the history of furniture. Mirrors were also used for decoration with inlaid bevelled drawings. Marquetry was very much in fashion and enriched with mother-of-pearl, shells, ivory, ebony and bronze appliqués. In some towns, especially Turin, pieces by the famous woodworker and marquetry artist P. Piffetti are still preserved (figs. 729, 735).

In the region of Naples pieces were made of shell on gold backgrounds, with continuous lines and nails reinforcing the expressivity of the lines. Later all these ornamental procedures were adopted by the French.

STRUCTURES

At the beginning the Renaissance structures endured with new decoration superimposed on them. But little by little this decorative style took over the architectural aspects until the structural lines became an intrinsic Baroque expression, with the great sincerity and simplicity that came from getting rid of superfluous adornments and reducing them only to certain parts. It was then that the line broke in the split pediments, the twist-turned columns and S-shaped legs. But Italian art was too classical and imbued with the esthetic principles of antiquity, and it required foreign influence to make strictly Baroque pieces. We can see how French and English models already incorporated into the European movement were copied. For this very reason Italian art could not compete with them, except in some isolated cases, and these precisely for the purity and proportion of their motifs and moldings.

KINDS OF FURNITURE

The pieces of furniture used in Italy during this period were the same as in the rest of Europe, and they were in the process of transformation and evolution from the last Renaissance forms.

The chest had almost completely disappeared as a characteristic piece and was replaced by cupboards and credences. We can still see the cabinet wardrobe, the traditional *stipo* with Baroque elements but without any basic structural changes, as we can see in the photographs. Its structure was always architectonic, with small subdivisions slowly replaced at the end of the style by large surfaces that show greater movement.

Chairs and tables

The *casapanche* was replaced by sofas and couches known as *da portego* divans with four or five chair backs. We can see in them the English influence of the Georgian style and the French Louis XV influence (fig. 718).

With the new pompous art, the severe tables and chairs changed. Table legs were twist-turned or carved with rolls, scrolls or brackets. Chair decoration was based on the same elements and we can see even French rocaille and the cabriolet leg. Backs that were wider in the upper part with a slightly trapezoidal shape were very characteristic. In the commodes, much less important than in central Europe, bombés began to appear. The pediments and the old, classical split pediments on cupboards were replaced by looped designs, asymmetrical in French Rococo, so contrary to the Italian Baroque in its imperturbable symmetry (figs. 732, 733, 734, 737).

National art, in sum, produced few models and even these were usually mere copies of French pieces, even those used to furnish Italian palaces. Some types of tables with lyre legs with safety catches were doubtless products of Spanish influence.

Beds

There were also beds with hangings like the French ones, or with the head outlined in carved and gilded Baroque molding and a background of carved or upholstered wood. The footboard had twist-turned columns or inverted cabriolet legs.

Among the different pieces of furniture, the bed was very original, with the rich Baroque silhouette of its headboard, usually painted and without canopy. It was precisely this type, on which the footboard usually had two highly ornamental feet, that is copied even today along the entire Spanish seaboard, the Levant and Majorca, with this clear Italian influence.

Other pieces

A group of interesting and original pieces of furniture were the Venetian lacquered pieces, that began as an imitation of Chinese lacquer. But the typical Venetian lacquer was completely different. The backgrounds were light colors like turtledove, ivory and light green shades, and the decoration superimposed on them consisted of realistic drawings of flowers and small landscapes. There were pieces that were inferior but with highly feigned decoration, the so-called *arte povera* (figs. 732, 733, 741), because the decoration was made with simple colored stamps that gave an effect similar to the lacquers.

The painted pieces had themes, sometimes inlaid, in bevelled mirrors that were purely decorative. Some, like the *trumeaux*, with their undulating lines, had drawers in the lower section, a drop-top for a writing desk in the center and a showcase for the top section. Some very beautiful pieces are preserved today (figs. 758, 739).

Finally, we should say that Italian furniture, if it was not universally Baroque or Rococo like French furniture, but rather in isolated pieces, on the other hand was characterized by its elegant lines (we are reminded of the backs of Italian Louis XIV armchairs that are somewhat open at the top, as seen in figs. 713, 720), and by the careful choice of ornamental motifs. These were always classical and very well proportioned; their rich carvings were, in many cases, truly important works of sculpture.

There were numerous interiors of Lombard, Venetian and Roman palaces, as well as many others. Especially beautiful were those of the Stupinigi hunting Palazzina in Turin, the magnificent interiors of the Roman palaces like the ones in Doria or Colonna, the celebrated Ca Razónico of Venice, all found in a museum of 18th-century Venice or the Neapolitan Capo di Monte palace.

SPAIN AND PORTUGAL

Baroque appeared in Spain in the middle of the 17th century. All the arts influenced by Italian styles continued their evolution and in architecture there is a very marked national character in the other European countries. Within this movement the industrial arts, and consequently furniture design, took on this same character.

As in Italy, furniture design can be categorized in various regional schools: Galician, influenced by England and Portugal; Catalan, Levantine and Majorcan, with the luminous and decorative Italian and especially Venetian tradition; Salamancan, otherwise known as Churrigueresque (a name that is doubtless the most representative of Spanish Baroque style), of which there are a number of notable examples we will mention shortly; Andalusian, in which the relationship with England can be seen but in a more homespun, decorative and popular sense. Castile represented the most traditional school in which not only Renaissance models were copied with their consequent evolution, but because the Court resided here the influence of the Louises and Italian Rococo could be seen. Finally there were the northern schools where 16th-century models persisted in popular furniture, although with the distinct mark of the new themes.

The reigns of Charles II, Philip V and Charles III marked the prime moments of Spanish Baroque. In the first period a very national Baroque style was developed, which was linked to the name of José Churriguera, a Salamancan architect (1650-1723) as well as woodworker and carver. Although he was neither initiator nor author of the most representative Baroque works, it was his disciples and followers who spread it throughout Spain. He was, however, the designer of the 1689 catafalque for Queen Marie Louise, wife of Charles II, a work awarded a prize which made him famous and raises him to the category of arbiter in the field of architecture.

With Philip V, the French prince who began the Bourbon dynasty in Spain, the trophies, angels, hangings and national and Italian motifs used in decoration are replaced by French rocaille, an influence seen mainly in court furnishings.

Finally, Charles III (Charles VII of Naples) in 1759 brought from Italy artists and furnishings for his palaces in the Louis XV style. We should remember also that Charles III was impressed by the recent discoveries at Pompeii (1755) and because of this at the end of his reign he initiated in Spain, as in the rest of Europe, a return to Neoclassicism.

During these reigns, with clear influence first from France and later from Italy, Spanish furniture slowly lost the rigidity and austerity that had characterized it, although models of a universal nature were not created.

The foreign fashions with their superfluous pieces, upholstery and emphasis on comfort did not penetrate into Spain until well into the 18th century. Furniture of the court and the aristocracy was usually imported (Boulle, Martin and the Goebelin tapestries), especially from France. National furniture production was limited to copying and repeating these imported pieces, but it was of inferior quality and lacked the fineness of the originals. Other times bourgeois furniture was a continuation of the Renaissance types, influenced by the new styles only in details, in which the delicacy of the construction, the choice and harmony of the proportions was supplanted with great originality and surprising imagination, which gave rise to isolated pieces that do not form a school.

As always, popular pieces were very interesting (the same as in the rest of Europe), within a great simplicity of lines and an ingenuous interpretation of the new motifs and elements. On the other hand, we should not forget that the Moorish influence did not disappear altogether from Spain. The Mohammedan tradition, the inlays with geometric designs, the inclination toward pictorial decoration, endured until well into the 19th century.

In sum, we see in Spain three types of furniture: court furniture, usually imported; bourgeois pieces, copies of the former or also imported when they were not Renaissance type with its natural evolution; and the popular models that, like in the rest of Europe, repeated the old types with slight variations, more in the details than in the structure.

With reference to Portugal, we can make the same general observations. Here the English influence was greater for political, historical and geographical reasons. Portugal's Oriental colonies also exercised great influence in ornamentation and materials (figs. 832, 833, 834). With this ascendancy, these means, this efficient environment, a series of pieces with clearly defined characteristics were produced, which make up the so-called Portuguese style, with its looped moldings, violent and exaggeratedly turned elements and highly ornate high relief carvings (figs. 827, 842). The lack of purity in the lines was compensated by the great originality and highly charged motifs that define Portuguese Baroque furniture.

MATERIALS

In addition to the enormous variety of woods found in Spain, of which the most important

Forked iron braces

were walnut, oak and chestnut (in this order), and pine, used for pieces to be painted or covered, the use of new exotic woods began at this time, but only for appliqués and veneers. In Spain also, before the rest of Europe, mahogany was so widely accepted that it soon spread to France and England and was known as "Spanish mahogany".

The number of materials used to enrich and embellish these pieces was enormous: shell, ivory, bronze and hard stone or marble alternate with pained glass, marquetry in exotic wood, repoussé leathers and rich tapestries, often coming from France, where the specialized masters also come from.

At the beginning the motifs were scrolls, angels, twisted columns, etc., which we have already seen in Italy before they spread to the rest of Europe.

Velázquez, in his travels as the king's courtier and to bring works of art to the palaces in Madrid, went to Italy in 1649. It was perhaps then that he brought back, or pointed the way to, the decorations in vogue. On the other hand, Boulle sent pieces from the French court, Martin sent hand chairs and La Cotte, in 1712, decorative engravings. It is not difficult to see how French influence became so important in Spain in the time of Philip V, until with Charles III, although the Louis XV Rococo continued, a certain Neapolitan and Italian fashion began to appear.

Furniture was carved, gilded and enriched with shells, bronzes, etc., and tapestries achieved their maximum importance. Charles III brought from Naples numerous artists (it is enough to mention Gasparini) and created various artistic and decorative industries in Madrid. The most important were Buen Retiro, an imitation of Capo di Monte in Naples, and the royal workshops where palace furniture had been made a century before.

The prototypes slowly changed their structural elements. In decoration the legs were no longer simply square or turned but twist-turned or with highly complicated turned shapes, with large rungs and crossed scrolls. Later, shells, characteristic of the Louis XIV style, appeared on these scrolls. On the so-called lyre tables, the legs also ended in scrolls and on this very national type of table the rungs were, as we already said in the Renaissance, replaced by iron supports, double or forked. The slanting table legs were another sign of their Baroque style. National decoration was generally more coarse than on the original models, but the result was a certain vigor and drama that was intrinsic to Spanish art. What better example than the armchair by Fray A. de Sotomayor to study these features? The lines were violent, tortured and dynamic, neither studied nor balanced, as in the contemporary French models of the Louis XIV style. If we had to choose a specimen of the style, we could not find a more representative national model (fig. 762).

We should point out at the same time the details characteristic of Portuguese furniture with their turned parts with sudden widening and strangulation, moldings with undulating and looped profile made of ebony and lignum, and drawer bottoms with their semicylindrical shapes. On dark and reddish pieces, lignum and other colinial woods were used. The examples are of great decorative value and are abundant. Especially interesting and curious, for example, are the furnishings of the Cintra, Pena and Queluz palaces.

STRUCTURES

We have already said that the pure Renaissance lines were gradually mixed with curved elements such as pediments on the tops of various pieces, the use of twist-turned elements, etc., and the richness and exuberance of the decoration of backgrounds for carvings and paintings. But in spite of the absorption of the national Baroque style by the various fashions, there was still a feeling of uncertainty in the face of the asymmetry imposed by the Louis XV style.

It is interesting, for example, to see this evolution of types of legs. The completely prismatic and straight legs of the friaries, or turned legs on tables, became curved or undulating and ended in scrolls. The rungs and arms of chairs repeated the same curved line. From this typical French style the lyre table was undoubtedly derived, and its evolution can be seen clearly in the elegant example in the cathedral of Gerona (fig. 784). We can see how that characteristic rigidity, lack of flexibility and austerity of Spanish styles began to disappear with the foreign influences, and we see models with legs curved at the top and ending at the bottom in scrolls. There are cabriolet legs (that was the great 17th-century revolution in all of Europe) and legs with pyramidal and quadrangular balusters, carved as in the Louis XIV period. There are also legs with angels, scrolls and caryatids of Italian influence, and lyre legs on tables, whose origin we have already mentioned. In sum, the structural rigidity of the 16th century took on a greater flexibility, although it did not have the elegance of French models.

KINDS OF FURNITURE

Chairs

As in the Renaissance, the friary continued with its multiple variations in chairs and benches, applying the new ornamentation to all of them (figs. 749, 753) in crestings, rungs and general curved lines. This type persisted, becoming more Baroque first in its carvings, especially on the front rung, and with rich quilted fabrics on the back and seat. There was a multitude of chairs, from the most luxurious (with foreign influence) to the popular models. Not only in Andalusian chairs but in those from Galicia as well, there was a greater English influence, that is, of the Queen Anne period rather than Louis XV (fig. 761).

In the last third of the 17th century we begin to find the so-called Portuguese chairs, contemporaneous with and similar to those of the Louis XIII period, with back and seat of embossed leather (*guadamecil*) tacked to the frame and with bronze pieces in the form of urns. The top was not straight but had a high curve. The vertical elements were turned and highly varied, with a large rung of crossed S-shaped scrolls. Portuguese chairs (the most original of the period) were exported in large numbers to the rest of Europe. The total evolution of this type is curious and graphic and can be fully studied in the Museum of Janelas Verdes in Lisbon. It is reproduced here in a series of photographs (figs. 822-829).

The first type was the interpretation of the friary chair with a low leather back and straight back legs. The first variation was the fall in the back. Afterward came the curved top and the variation in the legs with turned elements and a curve in the back.

The same model continued with other more important elements tending gradually toward Baroque until we come to the variation in the leg, that ended in a stylization of the cabriolet leg of English influence.

At the end of the 17th century, the crossed S-shaped rungs that we see on all the previous models disappeared and the cabriolet leg appeared, reinforced at the beginning by lateral rungs. The last fully Baroque model had cabriolet legs with claws and a high, amply curved back with a highly curved crest. Another chair with gently curved elements ending in scrolls was the model common on the penninsula and contemporary to the Louis XIII and XIV styles, which we have already mentioned.

The Majorcan chairs were very interesting and original. They were usually made of polychrome pine with ladder backs. The high back ended in a circular crest with coarse carvings, both simple and graceful. It was a very Spanish type, the equivalent of the Louis XIII style and a very popular piece. The chair with rush seat and ladder back was also a popular model; it was none else than an interpretation of the so-called French *capuchine* (fig. 772).

We can see that nearly all the more or less interesting and original models were examples of popular art. In France furniture was very much a court art, in England it was more bourgeois and in Spain it was pre-eminently popular.

We have already mentioned the representative and famous Sotomayor armchair, pre-

Showcase

viously preserved in Salamanca, although because of its exaggerated lines and carvings it can be compared to the pure French styles since it is a mixture of the Louis XIII and XIV styles. There were various Salamanca chair models inspired in this one, which was characteristic of the region and which, unfortunately, was sold to a Cuban collector.

There were very beautiful benches with a national interpretation of the Louis XV or Italian styles, with arches on the back like the chairs, some of which were exuberant and fantastic, like the one in the Municipal Museum in Madrid.

Tables

In addition to the lyre table and the small rectangular models with turned and slanted legs, wide aprons, drawers and carvings in the popular style, there were refectory tables with the same structure but new details in ornamentation, such as twist-turned legs (figs. 783, 785, 786) or counterserrate legs, and cabriolet legs in highly exaggerated interpretations.

Whereas the rungs in the Renaissance period were continous or H-shaped, now they were crossed and made with curved and broken elements.

The court table was not lacking either, carved and gilded like its French and Italian counterparts, but cruder.

The tables with lyre-shaped legs were completely national, to the extent of being called Spanish in the rest of Europe. Their legs were highly varied in form, with turned or twist-turned elements sometimes ending in scrolls, but always slanting. One of their distinguishing characteristics was the use of brackets or braces instead of rungs.

There were also tables inspired in French models, especially in Spanish palaces. Others had only two legs or lateral supports, like the Italian models of the 17th century, inspired in the old stone tables. Tables covered with large and richly adorned tapestries were also found.

Consoles, inspired in the Louis XV style, were usually gilded or painted. The most popular ones were from the Levant region.

Cornucopia

They were profusely carved, with cabriolet legs and with the same themes of shells and rocaille we saw in the French Baroque (figs. 790-798).

Cupboards

The *bargueño*, a kind of cabinet for keeping papers, continued in use with a multitude of variations of the preceding style. For example, the table it rested on no longer had arched legs nor was of the friar type, but had lyre-shaped legs, as we shall see further on. The *bargueño* itself continued the architectonic composition of the new Baroque trends with curved and split pediments, twist-turned columns, figures carved all around, very dynamic bronze figures, broken and active galleries and moldings. The drawer fronts had many shapes: looped moldings framing tortoise-shell or marquetry backgrounds with ebony or lignum moldings, backgrounds of painted glass (*eglomisé*), all in the Flemish or Italian style. Plain backgrounds were enriched with cast bronze appliqués, tortoise-shell plaques, velvet, etc. These pieces, representing an evolution of the *bargueño* and the French and Italian cabinet, no longer had drop-tops and were known as *arquimesas* or writing desks. They were crowned with a metal gallery of small balusters with small figures and topped with bronze claws that rested on the table, which was nearly always lyre-shaped with twist-turned legs. This model, with slight variations in composition, was found all over the peninsula (figs. 800, 806).

The chests of prior centuries were still found, nearly always of popular styles with crude Baroque carvings on the legs or influenced by rocaille and covered with rich tapestries. Especially interesting were the so-called bride's chests, similar to those of the Renaissance period, found in the Levant region. They had double covers and the top one could be left open. The interior cover was decorated with paintings, marquetry or carvings, and there was a small drawer for the bride's jewels.

There were also tall cupboards (fig. 805), others with a desk as the lower part, pieces that belonged to the foreign tradition (fig. 803) like the commode that finally appeared well into the 18th century and replaced the large chest (fig. 800). The bureau with inclined top and carved bombé front with drawers was readily accepted in Spain and interpreted by regional artists in the popular style (fig. 805). One example is the *cantarano*, a model commonly seen in Catalonia, whose Italian influence is undeniable.

The so-called showcase was, on the other hand, very much a national piece. It was a sort of cupboard on a table with glass front and sides; it was used to exhibit objects of art or religious images and could be found in an old Spanish house.

Finally, we should mention the cornucopia, a mirror with curved frame and highly varied showy ornamentation with an abundance of motifs and horns of plenty (from which it takes its name; some people call Spanish Baroque the "cornucopia style"), shells, birds, etc. It was an indispensable object in any national interior, to the extent that its name must be added to Spanish Rococo because it was such a common theme (fig. 796).

Clocks

The tall grandfather clock, so characteristic of England, also had national examples, nearly always copies of English models. Nevertheless, there were some whose lines were purely Spanish Baroque.

Beds

There was a wide variety of beds that can be divided into several groups. The first included Italian-style beds, with turned legs and arcaded headboards, cut brass appliqués and high, turned legs on the footboard.

The second group was made up of Portuguese turned beds from Galicia and Salamanca. The headboards were not arcaded but are often finished with intertwined pieces and carved scrolls, and sometimes with bronze appliqués reminiscent of Gothic railings. The third group, with solid headboards raised in the center and very dynamic lines, was nearly always painted with a religious motif in the center. It was a very common model of Venetian tradition and was found throughout the regions of Valencia, Catalonia and Majorca. The fourth group was characterized by carved backgrounds with rocaille, shell, etc., cabriolet legs and balusters, and had a rather English flavor. Finally, we come to the group composed of beds with tall turned columns to support a canopy and covered with hangings like their counterparts of the Louis XIV style and the English beds of the same period. It is curious to see in the photographs, by way of summary, the Spanish version of European models, made by national artists from original pieces brought to the penninsula (figs. 808, 815, 819). Among them we might point out those with Majorcan turned and twist-turned elements, in which we can see Portuguese influence.

Although many names of woodcarvers and woodworkers are known, especially with regard to sacristy pieces, like the Commemorators of Santiago in Madrid, Francisco Delgado (fig. 811), none of them created a school or a style like Boulle or Chippendale. As in the Renaissance, furniture was impersonal. In the archives of the National Palace, names of many woodcarvers in the service of the royal house from the beginning of the 18th century to the middle of the 19th are preserved. But the most original and interesting pieces of furniture are those belonging to the popular group, the works are done by educated Castilian artists acquainted with the Renaissance. The new art and French Rococo filtered through slowly and produced interesting pieces of times past (chests, friar's chairs, *bargueños*) with a purely regional stamp.

There are numerous examples of court furniture in national and private palaces. To give a single example of national characteristics, we might mention the famous Gasparini Salon of the Royal Palace of Madrid, whose designer, brought from Naples by Charles III, was also the designer of the furniture, marbles and scagliolas in the room.

Villa-Real salon

These are some of the most important, perfect and original pieces of Spanish Baroque court furnishings. It is also a curious example in that we see the combination of an order given by a Spanish monarch (Charles III) for his dressing chamber to an Italian artist (M. Gasparini) who designed the furniture with the characteristics of the Louis XV style, and Joseph Canops, master Dutch woodworker (figs. 781, 782), who made them in the royal workshops. The interpretation of the arms of the chairs is interesting and original, with their double curve that gives the model a special elegance, and the marquetry with exquisite metal fillets.

There are abundant examples of bourgeois or aristocratic pieces in the salons and palaces of the Spanish nobility. Very representative, and not chosen by chance, is the salon in the palace belonging to the marquis of Villa-Real in the port of Santa Maria, with ornate consoles in the corners and large, richly adorned mirrors over them. There are examples of the cornucopia mirrors (figs. 816, 817). This combination has gradually disappeared in recent years. Many very beautiful interiors are still preserved in numerous Catalan and Majorcan palaces.

With regard to popular furniture, there is a collection containing many carefully selected pieces in the National Museum of Decorative Arts, which can be taken as an example of the Baroque style as interpreted in Spain.

We add to this chapter, without studying them in detail, a few photographs of South American colonial furniture, in which we can easily see the interpretation of Spanish styles by indigenous artisans (figs. 774, 775, 842) and whose study would be interesting to undertake.

ENGLAND

It was now that England arrived at her moment of grandeur in furniture art. It was a propitious occasion influenced by three important factors: in the first place it was a time of peace in the nation; in the second place the introduction of mahogany, whose malleability, fineness and beauty made it irreplaceable for making furniture; and finally, the advent of a great artist, T. Chippendale. Up to this time the various styles were always known by the name of the monarchs or eras that set their standards. On the contrary, from now on they would be known by the name of the creative artists who best characterize them. In this way the name of Chippendale, who belonged to an old family of woodworkers (his father worked at the beginning of the 18th century) characterized an entire period of English furniture design, elevated by him to its maximum expression. Before him the continental influences were constant and there was little reciprocity. But with Chippendale bourgeois art was carried not only to France and the Netherlands, but to all the continent. European bourgeois furniture, that up to now revolved around the court of the Louises, suddenly discovered a fountain of youth in the sense of inspiration in the English artist and his name is even today the most popular in the history of furniture, even in America.

The transition from the Jacobin Renaissance to Baroque began around 1600 during the reign of Charles II. The era of Charles I, in spite of his friendship with Rubens and his furniture, in all its decorative richness, belonged to the Renaissance period. In the middle of the 17th century, English furniture evolved toward autonomy. If at the beginning it was influenced by French and Italian fashions, later it was to undergo a transformation until it became characterized by an infinitely more practical sense and a perfect assimilation of the continental forms converted to the purest national character. However, the Charles II style was not yet true Baroque; there was still another undefined transition period reflected in James II in 1665. Specifically, it can be said that the first truly English style is the so-called William and Mary. William, Dutch by birth, surrounded himself with continental artists and placed them in contact with English artists. Among these the architect Christopher Wren and the sculptor G. Gibbons contributed the Oriental flavor of porcelain and lacquer, large marquetry compositions with flowers and birds, Dutch cabinets and cupboards also with marquetry and gentle bombés that were constantly copied. Alternating with these bourgeois pieces, constantly increasing in number, were the court furnishings—heavy consoles, armchairs, beds with high columns, Louis XV hangings and large, curved headboards in the shape of a reverse C, adorned with scrolls and angels and showing a far greater continental inspiration. Thus in 1712 we come to the Queen Anne style, the first pure Baroque, somber and elegant. With it we see the first use of lacquer and marquetry, both with a more national character than in the time of William, and the constant use of the cabriolet leg (claw and ball), Oriental in origin, whose appearance can be placed at about 1700.

The following reign of George I and the contribution of the artist William Kent, architect and furniture designer (1714), represented in English furniture design an era and a style that was undeniably parallel to the French Regency. In it we can see clearly the influence of the Louis XIV style and at the same time a prelude to the George II, full and true English Baroque—the Georgian style—that would be characterized and absorbed by the great furniture maker Chippendale, whose fame began in the first third of the 18th century. It is at this time when English furniture, so different from continental models, acquired once and for all its peculiar stamp of practical correctness with a bourgeois and comfortable nature.

Chippendale not only made furniture but also created models and prototypes and even introduced new styles and fashions. He evolved with great malleability toward these currents. His famous illustrated books with original drawings, dedicated to the public at large as well as to the specialist, established the fashion of his time, extending new forms and with them, naturally, his personal fame and style. His primary talent was his ability to see how to link pure furniture art to industrialization processes, and although he made all types of pieces, he achieved his greatest heights with chairs. His facility for capturing the essential ideas of all styles is admirable, and we can see how he not only evolved from Baroque toward Rococo but even entered into the Neoclassical style. Although he used the characteristic claw-and-ball feet of the George I style, his personality is easily perceived in the curves of the arms as well as in the sloping backs and the decorative compositions of cupboard fronts, pediments and drawers. When R. Adam appeared in the reign of George III and with the Neoclassical style, we see Chippendale making new models, attracted by the serene and somewhat cold beauty of the return to classical ways. A true artist, his creative powers did not diminish or die as long as he was physically able to bear up under the weight of a truly astounding creative labor, which perhaps came closer to the ephemeral notion of universality than that of many other artists.

Chippendale was born in 1710; he worked during the reigns of George II and III and died in 1779. He represented an entire era in the history of furniture and belonged to the highest plane as a pace setter of good taste. He was copied by the best furniture makers to the extent that many pieces considered to be his were actually made by his imitators. His art crossed the channel and the continent adopted the English fashion.

The artistic fervor of the most celebrated English furniture maker, brought to life in different manners and styles, can be followed step by step today. In the first period, Chippen-

Bell leg

dale followed the influence of the Queen Anne and Dutch styles, mixed later with Louis XV. In the middle of the century new decorative motifs penetrated his technique; this was his Chinese period, original and firmly fixed in European elements, which demonstrated his extraordinary ability. Finally, around 1760, in his desire for variety and perfection, he began a new decorative style with a conventional Gothic mode that was surprisingly ephemeral. In the last quarter century he followed the Neoclassical fashion, to which he was attracted by the most representative personality of the style, the architect R. Adam.

MATERIALS

In the first period we see how Renaissance oak was replaced by walnut, easier to carve and turn. This was in the reign of the William and Mary style. Its use continued in the Queen Anne years, but from 1720 when mahogany was introduced, this wood predominated immediately and with Chippendale was adopted everywhere. It became the wood of the period, and various types of mahogany were distinguished: one from Cuba, another from Santo Domingo and a third continental variety. The first was the finest and most malleable. Large surfaces were panelled with exotic woods or were lacquered and gilded. Marquetry was a mixture of Dutch flowers and Italian geometry. Art was essentially bourgeois and, instead of the rich and expensive silks and wall tapestries, used decorative wallpaper in harmony with them and the economic and decorative fabrics of the Orient. Curiously, mahogany was not used in Dutch furnishings.

DECORATION

In interior decoration, as in the Louis XIV style, the architect Christopher Wren used mantelets, tapestries, squared spaces and opulent cornices. In furniture the legs, arm brackets and rungs were fluid and characteristic of the James II style, which marked the beginning of Baroque. The seats were wider and more square, and backs higher. The decorative motifs were marquetry and lacquer. Bronze appliqués for drawer pulls and keyholes were very typical and clearly defined, simple and fine. There were various characteristic details of the 18th-century English styles which we can define. In the William and Mary period, turned legs were often used with a large bell on the upper turned part, and the feet were onion-shaped or stylized claws ending in scrolls. Similarly, rungs were very typical, crossed and sinuous as in the Louis XIV style. The front rung was especially decorative, in the form of two crossed S's (figs. 844, 855, 856).

Chair and settee backs were very high, either upholstered or made of cane and with turned wood elements and large flat surfaces (figs. 843, 845).

With the Queen Anne style the use of the cabriolet leg spread. Furniture was made with little molding; pieces were plain and smooth, sometimes partly gilded or perhaps with a carved shell (figs. 857, 858, 871, 873). A new element was introduced on chair backs, whose lines were gentle and curved. This was the center splat or lyre, a wooden piece in the form of a stylized goblet, a solid piece at the beginning of the Baroque style (fig. 848). Perhaps the vertical bars in the backs of some Windsor chairs, a typical model with a similar but wider element, were the origin of this solid splat which became one of the characteristics of the Queen Anne style (fig. 847). On the other hand, these splats were carved with openwork by Chippendale and doubtless represent one of the differences between the chairs of these two periods, otherwise so difficult to distinguish in many cases (figs. 849, 859).

We have already said that legs in the Queen Anne style were of a simple cabriolet form (the first still have H-shaped rungs), ending first in a disk that rested on the floor and later in a claw and ball. In the upper part they also had carvings of acanthus leaves or shells, this last a very characteristic element and the one most commonly found on the tops and aprons of cupboards, writing desks, etc. As the century progressed, with the Georgian style, furniture became richer in carvings and decoration while, on the other hand, marquetry and turned elements disappeared altogether (figs. 896, 908).

Chippendale picked up all these elements and purified them to produce an enormous variety in his drawings on chair backs. He mixed Chinese with Rococo motifs (although we should not forget that it was Sir William Chambers who launched the fashion of Chinese motifs after a journey as tutor for George III) (figs. 867, 868).

In what we can call his Gothic period, seat backs were fine latticework pieces with a highly personal design. Toward the end he even replaced cabriolet legs with simple square ones, placing all the Baroque decoration on the backs which were of very definite types, some with latticework center splats with ingenious designs, like those with intertwined letters and pleated bands. In this latter type the French influence was evident; there were others with the back entirely carved in a fine filigree design with Chinese or Gothic patterns. Finally we have the ladderback type, typical of Chippendale, with finely carved parallel horizontal slats (figs. 859, 860, 862, 872, 874).

In the bookshelves the plain surfaces achieved their greatest expression in wood latticework superimposed on the glass doors, while square straight legs continued. On the round dressing tables, a piece created in the middle of the century, the silhouette of the leg was broken with the curves so typical of this artist (figs. 888, 894, 907).

There was also a so-called Irish Chippendale style, which was more coarse and had flatter surfaces and less finely carved bas reliefs. There were a large number of these pieces inspired in the English originals. The mahogany used in them was the darkest variety that comes from the island of Santo Domingo.

STRUCTURES

At the beginning, still in the low Renaissance style, there was little variation. Armchair backs were exaggeratedly high, seats were upholstered and the design of arms and legs was very fluid. Design was somber and no molding was used; separations between drawers and doors were flat and architectonic elements were not used on them, contrary to the continental custom. Turned or twist-turned legs ended in scrolls and began to evolve toward the double C form with a natural curve, until the curved or cabriolet form appeared with the purity of the style itself.

At the beginning, these cabriolet legs preserved the H-shaped rungs out of timidity, but these did not respond to a clear decorative composition with the simple curved line of the leg and gradually disappeared.

Backs curved horizontally and vertically to adapt better to the shape of the human back; they were no longer so high and narrow as at the beginning of the style. The back legs were not vertical but slightly inclined. In general, English Baroque furniture was characterized by its logical structural line, the elegance of the whole and the continuity of the silhouette more than by the richness and profusion of its carvings which never reached the heights of fluidity and ornateness of the continent. All the elements of continental Baroque—split pediments, floral exuberance, convoluted and broken panels, twist-turned elements, bombé pieces—were used in England, but their dynamism was much more contained. We can see a deep aversion not only to symmetry but also to the exaggerated movement of some elements, such as the twist-turned elements, and on the other hand, the cabriolet leg imported from China was captured and made such an important characteristic in England that it is a defining feature of the Queen Anne and Chippendale styles.

The legs of commodes and cupboards were a prolongation of the supports from which the socles extended. The bronze drawer pulls were also an interesting feature of the period.

The preoccupation with proportion in furniture was expressed in numerous books with details and measurements. In the grandfather clocks, for example, the proportion of height and width were carefully studied and chair proportions were also highly rigorous.

KINDS OF FURNITURE

A multitude of pieces were created which were practical as well as elegant, precisely the same ones that are used today and that serve as prototypes. Luxury and comfort became increasingly important. The sale of mass-produced sets began for the growing middle class that made up English society, as each room formed a unit. Wallpapers decorated with Chinese drawings were substituted for expensive tapestries.

Chairs

The upholstered James II chair, with its high square back and legs with original lines and carvings, prepared the maturity of the Baroque style. With William and Mary a type of chair appeared with an oval cane back surrounded by a carved frame, with carved arms and legs also. In this period sofas made of three or more chairs joined together were very characteristic. We need say no more here about the Queen Anne and Chippendale chairs and sofas as we have already discussed them (figs. 843–889).

Although they were a popular and somewhat peasant style, we should mention here the Windsor chairs, with their curved wood, backs made of turned vertical posts, the center one wider, and wooden seat. Because of their beauty they have been copied by numerous English, American and even continental furniture designers, each one giving them his own character (figs. 846, 847).

Tables and cupboards

Tables, which at the beginning were made with twist-turned legs due to Dutch and Italian influence, adapted to national tastes and the gate-leg table appeared, so named because its eight legs were made in such a way that they swung aside like a gate. This model, which began with the William and Mary style, was later taken to the Netherlands and even today is very common on all the continent. There were study tables with side drawers and claw feet, still seen today, that were designed by Chippendale himself (figs. 888, 889, 890). Round tables were large, supported on a single center leg in the shape of a turned and carved goblet which in turn rested on three cabriolet legs (figs. 875, 876). This model has lasted until today and is a true specimen of the period. At the same time, the great interest in entertainment and diversion during this period gave rise to the construction of a large number of game tables.

Consoles copied the continental court models with gilded carvings (figs. 884, 885, 886), although at times they were simple rectangular tables on cariolet legs, usually with marble tops (figs. 882, 886).

Among the new models the most exquisite was undoubtedly the highboy or tallboy, a large, tall cabinet in two sections. The upper part sometimes had glass doors for exhibiting fine china or books, so much in vogue throughout the century, and the lower one had drawers like a commode. Variations on this theme were the bureaus with inclined top, models in which nobody has surpassed the English, crowned with curved and broken pediments, sometimes lacquered and always beautiful (figs. 898, 903, 906). On all of them the handles and hinges were carefully made of gilded bronze.

The secretary was a typical piece of this period, sometimes with marquetry and other times lacquered and varnished. The commode, imported from France, replaced completely the chests and credences. They were simple, with extended socles and bronze appliqués (figs. 908, 909, 910).

Clocks

Lacquered furniture became very common. Chippendale made all kinds of pieces of which he left a multitude of models in his publications. He composed dining room, bedroom and study sets in which the proportions were always perfect and renovation constant. A highly interesting model was the grandfather clock which at the beginning of the Baroque period was covered with marquetry and later lacquered. Chippendale perfected the type, making it of mahogany, ornamented with his characteristic fretwork, bronze appliqués, split pediments, etc. In general clocks follow, with respect to materials and ornamentation, the same evolution as other pieces of furniture. The most famous clocks were those by Tompion, father of the art of clockmaking, and his disciple Graham (figs. 913, 915). But the number of artists was infinite.

Beds

Beds were of large proportions with columns on the ends. These bed pillars or columns were very interesting; Chippendale shows us numerous models in his books, as well as instructions for placing the canopy. This and the headboard were usually upholstered, sometimes with colored print fabrics (figs. 917, 918, 919, 920), instead of being made of wood, as on the continent. Other times the headboards had highly Baroque silhouettes. The fabrics, as we have already said, were not comparable in richness to the French ones but, like the print bedspreads, were highly pleasing.

The number, use and property of each piece of furniture were interminable and we cannot possibly list them all here. But in the photographs we have attempted to choose the most characteristic models so that a simple examination makes explanation unnecessary.

We can observe also that many interiors of this period, doubtless because of their more human nature, the proportions of the rooms, the very placement of the furniture with the simple and pleasing lines of the pieces, were practical and useful and are still used today with a constant demand for comfort.

GERMANY

Baroque did not begin in Germany until the middle of the 17th century, later than in Italy, France and the Netherlands, and it did not penetrate by way of southern Germany, so close to Italy, but across its borders with France and the Netherlands. It was perhaps the constant exchange of artists between these nations that best explains this phenomenon.

As in France, German Baroque was divided into three periods that coincided with the French ones: Baroque itself, the equivalent of the Louis XIV style; Regency, which is the French style of the same name; and Rococo, corresponding to the time of Louis XV. Schluter in the first period, Effner, contemporary of Cressent in the second, and Kambly, Hoppenhaupt and Cuvilles in the third were the artists who characterized most strongly and personally these three moments of German Baroque.

In general, German Baroque contributed very few new models, and these were exclusively influenced by French types or vice versa, especially in those pieces or bronze appliqués which, like all luxury pieces, were ordered directly from France. There was also some English influence, especially in pieces we might call Georgian and Chippendale of the period (figs. 923, 925). In spite of these relations and the knowledge of a greater number of prototypes within the group of cupboards and their variations (the cupboard is still the national piece of furniture *par excellence*), many highly original and interesting types were produced (figs. 939, 941).

One of the most characteristic features of German Baroque was the unfortunate exaggeration of French models. We can see the excessive twisting of the elements that in France had achieved a delicate and difficult balance of a highly dynamic style. The same occured with the bourgeois models of England, with their studied and perfect lines, that here were made more coarse and heavy. Even in the cupboards, directly influenced by the Dutch, the moldings and reliefs were violent and protruding, although in many cases pieces of great beauty were achieved (fig. 945).

The old Renaissance pieces based on small architectonic subdivisions were now large compositions that in general produced a whole which was an excellent piece of carpentry work.

Within the Baroque style there were not such great regional differences as we saw in the Renaissance period between the north and south. However, there were local schools at Nuremberg, Frankfurt, Dantzig, Hamburg, etc. (figs. 943, 944, 947), each with its peculiar characteristics in moldings, carvings, use of veneer, marquetry, etc., which can be clearly seen in the photographs. But in the Rococo period furniture did not respond to the influence of these local schools. It was rather the artists themselves who were the creators of types.

Between 1760 and 1770 there was also in Germany a return to classical styles that, similarly to other European countries, made itself felt in a breath of inspiration from the past.

MATERIALS

Walnut and national woods from the south were still used as raw materials, although they were enriched with marquetry and inlay made not only of exotic woods but of metal, imitating Boulle, with a greater proportion of tin, mother-of-pearl, ivory, shell and hard stones. The use of tapestries became important and innumerable types of fabric and luxurious tapestries adorned, preserved and made of furniture and rooms new expressions of the nascent feeling of intimacy.

STRUCTURES

As in France, the end of the Renaissance moved and complicated structures in abundant subdivisions that the Baroque style now simplified to convert a piece of furniture into a truly unified whole. The elements were fully Baroque: twisted columns, split pediments (replaced at the end of the style by crestings with Rococo forms) and, especially, moldings on the surfaces, cornices and socles. These, with their violent lights and shadows, gave extraordinary life to furniture. This was perhaps one of the most characteristic features of German furniture. Although it was found on Dutch pieces as well, it was in Germany where its profiles took on a more exaggerated and unmistakable line. The S-shaped curved leg we saw introduced into Europe from the Netherlands also appeared here. In the full Rococo period, in the bombé commodes or in the lower part of cupboards, furniture makers did not stop at curves like those of the highly balanced French art, but complicated the fronts of their pieces with two or three concave and convex undulations, still achieving models of great beauty and originality (fig. 933).

DECORATION

Decoration was highly varied. There were profusely carved pieces and others with the undulating design we have described earlier. Still others were gilded and some, in the Rococo period, were painted in gold and white with profuse decoration or marquetry.

Sometimes the Baroque aspect of furniture decoration was obtained with great simplicity, only in terms of a daring and dynamic line. It was then enriched with bronze or copper appliqués as drawer pulls and keyholes in the form of stylized and careful motifs with obvious influences, as we have said before, not only of the Regency and Louis XV styles, but also of contemporary English Georgian and Chippendale styles.

We find a new originality in the opulent German Baroque. When the vertical elements and supports, especially on tables, were twist-turned, their profiles were large and voluminous, characteristic of the style and unique in the history of such ornamental elements (figs. 928, 929).

KINDS OF FURNITURE

Tables and cupboards

The cupboard was still the national piece of furniture, with slight variations according to its artistic origin. Those of Nuremberg, an important and well known manufacturing center, were classical in line and enriched with garlands and Baroque motifs. Interesting also were those from Frankfurt with their violent moldings and socles on balls. To the north, in the cupboards of Hamburg, we can easily see the relation to Holland in the carvings. These cupboards were finished with a pediment on the cornice, whereas the pediments on the Dantzig cupboards were split. As in the Renaissance, all the cupboards had two or four doors of large and heavy proportions (figs. 939, 947).

Study tables with drawers and spiral legs now began to appear. Chairs and sofas, similar to French, Dutch and English models, also had this type of leg, as well as round and square tables whose twist-turned legs gave them a highly original aspect. Consoles, commodes, tables and chairs of the Regency period, very similar to the French type (we should not forget that Cotte, Oeben and other French decorators come from Germany) were exuberantly decorated and carved and "not very distinguished" (fig. 935).

The most beautiful piece of the period was the commode-writing desk with a two-door showcase or cupboard, whose origin and development were rooted not only on the continent but also in England (figs. 937, 940). Rococo chairs and sofas were, like their predecessors, influenced by the French. Nevertheless, there was a group of bourgeois chairs and armchairs of the 18th century that were directly influenced by the great English furniture maker Chippendale, models almost as pure, perfect and delicate as the English ones of universal fame.

Numerous German palaces possessed many Rococo pieces similar to French ones, although not always as well done. The types were the same, and the Regency writing desk now achieved its maximum importance and perfection, obtaining a great unity with its diverse elements—cupboard, commode, bureau. There were very beautiful pieces with variations in the upper part of the showcase and the lower in bombé form, as we have already mentioned. Beautiful examples of the three periods—Baroque, Regency and Rococo—are still preserved, such as those of the Berlin and Potsdam palaces, designed by Schluter at the beginning of the 18th century. There are also models by Effner and Schleisheim, others by Cuvilles and Hoppenhaupt in Munich and others by Kambly in Frederick the Great's palace in Potsdam (fig. 950).

Potsdam showcase cupboard

LOW COUNTRIES

At the beginning of the 18th century, Rubens, personally overseeing the decoration of his house in Antwerp, pointed the way to the beginning of the Baroque style in furniture and interior decoration. The development of the style can be followed perhaps better in the paintings of the Flemish masters than in the pieces of furniture that have been preserved. Some very interesting pieces can be studied in paintings by Rubens himself as well as others by Van Dyck, Jordaens, etc.

It was in this period when rooms began to be considered as a whole, with unity in decoration and furnishings. In these decorative schemes with their marble fireplaces, doors crowned with split pediments, adorned with leaves and scrolls, and in their rich panelling we can see the first Baroque elements.

At the beginning, as always occurs in transition periods, there was little variation in furniture from the Renaissance models, which persisted in the face of change. For example, turned elements, which were stronger, were replaced by twist-turned pieces. Ebony, lignum and other exotic woods were superimposed on oak or walnut panels, just beginning to appear, and at the same time the angles began to break and new motifs appeared in carvings.

Among the pieces of furniture characteristic of this period the cupboard was the most important. It was crowned with large cornices on columns or caryatids. It had two or four doors covered with carvings that always followed Biblical or historical themes. The credenzas, a type of low cupboard between columns and brackets, had two doors. On the first commodes that appeared in these bourgeois interiors, the drawer fronts began to curve.

Tables were rectangular and were still made of large pieces supported on round and oval balusters. Armchairs had the same shape as those of the Louis XII style, with upholstered seats and nails of Spanish Renaissance type but larger and rounder, doubtless because of the profusion of pleats in the clothing of the time (figs. 966, 967, 972).

When all the elements of the early Baroque style had infiltrated the structure of furniture, decoration became simpler. It was reduced exclusively to the movement of the line, a characteristic which especially influenced the nascent French Baroque style.

In Holland, to the northeast of the Netherlands, the importance of furniture making coincided with a general resurgence of the arts and a natural Flemish influence, even more important because of the complex political and frontier problems of the time.

The bourgeois atmosphere of the nation exerted a great influence on this development, as can be observed, for example, in the Dutch paintings showing interiors of the period (fig. 968). Houses were built and rooms were decorated with the unity that is characteristic of the style, but they were more frugal and simpler than the French ones. Persian tapestries and fabrics appeared at this time and were not only used for decorating floors and walls but for upholstering furniture as well. The Oriental influence penetrated also with its porcelain and lacquers, and the height of this fashion was clearly reflected in the lacquered two-door cupboards with inside drawers imported from the Orient.

Nevertheless, the Renaissance forms continued and refused to disappear, although there was less carving, to the benefit of the structural line, which was now purer. At this time, toward the end of the 17th century, Quelinus founded the Dutch School of Decorative Sculpture.

We have already said that the cupboard, as in all of central Europe, was the most important piece of furniture. Its doors were subdivided into octagonal shapes with inlay of other kinds of wood and ivory, and they were adorned with looped moldings. The twist-turned column, a typically Baroque element, was commonly used on the lengthwise parts of cupboards and on chairs and tables. Among the various types of wood used in furniture making, oak predominated at first and ebony and lignum were nearly always used for veneer decoration. Around 1660 walnut became as common as oak and toward the end of the century ebony furniture came into style, a fashion which passed into France. The vertical elements were turned, highly fluid or twist-turned; moldings were usually looped (fig. 974) and carvings were discreet within the dynamic lines of the pieces.

At the beginning of the 17th century cupboards were made with even more protruding moldings but with rounded angles.

Dutch relations with the Orient made it possible for their furniture makers to copy the legs of Chinese furniture, curved in the shape of an S, and cabinets with inside drawers and lacquered doors, made in China, were imported.

In general, the Dutch accentuated the width and solidity of Flemish lines. There are many examples of this in the paintings of Terborch,

Gerard Dou, Franz Hals, etc. And thus we come to the 18th century.

Furniture was very simple, but its structural lines were curved, continuous, fluid—that is, Baroque. Pieces were decorated with beautiful marquetry works of flowers and fruit (figs. 960, 965, 968), especially large cupboards with bombé doors and drawers, many of them attributed to the Moraves brothers. These works of marquetry, which cover the surfaces of all types of furniture, were taken to England by Prince William on the occasion of his marriage to Queen Mary. They were received with such enthusiasm that their continental origin was forgotten and they took on a fully English nature. Prince William, however, surrounded himself with Dutch artists and, in the same way that the Baroque style penetrated into France through Flanders, in England it came by way of Holland.

In this way it arrived in France and England, the two countries in which the Baroque style found its most perfect development. In France this was accomplished in court and luxury furnishings and in English in bourgeois furniture.

Similarly in Spanish furniture, with floral inlay in the drawers of writing desks covered with shells and in ornamentation with looped moldings and painted crystal, we can see its even more natural origin because of the political relations with the Netherlands.

NEOCLASSICAL AND EMPIRE

FRANCE

NEOCLASSICAL

In 1738 and 1748 under the patronage of Charles of Bourbon, king of the two Sicilies, excavations of Herculaneum and Pompeii were begun.

Some years later, in 1761, the writings of Winckelmann and Barthelemy on ancient art began to shed light, if not on the pure art of Greece, at least on that of Imperial Rome. These events coincided with, and stimulated, a cult of antiquity which architects, sculptors and painters translated into works of great purity of line, although the results were less spontaneous, cold and academic, and somewhat affected.

It was a natural reaction after the wantonness of the Rococo style, whose historical evolution and study in depth we cannot enter into here.

In the development and production of furniture throughout these years, a transformation began that was similar to the reaction produced by Neoclassicism in the plastic arts at the end of the 18th century in the final years of the reign of Louis XV with the construction of the Trianon palaces at Versailles.

France continued to be the most important center of furniture production. Its study, as well as the standards that define and characterize it, can be generalized to the entire continent, with certain national features that, although resulting in pieces luxurious on the one hand and charming and interesting on the other, were certainly less pure in line and proportion.

Simultaneously in England, this expected evolution of the Baroque style was evidenced in a clear bourgeoisie feeling in English furniture, and the styles—as in all the 18th century—bore the names of the creating artists, in contrast to the rest of Europe where they continued to be identified with the kings of each period.

In the last years of Louis XV, the Pompadour style represented the beginning of a reaction against the dislocated dynamism of the Rococo and we can see how, from 1775 on, furniture designs were more restful and balanced. Even before the death of the king, the first signs of the new style that would bear the name of the Delphin are evident, although in reality it should be called Marie Antoinette, after that delicate, restless and elegant woman, since there is nothing in its slender and graceful forms to suggest the large, rotund man that Louis XVI was, as one of the queen's biographers has pointed out.

Toward the end of the 18th century, furniture was produced in increasing quantities and the technique achieved its maximum perfection.

With the nascent classical cult, the lines became straight and restful and the decoration austere and classical. Thus the Louis XVI or Neoclassical style came to have its own features that distinguished it from preceding ones and from the Empire style that followed it after the Revolution. Its elegance, lightness and delicacy were in no way overdone but natural, and it was not without coquetry and femininity, although less so than the style of Louis XV which was more graceful and fluid. The purity and rigidity of its lines contrasted with the heaviness of Louis XIV and Regency styles although like them, it was a severe style, so much so that the two are sometimes confused, especially in Boulle pieces, which reappear, and in the use of some of the typical elements of those styles, such as hound's feet—not cabriolet legs with their gentle curves—slightly bombé surfaces and bronze appliqués, etc. We should note that these three details are not characteristic of the style.

On the other hand, Louis XVI is differentiated from the Empire style, which we shall analyze further on, in that it was a more original and elegant adaptation, although sometimes affected, of the older forms, but always with a more feminine feeling. If there was any artist who characterized this era, it was undoubtedly the sculptor Houdon, creator of the statue of Voltaire. But in furniture art it is interesting to note that the artists were the same ones of the preceding period, even lasting into the 19th century, who themselves continued the new styles, such as the Directoire and Empire. This is why we find pieces of doubtful or transitional style because some of the preceding decorative elements were still used, such as some examples of Empire style with Louis XVI motifs, and pieces featuring Louis XVI lines and Empire bronze appliqués.

We could study this evolution and mixture of styles, complete with the survival of various motifs of both, in the work of a genial artist of the second half of the 18th century, George Jacob. In this way we see the changes that came about in furniture from the end of the Louis XV period until the Empire, that is, in a space of forty years.

It is also interesting to observe that although many artists were German (perhaps the queen's nationality exerted some influence here), furniture designs did not for this reason lose their French character and they were perfect and pure of line, balance and proportion. For all these reasons, the return to the old forms was not brusque and was always linked to the preceding style. Thus we see the gentle bombé of the commodes, the slightly cabriolet leg—now softer—the metal appliqués of classical drawings and other details we shall analyze further on, which gave rise in this moment of transition to the most beautiful pieces of the style.

In the revolutionary period, when the guillotine finished off the monarchy and the desire to renew the customs of the ancient Greek and Roman republics was born, furniture designs became more severe and less rich. Marquetry, mosaics and chiselling were brushed aside to adapt the new models to this intermediate era, which uses phrases such as "in the Greek style", "the Etruscan mode", "revolutionary". All of them were nothing more than a simplified Louis XVI ornamented with revolutionary symbols, even the Consulate and Directoire. Later on, with the Empire style, luxury returned and furniture designs took on an imperial look, instead of reviving the old national forms of the 18th century that marked the height of grandeur in furniture. The new classical tradition continued its tyranny with a more architectonic and imitative sense, although its lines were careful and exquisite, and everywhere across the nation the furnishings of whole homes were changed and replaced with the new style that, with Napoleon, bore the name of Empire.

MATERIALS

Around 1670 mahogany appeared in France and from then on became irreplaceable. At the same time the use of exotic wood veneers, such as *sapeli*, mahogany panels, tulip wood, *palo santo* and *bois de roi*, became popular. The dark edges of large flat surfaces were covered with *palo santo* and ebony, and fillets with light and rose-colored woods. In the centers were flowers in marquetry with designs by Riesener, the great woodworker of German and French origin, or a variety of geometric designs. Upholstery was done with tapestries by Gobelin, Bauverais and Aubousson, delicately worked and in soft colors. The drawings often showed scenes from Pompeii, always somber and classical. Bronze appliqués were still used although they were much lighter but finely gilded and chiselled. Their importance was now only secondary, as compared to the Louis XV style, and marquetry, which reappeared at the end of this king's reign, was now more highly developed.

DECORATION

There were several decorative elements that defined pieces of the Louis XVI style. However, since the change was not brusque and the artists were the same as in the final years of Louis XV, there were pieces that seemed to belong to the former period and others characteristic of the Empire style and even Louis XIV either because of the predominance of straight lines or their general rigidity. A characteristic that clearly distinguished the two Louises was the heavy masculinity in the case of Louis XIV pieces, as compared with the somewhat feminine lines of Louis XVI. The latter tended to be small and easily carried whereas the former were heavy and difficult to move.

Let us look now at the most characteristic elements of decoration. Marquetry was either geometric, like the peculiar rhombus or flower centers of Riesener, one of the most important woodworkers of the period. Gold was no longer used except in fillets or isolated decorative motifs, and a new fashion of painted furniture became popular. Predominating in these pieces were "delicate and pale shades, soft cream, rose-peach and spring blue", according to a description by S. Zweig. The resulting ornamentation replaced the Rococo style with classical capitals, especially Ionic, and repeated motifs with laurel and evergreen oak leaves, fruit, leaves and chains of pearls. Other Neoclassical features were multi-folded fabrics, medallions and ruffled bands with characteristic intertwinings or grooved legs, and X-shaped bands. Another popular motif was a leaf carved inside a rectangle or a rhombus, usually gilded or made of bronze and found on socles amid classical designs. Little by little ornamentation became rigid, balanced and symmetrical, with right angles predominating. The garlands no longer showed the disorderly gaiety of the Louis XV style but were now somber and inflexible, as dictated by the new academic standards. Pastoral scenes were still used, such as quivers, bird nests, flowers, doves and Cupids, all intertwined with musical instruments, horns of plenty, rams' heads, etc., in groups, circular or oval medallions and festooned with the classical pleated and intertwined band. Animal themes were frequently used also, such as dolphins and the allegorical eagles of the royal houses, and sphinxes, lions, etc. Bronze was no longer used in such profusion that it nearly became part of the structure as in the Rococo style, but is used for its color and quality to enhance the ornamentation. Typical metal elements were the banisters or fretwork found on the upper part of pieces such as secreteries, bureaus or *chiffonniers*. The grooves and striations on uprights and legs were another characteristic feature of the period, as well as the gilt bars or finely chiselled bronze, often in the form of asparagus stalks, found in the grooves.

Sometimes the legs were still curved, evoking the graceful cabriolet. Others were tapered or turned, ending in a small hoof-shaped foot which gave them a very elegant line. Turned legs, unused since the time of Louis XIII, returned now decorated with small bronze appliqués in the form of raindrops, capitals, spiral-shaped laurel branches and, especially the typical carved grooves we mentioned before. We should not forget, finally, the characteristic appliqués in oval, octagonal and other geometric shapes, some made of painted and gilded crystal called *eglomisé* and frequently of Sèvres porcelain—Wedgwood in England, Retiro in Spain, Capo di Monte in Italy—that were an important decorative element used so lavishly in the 19th century, repeating models of the 18th century as influenced by the disorientation and artistic eclecticism of the time.

STRUCTURES

The highly organized guilds in the time of Louis XV, and even more rigorously ordered around 1770, imposed rigid conditions on the woodworking profession and took this industrial art to its great technical perfection. All work was controlled by the guilds and pieces were generally signed or stamped. A listing was published annually, thanks to which we can follow today the history of furniture throughout nearly the whole of the 18th century. Pieces were technically perfect. Techniques such as the use of dowels, tongue-in-groove, glede or swallow tail were followed by variations on these same methods that become more and more complex as dictated by the quality of the work and technological advances. As examples we can mention the mixed assemblies of angle and dowel, or the so-called bastard dowels or flute tip, using the decorative lines themselves to hide the joints. Furniture in general was of finely rigid lines, softened by ornamentation, for example, on the legs which were straight with slight tapering and a gentle curve. The old decorative pieces used to cover chair legs had disappeared, in spite of the return of the straight line, and now were seen only on large tables or consoles, crossed over and with large decorative elements at the point of crossing. Surfaces were generally flatter; the drawers of commodes were flush with the front and formed a single whole with bronze appliqués and other decorative elements concealing them. Vertical supports stood out, although they might be curved and the horizontal lines molded. These two directions, vertical and horizontal, were accented with channels and grooves and, although they were sometimes spiral, right angles and verticals predominate. Bronze, which in preceding styles was part of the structure, here was used only to accentuate the vertical lines. And finally, the lines that in the Louis XV style were veiled and concealed by decorative elements typical of Baroque, now stood out clearly.

KINDS OF FURNITURE

It may be said that all of the Louis XVI style is contained in the Petit Trianon, the private palace built by Marie Antoinette in Versailles. The music salon was never empty (the Austrian queen known as "La Toinette", as a child in Schoembrunn was taught by Bluck); we can see and study the finest models of the style in its furnishings. But in addition, the number of pieces multiplied and models for new uses were created. The variety of beds, all types of tables, chairs, as well as totally useless pieces, was enormous. We have already said that the artists were often foreigners, but the architects, draughtsmen and decorators were French. In this way furniture did not lose its national character and the names of the latter were not so well known as the former. The first and most important was undoubtedly Riesener, of German origin but educated in Paris with Oeben. After him came Carlin, Leleu, Beneman and too many others to mention here—well over a hundred and all important.

Beds

Beds, as in previous reigns, were placed in large salons either lengthwise, sideways, in special niches, or in alcoves separated by balustrades. They were called, in order of importance, "duchess", "crown" and *parade*, with canopies in varied forms or without them (figs. 1008, 1009, 1010). The upholstered headboards and footboards were made of wood and were similar in line to the chairs, between turned and grooved columns on the sides. The top pieces were usually straight, with slight arches and especially in the form known as *chapeau*. The best examples of this type were those of Marie Antoinette in the Petit Trianon, and the best of the *parade* type can be found in the Fontainebleau Palace, as drawn by Philippe

Lasalle. We can see the eiderdown coverlets on them, after the Austrian and German custom.

Tables

In the 17th century the table was similar to the console. The latter was placed along the wall and often attached to the table. The top was made of marble and the legs were bracket shaped, set in and richly gilded. Toward the end of the 18th century consoles appeared with crossed rungs decorated in the center with a goblet, urn, vase with flowers or figures of sphinxes, dragons, etc. (fig. 990).

On the other hand there was an infinite variety of small work tables, tables for sewing or games, and small desks and *gueridon*—a name dating back to the 17th century describing a small end table for a lamp and probably a word used to refer to a slave or servant who performed this service. The examples of *bonheur de jour*, small *bureaux* or *secrétaries* feminine and delicate of line, are numerous. The most famous are those by Riesener, Levasseur, Weisweller and Schwerdfeger (fig. 993).

The old dressing tables, which were nothing more than simple covered wooden tables, were replaced by authentic dressing tables that were used in the same form until the 19th century. These *toilettes*, with slender turned or tapered legs, sometimes had two lyre-shaped supports which were so common in Romanticism and in the Second Empire style. At the end of the 18th century this piece assumed great importance. It was usually made with a vertical mirror in the center that folded down into the top of the table. The *poudreuse*, so called because it was used for powdering wigs, was derived from the dressing table. Later the mirror was no longer hidden but rotated between two posts. We shall see elegant examples of this in the English Neoclassical style.

In the latter case these mirrors were placed on top of a set of small drawers, forming a separate piece of furniture which could be placed on top of a table. These were the small *coiffeuses*.

From here we go to the *psique* later on in the Empire style, on which the mirror and the posts were very large.

Cupboards and chairs

This period was characterized by numerous pieces of Oriental lacquered furniture. Carlin used these lacquers in his *chiffonnier* commodes, corner cupboards, *encoignures*, *bureaux* and small tables. There were a number of representative works of this famous woodworker in the Louvre. A close collaborator of all woodworkers is the bronze worker. Of these the most famous of the period were Gouthière, who worked in France and other European courts, and Clodion, the sculptor whose hand can be seen in many pieces dating from the end of the 18th century (fig. 1000).

Commodes, severe and majestic, were the richest and most commonly seen pieces. The commodes by Leleu, who apparently did no work in marquetry, are among the best known, as well as those by the German Beneman in palaces and national museums (figs. 1001, 1005). We should remember that Boulle pieces also appeared in this period; Montigny, assisted by Levasseur, reproduced these models by official request. His work, nevertheless, did not have the same quality as the originals.

Let us go on now to chairs. We should mention first G. Jacob, founder of the house that continued in existence until the middle of the 19th century and in which we can follow the evolution of the chair. A wide variety of models were created by him. The *cabriolé*, *violoné* and curved types of the preceding style were softened and, like other pieces of furniture, became somewhat more rigid (figs. 979, 985).

The backs were highly varied: medallion type (for the queen) (fig. 981) and the oval shape of Louis XV. The rectangular back returned and we sometimes see arch-shaped tops. The most typical of these was the so-called *à chapeau* (fig. 982), straight in the center with two quarter circles on the sides. The wood was decorated, carved, gilded or painted and the backs were either upholstered or made of cane or carved wood. Sometimes the upholstering was done in the shape of a gondola, that is, joining the back and the arms, especially for bureaus and dressing tables. When the backs were made of open-worked wood, the chairs were lighter and adorned with original designs, like the famous chairs from Marie Antoinette's music salon, with her monogram. Other decorative motifs were the lyre (known as *voyeuse*), the open work of Fontainebleau (figs. 977, 985) or the so-called balloon of the Carnavalent Museum in which the Montgolfier was the decorative motif (fig. 980) (the Montgolfier brothers sent up their balloon in 1783). Couches, settees, ottomans, *confessional duchesses* and small footstools were made according to the same standards.

Among the finest and most delicate examples were the famous *chiffonnier* by Saunier and the cupboards and roll-top writing desks known as Kaunitz, the name of the famous Austrian ambassador in France who used this type of cover for the desks in his study. Of these, the four created by Riesener are the best known (figs. 996, 997, 998, 999).

One of the most representative pieces of furniture was the well known jewel chest that belonged to Marie Antoinette, by the German artist Schwerdfeger. It was one of the last pieces of the style and was richly designed and decorated. Mentioning it here reminds us of another jewel chest that belonged to Queen Marie Louise, in the Empire style, more architectonic and heavier than the former (fig. 1033). Another excellent example is the famous bureau of King Louis that took nine years to make—from 1760 to 1769. It was begun by Oeben and finished by Riesener. It is an example of the transition of the final period of Louis XV with details in the marquetry and bronze work introduced by Riesener. Its careful and studied shapes and its original and admirable composition make it the finest example of the last third of the 18th century.

TRANSITION TO THE EMPIRE STYLE

A lapse of 24 years was sufficient to forget completely the Baroque style and adapt to a new fashion, with the necessary transition. It was a period characterized by the cult of the straight line and exaggerated, if not extravagant, return to classical antiquity, and is at the same time the antithesis of Rococo.

France—after all is said and done, the center of Europe at the end of the century because of her all-important political circumstances—with the Louis XVI style was nothing more than the first phase of the Neoclassical style. After years of inactivity because of the Revolution, it was oriented, first with the Directoire and later with the Consulate, toward the pagan art of Rome and culminated in the Empire style. These years from 1789 to 1795 were a kind of pause or waiting period. The first stirrings of artistic interest, beginning with the Directoire or Mesidor in 1795, the year that marks the beginning of the Empire, were developed later with Napoleon in the Consulate and achieved their greatest heights from 1804 to 1814. These same decorative formulas were maintained throughout the first third of the 19th century. During the Revolution, interest in works of art disappeared and nearly all the artists left the country or remained in hiding until the end of the century. The Revolution inspired by the pagan republic of Rome tore down, uprooted, changed and muted the form and even the substance of things. David, "one of the most cowardly souls and at the same time one of the greatest artists of the period", was the man of the moment and left his personal mark on the newly emerging style. His art was in reality a cult of pagan antiquity and pointed out the road to follow. In the first moments of the Revolution, Percier and Fontaine, "the Siamese twins of architecture", according to a well-aimed remark by Bayard, found occasion to initiate this new fashion. It should not seem strange to us to see a repetition of the same Louis XVI models, although they were simpler with less carving and gild and, naturally in the frank revolutionary feeling, replaced the royal emblems with the new symbols. In all this we find models showing the wildest flights of fantasy or, at the opposite extreme, almost vulgar simplicity. The old designs of *fleur de lis*, intertwined initials, eagles and dolphins—all realized after careful study and decorative

Etruscan chair

stylization—were replaced by serpents, cocks, the eye of reason, the Phrygian cap, the thyrsus and intertwined hands. Simplicity predominated, although we might rather call it simplicity in republican fantasy. It was the time of patriots and, naturally, patriotic furniture was made, such as "revolution" and "federation" beds with grooved posts painted in grey or gilded. The legs were usually in the old style and made of solid polished copper. These beds nearly always had a canopy in the shape of a shield or tent with red and white curtains. Others feature different symbols of liberty, such as the typical Phrygian cap, etc.

The "antique-style" chairs, with upholstered back and seat, date from this period, as well as the so-called "Etruscan" and "Greek" styles with carved wooden backs. The legs were of the so-called "old style", conical and made of bronze, and the upper parts of the back were gracefully twisted in volutes, an idea already begun in the time of Louis XVI that characterized the Directoire style (figs. 1011, 1012, 1017).

Chair backs were wide, like a cameo. The wood most commonly used was mahagony and the legs were straight, turned, or "in the old style". But these pieces, as well as the decoration of rooms, were lacking in originality and logic. They were finished with no sense of composition and were painted in violent and unharmonized colors. Because of their obvious defects they were easily forgotten once the moment of political furor was past. On the contrary, the simpler pieces, whose lines represented the purer origins of the Louis XVI style, endured. The elegance of the period continued in numerous tables, commodes, cupboards and chairs. A short time later, in the Mesidor period, this chaos began to take on some sense of order and direction. It was the second step taken by Neoclassical furniture toward its new goal. It was 1793 when the Directoire style began to take shape.

The Directoire was somewhat like a second phase of the Neoclassical style. Directed, as we have said, by the current of the cult that, inspired in Rome, led to the Empire style, from which the seed arose, it lasted only ten years from 1790 to 1800. It included not only the years of the Directoire, 1793-96—short for the development of a style—but those immediately before and after, that correspond to the Revolutionary and Consulate period. These periods were all brief and difficult to determine. Furniture styles followed not only the evolution of the esthetic Neoclassical style but, because of the pagan significance, fit perfectly into the historical moment. The Empire style as well, the final phase of the Neoclassical, found this character favorable in its imposition by Napoleon, lover of antiquity, and the environment from which it must have arisen. We can easily see in the last quarter of the 18th century the great desire for renovation in the arts, for simple and serene lines, that coincided first with the discoveries of Pompeii and Herculaneum and later with the studies of classical Rome, with the Revolution in which the styles of the Greek and Roman republics were further accentuated like a symptom of admiration of paganism, and finally with the Empire style, following the example of Imperial Rome with her proud Caesars. All these innovations crystallized in an obvious esthetic order. It was only in this way and by taking these steps that the Empire style could be fully developed.

MATERIALS

Mahagony, which had been used since 1770, was practically irreplaceable. It was now used nearly always in its natural color, although there were numerous examples of pieces painted in light colors. Furniture styles preserved some of their own characteristics and features that, in the Empire style, we will see completed and totally developed. At any rate, and although it is not easy to distinguish the pieces of this second phase, the Directoire style had its own personal details and elements that made it eminently recognizable, as we can see in the following paragraphs.

ORNAMENTATION

In the first place, the pieces were not as

delicate as those of the Louis XVI style nor as heavy as those of the Empire. They were the result of great simplicity as in the Revolutionary period, but in their more careful and studied lines and profiles we can detect the influence of the great artists of the period.

There were three characteristic motifs that appeared constantly in the furniture of this period: the daisy, the ferule of Greek origin (see the acroteria and funereal steles of Athens) carved in the arm joints and backs of armchairs, and the rhombuses on the blocks of the leg joints and on the aprons of various pieces, which replaced the rectangles and acanthus leaves of the preceding period. In addition to these ornamental details, the bars of the back legs of chairs were attached to the top in a volute and their graceful descent and gentle curve, like the front legs, revived the forms of Greek and Roman chairs.

Other concave chair backs known as "gondolas" (fig. 1013), curved around the sides to the front legs to form the arms. At times the back legs supported wide concave comb-shaped piece that evoked the classical forms of the Greek *klismos*. Plain and unpolished conical pieces, reminiscent of the three ancient empires of Egypt, Greece and Rome, were also seen on the front legs.

Chair backs were often open-worked with rhombuses, squares, diagonals (figs. 1011, 1013, 1015), and brought to mind the contemporary English models by Adam and Hepplewhite. At this time, as we have seen, furniture followed the styles of the Louises, and when they were done "in the old style", they were exaggerated. For this reason we see grooved columns with more and more exaggerated curves and molding, on the other hand, becoming increasingly flatter.

KINDS OF FURNITURE

All the art of furniture in Europe revolved around France, since the destiny of the continent was fatally linked to her. This dependence can be seen even more in the Empire style. It is not strange, then, that we find Directoire pieces, a wholly French style, in all of Europe. The *curule* chair, in the shape of an X, was now typical and we see it often in Italy, Spain and Germany. In this period the gondola and boat forms arose—settees, chairs, couches—and we see also backs with a cabriolet silhouette. Tables were often round—like the old *gueridon* or the Roman or Pompeyan tables—and rested on tripods with legs in the shape of animals, sphinxes, dragons, etc., ending in hooves and claws, or simple turned pieces or classical columns. We shall see all these motifs fully developed in the Empire style. The commodes, roll-top desks, cupboards, etc., showed the same simplicity and mahogany continued to dominate, although metals were not used because of their excessive cost and difficulty of fabrication. Beds were characteristic, with lines similar to the Louis XVI style, in the projecting side columns and a headboard with an antique goblet in the center. The moment was marked by the celebrated portrait of Madame Recamier, painted by David, reclining on a beautiful *lit de repos*.

THE EMPIRE STYLE

Thus we come, in 1804, to the Empire style, pompous and solemn. All these currents were gathered together and channelled according to the standards and paintings by David. His inspiration, or dictatorship, embodied the Empire style in the same way that Le Brun oriented the Louis XIV. The architects Percier and Fontaine illuminated this movement; their highly varied paintings, drawings and designs and their diverse works of architecture, painting and furnishings gave it a marked national character and spread it not only all over France, but throughout Europe. Esthetics became a State matter because art was a constant evocation of Imperial Rome. At this particular time the destiny of Europe was in the hands of Napoleon, and kings, politics, customs, atmosphere and fashion revolved around him. Consequently, it was not unusual that furniture all over the continent should show a similarity to French styles and that French artists should

Madame Recamier

work outside their own country. Much of the interior decoration of Spanish, Italian and Russian palaces was the work, in one way or another, of Percier, Fontaine, Proudhon, etc.

The new style, in its eagerness to adapt to the old forms, lacked personality, although not originality. But its influence and scope became so wide that, after Napoleon's abdication in 1814, it endured for another fifteen years. It may be said that it represented the end of the so-called historical furniture styles in France and Europe.

MATERIALS

Mahagony, usually solid, continued to be the only material used, and veneer was found only on large panelled surfaces. The lines were Roman and the decoration cubic, and gilded and chiselled bronze appliqués were used on top of the wood. Marquetry and inlay of light-colored wood—boxwood and satinwood— appeared from time to time, especially in Italy where the technique had not been lost. The materials used were of the highest quality and resistance, as opposed to the weakness characteristic of those of the Second Empire, as we will see further on. We have said that the Empire style brought order to the decorative chaos of the 18th century, which at times during the first third of the century even went back to the Gothic style itself. In England also, for example, we saw how Chippendale pieces returned to the extravagant shapes of a fleeting Gothic style. But it is true that all the inexhaustible material of Roman, Greek and Egyptian art in wood, bronze, fabrics and wall decoration was used abundantly: Garlands, Doric and Corinthian columns, with bronze capitals and bases—this metal being commonly found on table legs—rose and laurel wreaths, acanthus leaves and ferns, ferules like the ancient acroteria of Greek temples and stelae, stars, bees symbolizing work (reminding us of Napoleon's cloak decorated with golden bees, like those found in the tomb of Childric), arches, thyrsus, lyres, cameos, animals inspired in Egyptian mythology, imperial Roman eagles, chariots and swans, allegories of war and sphinxes with women's bodies, Venus, Bacchantes, Graces, mythological muses, etc. An oval-shaped decorative theme, that is goblets, was constantly used, as well as scrollwork and Greek-style decoration. Episodes like the battle of the pyramids were reproduced over and over again on hangings and wallpapers. At the same time the white, ivory and gold tones of the Louises fell into disuse. Napoleon, son of the Revolution, did not go back to the traditional French styles that end with Louis XVI, but looked ahead and was inspired in the cult of Rome and in the victories of his Egyptian and Italian campaigns which became the themes of his decoration. Ornamentation took on a more decorative and at the same time colder feeling, but this in itself gave it a great sense of luxury and majesty. The main decorative element was bronze, marvelously chiselled and fire-gilded in bas-relief plaques. At the same time, daisies, rhombuses, stars, acanthus leaves, etc., were carved in the wood, but only as decoration and never as a part of the structure.

STRUCTURES

Furniture was exaggeratedly symmetrical. The general lines, as in all the Neoclassical style, was straight and the clear and simple silhouettes became heavier and more solid than in the Directoire style and, naturally, much more than in the Louis XVI. Structures commonly used were cubes, prisms, closed blocks, flat surfaces with almost no molding, superimposed to give them a sense of lightness, and with a highly esthetic sense of decoration, with gilt bronze pieces and pleated draperies. The feminine profiles of the Louis XVI style were no longer seen. Pieces now were cold, monotonous, with the same motifs repeated, although it was precisely in this way that a truly monumental grandeur and majesty were created, as much in a large palace table as in a simple bed-side table, which resembled an altar. And this was brought about not only by the adequate use of superb materials—bronze and mahogany— but also by proportion, care of the lines and symmetry, which gave an uncommon richness to individual pieces of furniture. Part of the piece was upholstered and, harking back to the Roman style, these tapestries were attached without springs, as though they were rigid, and were less comfortable than in the time of Louis XV and XVI. Only toward the end of the Empire period did they become softer again. Some of the materials and themes of the Louis XVI style were forgotten or are not used, such as, for example, cane seats and backs which fell into disuse because of their lack of classical antecedents.

The Empire style ignored roundness, but its very simplicity and sobriety were imposing and captivating, and created the novelty of the style. We should point out that many pieces had nothing but volume; without the sheets of fine wood that covered them and the chiselled bronze appliqués, we would see nothing more than a geometric block with no grace or intrinsic value.

KINDS OF FURNITURE

Tables

The same anachronism of the Empire style in the middle of the 19th century, and by virtue of its very originality, created a multitude of useless pieces of furniture. Such was the case of the varied and innumerable types of tables, from circular ones with legs in the shape of Tuscan columns, to sphinxes and mythological animals ending in claws or hooves where it is easy to see the Roman influence. The most interesting of the rectangular tables are those with legs in the shape of bronze caryatids, the work of the excellent sculptor Desmalter, and small tripods, or small three-legged tables—like the Pompeyan tables of the 1st century—some used for flower vases and others for wash basins. These were called "Athenian" because of their marked Greek imitation. Then there were the *gueridon* using the same themes in widely varied types, dressing tables, *poudreuses* and the so-called *bonheur de jour*.

Beds

Beds became exceptionally important at this time. Since they were usually placed parallel to the wall, the head and foot pieces were of the same height to comply with the exaggerated law of symmetry. The so-called Napoleonic beds of the French palaces were especially famous, and others similar to them can be found in nearly all the palaces of Europe. Equally well known were the gondola and boat-shaped beds with curved back, ending in the form of a volute, like the chairs. Many had canopies that look like tents with war and military trophies (figs. 1028-1032, 1034). Especially interesting were the cradles, among them that of the king of Rome by Proudhon. The various sorts of seats and reclining pieces were always voluminous, cubic and varied, ranging from gondola chairs and couches (among them the so-called *meridienne* (fig. 1024) with one arm higher than the other) to the *chaiselongue* with its low, curved back, swan-shaped arms and turned legs and elbow rests.

Chairs

We already encountered Roman X-shaped chairs (fig. 1020) and those with mythical animals (fig. 1019) in the Louis XVI period, but not in such a romantic and imperial sense. Among all these models, some of the most outstanding were the celebrated projects by Percier and Fontaine (figs. 1032, 1023) and those by the famous G. Jacob, that great maker of chairs of whom we have already spoken. When he was given the task of decorating the Convention salon, after having remained in hiding during the Revolution, he called on Percier and Fontaine to assist him. Jacob's son Desmalter was considered the best woodworker of the Empire style and made furniture not only for France but for other European courts as well, among them Spain and Russia. Perhaps his most famous piece was the jewel chest made for the Empress Marie Louise, which was preferred by the Emperor over another by Riesener. He had previously made a simpler one for the Empress Josephine.

Other pieces

Bedside tables were very simple, cylindrical, solemn and imposing, exaggerated in appearance. New pieces to appear were the *psique* (fig. 1026), large mirrors between two columns, in geometrical shapes of large and monumental proportions, derived from the small dressing tables at the end of the century. The mirror, already known in Egypt and Greece, was made of metal until the 15th century with the discovery of *étamage* which became more common, especially among the Venetian glassmakers. In 1673 Colbert introduced the manufacture of mirrors (in France), and Saint-Gobain even today monopolizes the manufacture of mirrors and surpasses the fame previously enjoyed by Venice. These large mirrors were the origin of the unesthetic mirrored wardrobes that were so common during the second half of the 19th century and the first part of the 20th.

Pieces typical of the era were harps and pianos, like that by Godoy—now found in England—decorated with Wedgwood porcelain plaques, and showcases, consoles, small tables with several levels, bookcases, study tables (the Emperor's were especially interesting). Furnishings and decoration, so rich and numerous in the French palaces, are not difficult to select (figs. 1019, 1020, 1029, 1034).

ENGLAND

Contrasting to French furniture—luxurious and courtly in the gallantly feminine Pompadour style or the more serene Marie Antoinette—was the style developed in the 18th century in England, with its bourgeoisie character that achieved its maximum expression during this century. We can also see here the same movement as on the continent. The designs began with the dynamic and unbalanced silhouettes of the Baroque style to become more classical and correct with fine, vigorous lines. The decoration was scarce and somber, characteristic of a natural evolution, with little relation to the continent.

Chippendale himself, who was undoubtedly the most representative Baroque artist, was influenced by the environment and instinctively made pieces according to the new standards. But his moment had already passed and his name was forgotten by the innovators and creators of the new style, especially the Adam brothers, Hepplewhite, and Sheraton.

From 1758 to 1762 the architect Robert Adam worked in Italy and France with his colleague Clerisseau. It was then that he adopted and captured the new forms and fashions and introduced them in England. Later his brother James joined him. During these years they were known in London under the name of Adelphi (who does not remember the Adelphi quarter, along the Thames, begun by them?) and together they developed and spread the new style, not only in the pieces and decoration created by them, all highly select, but through their numerous and interesting publications.

The years spent by Adam in France and Italy can be clearly seen in the two phases of his work, the French and the Italian. The first phase, more superficial, was that of the Louis XVI style, but the second was more important and profound if we observe that, in addition the artists he so intelligently surrounded himself with were either Italians (Zucchi, Pergolesi,

Peranesi) or educated there, like the painter A. Kauffman or the sculptor Flaxman.

It is easy in this era—the inspiration of 19th century English furniture—to confuse the works of Adam with those of other artists such as Hepplewhite and Sheraton, and this not for lack of personality. Hepplewhite had an exquisite and flexible temperament that linked him more with Chippendale, while Sheraton showed greater rigidity and severity that harkens more to the Directoire and Empire styles. But all of them were contemporaries. They published three books on furniture with engravings; they saw and studied the works of the great classical and Italian Renaissance artists. Their sources were the same and the interchange of influences was constant. The Adam brothers took the French and Italian forms, adapted them to the bourgeoisie taste of the English and ably surrounded themselves with artists such as Angelica Kauffman, an excellent painter (1741-1807), the sculptor Flaxman, correct but cold who, although not at the forefront as a sculptor, nevertheless was one of the foremost decorators and illustrators, and other Italian decorators such as Zucchi, Pergolessi, etc. But these were adaptors and innovators or decorators, rather than creators.

Hepplewhite, with his great sensitivity, perfected his own models with the introduction of gentle, rippling curves instead of the excessively rigid and straight lines of the Adelphi. It is not difficult to find models by Adam carried on to greater perfection by Hepplewhite, with a highly personal sense.

Sheraton had his own character and was more of a slave of the straight line. He interpreted in this fashion, for example, the delicious heart-shaped backs of Hepplewhite. His severity and simplicity found a broad field with the currents coming from the continent in the first years of the 19th century that climaxed in the Empire style. Of the three only Sheraton, who lived until 1806, saw the complete evolution from the Neoclassical to the Empire style. R. Adam and Hepplewhite had already died in 1792 and 1786 respectively, and Sheraton ended up making furniture with this Empire influence. He was the furniture maker who gave the tone to English designs at the end of the century. But the Empire style—indissolubly linked to Napoleon and known throughout Europe in this unique French and imperial character—in England was more original and kept ahead of the whims of the public. It created here a special Empire style with a certain English character, as always, bourgeois and therefore closer to the Directoire style, which soon came to be known by the name of "Trafalgar". Like a symbol of the times it penetrated into official spheres (figs. 1085, 1086), although in court furniture it was more subject to continental styles.

MATERIALS

So-called Spanish mahogany was introduced around the middle of the 18th century and was used without the superimposed bronze decorations of past eras. It was enhanced only by marquetry, forgotten since the times of Queen Anne, but used only in a geometric and architectonic sense.

Another type of wood, used generally for veneer and alternating with mahagony, was satinwood. It was a light wood, bright and with a flat grain, that was usually decorated and enhanced with inlays of other dark-colored woods or by painting. Sycamore, tulipwood and pearwood were used as veneer, and even exotic Asian and American woods were employed. On the other hand, bronze was used only in some cases as molding on handles to underline the general lines of structure and composition.

The Adam brothers, to reproduce and repeat the bas reliefs finely carved and drawn by the Italian decorators, used a new material known as "compo", derived from scagliola mixed with glue (a type of *papier maché*). Its composition was kept a secret. It allowed industrial production in all detail in a hard, permanent and fine material, easily applied on the surfaces of ceilings and walls (fig. 1087).

Cane, unused since the beginning of the 18th century, was again used by Sheraton and Hepplewhite (figs. 1045, 1046) in the last years of the century.

STRUCTURES

Furniture design achieved great simplicity of line and a very somber and studied decoration.

The structure was always visible, constructive and esthetic at the same time that it was frank, utilitarian and beautiful. The lines were fine. The dimensions of chairs were studied, exact, and minimum, to the point of appearing fragile. The curves, when they existed, were gentle, simple and natural.

In the books published by all these artists, furniture dimensions were given. Thus for certain chairs by Hepplewhite, the following measurements were given: 50 cm wide at the front of the seat, 42 cm at the seat back and 92 cm total height. The structural skeleton was sometimes so simple that, to enrich and distinguish it from more economical models, the use of marquetry and paint was required. But above all, the very careful proportions were their greatest asset (figs. 1040, 1050).

Adam, still used the curve, always following classical and geometrical standards and lines. His notable and original semi-cylindrical commodes featured geometrical marquetry and were a good example. Hepplewhite, on the other hand, used curved lines and surfaces, "by feeling". These bombé shapes followed no geometrical law, but were a response to a simple esthetic sense, since in his commodes the silhouette was no longer semicircular but undulating, even semi-elliptical—with a certain reminiscence of the Baroque style—but always restful and continuous.

Finally, Sheraton turned to richness and his melodious lines were translated into more rectilinear and drier shapes. These two artists, Hepplewhite and Sheraton, revived the turned legs, abandoned since the beginning of the century for the cabriolet line, using very careful and fine profiles and dimensions (fig. 1049).

DECORATION

R. Adam, initiator of the style, and his collaborators introduced motifs that were imitated by others: hangings with flowers and leaves, goblets or ellipses decorated with radial lines in the shape of fans, oval rosettes, sphinxes, goblets and urns of classical shape (this last a very common motif). Pleated and gathered hangings were also used, with grooves or fine lines of acanthus leaves. Cane was also used in radial form in chair backs with a central wood motif, sometimes decorated with a small painting. All these ornamental details were finely drawn by the previously mentioned artists and decorators. On occasion, Angelica Kauffman with her paintings or Flaxman with his bas reliefs and drawings enriched the pieces of the most important furniture makers of the end of the century. The marquetry designs were no longer flowers, but radial or fan-shaped figures, like all ornamentation in general, or with garlands and Grecian frets in geometric forms, interpreting the motifs and friezes of classical times in oval and circular centers (figs. 1038, 1039).

The same influences were found in all the industrial arts. For example, Wedgwood ceramics worked with white figures on a light blue background, adopted the drawings of Flaxman and his school. This era of rigidity and coldness was the antithesis of Chippendale, with its greater decorative and structural freedom. In spite of this, designers continued using curved motifs, gently curved legs, bombé commodes and serpentine lines on sideboards and chair backs. We must not forget the importance of painted pieces, not in the sense of French and Italian, but more ornamental and decorative with landscapes, figures, etc. They were signed by Kauffman, her disciples or her imitators and followers (figs. 1055 1061).

KINDS OF FURNITURE

It was at this time that English furniture reached its greatest heights. Its beauty and utility were combined with simplicity. From 1788 until the beginning of the following century, books and furniture guides were published by the Adam brothers, Hepplewhite and Sheraton. Woodworkers reproduced these models or varied them to create new ones. It was a time when the nascent bourgeoisie continuously ordered new furniture, from the most practical to totally useless pieces. But rooms themselves, because of the requirements of the bourgeoisie itself, projected a certain unity. The number of pieces and types of furniture was extraordinary. It is not our purpose to list them all here, but to point out the most important and characteristic.

Cupboards

One of these was the sideboard, horizontal in line, generally with three sections (the center one being the most important) and with straight or gently curved lines, like the Hepplewhite models. Complementary to these pieces were the original pedestals with boxes for knives or wine glasses.

These boxes, truly characteristic, did not pass over to the continent. They were usually in the shape of a goblet, amphora or urn, with a classical and simple silhouette. We have already seen that the goblet was an element much used by Adam and their followers, from very large ones to those used as the central element in split pediments or on elbow rests, or simply in decorative bas-reliefs, friezes, centers, etc. (figs. 1056, 1057, 1058, 1074, 1075).

The top of this box lifted up on a hinge and the goblets or knife handles were arranged in the shape of a stepped pyramid. Hepplewhite and Sheraton used these original cutlery boxes constantly (fig. 1059). In all the elements of interior architecture, and especially in fireplaces, we can see all the decorative forms we have been speaking of. Many of them were designed by the Adelphi and highly adorned with bas-reliefs and Wedgwood porcelain plaques in the style of Flaxman. The pieces from this period were very beautiful.

Cupboards and bookcases followed these forms already adopted by Chippendale himself. They were usually in two sections: the upper one with lattice-worked glass doors and the lower one with doors or drawers decorated with marquetry or plain. They were nearly always topped by split pediments with delicate modulations and cornices. All these pieces were simply adorned. Especially interesting were the double curved lines of the pediments, ending in volutes. Bronze appliqués were used only on keyholes and handles in simple geometric forms. Commodes took on semi-cylindrical. circular or elliptical curves with the Adam brothers, while Hepplewhite's surfaces were freer. The legs were tapered or with socles, similar to those of the Queen Anne era.

Although furniture was frequently adorned with painted designs, their beauty lay rather in the perfection and proportion of line and surfaces, and varying thicknesses of wood were used.

An example of this decoration, possibly one of the most characteristic, was the dressing table in the shape of a central shield between two lateral sections, decorated with painted designs in the Pompeyan style.

There were also beautiful examples of consoles, especially those by Adam, whose lines were similar to the Louis XVI style (fig. 1062).

Chairs

Of all pieces of furniture, the greatest originality and personality was to be found in chairs. Their models and forms were highly varied. Of note were those with circular backs, harking back to the so-called "queen's models" of the Louis XVI style, and those with finely carved horizontal cross-pieces and rolled top and back supports, a feature that continued throughout all the Romantic period. The legs were usually straight and tapered or turned, simple and without rungs, although at times we also see them in more original forms. Other times we find the classic X-shaped legs of the Roman curule chair.

The chairs of the Adam brothers, although of the highest quality, were surpassed especially by those of Hepplewhite and Sheraton.

Hepplewhite introduced the curve in the top of the back. He used shield or heart shapes and the backs were humped or diaphanous with latticework and delicate wood carvings (figs. 1051, 1052). Among the most typical were those known as the Prince of Wales (because of the three symbolic ostrich feathers in the backs), the so-called wheat spike chairs, and those with three intertwined ovals (fig. 1042). Others had delicately carved goblets in the center, draperies and arbitrary silhouettes, and curved radii in those with round backs. The legs were generally tapered or turned, but nearly always curved gracefully outward at the bottom.

With Sheraton the straight line became more rigid and dry, and Hepplewhite's oval backs were transformed in this sense. But this did not make Sheraton any less important. Already in the 19th century, influenced by the French Directoire style, he curved and twisted the tops of his chair backs. He adapted and assimilated new classical forms and made his Nelson chairs, with the influences and characteristics of the moment (Trafalgar) mixed with those of the ancient Roman republic. Even the popular Windsor chair, which we find in all styles and periods, appeared now with its legs adapted to the turned and tapered shapes of the end of the century.

Hepplewhite's Duchess sofas and couches, as well as his beds—still with draperies and canopies—are widely known not only by the models that still remain in palaces and homes of the wealthy and the bourgeoisie, but also by the excellent drawings contained in his *Guides*.

In all these pieces we constantly see goblets as well as rhombuses, grooves, amphoras, draperies and wreaths, all characteristic of the Adam brothers.

The simple and beautiful dressing tables or small table-top *psiques* were similar in shape to Hepplewhite's chair backs. This was a piece that retained the same form throughout all the 19th century and reached its maximum development in the French Empire style in very large pieces (figs. 1082, 1083)

Tables

We end this chapter by mentioning the multitude of rectangular tables, sometimes with lyre-shaped legs, circular, in the style of dressing tables, tables with shelves or leaves of decreasing diameter as we saw in the Baroque Chippendale style. The *gueridon*, a small circular table with a central leaf, developed into a larger table with three legs of extended cabriolet type. It was used generally as a dining table at the end of the 18th century and throughout all the 19th century, first on one central leg and later on two, with circular or oval leaves respectively (figs. 1063, 1073).

Certainly at this particular moment, furniture design achieved a level that is difficult to surpass, associating a perfect technique and utilitarian nature with an exact sense of proportion and great artistic value. Prototypes of great beauty were produced, always inspired in themes well known in the industrial arts.

Even in England itself, traditional and attached to her national art so intelligently oriented by Sheraton, the French Empire Style penetrated by virtue of the whim of the people and the suggestion of the moment. Its interpreter in the British Isles was Tonis Hope, although his originality, we can assure, was almost nil. Although his drawings were influenced by David or by Percier, he could not altogether rid himself of the style of the Adam brothers, which persisted in all its elegant ornamental elements: hangings, goblets, ferules and other decorative details.

ITALY

The development of Neoclassical furniture in Italy followed, above all, the standards of the Louis XVI style, and secondarily Pompeyan influences. Thus there is nothing new to be said about its structure, decoration, materials.

With the discovery of Pompeii, but without forgetting the French teachings, the new Neoclassical style began in Naples, although almost from the beginning, as in earlier times, the Piedmont and Venetian regions became the most important centers. Furniture designs were still eminently decorative and followed the standards of the continent, in addition to those of the English Neoclassical style. One commonly sees chairs, tables and commodes in the Adam or Hepplewhite style (figs. 1091, 1095). In all these pieces two characteristics stand out: the tendency of the backs to open out or widen toward the top in the form of a trapeze, and the use of decorative motifs—Pompeyan arabesques—with great purity of line. Large surfaces were covered with marquetry with landscape designs and drawings of architectonic type, such as ruins and views of the Renaissance cities (fig. 1099).

The pieces found in Venetian palaces and in northern Italy, many of them painted, show characteristics peculiar to each region which are beyond the scope of this work (figs. 1093, 1094, 1103) and we illustrate them with only a few examples.

Later, as in all of Europe, Empire models were repeated with no national feeling to disrupt the style imposed by the Emperor. And we refer not only to the small German states nor to his father-in-law's Austria, but to the very Russia of Tsar Alexander, who followed the whim of the style of this man who left his mark on two centuries. Even in Italy, where the classical tradition was never lost, we find Empire pieces with the same French characteristics.

CENTRAL EUROPE

By virtue of its geographical location bordering on France and because it is the cradle of the first woodworkers of the style who were constantly passing between the two countries, Germany occupied the most important place on the continent after France.

In the countries of central Europe we see court furnishings of two types: those imported from France, executed paradoxically by German artists, and the national type. The latter, like all Germanic art, was heavier and more vigorous, and lacked the grace and femininity of the Louises. Röntgen was the most representative artist of the Neoclassical style in Germany. He was educated in France and worked not only for Germany but all of Europe, even for Russia. He was the protegé of Frederick William II and, for this reason, many of his pieces can still be found in the Potsdam and Charlottemburg palaces. His best period was from 1780 to 1790, and his fame is due especially to his work in marquetry. His pastoral and mythological scenes were as important as his work in stone.

His commodes and cylindrical bureaus are famous. But his work as a whole is less elegant than that of his French contemporaries and his bronzes are poor and of little significance.

Röntgen was known by the name of David and in England as David Luneville. He died in 1807.

The main interest of the moment lay especially in the appearance, as in England, of bourgeoisie furniture, which gave rise to the *biedermaier* pieces of the 19th century. It clearly showed English influences and characteristics (both are Saxon countries), less rich than the Louis XVI style and, like it, using national woods such as birch, pearwood, etc., in their natural colors and often painted or veneered (figs. 1114, 1116).

We are now in the period of the height of the bourgeoisie that tried to emulate luxurious interiors with a theatrical and modest appearance using decorative wallpapers. The rich tapestries were replaced by cretonnes, wall hangings and draperies by wallpaper, and upholstering was done over horsehair stuffing. All these details with their lack of taste and elegance presaged the arrival of the so-called Biedermaier style, represented simultaneously in England by the Victorian style, in Spain by the Isabeline and in France by the Second Empire (figs. 1117, 1123). We must not fail to mention a certain number of Neoclassical pieces, beautiful examples of the interpretations of ancient Rome, in Denmark. These were various models styled on the ancient chairs of Rome and Greece, made by Danish artists of the 19th century, like the chairs by Bindesboll, Abilgaard and C. Hausen. All were preserved in various collections in Denmark (figs. 1108, 1111, 1113).

SPAIN

Charles III brought the Neoclassical style to Spain when he returned from Naples after seeing the discovery of Pompeii. For this reason the first pieces of the style date from the end of this reign and perhaps the best examples are to be found in the Prince's House at El Pardo and the Farmer's House in Aranjuez. Most of the pieces are chairs and seats of one sort or another, but there are also consoles. All the models are of great beauty and originality, with upholstery and silk embroidered in Pompeyan designs forming a unified whole. It was, however, with Charles IV that the style reached its fullest development in Spain. During this period furniture workshops became highly important. The royal family had its own workshop in which not only furniture was made, but also metals and upholstery. Charles IV himself, for example, worked in the furnishings of the royal chambers of El Escorial. These pieces are among the few whose creators are known. From the existing documentation, we know that Angel Maeso, master of the royal workshop, worked on them and presented his bill in 1828. The group made up of a study, ante-oratory, oratory and alcove is of the best known in Spain and is of great beauty and interest, tecnically as well as artistically (figs. 1151, 1157, 1158). These four rooms occupy the second floor of the eastern tower. The furniture, floors, panelling and walls are covered with fine inlays. The furniture is covered with finely chiselled and gilded bronze appliqués, some with themes inspired by the return of Ferdinand VII to Madrid, a fact that helps us place its completion geographically and in time.

Not only El Escorial but all the royal palaces were now furnished in the new style, which was naturally taken over by the aristocrats as well. In the Andalusian provinces and the palaces of Castile and Majorca one can still see interiors decorated in this style. Much of the furniture was imported, but other pieces were copies or were inspired by the imported ones and always show the usual national characteristics (figs. 1144, 1155, 1156, 1159, 1201).

The following observations are of interest at this point: On the one hand popular art, of which we have so many examples on the penninsula, did not adapt to this cold, simple and rigid Neoclassical style with its inflexible academic laws, and produced pieces with no determined style. On the other hand, a middle-class furniture style arose in Spain, as in all of Europe, with unrefined and broken lines, cruder and much less richly decorated than the court styles and, therefore, more economical (figs. 1151, 1168, 1176).

We have characteristic examples of those court furnishings and the bourgeoisie styles. Of the first type we have tables with marble tops on legs without the well-known rungs—French and English—turned, grooved, with sphinxes, sometimes of mahogany and other times painted and gilded. There are round tables with Pompeyan-style or square, tapering legs; simple commodes with geometrical inlays; an enormous variety of chairs, nearly all of them creations or copies of the royal chair works and some in the popular style, as shown in the photograph on this page; pianos in which the industry reached great heights of fame (those signed by Flórez competed with the English ones) and many other examples of which we have chosen the most interesting and representative pieces. In them the reader can get an idea of the development of the Empire style in Spain, although a complete study of it would require a book devoted exclusively to Spain.

The manufacture of Empire furniture continued when Ferdinand VII returned to Spain. As always in our furniture art and because of its pecular national character, the pieces are cruder and more imaginative and therefore less pure than the French Empire style (figs. 1173, 1176, 1179, 1186). The bronze chiselling, for example, was replaced by carved and gilt wood and the piece is consequently less fine and somewhat more crude. We have an example of this phenomenon in the chairs illustrating this chapter, in that the carved and gilt wood appliqués are exaggerated.

We may mention among the first of our authentic Empire pieces a bedroom group given by the Emperor to King Joseph when he came to Madrid and which today can be seen in the Malmaison. Of great beauty and purity are the pieces in the so-called Platinum Room of the Farmer's House (fig. 1201) of Aranjuez, perhaps designed by Percier and Fontaine themselves. On the other hand, other pieces of the El Pardo palace, the Eastern palace and El Escorial, a collection of armchairs in the National palace and La Granja, and study tables, for example, are typically "Fernandine", made in Spain by woodworkers appointed by the royal family. They show the lack of personality characteristic of Europe at this time, but capture the flavor imposed by the era and interpreted in their own way by the Spanish artists (figs. 1186, 1187).

Popular chair

MID 19TH CENTURY

ISABELINE, VICTORIAN AND EMPIRE STYLES

In the 19th century furniture design, still influenced by the Empire style, continued with its more bourgeoisie character and evolved toward an untranscendant art, dulled by mechanization—the true revolution of the 19th century—and industrialization. This is why Oeben and Riesener, like so many other great artists, were hostile to the art style of the *petite bourgeoisie* that was increasingly utilitarian and simple.

It was the triumph of the impersonal. The middle classes overcame the old majesty. It was the century of the great bourgeoisie inventions, the practical and comfortable life that gave rise, with comfort and artificial elegance, to the mirrored wardrobe and the *capitoné* armchair, for not other reason than their utility. It was also a century of great political and social struggles and, on the other hand, the great romantic movement that idealized the things

Chair with X-shaped legs in the Farmer's House

of other centuries, such as feudalism, gothicism, etc. In every country there are movements and new currents whose intention is to return to the ideal of a false Middle Ages. We remember the young England of Disraeli and Byron, Goethe and Heine in Germany, Chateaubriand and Victor Hugo in France, and Viollet le Duc, a central figure of this movement in architecture, with his restorations and studies of Gothic cathedrals and, finally in Spain, Larra and Espronceda. Simultaneously with this movement, pseudo-Gothic pieces of furniture reappeared with modern structures and false moldings, with carvings and lattices that later attempted to appear as Neo-renaissance or Neo-rococo. The Gothic pieces of the French Renaissance and the Louises were copied—badly—and the result was a true potpourri. Pieces lacking in interest and sense of composition were produced, not created by true artists, and there was a constant parade of *dressoirs*, footstools, wardrobes, etc., adapted to modern needs. Thus we arrive at a mediocre and ridiculous style known as the Troubadour in which, for example, a piano was covered with Gothic decoration. And so the century progressed with these fashions.

In England it was the era of Queen Victoria, that began in France with the restoration of Louis XVII, followed with Louis Philippe and ends with the so-called Second Empire style of Napoleon III (1870). In Germany it was the so-called *biedermaier* bourgeoisie period, a name that comes from a political caricature of the good middle-class man and that in Vienna resulted in some interesting pieces at the end of the century.

And finally, in Spain, we have what is known as the Isabeline style of the era of Isabel II from 1830 to 1870. Here, although the Empire style lasted longer since its representative, Ferdinand VII, died in 1833, in its final period it was also crude and feigned. The bronze appliqués were no longer the same works of art as those used on French pieces, gilt and chiselled, but were unchiselled or die-cut cast pieces or plates.

There were three moments that stand out in our Isabeline period from 1833 to 1870. The first was that of the ruling queen during the childhood of Isabel II; the second was the first part of her reign; and the third—parallel to the second French Empire and Queen Victoria in England—included the long period until Isabel was dethroned.

In the first phase, furniture types and characteristics were similar to the Empire period and were usually made of mahogany covered with decorative veneer. The bronze appliqués were nothing more than highly schematic drawings and were frequently replaced by simple borders, fillets and marquetry, and cane and reeds that served as decoration. Likewise corners on tables, grooves and some carvings on legs—sphinx heads, claws—reappeared like golden reminders of the Empire style. This period, easily characterized by these details, is known as the Ruling Queen period. In the following phase, up to the second half of the century, the forms whose origins were not only in the new degenerated Empire style, but in the French Directoire itself, were perpetuated. Silhouettes like the gondola, swans, dragons, etc., and even more romantic ones were common and become irreplaceable and characteristic (fig. 1210). And on the other hand, the more classical columns and bronze appliqués, with chariot or Pompeyan motifs, disappeared and were forgotten. Furniture was solid and cubic with thick moldings and simple profiles, finished in socles, with turned front legs and sweeping back legs, like the classical motifs that were their origin and like not a few Gothic elements that had already begun in the last years of Ferdinand VII in full Empire period, and which we see in use throughout all of Europe in an expression of Romanticism when the restoration of the Gothic cathedrals began (fig 1208).

Finally, when these last forms of the Empire style began to fall into disuse, increasingly crude and degenerate, a reaction started—parallel to France—that repeated the models of the Louises (Louis XIV, XV and XVI) (figs. 1202, 1204, 1205).

Furniture was made in the Boulle mode, pieces with cabriolet legs, bronze appliqués, marquetry in the centers and without separating styles but mixing the motifs of one and another. In addition, the bronzes were no longer works of true artists nor was the line of the pieces so careful. They were covered with the elements of ostentatious luxury that characterized the Second Empire and this era that was parallel to the Isabeline period. They were pieces with wide curves, bombé commodes, cabriolet legs, bronze appliqués and fronts covered with marquetry, in the Boulle or Riesener modes, with a marked Baroque sense. The hangings and curtains were full of pleats, falls, tufts, fringes and bows, like the queen's dressing room and bedroom in Aranjuez that so well reflect the period and the person who inspired it. In sum, furniture designs were more and more middle class and modest, and a model often lost its value since it was repeated constantly.

MATERIALS

The materials were also poorer. The solid mahogany of the Empire style was replaced by pine with mahogany veneer or overlay, according to whether the piece was plain or carved. In the first case, the veneer was nearly always mahogany and in the second, the carvings of dragons, feathers or simple cane were crude but, nevertheless, pleasing as an expression, after all, of a truly popular art.

The chiselled bronzes were now simple brass plates with die-cut embossing. The silks in the rooms were replaced by wallpaper—so typical of the last Fernandine era—like the ones that can be seen today in La Quinta at El Pardo, in the Zarzuela, those of Aranjuez Palace or private country houses, and the silk and damask tapestries continued the repetition of old drawings.

There was a very rich wood that alternated with and replaces mahogany in its nearly universal use. This was *palo santo*, which returned to furniture a great nobility and richness.

Only occasionally in the furnishings of the court and wealthy families do we see marquetry and the backgrounds of ebony and *palo santo* and cast bronze appliqués that form a whole that summarizes Romanticism and constitutes the most intelligible pages of the history of our grandparents. Never lacking were the simple inlays of boxwood or mahogany on elliptical boxwood or satinwood backgrounds, reproducing modest drawings that were a distant reminder of the delicate and pure Empire themes.

STRUCTURES

Construction methods and techniques, developed and perfected to the maximum in the 18th century, were industrialized and, with the mass production of economical models, handiwork and perfection of finish were lost.

A decorative element whose use now became common was fluted molding, so characteristic of Dutch furniture at the end of the Renaissance and the beginning of the Baroque in framing panels and mirrors, always in dark colors.

As we have already noted, furniture was made of pine covered with veneer, and bronze appliqués were replaced by brass plates. The fine Neoclassical or Egyptian style carvings were now coarse, with necks of ducks, swans and dragons, urns with fruit, not perfect, obviously, but neither grotesque because the charm of popular art palpitates in all of them.

DECORATION

Everything was overdone and fatuous: furniture with wide curves, marquetry, bronze appliqués and plates. But how different from the delicacy of the Empire pieces, in their elegance and sensitivity! The legs were turned, as in the Louis XVI style, or curved as in the Louis XV. Chair backs were curved "in the queen's mode" or twisted in Directoire volutes and open work. The simple forms of furniture were inspired (as we have already said) in the style of the Empire or of the Louises. Numerous pieces were upholstered with springs, and the arms of sofas were softly curved in the shape of swans and mythical animals.

The queen's dressing room

Wallpaper

Fabrics were highly embossed and grandly pompous and ingenuous, covering the pieces almost entirely. The visible parts were sometimes gilded and other times with covered marquetry or inlays of metal and boxwood. The backgrounds were light in color and drawings of satinwood or boxwood were usually done on mahagony.

Handles and metal appliqués were cast, seldom chiselled, and were usually brass plate. Even these, however, lacked the fineness of the 18th century styles. Although in general they were cruder, in all pieces of furniture we find charming and original characteristics, especially in bourgeoisie or popular pieces, with unstudied and disproportionate lines and even badly made by popular artists and workshops, but of unquestionable value as craftwork.

KINDS OF FURNITURE

The pieces of furniture most commonly used were the same as in all of Europe, inherited from previous periods. Only the *psique* was replaced by the mirrored wardrobe, a more practical piece but of less artistic interest, and the low commodes or cupboards became pompous lavatories which are not only unesthetic (like the wardrobe) but impractical. On the other hand, however, there were wardrobes whose proportions were similar to those of the Dutch ones of the 17th century with their simple and noble lines, a multitude of chairs, armchairs and sofas, more and more in the capitoné style and completely upholstered. Although utilitarianism and practicality were the predominating characteristics, these pieces still possessed a certain artistic value in their graceful and charming silhouettes.

For example, pieces characteristic of this period and not lacking in elegance were the gondola sofas with carved arms, and beds, also gondola-shaped, that were adorned with similar motifs. Also of interest were the small tables on one center leg in the form of a goblet, either turned or polygonal, or on three legs, with flowing lines, and even on a hexagonal or triangular platform. There were also consoles supported on flat legs, carved with fruit or bird motifs or in the form of brackets rolled in volutes. There were beds with marquetry and even metal beds with graceful canopies.

Before 1870 furniture lost all its interest. Styles of the past were repeated senselessly and adapted to fixed patterns that regulated the use of furniture. Thus we have the study, which must of necessity be in the style of Henry II, the Louis XV sitting room, the French Renaissance dining room, all with their incomprehensible crowning of railings with turned balusters. There was even a group of *papier maché* pieces in which many parts are made of this material, also known as "stone carton", painted and inlaid with mother-of-pearl in gilt drawings on a black background. Their success was ephemeral, but they are worth mentioning.

Furniture art lost its link with tradition because of the poor use of the classical models in the mechanical workshops at the end of the century. We end this section with a few photographs of Isabeline and Romantic pieces, exclusively Spanish since the European examples would be innumerable and would require a whole volume, and a group of palace and upper middle-class interiors.

This is only a small sample but in it we can appreciate the features we have mentioned earlier as most characteristic of the Isabeline period.

We close this last chapter with a group in the Neogothic style, inspired in a fashion promoted by the new Parliament in London in 1866. The work we refer to is the Senate library, designed by the architect Ayuse in 1882, a good example of the prevalent styles toward the end of the 19th century.

CONTEMPORARY FURNITURE

With the Isabeline style, which lasted until the last third of the 19th century, it could be said we have come to the end of our *A History of Furniture*. But we would like to touch briefly on the continued evolution of furniture styles that has led to contemporary models.

During the second half of the 19th century, and in the present century, we see a series of creative movements in furniture art. Such is the importance and the number of these variations and minor schools that a complete analysis and study of them would require a volume on the *History of Contemporary Furniture*, a very necessary work but beyond the scope of our possibilities here.

The great industrial revolution we referred to in the previous chapter occured in England years before it reached the continent. The machine converted the delicate craftwork of furniture art into an industry with mass production of models and vulgar interpretations of historical styles. We can compare, for example, the simple carpenter's lathe or the modest hand loom with today's machines. There are lathes that work the wood not in straight lines, but in broken ones that are required especially for the rear bars of chairs, and with such minimal error that, in comparison to the old woodworkers who allowed an error of one, two or even three mm., now it is possible to get as little as a few tenths of a mm. In the past it was necessary to number the legs and each peg fitted into its corresponding hole, with the resulting loss of time and labor. Now all the pieces are identical and fit anywhere.

The evolution of the loom has gone even further, until we come to the shuttle loom and the mechanical looms of the end of the century. Upholstery is also enriched with the invention of spiral steel springs by Samuel Pratt in 1828, which make backs and seats more comfortable and adaptable to the body. Nothing more need be added to this point.

With the use of iron in construction, and steel later on, the evolution of this industry became even more radical and the collaboration and influence of the engineer was now indispensable. All this had as a consequence the industrialization of building processes, very slowly of course, and furniture building as well since it is closely linked to the sector as a whole.

For the writers and artists at the end of the 19th century, engineers were like "our Hellenes" (as Adolph Loos called them in 1897), although polemics and nostalgic attitudes were never lacking in the face of the undeniable, precise and imperious necessity of this evolution.

The old craftwork in furniture art disappeared, replaced by those new methods that used only machines, eliminating specialized labor. The possibilities of the machine itself were not studied, except by groups of artists, architects and designers who had a clear idea of the change and devoted themselves to the study of the possibilities offered by the new methods and materials.

The aristocracy was replaced by the plutocracy. Furniture was no longer for the court nor the upper classes who created the great styles of the 18th century. A new type of furniture design emerged that was especially for the middle classes, who demanded a better standard of living. We should not be surprised to see, in the middle of the last century, a natural reaction against this mechanization fever.

Both movements, renovation and reaction, were stimulated with the still traditional styles (the Second Empire, Victorian, Biedermaier and our popular Isabeline) that, with the advances of the era, were utilized and improved by the designers.

In England in the second half of the 19th century, William Morris, an artist who continued the ideas of the great thinker Ruskin (who in 1849 published his celebrated book, *The Seven Lights of Architecture*, and for whom ornamentation is fundamental), attempted to bring about a pleasant and dignified environment for the middle class. To accomplish this, he created and oriented a new method of furniture manufacture and applied arts. In this way he attempted to fight against this first phase of "anti-art" mechanization. He incorporated into the movement, called *Art and Crafts*, painters, sculptors and architects and "raised up artisans to make true artists of them and converted artists into artisans", since "art should not be for just a few", as W. Morris said in his conferences throughout the entire country. But with his followers and disciples he evolved toward a paradoxical socialism in that he ended up working with a select minority and came to recognize that "cheap art is impossible". In spite of this, it is without a doubt true that *Art and Crafts*, the movement created by them, gave a great impulse to the industrial arts and these new currents soon spread to the continent. William Morris was fighting against the machine and the vulgar imitation of noble materials. For example, beech imitated mahogany, brass plates were an imitation of cast bronze, and wallpaper replaced silk tapestries. In furniture, proportion was deformed and careless because more and more pieces had to be made to satisfy the needs of a growing population. And this occured throughout these years not only in Spain but in all of Europe. W. Morris created, with his followers, a company dedicated to an excessively Utopian idea that was naturally criticized by his contemporaries.

W. Morris, as Pevsner says, "is the prophet of the 20th century and the father of the modern movement". But his disciples and followers, among them C. R. Ashbee (1863-1942), who "did not reject the machine but dominated it", not only accepted and incorporated the machine into their organizations, but used it, dominated it and applied it rationally. *Art and Crafts* can be considered a transition art in the second half of the 19th century. When it arrived on the continent and in the U.S.A., it took on different characteristics and directions. At the end of the century it slipped away from *Luddism* (an English workers' movement that attempted to bring about the destruction of the machine because its adherents saw it as the enemy of labor). At this point it is useful to mention some of the complex causes that stimulated the creation of a new art. Among them undoubtedly the most important was the dependency and relation of furniture to architecture. Others were the use of cast iron first and steel later, and toward the end of the century of reinforced concrete, factors which require a study in themselves. Finally we see the incorporation of the machine in all the industrial arts (natural consequence and evolution of the old schools of art), the rationalization of work, economic studies and organization, technological advance and the use of new materials.

A group of architects, around the end of the 19th century and in the 20th, began a new movement that included not only architecture but its collaboration with industry and the plastic arts, united to the new concepts of

Chair by Van de Velde

Couch by Gaudí

Dressing table by Gaudí

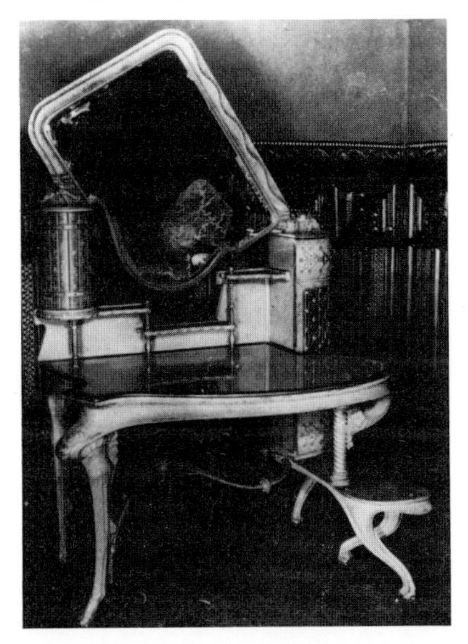

volume and space, of the beauty of the machine itself, of exteriors as a prolongation of interior environments, new materials and their application to ordinary objects and, finally, to furnishings.

In the final years of the 19th century and the first part of the 20th, these concepts gave rise to a new art. In France it took the name of *Art Moderne*, which in Belgium corresponds to *Art Nouveau*—the name by which it became most commonly known—*Jugendstil* in Germany, *Modernismo* in Spain, *Liberty* in Italy, *Sezession* in Austria, while in England the name of *Art and Crafts* continued in use.

However, *Art Nouveau* was not a cultural movement. The essence of this new style was in the personalities of its creators and their magnificent works because at the same time we find coexistence of the woodworker who repeated, more or less true to form, the old historical styles. Both movements were simultaneous. Frank Lloyd Wright, one of the greatest North American architects of the time 1869-1959), is a eulogist of the machine, but his contribution to *Art Nouveau* is not clear, and likewise that of his countrymen L. Sullivan, except in a return to inspiration in nature but with no more clearly defined or firmer link. H. Van de Velde in Holland (1863-1957) in all his creations shows us a continuation of *Art Nouveau* and admiration for the machine, without the artist losing his individualism. In fact, in his pieces we see the characteristics of *Art Nouveau*, simple lines with nearly total absence of carving and a special ornamentation. The surfaces and forms are strong and simple, the colors light and, in general, the construction is more rational and the technique perfected. The Belgian decorator Victor Horta (1861-1946), contemporary of Van de Velde, struggled constantly in favor of the new style. The latter of these two was more abstract and the former more of a naturalist because, as we should point out, there was a singular theme in all the continental *Art Nouveau* which was a simple interpretation of a lily stem and a water lily in a long, gently undulating symmetrical line. A clear example of this typical ornamentation can be seen in the Paris Metro stations of 1900, drawn by H. Guimard. It is not necessary to point out in this chapter any particular examples of the style in which, undoubtedly, France did nothing more than continue the work begun in Belgium by Van de Velde and Horta and, in this line, the pieces of furniture by Grasset and Gallé, founders of the so-called Nancy school, are very characteristic. In Spain it is in Catalonia where most of the elements of the new style are preserved and which today have a particular charm. The exhibitions of 1890 and 1891 by the painters Casas, Rusiñol and Clarasó are an important landmark in the history of modernism. But for us the architects Domenech and Montaner, Martorell and Puig y Cadafalch are more interesting in that they are representative of the moment and have so greatly influenced their collaborators who applied *Modernismo* to the industrial arts.

Good examples of decoration and ornamentation typical of *Modernismo* in Barcelona are the Salon of the Hotel Internacional of 1898 and the Hotel de España in 1900, both by Domenech, or the Bar Torino on the Paseo de Gracia, by Eusebio Arnau and Puig y Cadafalch.

But the most unusual image with its singular personality, that remains outside the more or less common standards in all of Europe within the style of *Modernismo*, is the Catalan architect Gaudi (1852-1926) whose furniture designs are highly original, with some of the characteristics of international *Art Nouveau*. These, together with his architectural designs, place him among the most outstanding creative artists.

What cannot be denied is that France, from this time on, lost her position of first place in the art of woodworking. Neither the pure and refined pieces by E. Ruhlman nor the expected originality of the Decorative Arts Exposition in Paris in 1925, nor the exceptional personality of Le Corbusier, whose influence revolutionizes and reaches all fields of the new industrial arts, can recapture the old position. It is the countries of Central Europe that have taken the initiative in contemporary furniture.

In Germany Peter Behrens (1888-1940) and Max Berg were the main propagators of *Art Nouveau*, which soon became transformed and took on other characteristics, not only in ornamentation but in proportions, materials, the relation of each of the parts with the utilitarian nature of the whole; not only with the interior environment and its volume but with light and space.

In Austria the new art, *Sezession*, was defined bv two celebrated architects, Olbrich (1867-1908) and J. Hofman (1870-1956). The latter was the creator of very simple and charming pieces that move (going beyond *Sezession*) toward cubism. We cannot fail to point out the advance, in the second half of the 19th century, represented by the creation and fabrication by the Viennese M. Thonet (1796-1871) and his five sons of curved beech pieces, in whose ample curves we can see the beginnings of *Art Nouveau.*

In Italy the pieces of this period are usually known as the *Liberty* style. This name is also applied to the English creations in the shop of the same name in London, with Chinese and Oriental themes, whose influences were felt in all of Europe at the end of the 19th century.

In England *Art and Crafts*, begun by Morris and spread by his followers with its natural evolution and change, saw the creation of the so-called Glasgow school, whose most representative artists were Mackintosh (1868-1928), his wife, daughter, and son-in-law. Pevsner relates Mackintosh with the *Sezession* style as he left a deep impression on it.

The predominance enjoyed by England passed on to Central Europe at the beginning of the 20th century, as had previously occurred with France.

All these minor styles brought about a revolution in furniture, as determined by the new techniques, and coalesced at the end of World War I in cubism and expressionism. Magazines and expositions devoted to decoration propagated and interchanged these currents and the style became international.

It was then that, simultaneously with architecture, which at that time was considered functional, what we can call contemporary furniture developed.

Germany and the Central European countries were now in the lead in these decorative arts. The Weimar School of Applied Arts became, in 1919, the Bauhaus School, a unique school of decorative and industrial arts which was considered suspicious by some because it was supposedly linked somewhat falsely to a certain rationalism. Nevertheless, the Bauhaus School, founded by W. Gropius, was an institution which brought about the synthesis of the preceding movements. This educational center was like a laboratory where architects, artists, artisans and technicians collaborated and performed a common task in construction, decorative arts, various types of craftwork, and all this in the manner of an evolution and continuation of the *Art and Crafts* created by W. Morris. Undoubtedly it is from here that the first currents of contemporary furniture came.

Although the Bauhaus was closed in 1933 with Hitler's National Socialism, in its mere 14 years of existence it carried on an intense labor that lasted much longer and, although it has been much criticized, its importance cannot be doubted. The phenomenon of the socialization of furniture now achieved its maximum interest, joined to the development of national economies, because the needs of the various social classes have many points of contact. Decorators, who are frequently architects, must take into account this new situation that is more clearly defined day by day. New types of housing and their smaller size, as well as the simplification of interior distribution, are all factors that powerfully influence furniture development. If we analyze these reasons, it is easy to understand that the chair is still the most important piece, since other pieces—tables, cupboards, beds, etc.—are often built-in units and others are transformable and variable in form and function.

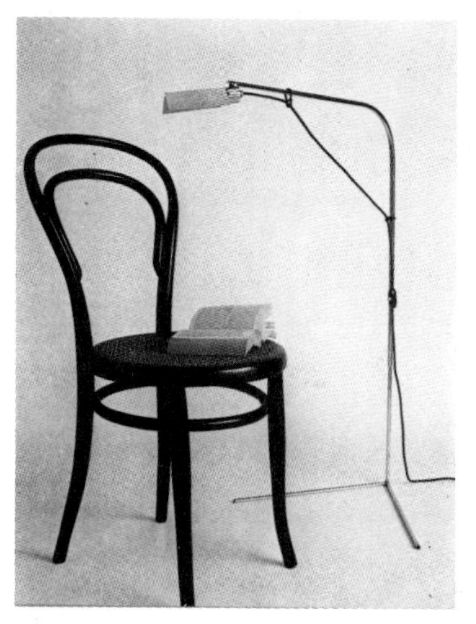
Chair by Thonet

In the chair, as we have said, technical advances and the use of new materials exert a great influence. But in this brief chapter we can include only a brief listing: (a) the use of metals, like iron, steel, aluminum (pieces with iron plates, tubes, laminated profiles, metallic fabrics, etc.); (b) the application of plastics, at the height of their development, not only as structural elements but also as rigid or elastic coverings, as well as rubber, new types of

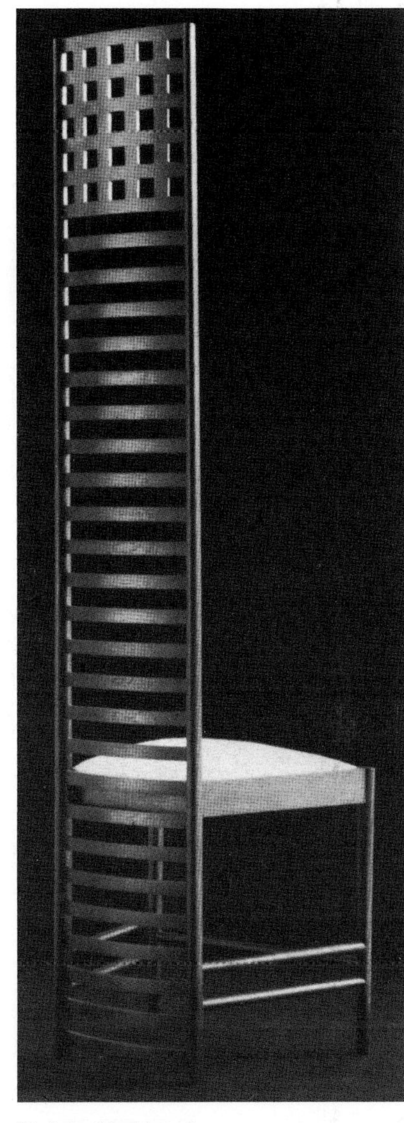

Chair by Mackintosh

springs or pneumatic elements; (c) the use of wood in the form of plywood, pressed wood or fibers; (d) various types of wood treatments such as drying, sterilization, waterproofing, etc., and the use of African and Asian woods; (e) new techniques in impermeable paint and varnish and their means of application.

This short listing, together with the introduction of certain mechanisms in some pieces to allow them to change their shape and use, is sufficient to be able to understand their importance.

There are numerous international decorative arts expositions in Europe and America that, with specialized magazines and books, design contests and international furniture patents, as well as new commercial methods arising out of political communitues, create an international furniture market. This has required a perfected study of design to resolve problems of construction, utility, economy, space, transportation, etc., far removed from the old concept of design. All this industrial organization is achieved through an enormous mechanization process with the consequent phenomenon of the almost total disappearance of the woodworker and his traditional working element: the carpenter's bench.

Consequently we see that the chair is the most representative piece, and we can take it as an example of the models created by designers, who create truly significant innovations that have served as the basis for the most important piece of the present moment. New models of chairs, armchairs, easy chairs, etc., appear constantly in magazines. But it may be said that they all have a predecessor in those who created the pioneering models of today's contemporary furniture and which we have chosen to illustrate here as objectively as possible.

From our point of view, which we can call evolutionary, the history of the contemporary chair begins first with the models by Thonet in the middle of the 19th century, with his innovations in curved beechwood in a multitude of models that flooded the international market.

Wood has been curved before (for example, the wheels of Egyptian carts), but never with the intent and wisdom of M. Thonet and his followers.

The second examples chosen for illustration here are the celebrated chairs by Mackintosh, one of the group known as "The Glasgow Four". They also belong to the 19th and 20th centuries and have a personality very much their own in the purity of their geometric lines and their perfect pleasing texture and finish.

But true contemporary chairs, nevertheless, begin after World War I, as a consequence of the enormous political, economic, technical and artistic changes brought about by this conflict.

We begin this group with a chair by the Dutch architect Gerrit Rietveld (1884-1964), the so-called "red and blue chair" (1908-1919). It appeared recently in an exhibition of chairs in England in 1970 that included more than one hundred models and was directed by Carol Haghen and a team of collaborators. This chair was presented here; it is a structural prototype, straight and rigid with no ornamental or decorative elements. At the beginning it was made simply of natural beech, but in 1925 the ends of the bars were painted yellow, the back and seat in red and blue and the rest in black. As Haghen has pointed out, when the chair is placed against a black wall, the legs disappear and the back and seat stand out in exaggerated fashion and appear to be floating in the air. This effect greatly influenced the evolution of future chair designs through the years, as we shall see.

In these years after the War, with the resulting labor shortage and, consequently, scarcity of craftwork in chairs, simplicity assumed great importance. But these highly simple forms required the use of more select materials and greater purity of style, and it is easy to see the difference between a piece of this period (cheap and made of cheap materials with little craftwork) and the models of the great masters (with carefully selected materials and pure craftwork, although they were mass produced following industrial designs).

Recently, in 1974, another exhibition of chairs was held in the museum of Grenoble. The name *S'Asseoir* is sufficiently expressive of its content. More than 300 models by the best designers were presented at this exposition, which was conceived and planned by Bérard Ifert and Béatrice Simon. We refer to these two expositions only because we can do no more in this chapter than present a summary and selection of the most outstanding models.

In the second half of the century we are undoubtedly in a period of changing social, political and economic concepts, and these transcend and are reflected in housing designs and, naturally, in furniture as well—and especially in the chair, the most expressive and morphological piece, as we have said before.

The classical methods of mass production of wooden chairs are now succeeded by the revolutionary incorporation of new materials that are in full evolution and production.

Contemporary furniture was begun by small groups of architects and designers in Central Europe with the architect Marcel Breuer, who was born in 1902 and worked in the Bauhaus School. In 1923 he designed the furniture for an experimental house built by the Bauhaus, and for a house planned by its director and creator Gropius, in Weissenhof. But his greatest success was, undoubtedly, the armchair made of steel tubes and canvas strips, which he designed in 1925 and which is accepted even today as a truly modern style.

The Bauhaus magazine in 1925 wrote about the use of steel for the first time in this chair (which was called the Wassily chair as it was made for the painter Wassily Kandinsky, who also worked in the Bauhaus). It is even surmised that M. Breuer was inspired by the handlebars of a bicycle, as Haghen says, a theme used much later by Picasso in his bull. The silhouette is a broken line, but at the same time continuous. Taking advantage of the properties of the steel tube in 1926, Mies van der Rohe and Breuer made several models, all with four legs or vertical bars because up to this time chairs required four legs for adequate support. The few made with three legs—nearly all popular—were badly balanced, but no one had ever attempted to make a chair supported only on two vertical bars. This was one of the most successful innovations in the making of chairs, and its first creator was the Dutch architect Mart Stam, born in the last year of the 19th century. It was he who designed, in 1926, the first chair suspended on two legs, joined at the bottom as well as at the top in perfect continuity, and called "the endless chair". Its structure is very similar to the chairs by Van der Rohe and Breuer, but is in a somewhat reclining position, supported on two bars. This produces an original optical effect and at the same time a guarantee of safety with no danger of upsetting, thanks to the elasticity and resistance of the curved steel tube.

Another beautiful example of this type was the design by Mies van der Rohe, on two semicircular front legs, and the one by Marcel Breuer, very similar to M. Stam's chair. The chair designed by Mies van der Rohe for the Barcelona Exposition, very wide and supported on steel plates, after 30 years is still considered a modern piece. In France also the great architect Le Corbusier, in 1928, transformed the traditional concept of the upholstered sofa, heavy and solid, into a lighter shape—doubtlessly inspired by the metallic structures of the Breuer and M. van der Rohe chairs—using loose cushions of more natural and lighter forms.

But in spite of the use of metals, that make possible designs with floating and springy seats, the use of wood was not abandoned.

In 1934 Gerrit Rietveld designed his wooden Zig-Zag chair which, although appearing irrational to the eye, advances the progress in technique and design. In these years the Nordic countries produced pieces in wood that adapted easily to human anatomy. Besides being interesting, they are very beautiful and their texture and general feeling are warmer than the metal pieces.

The wood used is teak, resistant and beautiful of grain and color. At the same time the use of structural metals continued, with backs and seats made of wood or upholstered, like the models by Wegner, Hansen and Finn Juhl.

Alvar Aalto, who in his first years designed a few models in metal, later used plywood with thicker and more resistant sections in the various elements of chairs. He obtained con-

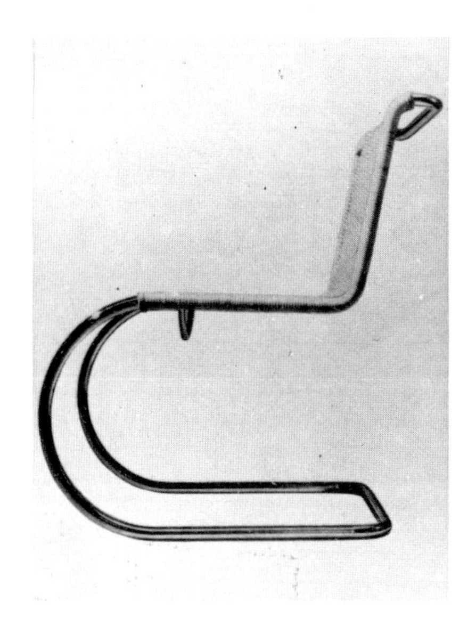

Chair by Mies Van der Rohe

Chair by Eames

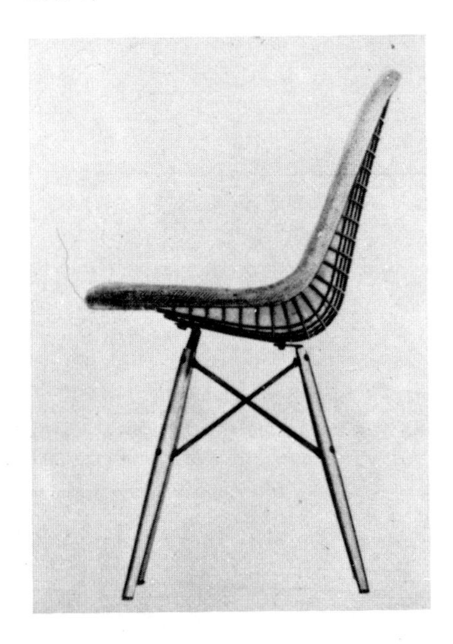

tinous pieces in the seat as well as in the back and even in the arms in a single piece ably fret-sawed and pressed. These models have been repeated and have brought about the evolution of techniques and the old concepts of classical woodworking. Even today the celebrated Finnish architect is still creating new and interesting models.

Among these designs in wood, the so-called "Tripolina" chair, a folding chair used by the Italian army and already known in the years from 1870-80 with its wood frame and canvas covering, was interpreted in 1938 by Hardoy, the Spaniard A. Bonet and other collaborators using a fixed metal frame and leather covering in the form of a hammock. It was known as the AA type and was highly successful for many years.

In 1940 the Museum of Modern Art in New York held a contest that was won by C. Eames and Eero Saarinen with a plywood chair in three dimensions, that is combining the seat and back in a single piece with waves and concave forms to adapt them better to the human body. These were the same concave forms already tried by A. Gaudí many years before in his solid wooden chairs and benches, to make them more adaptable to the human body. In New York the piece was made on a mold or box of cast iron. In 1949 the Museum held another contest in which Eames won a second prize with an armchair made of fiber-glass which, with Saarinen, he had presented at the 1940 contest. From then on molded plywood was used extensively, alternating this technique with polyester, polyurethane, etc. The latter of these two plastics is more flexible than the former. In 1948 foam rubber furniture was put on the market. All these procedures have changed the methods of attaching up-holstery, making them more mechanical and faster above all to reduce the amount of labor necessary as this is an increasingly difficult problem.

But the models are not always perfect and comfortable. The designers study meticulously the average height of a person and adapt their designs to it. They are comfortable, but they do not always coincide with the user; there are persons who are taller, shorter, heavier or thinner, and the result is physical strain after sitting too long in such a chair. Perhaps this is why the best models are the ones with ample measurements and loose cushions on a metal or wood frame.

According to Dermih Yomig, the beautiful armchair by Mies van der Rohe, known as the "Barcelona chair", satisfies these requirements.

It is curious to note the constant desire of the designers to eliminate legs from chairs. We have seen how the four legs have become three since the Middle Ages and how, with extra-ordinary ingenuity, they are reduced to two and how, in addition, the chair can be made to rock or swing gently on its two legs. The next step is to go to one leg, such as seen on 19th-century piano stools. Now we see the same design in a chair by Saarinen, called the "tulip chair", an elegant model consisting of a back and seat of a single piece of plastic, supported on a single center leg that opens outward at the base to form a cone. Mies van der Rohe takes this even further with a cinematographic effect that appears to suspend the person in the air. What then was like a dream, a wish expressed more or less ironically, is still far in the future although closer today. We are talking about houses suspended in air, aerospace cities, as indicated by Horacio Cabral in a recent article.

In the succession of wooden models, of special interest is the 1961 chair by B. Rasch, made of two pieces of plywood that looks somewhat like an unfinished frame. Another is the one by Gio Ponti, the famous Italian architect, creator of *Domus* magazine, who in 1956 designed a very light chair of wood with very careful lines that reminds us of the chairs made in Chiavari, the little Italian town where many of these types of chairs were mass produced in the 19th century, many with straw or cane seats very similar to Ponti's chair.

Many new models merely follow previous lines, such as the one inspired by Eames's chairs with combinations of steel legs and continuous rattan, laminated or plywood back and seat. Another original model that solves the technical problems of making a two-legged chair of wood is the one by A. and D. Heat in Denmark in 1968.

Another idea is the manufacture of stacking chairs to save space. This was done in the Middle Ages with the X-shaped chairs that were reduced to minimum size. Now it is done with the total volume and rigidity of the chair. Jacobson, Eames, Ilmari Tapiovara of Finland make chairs entirely of fiberglass. Others working with this medium are Verner Panton, with an outstanding model in 1960, Magistretti of Milan in 1968 or Sergio Mazza, also of Milan. All these are stacking chairs.

With the appearance of inflatable plastics, some of them transparent, comfortable and ingenious chairs are designed, easily carried and lightweight, like those by Scolari, D'Urbino, Lomazzi and De Pas, or the polyurethane chairs designed by Gaetano Peisce in 1969.

As the reader can see from this brief summary, Italy again occupies a leading position after having been somewhat outside the Central European movement, dominated especially in the bourgeois furniture market first by the Germans and later by the Nordic countries. Her artists, architects and designers invade the world market and flood it with their products.

With them, the American C. Eames, the Dane Jacobson and P. Paulin in the Netherlands design notable and daring models, such as Paulin's chair in 1965 consisting of a sheet of rubber stretched over a tubular metal frame covered with latex.

The Dane J. Utzon also designed an armchair of foam rubber on an aluminum frame, a highly comfortable piece but of less eccentric shape.

Rosselli of Milan molds a solid armchair of fiberglass. But perhaps the most original of all, following this concept, is the ovoid shape designed by E. Aarnio of Finland.

Using polyurethane on aluminum frames, the Italian J. Colombo created several somewhat strange models in 1968. The Japanese architect Motomi Kawa Kami made a fiberglass armchair with a highly original shape and a slight rocking motion (in 1960 in Italy). Thus we come to the last examples shown on these pages.

The models by Eames and Saarinen, with a central leg on four crossed feet, nearly flat or slightly inclined and using wheels and springs for perfect levelling, are especially designed for offices. They are swivel chairs upholstered with leather or plastic fibers over rubber. They were presented in 1956 and are still popular on international markets.

The famous "sack chair" was created by the Italians Gatti, Paolini and Teodoro in their study in Milan. This is a bag filled with grains of polystyrene and covered with imitation leather. It adapts easily to the form of the human body, always in a restful posture. All these chairs and armchairs, as might be deduced, have diverse uses, like this last one, and are highly stable and appropriate for relaxing.

The chair is one of the most fundamental pieces of furniture used by man.

Its relation to man implies a series of conditions very different from other pieces of furniture. Although it is very elementary—a chest or basket or some similar piece may be used among Oriental peoples, even the most primitive—we should remember that sitting on the floor or simply on a cushion is an Oriental custom. On the other hand, in our world with its different culture, the use of the chair has existed from the time of Egyptian civilization. Its purpose is to take an intermediate position between vertical and horizontal. As Sheban Cantacocino has suggested, "the chair is joined to man and is closely identified with him, even to the extent of becoming almost a personal object". Or as Neruda has defined it in his ode to the chair: "the supreme dignity of repose".

We have given a rapid overview of the advances in technique and the corporal needs of man, i.e. comfort and relaxation. Both have made the designer seek new paths in the design and construction of chairs. The sack chair by Gatti, Paolini and Teodoro is perhaps one way. But in the past quarter century, the chair has become irreplaceable and new models will be seen for many years to come before we attain the Utopian dream of Mies van der Rohe in the Bauhaus.

Woman "seated in the air"

Stacking chair by Albingon

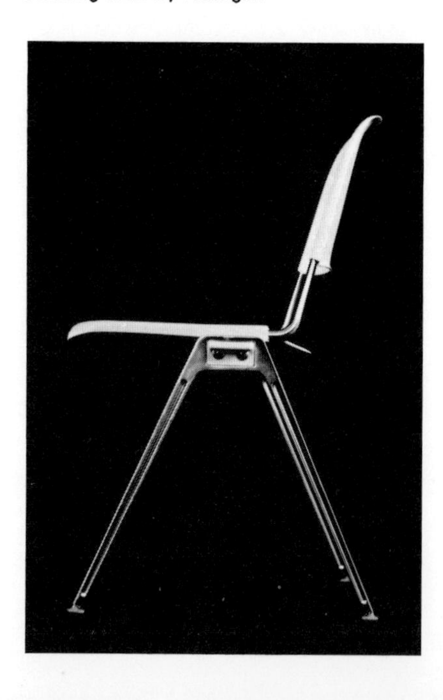

ILLUSTRATIONS

EGIPTO

EGYPT

1. Silla popular con refuerzo vertical en la parte posterior del respaldo. Museo del Cairo

1. A Popular chair with vertical strengthener behind the back. Cairo Museum

2. Silla con aplicaciones de marfil. Altura 90 cm. Museo del Louvre, París

2. Chair with ivory appliqués. Height 90 cm. The Louvre, Paris

3. Trono chapeado de oro y pastas vítreas. Pies en forma de pata de animal y asiento para almohadones sobre rejilla. Altura 104 cm, frente 53 cm, fondo 64 cm. Museo del Cairo

3. Throne decorated with gold and vitreous compositions. Legs of animal form, seats for cushions on canework. Height 104, front 53, depth 64. Cairo Museum

4. Silla egipcia de madera de cedro, con aplicaciones de oro. Tumba de Tutankhamen. Dinastía XVIII (1400 a. de J.C.). Museo del Cairo

4. Cedar wood Egyptian chair with gold appliqués. Tomb of Tutankhamen. XVIII dynasty. (1400 B.C.). Cairo Museum

5. Silla en el respaldo del sillón representado en la figura 3, en la cual se puede apreciar la colocación de almohadones sobre el asiento y el respaldo. Museo del Cairo

5. Chair design on the back of the illustration 3, which clearly shows the location of the cushions on the seat and back. Cairo Museum

6. Taburete de Tutankhamen. Pies en forma de pata de animal, pintado en blanco y oro; asiento muy cóncavo. Frente 45 cm, costado 43 cm, altura 45 cm. Museo del Cairo

6. Tutankhamen's stool. Legs of animal form painted in white and gold. Deep concave seat. Front 45, side 43, height 45. Cairo Museum

7. Taburete de tres patas rematadas en garras, chambranas talladas que simbolizan la unión de Egipto. Tumba de Tutankhamen

7. Three-legged stool with legs ending in talons. Carved crosspieces represent the union of Egypt. Tomb of Tutankhamen.

8. Sillón de carácter religioso, utilizado por el faraón en sus funciones de sacerdote. Respaldo y asiento cóncavos, pies en forma de tijera, con cabezas de pato. Chapeado en oro, marfil y piedras. Museo del Cairo. Altura 102 cm, frente 70 cm, fondo 44 cm

8. Chair of a religious nature used by the Pharaoh in his functions as a priest. Concave back and seat, X-shaped legs with duck heads. Covered with gold, ivory and stones. Height 102, front 70, depth 44. Cairo Museum

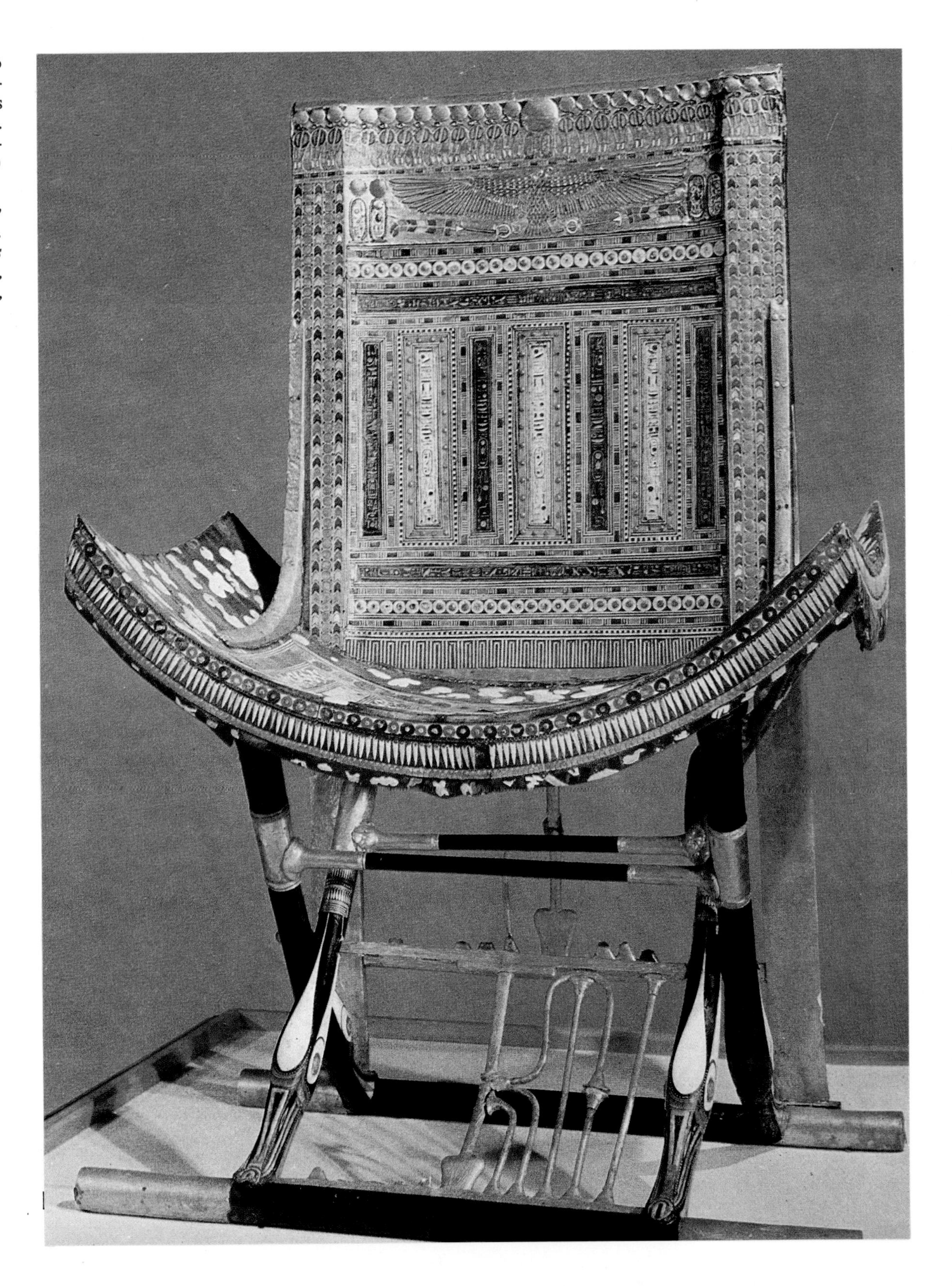

9. Cama fúnebre. Tumba de Tutankhamen

9. Burial bed. Tomb of Tutankhamen

10. Cofre policromado. Museo del Cairo

10. Polychrome coffer. Cairo Museum

11. Mueble-arca, de madera roja y ébano, con bisagras de bronce. Altura 58 cm. Museo del Cairo

11. Chest in redwood and ebony with bronze hinges. Height 58. Cairo Museum

12. Cofre-ataúd policromado de la época saíta. Dinastía XXVI. Metropolitan Museum, Nueva York

12. Polychrome coffer-coffin of the Saita era. XXVI dynasty. Metropolitan Museum, New York

13. Cofre de cedro, ébano y marfil. En el cajón ensambles a cola de milano. Dinastía XII. Tebas

13. Coffer in cedar, ebony and ivory. The drawer has dovetailed joints. XII dynasty. Thebes

14. Arqueta estucada y pintada, con tapa en forma de teja. Altura 44 cm, largo 61 cm. Museo del Cairo

14. Painted stucco chest with lid in the form of a tile. Height 44, length 61. Cairo Museum

15. Cama plegable, desplegada. Museo del Cairo

15. Folding bed, open position. Cairo Museum

16. Cama anterior plegada

16. The same bed folded

17. Cama con incrustaciones en el cabecero y patas en forma de garras de animal. Tumba de Amenofis III (s. XV a. J.C.).

17. Bed with inlaid head and legs of animal form with claws. Tomb of Amenophis III (XV century B.C.)

18. Cama. Detalle de patas de marfil

18. Bed. Detail of ivory legs

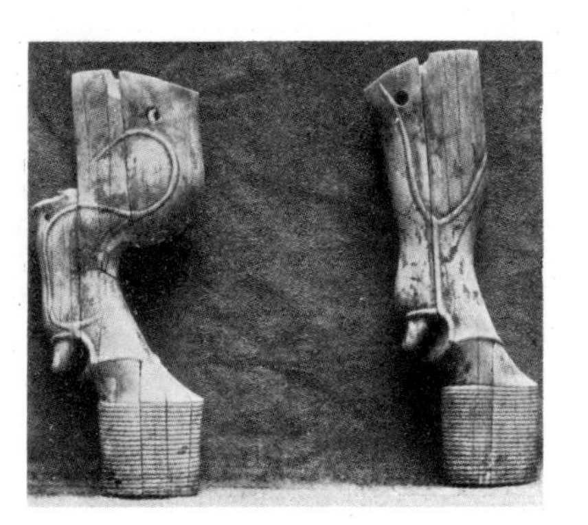

19. Cama de la reina Hetepheres recubierta de oro y cerámica vidriada. El uol chapeado en oro y plata. Museo del Cairo

19. Queen Hetepheres'bed, covered with gold and glazed ceramic. The uol, or headrest, is plated with gold and silver. Cairo Museum

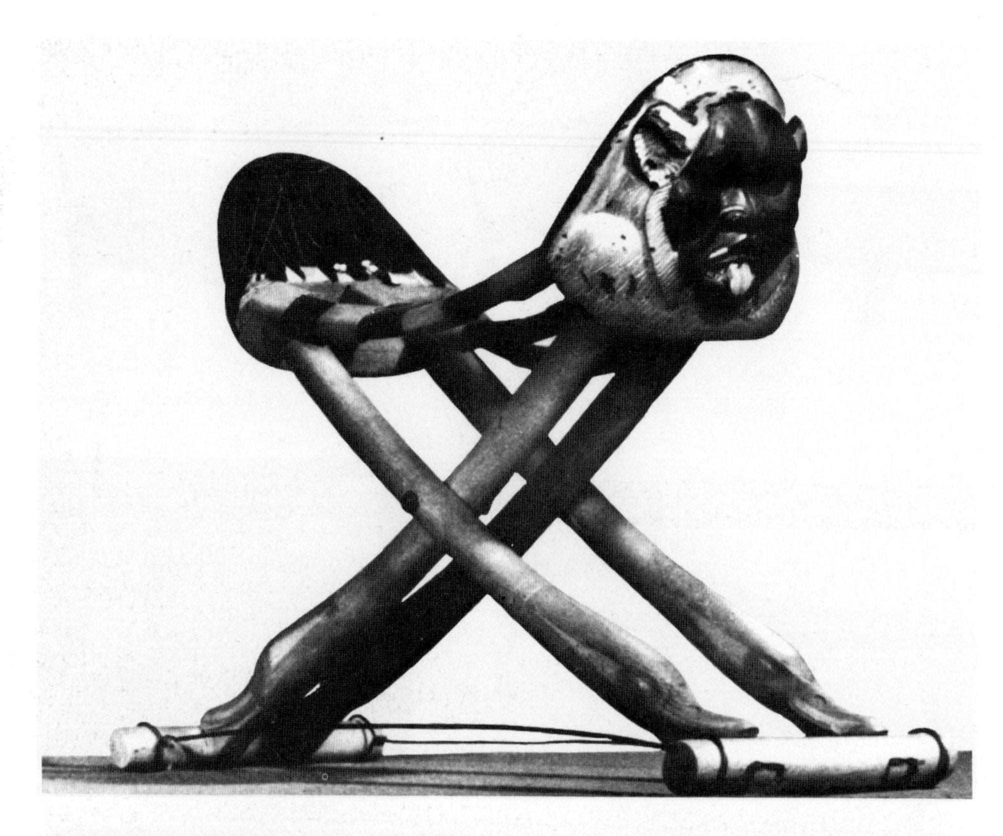

20. Uol o cabecero de cama en forma de asiento de tijeras con pies de cabezas de pato. Altura 20 cm, largo 19 cm, fondo 10 cm. Tumba de Tutankhamen. Museo del Cairo

20. Uol or bed head of X-shaped seat form, legs with duck heads. Height 20, length 19, depth 10. Tomb of Tutankhamen. Cairo Museum

21. Uol o cabecero de pasta vítrea azul. Altura 18 cm, largo 28 cm

21. Uol or bed head in blue vitreous composition. Height 18, length 28

GRECIA

GREECE

22. Trono de piedra del palacio real de Cnosos. Arte prehelénico. Creta

22. Stone throne from the Royal Palace of Knossos. Pre-Hellenic art. Crete

23. Trono Ludovisi, de piedra, con el asiento de madera. Siglo VI a. de J.C.

23. Ludovisi throne in stone with a wooden seat. VI century B.C.

24. Trono Ludovisi. Parte posterior que representa el nacimiento de Venus. Museo de las Termas, Roma

24. Ludovisi throne. The back part depicting the birth of Venus. Museo delle Terme, Rome

25. Estatuilla de mármol representando una arpista sentada. Cultura cicládica, 2500 a. de J.C. Museo Nacional de Atenas

25. Marble statuette representing a seated harpist. Cycladic culture, 2500 B.C. National Museum of Athens

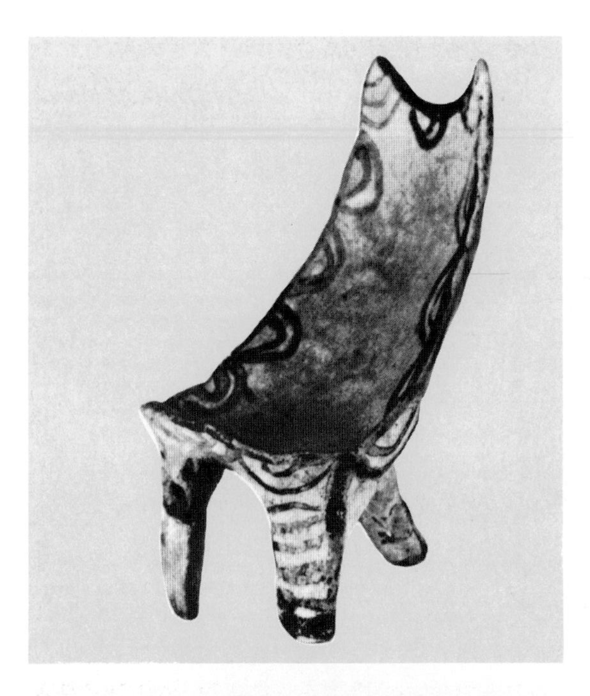

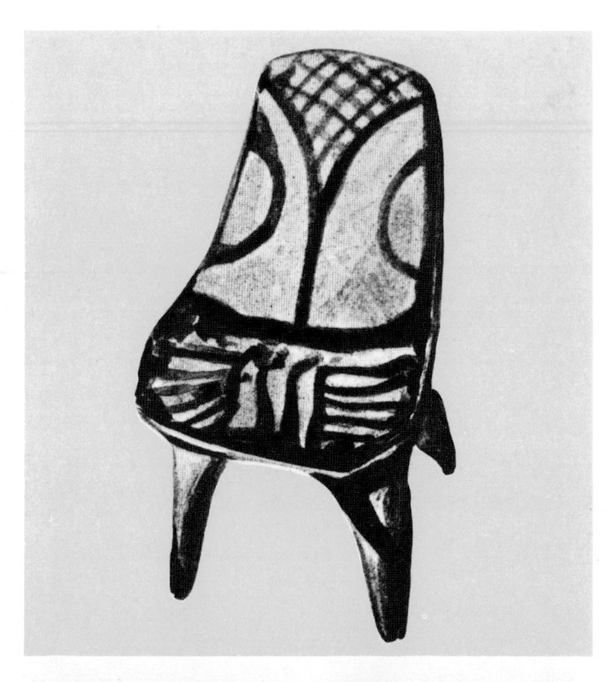

26. Trono de miniatura, de terracota. Museo Nacional de Atenas

26. Miniature throne of terra cotta. National Museum of Athens

27. Trono en terracota. Cultura egea. Museo Nacional de Atenas

27. Terra cotta throne. Aegean culture. National Museum of Athens

28. Diophros, banqueta en una estela funeraria. Siglo IV a. de J.C. Museo del Estado, Berlín

28. Diophros, stool on a funerary stele. IV century B.C. Berlin State Museum

29. Banqueta o diophros en una estela sepulcral. Museo Nacional de Atenas

29. Stool or diophros on a sepulchral stele. National Museum of Athens

30. Silla de tijera en una copa con figuras blancas. Siglo IV a. de J.C. Museo del Estado Berlín

30. X-shaped chair on a vase with white figures. IV century B.C. Berlin State Museum

31. Sillón en una metopa del templo de Thesauros de Paestum

31. Armchair in a metope of the Temple of Thesauros in Paestum

32. Klismos, silla de patas y respaldo muy curvados, en una estela sepulcral. Siglo V a. de J.C. Cementerio del Cerámico de Atenas

32. Klismos, chair with deeply curved legs and back, on a sepulchral stele. V century B.C. Cemetery of Ceramics, Athens

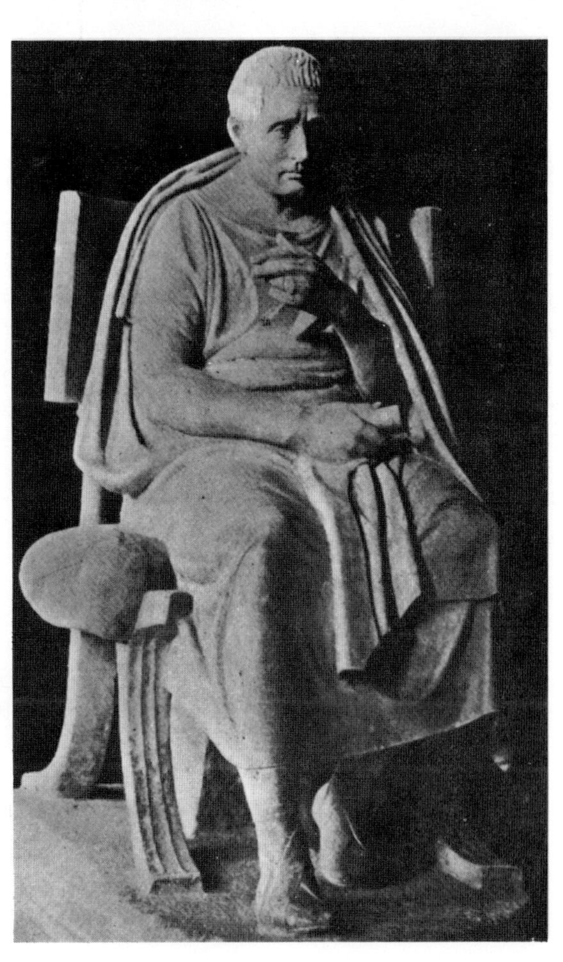

33. Silla o cátedra tipo klismos. Siglo IV a. de J.C. Museo Vaticano

33. Chair or cathedra, Klismos type, IV century B.C. Vatican Museum

34. Sillón de piedra con patas de león. Siglo III a. de J.C. Gliptoteca de Copenhague

34. Stone armchair with lion's paws. III century B.C. Glyptotheque of Copenhagen

35. Trípode de bronce, el más antiguo mueble de Grecia. Metropolitan Museum, Nueva York

35. Bronze tripod. The most ancient piece of furniture of Greece. Metropolitan Museum of Art, New York

36. Sillones de piedra en el teatro Dionisos, a los pies de la Acrópolis de Atenas. Patas de león y respaldo con alegorías solares

36. Stone armchairs in the Dionysus theatre at the foot of the Acropolis of Athens. Lion's paw legs and back with solar allegories

37. Sillón de mármol conservado en el teatro Dionisos, Atenas

37. Marble armchair preserved in the Dionysius theatre. Athens

38. Triclinio. Escena de gineceo. Villa imperial, Pompeya

38. Triclinium. Gynaeceum scene. Imperial Villa, Pompeii

39. Costado del sarcófago de Alejandro

39. Side of Alexander's sarcophagus

40. Lecho en el fresco "La boda de Aldobrandini", copia de un original griego del siglo IV a. de J.C. Museo del Vaticano, Roma

40. Bed in the fresco painting "The wedding of Aldobrandini", copy of the Greek original of the IV century B.C. Vatican Museum

41. Lecho griego representado en un vaso ático del siglo VI a. de J.C. Metropolitan Museum, Nueva York

41. Greek bed represented on an Attic vase. VI century B.C. Metropolitan Museum of Art, New York

42. Sarcófago de Hagia-Triada. Museo Herakleion, Creta. Estructura semejante a las arcas españolas del norte. Arte cretense. 137 cm de frente

42. Sarcophagus of Hagia-Triada. Museum of Herakleion. Crete. Structure similar to the chests of Northern Spain. Cretan Art. Front 137

43. Sarcófago de terracota en forma de arca Kamilari, Herakleion. Cultura micénica

43. Terra cotta sarcophagus in the from of a chest. Kamilari, Herakleion, Mycenaean culture

ROMA, PALEOCRISTIANO Y BIZANTINO

ROMAN, PALEO-CHRISTIAN AND BYZANTINE

44. Sillón de paja o mimbre en un relieve de Neumagen. Siglo III a. de J.C. Museo Provincial, Tréveris

44. Straw or wicker armchair in a relief of Neumagen. III century B.C. Museum of Trier

45. Sillón de bronce cincelado. Arte etrusco del s. V a. de J.C. Museo de Villa Julia, Roma

45. Chased bronze chair. Etruscan art. V century B.C. Museum of Villa Julia, Rome

46. Trono etrusco de bronce, reconstruido: proviene de la tumba Regulini-Calari, Cerveteri. Museo Vaticano

46. Bronze Etruscan throne, restored. From the Regulini-Calari tomb, Cerveteri. Vatican Museum

47. Silla en una pintura de la Villa Farnesio de Roma. Museo Nacional de las Termas, Roma

47. Chair in a painting of the Villa Farnesina, Rome. Museo delle Terme, Rome

48. Lecho etrusco representado en un sarcófago cerámico procedente de Cerveteri. Siglo VI a. de J.C. Museo de Villa Julia, Roma

48. Etruscan bed depicted on a ceramic sarcophagus from Cerveteri. VI century B.C. Museum of Villa Julia, Rome

49. El mismo lecho anterior

49. The same bed as above

50. Sillones de respaldo curvo en un relieve funerario de Neumagen. Siglo III a. de J.C. Museo Provincial, Tréveris

50. Armchairs with curved back on a funerary relief of Neumagen. III century B.C. Provincial Museum of Trier

51. Trípode con sátiros de bronce. Museo de Nápoles

51. Tripod with bronze satyrs. Naples Museum

52. Sillón de piedra de la necrópolis estrusca de Cerveteri

52. Stone armchair of the Etruscan Necropolis of Cerveteri

53. Silla honorífica de piedra de la época republicana. Palacio Corsini, Roma

53. Honorary chair in stone of the Republican era. Corsini Palace, Rome

54. Sillón romano de mármol, con leones alados en los brazos. Siglo I. Museo del Louvre

54. Roman armchair in marble with winged lions on the arms. 1st century. The Louvre, Paris

55. Reconstrucción de un *bisellium* en bronce cincelado, con damasquinados de plata y banqueta para los pies. Museo Capitolino, Roma.

55. Rebuilt bisellium in chased bronze with silver damaskeening and footstool. Capitolino Museum, Rome

56. Trípode de bronce cincelado, Pompeya

56. Chased bronze tripod. Pompeii

57. Mesa reconstruida Diophros "okladia", con bronces originales de una tumba etrusca de Felsinae, Bolonia

57. A rebuilt Diophros "okladia" table of original bronze work from an Etruscan tomb of Felsinae, Bologna

58. Silla klismos, de origen griego. Retrato de la segunda Agripina. Museo Capitolino, Roma

58. Klismos chair of Greek origin. Portrait of the second Agrippina. Capitolino Museum, Rome

59. Sillón de pórfido con patas en forma de ménsula. Museo del Vaticano, Roma

59. Armchair in porphyry with legs of bracket form. Vatican Museum, Rome

60. Mesa circular de mármol sobre tres patas en forma de grifos. Museo de Nápoles

60. Round table in marble standing on three legs of griffin form. Naples Museum

61. Mesa de campo plegable, de bronce. Las patas, en forma de garra, representan faunos. Museo de Nápoles

61. Folding campotable in bronze. The legs with claw feet represent fauns. Naples Museum

62. Silla honorífica *bisellium*, posiblemente mal restaurada. Museo de Nápoles

62. Bisellium honorary chair (possibly badly restored). Naples Museum

63. Trípode de bronce cincelado de estilo griego, Pompeya

63. Chased bronze tripod in the Greek style. Pompeii

64. Mesa de mármol. Costado o tropezóforo. Peristilo de la casa de Cornelio Rufo, Pompeya

64. Marble table. Side or trapezophrum. Peristyle of the house of Cornelius Ruphus. Pompeii

65. Lecho-triclinio de madera, semejante a un diván. Casa del mueble carbonizado, Herculano

65. Triclinium bed in wood similar to a divan. The house of carbonished furniture. Herculaneum

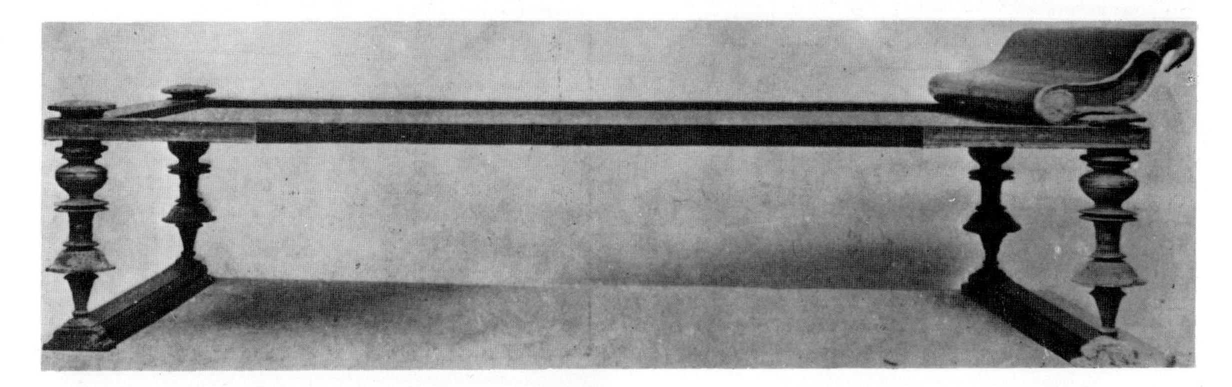

66. Lecho de bronce cincelado, Pompeya

66. Chased bronze bed, Pompeii

67. Larario de madera carbonizada de composición arquitectónica. Casa en Herculano

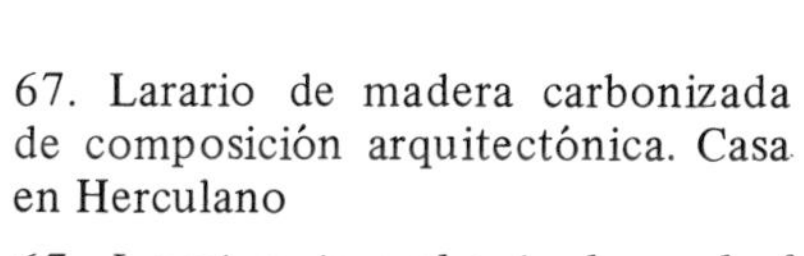

67. Lararium in carbonized wood of architectural composition. House in Herculaneum

68. Puertas de armario de madera, Herculano

68. Wooden closet doors. Herculaneum

69. Modelo de lecho en las tumbas etruscas. Siglo III a. de J.C. Cerveteri

69. Model of burial bed in Etruscan tombs. 3rd century B.C. Cerveteri

70. Triclinio en un relieve arcaico, con patas torneadas y brazos curvos

70. Triclinium in an ancient relief; with turned legs and carved arms

71. Lecho con patas torneadas y brazos curvos. Frente de un sarcófago. Siglo III a. de J.C.

71. Bed with turned legs and curved arms. Front of a sarcophagus. III century B.C.

72. Triclinio. Dibujo de un relieve

72. Triclinium. Drawing of a relief

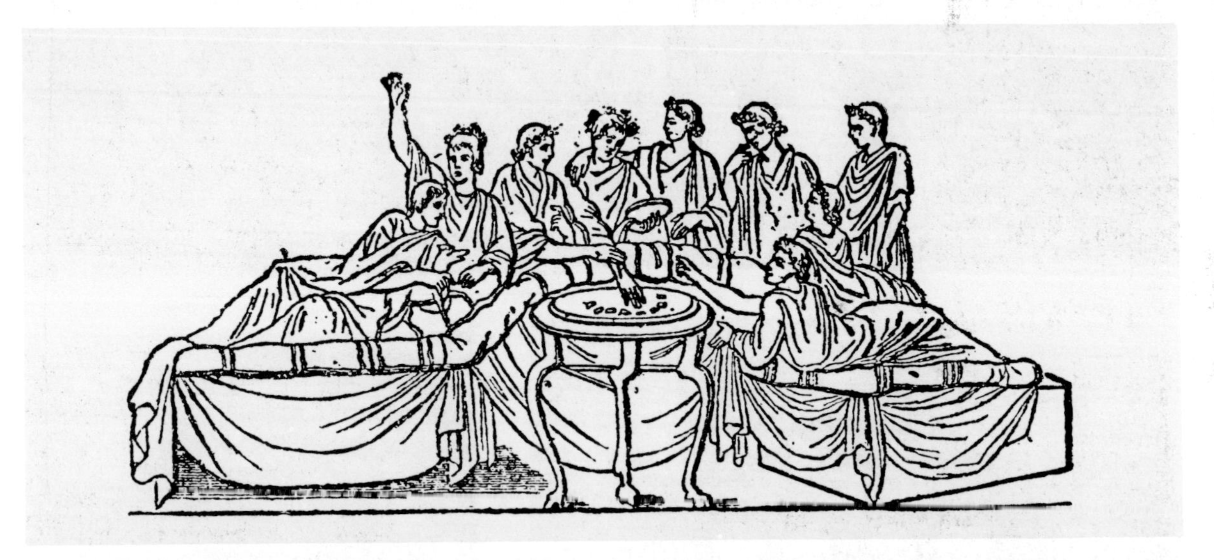

73. Triclinio de la casa del Moralista, Pompeya

73. Triclinium in the house of the Moralist. Pompeii

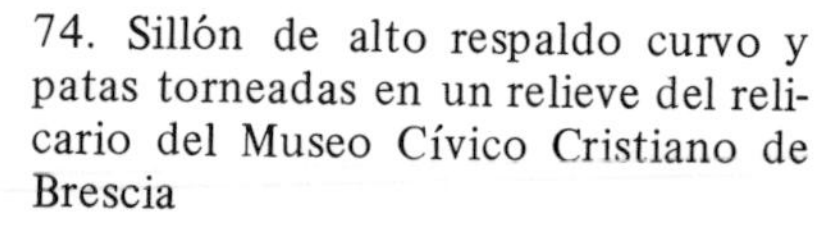

74. Sillón de alto respaldo curvo y patas torneadas en un relieve del relicario del Museo Cívico Cristiano de Brescia

74. Armchair with high back and turned legs in a relief of the reliquary of the Christian Civic Museum of Brescia

75. Cátedra de Maximiano. Detalle de relieves en los que se ve representada una cama de patas torneadas y dosel. Siglo VI. Rávena

75. Cathedra of Maximian. Detail of reliefs in which a bed with turned legs and canopy are represented. VI century. Ravenna

76. Silla de tijera y lecho en un relieve del relicario del Museo Cívico Cristiano de Brescia

76. X-shaped chair and bed in a relief of the reliquary of the Christian Civic Museum of Brescia

77. Cátedra o silla de San Pedro. Siglo IV. Basílica de San Pedro

77. Cathedra or chair of St Peter. IV century. Basilica of St Peter, Rome

78. Sillón de respaldo curvo representado en el cáliz de Antioquía. Siglo IV. Metropolitan Museum, Nueva York

78. Armchair with curved back represented on the Chalice of Antioquia. IV century. Metropolitan Museum of Art, New York

79. Cátedra de Maximiano, en madera chapeada de marfil. Siglo VI. Museo de la catedral, Rávena

79. Cathedra of Maximian in ivory covered wood. Ravenna. VI century. Cathedral Museum, Ravenna

80. Mesa de tres patas curvas, representada en un fresco de las catacumbas de san Calixto, Roma

80. Table with three curved legs in a fresco of the Catacombs of St Calixto, Rome

81. "La Magdalena", pintura copta. Museo copto del Cairo. Epoca indeterminada

81. "The Magdalene", Coptic painting. Coptic Museum of Cairo. From an unknown period

82. Silla de tijera de hierro cincelado y damasquinado con oro en estilo bizantino. Siglo XII. Victoria and Albert Museum, Londres

82. X-shaped chair in chased iron and damåskeened with gold in the Byzantine style. XII century. Victoria and Albert Museum, London

83. Interpretación de triclinio bizantino. Siglo X al XIII. Esmalte de la Pala d'Oro. San Marcos de Venecia

83. Example of Byzantine triclinium. 10th-13th century. Gold leaf enamel. Saint Mark of Venice

84. Sillón representado en un fresco de las catacumbas de santa Priscila, Roma

84. Armchair depicted in a fresco of the Catacombs of St Priscila, Rome. III century

85. Sillón de alto respaldo, con brazos en forma de pez y patas de tijera. Marfil de la cátedra de San Marcos. Grado. Siglo V

85. Armchair with high back and arms of fish form and X legs. Ivory of the catedra of St. Mark. Grado. V century

86. Armario representado en un mosaico del mausoleo de Gala Placidia, Rávena. Siglo VI

86. Cupboard represented in a mosaic of the Mausoleum of Gala Placidia. Ravenna. VI century

87. Cama vestida, representada en un mosaico de la iglesia de Daphni, que figura la natividad de la Virgen. Siglo XI. Atenas

87. Bed with hangings represented in a mosaic of the Church of Daphni representing the Birth of the Virgin. XI century. Athens

88. Trono de oro y piedras incrustadas en un esmalte bizantino. Colección Sachs, Nueva York

88. Throne with gold and stone inlay on a Byzantine enamel. Sachs Collection. New York

ROMANICO

ROMANESQUE

89. Cassone de Terracina. Siglo XI. Museo del palacio de Venecia. Roma

89. Cassone de Terracina. XI century. Museum of the Palace of Venice. Rome

90. Atril y silla de tijera de un evangeliario de la escuela de Reims. Siglo IX. Biblioteca Morgan, Nueva York

90. Lectern and X chair in an evangelistary of the Rheims School. XI century. Morgan Library, New York

91. Sillón de plata repujada, con piedras incrustadas. Epoca carolingia. Siglo VIII. Sainte-Foy de Conques, Auvernia, Francia

91. Armchair in repoussé silverwork with inlaid stones. Carolingian period. VIII century. Sainte-Foy de Conques, Auvergne, France

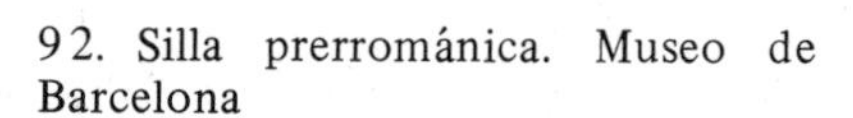

92. Silla prerrománica. Museo de Barcelona

92. Pre-romanesque chair. Museum of Barcelona

93. Sitial y atril (analoquium) representados en el Códice Emilianense. Siglo X. Biblioteca del Escorial

93. Presiding chair and lectern (analoquium) represented in the Emilianensis Codex. X century. Biblioteca del Escorial

94. En esta miniatura el armario, representado en la Cantiga LVI, tiene unas armaduras muy anchas y una ornamentación como los armarios de Santa Ursula de Toledo. Biblioteca del Escorial

94. In this miniature, ilustrating Cantiga LVI, the cupboard has a thick framework and decoration like that found in the cupboards of Saint Ursula in Toledo

95. Cama representada en un relieve de la catedral de Chartres. Siglo XII. Barandilla interrumpida en el centro para hacer más cómodo el acceso

95. Bed represented in a relief of Chatres Cathedral. XII century. (Balustrade cut in the centre to allow easier access)

96. Arcón con refuerzos de hierro. Al fondo, silla de asiento triangular con elementos torneados de origen nórdico. Museo de Artes Decorativas. París

96. Chest with iron strengtheners. In the background, a chair with triangular seat and turned elements of Nordic origin. Museum of Decorative Arts. Paris

97. Trono del rey Dagoberto, de bronce. Siglo VIII. El respaldo fue restaurado en el siglo XIII. Biblioteca nacional. París

97. Bronze throne of King Dagobert. VIII century. The back was restored in the XIII century. National Library. Paris

98. Sillón representado en una escultura, con elementos torneados muy simples

98. Armchair represented in a sculpture with very simple turned elements

99. Trono de la Virgen de Orcival, de madera, recubierto de láminas de plata cincelada. Auvernia. Francia

99. Throne of the Virgin of Orcival, in wood covered with chased silver laminates. Auvergne. France

100. Armario con refuerzos de hierro. Siglos XII-XIII. Catedral de Noyon. Francia

100. Cupboard with iron strengtheners. XII-XIII century. Noyon Cathedral. France

101. Puertas de armario románico, con refuerzos de hierro forjado. Siglo XII. Obazine (Corrèze). Francia

101. Doors of a romanesque cupboard with forged iron strengtheners. XII century. Obazine (Corrèze). France

102. Armario románico de Obazine (fig. 101). Tipo arquitectónico con refuerzos de hierro. Dibujo según Viollet le Duc

102. Romanesque cupboard of Obazine (fig. 101). Architectural type with iron stengtheners. Drawing after Viollet le Duc

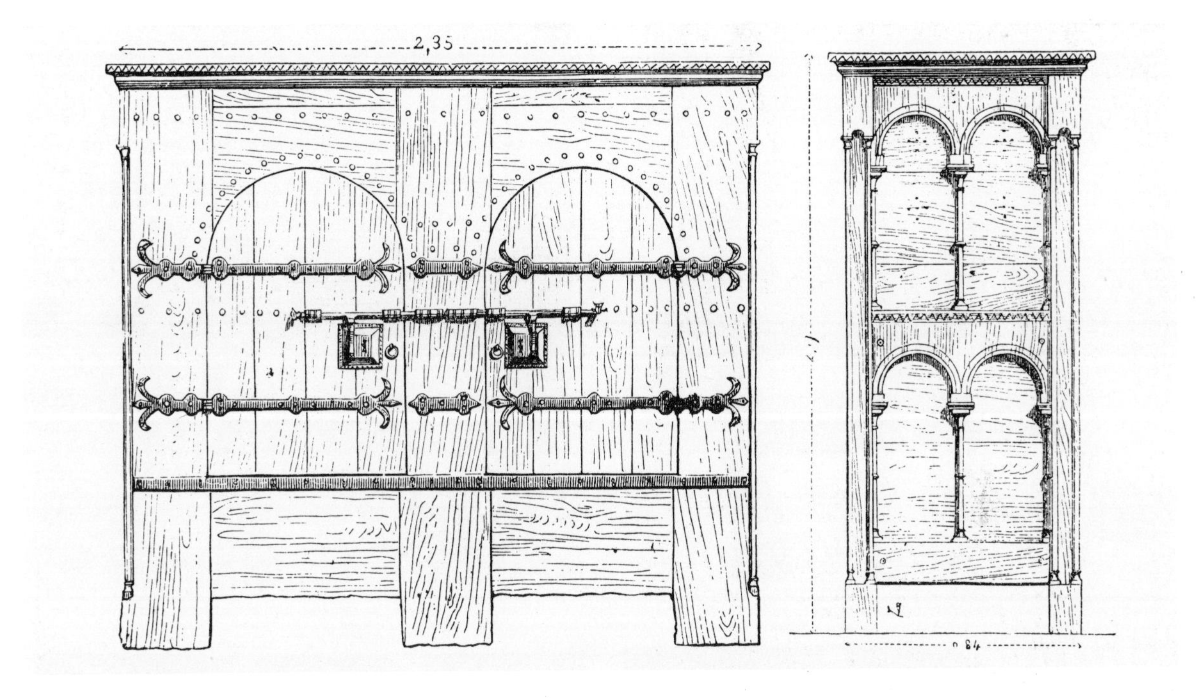

103. Dibujo, por Viollet le Duc, de una mesa representada en el festín del rey Baltasar. Biblia de la Biblioteca Imperial

103. Drawing by Viollet le Duc, depicting a table at the banquet of King Balthazar. Bible of the Imperial Library

104. Interpretación de un interior románico por Viollet le Duc. Siglo XIX

104. Interpretation of a Romanesque interior by Viollet le Duc. XIX century

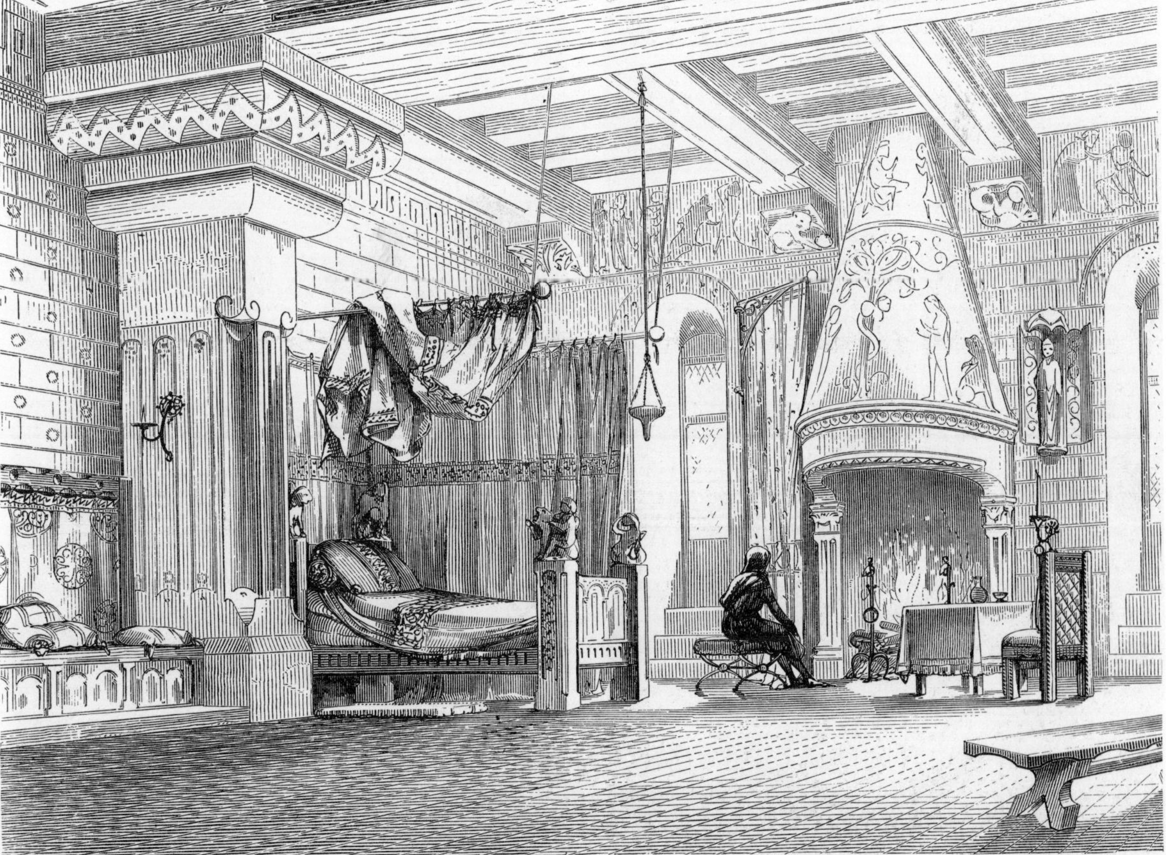

105. Faldistorio de la catedral de Roda, con patas cruzadas en forma de tijera, talladas en madera de boj. Siglo XI. Museo de la catedral de Roda de Isabena (Huesca)

105. Faldstool of Roda Cathedral, with X-shaped legs in boxwood. XI century. Museum of the Cathedral of Roda de Isabena, (Huesca, Spain)

106. Detalle del banco de la figura 107

106. Detail of the bench of the figure 107

107. Banco de presbiterio, de la iglesia de Tahull (Lérida), en madera de pino, con detalles mozárabes, tallas planas, celosías, arcos de herradura. Museo de Montjuich, Barcelona

107. Presbytery bench of the Church of Tahull (Pyrenees), in pine with Mozarabic details, chip carving, lattice-work, arcading. Montjuich Museum, Barcelona

108. Silla episcopal de madera policromada. Siglo XIII. Catedral de Roda de Isabena (Huesca)

108. Episcopal chair in polychrome wood. XII century. Cathedral of Roda de Isabena (Huesca, Spain)

109. Arqueta románica cubierta de tejadillo, policromada. Museo Episcopal, Astorga

109. Romanesque chest covered with roof. Polychromed. Episcopal Museum, Astorga

110. Cofre del Cid, de madera con refuerzos de hierro. Museo de la catedral, Burgos

110. Coffer of the Cid in wood with iron strengtheners. Museum of the Cathedral, Burgos

SIMON
ANDREAS
PETRVS
IACOBVS
IOANNES
PHILIPVS
THOMAS
MARCVS

111. Escena de la Sagrada Cena, relieve que nos muestra una mesa cubierta. Arca de San Felices. Siglo XI. San Millán de la Cogolla, Logroño

111. Scene from the Last Supper. Relief showing a prepared table. Chest of St Felices. XI century. San Millán de la Cogolla (Logroño).

112. Representación en la Cantiga CXXVI de una cama con gruesos montantes torneados en los que se ven las espigas y las cañas. Biblioteca del Escorial

112. In Cantiga CXXVI, picture of a bed with thick, turned posts in which the tenons and pins can be seen. El Escorial Library

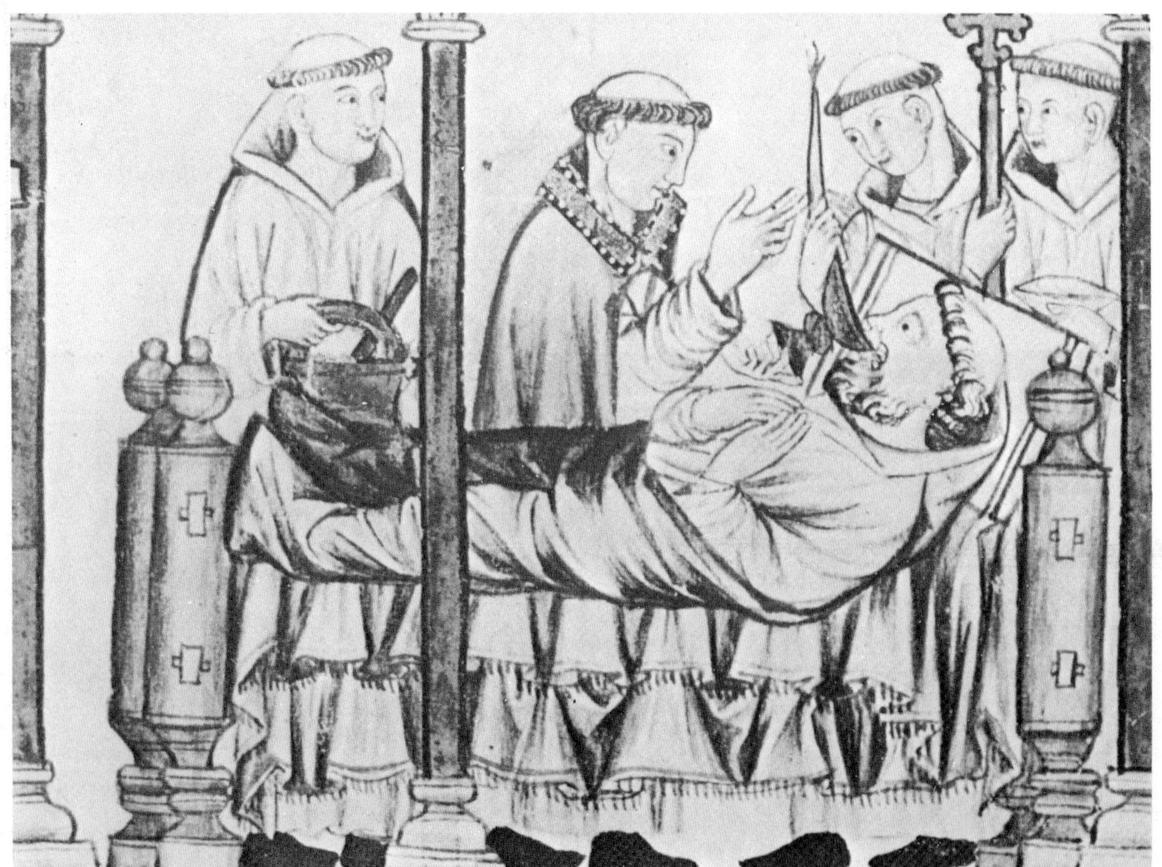

113. Sillón y armario de la Cantiga II; ornamentación con arquerías lobuladas de ascendencia árabe, así como las taraceas del armario. Biblioteca del Escorial

113. Armchair and cupboard from Cantiga II decorated with foliated arcade of Arabian derivation. The same is true for the inlaid work on the cupboard. El Escorial Library

114. Trono románico de San Nicolás de Bari. Obra de piedra, siglo XI (1098)

114. Romanesque throne of San Nicolas de Bari. Stonework of the XI century (1098)

115. Silla episcopal de Canosa. Siglo XI. Italia

115. Episcopal chair of Canosa. XI century. Italy

116. Banco de Alpirsbach. Largo 6.70 m. Siglo XIII

116. Bench of Alpirsbach. Length 6.7 m. XIII century

117. Banco de Alpirsbach. Costado. Siglo XIII. Schlossmuseum, Stuttgart

117. Bench of Alpirsbach. Side view. XIII century. Schlossmuseum, Stuttgart

118. Sillón con torneados característicos. Museo de Königsberg

118. Armchair with characteristic turnings. Könisberg Museum

119. Trono románico del palacio real de Goslar. Siglos XII-XIII

119. Romanesque throne of the Royal Palace of Goslar. XII-XIII century

120. Silla de tijera, de madera, con incrustaciones de marfil. Siglo XIII. Salzburgo

120. Wooden X-shaped chair with ivory incrustations. XIII century. Salsburg

121. Sillón con elementos torneados de estructura románica

121. Armchair with turned elements of Romanesque structure

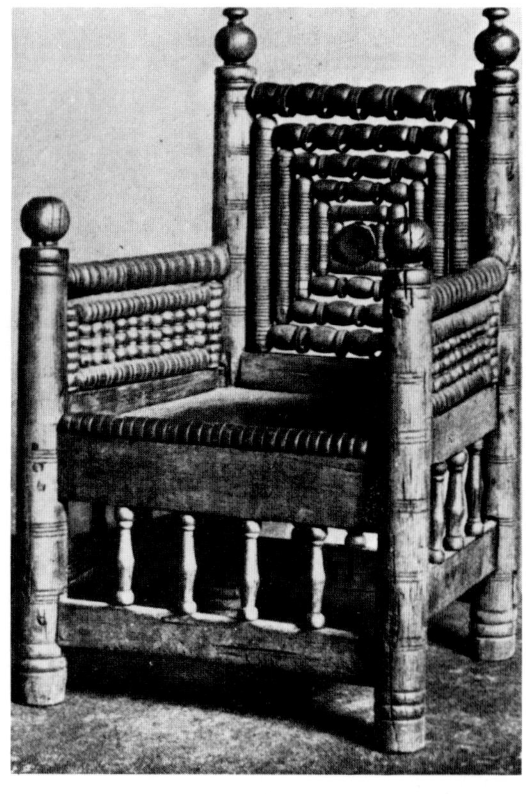

122. Arca de composición arquitectónica. Siglo XII. Museo de santa Valeria de Sión, Suiza (véase fig. 127)

122. Chest of architectural composition. XII century. Museum of St Valeria of Sion, Switzerland (see fig. 127)

127. Arca de composición arquitectónica. Siglo XII. Museo de Santa Valeria de Sión, Suiza (véase fig. 122)

127. Chest of architectural composition. XII century. Museum of St Valeria of Sion, Switzerland (see fig. 122)

128. Arca de roble con tallas planas. Románico tardío. Siglo XIV

128. Chest with chip carving. Late Romanesque. XIV century

129. Silla de Valdres (Noruega), de 1685, que repite el tipo de sillas escandinavas del medioevo

129. The Valdres Chair (Norway), 1685, following the pattern of medieval Scandinavian chairs

130. Sillón escandinavo con tallas planas características

130. Scandinavian armchair with characteristic flat carving

131. Silla de líneas románicas y bizantinas

131. Chair of Romanesque and Byzantine lines

132. Banco de roble. Siglo XIII

132. Oak bench. XIII century

133. Armario de roble con refuerzos de hierro. Siglo XIII. Catedral de Chester, Inglaterra

133. Oak cupboard with iron strengthening. XIII century. Chester Cathedral, England

134. Arqueta de Hälsingland, con tallas de lazo rúnico de los vikingos, de época indeterminada pero con los caracteres del medioevo. Museo Nordiska. Estocolmo

134. Small chest from Hälsingland, with carved knots of Viking runes. Date unknown, but the characters are medieval. Nordiska Museum. Stockholm

135. Arcón de roble con refuerzos de hierro. Románico. Iglesia de Milton. Bryant, Inglaterra

135. Oak chest with iron strengthening. Romanesque. Milton Church, Bryant, England

GOTICO

GOTHIC

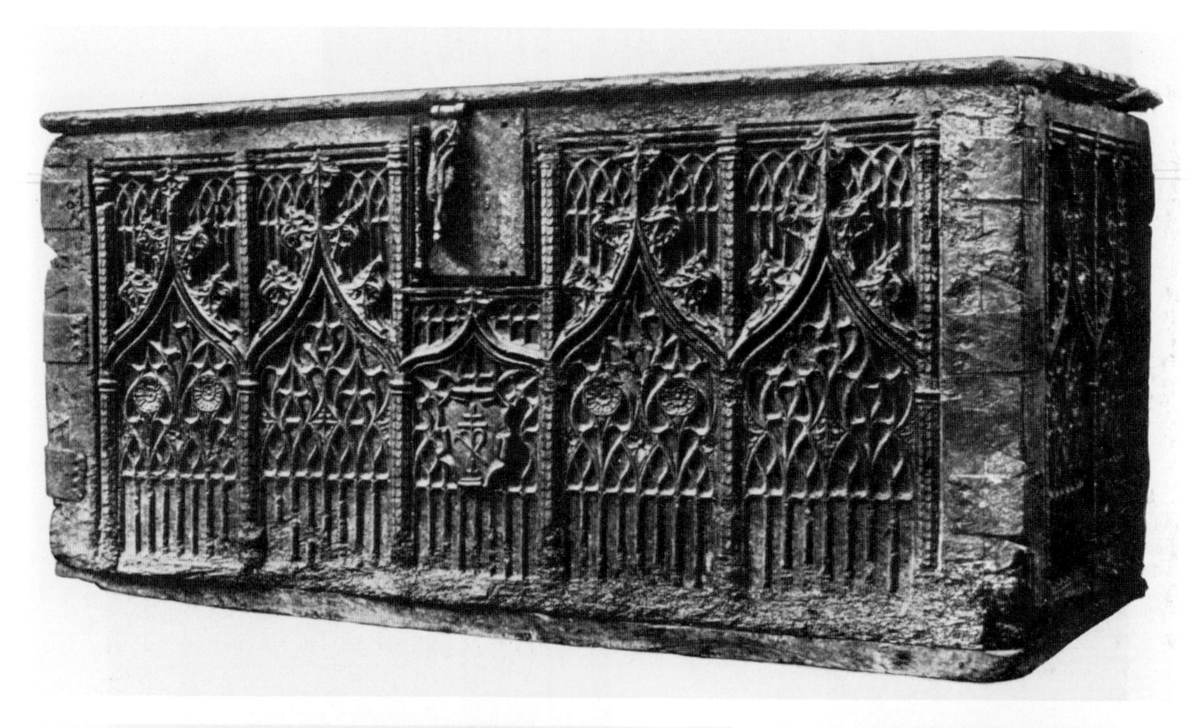

141. Arcón gótico francés de finales del siglo XV

141. French Gothic chest, late XV century

142. Credencia de fines del siglo XV. Museo de Artes Decorativas, París

142. Credence, late XV century. Museum of Decorative Arts, Paris

143. Bufete de roble con la parte superior tallada. Siglo XV. Altura 115 cm, frente 85 cm

143. Oak buffet with carving on the upper part. XV century. Height 155 cm, front 85 cm

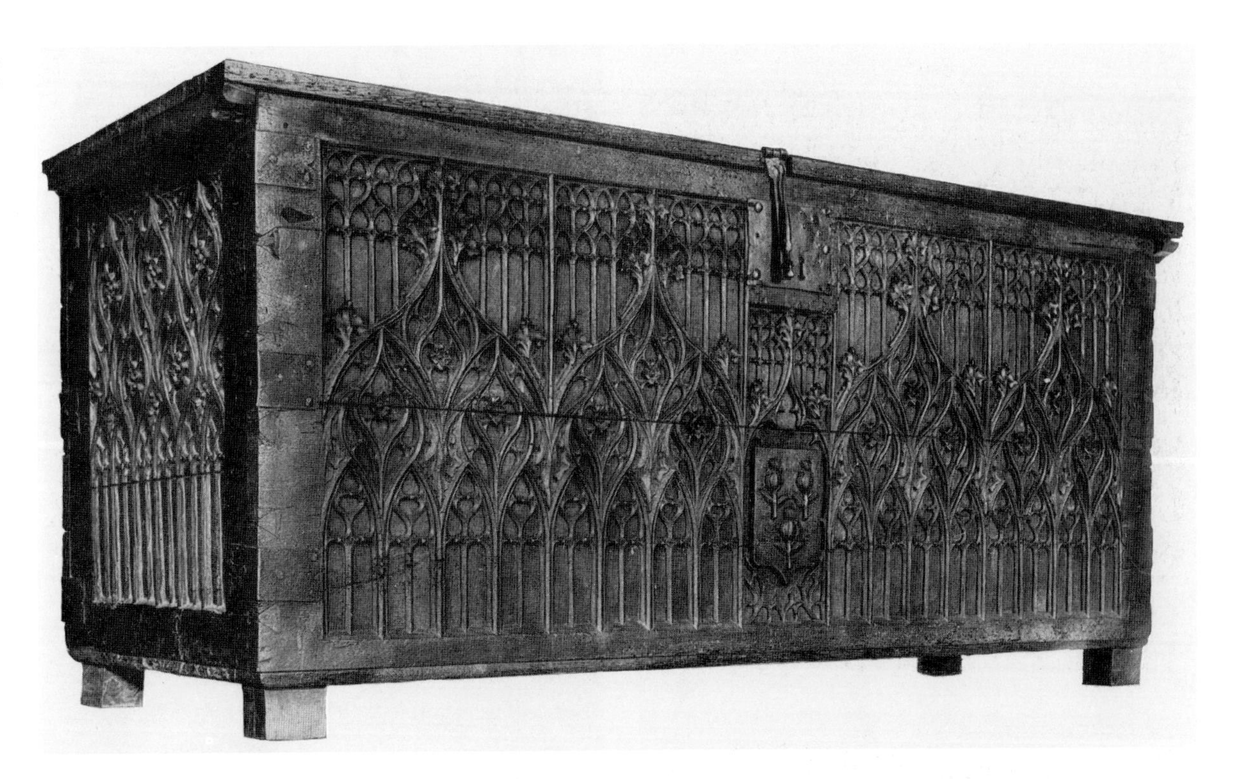

144. Arcón de nogal con decoración gótica. Siglo XV. Frente 175 cm, altura 77 cm, Francia

144. Walnut chest with Gothic decoration. XV century. Front 175, height 77, France

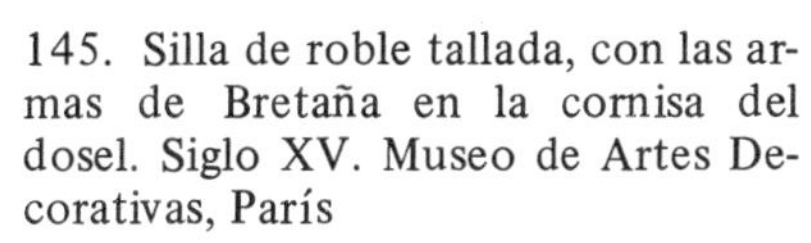

145. Silla de roble tallada, con las armas de Bretaña en la cornisa del dosel. Siglo XV. Museo de Artes Decorativas, París

145. Carved oak chair with the arms of Brittany on the cornice of the canopy. XV century. Museum of Decorative Arts, Paris

146. Arca con decoración de escena de guerra, tallada en su frente. Siglo XV. Museo de Cluny, París

146. Chest with battle scene decoration on the front. XV century. Museum of Cluny

147. Arcón gótico típicamente francés, de finales del siglo XV

147. Gothic chest typically French of the late XV century

148. Cama con las armas de Rigaud d'Auselhe, de finales de siglo XV. Museo de Artes Decorativas, París

148. Bed with the arms of Rigaud d'Auselhe, end XV century. Museum of Decorative Arts, Paris

149. Armario con cubierta en forma de tejadillo y pinturas góticas en sus puertas perteneciente a la actedral de Noyon, Francia

149. Cupboard with roof form and Gothic paintings on its doors. Property of Noyon Cathedral. France

150. Puertas de armario con tallas de pergamino en sus tableros. Sala del Tesoro de la catedral de Noyon, Francia

150. Cupboard doors with parchment carving on its panels. Treasure Room of Noyon Cathedral, France

151. 152. Interpretación de interiores de la época. Dibujos de Viollet le Duc

151. 152. Interpretation of interiors of the period. Drawing by Viollet le Duc

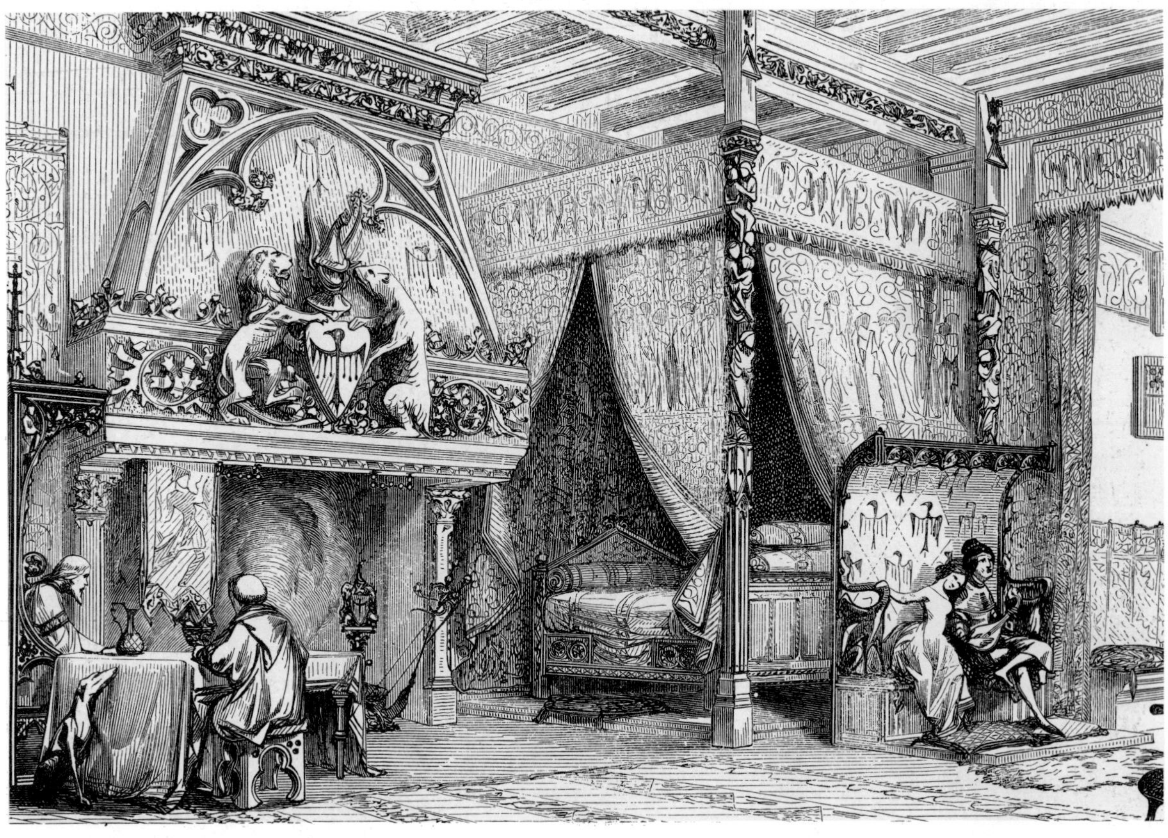

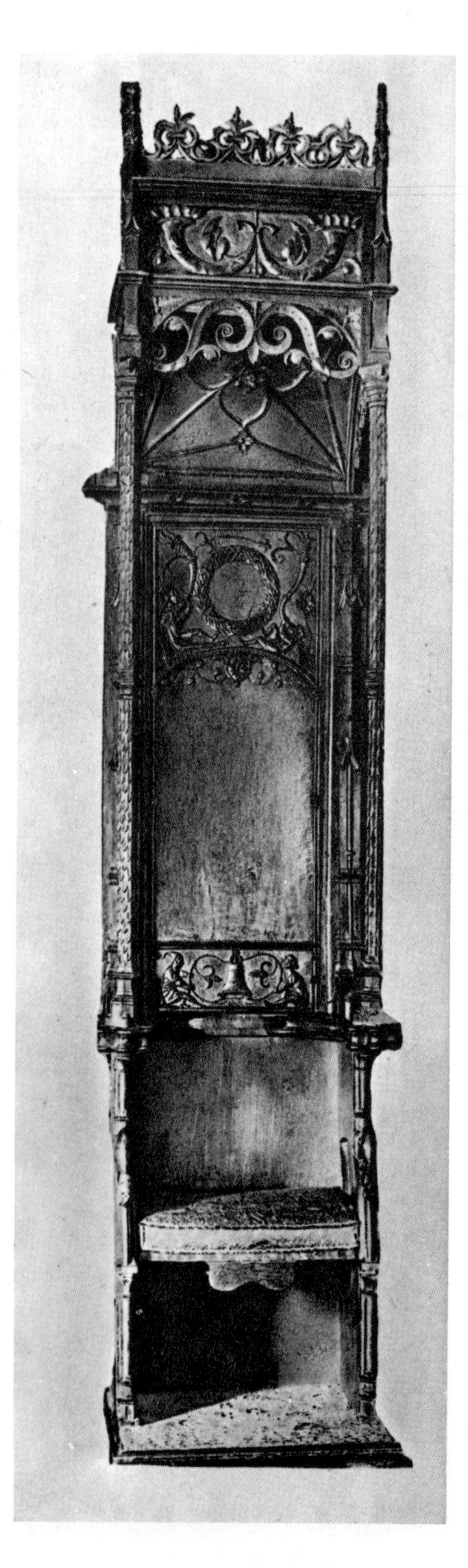

153. Sitial de coro del siglo XVI en el que se alternan los elementos góticos con los renacentistas

153. Presiding choir chair, XVI century, in which Gothic elements alternate with the Renaissance

154. Sitial de coro de madera de nogal. La crestería gótica alterna con la incipiente decoración renacentista. Principios del siglo XVI

154. Presiding choir chair in walnut. The Gothic cresting alternates with incipient Renaissance decoration. Early XVI century

155. Sitial de madera policromada decorado con tallas góticas. Siglo XV. Se conserva en el claustro de la catedral vieja de Salamanca, capilla de Santa Catalina

155. Presiding chair in polychrome wood with Gothic carving. XV century. It is conserved in the cloister of the old cathedral of Salamanca, chapel of St Catalina

156. Silla de plata cincelada llamada del rey Don Martín. Primera mitad del siglo XV. Catedral de Barcelona

156. Chased silver chair known as that of King Don Martin. First half XV century. Barcelona Cathedral

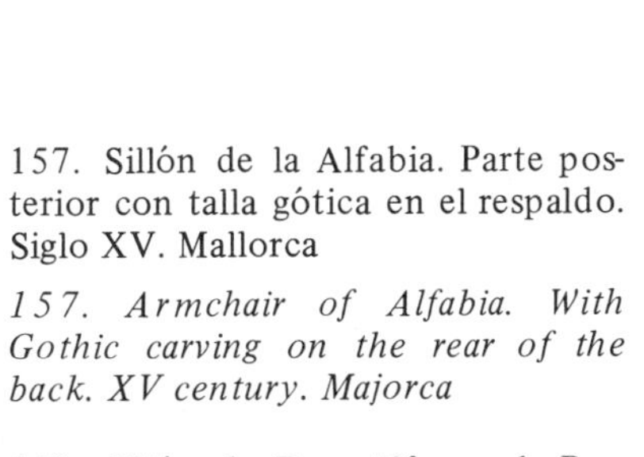

157. Sillón de la Alfabia. Parte posterior con talla gótica en el respaldo. Siglo XV. Mallorca

157. Armchair of Alfabia. With Gothic carving on the rear of the back. XV century. Majorca

158. Sillón de Don Alfonso de Portugal con trabajo de talla gótica. Siglo XV. Museu das Janelas Verdes, Lisboa

158. Armchair of Don Alfonso of Portugal with Gothic carving. XV century. Museu das Janelas Verdes, Lisbon

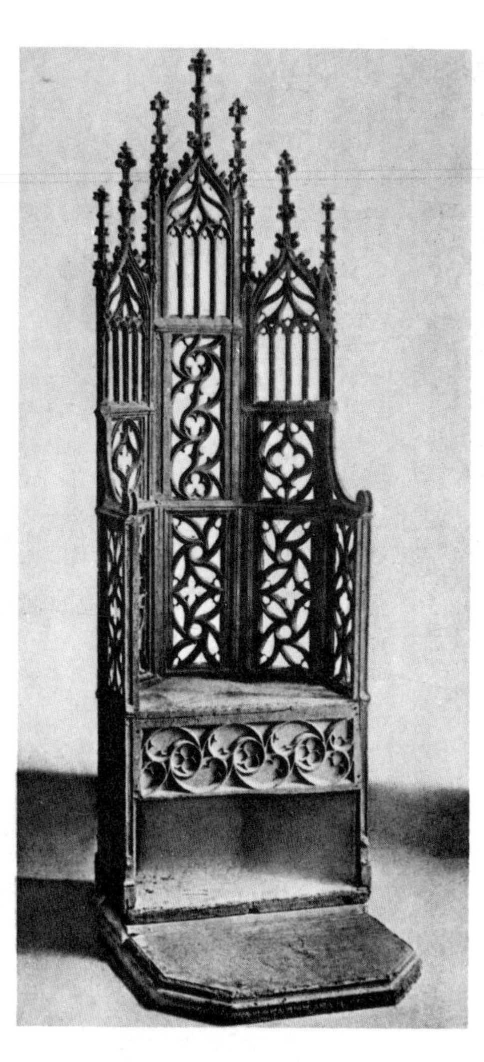

159. Sillón prioral de madera de roble con tracerías góticas. Procede del convento de Santiago de Uclés. Siglo XV. Museo Arqueológico Nacional, Madrid

159. Prior's armchair in oak with Gothic tracery. From the convent of Santiago de Uclés. XV century. Archeological Museum, Madrid

160. Sillón prioral de la cartuja de Valldemosa (hoy en la celda de Chopin). El respaldo es de tracería gótica tallada. Mallorca

160. Prior's armchair of the Carthusian monastery of Valldemosa (now in Chopin's cell). The back with carved Gothic tracery

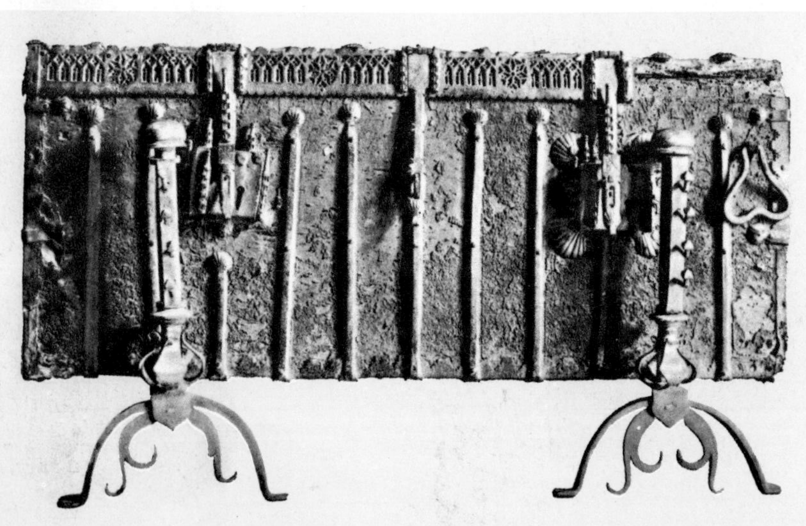

161. Arcón encorado, guarnecido con hierros forjados y calados de estilo gótico. Siglo XV. Propiedad de D. Pedro Ruiz. Madrid

161. Chest covered with leather, garnished with forged iron pieces and fretwork in the Gothic style. XV century. Property of Pedro Ruiz. Madrid

162. Sillón de "cajón", con tableros decorados con tracerías talladas. Se conoce con el nombre de "sillón de la familia Enríquez". Siglos XIV-XV. Museo Valencia de Don Juan, Madrid

162. Boxchair with panels decorated with carved tracery. It is known under the name of the armchair of the Enríquez family. XIV-XV centuries. Valencia de Don Juan Museum. Madrid

163. Banco gótico tallado en madera de pino y de nogal. Procede de la catedral de Cuenca. Siglo XV. Museo Lázaro Galdeano

163. Gothic bench carved in pine and walnut. From Cuenca Cathedral. Lázaro Galdeano Museum. Madrid

164. Arcón de estilo "perpendicular", con decoración de tracerías flamígeras, del siglo XV. Mallorca

164. Chest in the "perpendicular" style with decoration of flammiferous tracery. XV century. Majorca

165. Banco-arcón con talla gótica de pergamino en todos sus tableros

165. Box bench with Gothic parchment carving on all its panels

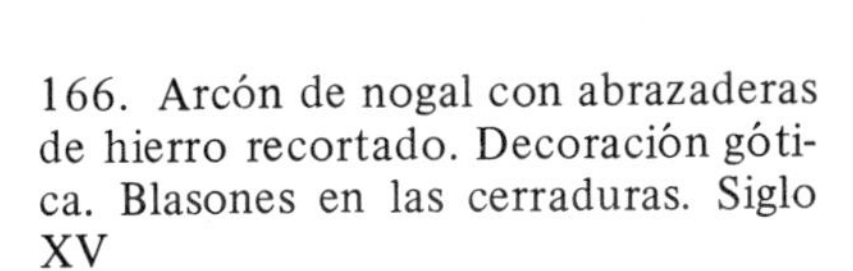

166. Arcón de nogal con abrazaderas de hierro recortado. Decoración gótica. Blasones en las cerraduras. Siglo XV

166. Walnut chest with trimmed iron clasps. Gothic ornamentation. Armorial bearings on the locks. XV century

167. Armario bajo con tallas góticas, muy restaurado. Museo Lázaro Galdeano

167. Low cupboard with Gothic carving extensively restored. Lázaro Galdeano Museum

168. Arcón tallado en madera con aplicaciones de cuero y hierro. Siglo XIV. Museo de Vich (Barcelona)

168. Carved wooden chest with leather and iron appliqués. XIV century. Museum of Vich (Barcelona)

169. Armario bajo o credencia con tallas. Siglo XV. Museo Lázaro Galdeano, Madrid

169. Low cupboard or credence with carving. XV century. Lázaro Galdeano Museum, Madrid

170. Arcón de estilo gótico tardío con celosías caladas. Siglos XV-XVI. Museo de Artes Decorativas, Madrid

170. Chest in the late Gothic style with pierced lattice-work. XV-XVI centuries. Museum of Decorative Arts, Madrid

171. Arcón con tallas góticas y guarnición de hierro. Las tracerías semejan las más puras francesas. Siglo XV

171. Chest with Gothic carving and iron ornamentation. The tracery is similar to the purest French style. XV century

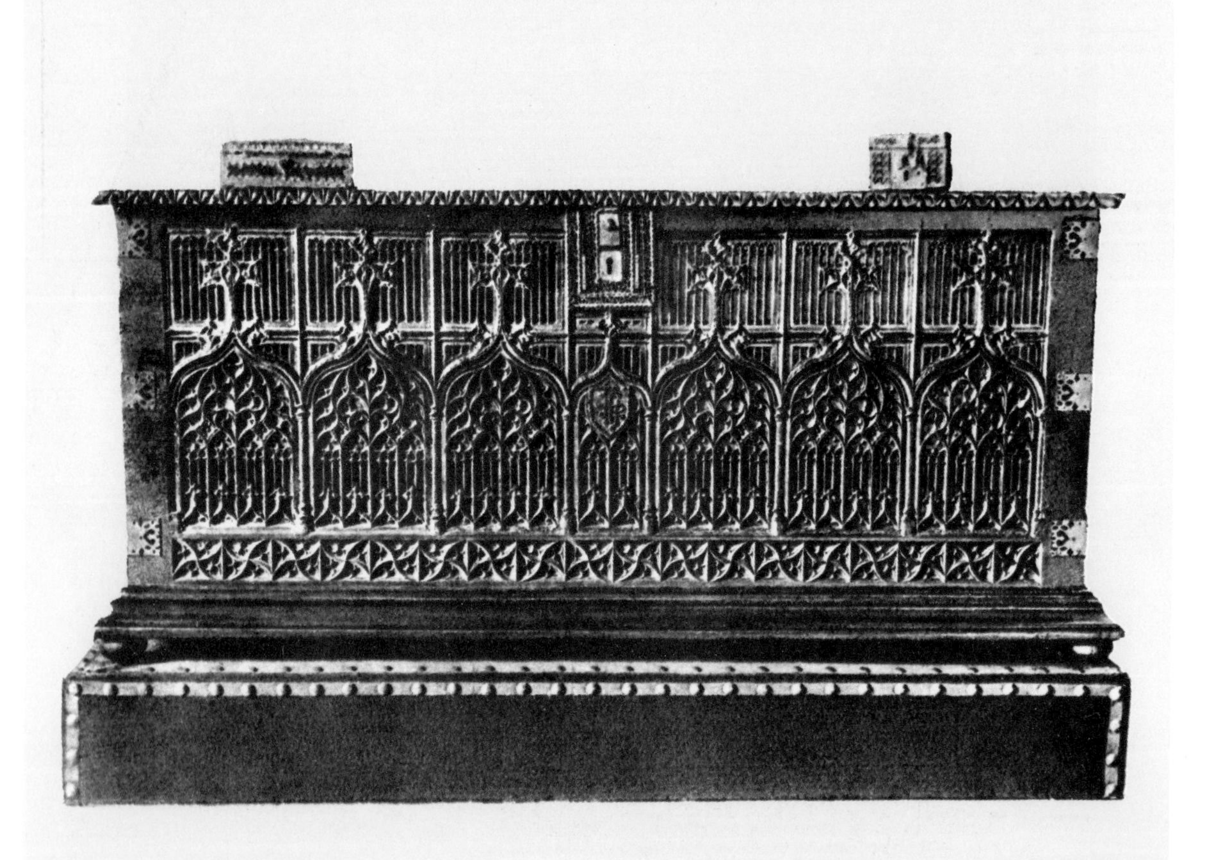

172. Arcón con tracerías góticas y guarniciones y cerraduras de hierro. Monograma de Jesús en el escudo central. Su decoración es de época muy avanzada dentro del estilo gótico

172. Chest with Gothic tracery, iron garnishing and locks. Monogram of Jesus on the central shield. The decoration is of a very advanced period within the Gothic style

173. Arqueta gótica. Vich (Barcelona)

173. Gothic chest. Vich (Barcelona)

174. Arca con tapa de tejadillo, forrada de terciopelo, guarnecida con hierros y tracerías góticas. Finales del siglo XV

174. Chest with roof top. Lined with velvet, ornamented with iron and Gothic tracery. End XV century

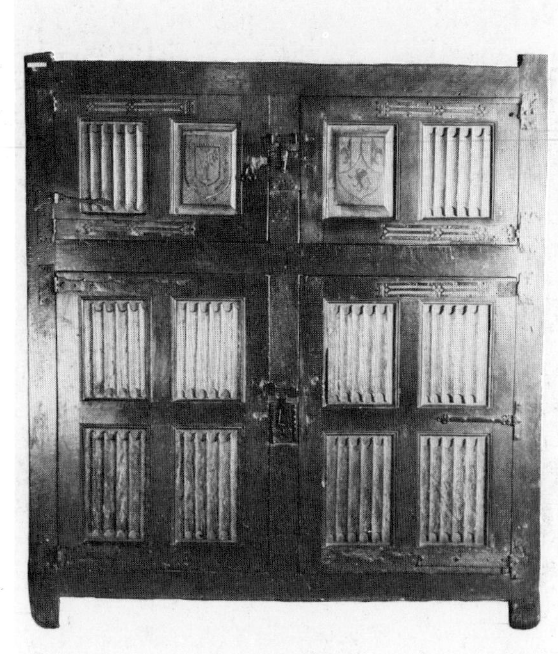

175. Armario gótico con tallas planas geométricas. Siglo XIII. Cornellá de Conflent (Pirineos Orientales)

175. Gothic cupboard with geometrical chip carving. XIII century. Cornellá de Conflent (Eastern Pyrenees)

176. Armario gótico con decoración de pergaminos. Finales del siglo XV

176. Gothic cupboard with linenfold decoration. End XV century

177. Puerta de armario gótico. Siglo XV. Colección particular

177. Gothic cupboard door. XV century. Private Collection

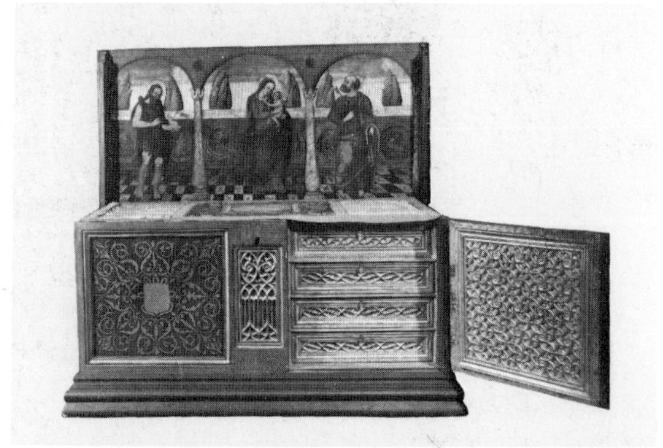

178. 179. Arcones de transición del gótico al Renacimiento: composición típica del frente, con dos recuadros a los lados y tracería gótica en el centro. Al levantar la tapa se ven pinturas renacentistas de influencia italiana. Estos arcones, llamados "caixes de nuvia", llevan un cajoncito interior donde la novia lleva la dote y las joyas. Son muebles característicos de la región catalana. Son muebles difíciles de clasificar por ser de principios del siglo XVI, con elementos y estructura aún gótica. Colección Muntadas (Museos de Barcelona)

178. 179. Chest from the period of transition from Gothic to Renaissance. The front is of typical composition with two panels and Gothic tracery in the middle. Inside the lid there are Renaissance paintings of Italian influence. These chests, called "caixes de nuvia" (bride's box), have a small drawer inside where the girl kept her dowry and jewelry. They are typical of Catalan region. They are difficult to classify because they date from the beginning of the 16th century but still retain Gothic elements and structure. Muntadas Collection (Museums of Barcelona)

180. Armario gótico de estilo transición, con decoración de pergaminos. Siglo XVI. Colección particular

180. Gothic cupboard, transition style, with linenfold. XVI century. Private Collection

181. Miniatura del libro coral con representación de cama, banco, sillón y arquilla góticos. Siglos XV-XVI. Monasterio de Guadalupe, Cáceres

181. Miniature of choral book depicting a Gothic bed, bench, armchair, and small chest. XV-XVI centuries. Monastery of Guadalupe, Cáceres

182. Sillería de coro del convento de Santa Clara de Moguer, Huelva

182. Choir stalls of the Convent of Santa Clara de Moguer, Huelva

183. Sillería gótico-mudéjar de Santa Clara de Astudillo. Museo Arqueológico Nacional, Madrid

183. Gothic-Mudejar stalls of Santa Clara de Astudillo. Archaeological Museum, Madrid

184. Sillería de Gradefes. La línea es románica pero la decoración es mudéjar con carácter gótico. Siglo XIII. Museo Arqueológico Nacional, Madrid

184. Stalls of Gradefes. The line is Romanesque but the decoration is Mudejar with Gothic features. XIII century. Archaeological Museum, Madrid

185. Silla de cadera, de estructura gótica y decoración mudéjar, con taracea. Colección particular

185. X-shaped chair of Gothic structure and Mudejar decoration with inlay. Private Collection

186. Armario procedente de Perpiñán, hoy en el museo de la Ciudadela, Barcelona. Puertas con decoración mudéjar

186. Cupboard from Perpignan, now in the Museo de la Ciudadela, Barcelona. Doors with Mudejar decoration

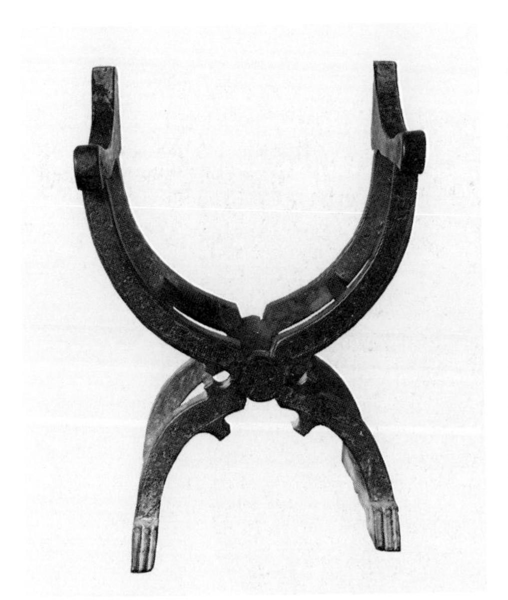

187. Arquilla con tapa superior elevable y delantera abatible; trabajo de taraceas granadinas del siglo XV. Procede de Zaragoza. Museo Valencia de Don Juan. Madrid

187. Small box with lifting cover and collapsable front, 15th century, Granada inlays. From Saragosa. Valencia de Don Juan Museum. Madrid

188. Arqueta mudéjar con tallas geométricas a bisel. Se advierten bien los lazos de la ensambladura. Museo de Artes Decorativas, Madrid

188. Mudejar chest with geometrical bevel carving: the jointing is well visible. Museum of Decorative Arts. Madrid

189. Arcón gótico de influencia italiana, con los frentes y la parte oculta de la tapa pintados. Siglo XV-XVI. Cataluña

189. Large Gothic chest, of Italian influence, with the front and hidden part of the cover painted. 15th-16th century. Catalonia

190. Armario mudéjar de la catedral de León. Pieza de extraordinario valor por su trabajo y dimensiones. Frente 4 m. Siglo XIII

190. Mudejar cupboard of Leon Cathedral. A piece of extraordinary value for its work and dimensions. Front 4 m. XIII century

191. Costado izquierdo del armario de la catedral de León. Siglo XIII. En él se advierte la profusión de la talla mudéjar

191. Left side of the cupboard of Leon Cathedral, showing the profusion of Mudejar Carving. XIII century

192. Costado derecho del armario mudéjar de la catedral de León. Siglo XIII

192. Right side of the Mudejar cupboard of Leon Cathedral. XIII century

193. Frente de bargueño mudéjar abierto. Propiedad particular

193. Open front of Mudejar inlaid, gilt secretary. Privately owned

194. Costado del bargueño anterior con una taracea muy menuda que lo cubre totalmente

194. Side of the same secretary completely covered with minute inlays

195. Frente del armario gótico-mudéjar de la figura 196

195. Front of Gothic-Mudejar cabinet seen in figure 196

196. Armario gótico-mudéjar con seis puertas. La decoración exterior de tracerías y el interior policromado. Procede del convento de Santa Ursula de Toledo. Museo Arqueológico Nacional, Madrid

196. Gothic-Mudejar cupboard with six doors: decorated with tracery on the outside and polychrome inside. From the convent of Santa Ursula, Toledo. Archaeological Museum, Madrid

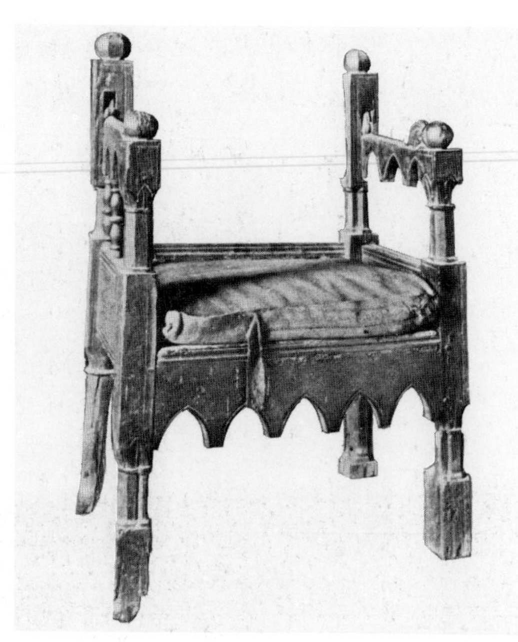

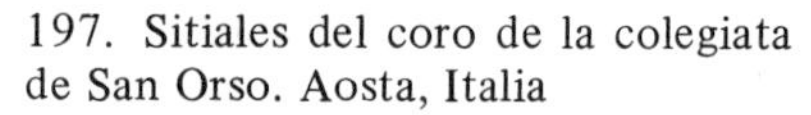

197. Sitiales del coro de la colegiata de San Orso. Aosta, Italia

197. Ceremonial chair of the choir of the colegiata of San Orso. Aosta, Italy

198. Sitial de la catedral de Anagni, Italia

198. Ceremonial chair of Anagni Cathedral, Italy

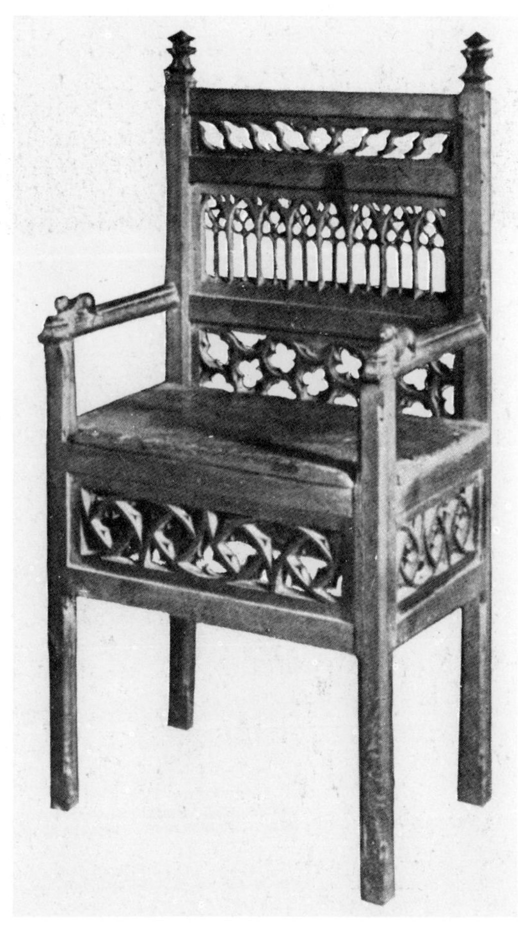

199. Mesa representada en una pintura de la escuela de Umbría. Siglo XIV. Monasterio de Subiaco, Roma

199. Table depicted in a painting of the Umbria school. XIV century. Monastery of Subiaco, Rome

200. Silla con talla de celosía. Siglo XV. Academia de San Anselmo. Aosta, Italia

200. Chair with lattice-work. XV century. Academy of San Anselmo. Aosta, Italiy

201. Sillón de cadera con respaldo de terciopelo. Siglo XIV. Al fondo chimenea de ángulo. Palacio Davanzati, Florencia

201. X-shaped armchair with velvet back. Note the corner fireplace in the background. Davanzati Palace, Florence

202. Arcón con tracerías góticas. Mesa con decoración semejante en sus faldones, y sillas de estructura gótica con patas de tijera. Siglo XIV. Salón del Papagayo en el Palacio Davanzati, Florencia

202. Chest with Gothic tracery. Table with similar decoration on its frieze panels and Gothic style chairs with X-shaped legs. XIV century. Salone del Papagallo. Davanzati Palace, Florence

203. Armario lombardo con tracerías góticas. Norte de Italia. Siglo XIV

203. Lombard cupboard with Gothic tracery. Northern Italy. XIV century

204. Silla en forma de cajón. Siglo XV. Fundación Horn, Florencia.

204. Box chair. XV century. Horn Foundation, Florence

205. "Cassone" con tarsia y talla de tracería gótica. Siglo XV. Museo Nacional, Florencia

205. "Cassone" with tarsia and Gothic tracery carving. XV century. National Museum, Florence

206. Cofre con talla gótica en sus tableros. Siglo XIV. Colección particular

206. Coffer with Gothic carving on its panels. XIV century. Private Collection

207. "Cassone" decorado con "pastiglia". Siglo XV. Colección particular. Florencia

207. "Cassone" decorated with "pastiglia". XV century. Private Collection. Florence

208. Mueble religioso de planta cuadrada rematado por una pirámide que proviene de una capilla privada. Es un pequeño oratorio o coro destinado a la meditación, decorado con intarsias. Siglo XVI. Florencia. Victoria and Albert Museum. Londres

208. This piece of religious furniture comes from a private chapel. It is square in shape and is topped with a pyramid. It is a small oratory or choir used for meditation. 16th century, Florence. Victoria and Albert Museum

209. Angulo del Salón del Papagayo. Siglo XIV. Palacio Davanzati, Florencia

209. Corner of the Salone del Pappagallo. XIV century. Davanzati Palace, Florence

210. "Cassone" con decoración de tracería gótica. Siglo XV. Museo Cívico, Turín

210. "Cassone" with Gothic tracery decoration. XV century. Civic Museum of Turin

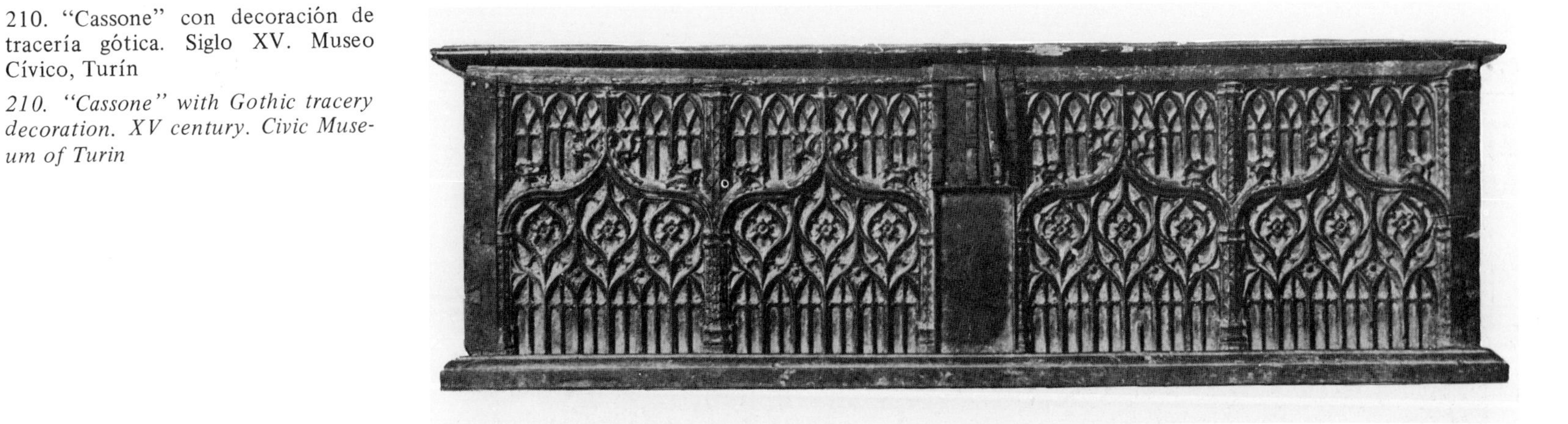

211. "Cassone" decorado con figuras simbólicas en "pastiglia". Siglo XV. Colección Bassanti, Roma

211. "Cassone" decorated with symbolic figures in "pastiglia". XV century. Bassanti Collection. Rome

212. "Cassone" decorado con "pastiglia" y dorado. Siglo XV. Villa "I Collazzi", Florencia

212. "Cassone" decorated with "pastiglia" and gilt. XV century. Villa "I Collazzi", Florence

213. Banco de roble de estructura gótica primitiva. Catedral de Winchester

213. Oak bench of primitive Gothic structure. Winchester Cathedral

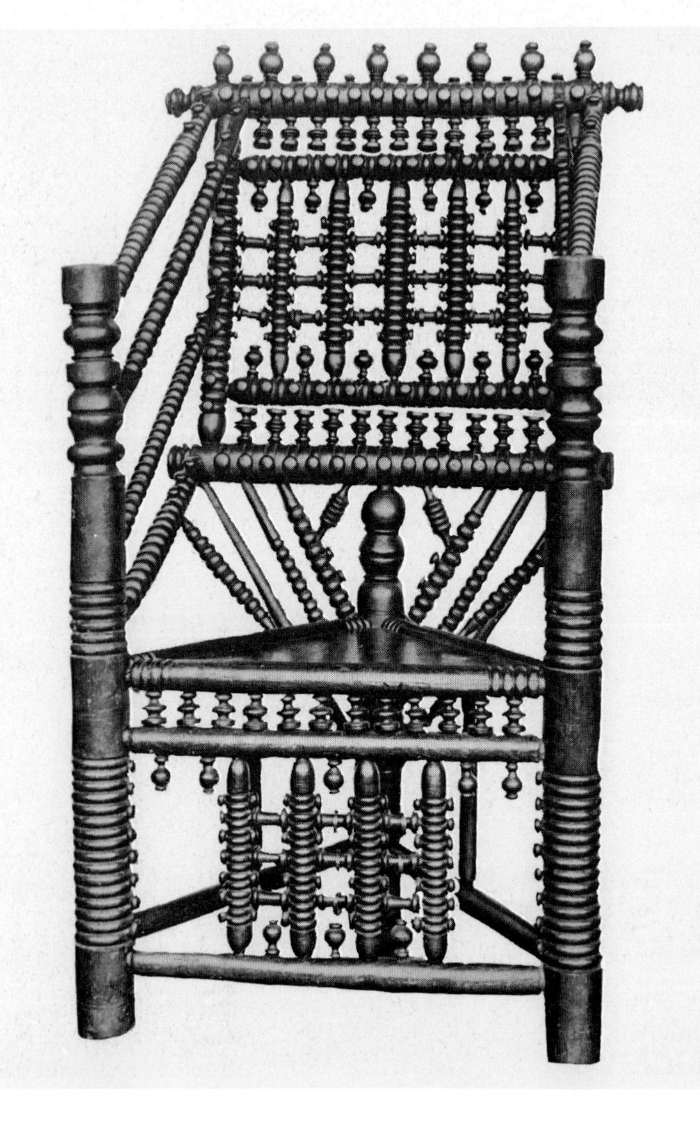

214. Silla torneada de tipo nórdico. Siglo XVI. Victoria and Albert Museum, Londres

214. Turned chair of Nordic style. XVI century. Victoria and Albert Museum

215. Silla "joyned", con algunos paneles ya renacentistas. Siglo XVI. Victoria and Albert Museum, Londres

215. "Joyned" chair with some panels already in the Renaissance style. XVI century. Victoria and Albert Museum

216. Silla plegable de tijera cubierta con terciopelo claveteado. Siglo XVI. Catedral de Winchester

216. Folding X chair covered with nailed velvet. XVI century. Winchester Cathedral

217. Trono de la coronación, Westminster Abbey, en madera de roble policromada, con el asiento sobre la legendaria piedra de la coronación de los reyes

217. Coronation Chair, Westminster Abbey, in polychrome oak with the seat on the coronation stone of the Scottish Kings

218. Banqueta de roble con recorte en su faldón. Siglo XVI. Victoria and Albert Museum, Londres

218. Oak stool with designs cut out in the apron piece. XVI century. Victoria and Albert Museum

219. Banqueta de roble con recorte en su faldón. Siglo XVI. Colección particular

219. Oak stool with design cut in the apron piece. XVI century. Private Collection

220. Banco de roble con silueta de arquería gótica en el faldón. Siglo XV. Victoria and Albert Museum, Londres

220. Oak bench with Gothic arcading cut out in the apron piece. XV century. Victoria and Albert Museum

221. Banco de roble con tallas de "pergamino" en los paneles. Siglos XV-XVI

221. Oak bench with linenfold carving on the panels. XV-XVI centuries

222. Arcón de roble con refuerzos de hierro forjado de volutas terminadas con flores de lis. Siglo XVI. Iglesia de Icklingham

222. Oak chest with forged iron voluted strengtheners terminating in fleur-de-lis. XVI century. Icklingham Church, Suffolk

223. Mesa conventual de roble del estilo gótico tardío, con tres pies en forma de cruz. Siglo XVI. Penshurst Place

223. Covent table in oak, late Gothic style, with three legs in cross form. XVI century. Penshurst Place

224. Mesa de roble con algunos paneles tallados con celosías góticas. Siglo XVI. Victoria and Albert Museum, Londres

224. Oak table with Gothic tracery on some panels. XVI century. Victoria and Albert Museum

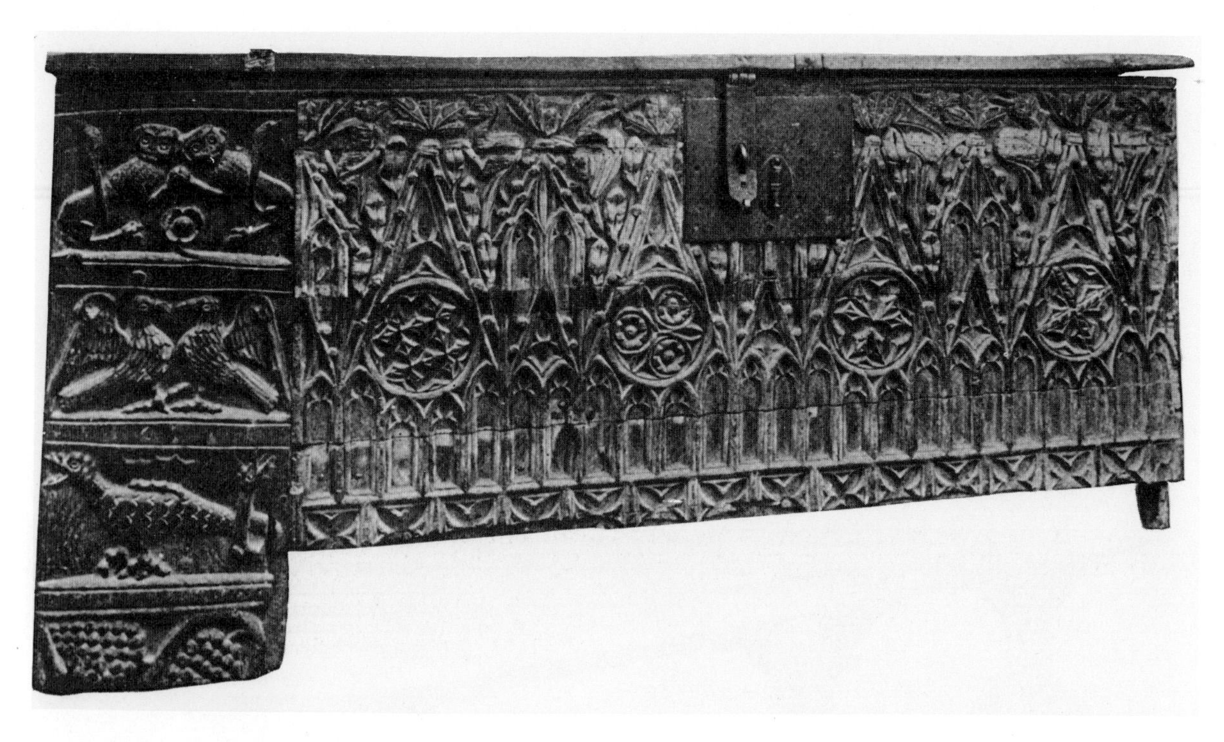

225. Arcón de roble con talla de estilo "perpendicular" en su frente. Siglo XIV. Iglesia de Chevington, Suffolk. Nótese la semejanza con el de Palma de Mallorca (fig. 164)

225. Oak chest with "perpendicular" style carving on the front. XIV century. Chevington Church, Suffolk. Note the similarity with that of Palma, Majorca (fig. 164)

226. Cofre de roble con tallas de la rosa Tudor en los laterales. Finales del siglo XV. Victoria and Albert Museum, Londres

226. Oakcoffer with Tudor rose carving on the sides. Late XV century. Victoria and Albert Museum

227. Armario con celosías góticas en las puertas (para ventilar la comida). Siglo XVI. Victoria and Albert Museum, Londres

227. Cupboard pierced with Gothic lattice-work on the doors (for ventilation purposes). XVI century. Victoria and Albert Museum

228. Credencia gótica con celosías caladas. Siglo XVI. Victoria and Albert Museum, Londres

228. Gothic credence with pierced lattice-work. XVI century. Victoria and Albert Museum

229. Armario de roble con cornisa almenada y refuerzos de hierro forjado. Siglo XV. York Minster

229. Oak cupboard with battlement form cornice and forged iron strengtheners. XV century. York Minster

230. Armario de roble con tallas muy finas de "pergamino", Siglo XVI. Iglesia de Parish Woodbridge

230. Oak cupboard with very fine linenfold carving. XVI century. Woodbridge Parish Church

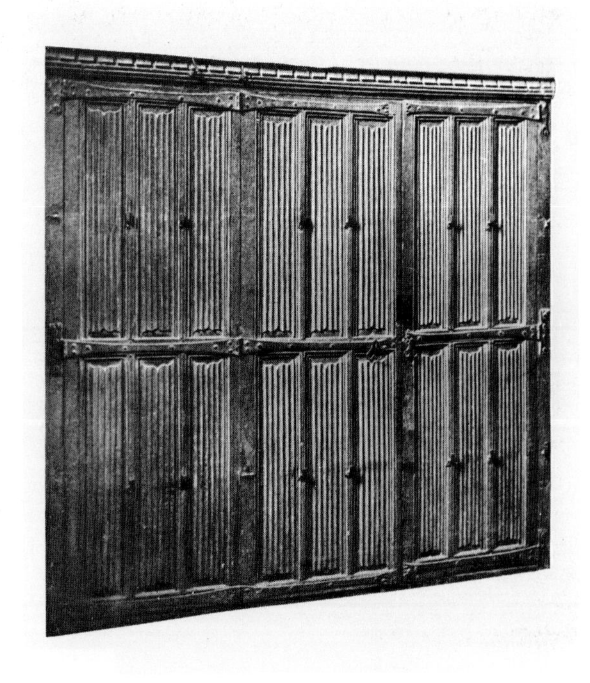

231. Cama de roble; cabecero con paneles de "pergamino" y columnas renacentistas. Siglo XVI. Victoria and Albert Museum

231. Oak bed, the head with linenfold carving and Renaissance posts. XVI century. Victoria and Albert Museum

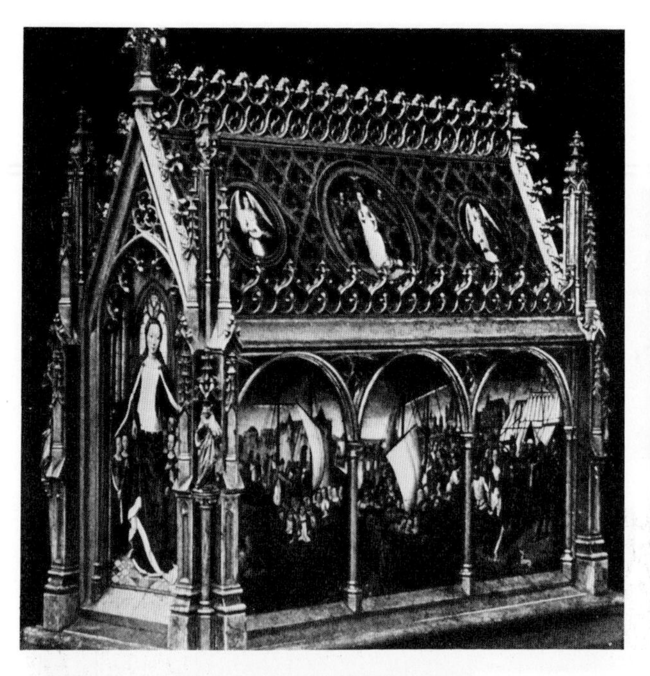

237. Arqueta de estructura metálica llamada de Santa Ursula con pinturas de Memling. Siglo XV. Hospital de San Juan. Brujas

237. Chest of metal structure known as that of St Ursula with paintings by Memling. XV century. St John's Hospital, Bruges

238. Sillón llamado "Cuna del Niño Jesús" del convento de Beguinas, Lovaina

238. Armchair called "Cradle of the Infant Jesus" of Beguinas Convent, Louvain

239. Sillas de distintas épocas representadas en un relieve del retablo de la iglesia del Salvador de Valladolid. Siglos XV-XVI

239. Chairs of different periods represented in a relief of the retable of the Iglesia del Salvador, Valladolid. XV-XVI centuries

240. Silla de tijera de hierro plegable con asiento de cuero representado en "La Adoración del Cordero Eucarístico", J. Van Eyck ,Gante. Siglo XV

240. Folding X chair in iron with leather seat, depicted in "The Adoration of the Eucharistic Lam", J. Van Eyck. Ghent. XV century

241. Mesa, bancos y credencia góticos representados en un relieve del retablo de la iglesia del Salvador, Valladolid. Siglos XV-XVI

241. Gothic table, bench and credence represented in a relief of the retable of the Church del Salvador, Valladolid. XV-XVI centuries

242. Armario de estructura gótica con talla de pergamino en sus tableros. Siglo XVI

242. Cupboard of Gothic structure with parchment carving on the panels. XVI century

243. Varios tipos de muebles representados en una miniatura de las Crónicas de Inglaterra ejecutada en Brujas. Siglo XV

243. Various types of furniture depicted in a miniature of the Chronicles of England executed in Bruges. XV century

244. Interior flamenco. Sta. Bárbara, por el maestro de Flemalle, Museo del Prado. Madrid

244. Flemish interior. St Barbara, by the Maestro de Flemalle. Museo del Prado. Madrid

245. Cama gótica y sillón representados en un relieve del retablo de la iglesia del Salvador, Valladolid. Siglos XV-XVI

245. Gothic bed and armchair represented in a relief of the retable of the church del Salvador, Valladolid. XV-XVI centuries

246. 247. Interiores con diversos muebles. "Los siete pecados capitales", por J. Bosch. Museo del Prado. Madrid

246. 247. Interior with various pieces of furniture. "The Seven Deadly Sins", by J. Bosch. Museo del Prado. Madrid

Accidia

248. Armario gótico con talla de pergamino en sus tableros. Siglo XVI. Brujas

248. Gothic cupboard with linenfold carving on its panels. XVI century. Bruges

249. "Dressoir" con talla gótica. Siglo XVI. Rijkmuseum. Amsterdam

249. Dresser with Gothic carving. XVI century. Rijkmuseum, Amsterdam

250. Cama, arcón y credencia representados en "El Nacimiento de la Virgen", anónimo. Siglo XV. Museo de Munich

250. Bed, large chest and credence depicted in the "Birth of the Virgin", anonymous. XV century. Munich Museum

251. Sillón saboyano, hacia 1500. Colección Figdor. Viena

251. Savoy armchair, c. 1500. Figdor Collection. Vienna

252. Sillón popular gótico tardío. Colección Figdor. Viena

252. Popular armchair, late Gothic. Figdor Collection. Vienna

253. Mesa de estilo gótico tardío del sur de Alemania. Siglo XVI

253. Table, late Gothic style of Southern Germany. XVI century

254. Mesa popular del sur de Alemania

254. Popular table of Southern Germany. XVI century

255. Mesa popular, gótico tardío. Siglo XVI. Colección Figdor. Viena

255. Popular table, late Gothic. XVI century. Figdor Collection. Vienna

256. Mesa popular circular sobre pie central y seis patas de estructura gótica, por Tilman Reimenschneider (1500). Museo de Wurzburg, Baviera

256. Popular round table on central leg and 6 Gothic structure feet, by Tilman Reimenschneider (1500). Museum of Wurzburg, Bavaria

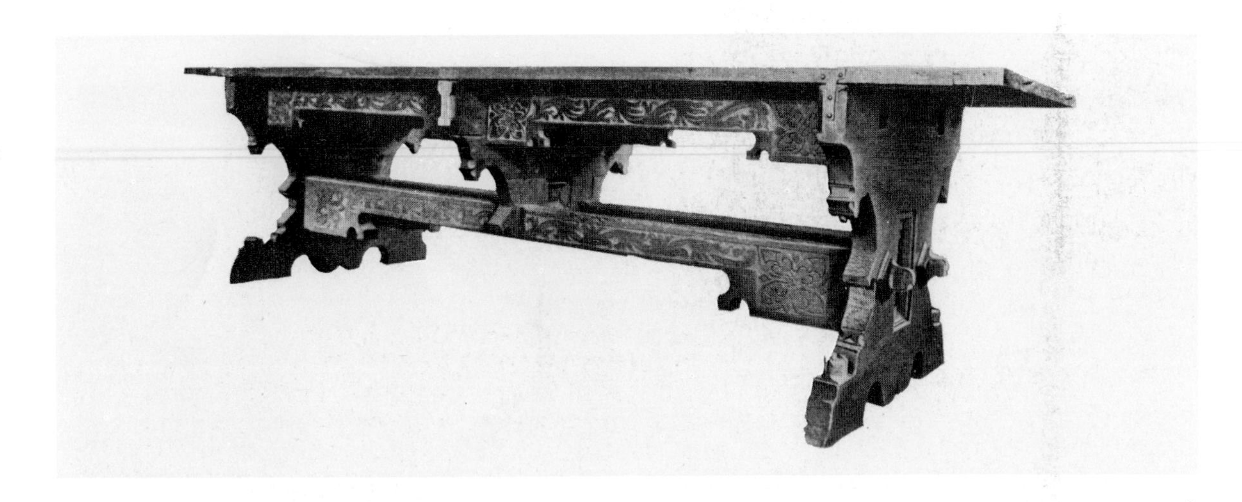

257. Mesa gótica con chambrana central desarmable. Siglo XV. Ayuntamiento de Goslar

257. Gothic table with detachable stretcher. Goslar Town Hall. XV century

258. Banquetas con talla calada en el faldón. Siglo XV. Colección Figdor. Viena

258. Stools with fretwork carving on the apron piece. XV century. Figdor Collection. Vienna

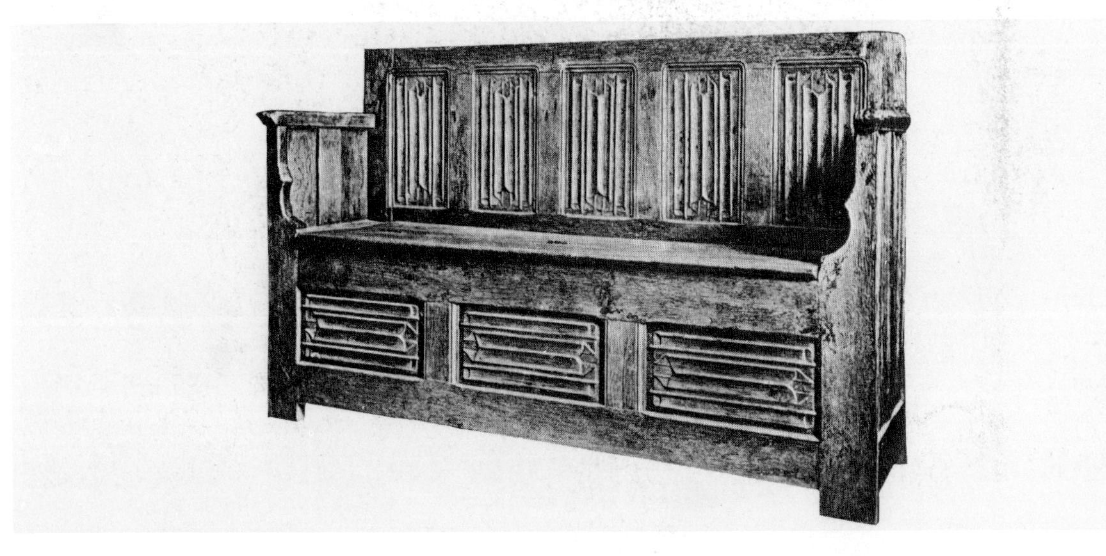

259. Banco-arca con decoración de pergaminos. Siglo XV. Viena

259. Box settle with linenfold. XV century. Vienna

260. Banco con decoración de pergaminos y respaldo reversible. Schlossmuseum, Berlín

260. Settle with linenfold decoration and reversible back. Schlossmuseum, Berlin

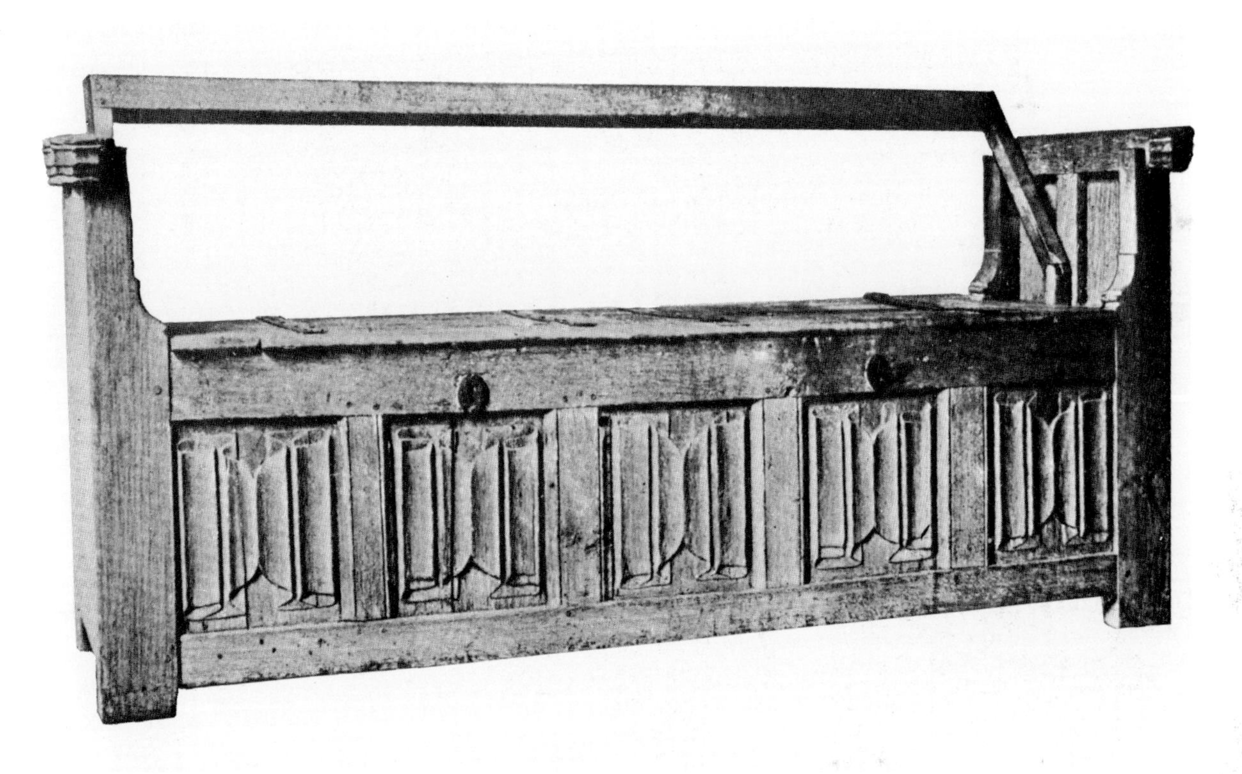

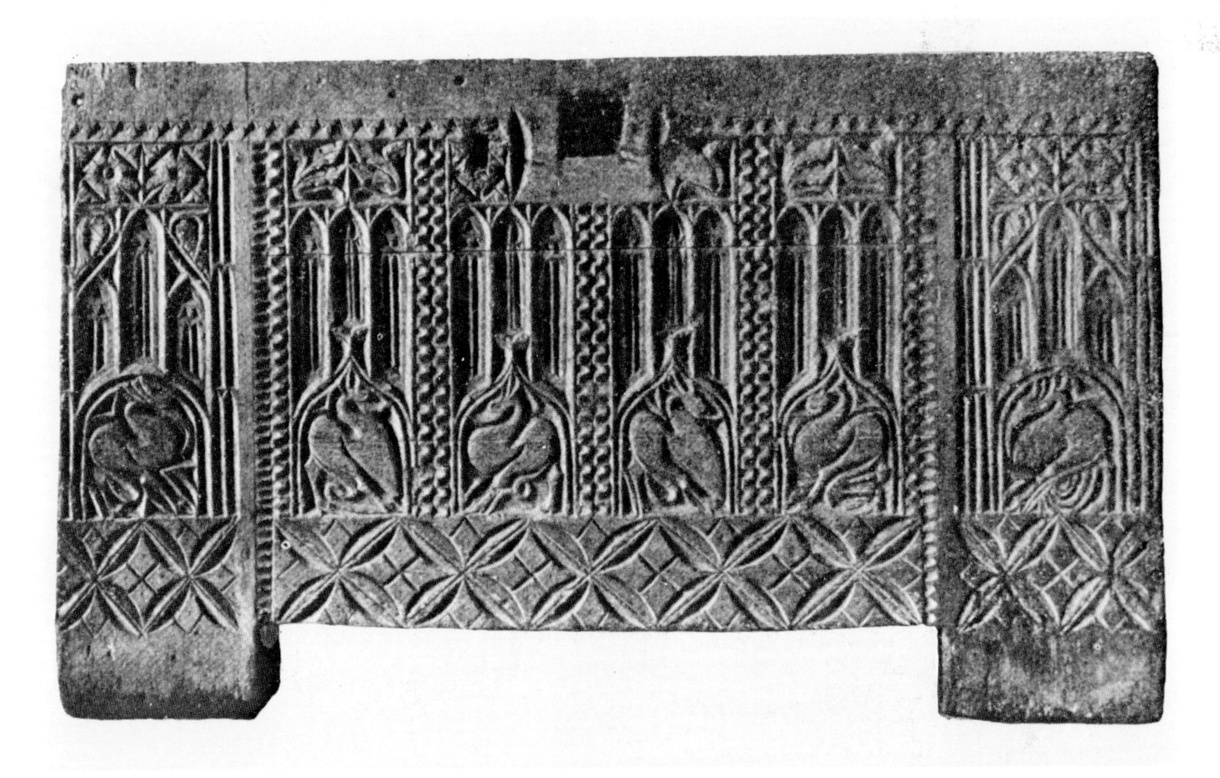

261. Arca de roble con tallas planas

261. Oak chest with flat carving

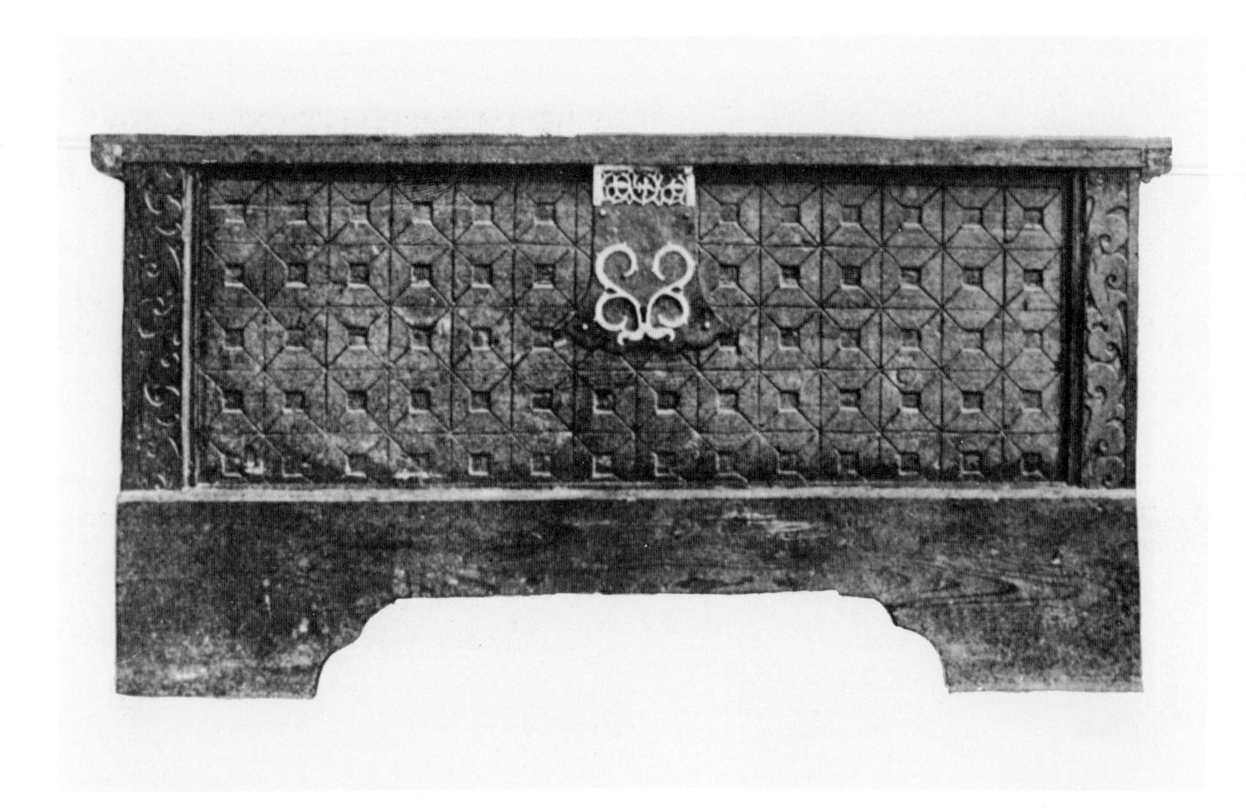

262. Arca con decoración de talla imitando pequeños casetones. Siglo XVI. Museo Histórico de Berna

262. Chest decorated with carving imitating small lacunas. XVI century. Historial Museum of Berne

263. Armario con cubierta en forma de tejadillo y gabletes de roble con refuerzos de hierro. Siglo XIV. Catedral de Brandenburgo

263. Cupboard with roof form cover and oak gables with iron strengthening. XIV century. Brandenburg Cathedral

264. Armario de tejadillo. Tallas planas populares. Siglo XIII. Hannover

264. Cupboard of roof form. Chip carvings. XIII century. Hannover

265. Armario de tejadillo. Siglo XIII. Tallas populares y refuerzos de hierro. Catedral de Halberstadt

265. Cupboard of roof form. XIII century. Popular flat carving and iron strengthening. Halberstadt Cathedral

266. Armario con decoración de tallas planas y cornisas de almenas, fechado en 1539. Schlossmuseum, Berlín

266. Cupboard with flat carving decoration and battlement cornice. Dated 1539. Schlossmuseum, Berlin

267. Armario con decoración de celosías sobre las armaduras y los paneles lisos

267. Cupboard decorated with tracery on the framework and flat panels

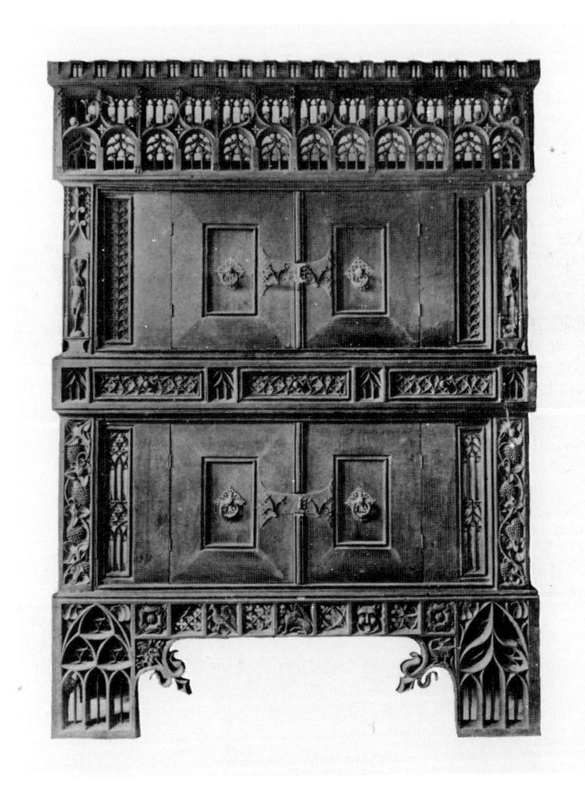

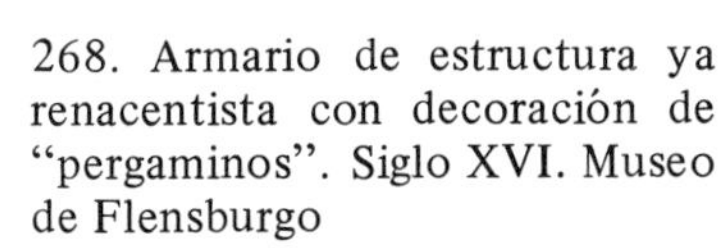

268. Armario de estructura ya renacentista con decoración de "pergaminos". Siglo XVI. Museo de Flensburgo

268. Cupboard of Renaissance structure with linenfold decoration. XVI century. Flensburg Museum

269. Armario de talla plana en las armaduras. Siglo XV. Museo Nacional de Munich

269. Cupboard with flat carving on the framework. XV century. Munich National Museum

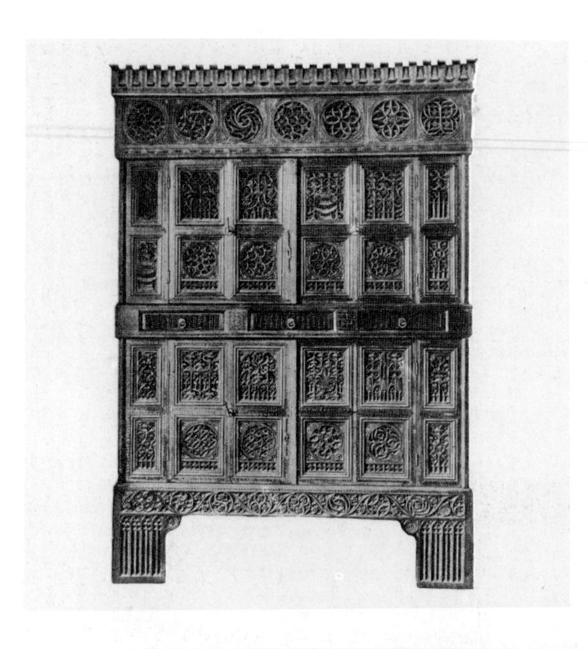

270. Armario cubierto totalmente con decorado de celosía calada sobre madera. Siglo XV. Wimpfen

270. Cupboard completely covered with tracery work carved on the wood. XV century. Wimpfen

271. Armario del Ayuntamiento de Kreuzenstein (Viena). Procedente del monasterio de Neustift. Hacia 1500

271. Cupboard of the Kreuzenstein Town Hall (Vienna). From the monastery of Neustift, c. 1500

272. Armario de estructura gótica. Siglo XV. Brujas

272. Cupboard of Gothic structure. XV century. Bruges

273. Cama con decoración de celosía calada en el cabecero y dosel. 1470. Museo Nacional de Munich

273. Bed with pierced tracery on the head and on the canopy. 1470. National Museum of Munich

274. Armario-archivo con decoración de celosía. 1518. Museo Histórico de Basilea

274. Cupboard-archive with tracery decoration. 1518. Historial Museum of Basle

275. Sala gótica del Tirol. Hacia 1500. Las sillas, del norte de Italia plegables tipo "Savonarola"

275. Tyrolese Gothic room, c. 1500. "Savonarola" type folding chairs from Northern Italy

276. Interior gótico tirolés. Siglo XV. Museo germánico de Nuremberg. Muebles alemanes y sillas del norte de Italia, ya renacentistas

276. Tyrolese Gothic interior. XV century. Germanic Museum of Nuremberg. German furniture and Renaissance chairs from Northern Italy

RENACIMIENTO

THE RENAISSANCE

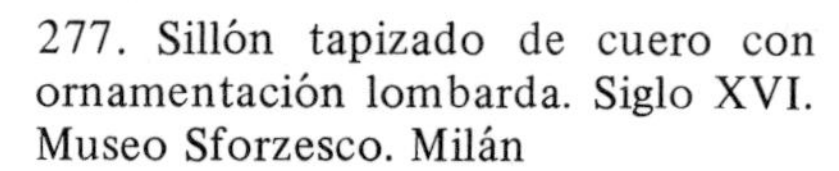

277. Sillón tapizado de cuero con ornamentación lombarda. Siglo XVI. Museo Sforzesco. Milán

277. Armchair upholstered in leather with Lombard ornamentation. XVI century. Sforzesco Museum. Milan

278. Sillón con el respaldo y chambrana con tallas de entrelazos; trabajo veneciano. Siglo XV. Colección Bagatti Valsecchi. Milán

278. Armchair with braided carving on the back and stretcher. Venetian work. XV century. Bagatti Valsecchi Collection. Milan

279. Sillón de nogal tallado y tapizado con terciopelo rojo. Siglo XVI. Colección Bardini. Florencia

279. Armchair in carved walnut and upholstered in red velvet. XVI century. Bardini Collection. Florence

280. Sillón tallado de la región de Venecia. Chambrana de lazo de influencia oriental. Siglo XVI. Venecia

280. Carved armchair of the Venice region. Stretcher with bow shape of oriental influence. XVI century. Venice

281. Sillón con respaldo de cuero repujado. Chambrana con el "nudo de amor". Clara influencia del "frailero". Siglo XVI. Piamonte

281. Armchair with repoussé leather-work back. Stretcher with "love-knot" carving. Clearly showing the "frailero" influence. XVI century. Piamonte

282. Sillón episcopal. 1560. Museo del Duomo, Siena

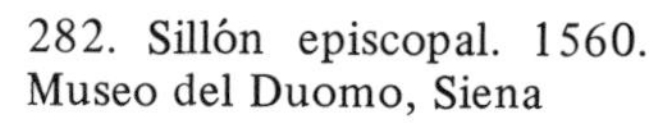

282. Episcopal chair. 1560. Duomo Museum, Siena

283. Silla de tijera "Savonarola". Castillo de Monselice. Toscana

283. "Savonarola" X-shaped chair. Monselice Castle, Tuscany

284. Sillón de los Dux, de nogal tallado. Obra probable de Tullio Lombardo. Museo de San Marcos. Venecia

284. Armchair of the Doge, in carved walnut. Probably the work of Tullio Lombardo. St Mark's Museum, Venice

285. Silla plegable y desmontable con tallas planas del norte de Italia. Mediados del siglo XV. Turín

285. Folding and demountable chair with flat carving of Northern Italy. Mid XV century. Turin

286. Interior. Cámara de estudio de San Jerónimo por Carpaccio. Siglo XVI. S. Jorge de Schiavoni. Venecia

286. Interior. Study of St Jerome by Carpaccio. XVI century. S. Jorge de Schiavoni, Venecia

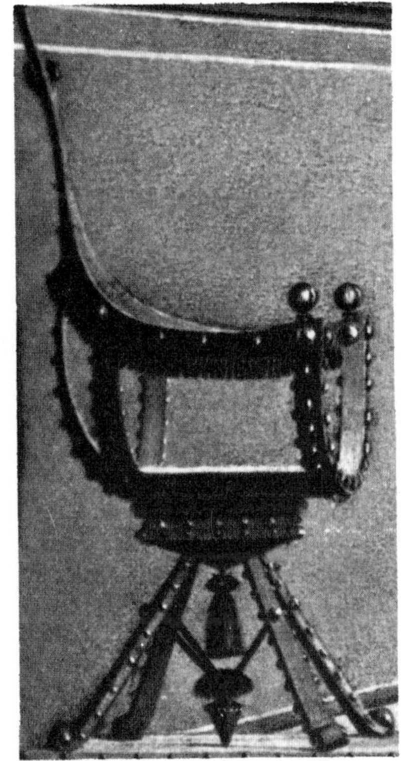

287. Sillón en el despacho anterior

287. Armchair in the above study

288. Sillón lombardo con tallas de tipo popular. Siglo XV. Museo Cívico. Padua

288. Lombard armchair with popular type carving. XV century. Civic Museum. Padua

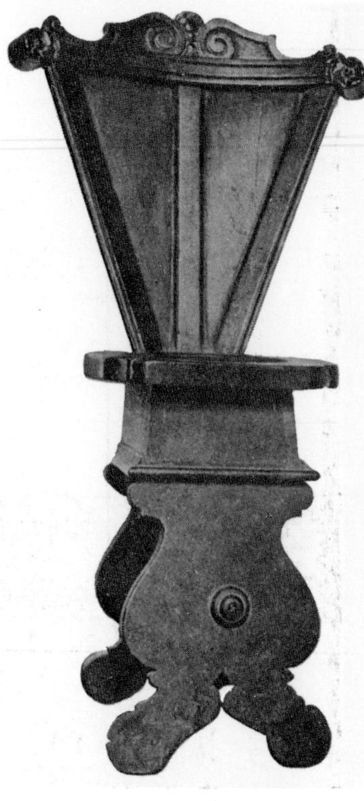

289. Silla con la típica decoración florentina de lises en las aldabas caladas. Siglo XVI. Bolonia

289. Chair with typical Florentine lily decoration on the fret-cut cross rails. XVI century. Bologna

290. Silla de tipo florentino. Siglos XVI-XVII. Museo Sforzesco. Milán

290. Florentine type chair. XVI-XVII centuries. Sforzesco Museum, Milan

291. Silla o sgabello de nogal. Siglo XVI. Palacio de la Señoría. Florencia

291. Walnut chair. XVI century. Palazzo della Signoria. Florence

292. Silla "pancheto" policromada y tallada. Palacio Strozzi. Florencia

292. Polychromed and carved "pancheto" chair. Strozzi Palace, Florence

293. Silla de tres patas de la región de Cremona. Museo Sforzesco. Milán

293. Three-legged chair of the Cremona region. Sforzesco Museum, Milan

294. Silla de nogal tallada. "Sgabello". Siglo XVI. Castillo de Monselice

294. Carved walnut chair or "sgabello". XVI century. Monselice Castle

295. Silla "pancheto" de tres patas con asiento y respaldo con tallas populares. Finales del siglo XVI. Museo Sforzesco. Milán

295. Three-legged "pancheto" chair with seat and back with conventional carvings. Late XVI century. Sforzesco Museum. Milan

296. "Cassapanca" toscana de nogal. Siglo XVI. Florencia

296. Tuscan "cassapanca" in walnut. XVI century. Florence

297. "Cassapanca" toscana. Siglo XVI. Colección Bellini. Florencia

297. Tuscan "cassapanca". XVI century. Bellini Collection. Florence

298. "Cassapanca". Siglo XVI. Palacio Davanzati. Florencia

298. "Cassapanca". XVI century. Davanzati Palace. Florence

299. "Cassapanca toscana. Siglo XVI. Colección Bellini. Florencia

299. Tuscan "cassapanca". XVI century. Bellini Colection. Florence

300. Mesa toscana sobre patas torneadas. Colección Basanti. Roma

300. Tuscan table on turned legs. Basanti Collection. Rome

301. Mesa sobre dos pies. Colección M. V. Parenti. Florencia

301. Table on two legs. M.V. Parenti Collection. Florence

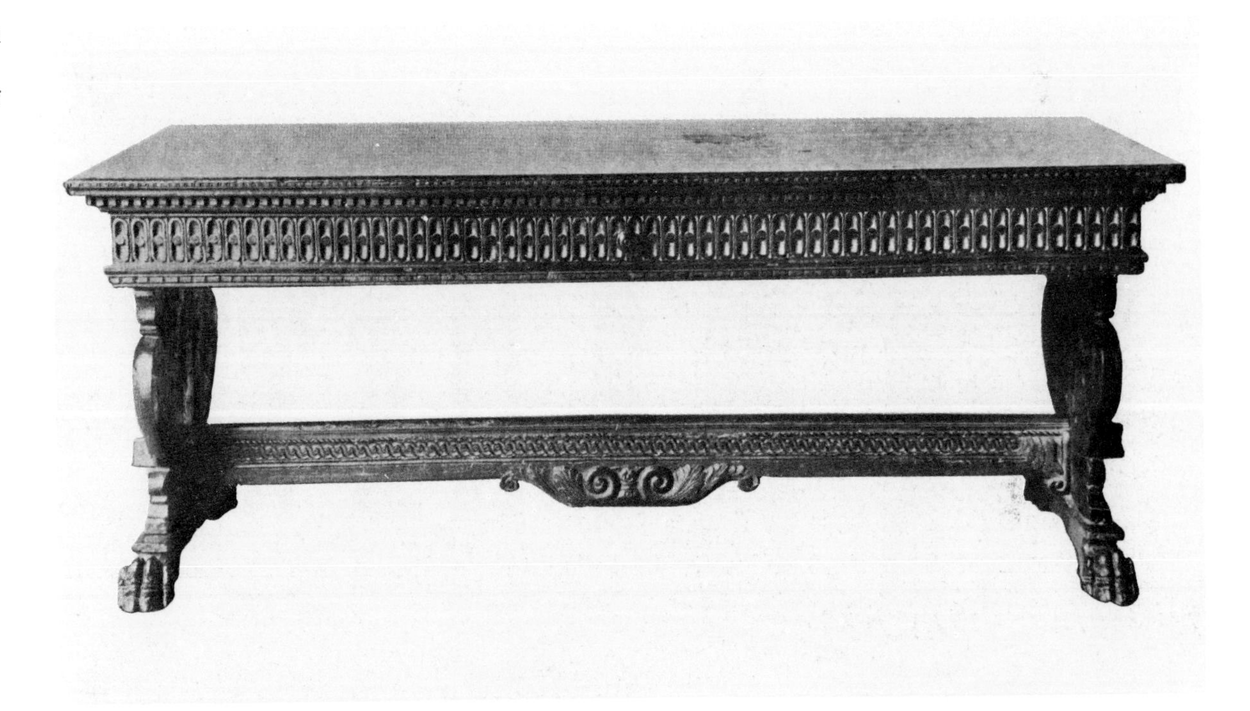

302. Mesa circular con patas torneadas de nogal. Siglo XVI. Bolonia

302. Round table with turned walnut legs. XVI century. Bologna

303. Mesa sobre patas de tipo columna. Tapa ampliable. Liguria. Colección privada. Nueva York

303. Draw leaf table on column type legs. Liguria. Private Collection. New York

304. Mesa italiana con aplicaciones de metal y piedras duras. Museo de la catedral. Burgos

304. Italian table with metal and hard stone inlays. The Cathedral Museum. Burgos

305. Mesa de nogal. Primer Renacimiento toscano. Museo Lázaro Galdeano. Madrid

305. Walnut table; first Tuscan Renaissance. Lázaro Galdeano Museum. Madrid

306. Mesa toscana con costados calados y decoración grabada. Colección Grassi. Florencia

306. Tuscan table with fretwork and engraved decoration on the sides. Grassi Collection. Florence

315. Arcón decorado a la "pastiglia", arte toscano. Siglo XV-XVI

315. Chest decorated with "pastiglia", Tuscan art. XV-XVI centuries

316. "Cassone" nupcial en "pastiglia" policromada. Principios del siglo XV. Proviene del Castillo de Monselice. Toscana

316. Nuptial "cassone" in polychromed "pastiglia". Early 15th century. From Monselice Castle. Tuscany

317. "Cassone" con pinturas. Siglo XIV. Museo Nacional. Florencia

317. "Cassone" with paintings. XIV century. National Museum. Florence

318. Arcón de composición clásica renacentista con cartelas heráldicas y cariátides. Siglo XVI. Saluzzo. Colección R. Cerutti

318. Chest of classic Renaissance composition with heraldic modillions and caryatids. XVI century. Saluzzo. R. Cerutti Collection

319. Arcón tallado. Arte toscano. Siglo XVI

319. Carved chest. Tuscan art. XVI century

320. "Cassone" con tarsias geométricas policromadas. Colegiata de Montevarchi. Arezzo

320. "Cassone" with polychromed geometrical tarsias. Colegiata di Montevarchi. Arezzo

321. "Cassone" nupcial florentino, dorado, tallado y pintado. Museo Arqueológico Nacional. Madrid

321. Florentine nuptial "cassone", gilded, carved and painted. Archaeological Museum. Madrid

322. Arcón monumental con escudo italiano. 165 largo, 63 alto y 47 ancho. Museo Arqueológico Nacional. Madrid

322. Monumental chest with Italian escutcheon. Length 165, height 63 width 47. Archaeological Museum. Madrid

323. "Cassonne" toscano con tarsias policromadas. Palacio Corsini. Florencia

323. Tuscan "cassone" with polychromed tarsias. Corsini Palace. Florence

324. Arcón tallado. Alto 79, largo 179, ancho 60. Siglo XVI

324. Carved chest, height 79, length 179, width 60. XVI century

325. Arcón con tallas planas. Siglo XVI. Museo Sforzesco. Milán

325. Chest with flat carving. XVI century. Sforzesco Museum. Milan

326. Armario con tarsias, por fray Giovanni da Verona Monte Oliveto. Siena

326. Cupboard with tarsias, by fray Giovanni da Verona Monte Oliveto, Siena

327. Armario de dos cuerpos de composición arquitectónica. Siglo XVI. Florencia

327. Cupboard in two sections of architectural composition. XVI century. Florence

328. Armario de dos cuerpos con decoración arquitectónica tallada de perspectivas. Siglo XVI. Florencia. Villa "I. Collazzi"

328. Cupboard in two sections with architectural decoration carved in perspective. XVI century. Florence. Villa "I. Collazzi"

329. Armario policromado y taraceado con grabados pegados en los cajones. "Arte Povero" veneciano. Museo Arqueológico Nacional. Madrid

329. Chest, polychromed and decorated with inlaid engravings glued on to the drawers. Venetian "Arte Povero". Archaeological Museum. Madrid

330. Armario o stipo con ornamentación de piedra dura. Composición arquitectónica. Siglo XVII. Palacio Pitti. Florencia

330. Cupboard or "stipo" ornamented with hard stone. Architectural composition. XVII century. Pitti Palace. Florence

331. Armario-cabinet con cajonería pintada sobre vidrio. Siglo XVII. Victoria and Albert Museum. Londres

331. Cabinet-cupboard with drawers painted on glass. XVII century. Victoria and Albert Museum

332. Cajonería damasquinada de Carlos V. Habitaciones de Felipe II. Hoy en el museo de pintura. Palacio del Escorial

332. Damaskeened chest of drawers of Carlos V. Rooms of Philip II. Now in the Pictoric Museum. Palace of the Escorial

333. Frente de uno de los cajones en el que se aprecia el trabajo damasquinado

333. The front of one of the drawers in which the damaskeen work can be appreciated

334. Bargueño que fue escritorio de Felipe II, forrado de bronce y damasquinado con oro y plata. Hoy sagrario. Monasterio de Guadalupe (Cáceres)

334. "Bargueño" which was the secretaire of Philip II, lined with bronze and damaskeened with gold and silver. Now a ciborium. Monastery of Guadalupe (Cáceres)

335. Bargueño de hierro damasquinado. Detalle de la puerta central. Siglo XVI. Monasterio de Guadalupe (Cáceres)

335. "Bargueño" of damaskeened iron. Detail of the central door. XVI century. Monastery of Guadalupe (Cáceres)

336. Credencia de composición arquitectónica. Museo del Duomo. Siena

336. Credence of architectural composition. Museum of the Duomo. Siena

337. Bancos y pupitres de la Biblioteca Laurenziana, tallada por Ciapino y Battista del Cinque, según dibujo de Miguel Angel. Siglo XVI

337. Benches and desks at the Laurentian Library, carved by Ciapino and Battista del Cinque, after a design by Micelangelos. XVI century

338. Otro aspecto de la Biblioteca Laurenziana

338. Another aspect of the Laurentian Library

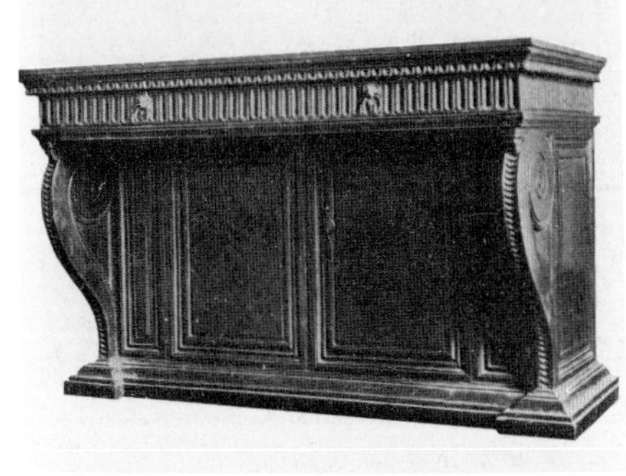

339. Credencia toscana. Siglo XV. Colección Ugo Jándolo. Roma

339. Tuscan credence. XV century. Ugo Jandolo Collection. Rome

340. Credencia de composición arquitectónica. Siglo XVI. Colección Bellini. Florencia

340. Credence of architectural composition. XVI century. Bellini Collection. Florence

341. Credencia con pilastras en estípite. Siglo XVI. Colección Bardini. Florencia

341. Credence with pilasters in the form of a reversed pyramid. XVI century. Bardini Collection. Florence

342. Credencia con paneles de ornamentación prebarroca. Colección Grassi. Florencia

342. Credence with panels of prebaroque ornamentation. Grassi Collection. Florence

343. Cama con dosel y columnas talladas y doradas procedente de Pistoia. Siglo XV. Colección Bossi. Génova

343. Bed with canopy and carved and gilt posts from Pistoia. XV century. Bossi Collection. Genoa

344. Cama con baldaquino. Cabecero de composición del Piamonte. Siglo XVI. Castillo de Pavone. Ivrea

344. Bed with canopy, headboard of Piamonte composition. XVI century. Pavone Castle. Ivrea

345. Cuna de nogal tallado. Siglo XVI. Florencia

345. Carved walnut cradle. XVI century. Florence

346. Cama con baldaquino en "Las bodas de Rossana y Alejandro" por el Sodoma. La Farnesina. Roma

346. Bed with canopy in "The Wedding of Rossana and Alexander" by Sodoma. La Farnesina. Rome

347. Cama tallada y dorada conservada en el castillo de Sant'Angelo. Siglo XVI. Roma

347. Carved and gilt bed conserved in the Castle of Sant'Angelo. XVI century. Rome

348. Interior veneciano "Sueño de santa Ursula" por Carpaccio. Finales del siglo XV

348. Venetian interior "Dream of St. Ursula" by Carpaccio. End 15th century

349. Cama de cuatro columnas talladas. Museo Sforzesco. Milán

349. Carved four-poster bed. Sforzesco Museum. Milan

350. Banco convertible en lecho. Siglo XVI. Palacio de la Señoría. Siena

350. Bench convertible into bed. XVI century. Palazzo della Signoria. Siena

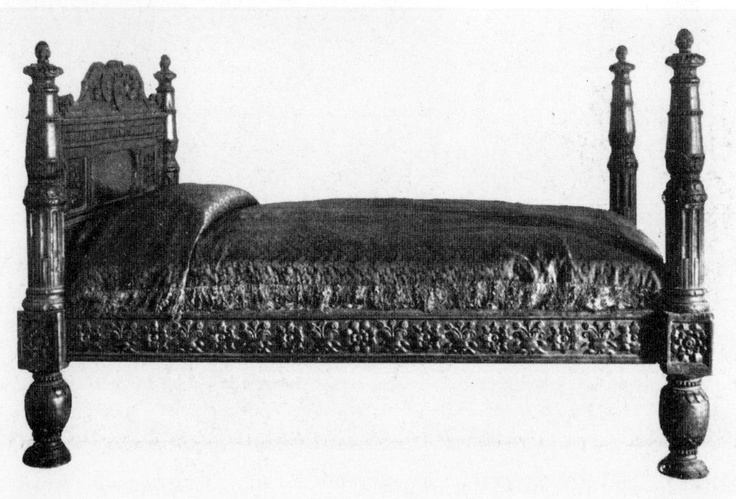

351. Cama tallada y dorada. Siglo XVI. Castillo de Monselice

351. Carved and gilded bed. XVI century. Castle of Monselice

352. Dormitorio. Siglo XIV. Palacio Davanzati. Florencia

352. Bedroom. XIV century. Davanzati Palace. Florence

353. Ambiente del Palacio Davanzati de Florencia. Siglo XIV

353. Environment of Davanzati Palace. Florence. XIV century

354. Despacho de Francisco de Médicis. Palacio Vecchio. Florencia

354. Study of Francesco de Medici. Vecchio Palace. Florence

355. Detalle del coro de la cartuja de Pavía. Tarsias de Pietro da Vallate. 1498

355. Detail of the choir of the Carthusian monastery of Pavia. Tarsias by Pietro da Vallate. 1498

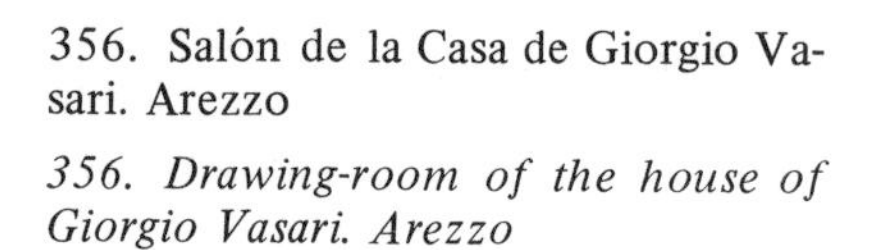

356. Salón de la Casa de Giorgio Vasari. Arezzo

356. Drawing-room of the house of Giorgio Vasari. Arezzo

357. Sala de audiencia del Colegio di Cambio de Perusa por Doménico Tasso. 1490

357. Audience-chamber of the "Colegio di Cambio" of Perusa by Domenico Tasso. 1490

358. Despacho-celda de fray J. Savonarola. Museo de S. Marcos. Florencia

358. Study-cell of fray J. Savonarola. St. Mark's Museum. Florence

359. Sillón frailero del arzobispo Sandoval y Rojas

359. "Frailero" armchair (friar's armchair) of Archbishop Sandoval y Rojas

360. Sillón frailero del arzobispo Salazar con aplicaciones de vidrio pintado. Alcalá de Henares

360. "Frailero" armchair of Archbishop Salazar with appliqués of painted glass. Alcalá de Henares

361. Sillón de tijera tipo curul con tapicería antigua de terciopelo bordado. Salón del trono. Habitaciones de Felipe II. El Escorial

361. X chair, curule type, with old upholstery in embroidered velvet. Throne Room. Rooms of Philip II. El Escorial

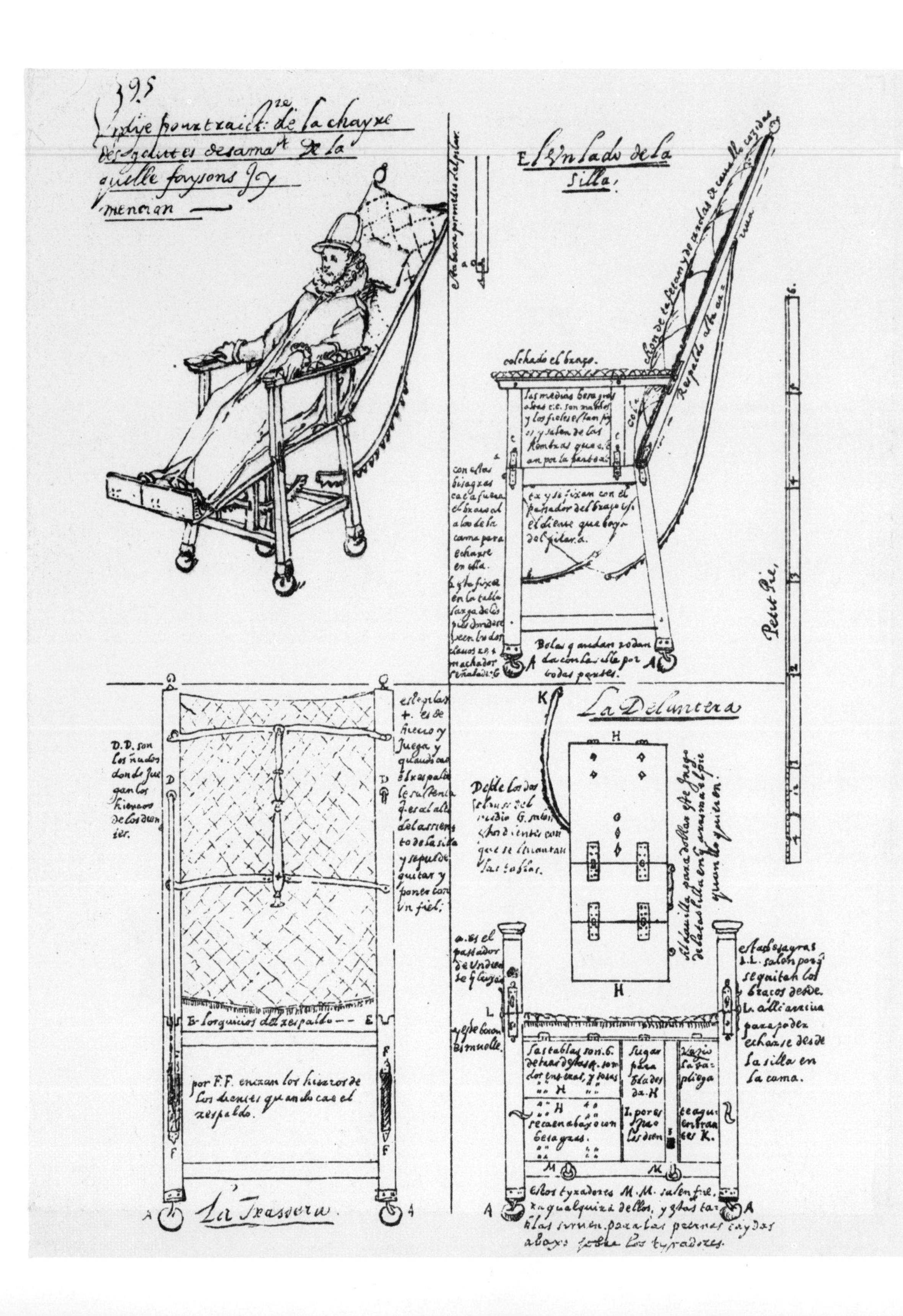

362. Dibujo de la silla de gota de Felipe II hecho por su mayordomo Jean Lhermite y que sin duda sirvió de base para la de la figura 363

362. Sketch of Philip II's reclining chair designed by his steward Jean Lhermite and doubtless served as a basis for the one in figure 363

363. Sillón frailero de Felipe II, con toldo y respaldo abatible. Abrazaderas para ser llevado a mano. Cuero acolchado. Palacio de Felipe II. El Escorial

363. "Frailero" chair of Philip II, with awning and drop back, and clamps by means of which it could be carried. Quilted leather. Palace of Philip II. El Escorial

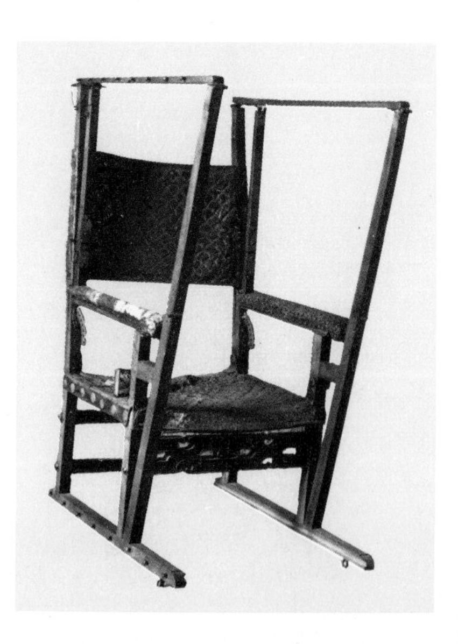

364. Sillón de cadera con terciopelo de seda. Museo Valencia de Don Juan. Madrid

364. X chair with silk velvet. Valencia de Don Juan Museum. Madrid

365. Silla de tijera tipo "Savonarola" de influencia italiana, con incrustaciones de nácar

365. X Chair, "Savonarola" type with Italian influence, mother-of-pearl incrustations

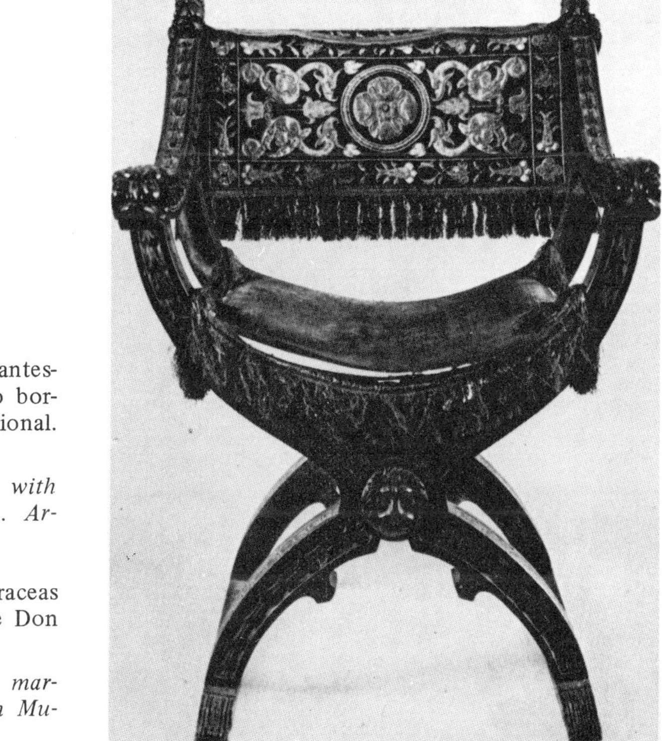

366. Sillón de cadera. Sillón dantesco con tapicerías de terciopelo bordado. Museo Arqueológico Nacional. Madrid

366. X chair. Dantesque chair with embroidered velvet upholstery. Archaeological Museum. Madrid

367. Sillón de cadera con taraceas granadinas. Museo Valencia de Don Juan. Madrid

367. X chair with Granada marquetry. Valencia de Don Juan Museum. Madrid

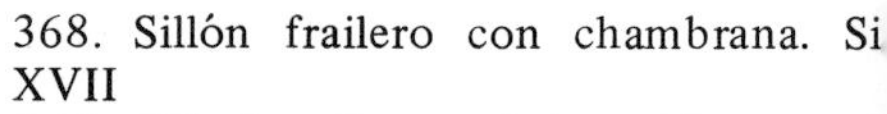

368. Sillón frailero con chambrana. Si
XVII
368. "Frailero" armchair with stretch
XVII century

369. Sillón frailero. Tapicería acolchada
369. "Frailero" armchair, with quil
upholstery

370. Sillón de nogal levantino, con respa
de arquerías de influencia italiana
370. Walnut Levantine armchair with arc
back of Italian influence

371. Frailero con respaldo de cuero go
do; clavos de gota de sebo
371. "Frailero" (friar's chair) with g
ffered leather back, wax-drop nails

372. Sillón frailero de proporción muy b
372. "Frailero" armchair with low seat

373. Sillón de cadera con marquetería mudéjar y cuero, con ornamentación renacentista

373. Hip chair with Mudejar carvings and Renaissance decoration on leather parts

374. Sillón de cadera muy simple

374. Very simple hip chair

375. Sillón interpretación popular del frailero

375. Popular versión of "frailero" (friar's chair)

376. Sillón muy rico en taraceas. Museo Valencia de Don Juan. Madrid

376. Armchair, richly decorated with marquetry. Valencia de Don Juan Museum. Madrid

377. Sitial de un coro en nogal con tallas renacentistas. Colección de Don Juan Lafora. Madrid

377. Presiding chair of a choir, in walnut with Renaissance carving. Juan Lafora Collection. Madrid

378. Sillón o faldistorio tipo curul de hierro, bronce y cuero repujado (paso del gótico al Renacimiento). Museo de Arte Antiguo. Lisboa

378. Faldstool, curule type, in iron, bronze and repoussé leather (transition from Gothic to Renaissance). Museum of Antique Art. Lisbon

379. Sillón de cadera con asiento y respaldo de cuero repujado (cordobán). Museo Lázaro Galdeano. Madrid

379. Hip chair with embossed Cordovan leather back and seat. Lázaro Galdeano Museum, Madrid

380. Sillón frailero de línea y chambrana clásica; respaldo y asiento de vaqueta; las patas son plegables para su más fácil transporte. Museo de Vich (Barcelona)

380. "Frailero" (friar's chair) with classical lines and trim, leather back and seat. The legs are collapsable for easier carrying. Vic Museum (Barcelona)

381. Frailero con chambrana delantera característica

381. "Frailero" with characteristic front stretcher

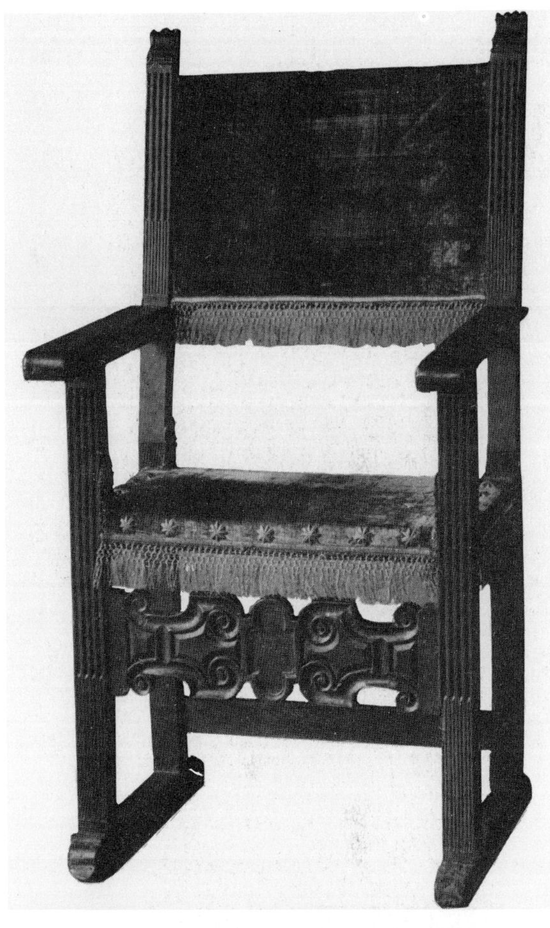

382. 383. Sillones fraileros plegados

382. 383. Folded "frailero" chairs

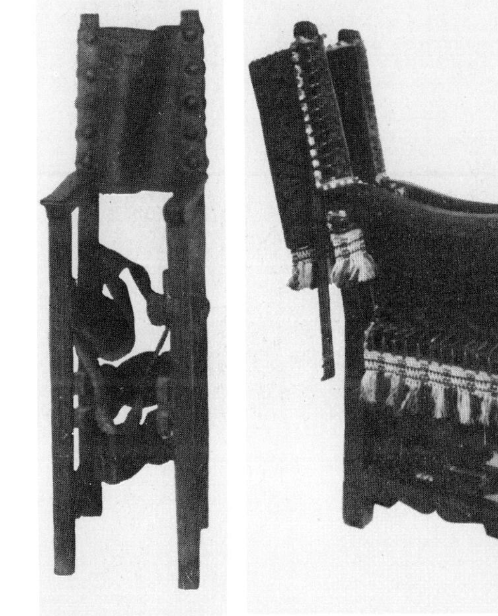

384. Banco con taraceas; respaldo abatible sobre el asiento. Museo Valencia de Don Juan. Madrid

384. Marquetry bench; the back frops down on to the seat. Valencia de Don Juan Museum. Madrid

385. Silla derivada del frailero; tapicería con flecos y clavos piramidales; respaldo ligeramente inclinado. Palacio de Felipe II. El Escorial

385. Chair derived from "frailero". Fringed upholstery and pyramid-shaped nails. Back is slightly inclined. Palace of Philip II. El Escorial

386. 388. 389. Sillas de tipo popular del norte de España, con tallas muy sencillas a golpes de gubia

386. 388. 389. Chairs of a popular type from northern Spain with very simple carvings made with a gouge

387. Banco con decoración de cuero trenzado

387. Bench with decoration of braided leather

390. Banco con tapicería de terciopelo y patas con fiadores. Museo de Afuera. Toledo

390. Bench with velvet upholstery and braced legs. Afuera Museum. Toledo

391. Banco de Medinaceli por Adrián Lombart. 1553. Ejemplar muy importante del Renacimiento español

391. Medinaceli bench by Adrián Lombart. 1553. Outstanding example of Spanish Renaissance work

392. Banco con cuero acolchado. Patas de recorte, fiadores. Museo Arqueológico Nacional. Madrid

392. Bench, with quilted leather; profile legs and stretchers. Archaeological Museum. Madrid

393. Mesa de nogal con tapa ampliable, de influencia francesa. Con torneados muy típicos

393. Walnut draw table with French influence. Typically turned legs

394. Mesa vestida en las habitaciones de Felipe II. El Escorial

394. Covered table in Philip II's rooms. El Escorial

395. Mesa de nogal compuesta por un tablero sobre patas laterales oblicuas talladas con fiadores. Siglo XVI-XVII

395. Walnut table composed of a top resting on slanting carved legs with braces. 16th-17th century

396. Mesa del tipo llamado de refectorio; tablero estrecho y largo sobre ancho faldón con cajones y cuatro patas torneadas con chambranas. Museo de Artes Decorativas. Madrid

396. Table of the Kin known as refectory tables: a long, narrow top with deep drawers and four turned legs with crosspieces. Museum of Decorative Arts. Madrid

397. Mesa plegable de campaña con taraceas. Marqués de Santillana. Madrid

397. Folding camp-table with marquetry decoration. Marqués de Santillana. Madrid

398. Mesa vestida de terciopelo rojo en el "San Ildefonso" del Greco. Hospital de Illescas. Toledo

398. Table with red velvet hangings in "San Ildefonso" by el Greco. Hospital de Illescas. Toledo

399. Mesa de nogal. Faldón con cajones tallados. Columnas corolíticas

399. Walnut table with carved drawers in the apron piece. Spiral carved supports

400. Mesa sobre patas torneadas y estriadas con fiadores

400. Table with turned and fluted legs with braces

401. Mesa popular, de nogal, de influencia francesa

401. Popular type walnut table with French influence

402. Mesa de tipo popular, muy estilizada; patas laterales sobre zapatas

402. Popular type table, greatly stylised; splay-foot supports

403. Mesa de nogal de tipo refectorio. Museo Lázaro Galdeano. Madrid

403. Refectory type walnut table. Lázaro Galdeano Museum. Madrid

404. Mesita de nogal con patas acanaladas en estípite y contraserradas. Palacio de Felipe II. El Escorial

404. Small walnut table with legs in reversed pyramid form and counter-sawn. Palace of Philip II. El Escorial

405. Arcón encorado con refuerzos de hierro. Siglo XVI. Palacio de Felipe II. El Escorial

405. Large leather covered chest with iron strengtheners. XVI century. Palace of Philip II. El Escorial

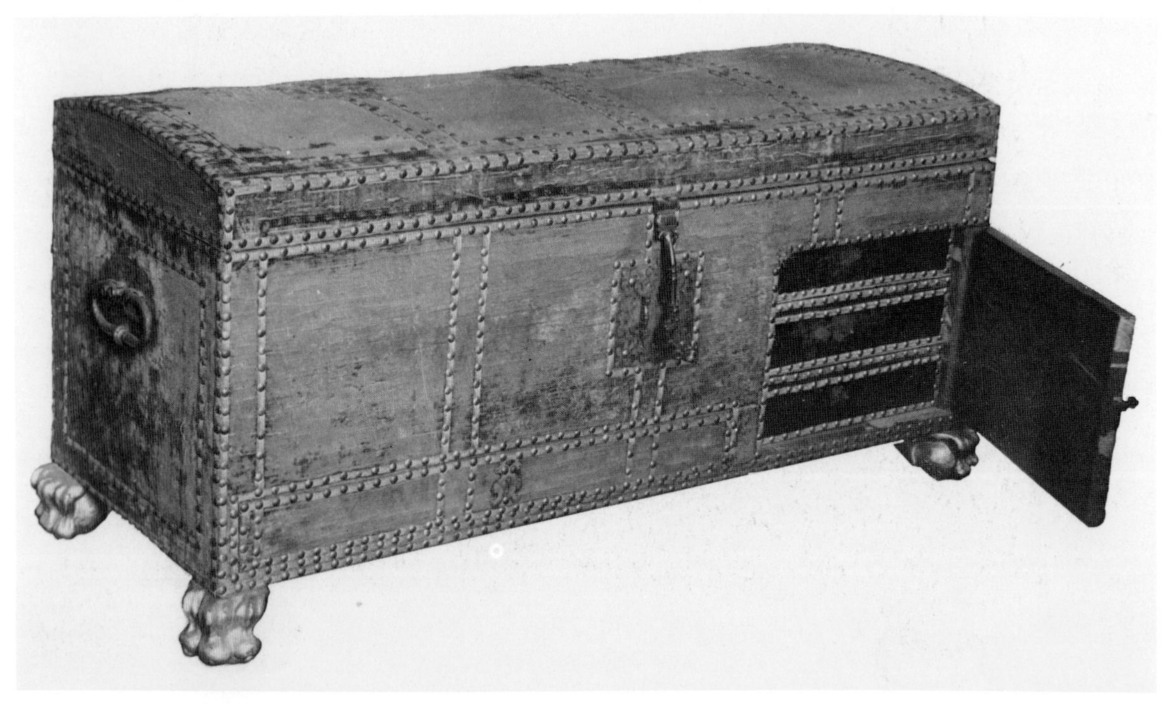

406. Arca de novia ensayalada de seda verde y puertecita lateral con gavetillas; dibujos con pasamanería y tachuelas a cordón. Casa Oleza. Palma de Mallorca.

406. Bride's chest covered with green silk. Small side door hides tiny drawers. Lace figures and tacked ribbon. Oleza House, Palma de Majorca

407. Arca "de novia" de talla popular y composición de influencia italiana. Siglo XVI. Museo de Artes Decorativas. Madrid

407. Bride's chest with popular carvings. Composition reveals Italian influence. 16th century. Museum of Decorative Arts. Madrid

408. Arcón con tallas populares. Museo de Artes Decorativas. Madrid

408. Chest with popular carvings. Museum of Decorative Arts. Madrid

409. Arcón-armario de roble tallado en madera de nogal, con tallas de la escuela de Berruguete. Capilla del Condestable. Catedral de Burgos.

409. Cupboard-chest in carved oak on walnut, with carvings of the Berruguete school. Chapel of Constable. Burgos Cathedral

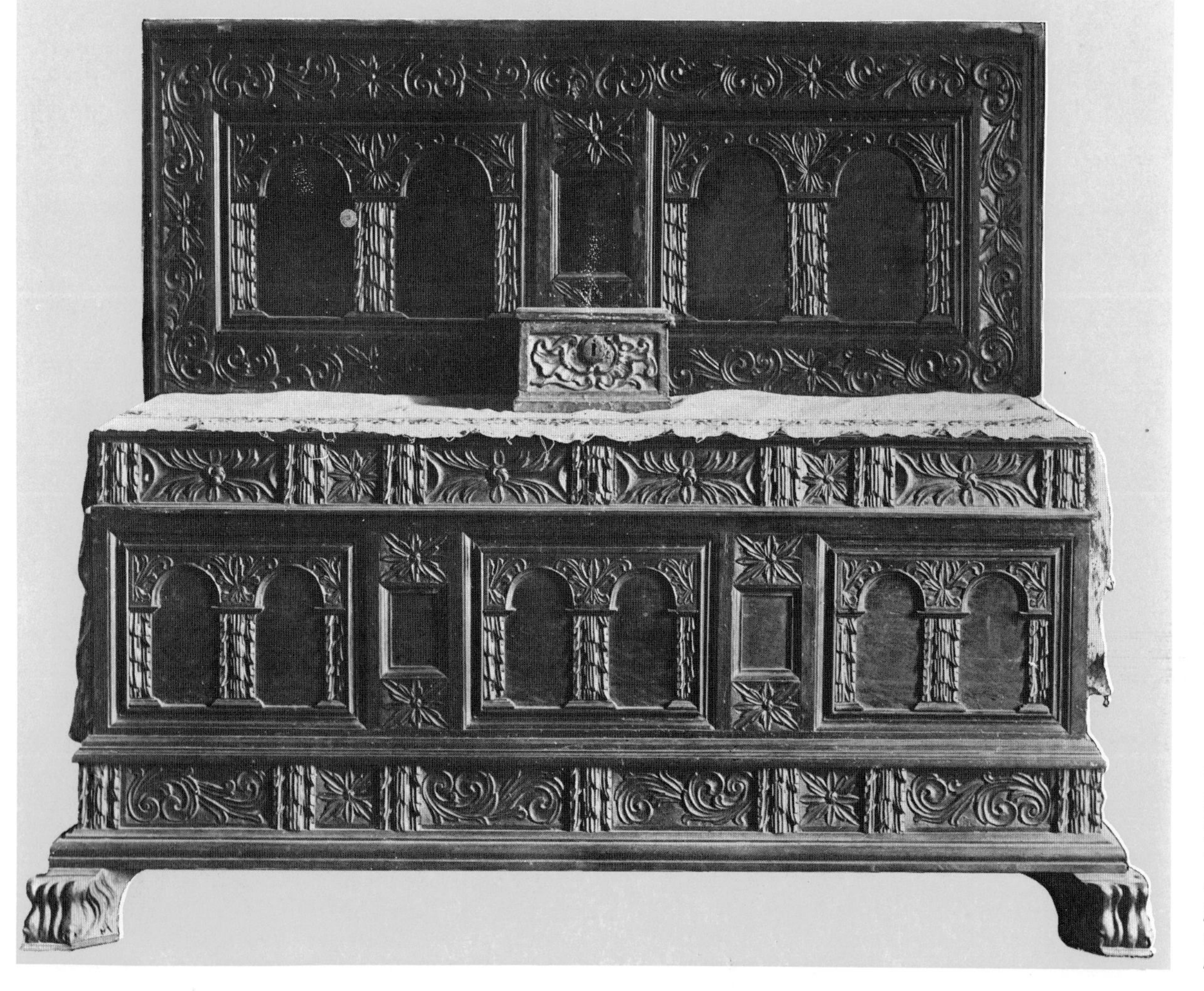

410. Arcón de nogal con tallas populares y levantinas arquerías de influencia italiana. Museo de Artes Decorativas. Madrid

410. Large walnut chest with popular carving and Levant arcading with Italian influence. Museum of Decorative Arts. Madrid

411. 413. Arcones tallados en madera, de estilo mudéjar y tallas a bisel. Siglo XVI

411. 413. Chests in Mudejar style with chamfer carvings. XVI century

412. Costado del Arcón-armario de la capilla del Condestable. Catedral de Burgos (véase fig. 409)

412. Side of cabinet-chest from Chapel of Constable, Burgos Cathedral (see figure 409)

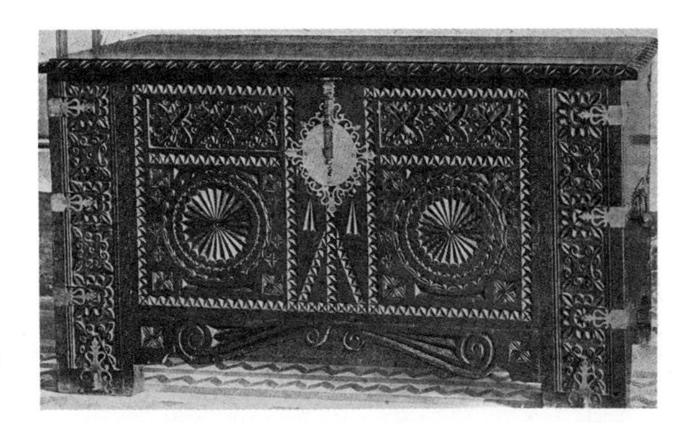

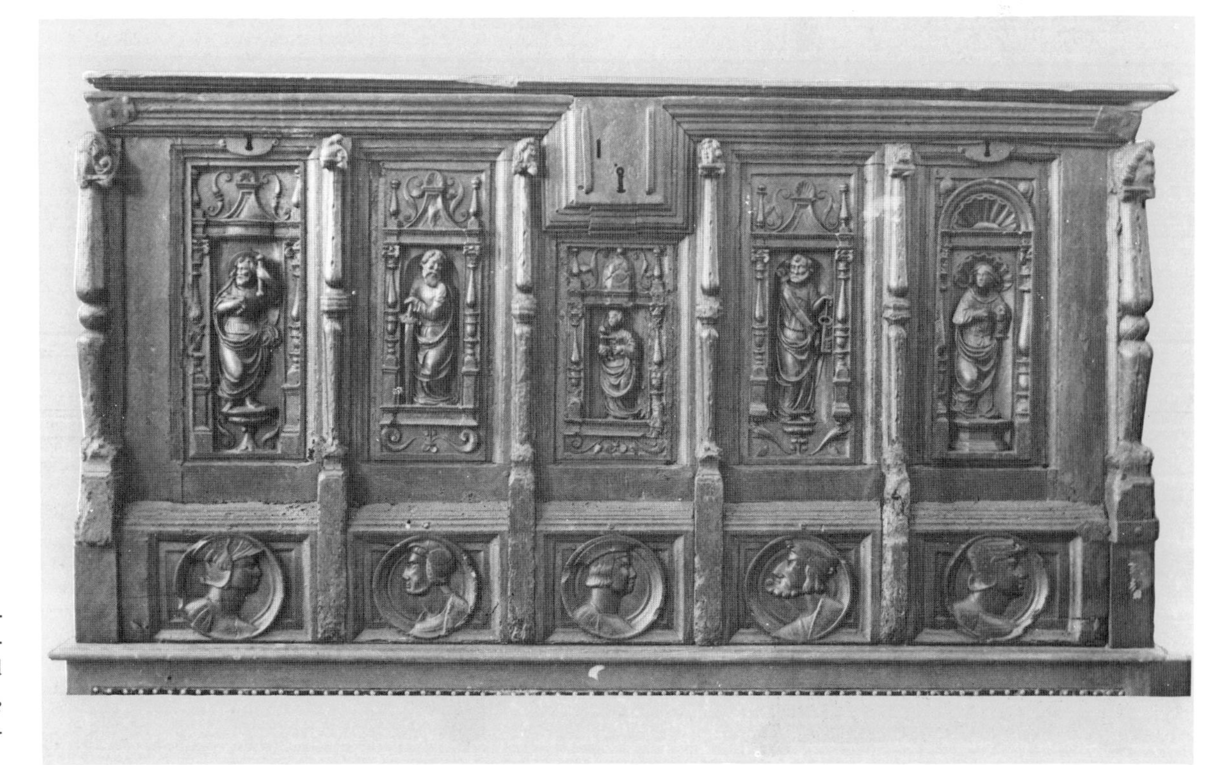

414. Arcón de nogal con tallas renacentistas de influencia italiana. Museo Arqueológico Nacional. Madrid

414. Walnut chest with Renaissance carvings with Italian influence Archaeological Museum. Madrid

415. Armario con cuatro puertas coronado por un frontón, tallas platerescas

415. Cupboard with four doors and crowned by a pediment; plateresque carvings

416. Armario tallado en madera de nogal. Iglesia parroquial de Paredes de Nava. Palencia

416. Carved walnut cupboard. Church of Paredes de Nava. Palencia

417. Armario llamado de los Evangelistas, profusamente tallado y coronado con un frontón

417. Cupboard called that of the Evangelists, richly decorated and crowned with a pediment

418. Taquillón o armario bajo de roble con cartelas talladas en la cajonería y puertas y refuerzos de hierro arcaizantes; principios del barroco. Palacio del Marqués de Viana. Córdoba

418. Low cupboard or file cabinet made of oak with carvings in the drawers and doors. Obsolescent iron reinforcements. Beginning of the Baroque period. Palace of the Marquis of Viana. Cordova

419. Armario, de nogal uno de los elementos. Ejecutado por Gregorio Pardo, 1549-1551. Sala capitular de la Catedral de Toledo

419. Cupboard, one of the elements being walnut. Executed by Gregorio Pardo, 1549-1551. Chapter-house of Toledo Cathedral

420. Armario renacentista con cuatro puertas

420. Renaissance cupboard with four doors

421. Armario de composición italiana con cuatro puertas y dos cuerpos. Tableros con cartelas y escudos catalanes

421. Cupboard of Italian composition, with four doors and two sections. Paneles with cartouches and Catalan shields

422. Armario con tallas renacentistas. Ornamentación de celosías en la parte superior y pergaminos en la inferior. Colección particular

422. Cupboard with Renaissance carvings. Lattice-work decoration in the upper section and parchment on the lower. Private Collection

423. Credencia de nogal. Cajones con taraceas mudéjares y modillones en los montantes. Museo Lázaro Galdeano. Madrid

423. Credence in walnut. Drawers with Mudejar inlay and brackets on the stiles. Lázaro Galdeano Museum. Madrid

424. Credencia de nogal con modillones en los montantes verticales y cuatro cajones. Hospital de Afuera. Toledo

424. Credence in walnut with modillions on the stiles and with four drawers. Afuera Hospital. Toledo

425. Credencia de nogal muy restaurada. Museo Lázaro Galdeano. Madrid

425. Walnut credence, extensively restored. Lázaro Galdeano Museum. Madrid

426. Bargueño de tipo granadino. Caja superior con decoración de hueso

426. Granada type "bargueño". Upper section with bone decoration

427. Bargueño tipo Carlos V, en nogal sobre taquillón con la tapa abatida. Hospital de Afuera. Toledo

427. Carlos V type "bargueño" in walnut, on cabinet with the door lowered. Afuera Hospital. Toledo

428. Taquillón o credencia de nogal tallado. Museo Arqueológico Nacional. Madrid

428. Credence in carved walnut. Archaeological Museum. Madrid

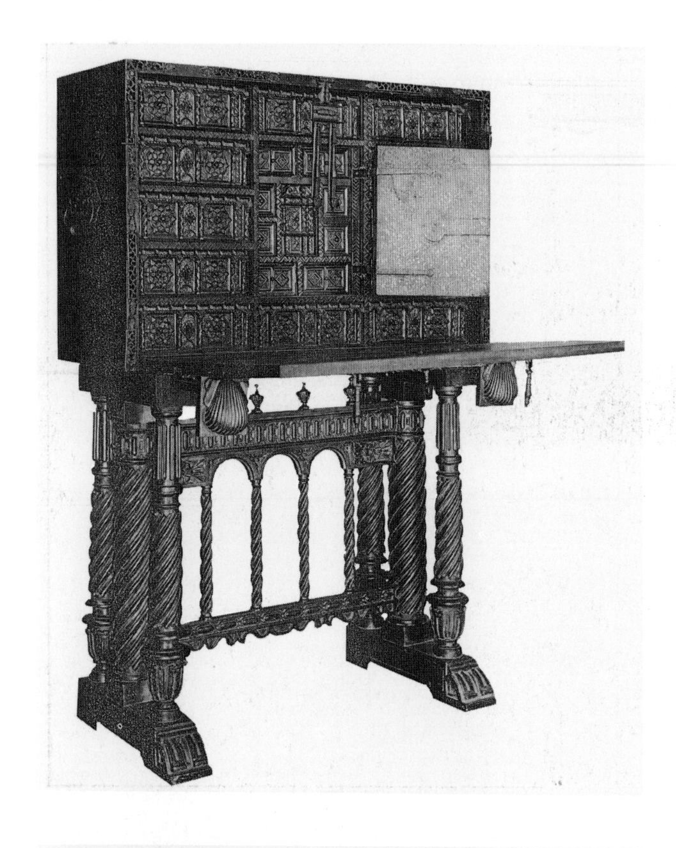

429. Bargueño de pie de puente de nogal con la puerta abatida. Interior con cajones tallados y policromados. Conde de las Almenas

429. Walnut "bargueño" on stand with arcaded stretcher, with the door lowered. Interior with carved and polychromed doors. Conde las Almenas

430. Bargueño tipo Carlos V de nogal sobre mesa tallada y patas con fiadores

430. Carlos V type walnut "bargueño" on carved table and legs with stretchers

431. Bargueño de pie de puente con el frente interior de nogal. Tapa abatida

431. "Bargueño" on stand with arcaded stretcher, with the inner front in walnut. Door lowered

432. Bargueño de pie de puente con el frente de nogal. Hierros calados sobre terciopelo rojo

432. Secretary on bridged legs with walnut front. Iron openwork over red velvet

433. Bargueño con decoración tallada y dorada gótico-mudéjar. Museo Lázaro Galdeano. Madrid

433. Secretary with Gothic-Mudejar carved and gilt decoration. Lázaro Galdeano Museum. Madrid

434. Bargueño de pie de puente, dorado y policromado. Museo Lázaro Galdeano. Madrid

434. Secretary on bridged legs, gilt and polychromed. Lázaro Galdeano Museum. Madrid

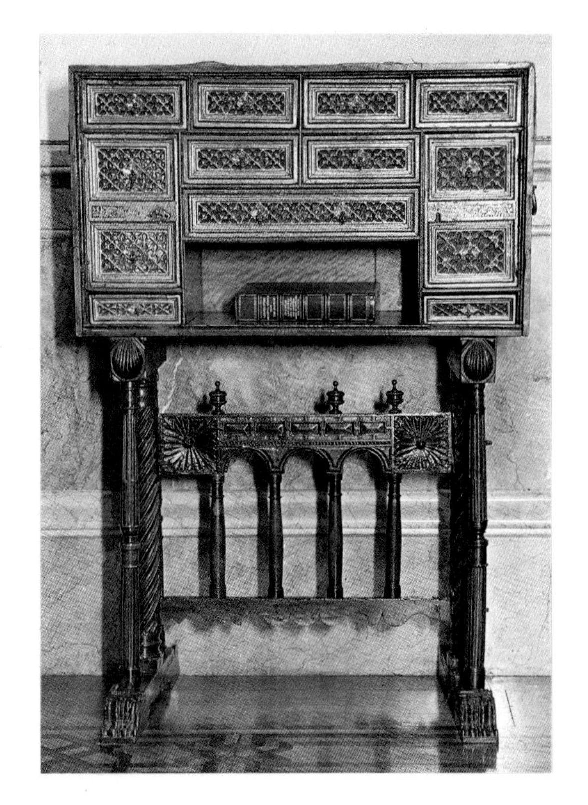

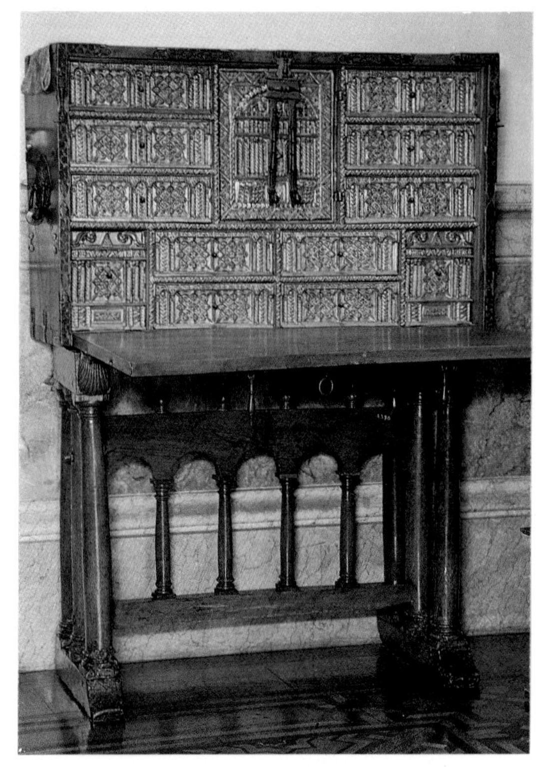

435. Armario finamente tallado con madera de nogal, existente en la sacristía de la Catedral de Huesca. Siglo XVI

435. Cupboard with fine walnut carving, in the sacristy of Huesca Cathedral. XVI century

436. Bargueño de taquillón sin la puerta. Ejemplar muy característico con tallas doradas y policromadas

436. "Bargueño" and cabinet without door. A very characteristic example with gilded and polychromed carvings

437. Bargueño de pie de puente abierto con tallas de boj. En la cajonería la tapa se eleva y va tallada interiormente

437. "Bargueño" on stand with arcaded stretcher, in the open position, with boxwood carvings. In the drawers section the flap, with carving on the inner face, can be raised

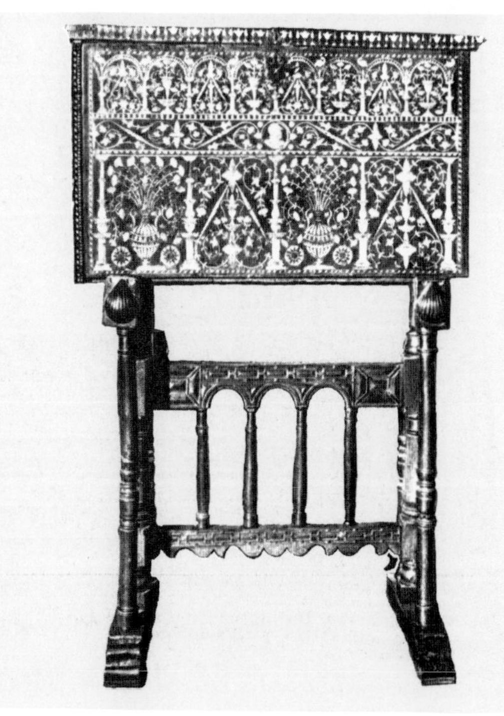

438. Bargueño sin tapa sobre mesa con fiadores, dorado y policromado. Tallas a bisel muy populares

438. "Bargueño" without door, on table with iron stretchers, gilded and polycromed. Very popular chamfer carvings

439. Bargueño de pie de puente sin tapa, taraceado. Museo Valencia de Don Juan. Madrid

439. "Bargueño" on stand with arcaded stretcher, without door: inlay work. Valencia de Don Juan Museum. Madrid

440. Bargueño con frente de cajonería con taraceas de hueso. Dibujos populares

440. "Bargueño". Drawer fronts with bone inlay. Popular designs

441. Bargueño con decoración mudéjar tallada y dorada. Caja superior sin tapa. Museo de Artes Decorativas. Madrid

441. "Bargueño" with Mudejar carving and gilded decoration. Upper section without cover. Museum of Decorative Arts. Madrid

442. Bargueño con frente de cajonería con tallas planas vermiculares

442. "Bargueño". Drawer fronts with vermicular flat carvings

443. Bargueño. Caja superior sin tapa: trabajo popular dorado y tallado con elementos de hueso

443. "Bargueño". Upper section without cover: popular gilded and carved work with bone elements

444. Bargueño. Frente de cajonería de influencia italiana

444. "Bargueño". Drawer fronts with Italian influence

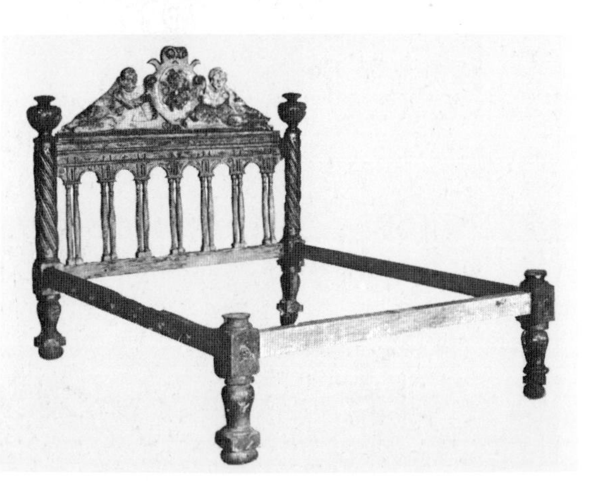

445. Cama popular de la región toledana. Colección particular

445. Popular bed of the Toledo region. Private Collection

446. Cama de influencia italiana

446. Bed with Italian influence

447. Cama de Isabel Clara Eugenia. Colgaduras bordadas sobre un esqueleto de madera. Habitaciones del palacio del Escorial

447. Bed of Isabel Clara Eugenia. Embroidered hangings on a wooden frame work. Rooms of the palace of the Escorial

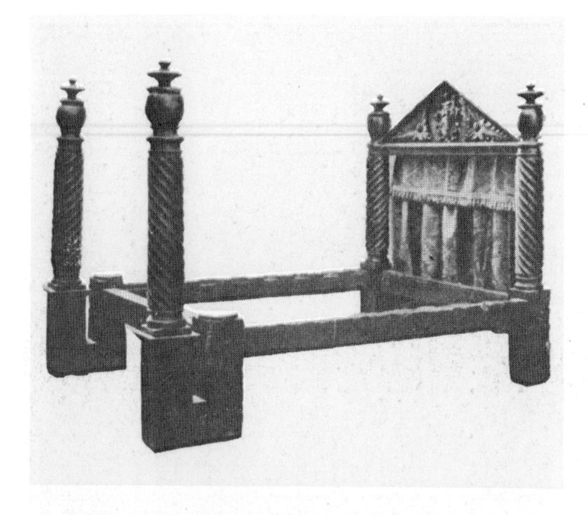

448. Cama renacentista herreriana

448. Renaissance bed. Herrera's style

449. Cama renacentista herreriana

449. Renaissance bed. Herrera's style

450. Comedor. Palacio de Tavera. Hospital de Afuera. Toledo

450. Dining-room. Palacio de Tavera. Afuera Hospital. Toledo

451. Habitaciones de Felipe II. Palacio del Escorial

451. Rooms of Philip II. Palace of the Escorial

452. Salón del trono. Restaurado a principios de siglo. Habitaciones de Felipe II. El Escorial

452. Throne Room. Restored at the beginning of the century. Rooms of Philip II. El Escorial

453. Habitaciones de Isabel Clara Eugenia. Palacio del Escorial

453. Rooms of Isabel Clara Eugenia. Palace of the Escorial

454. Cama de hierro forjado. Museo de Cau-Ferrat. Sitges. Barcelona

454. Forged iron bedstead. Cau-Ferrat Museum. Sitges. Barcelona

455. Biblioteca del Escorial proyectada por J. de Herrera

455. Library of the Escorial, projected by J. de Herrera

456. Detalle. Biblioteca del Escorial

456. Detail. Library of the Escorial

457. Cama de madera tallada, dorada y policromada. Museo de Artes Decorativas. Madrid

457. Bed of carved wood, gilded and polychromed. Museum of Decorative Arts. Madrid

458. Ambiente de la casa de Lope de Vega. Madrid

458. View of the inside of Lope de Vega's house. Madrid

459. Interior de un salón renacentista con chimenea y yesería plateresca. Palacio del marqués de Peñaranda. Córdoba

459. Interior of a Renaissance room with a chimney illustrating plateresque plastering. Palace of the Marquis of Peñaranda. Cordova

460. Sitial de transición con tallas góticas y renacentistas

460. Presiding chair, transitional period, with Gothic and Renaissance carving

461. Sitial renacentista con estructura vertical aún gótica

461. Presiding chair. Renaissance lines with vertical structure still in the Gothic style

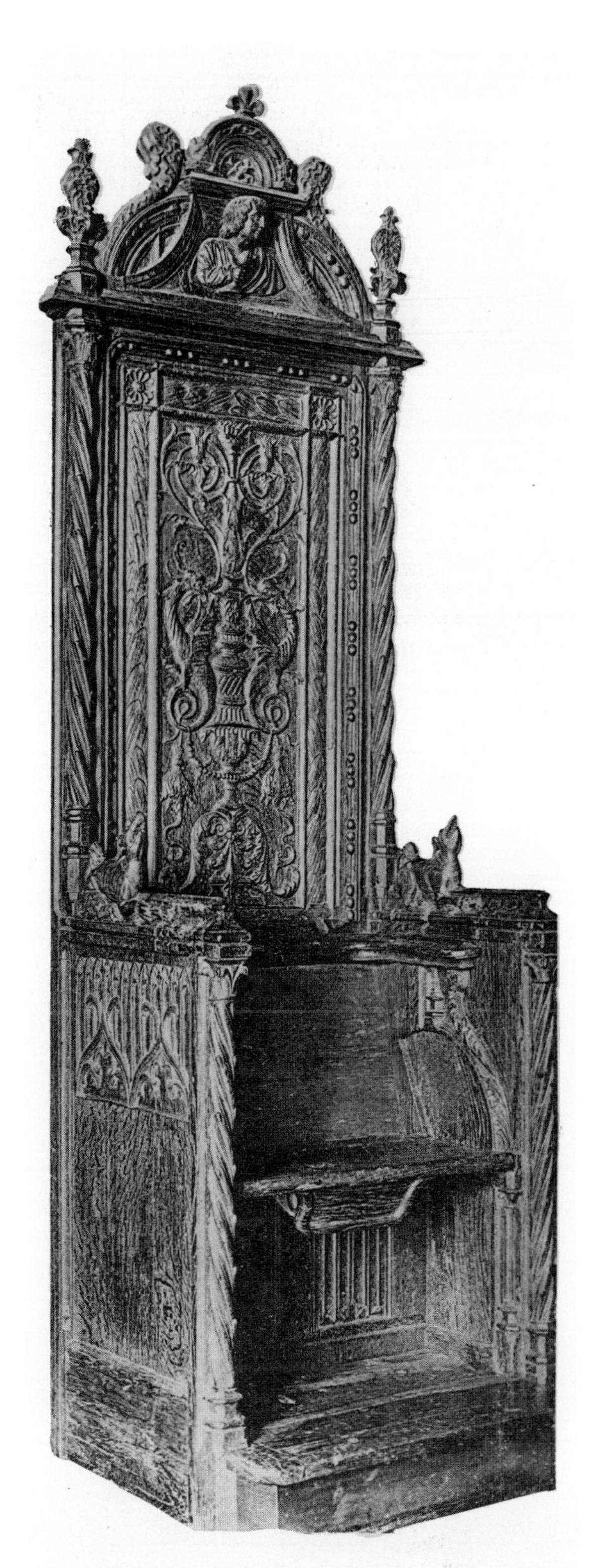

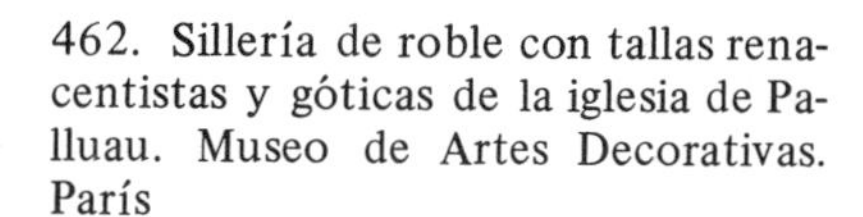

462. Sillería de roble con tallas renacentistas y góticas de la iglesia de Palluau. Museo de Artes Decorativas. París

462. Sedilia in oak with Renaissance and Gothic carvings. Palluau Church. Museum of Decorative Arts. Paris

463. Sillón de cadera, plegable, de nogal

463. Folding walnut X chair

464. Sillón "caqueteusse". Siglo XVI

464. "Caqueteusse" armchair. XVI century

465. Sillón "caqueteusse". Siglo XVI

465. "Caqueteusse" armchair. XVI century

466. Silla plegable de tipo italiano. Principios del siglo XVI

466. Italian type folding chair. Early 16 th century

467. "Caqueteusse" de nogal. Museo del Louvre. París

467. "Caqueteusse" in walnut. Louvre. París

468. Sillón renacentista tipo "Francisco I", con tallas de influencia italiana

468. Renaissance armchair, "Francis I" type; carving with Italian influence

469. Sillón "caqueteusse". Siglo XVI

469. "Caqueteusse" armchair. XVI century

470. Sillón de nogal con incrustaciones de ébano y cajón bajo el asiento. Museo del Louvre. París

470. Armchair in walnut with ebony incrustation and a drawer under the seat. Louvre. Paris

471. Sillas con tapas cruzadas "de tijera"

471. X-shaped chair

472. Silla popular con arquerías de influencia italiana

472. Popular chair, arcading with Italian influence

473. Sillón "caqueteusse", en roble. Museo Cluny. París

473. "Caqueteusse" armchair in oak. Cluny Museum. Paris

474. Banco-arcón de roble, de 175 de largo, 100 de alto y 58 de fondo

474. Box-bench in oak; 175 length, 100 height and 58 depth

475. 476. 477. 478. Mesas. Dibujo de costados de mesas por Ducerceau

475. 476. 477. 478. Tables. Drawing of table sides by Ducerceau

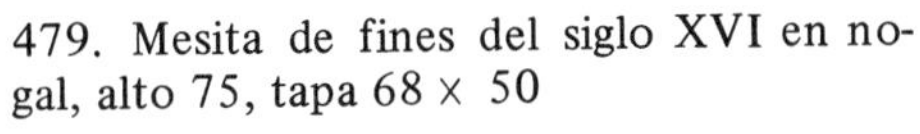

479. Mesita de fines del siglo XVI en nogal, alto 75, tapa 68 × 50

479. Small walnut table, late 16th century; height 75, top 68 × 50

480. Mesa de roble con tallas renacentistas de influencia italiana. Museo Lázaro Galdeano. Madrid

480. Oak table, Renaissance carving with Italian influence. Lázaro Galdeano Museum. Madrid

481. Mesa de influencia italiana. 80 de alto, 115 de largo y 75 de ancho

481. Table with Italian influence; height 80, length 115 and width 75

482. Mesa a la italiana, 88 de alto, 148 de largo y 55 de ancho. Siglo XVI

482. Table in the Italian style; height 88, length 148 and width 75

483. Mesa. Dibujo de Ducerceau

483. Table. Drawing by Ducerceau

484. Mesas circulares de influencia italiana. Esquema por Ducerceau

484. Round tables with Italian influence. Drawing by Ducerceau

485. Arcón de nogal. Alto 68, largo 130 y ancho 55

485. Large walnut chest. Height 68, length 130 and width 55

486. Arcón de roble con tallas muy primitivas. 75 alto, 155 largo, 65 ancho

486. Large chest in oak with primitive carvings. Height 75, length 155 and width 65

487. Arcón de roble con tallas renacentistas y góticas. Principios del siglo XVI. 85 de alto, 162 de largo y 70 de ancho

487. Oak chest with Renaissance and Gothic carvings. Early 16th century. Height 85, length 162 and width 70

488. Arcón lyonés. Alto 73, largo 135 y ancho 55. Segunda mitad del siglo XVI.

488. Lyonnais chest. Height 73, length 135 and width 55. Second half 16th century

489. Cofre decorado con alegorías. 80 cm de altura, 160 de largo y 62 de ancho. Finales del siglo XVI

489. Coffer decorated with allegories. Height 80, length 160, width 62. Late 16th century

490. Armario de nogal de dos cuerpos tallados, coronado por un frontón quebrado. Alto 215, ancho 110. Mediados del siglo XVI

490. Walnut cupboard in two stages with broken pediment. Height 215, width 110. Mid-16th century

491. Armario de roble de dos cuerpos. Escuela lyonesa. 117 de alto, 115 de ancho y 50 de fondo

491. Oak cupboard in two sections. Lyons school. Height 117, width 155 and depth 50

492. Armario. Parte superior. Alto 76, largo 113 y ancho 37. Siglo XVI

492. Cupboard. Upper part. Height 76, length 113 and width 37. XVI century

493. Armario de nogal de dos cuerpos con tallas vermiculares. 200 de alto y 133 de ancho. Escuela lionesa

493. Walnut cupboard in two sections, with vermicular carvings. Height 200 and width 133. Lyons school

494. Armario de dos cuerpos. 156 de alto y 110 de frente. Fines del siglo XVI

494. Cupboard in two sections, late 16th century. Height 156, front 110

495. Armario de dos cuerpos decorado con marquetería. 205 de alto y 121 de ancho. Finales del siglo XVI

495. Cupboard in two sections, decorated with marquetry. Height 205 and width 121. End 16th century

496. Armario de nogal de dos cuerpos con frontón partido. Siglo XVI. Museo de Artes Decorativas. París

496. Walnut cupboard in two sections, with broken pediment. XVI century. Museum of Decorative Arts. Paris

497. Armario de dos cuerpos coronado por frontón curvo quebrado. Clairveaux. Arte bourguignon del siglo XVI. Museo de Cluny

497. Oak cupboard in two stages with curved broken pediment. Clairveaux. Bourguignon art of the 16th century. Cluny Museum

498. Armario de roble de dos cuerpos profusamente tallados. Museo de Artes Decorativas. París

498. Oak cupboard in two stages, profusely carved. Museum of Decorative Arts. Paris

499. Armario de nogal de la época de Enrique IV. Cuerpo elevado sobre consola. 191 de altura y 110 de ancho. Principios del siglo XVII. Museo de Artes Decorativas. París

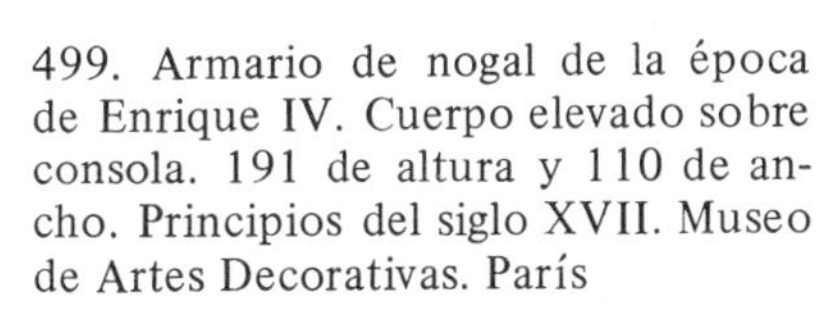

499. Walnut cupboard of Henry IV period. Section raised on a console table. Height 191, width 110. Early 17th century. Museum of Decorative Arts. Paris

500. Armario de madera tallada. Cariátides y figuras grotescas. Museo del Louvre. París. Atribuido a Hugues Sambin

500. Carved wooden closet. Caryatids and grotesque figures. The Louvre, Paris. Attributed to Hugues Sambin

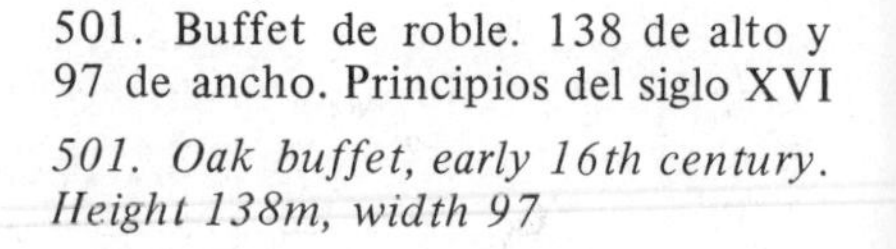

501. Buffet de roble. 138 de alto y 97 de ancho. Principios del siglo XVI

501. Oak buffet, early 16th century. Height 138m, width 97

502. Cama. Dibujo por Ducerceau

502. Bed. Drawing by Ducerceau

503. Buffet-dressoir en nogal. Escuela de Auvernia. 172 de alto y 151 de ancho

503. Dresser-buffet in walnut. Auvergne school. Height 172, width 151

504. Cama renacentista de estilo Ducerceau. Museo de Cluny. París

504. Renaissance bed in the Ducerceau taste. Cluny Museum. Paris

505. Cama de Jeanne d'Albret. Castillo de Pau

505. Bed of Jeanne d'Albret. Pau Castle

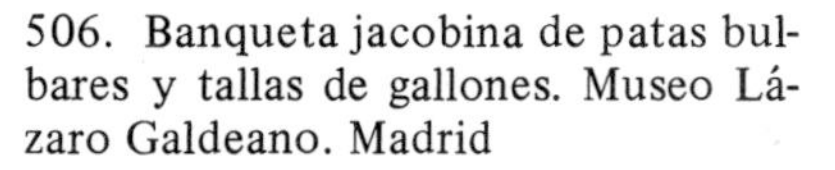

506. Banqueta jacobina de patas bulbares y tallas de gallones. Museo Lázaro Galdeano. Madrid

506. Jacobean stool with bulb supports and carved lunette decoration. Lázaro Galdeano Museum. Madrid

507. Sillón de Glawstombury, plegable, en roble, de influencia italiana. Hacia 1570. Victoria and Albert Museum. Londres

507. Folding armchair of Glawstonbury, in oak with Italian influence, c. 1570. Victoria and Albert Museum

508. Banqueta de tijera completamente tapizada de terciopelo claveteado. Knole Park, Kent. Hacia 1610

508. X-shaped stool completely upholstered in velvet garnished with nails; Knole Park, Kent. C. 1610

509. Sillón tipo "caqueteusse" francés. Hacia 1575. Castillo Hever, Kent

509. Armchair of the French "caqueteusse" type, c. 1575. Hever Castle, Kent

510. Sillón de cadera completamente tapizado con terciopelos claveteados, del arzobispo Juxon, llamado sillón de Carlos I. Principios del siglo XVII. Westminster Hall

510. X-shaped armchair, completely upholstered in velvet garnished with nails, of Archbishop Juxon, called the chair of Charles I. Early 17th century. Westminster Hall

511. Sillón de roble con marquetería en el respaldo. Hacia 1600. Victoria and Albert Museum. Londres

511. Oak armchair with marquetry on the back, c. 1600. Victoria and Albert Museum

512. Sillón de Derbyshire, de roble. Hacia 1655. Colección de C. G. Stirling

512. Derbyshire armchair in oak, c. 1655. C. G. Stirling Collection

513. Sillón con marqueterías en el respaldo. Hacia 1555. Castillo Hornby

513. Armchair with marquetry on the back, c. 1555. Hornby Castle

514. Sillón de respaldo abatible para hacerlo mesa. Tallas vermiculares. Epoca jacobina

514. Armchair with back which drops down to form a table. Vermicular carving. Jacobean period

515. Sofá en terciopleo rojo con los brazos abatibles. Hacia 1610. Knole Park, Kent

515. Setee in red velvet, with drop-wings, c. 1610. Knole Park, Kent

516. Sofá con orejeras abatibles en terciopelo rojo. Hacia 1610. Knole Park, Kent

516. Settee in red velvet, with drop-wings, c. 1610. Knole Park, Kent

517. Sofá de nogal. Hacia 1660. Colección M. F. Mallet

517. Walnut settee, c. 1660. M. F. Mallet Collection

518. Pata Elizabethan de mesa de roble. Hacia 1605. Victoria and Albert Museum. Londres

518. Elizabethan type leg, oak table, c. 1605. Victoria and Albert Museum

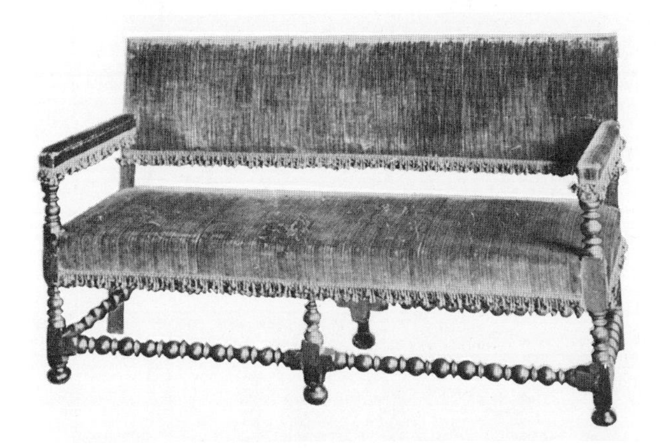

519. Mesa de roble semioctogonal ampliable, tipo jacobino. Mr. Fredskull

519. Jacobean type semi-octagonal gate-leg. Mr. Fredskull

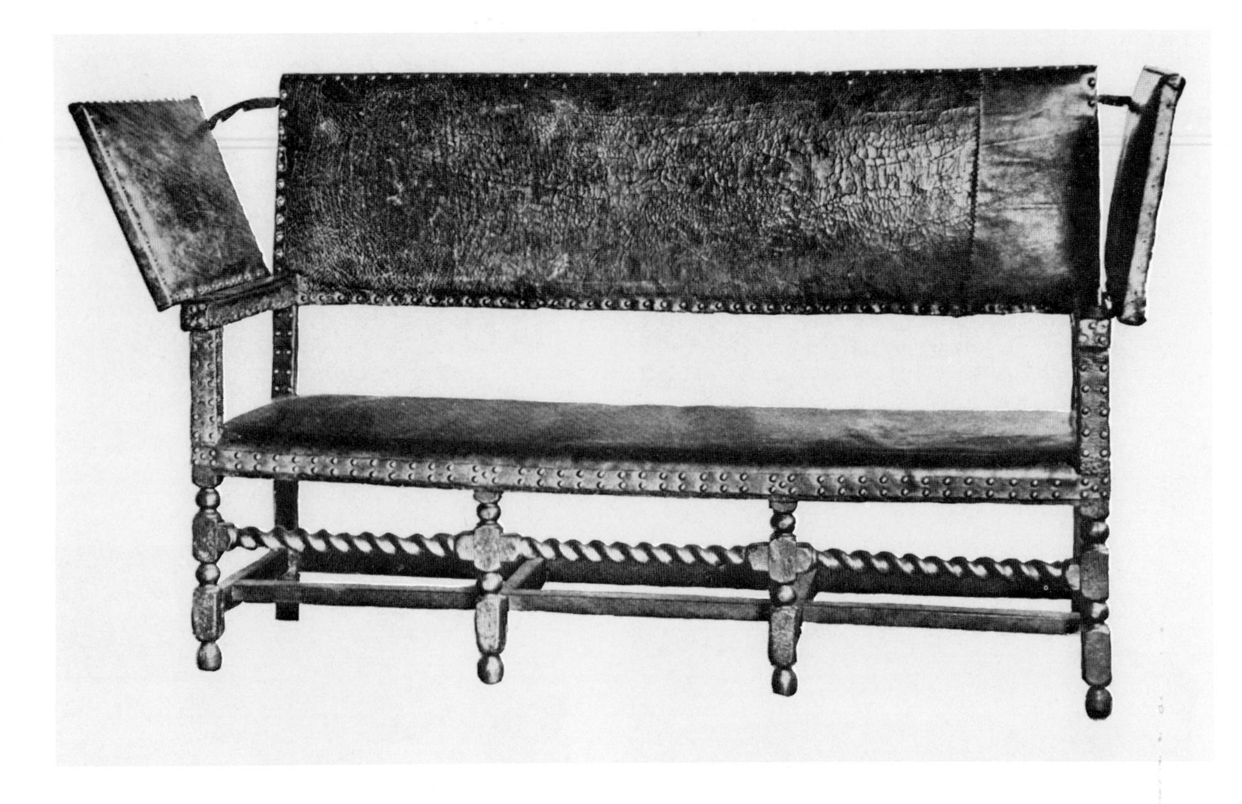

520. Sofá estilo jacobino de roble con costados abatibles, tapizado en cuero. Hacia 1660

520. Jacobean style settee in oak, with drop-sides, upholstered in leather, c. 1660

521. Aparador "dressoir", tipo jacobino. Hacia 1660

521. Jacobean type dresser-sideboard, c. 1660

522. Mesa de refectorio, de roble, taraceada en el faldón. Hacia 1630. Colección F.M. Leggeh

522. Oak refectory table, with inlay on the apron piece, c. 1630. F. M. Leggeh Collection

523. Mesita con patas plegables y tablero abatible tipo popular. Hacia 1660. Westwood Manor Wilts

523. Small gate-leg table with folding leaf, popular type, c. 1660. Westwood Manor Wilts

524. Arca de roble con tallas vermiculares. Firmado por E.B. en 1662. Ockwells

524. Oak chest with vermicular carving. Signed E. B. in 1662. Ockwells

529. Clavico
ward, de robl
Londres, 162

529. Clavicho
in oak with ve
don, 1622. Kr

525. Arcón de roble renacentista con tallas primitivas y estructura aún gótica. Hacia 1535. Victoria and Albert Museum. Londres

525. Renaissance chest in oak with primitive carving and structure still in the Gothic style, c. 1535. Victoria and Albert Museum

526. Arcón de roble con marquetería, escudos del Lord Mayor de Londres y arabescos de influencia italiana, hacia 1580. Catedral de Southwark

526. Oak chest with marquetry, arms of the Lord Mayor of London, arabesques with Italian influence, c. 1580. Southwark Cathedral

530. Virginal
Hacia 1641. C

530. Virginal,
1641. Brussel

561. Armario de Nuremberg con molduras rizadas. Hacia 1630

561. Cupboard, Nuremberg, with looped mouldings, c. 1630

562. Armario de Nuremberg con tallas planas. Mitad del siglo XVI

562. Cupboard of Nuremberg with flat carving, mid-16th century

563. Armario buffet con taraceas y tallas. Hacia 1600. Museo Rheydt. Colonia

563. Buffet-cupboard decorated with inlay and carvings, c. 1600. Rheydt Museum. Cologne

564. Armario cabinet de estilo Renacimiento; composición arquitectónica en madera de nogal con marqueterías Siglo XVI. Museo de Artes Decorativas. Madrid

564. Cabinet-cupboard in the Renaissance style: architectural composition in walnut with marquetry. XVI century. Museum of Decorative Arts. Madrid

565. Armario marqueteado. Siglo XVI. Colonia

565. Chest with marquetry decoration. XVI century. Cologne

566. Cama con baldaquino taraceada de influencia italiana. Hacia 1610

566. Bed with canopy, inlay decoration with Italian influence, c. 1610

567. Arcón de influencia francesa. Museo de Colonia

567. Chest with French influence. Cologne Museum

568. Arca de influencia hispano-italiana. Schlossmuseum. Berlín

568. Chest with Spanish-Italian influence. Schlossmuseum. Berlin

569. Arcón marqueteado y molduras rizadas. Museo de Flensburgo

569. Chest with marquetry and looped moulding. Late Renaissance. Flensburg Museum

570. Interior de Lucas Granach. Siglo XVI

570. Interior by Lucas Granach. XVI century

571. Arqueta de Pomerania. Augsburgo. 1617. Museo de Berlín

571. Small chest of Pomerania. Augsburg. 1617. Berlin Museum

572. Credencia con estructura gótica y decoración renacentista. 1540. Colonia

572. Credence of Gothic structure with Renaissance decoration. 1540. Cologne

573. Interior del Museo de Neldorf-Holstein. 1568

573. Interior of the Neldorf-Holstein Museum. 1568

574. Puerta de marquetería, regalo del emperador Maximiliano a Felipe II. 1567. Palacio del Escorial

574. Door with marquetry decoration, a gift from Emperor Maximilian to Philip II. 1567. Palace of the Escorial

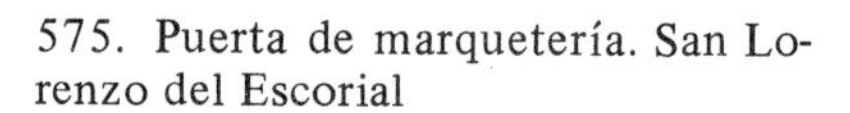

575. Puerta de marquetería. San Lorenzo del Escorial

575. Door with marquetry decoration. San Lorenzo del Escorial

576. Puerta de marquetería. Interior del Salón del Trono. Palacio del Escorial

576. Door with marquetry decoration. Interior of the Throne Room. Palace of the Escorial

577. 578. Detalles de las puertas anteriores

577. 578. Details of the preceding doors

579. Sillón de nogal con patas salomónicas y tallas. Principios del siglo XVI. Museo del Cincuentenario. Bruselas

579. Walnut armchair with twist-turned legs and carvings. Early 16th century. Jubilee Museum. Brussels

580. Sillón popular de pino. Colección Claes. Amberes

580. Popular chair in pine. Claes Collection. Antwerp

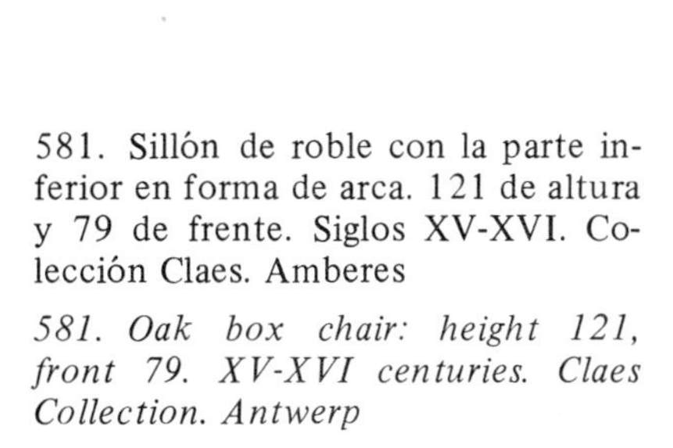

581. Sillón de roble con la parte inferior en forma de arca. 121 de altura y 79 de frente. Siglos XV-XVI. Colección Claes. Amberes

581. Oak box chair: height 121, front 79. XV-XVI centuries. Claes Collection. Antwerp

582. Sillón de nogal tallado forrado de terciopelo. 122 de alto y 58 de frente. Mitad del siglo XVII. Museo del Cincuentenario. Bruselas

582. Carved walnut armchair, upholstered in velvet. Height 122, front 58. Mid-17th century. Jubilee Museum. Brussels

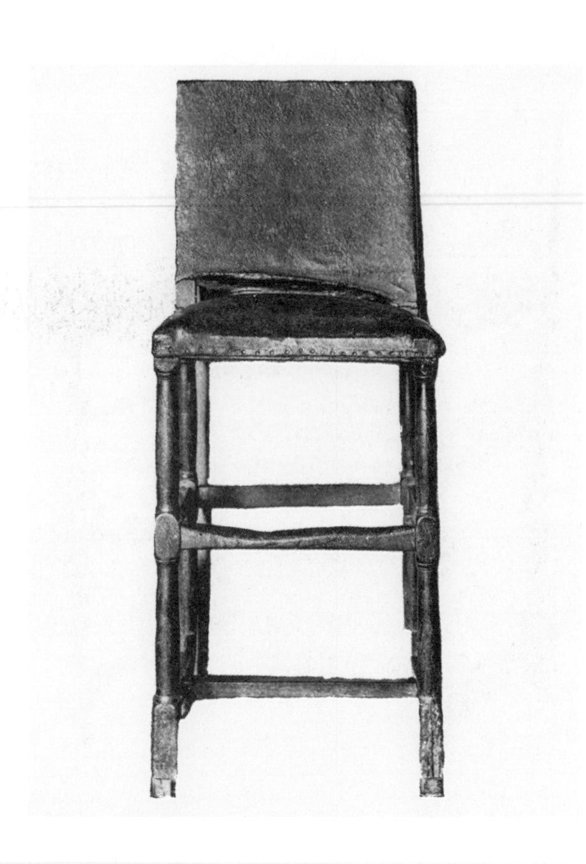

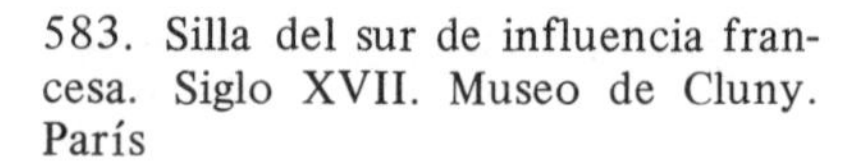

583. Silla del sur de influencia francesa. Siglo XVII. Museo de Cluny. París

583. Chair of the south, with French influence. XVII century. Cluny Museum. Paris

584. Silla de nogal de asiento alto. Rijksmuseum. Amsterdam

584. Walnut chair with high seat. Rijksmuseum. Amsterdam

585. Mesa de roble con patas bulbares y tableros deslizantes. 128 × 21 y 82 de altura. Principios del siglo XVII. Museo del Cincuentenario. Bruselas

585. Oak draw table with bulb supports. 128 × 81, height 82. Early 17th century. Jubilee Museum. Brussels

586. Mesa de nogal tallado de influencia francesa. 152 × 84, altura 82. Museo del Cincuentenario. Bruselas

586. Carved walnut table with French influence. 152 × 84, height 82. Jubilee Museum

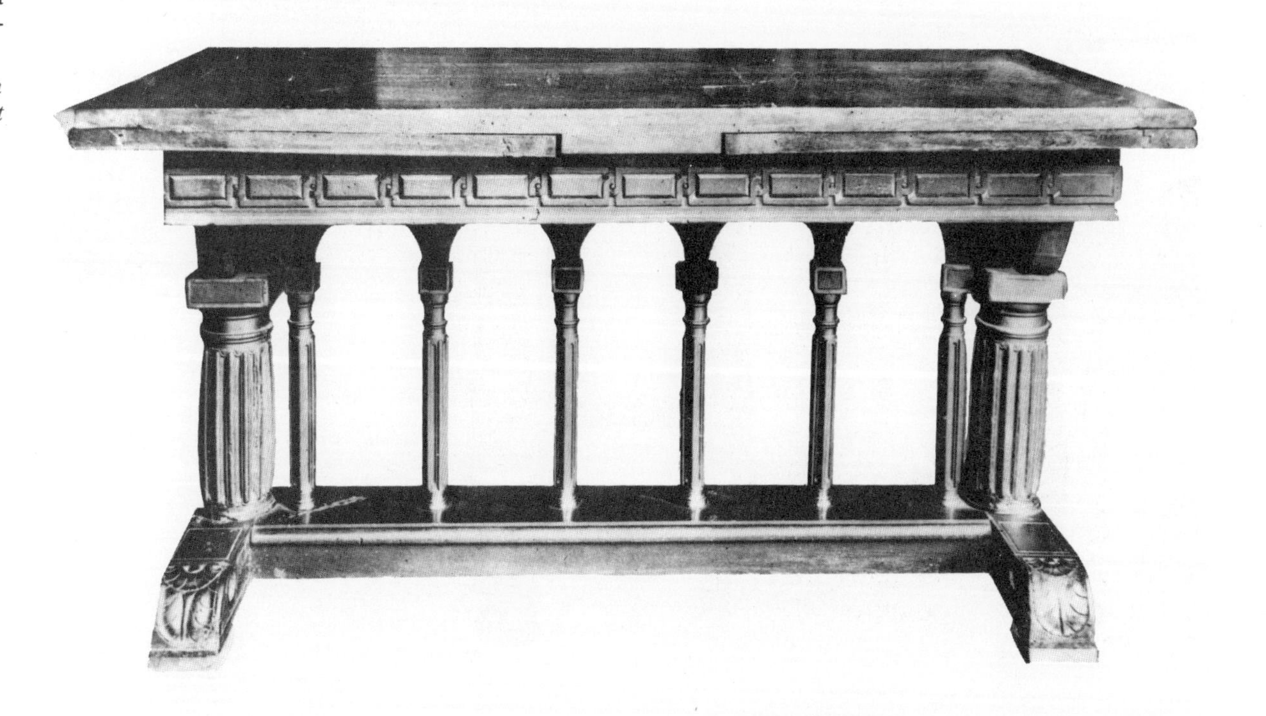

587. Mesa de nogal de patas torneadas en forma de bulbo. Siglo XVI. Amberes

587. Walnut table with turned bulb supports. XVI century. Antwerp

588. Mesa con tableros abatibles. Siglo XVII. Colección Claes. Amberes

588. Table with drop-flaps. XVII century. Claes Collection. Antwerp

589. Aparador-bahut de roble con tallas vermiculares y tableros con cuarterones. Siglo XVII. Museo Plantin. Amberes

589. Bahut-sideboard in oak with vermicular carvings and door panels. XVII century. Plantin Museum. Antwerp

590. Cabinet decorado con pinturas, sobre mesa con patas torneadas. 160 alto y 220 frente (con puertas abiertas). Principios del siglo XVII. Alcaldía de Bailleul

590. Cabinet decorated with paintings, on a stand with turned legs. Height 160, front 220 (with doors open). Early 17th century. Town Hall of Bailleul

591. Chimenea de madera tallada por Lancelot Blondeel. 1529-31. Palacio de Justicia de Brujas

591. Fireplace in carved wood by Lancelot Blondeel. 1529-31. Palace of Justice. Bruges

592. Armario de roble tallado. 220 altura y 76 de frente. Principios del siglo XVI. Hospital de Lierre

592. Carved oak cupboard. Height 220, front 76. Early 16th century. Lierre Hospital

593. Armario de roble de Valenciennes; 225 de alto y 146 de frente. Principios del siglo XVII. Colección de Thibeau-Motte. Roubaix

593. Oak cupboard of Valenciennes. Height 225, front 146. Early 17th century. Thibeau-Motte Collection. Roubaix

594. Cama. Siglo XVII. Museo Plantin. Amberes

594. Bed. XVII century. Plantin Museum. Antwerp

595. Cama con techo y costados de madera. Principios del siglo XVII. Colección Claes. Amberes

595. Bed with tester and sides in wood. Early 17th century. Claes Collection. Antwerp

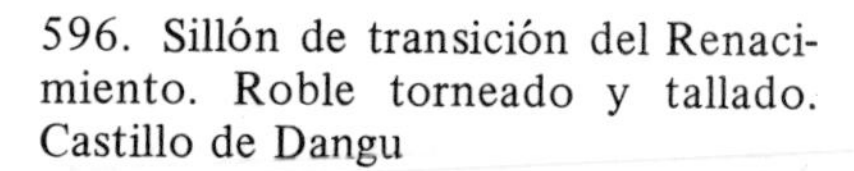

596. Sillón de transición del Renacimiento. Roble torneado y tallado. Castillo de Dangu

596. Armchair, transition from the Renaissance. Turned and carved oak. Dangu Castle

597. Sillón con elementos torneados y tapicería de cuero repujado. Transición del Renacimiento

597. Armchair with twist-turned elements and repoussé leather upholstery. Transition from the Renaissance

598. Sillón con asiento y respaldo de rejilla. Roble tallado y elementos salomónicos

598. Armchair with cane seat and back: carved oak and twist-turned elements

599. Sillón con asiento y respaldo de rejilla. Patas y ménsulas de los brazos características en forma de S y C

599. Armchair with cane seat and back. Characteristic legs and arm brackets in S and C form

600. Banqueta. Con patas salomónicas. Siglo XVII

600. Stool with twist-turned legs. XVII century

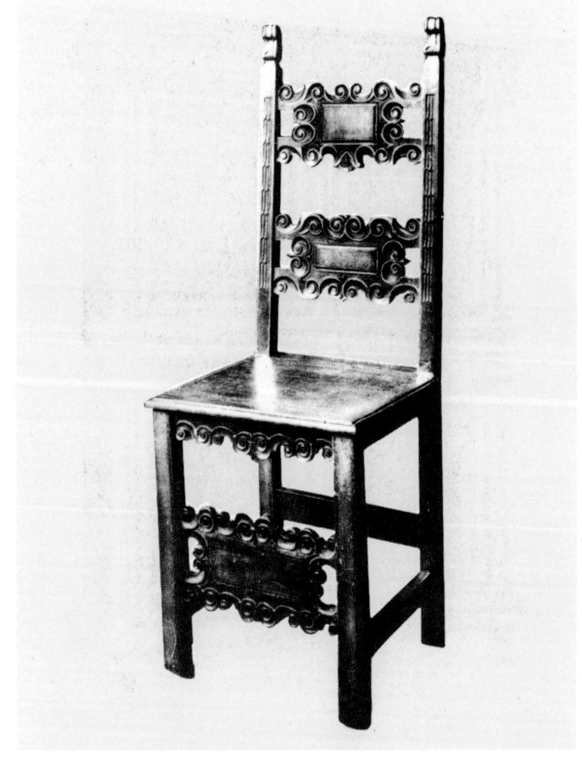

601. Silla de madera tallada. Arte franco-flamenco. De transición. Museo Vieille Boucherie. Amberes

601. Carved oak chair. Franco-Flemish art. Transition period. Vieille Boucherie Museum. Antwerp

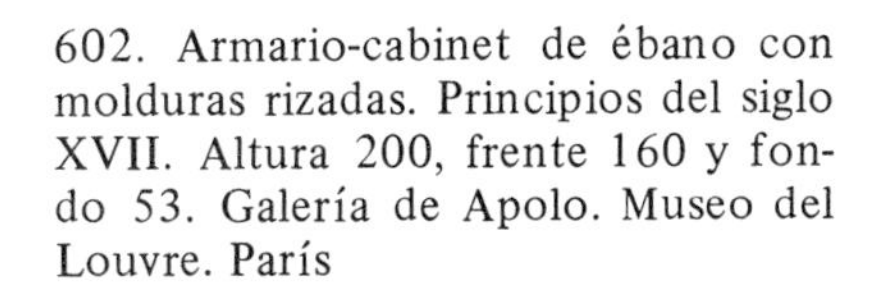

602. Armario-cabinet de ébano con molduras rizadas. Principios del siglo XVII. Altura 200, frente 160 y fondo 53. Galería de Apolo. Museo del Louvre. París

602. Cabinet-cupboard in ebony with looped mouldings. Early 17th century. Height 200, front 160 and depth 53. Apollo Gallery. Louvre. Paris

603. Armario-cabinet de ébano con molduras rizadas. Patas salomónicas. Altura 200, frente 160, fondo 53. Museo de Artes Decorativas París

603. Cabinet-cupboard in ebony with looped mouldings and twist-turned legs. Height 200, front 160, depth 53. Museum of Decorative Arts. Paris

604. Armario de nogal de dos cuerpos. Principios del siglo XVII. Museo de Artes Decorativas. París

604. Walnut cupboard in two stages. Early 17th century. Museum of Decorative Arts. Paris

605. Armario Luis XIII estilo de Gascuña decorado con puntas de diamante-roble. Colección particular. Murcia

605. Louis XIII cupboard in the Gascony style, with oak lozenge decoration. Private Collection. Murcia

606. Armario de ébano. Principios siglo XVII. Museo Lázaro Galdeano. Madrid

606. Ebony cupboard. Early 17th century. Lázaro Galdeano Museum. Madrid

607. Detalle del armario precedente. Frente de una puerta

607. Detail of the preceding cupboard. A door front

608. Armario de dos cuerpos y cuatro puertas. Transición. Alto 190, frente 140

608. Cupboard in two sections and four doors. Transition. Height 190, front 140

609. Interior del siglo XVII. Grabado por Abraham Bosse

609. 17th-century interior. Engraving by Abraham Bosse

610. Interior del siglo XVII por Abraham Bosse, "El tacto"

610. 17th-century interior. "Le Touche" by Abraham Bosse

611. Cabinet Luis XIII atribuido a A. Boulle; las aplicaciones de concha y plata. Propiedad de Mrs. T. Nichols

611. Louis XIII cabinet attributed to A. Boulle; appliqués in coquillage and silver. Owned by Mrs. T. Nichols

612. Interior del siglo XVII. "El invierno", por Abraham Bosse

612. 17th-century interior. "Winter" by Abraham Bosse

613. Interior del siglo XVII. "La vista" por Abraham Bosse

613. 17th-century interior. "The view" by Abraham Bosse

BARROCO

BAROQUE

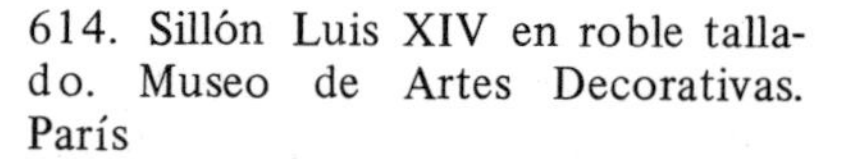

614. Sillón Luis XIV en roble tallado. Museo de Artes Decorativas. París

614. Louis XIV armchair in carved oak. Museum of Decorative Arts. Paris

615. Sillón Luis XIV, patas cabriolé y respaldo muy alto con tallas

615. Louis XIV armchair, cabriolet legs and very high back, with carvings

616. Sillón de rejilla. Siglo XVIII. Conchas y ornamentación Luis XIV. Altura 98, frente 61. Altura asiento 42

616. 18th century cane armchair, with shell carving and decoration in the Louis XIV style. Height 98, front 61, seat height 42

617. Sillón Luis XIV de la colección Perrin, madera negra tallada. Museo de Artes Decorativas. París

617. Louis XIV armchair of the Perrin Collection, carved black wood. Museum of Decorative Arts. Paris

618. Sillón con patas cabriolé y conchas talladas Luis XIV, tapicería de terciopelo bordado

618. Louis XIV armchair with cabriolet legs and decorated with coquillage, upholstery of embroidered velvet

619. Silla plegable estilo Regencia. Principio del siglo XVIII. Tallas de "rocalla" simétricas doradas

619. Early 18th-century folding chair in the Regency style. Symmetrical rococo gilded carvings

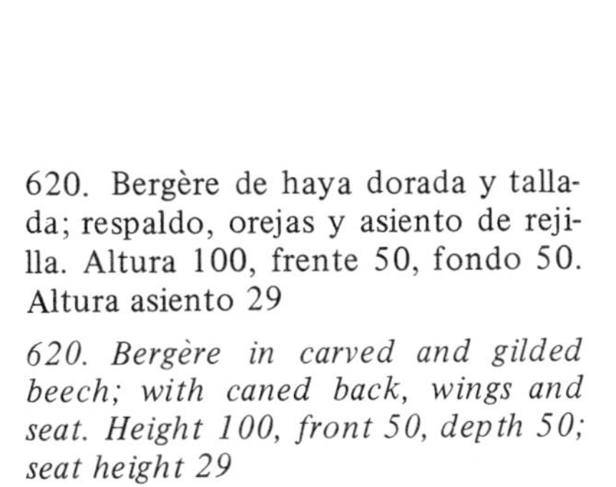

620. Bergère de haya dorada y tallada; respaldo, orejas y asiento de rejilla. Altura 100, frente 50, fondo 50. Altura asiento 29

620. Bergère in carved and gilded beech; with caned back, wings and seat. Height 100, front 50, depth 50; seat height 29

621. Silla Regencia de haya tallada. Principio del siglo XVIII. Almohadones sobre asiento y respaldo de rejilla

621. Early 18th-century Regency armchair in carved beech; cushions on the seat and caned back

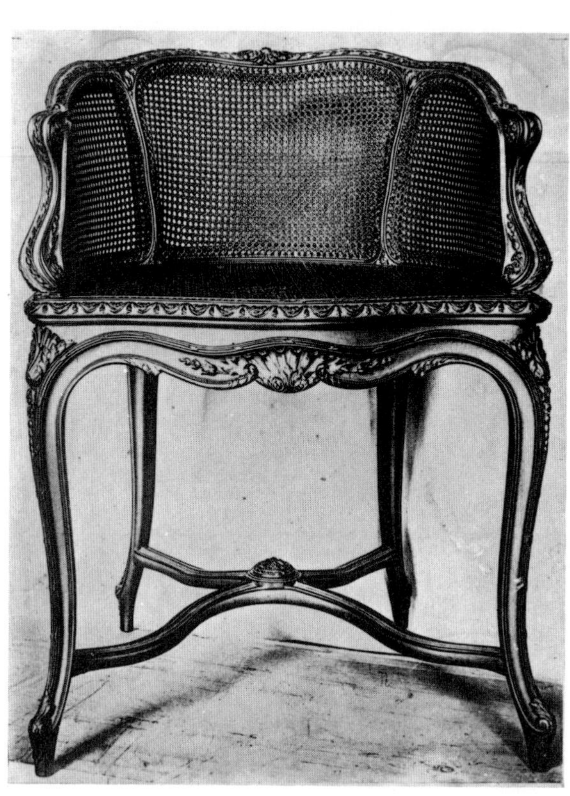

622. Butaquita para peinarse tallada, dorada y tapizada de cuero. Chambranas en X. Altura 75, frente 50, altura asiento 45

622. Toilet-armchair, carved and gilded with leather upholstery. X-form stretchers. Height 75, front 50, seat height 45

623. Silloncito de madera tallada y dorada Luis XV, ejecutada por M. Drouard. Museo de Artes Decorativas. Paris

623. Small armchair in carved and gilded wood in the Louis XV style. Made by M. Drouard. Museum of Decorative Arts. Paris

624. Silla de rejilla Luis XV. Museo de Artes Decorativas. París

624. Louis XV cane chair. Museum of Decorative Arts, Paris

625. Sillón Regencia tallado y dorado. Museo de Artes Decorativas. París

625. Regency armchair, carved and gilded. Museum of Decorative Arts. Paris

626. Sillón de despacho Luis XV. Respaldo en ángulo. Museo de Artes Decorativas. París

626. Louis XV study armchair, with sloping back. Museum of Decorative Arts. Paris

627. Butaca firmada por N. Q. Foliat (1706-1776), transición del Luis XV; dorada y tallada. Museo del Louvre. París

627. Armchair, signed by N. Q. Foliat (1706-1776), transition from Louis XV; carved and gilded. Louvre. Paris

628. Sillón con respaldo "a la reina". Mitad del siglo XVIII; tallado y dorado. Colección Aveline

628. Mid-18th-century armchair with sloping back carved and gilded. Aveline Collection

629. Sillón de madera dorada atribuido a J. B. Tilliard hacia 1750. Colección Niarchos

629. Armchair in gilded wood, attributed to J. B. Tilliard, c. 1750. Niarchos Collection

630. Bergère con orejas época Luis XV. Museo de Artes Decorativas. París

630. Louis XV "bergère" with wings. Museum of Decorative Arts. Paris

631. Silla de rejilla con pata cabriolé de nogal Luis XV. Hacia 1760. Altura 98, altura asiento 60, frente 48

631. Louis XV cane chair, with cabriolet legs, in walnut, c. 1760. Height 98, seat height 60, front 48

632. Bergère finamente tallada y dorada. Fin del siglo XVIII. Colección Seligmann

632. "Bergère", finely carved and gilded. Late 18th century. Seligmann Collection

633. Sillón cabriolé Luis XV. Haya moldurada. Respaldo muy inclinado

633. Lois XV armchair with cabriolet legs, in moulded beechwood; sharply sloping back

634. Silloncito, por J. Gourdin, 1750. Museo de Artes Decorativas. París

634. Small armchair by J. Gourdin, 1750. Museum of Decorative Arts. Paris

635. Sillón tapizado Luis XV. Museo de Artes Decorativas. París

635. Louis XV upholstered armchair. Museum of Decorative Arts. Paris

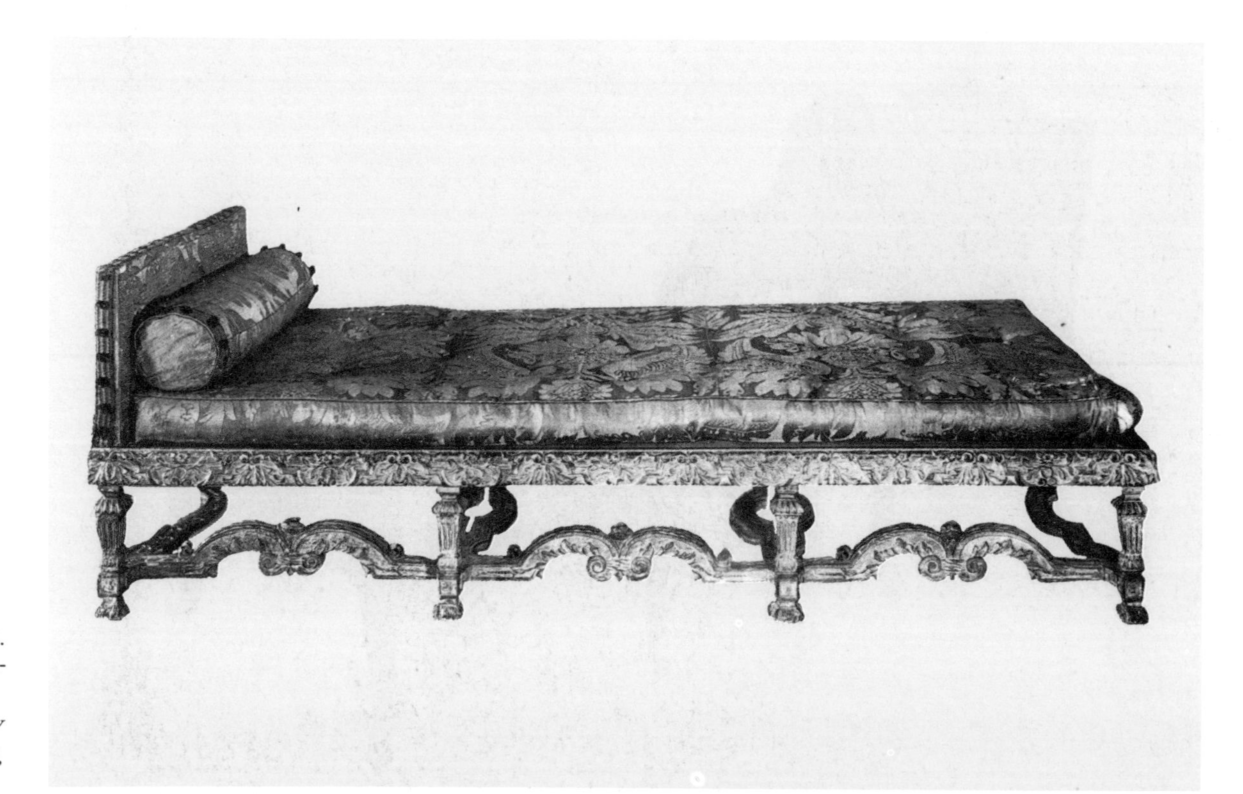

636. "Lit de repos" época Luis XIV. Altura asiento 40, longitud 190, ancho 80

636. "Lit de reposs" of Louis XIV period. Seat height 40, length 190, width 80

637. Duquesa estilo regencia. Haya con rejilla, patas cabriolé. Frente 135, fondo 48, altura 96, altura asiento 30

637. Regency style "duchesse". Beechwood with canework, cabriolet legs. Front 135, depth 48, height 96, seat height 30

638. Duquesa "en bateau" de rejilla y patas cabriolé Luis XV. Altura 58, altura asiento 37, longitud 185, ancho 78

638. Louis XV "duchesse en bateau", with canework and cabriolet legs. Height 58, seat height 37, length 185, width 78

639. Duquesa "en bateau". Haya tallada y dorada. Colección particular

639. "Duchesse en bateau", carved and gilded beechwood. Private Collection

640. Sofá duquesa en dos partes. Haya tallada. Colección Mme. Fraenckel. Fondo 92, frente 80, altura respaldo 105, altura asiento 32

640. "Duchesse" sofa in two parts. Carved beechwood. Mme. Fraenckel Collection. Depth 92, front 80, back height 105, seat height 32

641. Sofá de haya tallada, con las patas cabriolé y tapizado. Principios del siglo XVIII. Ornamentación simétrica Regencia

641. Sofa of carved beechwood, cabriolet legs and upholstered. Regency symmetrical decoration. Early 18th century

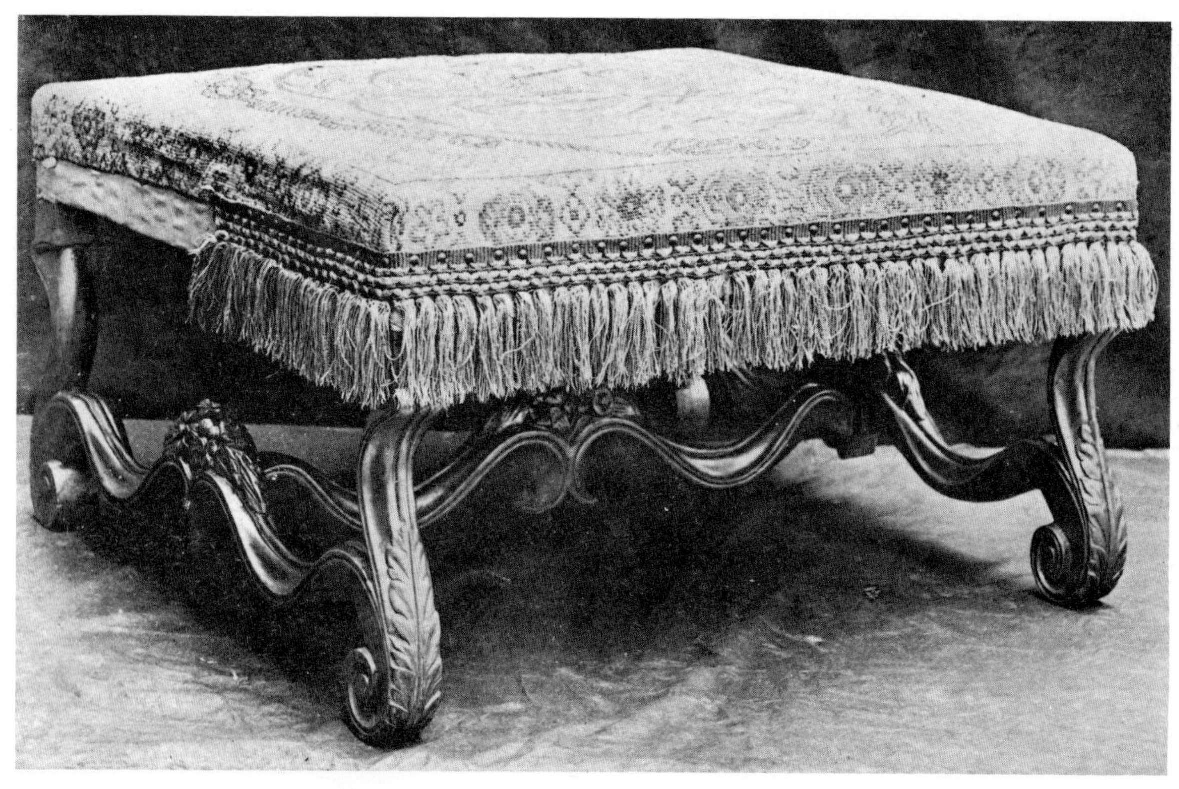

642. Banqueta Luis XIV, tallada y tapizada

642. Stool, Louis XIV period, carved and upholstered

643. "Veilleuse" mitad del siglo XVIII. Pintada y tallada. Colección particular. Altura respaldo 95, altura asiento 30, fondo 45, frente respaldo 175

643. Mid-18th century "veilleuse". Painted and carved. Private Collection. Back height 95, seat height 30, depth 45, back length 175

644. Sofá "sultana" o canapé de tres plazas. Línea muy elegante. Atribuido a J. Avisse. Museo Nissin de Camondó. París

644. "Sultana" three seat sofa in very elegant lines, attributed to J. Avisse. Museum Nissin de Camondó. Paris

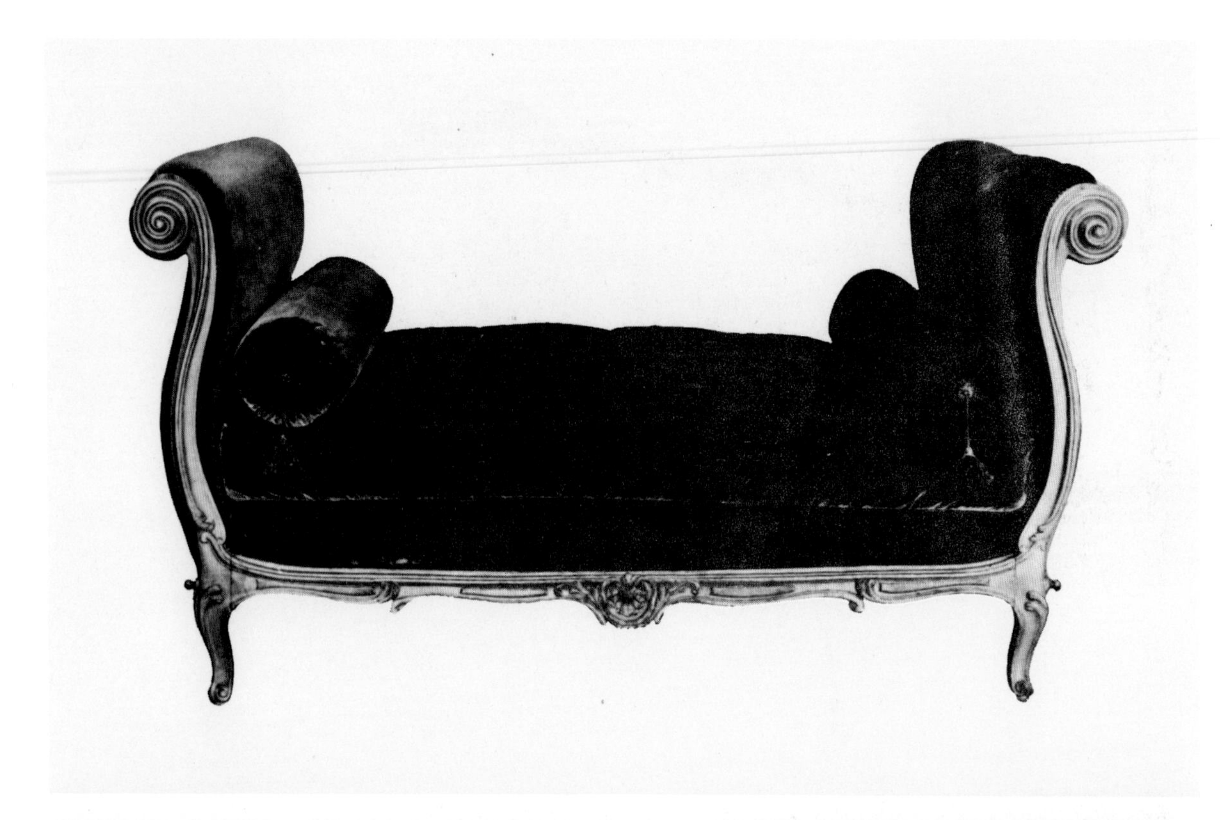

645. Cama a la "turca" fin del Luis XV. Costados enrollados en volutas. Línea elegante en los brazos y en el frente. Atribuido a J. Avisse. Colección S. Chalou

645. Couch in the Turkish style, late Louis XV period. Sides ending in scrolls, and elegant lines in the arms and front. Attributed to J. Avisse. S. Chalou Collection

646. Sofá "otomano" Luis XV. Mitad del siglo XVIII. Haya tallada y pintada en blanco. Patas cabriolé. Colección Serge Roche et Rothil

646. Louis XV ottoman sofa, mid 17th century. Carved and white painted beechwood, cabriolet legs. Serge Roche et Rothil Collection

647. Sofá, hacia 1760. Madera tallada y dorada. Museo Nissin de Camondó. París. Frente 200, fondo 80, altura respaldo 108, altura asiento 32

647. Sofa in carved and gilded wood, c. 1760. Museum Nissin of Camondó. Paris. Front 200, depth 80, back height 108, seat height 32

648. Mesa de despacho marqueteada, estilo Luis XIV. Museo Lázaro Galdeano. Madrid

648. Study table with marquetry decoration, Louis XIV style. Lázaro Galdeano Museum. Madrid

649. Mesita tallada, época Luis XIV

649. Carved table, Louis XIV period

650. Gueridón época Luis XV. Alto 65, frente 45, fondo 40

650. Gueridon, Louis XV style. Height 65, front 45, depth 40

651. Mesita Regencia de 78 de alto, 95 de frente y 63 de fondo

651. Small Regency table. Height 78, front 95, depth 63

652. Mesita tallada Regencia de 70 de alto, 80 de frente y 57 de fondo

652. Small carved Regency table. Height 70, front 80, depth 57

653. Escritorio por A. F. Delorme decorado con barniz Martin, grabado de las patas muy delicado. Propiedad de Waddesdon Manor

653. Writing desk by A. F. Delorme, decorated with Martin varnish, very fine etching on the legs. Property of Waddesdon Manor

654. Mesa, por Claudio Carles Saurnier. Museo de Artes Decorativas. París

654. Table, by Claudio Carles Saurnier. Museum of Decorative Arts. Paris

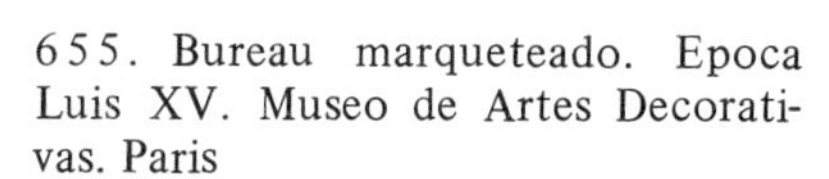

655. Bureau marqueteado. Epoca Luis XV. Museo de Artes Decorativas. Paris

655. Bureau with marquetry decoration, Louis XV period. Museum of Decorative Arts. Paris

656. Bureau de cilindro con marquetería de rombos y aplicaciones de bronce dorado, transición al Luis XVI. Museo Lázaro Galdeano. Madrid

656. Cylindrical top bureau with lozenge marquetry and gilt bronze mounts, transition to Louis XVI period. Lázaro Galdeano Museum. Madrid

657. Mesa escritorio de María Lekzinska, mujer de Luis XV, en madera de caoba con aplicaciones de bronce. Mueble de Riesener y bronces de Duplessis. Regalo del ayuntamiento de París a la reina

657. Writing table of Maria Lekzinska, wife of Louis XV, in mahogany with brass mounts. The table by Riesener and brasswork by Duplessis. A gift to the queen from the Paris Town Hall Council

658. Vista posterior del mueble anterior

658. Rear view of the preceding piece

659. Bureau con tapa abatible y parte posterior elevada, marqueteado y con aplicaciones de bronce Luis XV

659. Bureau with drop top and rear part raised, marquetry decoration with bronze appliqués in the Louis XV style

660. 661. "Bureau du Roi", mesa firmada por Riesener, con espléndidas marqueterías y aplicaciones en bronce. Obra comenzada por Oeben

660. 661. "Bureau du Roi", signed by Riesener, with splendid marquetry decoration and bronze appliqués. The work was begun by Oeben

662. "Bureau du Roi", mesa firmada por Riesener, con espléndidas marqueterías y aplicaciones de bronce. Museo del Louvre. París

662. "Bureau du Roi", signed by Riesener, with splendid marquetry decoration and bronze mounts. Louvre. Paris

663. Bureau por A. Boulle, ejecutado o realizado para Maximiliano Manuel, Elector de Baviera, 1715. Museo del Louvre, París

663. Bureau by A. Boulle, executed or made for Maximilian Manuel, Elector of Bavaria, in 1715. Louvre. Paris

664. Bureau de tapa inclinada en tres piezas independientes

664. Bureau with inclined front in three independent parts

665. Mesa con patas cabriolé y "spagnolettes" de bronce dorado, por Ch. Cressent. Siglo XVIII. Fundación Gulbenkian. Lisboa

665. Gilt bronze table with cabriolet legs and "spagnolettes", by Charles Cressent, 18th century. Calouste Gulbenkian Foundation Lisbon.

666. Mesa de despacho de Dubois. Bronce Luis XV. Museo del Louvre. París

666. Study table by Dubois; Louis XV bronze decoration. Louvre. Paris

667. Mesa de despacho de caoba y bronces Luis XV. Alto 80, frente 137, fondo 83

667. Study table in mahogany with Louis XV bronze mounts. Height 80, front 137, depth 83

668. Consola Luis XIV, tallada y dorada. Elementos característicos del estilo

668. Louis XIV console table, carved and gilded. The members are characteristic of the style

669. Consola de la época Luis XIV. Con tallas características

669. Louis XIV console table, with characteristic carvings

670. Consola de madera tallada Luis XV. Altura 80, frente 112

670. Louis XV carved console table in wood. Height 80, front 112

671. Consola Luis XV. Ornamentacion asimétrica

671. Louis XV consola table, with asymetrical decoration

672. Cómoda, dibujada por Jean Berain. París

672. Commode, drawn by Jean Berain. Paris

673. Cómoda atribuida a Boulle por sus aplicaciones de bronce y marquetería, chapeada con hojas de madera de amaranto, hacia 1715. Museo del Louvre. París

673. Commode, attributed to Boulle in view of the bronze and marquetry decoration, with amaranth veneers, c. 1715. Louvre Paris

674. Cómoda por A. Boulle, estilo Luis XIV, marqueteada con concha y cobre. Empiezan las cómodas panzudas, bombeadas con bronces cincelados de la Regencia

674. Commode, by A. Boulle in the Louis XIV style, marquetry in shell and copper. The bombé commodes with Regency chiselled bronze decoration now begin

675. Cómoda de A. Gaudreaux y bronces de Caffieri en 1739 para las habitaciones de Luis XV en Versalles. Colección Wallace. Inglaterra.

675. Commode by A. Gaudreaux and bronze work by Caffieri in 1739 for the rooms of Louis XV at Versailles. Wallace Collection

676. Cómoda con bronces cincelados estilo Luis XV. Atribuida a J. Dubois

676. Louis XV commode with chiselled bronze decoration. Attributed to J. Dubois

677. Cómoda Luis XV por P. Roussel con marquetería de flores y bronces cincelados. Museo del Louvre. París

677. Louis XV commode, by P. Roussel, with floral marquetry and chiselled bronze mounts. Louvre. Paris

678. Cómoda por Charles Cressent. Altura 85 cm, costado 143, largo 63

678. Commode by Charles Cressent. Height 85 cm, side 143, length 63

679. Cómoda con marquetería y bronces Luis XV. Galería Apolo. Museo del Louvre. París

679. Louis XV commode with marquetry and bronze mounts. Apollo Gallery. Louvre. Paris

680. Cómoda realizada para medallero de Luis XV en Versalles, por Gaudreaux y bronces de los hermanos Slodtz, 1739

680. Louis XV's medal commode at Versailles, executed by Gaudreaux with bronze work by the Slodtz brothers, 1739

681. Cómoda atribuida a Cressent. Hacia 1730. Estilo Regencia, figuras femeninas "espagnolettes". Colección Wallace

681. Commode, attributed to Cressent, c. 1730; in the Regency style with "espagnolettes" feminine figures. Wallace Collection

682. Cómoda de línea y silueta muy pura Luis XV. Museo de Artes Decorativas

682. Commode with very pure Louis XV lines and silhouette. Museum of Decorative Arts. Paris

683. Cómoda laqueada con temas orientales Luis XV. Museo de Artes Decorativas. París

683. Louis XV lacquered commode with oriental themes. Museum of Decorative Arts. Paris

684. Biblioteca por Charles Cresent, 1725. Aplicaciones de bronce y bustos representando las cuatro partes del mundo. Museo Gulbenkian. Lisboa

684. Library by Charles Cressent, 1725. Bronze appliqués and four busts representing the World Continents. Gulbenkian Museum. Lisbon

685. Mesa y papelera de roble tallado Luis XIV

685. Louis XIV writing-desk in carved oak

686. Cómoda marqueteada y con bronces cincelados por Pierre II Migeon. Museo de Artes Decorativas. París

686. Commode with marquetry and chiselled bronze decoration by Pierre II Migeon. Museum of Decorative Arts. Paris

687. Cómoda de roble estilo Luis XIV, provinciano, y bronces Luis XV. Colección particular. Murcia

687. Oak commode in the provincial Louis XIV style and Louis XV bronce work. Private Collection. Murcia

688. Armario bajo de roble con tallas Regencia. Obra normanda

688. Low cupboard in oak with Regency carving. Norman work

689. Escritorio de perfil combado, por J. F. Leleu. Museo de Artes Decorativas. París

689. Curved profile escritoire, by J. F. Leleu. Museum of Decorative Arts. Paris

690. Rinconera marqueteada con temas florales y bronces "rocalla" Luis XV

690. Louis XV "rocaille" corner cupboard with floral marquetry and bronze decoration

691. Rinconera Luis XV marqueteada y con bronces firmada por Roisell

691. Louis XV corner cupboard with marquetry and gilded bronze mounts, signed by Roisell

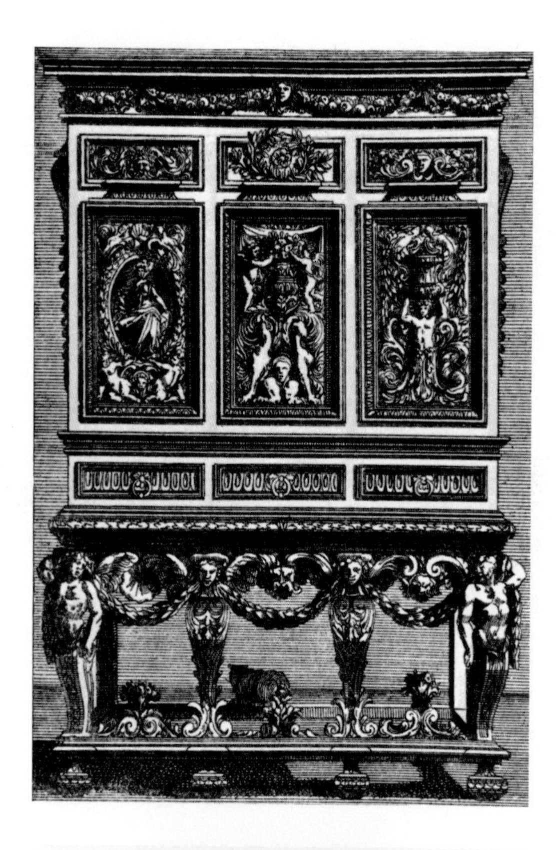

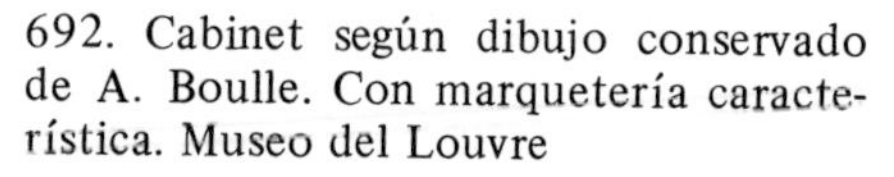

692. Cabinet según dibujo conservado de A. Boulle. Con marquetería característica. Museo del Louvre

692. Cabinet according to drawing conserved by A. Boulle, with characteristic marquetry. Louvre. París

693. Cabinet, dibujo de Jean La Poutre (1618-1682). París

693. Cabinet. Drawing by Jean La Poutre (1618-1682). Paris

694. Armario, por A. Boulle. Museo de Artes Decorativas. París

694. Wardrobe by A. Boulle. Museum of Decorative Arts. Paris

695. Armario, cuatro puertas de roble con decoración Luis XIV

695. Wardrobe, four oak doors with Louis XIV decoration

696. Armario según dibujo de A. Boulle que perteneció a Luis XIV, marquetería de concha y cobre y maderas finas. Museo del Louvre

696. Closet belonging to Louis XIV as drawn by A. Boulle. Inlays of shell, copper and fine wood. The Louvre

697. Armario con marquetería y bronces cincelados, por C. Cressent. Museo de Artes Decorativas. París

697. Wardrobe with marquetry and chiselled bronze decoration, by C. Cressent. Museum of Decorative Arts. Paris

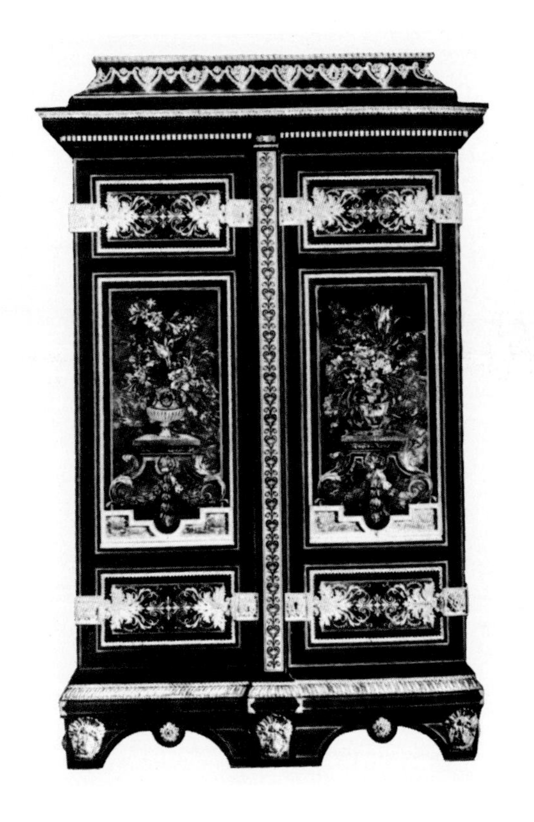

698. Armario de roble, Luis XIV provinciano, con herrajes de hierro. Colección particular. Murcia

698. Oak wardrobe in the provincial Louis XIV style, with iron mounts. Private Collection. Murcia

699. Armario de dos puertas en roble tallado Luis XIV. Altura 275, frente 165

699. Louis XIV two-doored wardrobe in carved oak. Height 275, front 165

700. Rinconera con un reloj. Interpretación de un dibujo de Nicolás Pineau por Jacobo Dubois, decoración de "rocalla" en los bronces cincelados Luis XV

700. Corner cupboard with clock. Execution of a drawing of Nicholas Pineau by Jacob Dubois; "rocaille" decoration on the Louis XV chiselled bronze mounts

701. Medallero por Charles Cressent (1685-1768) con aplicaciones de bronce dorado. Fundación Gulbenkian. Lisboa

701. Medal cabinet by Charles Cressent (1685-1768) with gilt bronze inlays. Calouste Gulbenkian Foundation. Lisbon

702. Reloj marqueteado y con aplicaciones de bronce. Estilo Luis XIV

702. Tall clock with marquetry and bronze appliqués. Louis XIV style

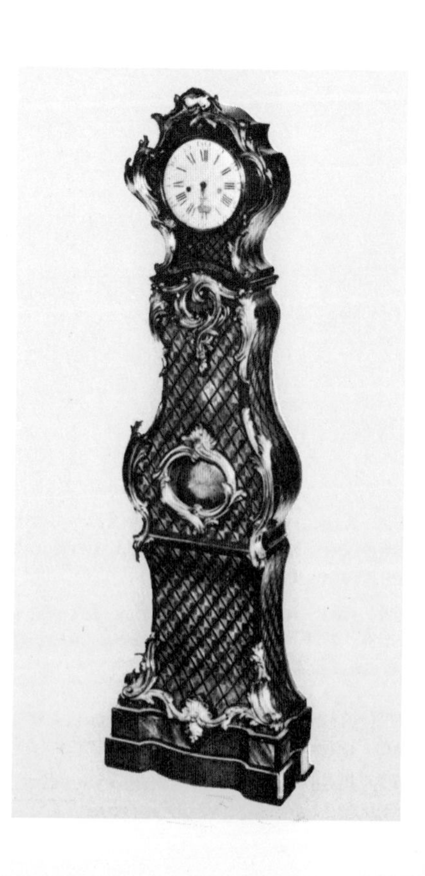

703. Reloj Luis XV por B. Lieutaud. Bronce, "rocalla" y marquetería

703. Louis XV tall clock, by B. Lieutaud. "Rocaille", bronze and marquetry decoration

704. Reloj con bronces estilo Luis XIV-Regencia. Versalles

704. Tall clock with Louis XIV-Regency style bronze decoration. Versailles

705. Reloj con marquetería y bronce estilo Luis XV

705. Tall clock with marquetry and bronze decoration in the Louis XV style

706. Dormitorio Luis XIV. Colección A. López Wilshaw. París

706. Louis XIV bedroom. A. López Wilshaw Collection. Paris

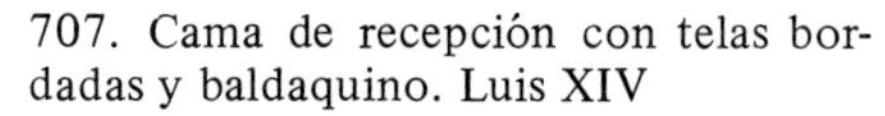

707. Cama de recepción con telas bordadas y baldaquino. Luis XIV

707. Louis XIV reception bed with embroidered fabric and canopy

708. Cama "a la turca" con los brazos del cabecero y piecero a la misma altura y vueltos en voluta

708. Bed in the Turkish taste with curved head and foot of the same height and scrolled ends

709. Cama Luis XV "a la polaca". Castillo de Rochecotte

709. Louis XV bed in the Polish taste. Rochecotte Castle

710. Cama recepción con telas bordadas y baldaquino, Luis XIV. Palacio de Oriente. Madrid

710. Reception bed with embroidered fabrics and canopy. Louis XIV. Oriental Palace. Madrid

711. Cama Luis XIV. Castillo de Dampierre

711. Louis XIV bed. Dampierre Castle

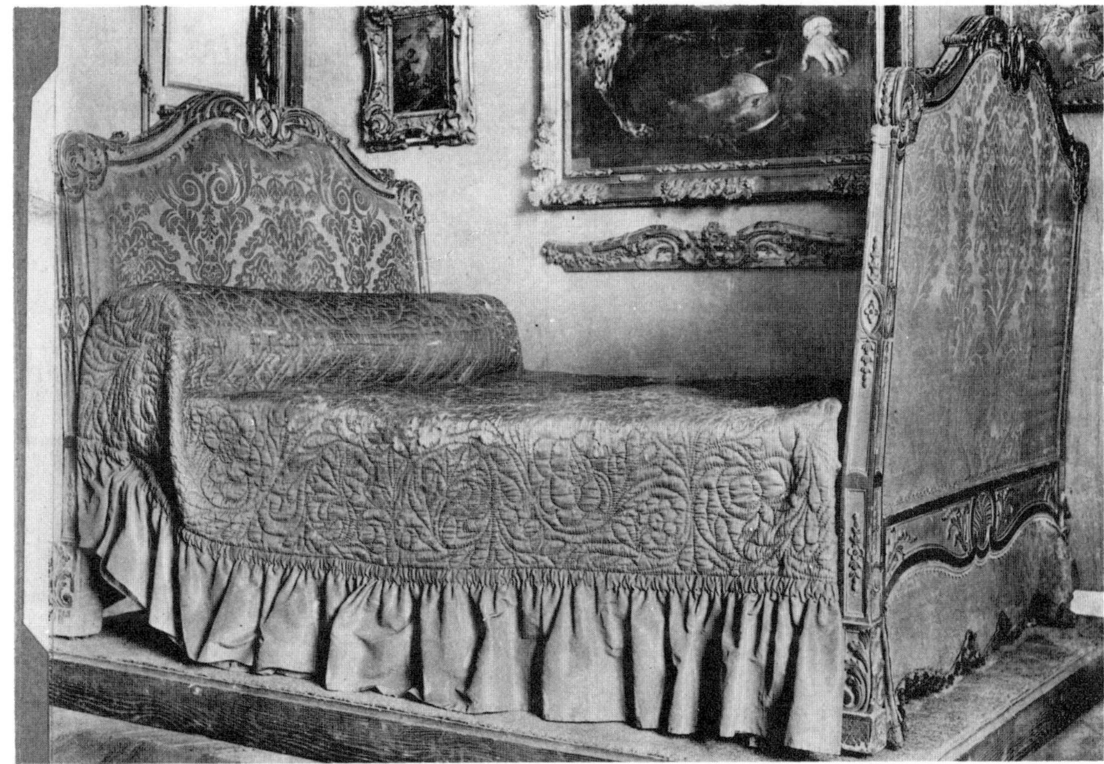

712. Cama con las armas de Rohan, principios del siglo XVIII

712. Early 18th century bed with the arms of Roham

713. Sillón tallado y dorado por Andrea Brustolon. Hacia 1700. Palacio Rezzonico. Venecia

713. Armchair, carved and gilded by Andrea Brustolon, c. 1700. Rezzonico Palace. Venice

714. Silla tipo Luis XIV con patas cabriolé sobre garras y con chambranas

714. Chair in Louis XIV style, with cabriolet legs on claws and with stretchers

715. Sillón veneciano lacado, pintado y tapizado con seda. Tipo Luis XV

715. Venetian armchair, lacquered, painted and upholstered in silk; Louis XV style

716. Sillón tapizado y pintado. Siglo XVIII. Arte veneciano. Museo de Arte antiguo. Milán

716. 18th-century carved and gilded armchair. Venetian art. Museum of Antique Art. Milan

717. Sillón de madera tallada y dorada tapizada con terciopelo de seda verde. Siglo XVII. Museo de Arte Antiguo. Milán

717. Armchair in carved and gilded wood, upholstered in green silk velvet. XVII century. Museum of Antique Art. Milan

718. Sofá de influencia francesa. Tipo Luis XIV

718. Settee with French influence; Louis XIV type

719. Sillón tallado y dorado, con tapicería de terciopelo rojo y galones dorados. Siglo XVIII. Palacio de España. Roma

719. 18th-century carved and gilded armchair, with red velvet upholstery and gilded gadroons. Palazzo di Spagna. Rome

720. Sillón de nogal tallado y dorado. Mitad del siglo XVIII. Milán.

720. Carved and gilded walnut armchair. Mid-18th century. Milan

721. Consola tallada, laqueada en color verde y oro, con tablero de mármol en la tapa. Siglo XVIII. Turín

721. Carved console table, lacquered in green and gold with marble top. 18th century. Turin

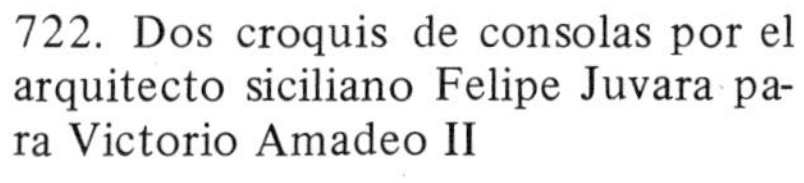

722. Dos croquis de consolas por el arquitecto siciliano Felipe Juvara para Victorio Amadeo II

722. Two sketches of console tables, by the Sicilian architect Filipo Juvara, for Victorio Amadeo II

723. Consola tallada y dorada, interpretación del Luis XIV

723. Carved and gilded console table in the Louis XIV taste

728. Consola por P. Piffetti con marquetería y bronces cincelados. Palacio de Moncalieri

728. Console table by P. Piffetti, with marquetry and chiselled bronze mounts. Palazzo di Moncalieri

729. Mesa de despacho por P. Piffetti con marquetería y bronces cincelados. Palacio de Moncalieri

729. Study table by P. Piffetti, with marquetry and chiselled bronze decoration. Palazzo di Moncalieri

730. Cómoda laqueada en verde y oro. Siglo XVIII. Palacio Rezzonico. Venecia

730. Console table lacquered in green and gold. 18th century. Palazzo Rezzonico. Venice

731. Cómoda cubierta con chapas de nogal. Asas de bronce. Siglo XVIII

731. Walnut veneered commode, bronze handles. 18th century

732. Cómoda tallada, pintada en marfil con temas florales policromados y oro. 1760. Turín

732. Carved commode, painted ivory with polychromed and gold floral decoration. 1760. Turin

733. Cómoda tallada y laqueada en diversos colores con tallas doradas. Mediados del siglo XVIII

733. Mid-18th-century commode, lacquered in various colours with gilt carving

734. Buró marqueteado con filetes de ébano sobre fondo de hojas de nogal

734. Bureau, marquetry decoration with fillets of ebony on background of walnut panels

735. Cómoda con vitrina alta por P. Piffetti. Palacio de Moncalieri

735. Commode with upper stage glass cabinet, by P. Piffetti. Palazzo Moncalieri

736. Cómoda cuebierta con chapas finas de nogal. Trabajo turinés del siglo XVIII. Altura 90, frente 137, fondo 63

736. Walnut veneered commode. 18th-century Turinese work. Height 90, front 137, depth 63

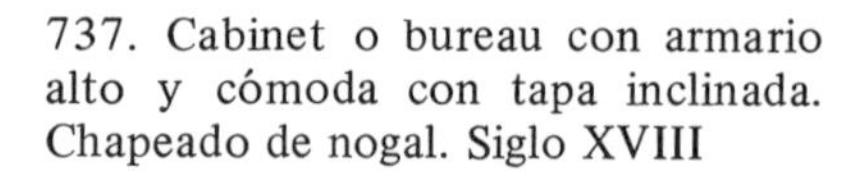

737. Cabinet o bureau con armario alto y cómoda con tapa inclinada. Chapeado de nogal. Siglo XVIII

737. Bureau with upper stage cabinet on commode with inclined front. Walnut veneered. XVIII century

738. Bureau con cuerpo alto en forma de "trumeau", con marquetería. Siglo XVIII

738. Bureau with upper stage in the form of "trumeau", with marquetry decoration. XVIII century

739. Cómoda con escritorio y cuerpo alto de librería. Chapeado de palo rosa con las vetas en cuadrifolio. Trabajo turinés. Altura 275, frente 118, fondo 57

739. Commode with escritoire and bookcase on top. Tulip wood veneered with the grain in quatrefoil. Turinese work. Height 275, front 118, depth 57

740. Bureau-vitrina de dos cuerpos. Madera laqueada en color claro; la tapa central inclinada se abate para formar el escritorio

740. Bureau-cabinet in two stages. Light colour lacquered wood; the central cover can be lowered to form the writing desk

741. Reclinatorio marqueteado del rey Carlos Alberto por P. Piffetti. Palacio Real de Turín

741. Praying-desk, with marquetry decoration, of King Charles Albert by P. Piffeti. Royal Palace of Turin

742. Mesa-mostrador de la farmacia del palacio Rezzonico. Venecia. Siglo XVIII (reconstrucción)

742. Counter of the pharmacy of the palace of Rezzonico, Venice. 18th century (reconstruction)

743. Cama y alcoba en el palacio Rezzonico. Venecia

743. Bed and alcove. Palace of Rezzonico. Venice

744. Cama en el apartamento de los Anazzi. Palacio Pitti. Florencia

744. Bed in the Anazzi apartment. Palazzo Pitti. Florence

745. Cama de la emperatriz Josefina en la Villa Borromeo; Isolabella (Lago Mayor)

745. Empress Josephine's bed at Villa Borromeo; Isolabella

746. Salón del palacio Borromeo en Isolabella

746. Salon of Palace of Borromeo at Isolabella

747. Sillón del trono. Palacio Borromeo de Isolabella

747. Throne. Palace of Borromeo, Isolabella

748. Espinetta del siglo XVII y armario pintado en el palacio Rezzonico. Venecia

748. 17th-century spinet and painted cupboard. Palace of Rezzonico. Venice

749. Sillón frailero abarrocado de la catedral de Córdoba

749. "Frailero" armchair. Cordova Cathedral

750. Sillón de nogal tallado, con terciopelo carmesí. Catedral nueva. Salamanca

750. Carved walnut armchair with red velvet upholstery. New Cathedral, Salamanca

751. Sillón barroco estilo Luis XIII. Casa Balmes. Olot

751. Baroque armchair in Louis XIII taste. Balmes House. Olot

752. Sillón de transición al barroco. Museo de Artes Decorativas. Madrid

752. Armchair, transition to the baroque. Museum of Decorative Arts. Madrid

753. Frailero de transición con elemento salomónico

753. "Frailero" of the transitional period, with twist-turned members

754. Interpretación española de una silla de Chippendale con respaldo de lira y patas cabriolé en garra sobre bola y chambranas curvadas. Las tallas rococó doradas

754. Spanish version of Chippendale chair with lyre back and cabriolet legs with talon and ball curved crosspieces. Carvings are gilt rococo

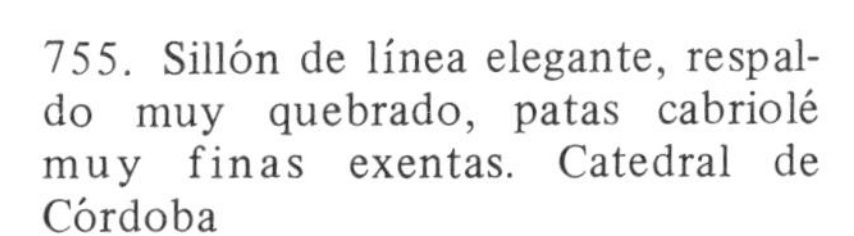

755. Sillón de línea elegante, respaldo muy quebrado, patas cabriolé muy finas exentas. Catedral de Córdoba

755. Elegant armchair with sharply curved back, very thin, widely spaced cabriolet legs. Cordova Cathedral

756. Sillón de orejas con mecanismo: el respaldo es abatible y el sillón se puede convertir en cama; chambranas en H; primeras manifestaciones del barroco. Casa Oleza, Palma de Mallorca

756. Mechanical armchair with "ears". The back is collapsable and the chair can be made into a bed. Crosspieces are H-shaped. First evidence of Baroque style. Oleza House. Palma de Majorca

757. Sillón Regencia, con patas cabriolé y chambranas erizadas. Siglo XVIII

757. Regency armchair, with cabriolet legs and crossed rungs. 18th century

758. Interpretación salmantina de una silla Chippendale. Museo Lázaro Galdeano. Madrid

758. Salamantine execution of a Chippendale chair. Lázaro Galdeano Museum. Madrid

759. Sillón de las mismas características de las de la silla anterior

759. Armchair with the same features as the preceding one

760. Interpretación del reina Ana, con un carácter muy popular; patas cabriolé con chambranas, pala de silueta quebrada; pintada con ornamentación oriental

760. A piece of Queen Anne furniture of popular style. Cabriolet legs with crosspieces, sharply curving uprights, painted oriental decoration

761. Sillón laqueado de tipo popular inspirado en el reina Ana. Museo de Artes Decorativas. Madrid

761. Popular type lacquered armchair in the Queen Anne taste. Museum of Decorative Arts. Madrid

762. Sillón barroco de fray Antonio de Sotomayor (Salamanca, ahora en Cuba)

762. Fray Antonio de Sotomayor's baroque armchair (Salamanca, now in Cuba)

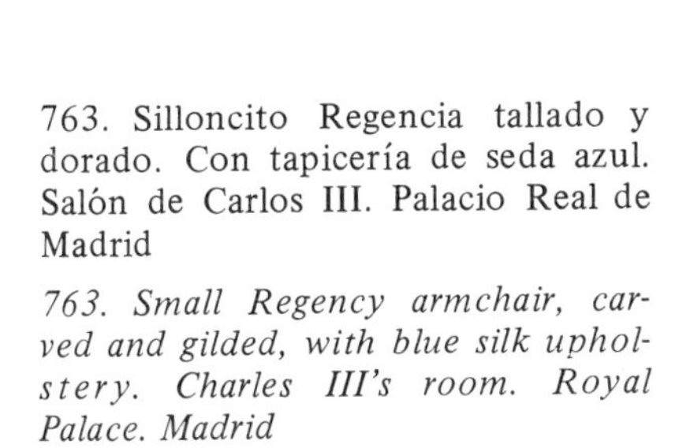

763. Silloncito Regencia tallado y dorado. Con tapicería de seda azul. Salón de Carlos III. Palacio Real de Madrid

763. Small Regency armchair, carved and gilded, with blue silk upholstery. Charles III's room. Royal Palace. Madrid

764. Sillón de estilo italiano Luis XV en madera pintada y dorada con tapicería de seda azul. Salón de Carlos III. Palacio Real de Madrid

764. Louis XV armchair in the Italian style, in painted and gilded wood with blue silk upholstery. Charles III's room. Royal Palace. Madrid

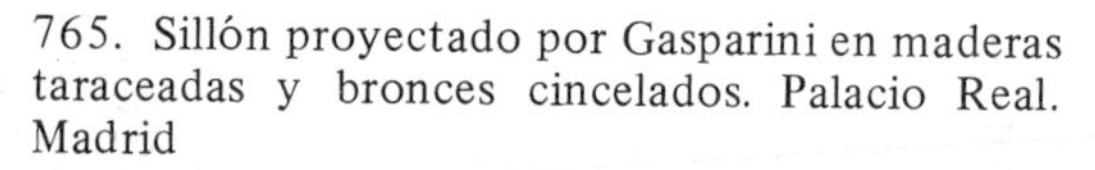

765. Sillón proyectado por Gasparini en maderas taraceadas y bronces cincelados. Palacio Real. Madrid

765. Armachair designed by Gasparini, wood inlay and chiselled bronze decoration. Royal Palace. Madrid

766. Sillón del Salón Gasparini, taraceado y con aplicaciones de bronce por Gasparini y Canops. Palacio Real de Madrid

766. Armchair in the Gasparini Room, inlay decoration and bronze appliqués by Gasparini and Canops. Royal Palace. Madrid

767. Detalle del brazo del sillón anterior

767. Detail of the arm of the preceding chair

768. Silla de caoba taraceada, tapizada en sedas bordadas de la Sala Gasparini. Palacio Real de Madrid

768. Mahogany chair with inlay work upholstered in embroidered silk in the Gasparini Room. Royal Palace. Madrid

769. Banqueta con las mismas características

769. Stool with the same feactures

770. Sillón barroco Carlos III. Salón del Trono. Palacio Real de Madrid

770. Charles III baroque armchair. Throne's Room. Royal Palace. Madrid

771. Silloncito plegable de tijera. Museo de Artes Decorativas. Madrid

771. X-shaped folding chair. Museum of Decorative Arts. Madrid

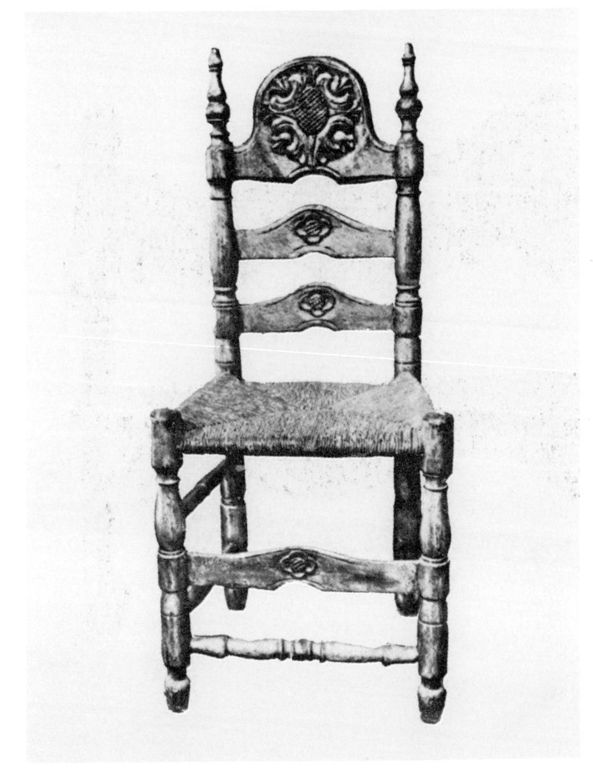

772. Silla. Modelo típico de Mallorca. Casa Oleza. Palma

772. Chair. Typical model of Majorca. Oleza House. Palma

773. Silla. Castillo de Sta. Florentina. Canet de Mar

773. Chair. St. Florentina Castle. Canet de Mar

774. Sillón barroco de la ciudad de Córdoba (Argentina)

774. Baroque armchair of Cordova, Argentine

775. Sillones de la sala capitular de la catedral de Córdoba (Argentina)

775. Armchairs of the Chapter-house of Cordova Cathedral, Argentine

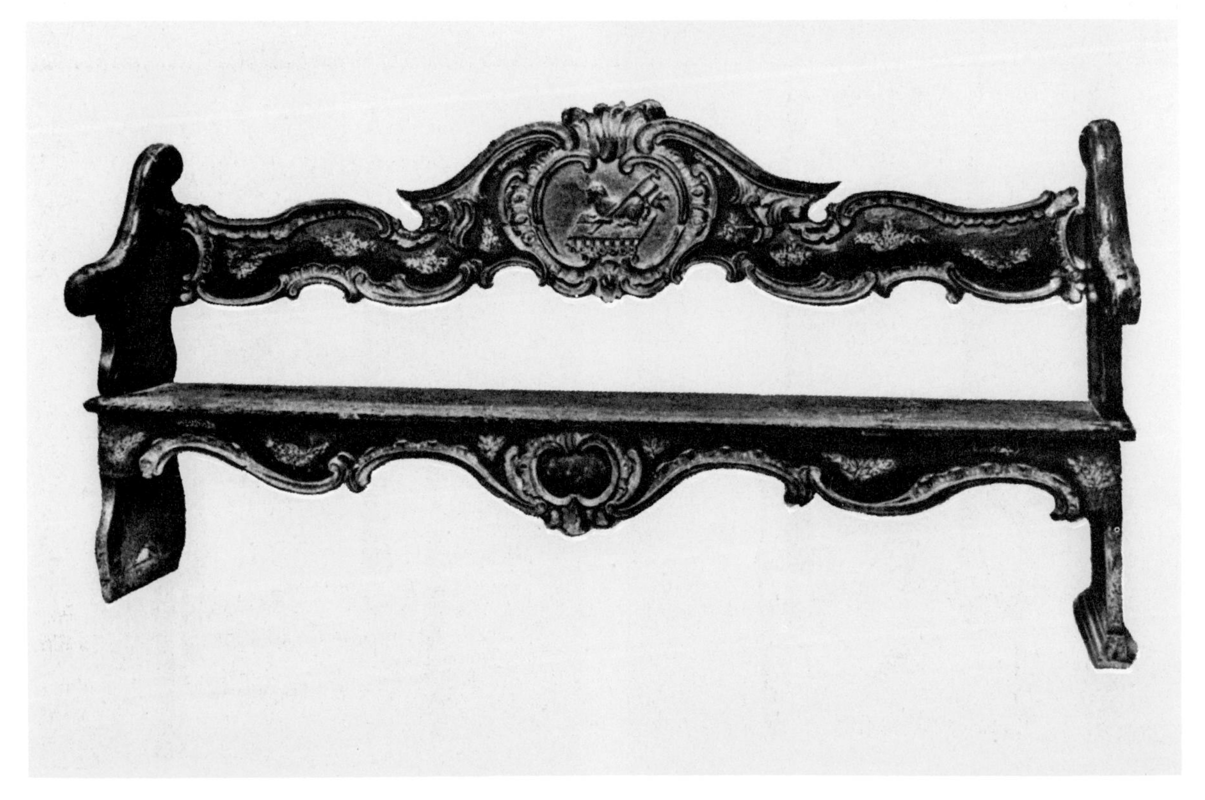

776. Banco tallado, dorado y pintado con tallas populares Luis XV. Sevilla

776. Carved, painted and gilt bench with popular carvings in the Louis XV taste, Seville

777. Sofá barroco rococó, tallado. Propiedad particular. Madrid

777. Carved rococo Baroque sofa. Privately owned. Madrid

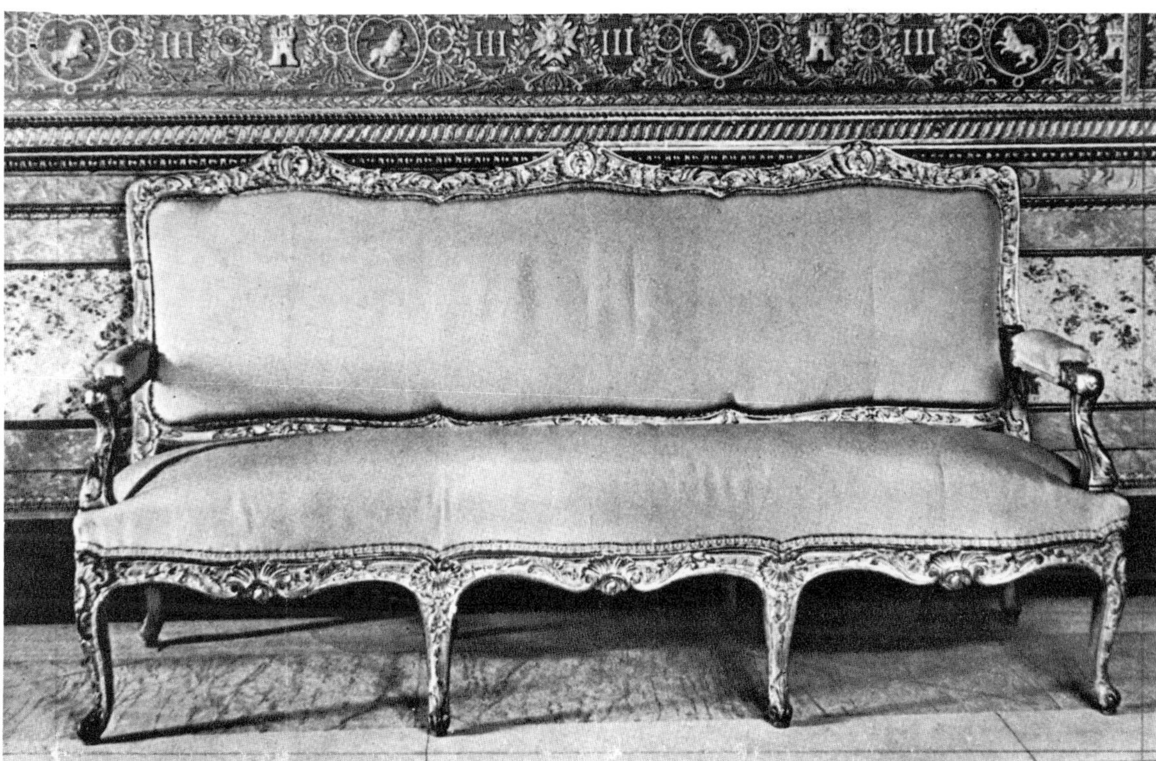

778. Sofá de tres plazas estilo Regencia, tallado y dorado. Palacio Real de Madrid

778. Regency style triple seat settee, carved and gilded. Royal Palace. Madrid

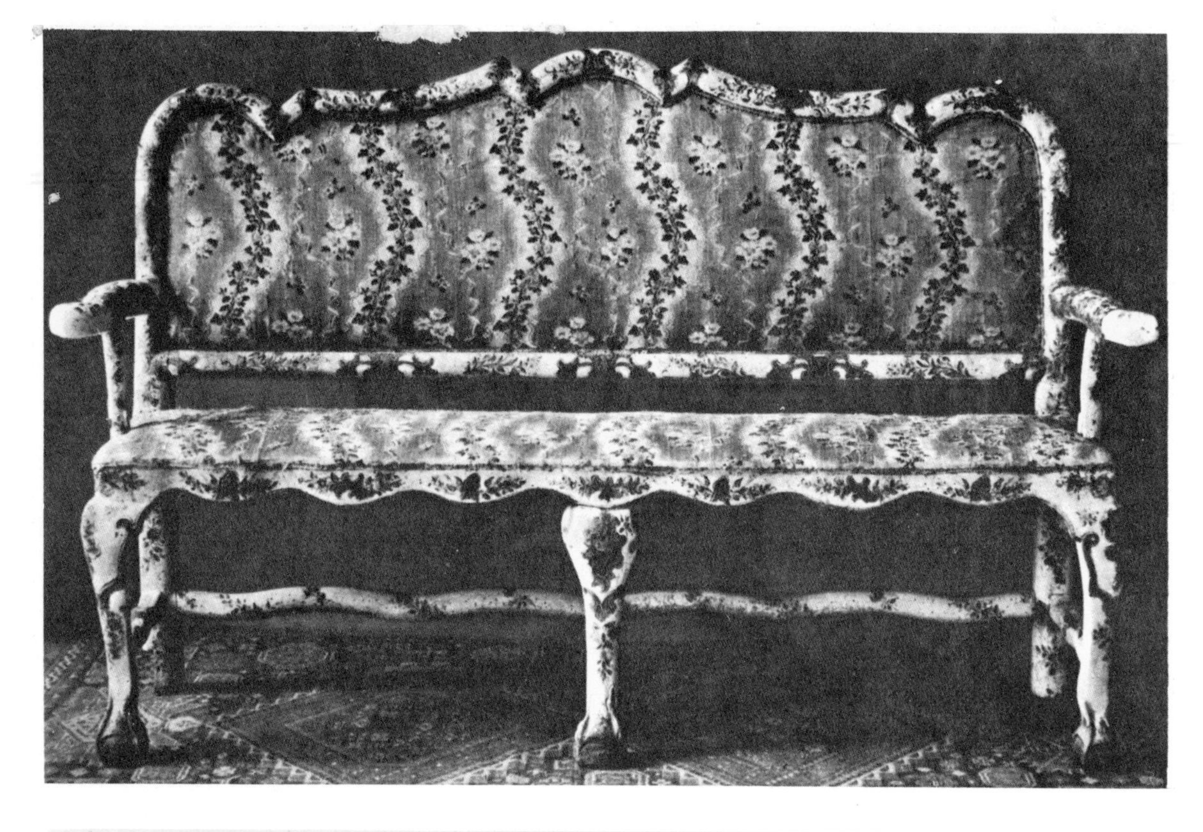

779. Sofá con las características tallas doradas rococó. Museo de Artes Decorativas. Madrid

779. Sofa, with characteristic rococo gilt carving. Museum of Decorative Arts. Madrid

780. Sofá más vulgar con líneas de características semejantes. Museo de Artes Decorativas Madrid

780. Sofa, more ordinary but of similar lines. Museum of Decorative Arts. Madrid

781. Salón proyectado por Gasparini, realizado por J. Canops en los talleres reales; bronces cincelados por Ferroni. Palacio Real de Madrid

781. State room projected by Gasparini, executed by J. Canops in the royal workshops; chiselled bronzework by Ferroni. Royal Palace. Madrid

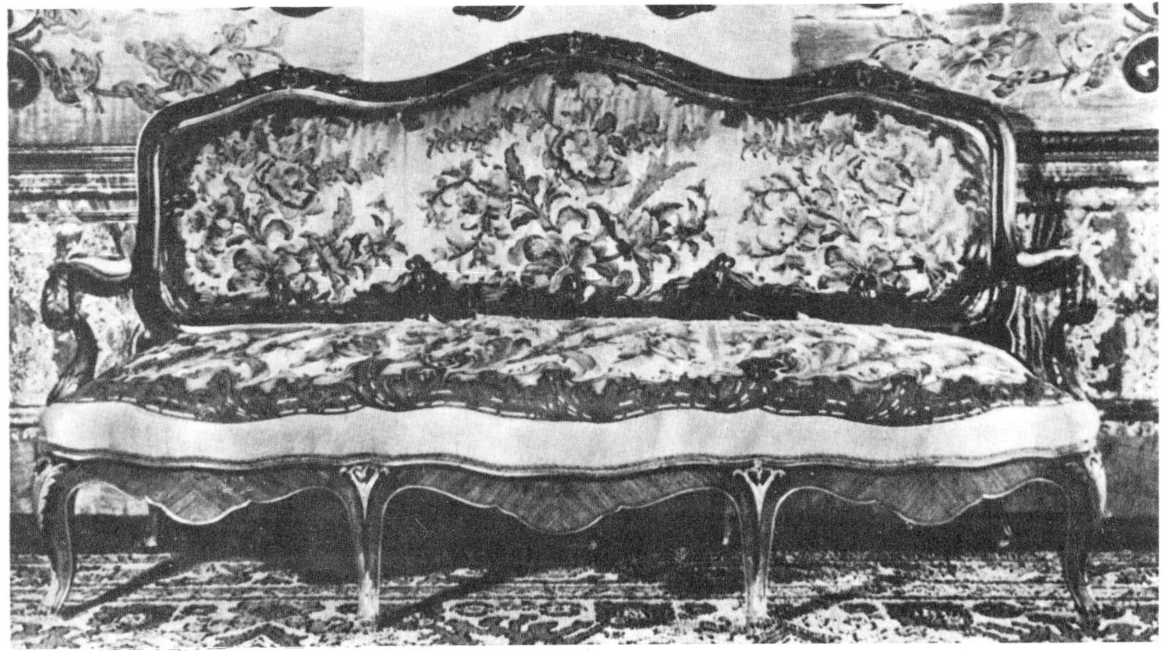

782. Sofá del salón Gasparini totalmente taraceado con bronces cincelados y tapicería bordada. Palacio Real de Madrid

782. Sofa in the Gasparini Room, completely inlaid, chiselled bronze decoration and embroidered upholstery. Royal Palace. Madrid

783. Mesa de nogal con tallas populares en los cajones y patas cabriolé. Museo de Artes Decorativas. Madrid

783. Walnut table with popular carvings on the drawer fronts and cabriolet legs. Museum of Decorative Arts. Madrid

784. Mesa barroca del siglo XVII en la sala capitular de la catedral de Gerona

784. 17th-century baroque table in the Chapter-house of Gerona Cathedral

785. Mesa recubierta de terciopelo con fiadores de hierro. Palma de Mallorca

785. Table covered with velvet and with iron stretchers. Palma, Majorca

786. Mesa con patas de lira y fiadores del siglo XVIII. Sacristía de la catedral de Sigüenza, Guadalajara

786. 18th century table with lyre form legs and stretchers. Sacristy of Sigüenza Cathedral, Guadalajara

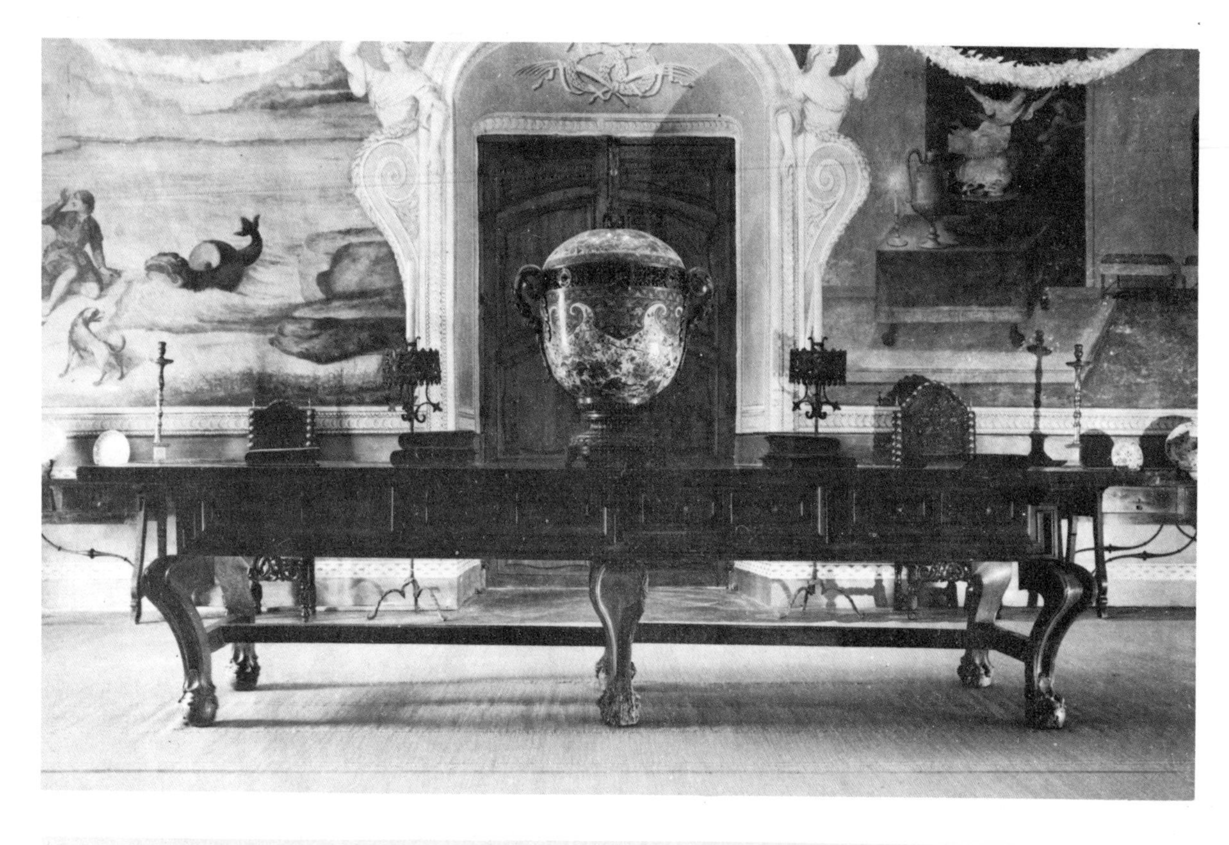

787. Mesa conventual o de refectorio, de roble, con ancho faldón; las patas cabriolé son muy estilizadas y exageradas, de marcado carácter popular. Palacio del Marqués de Viana. Córdoba

787. Refectory or conventual table made of oak with wide sides. Cabriolet legs are very stylized and exagerated. Very popular in character. Palace of the Marquis of Viana. Cordova

788. Mesa del tipo refectorio: interpretación de la región gallega. Talla de placas recortadas en el faldón. Museo de Pontevedra

788. Refectory table from the Galician region. Carved figures on side panels. Museum of Pontevedra

789. Mesa volante rectangular con patas de lira con silueta recortada y terminada en volutas. Palacio del Marqués de Viana. Córdoba

789. Rectangular table with carved lyre legs ending in scrolls. Palace of the Marquis of Viana. Cordova

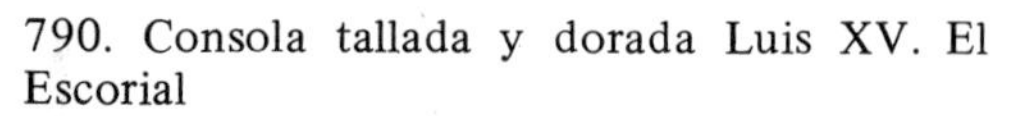

790. Consola tallada y dorada Luis XV. El Escorial

790. Louis XV carved and gilt console table. El Escorial

791. Consola, dibujo de Ventura Rodríguez

791. Console table. Drawing by Ventura Rodríguez

792. Consola levantina popular, tallada y pintada. Museo de Artes Decorativas. Madrid

792. Popular Levant console table, carved and gilded. Museum of Decorative Arts. Madrid

793. Consola levantina tallada, dorada y pintada. Museo de Artes Decorativas. Madrid

793. Levant console table; carved, gilded and painted. Museum of Decorative Arts. Madrid

794. Consola tallada y dorada estilo Luis XV. Patrimonio Nacional. Madrid

794. Carved and gilded console table in the Louis XV style. National Patrimony. Madrid

795. Consola dorada del Patrimonio Nacional. Madrid

795. Gilt console table. National Patrimony. Madrid

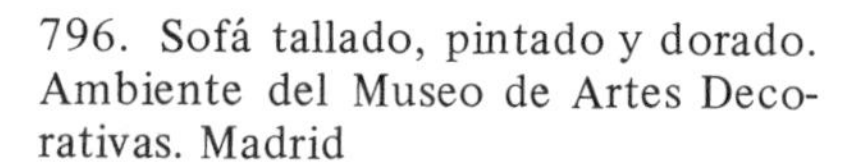

796. Sofá tallado, pintado y dorado. Ambiente del Museo de Artes Decorativas. Madrid

796. Carved, painted and gilded sofa. Environment of the Museum of Decorative Arts. Madrid

797. Consola pintada y dorada de tipo popular. Museo de Artes Decorativas. Madrid

797. Popular type painted and gilded console table. Museum of Decorative Arts. Madrid

798. Consola tallada y dorada estilo Luis XV. El Escorial

798. Carved and gilded console table in the Louis XV style. El Escorial

799. Bureau de tapa inclinada con marquetería sobre palmas de nogal y aplicaciones de bronce. Palacio de Campo-Franco. Palma de Mallorca

799. Bureau with sloping top covered with walnut branches and bronze inlays. Palace of the Marquis of Campo-Franco, Palma de Mallorca

800. Cómoda de la cajonería de la sacristía de las Comendadoras de Santiago. Madrid

800. Commode in the sacristy of the Comendadoras de Santiago. Madrid

801. Cajonería muy abarrocada. Sacristía de la Iglesia de San Gil. Ecija

801. Chest of drawers, very baroque. Sacristy of the Church of Saint Gil. Ecija

802. Bargueño abierto con cajonería de madera y aplicaciones de bronce. Museo de Artes Decorativas. Madrid

802. "Bargueño", open with drawers in wood with bronze appliqués. Museum of Decorative Arts. Madrid

803. Cómoda panzuda marqueteada. Patrimonio Nacional. Madrid

803. Bombé commode with marquetry decoration. National Patrimony. Madrid

804. Armario de sacristía con tallas policromadas y doradas; aplicaciones laterales con tallas inspiradas en el Luis XV. Catedral de Burgos

804. Sacristy cupboard with polychrome and gilt carvings. Lateral appliqués with carvings of Louis XV style. Burgos Cathedral

805. Papelera con cuerpo alto de cajones sobre mesa con patas salomónicas; aplicaciones de bronce. Museo de Artes Decorativas. Madrid

805. Cabinet for keeping papers, standing on table with twist-turned legs and bronze mounts. Museum of Decorative Arts. Madrid

806. Mueble alto de dos cuerpos: el inferior es un bureau de tapa inclinada con cajonería panzuda: el superior con dos puertas. Museo Municipal de Madrid

806. High bureau in two parts. The lower part has a sloping top and curved drawers: the upper part has two doors. Municipal Museum of Madrid

807. Uno de los más bellos tocadores de Mallorca, chapeado con hojas de caoba y ébano: en parte dorado. Palacio de Campo-Franco

807. One of the most beautiful boudoirs of Majorca, covered with mahogany and ebony, partly gilt. Palace of Campo-Franco

808. Cama con alto cabecero barroco, pintado y dorado; piecero con patas cabriolé. Casa Solá. Olot

808. Bed with high Baroque headboard, painted and gilt. Cabriolet legs. Solá House. Olot

809. Cama de tipo mallorquín del siglo XVII-XVIII con elementos torneados y salomónicos

809. Majorcan type bed from 17th-18th century with turned and Solomonic elements

810. Cama mallorquí en palo santo; cabecero con remate y patas con elementos torneados y salomónicos típicos de la región. Palma de Mallorca

810. Majorcan bed made of lignum. Crested headpiece and turned and Solomonic legs typical of the region. Palma de Majorca

811. Cama del siglo XVII

811. 17th-century bed

812. Cama imitación de ébano con inscrustaciones de marfil y bronce cincelado. Colección del Marqués de San Martín. Coruña

812. Bed in imitation ebony with ivory and chiselled bronze inlay. Marquis of St Martin Collection. Coruña

813. Cama del palacio de Villalonga, de línea portuguesa, en palo santo y bronce. Palma de Mallorca

813. Bed of the Palace of Villalonga. Portuguese taste in lignum vital with bronzework. Palma Majorca

814. Cama de madera tallada. Colección Beancharre. Pontevedra

814. Bed in carved wood. Beancharre Collection

815. Cama de madera tallada y metal cincelado. Palacio de Linares del Prado. Pontevedra

815. Bed in carved wood and chiselled metal. Palace of Linares del Prado. Pontevedra

816. Salón del palacio de Villa Real. Puerto de Santa María. Cádiz

816. Salon of the palace of Villa Real. Puerto de Santa María. Cadiz

817. Consola. Palacio de Villa Real. Puerto de Santa María. Cádiz

817. Console table. Palace of Villa Real. Puerto de Santa Maria. Cadiz

818. Interior de la casa Oleza. Palma de Mallorca. Las cornucopias son neoclásicas y la mesa de la parte central, llamada de "lira", del siglo XVIII

818. Interior of the Oleza House, Palma de Majorca. The cornucopias are Neo-classical, the table in the center, known as a "lyre table" is from the 18th century

819. Cama popular levantina pintada. Museo de Artes Decorativas. Madrid

819. Popular painted Levant bed. Museum of Decorative Arts. Madrid

820. Vista parcial de la sala capitular, obra del maestro Lucas Ferro Caveiro, año 1752. Catedral de Santiago de Compostela

820. Partial view of the Chapter-house, the work of master Lucas Ferro Caveiro, 1752. Cathedral of Santiago de Compostela

821. Salón Carlos III. Palacio Real de Madrid

821. Charles III salon. Royal Palace. Madrid

822. Evolución de la silla portuguesa: tipo primero, derivación del frailero; respaldo bajo de cuero repujado. Siglo XVII

822. Evolution of the Portuguese chair: the first type in the "frailero" style, low back with repoussé leatherwork. XVII century

823. Tipo segundo, respaldo inclinado

823. Second type, sloping back

824. Tipo tercero, respaldo más alto y copete curvo

824. Third type, higher back and curved cresting

825. Tipo cuarto, patas torneadas, respaldo más curvo, chambrana con tallas muy finas

825. Fourth type, turned legs, back more curved, with finely carved stretcher

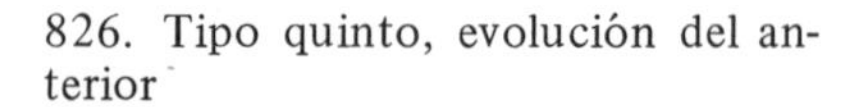

826. Tipo quinto, evolución del anterior

826. Fifth type, development of the preceding one

827. Tipo sexto, sillón con las patas rematadas en volutas

827. Sixth type, armchair with legs ending in scrolls

828. Tipo séptimo, patas cabriolé con chambrana

828. Seventh type, cabriolet legs with stretcher

829. Tipo octavo, patas cabriolé "tipo inglés" con garras sobre bolas: copete rococó de influencia francesa

829. Eighth type, cabriolet legs on claw-and-ball feet in the English taste: rococo cresting with French influence

830. Sillón de copete rococó, patas cabriolé en chambrana cruzada. Museo Valencia de Don Juan. Madrid

830. Armchair with rococo cresting, cabriolet legs with crossed stretcher. Valencia de Don Juan Museum. Madrid

831. Sillón característico, siglo XVIII. Museo Nacional de Arte Antiguo. Lisboa

831. Characteristic 18th-century armchair. National Museum of Antique Art. Lisbon

832. Sillón de despacho de características inglesas y realización portuguesa. Museo Nacional de Arte Antiguo. Lisboa

832. Study armchair in the English taste, Portuguese execution. National Museum of Antique Art. Lisbon

833. Silla de características inglesas semejantes. Museo Nacional de Arte Antiguo. Lisboa

833. Chair of similar characteristics in the English taste. National Museum of Antique Art. Lisbon

834. Sofá de inspiración inglesa. Museo Nacional de Arte Antiguo. Lisboa

834. Settee in the English taste. National Museum of Antique Art. Lisbon

835. Mesa con los característicos torneados portugueses y molduras rizadas. Museo Nacional de Arte Antiguo. Lisboa

835. Table with the characteristic Portuguese turned members and looped mouldings. National Museum of Antique Art. Lisbon

836. Mueble alto, cerrado y abierto; vitrina, buró-cómoda de palo santo. Museo Nacional de Arte Antiguo. Lisboa

836. Bureau-cabinet on commode in lignum, doors and flaps closed and open. National Museum of Antique Art. Lisbon

837. Interpretación del bargueño, en palo santo, con patas de torneados salomónicos y molduras rizadas

837. An interpretation of the "bargeño" in lignum, with twist-turned legs and looped moulding

838. Armario con molduras rizadas y decoración barroca. Museo Nacional de Arte Antiguo. Lisboa

838. Cupboard with looped mouldings and baroque decoration. National Museum of Antique Art. Lisbon

839. Mueble de influencia oriental con marquetería. Museo Nacional de Arte Antiguo. Lisboa

839. A piece with oriental influence and marquetry decoration. National Museum of Antique Art. Lisbon

840. Interpretación del bargueño. Museo Nacional de Arte Antiguo. Lisboa

840. An interpretation of the "bargueño". National Museum of Antique Art. Lisbon

841. Cama de influencia portuguesa del siglo XVIII, con cabecero calado. Colección particular. Galicia

841. Bed with Portuguese influence of the 18th century, with fretwork head. Private collection. Galicia

842. Cama barroca. Interpretación muy americana en las tallas y ornamentaciones. "El tránsito de la Virgen". Tema muy repetido en iglesias y casas particulares. Quito

842. Baroque bed, with marqued American taste in the carvings and decoration. "The Death of the Virgin". A much repeated theme in churches and private houses. Quito

843. Sillón tapizado con terciopelo de Génova, madera de nogal, 1685

843. Walnut armchair upholstered in Genoa velvet, 1685

844. Sillón de nogal y rejilla en el respaldo, 1685. Victoria and Albert Museum. Londres

844. Armchair in walnut, with cane panel in the back, 1685. Victoria and Albert Museum

845. Sillón tapizado de terciopelo, 1690

845. Armchair upholstered in velvet, 1690

846. Sillón Windsor, de palos torneados y salomónicos, tipo popular, 1685. Colección Mr. Fred Skull

846. Windsor armchair with turned and twist-turned members, popular type, 1685. Mr. Fred Skull

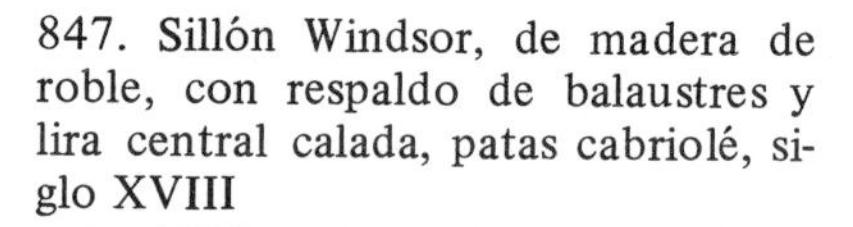

847. Sillón Windsor, de madera de roble, con respaldo de balaustres y lira central calada, patas cabriolé, siglo XVIII

847. 18th-century Windsor armchair in oak with baluster back, lyre-shaped splat and cabriolet legs

848. Sillón de caoba con pala tallada con hojas de acanto, patas con garra, 1730. Colección M. Percival Griffiths

848. Mahogany armchair, splat with acanthus leaf decoration, claw form feet, 1730. Mr. Percival Griffiths Collection

849. Silla de finas proporciones en caoba, 1750. Colección Mr. Percival Griffiths

849. Mahogany chair in fine proportions, 1750. Mr. Percival Griffiths Collection

850. Silla de caoba, llamada del Burgomaestre, 1725. Colección Lyme Park

850. Mahogany chair known as the Burgomaster's, 1725. Lyme Park Collection

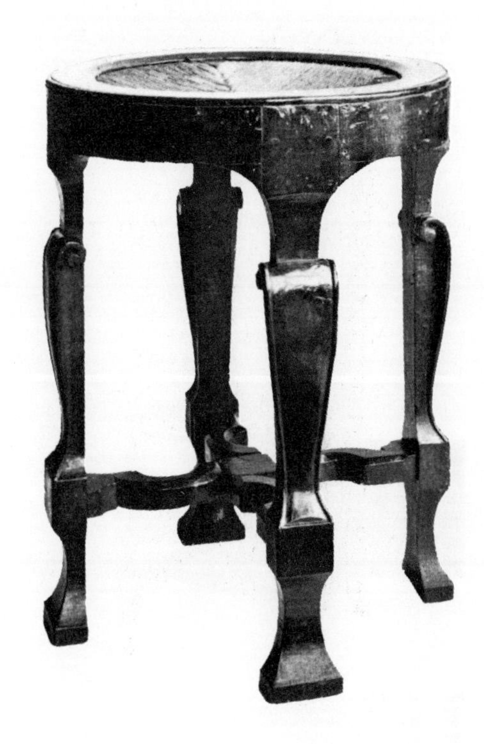

851. Banqueta tapizada en azul damasco, patas y chambranas William and Mary, 1685. Colección del duque de Buccleuch

851. Stool upholstered in blue damask, with legs and stretcher of the William and Mary period, 1685. Duke of Buccleuch Collection

852. Banqueta circular de nogal, 1710. Colección Canons Ashby

852. Circular stool in walnut, 1710. Canons Ashby Collection

853. Banqueta de nogal: patas William and Mary, con chambranas cruzadas y pie rematado en voluta, 1690. Hampton Court Palace

853. Walnut stool: legs with crossed stretcher and feet ending in scrolls, of the William and Mary period, 1690. Hampton Court Palace.

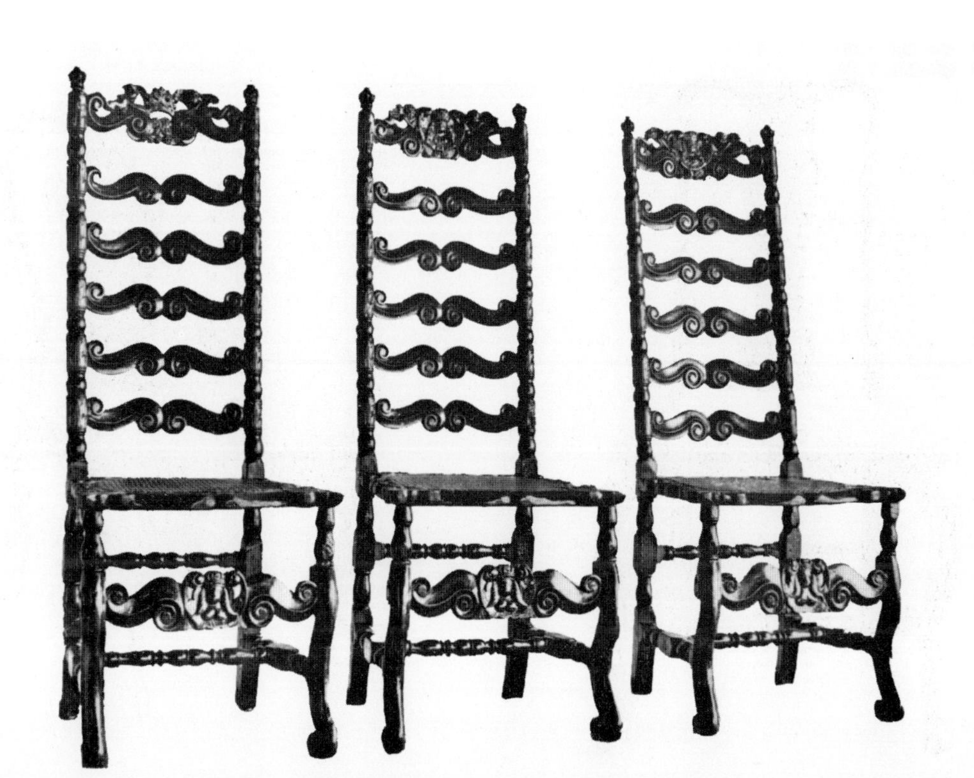

854. Sillas de nogal con respaldo con aldaba "de escaleras" estilo William and Mary, 1688. Colección Towers de Essex

854. Walnut chairs with ladder-back rails, typical of the William and Mary period, 1688. Colección Towers of Essex Collection

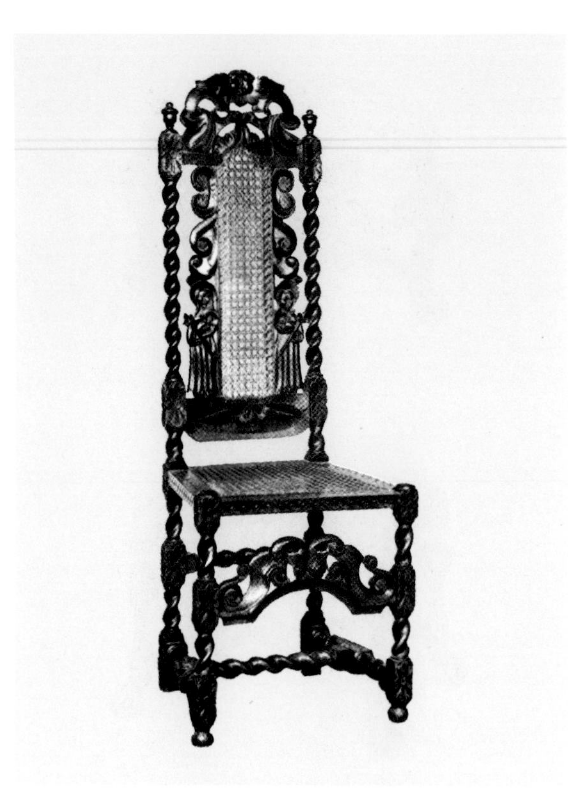

855. Silla de roble con asiento y respaldo con rejilla, tallas típicas del William and Mary, 1685

855. Oak chair with caned seat and back, carving typical of the William and Mary period, 1685

856. Silla de nogal tallada, 1688. Chilham Castle. Kent

856. Carved walnut chair, 1688. Chilham Castle. Kent

857. Silla de nogal con patas cabriolé y respaldo con palas planas y sencillas, chambrana entre las patas, características de la época de la reina Ana. Colección Mr. H. Avray Tipping

857. Walnut chair with cabriolet legs, back with simple panel splat and stretchers between the legs, characteristics of the Queen Anne period. Mr. H. Avray Tipping Collection

858. Silla de nogal con pala central, hacia 1720, patas sobre garra. Colección M. Percival Griffiths

858. Walnut chair with central spalt, claw form feet, c. 1720 Mr. Percival Griffiths Collection

859. Silla estilo Chippendale con aldabas en escalera, 1770. Colección Edward Hudson

859. Chippendale style ladder-back chair, 1770. Edward Hudson Collection

860. Silla de caoba con pala central ornamentada con cintas, 1755. Colección de Nostell

860. Mahogany chair, splat with ribbon decoration, 1755. De Nostell Collection

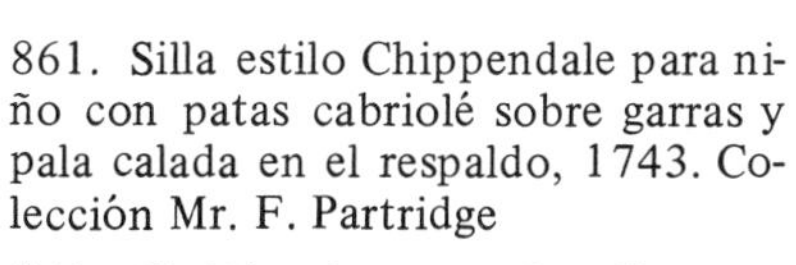

861. Silla estilo Chippendale para niño con patas cabriolé sobre garras y pala calada en el respaldo, 1743. Colección Mr. F. Partridge

861. Child's chair in the Chippendale style, with cabriolet legs and claw feet, fretcut splat, 1743. Mr. F. Partridge Collection

862. Silla de caoba con ornamentación de cintas, patas cabriolé rococó, 1755. Colección Leopold Hirsch

862. Mahogany chair with ribbon decoration and rococo cabriolet legs, 1755. Leopold Hirsch Collection

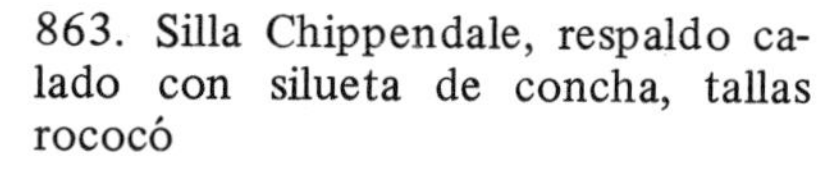

863. Silla Chippendale, respaldo calado con silueta de concha, tallas rococó

863. Chippendale chair with shell form back, rococo carving

864. Silla de caoba con pala calada, sobre pata cuadrada, 1755. Colección Percy Macquoid

864. Mahogany chair, with fretcut splat, on squared legs, 1755. Percy Macquoid Collection

865. Silla pintada con decoración caligráfica del 1765. Colección Edward Hudson

865. Painted chair with calligraphic decoration, 1765. Edward Hudson Collection

866. Silla, dibujo de Chippendale, de influencia francesa, "Director", 1753

866. Chair, designed by Chippendale, with French influence, 1753 edition of the "Director"

867. Silla de caoba, estilo Chippendale, época chinesca, 1765. Castillo Lulworth. Dorset

867. Chippendale style mahogany chair, Chinese period, 1765. Lulworth Castle. Dorset

868. Silla de caoba con dibujo chinesco, 1765. Colección Lannoxlove Haddington

868. Mahogany chair with Chinese drawings, 1765. Lannoxlove Haddington Collection

869. Silla, dibujo de Chippendale con influencia gótica, patas rectas caladas, primera edición de "Director", 1753

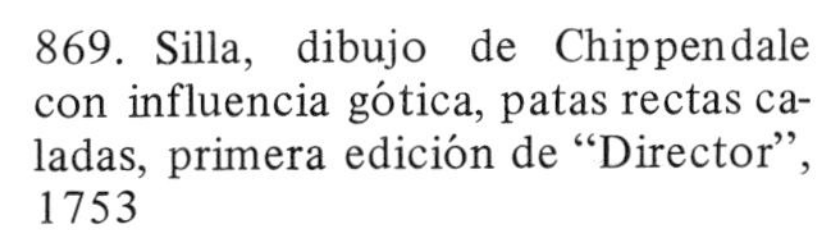

869. Chair, design by Chippendale, with Gothic influence, straight fret-cut legs, first edition of the "Director", 1753

870. Doble silla o canapé, principios del barroco William and Mary, 1685

870. Early baroque double-seat settee of the William and Mary period, 1685

871. Canapé o sofá de dos plazas, de nogal con patas cabriolé sobre garras: palas en el respaldo, hacia 1720. Colección Mr. Percival Griffiths

871. Walnut settee of double seat form, with cabriolet legs on claws, splats in the back, c. 1720. Mr. Percival Griffiths Collection

872. Sofá de caoba de dos plazas, patas cabriolé sobre garras, hacia 1750. Colección Mr. Percival Griffiths

872. Mahogany settee of double seat form, cabriolet legs on claw feet, c. 1750. Mr. Percival Griffiths Collection

873. Sofá de tres plazas, semejante al de la figura 871. 1730. Colección Mr. Percival Griffiths

873. Settess of triple seat form, similar to the figure 871. 1730. Mr. Percival Griffiths Collection

874. Sofá de tres plazas de caoba con patas rectas y palas caladas, 1770. Colección Bramshill Park

874. Mahogany settee of triple seat from with stright legs and fretcut splats, 1770. Bramshill Park Collection

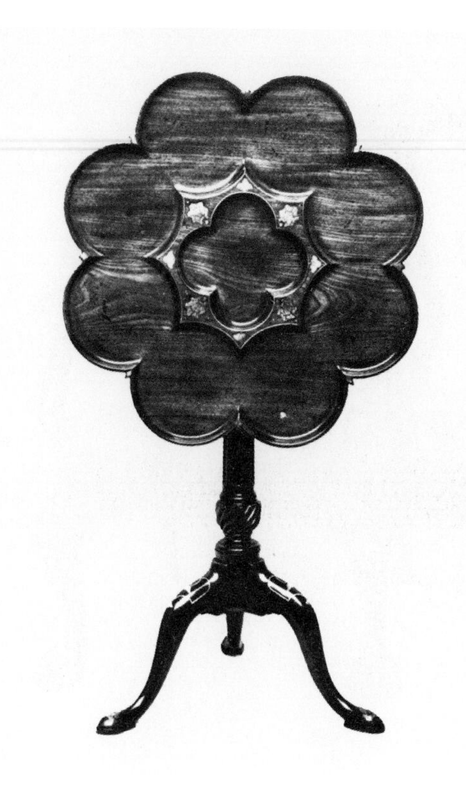

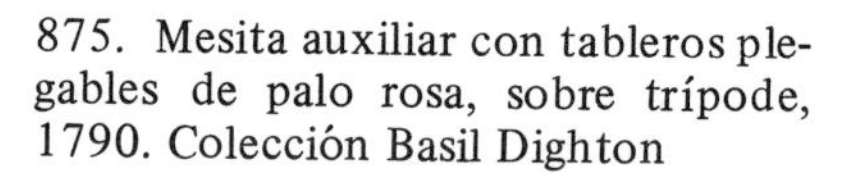

875. Mesita auxiliar con tableros plegables de palo rosa, sobre trípode, 1790. Colección Basil Dighton

875. Occasional tripod table with drop top, in tulip wood, 1790. Basil Dighton Collection

876. Mesa de caoba con compartimientos circulares para platos, trípode sobre patas cabriolé, 1760. Colección Frank Partridge

876. Mahogany tripod table with circular compartments for plates, cabriolet legs, 1760. Frank Partridge Collection

877. Mesa auxiliar de caoba con cuatro pisos, patas cabriolé, 1760.

877. Four-tiered dumbwaiter in mahogany, with cabriolet legs, 1760

878. Mesita de roble, patas y tableros abatibles, 1660. Colección Ernest Lawrence

878. Small gate-leg table in oak, 1660. Ernest Lawrence Collection

879. Mesa "gate-leg" con patas plegables, de roble, salomónica, principios del barroco, 1665

879. Oak gate-leg table with twist-turned members, early baroque, 1665

880. Mesa de patas plegables y tableros abatibles, de silueta salomónica, que señalan el principio del barroco, 1680. Colección Ernest Lawrence

880. Gate-leg table with twist turned supports, showing the early baroque period, 1680. Ernest Lawrence Collection

881. Mesa doble con patas y tableros abatibles. Principios del barroco, 1660. Colección N.R. Colville

881. Gate-leg table, early baroque period, 1660. N.R. Colville Collection

882. Mesa de nogal con dobles patas plegables y tablero abatible. Colección N.R. Colville

882. Walnut gate-leg table. N.R. Colville Collection

883. Mesa consola con tapa de mármol y tapas cabriolé con garras sobre bolas, 1760

883. Console table with marble top, cabriolet legs on claw-and-ball feet, 1760

884. Mesa de consola con tapa de mármol, 1745. Tallada. Colección Langley Park. Norfolk

884. Carved console table with marble top, 1745. Langley Park Collection. Norfolk

885. Mesa consola tallada y decorada, 1730. Colección Lady Capel Cure

885. Console table, carved and decorated, 1730. Lady Capel Cure Collection

886. Consola tallada y dorada, 1730. Colección St. Giles House. Dorset

886. Carved and gilt console table, 1730. St. Giles House Collection. Dorset

887. Dibujo para cómoda, por Chippendale, 1760, de "Director"

887. Commode, drawing by Chippendale in the "Director", 1760

888. Mesa de despacho con frentes abombados. Tableros planos y decorados, época Chippendale, bronces dorados, 1775. Colección Mr. Percival Griffiths

888. Serpentine-fronted writing-table; flat, decorated panels, Chippendale period, gilded brass mounts, 1775. Colección Mr. Percival Griffiths Collection

889. Mesa de despacho con frentes abombados, dibujo de Chippendale, en "Director", 1760. Colección Althorp Northamptonshire

889. Sepentine-fronted writing-desk, drawing by Chippendale in the "Director", 1760

890. Mesa de despacho con patas de garra, tiradores y bocallaves de bronce cincelado, 1760. Colección Mr. S. Joel

890. Writing-desk on claw feet, with chiselled bronze handles and key-plates, 1760. Mr. S. Joel Collection

891. Cómoda de caoba, frentes curvos, 1760. Colección Bayfordbury. Herts

891. Serpentine-fronted comode in mahogany, 1760. Bayfordury Collection. Herts

892. Cómoda de caoba, 1760. Colección Percy Dean

892. Mahogany commode, 1760. Percy Dean Collection

893. Cómoda, palmas de caoba, 1740. Colección Thursby Pelham

893. Commode, mahogany panels, 1740. Thursby Pelham Collection

894. Cómoda con panza de caoba, tallas planas de tipo Chippendale y bronces franceses estilo Luis XV. Colección Mr. Frank Partridge

894. Bow-fronted commode in mahogany, with low relief in the Chippendale taste, French bronze mounts in the Louis XV style. Mr. Frank Partridge Collection

895. Cómoda de panza. Frente abombado cubierto con chapas de maderas finas y bronces dorados. Colección Thursby Pelham

895. Bow-fronted commode with rich wood veneer and ormolu mounts. Thursby Pelham Collection

896. Cómoda de nogal con marquetería, época William and Mary, 1685. Colección Rev. Wiffred Brocklebank

896. Walnut commode with marquetry decoration, William and Mary period, 1685. Rev. Wiffred Brocklebank Collection

897. Cómoda-armario de dos cuerpos. El superior con puertas, el inferior, cómoda, cubierto con hojas de palma de caoba, frontón partido calado, 1770. Colección Mr. Percival Griffiths

897. Wardrobe-comode in two sections. The upper part with doors; the lower section, the commode, with mahogany veneers. The piece is topped with a fretcut broken pediment, 1770. Mr. Percival Griffiths Collection

898. Armario de dos cuerpos, el superior sobre cómoda, frente abombado rococó. Colección Mulliner

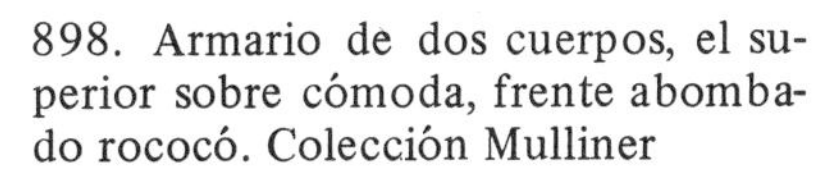

898. Wardrobe in two sections, the upper one on a rococo bombé-fronted commode. Mulliner Collection

899. Dibujo del armario precedente por Chippendale, en "Director", 1753

899. Drawing of the preceding wardrobe, by Chippendale, in the first edition of the "Director", 1753

900. "Tall-boy" estilo reina Ana, chapeada con palmas

900. Veneered tall-boy in the Queen Anne taste

901. "Tall-boy" mueble para vestirse, en madera de caoba, las patas cabriolé y la concha característica del reina Ana

901. Tall-boy in mahogany with cabriolet legs and shell decoration, characteristics of the Queen Anne period

902. Armario "tall-boy", 1760. Decoración de celosías chinescas. Caoba y bronce. Colección Mr. Percival Griffiths

902. Tall-boy. Chinese lattice-work decoration, in mahogany and bronze, 1760. Mr Percival Griffiths Collection

903. Armario de caoba de dos cuerpos, cubierto con palmas, 1770. Paso al neoclásico. Colección Mr. Percival Griffiths

903. Mahogany wardrobe in two stages, veneered. Transition to the neoclasical period, 1770. Mr. Percival Griffiths Collection

904. Armario-cabinet de nogal con marquetería de flores estilo holandés, hacia 1685. Colección M. F. Mallet

904. Wardrobe-cabinet in walnut with floral marquetry in the Dutch style, c. 1685. M. F. Mallet Collection

905. Cabinet laqueado sobre mesa tallada y dorada, 1685. Colección The Vyne

905. Lacquered cabinet on carved and gilded table, 1685. The Vyne Collection

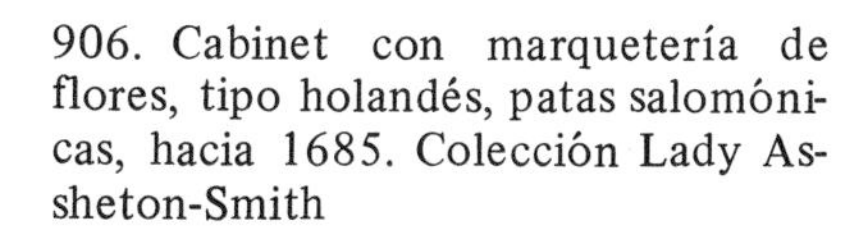

906. Cabinet con marquetería de flores, tipo holandés, patas salomónicas, hacia 1685. Colección Lady Assheton-Smith

906. Cabinet with Dutch type floral marquetry and twist-turned legs, c. 1685. Lady Assheton-Smith Collection

907. Cabinet-vitrina de caoba con decoración chinesca Chippendale, 1775. Penshurst Place, Kent

907. Chippendale mahogany china cabinet with Chinese decoration, 1775. Penshurst Place, Kent

908. Buró de tapa inclinada con cuerpo alto laqueado coronado por un frontón partido, 1715. Colección Mr. Percy Macquoid

908. Bureau with sloping flap, upper stage lacquered and topped with a broken pediment, 1715. Mr. Percy Macquoid Collection

909. Buró con cuerpo alto de nogal, reina Ana, 1720. Colección Mr. Percival Griffiths

909. Bureau with the upper section in walnut, in the Queen Anne style, 1770. Mr. Percival Griffiths Collection

910. Buró de caoba de Chippendale, 1748. Colección Mr. Percival Griffiths

910. Chippendale mahogany bureau, 1748. Mr Percival Griffiths Collection

911. Aparador de roble con patas cabriolé de tipo popular, hacia 1770. Colección Mayor Herbert Jenkins

911. Oak sideboard with popular type cabriolet legs, c. 1770. Major Herbert Jenkins Collection

912. Aparador de roble, popular, hacia 1755. Colección Edward Hudson

912. Oak dresser in the popular style, c. 1755. Edward Hudson Collection

913. Reloj abuelo de nogal con decoración de hoja, 1705. Colección Drummont Robertson

913. Long-case clock with inlay, 1705. Drummont Robertson Collection

914. Reloj abuelo de caja alta con marquetería, 1680. Colección Drummont Robertson

914. Longe-case clock with marquetry, 1680. Drummont Robertson Collection

915. Reloj abuelo, marquetería con nogal, 1680. Coleccción F. Garrett

915. Longe-case clock with walnut marquetry, 1680. F. Garret Collection

916. Virginal de Adam Leversidge de madera de roble, con pinturas del parque de St. James, 1670. Colección Mr Arthur F. Hills

916. Virginal by Adam Leversidge, in oak with painting of St James's Park, 1670. Mr. Arthur F. Hills Collection

917. Dormitorio del embajador veneciano en Knole, época de Jaime II, 1685-1688

917. The Venetian ambassador's bedroom at Knole, James II period, 1685-1688

918. Cama con dosel. Castillo de Leeds en Kent, año 1770

918. Bed with canopy. Leeds Castle, Kent, 1770

919. Cama de limoncillo y marquetería con colgaduras muy ricas, por Robert Adam, 1770

919. Bed in limewood and marquetry, with rich hangings, by Robert Adam, 1770

920. Dormitorio regencia hacia 1700, de la época de la reina Carlota. Sezincote House, Gloucestershire

920. Regency bedroom, c. 1700. Queen Charlotte period. Sezincotte House, Gloucestershire

921. Interior de Broughton House, Northamptonshire. Epoca posterior a Cromwell, 1680

921. Interior at Broughton House, Northamptonshire. Restoration period, 1680

922. Librería y mesa en Nostell, Yorkshire. Decoración de Robert Adam. Muebles Chippendale, 1770

922. Library and table at Nostell, Yorkshire. Decoration by Robert Adam; furniture by Chippendale, 1770

923. Sillón tallado y dorado, alto 110, frente 64. Schlossmuseum. Berlín

923. Carved and gilt armchair. Height 110, front 64. Schlossmuseum. Berlin

924. Sillón dorado con tallas rococó

924. Gilt armchair with rococó carving

925. Silla del norte de Alemania, de influencia inglesa, mediados del siglo XVIII

925. Mid-18th-century chair of north Germany, with English influence

926. Silla de nogal del norte, siglo XVIII. Schlossmuseum. Berlín

926. 18th-century walnut chair of the north. Schlossmuseum. Berlin

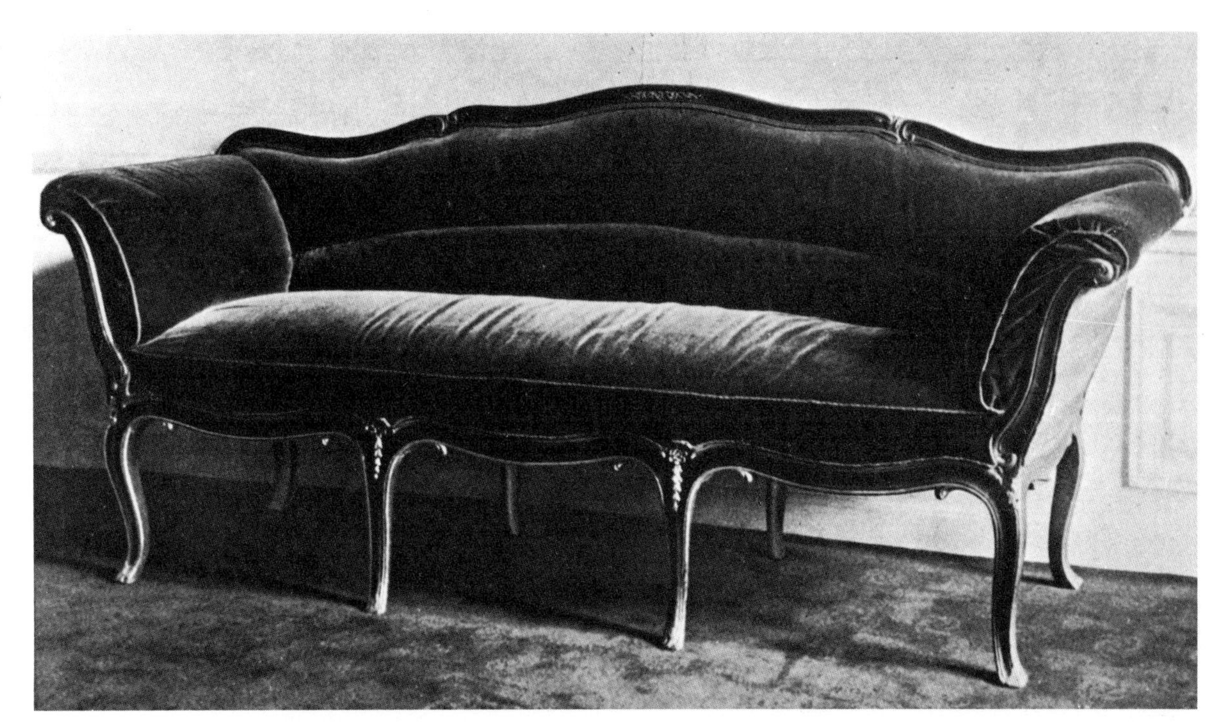

927. Canapé de tres plazas, mitad del siglo XVIII. Munich

927. Mid-18th-century settee of triple seat form. Munich

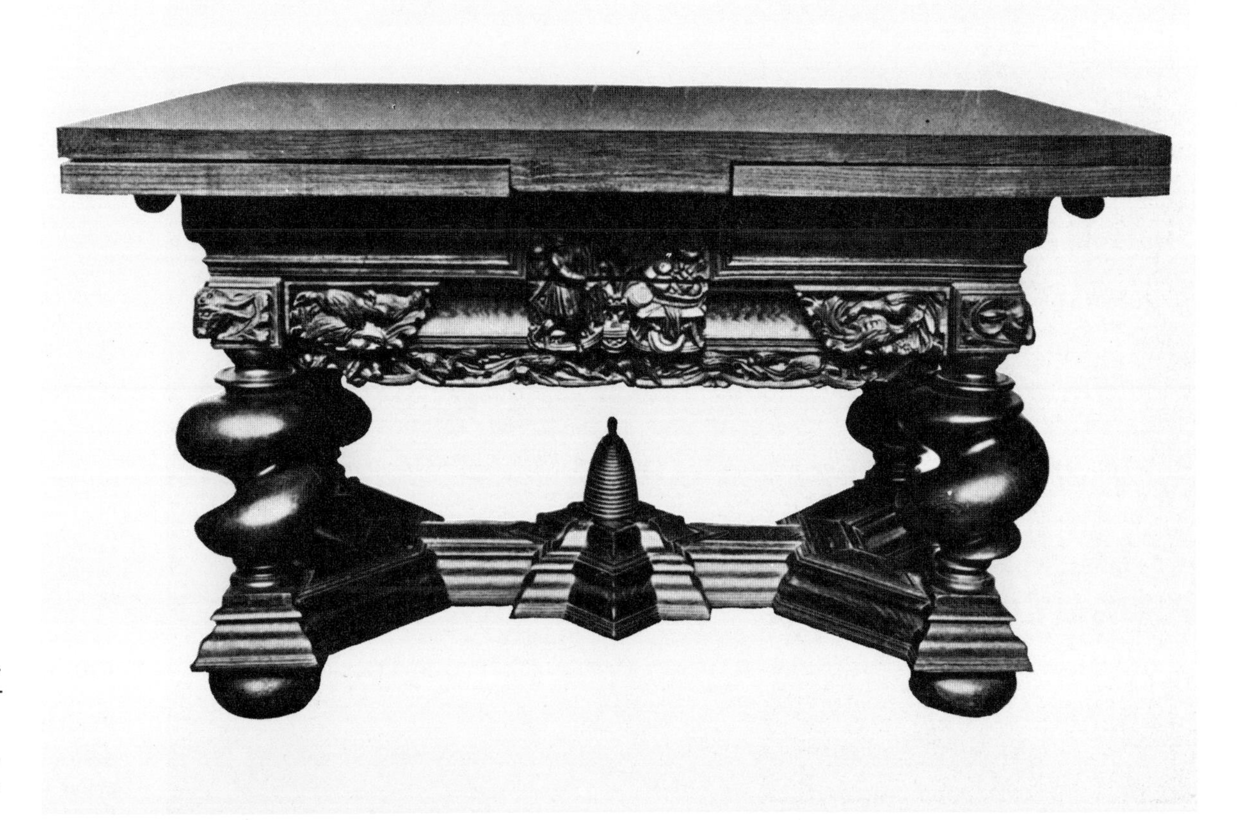

928. Mesa de nogal ampliable. Dantzig, hacia 1700. Altura 89, frente 149. Schlossmuseum. Berlín

928. Walnut draw-leaf table, c. 1700. Dantzig. Height 89, front 149. Schlossmuseum. Berlin

929. Mesa de despacho con marquetería y patas salomónicas. Charlottemburg. Berlín

929. Study desk with marquetry decoration and twist-turned legs. Charlottemburg. Berlin

930. Cómoda de Federico el Grande, de madera de cedro con incrustaciones de plata. Alto 93, frente 130; 1750. Stadtschloss. Potsdam

930. Commode of Frederick the Great in cedar wood with silver incrustations. Height 93, front 130. 1750. Stadtschloss. Potsdam

931. Cómoda laqueada y dorada. Influencia veneciana, mitad del siglo XVIII. Berlín

931. Lacquered and gilt commode, with Venetian influence, mid 18th century. Berlin

932. Cómoda pintada en azul claro, amarillo y oro. Altura 88, frente 150, fondo 80. Palacio nuevo de Potsdam

932. Commode, painted in light blue, yellow and gold. Height 88, front 150, depth 80. New Palace of Potsdam

933. Cómoda de panzas, con bronces y hojas de caoba, a mitad del siglo XVIII. Altura 82, frente 120. Stadtschloss. Potsdamm

933. Bombé commode, with bronze mounts and mahogany veneer, mid-18th century. Height 82, front 120, Stadtschloss. Potsdam

934. Armario de un barroco tardío, se compone de cuatro cuerpos, procede del norte de Alemania. Mediados del siglo XVIII

934. Mid-18th-century wardrobe in the late baroque style; it is made in four sections and comes from north Germany

935. Buró de David Roentgen en el Rijksmuseum. Amsterdam

935. Bureau by David Roentgen en el Rijksmuseum. Amsterdam

936. Vitrina para porcelanas, mitad del siglo XVIII. Altura 203, frente 114. Schlossmuseum. Berlín

936. Mid-18th-century china cabinet. Height 203, front 114. Schlossmuseum. Berlin

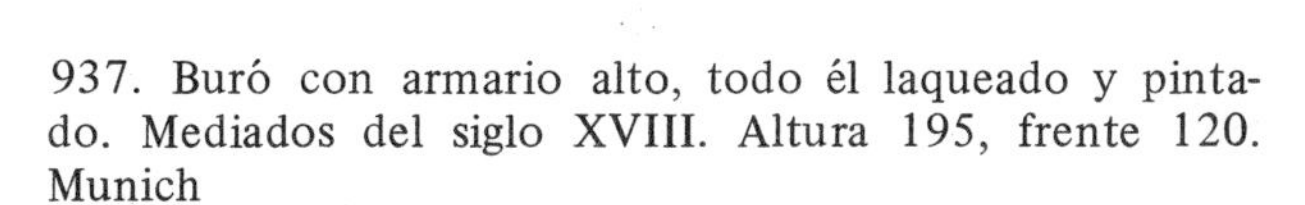

937. Buró con armario alto, todo él laqueado y pintado. Mediados del siglo XVIII. Altura 195, frente 120. Munich

937. Bureau with cabinet on top, all lacquered and painted, mid-18th century. Height 195, front 120. Munich

938. Armario con marquetería y celosía de bronce. Año 1720. Schlossmuseum. Berlín

938. Wardrobe with marquetry and pierced bronze work decoration 1720. Schlossmuseum. Berlin

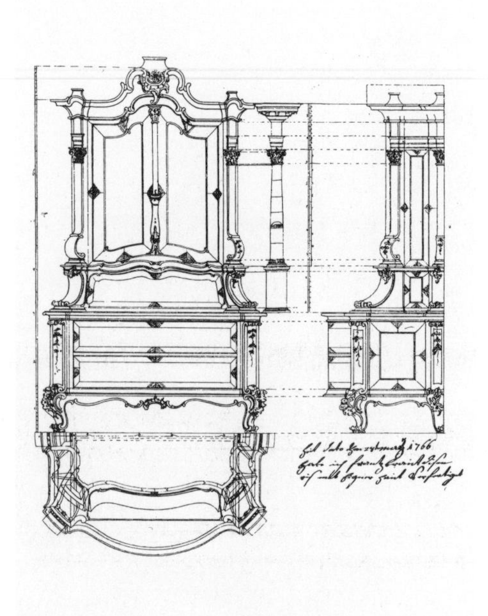

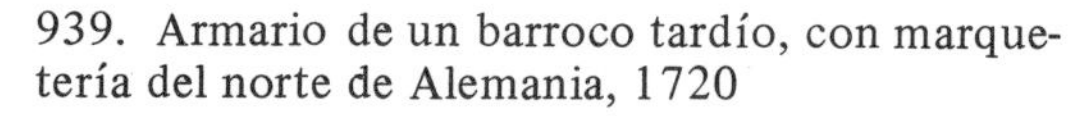

939. Armario de un barroco tardío, con marquetería del norte de Alemania, 1720

939. Late baroque wardrobe, with marquetry. N. Germany. 1720

940. Armario-escritorio, dibujo por Frantz Brandt, Mainz, 1766. Kunstbibliothek. Berlín

940. Escritoire-cabinet, drawing by Frantz Brandt, Maguncia, 1766. Kunstbibliothek. Berlin

941., Armario ropero en roble, de influencia francesa, 1758; alto 235, frente 154. Museo de Colonia

941. Oak wardrobe with French influence, 1758. Height 235, front 154. Cologne Museum

942. Armario-vitrina para porcelanas, madera de nogal, mediados del siglo XVIII. Altura 207, frente 120. Schlossmuseum. Berlín

942. Mid-18th-century china cabinet in walnut. Height 207, front 120. Schlossmuseum, Berlin

943. Armario del norte de Alemania, alto 251, frente 220. Madera de nogal, hacia 1700. Schlossmuseum. Berlín

943. Wardrobe of N. Germany in walnut. Height 251, front 220, c. 1700. Schlossmuseum. Berlin

944. Armario de Hamburgo, 1700

944. Wardrobe of Hamburg, 1700

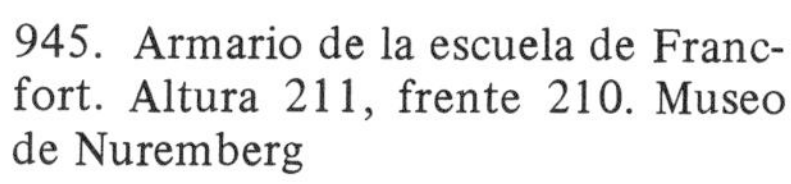

945. Armario de la escuela de Francfort. Altura 211, frente 210. Museo de Nuremberg

945. Wardrobe, Frankfort school. Height 211, front 210. Nuremberg Museum

946. Cabinet-armario, escuela de Dantzig, hacia 1700; cuerpo superior con dos puertas y molduras rizadas, mesa con patas salomónicas

946. Cabinet, Dantzig school, c. 1770. The upper stage has two door and looped mouldings, on stand with twist-turned legs

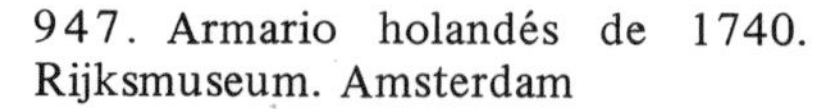

947. Armario holandés de 1740. Rijksmuseum. Amsterdam

947. Dutch cupboard, 1740. Rijksmuseum. Amsterdam

948. Cama de la fundación San Florian, Austria. Comienzos del siglo XVIII

948. Bed of St. Florian Foundation, Austria. Early 18th century

949. Cama de madera tallada y dorada de la fundación San Florian. Museo Nacional de Munich

949. Bed in carved and gilded wood of the St. Florian Foundation. Munich National Museum

950. Biblioteca de Federico el Grande; madera de cedro, tallas doradas, terminada en 1743. Palacio de Sanssouci

950. Frederick the Great's library; ceder wood and gilt carving, finished in 1743. Sanssouci Palace

951. Silla de influencia reina Ana, totalmente marqueteada con temas florales. Colección particular. Holanda

951. Chair in the Queen Anne taste, with floral marquetry all over. Private Collection. Netherlands

952. Silloncito popular, respaldo con aldabas en escalera y asiento de paja. Colección Claes. Amberes

952. Popular chair, with ladder-back and straw seat. Claes Collection. Antwerp

953. Sillón de tipo popular de influencia inglesa, asiento de anea. Colección Claes. Amberes

953. Popular type armchair with English influence, and rush seat. Claes Collection. Antwerp

954. Silla de influencia francesa, alto 78, frente 53. Hospital Saint-Sauveur. Lila

954. Armchair with French influence; height 78, front 53. Hospital Saint-Sauveur. Lille

955. Sillón de influencia francoespañola, estilo llamado de Rubens, tapizado con cuero estofado, siglo XVII, alto 93. Museo de Cluny. París

955. 17th-century armchair with French-Spanish influence, known as the Rubens style, upholstered in repoussé leather. Cluny Museum. Paris

956. Mesa con marquetería en la tapa y patas salomónicas

956. Table with marquetry top and twist-turned legs

957., Aparador de la escuela de Valenciennes, siglo XVII, frente 168, alto 110. Colección Thibeau-Motte. Roubaix

957. 17th-century sideboard of the Valenciennes school. Front 168, height 110. Thibeau-Motte Collection. Roubaix

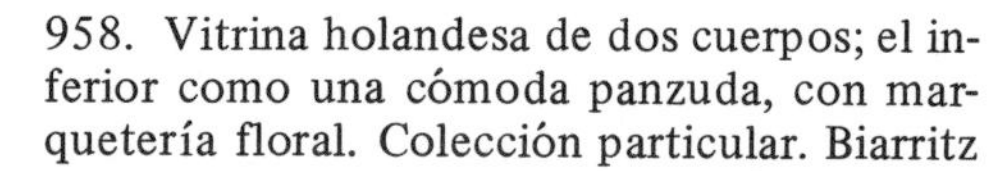

958. Vitrina holandesa de dos cuerpos; el inferior como una cómoda panzuda, con marquetería floral. Colección particular. Biarritz

958. Dutch display cabinet in two parts, the lower part like a paunchy commode with floral woodwork. Private collection. Biarritz

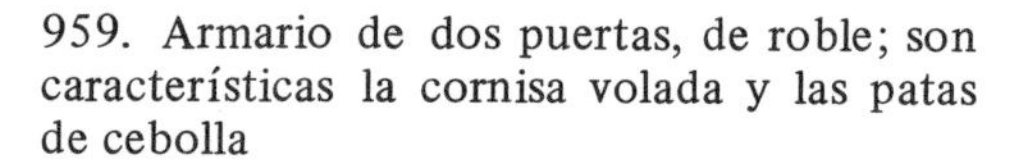

959. Armario de dos puertas, de roble; son características la cornisa volada y las patas de cebolla

959. Two-door wardrobe in oak; characteristics are the overhanging cornice and onion feet

960. Armario de dos cuerpos con marquetería, de influencia italiana. Colección particular

960. Two-stage cupboard with marquetry decoration, Italian influence. Private Collection

961. Armario flamenco del siglo XVIII con las características del estilo: cornisa volada, patas de cebolla y molduras violentas y rizadas

961. 18th-century Flemish cupboard with the features of the style: overhanging cornice, onion feet, marked and looped mouldings

962. Armario o bahut en nogal, de dos cuerpos, tallas del "Juició de París", altura 235, frente 204. Museo Vieille Boucherie. Amberes

962. Walnut cupboard or "bahut" in two section sand with carvings depicting the "Judgment of Paris". Height 235, front 204. Musée Vieille Boucherie. Antwerp

963. Armario o buffet flamenco de dos cuerpos en roble, fechado en 1664. Colección Claes. Amberes

963. Flemish two-stage cupboard, in oak. Dated 1664. Claes Collection. Antwerp

964. Buffett de dos cuerpos de ébano, con pinturas en cajones y puertas. Hospital Saint-Sauveur. Lila

964. Two-stage buffet in ebony, with paintings on the drawers and doors. Hospital Saint-Sauveur. Lille

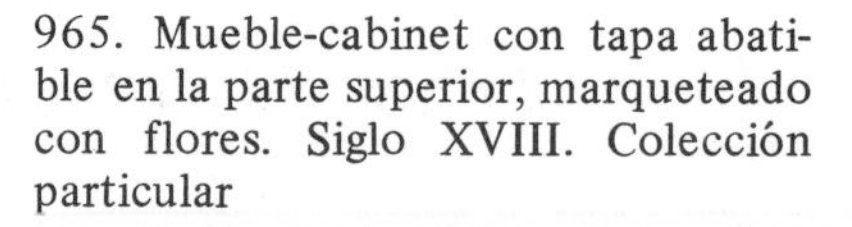

965. Mueble-cabinet con tapa abatible en la parte superior, marqueteado con flores. Siglo XVIII. Colección particular

965. Cabinet with drop flap in the upper part, floral marquetry decoration, 18th century. Private Collection

966. El mismo mueble abierto

966. The same piece with the flap down

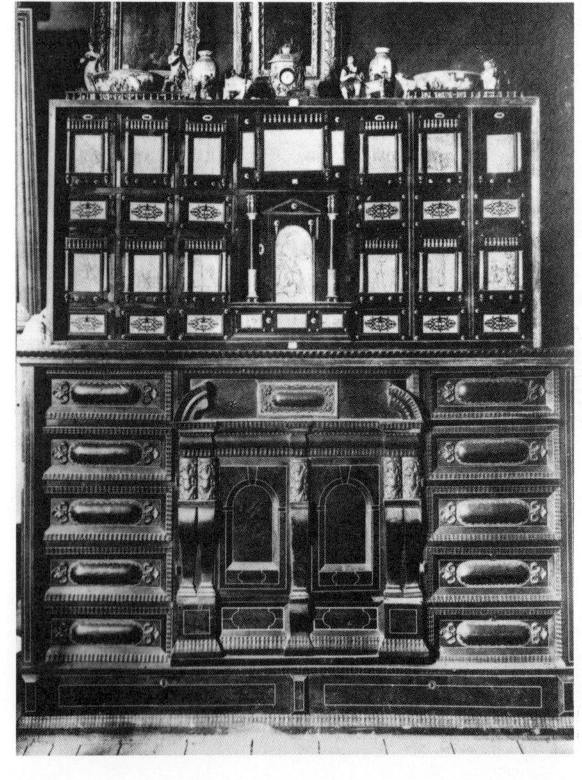

967. Cabinet de ébano con molduras rizadas y placas de marfil talladas; composición clásica. Siglo XVII. Alcaldía de Bailleul

967. Cabinet in ebony with looped mouldings and carved ivory panels, classical composition. 17th century. Town Hall of Bailleul

968. Cabinet de marquetería con patas en estípite. Tipo Luis XIV. Victoria and Albert Museum. Londres

968. Louis XIV type cabinet with marquetry decoration and legs of reversed pyramid form. Victoria and Albert Museum

969. Interior del estudio del pintor Jan Vermeer. Colección Czernin. Viena

969. Interior of the studio of the painter Jan Vermeer. Czernin Collection. Vienna

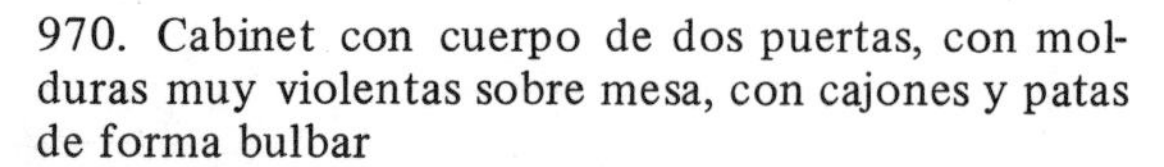

970. Cabinet con cuerpo de dos puertas, con molduras muy violentas sobre mesa, con cajones y patas de forma bulbar

970. Two-door cabinet with very marked mouldings supported on table with drawers and legs of bulbous form

971. Cómoda-escritorio con el esquema común de esta clase de muebles: parte inferior en forma de cómoda, parte central con cajonería y tapa abatible y parte superior en forma de armario

971., Commode-desk. The design is typical of this sort of furniture. The lower part is a commode, the central part has small drawers and a lid that opens out and down, and the top part is a cabinet.

972. Espejo holandés octogonal de ébano con moldura rizada y pintada. Hospital Tavera. Toledo

972. Dutch octogonal mirror in ebony with looped and painted mouldings. Hospital Tavera. Toledo

973. Reloj de influencia inglesa, siglo XVII. Nogal tallado; altura 240. Museo de Vieille Boucherie. Amberes

973. 17th-century long-case clock, with English influence, in walnut. Height 240. Musée de Vieille Boucherie. Antwerp

974. Reloj de nogal, siglo XVII; altura 260. Museo Plantin. Amberes

974. Long-case clock in walnut. 17th century. Height 260. Plantin Museum. Antwerp

NEOCLASICO E IMPERIO

NEO-CLASICAL AND EMPIRE

975. Bergère, por J. B. Boulard, pintada y dorada. Museo del Louvre

975. "Bergère", by J. B. Boulard, painted and gilded. Louvre

976. Bergère Luis XVI tallada y pintada. Colección Mlle. Rémy

976. Louis XVI "bergère", carved and painted. Mlle. Rémy Collection

977. Sillón Luis XVI. Caoba moldurada y tallada en su color. Asiento con cuero verde. Respaldo cuadrado con lira. Firmado por G. Jacob, en Mobiliario Nacional. París

977. Louis XVI armchair. Moulded and carved mahogany in its own colour, seat in green leather, back with lyre-shaped splat. Signed by G. Jacob. Paris

978. Sillón firmado por G. Jacob, tallado y pintado. Museo del Louvre

978. Armchair, carved and painted, signed by G. Jacob. Louvre

979. Butaca para el gabinete de María Antonieta en Saint-Cloud. Museo del Louvre.

979. Armchair from Marie Antoinette's boudoir at Saint-Cloud. Louvre

980. Silla Montgolfière, de madera pintada en blanco. Estampilla de J.B. Demay, 1780-1790. Colección Penard y Fernández

980. Montgolfière chair in white painted wood. Stamped by J.B. Demay, 1780-1790. Penard & Fernández Collection

981. Butaca, por J. B. Tilliard, tallada y dorada. Museo de Cleveland

981. Armchair, by J. B. Tilliard, carved and gilded. Cleveland Museum

982. Silla de María Antonieta en el Petit Trianon, tallada y pintada

982. Marie Antoinette's chair at the Petit Trianon, carved and painted

983. Silla del gabinete de "rocaille" del palacio de Rambouillet. Madera pintada de verde y rosa, asiento redondo

983. Chair of "rocaille" sitting-room at the Palais de Rambouillet, in green and rose painted wood.

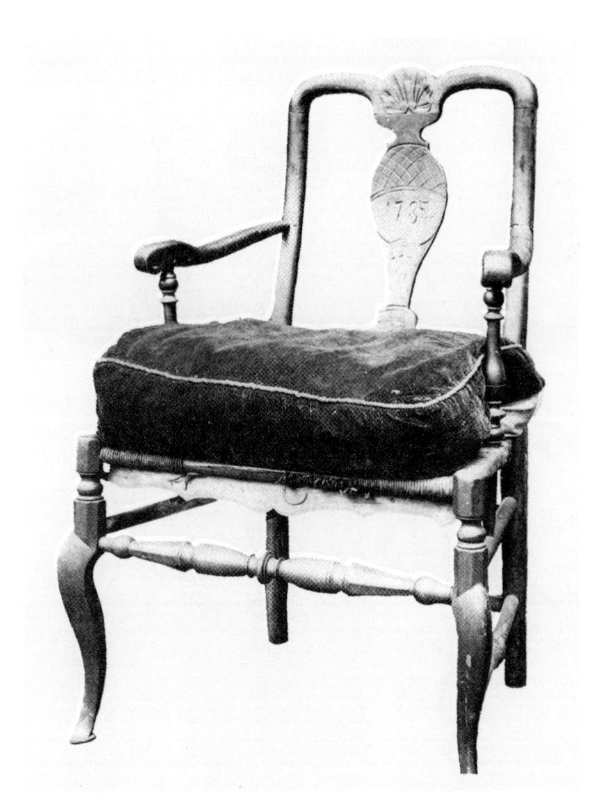

984. Silla popular con el tema Montgolfière, firmada en 1785

984. Popular chair with the Montgolfière theme, signed in 1785

985. Silla de tipo popular con respaldo de lira y asiento de anea

985. Popular type chair with lyre-shaped splat in the back and rush seat

986. Canapé Luis XVI. Madera pintada en gris, moldurada y esculpida. Estampilla de Pluvinet. 1780-1790. Colección Paul Louis Weiller

986. Louis XVI settee, grey painted, moulded and carved. Stamped by Pluvinet, 1780-1790. Paul Weiller Collection

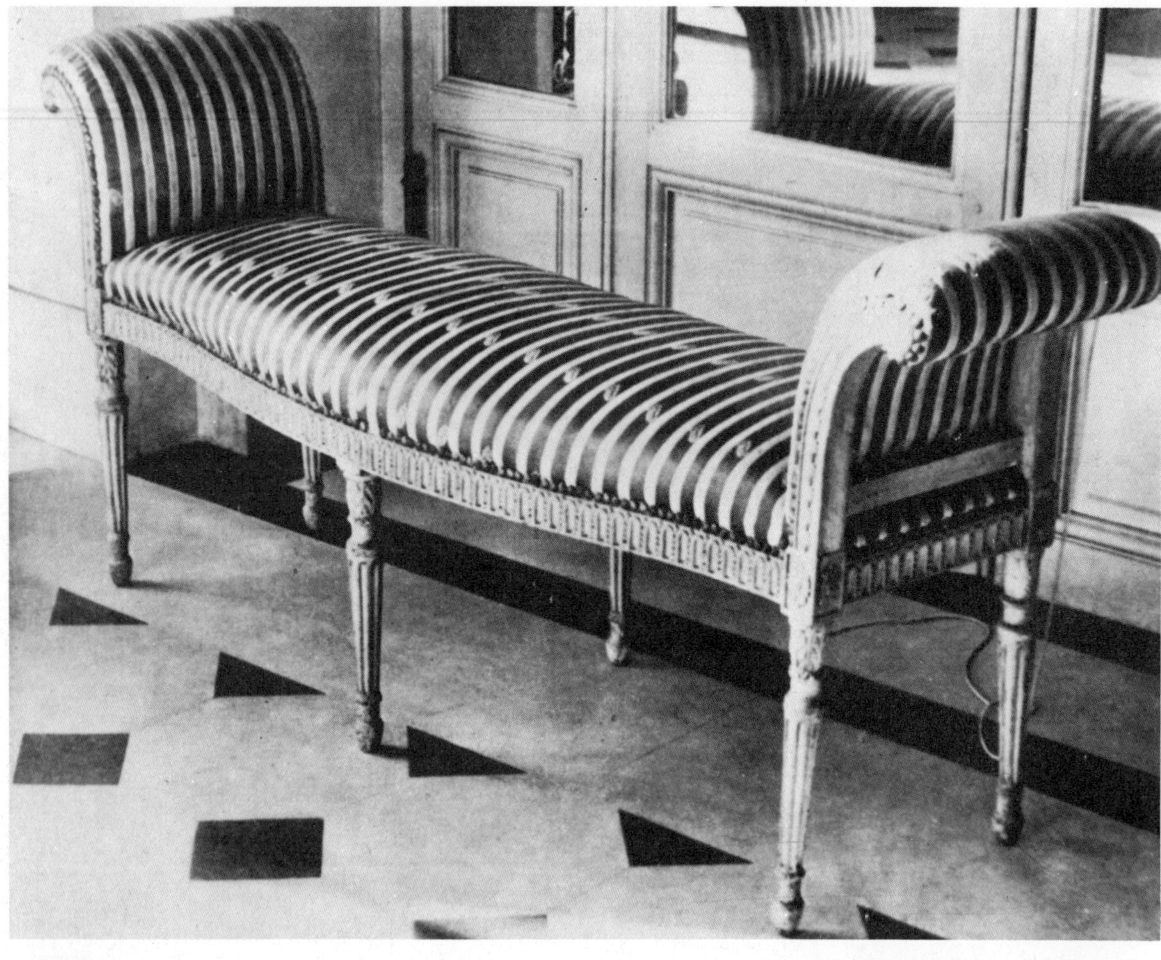

987. Banqueta con brazos vueltos, tallada y pintada. Museo Nissin de Camondó. Paris

987. Stool with curved arms, carved and painted. Musée Nissin of Camondó. Paris

988. Canapé Luis XVI en madera dorada, brazos vueltos en voluta. Castillo de Compiègne

988. Louis XVI couch in gilt wood, curved arms ending in scrolls. Château de Compiègne

989. Consola Luis XVI, tallas neoclásicas, pintada y dorada

989. Louis XVI console table, with neo-classical carving, painted and gilded

990. Consola tallada, pintada y dorada Luis XVI. Versalles

990. Louis XVI console table; carved, painted and gilged. Versailles

991. Secreter por Jean Henri Riesener (1734-1806). Altura 110, largo 105, ancho 58 cm

991. Secretaire by Jean Henri Riesener (1734-1804). Height 110, lenght 105, depth 58 cm

992. Mesa Luis XVI tallada y pintada. Versalles

992. Louis XVI table, carved and painted. Versalles

993. Mesa-tocador chapada en ébano, lacas de Japón y bronces cincelados con tapa abatible, por A. Weisweiler

993. Toilet-table, with ebony veneers, Japanesse lacquer and chiselled bronzework; the flap can be let down, by A. Weisweiler

994. Escritorio Luis XVI, de marquetería de rombos con partes de maderas claras y bronces con dibujos neoclásicos, por J. F. Oeben

994. Louis XVI secretaire with lozenge marquetry and parts in light-coloured wood, neo-classical design bronze decoration, by J. F. Oeben

995. Secreter, por Pierre Garnier (...1774); altura 107, largo 80, ancho 1.62 cm

995. Secretaire, by Pierre Garnier (...1774); height 107, length 80, depth 162 cm

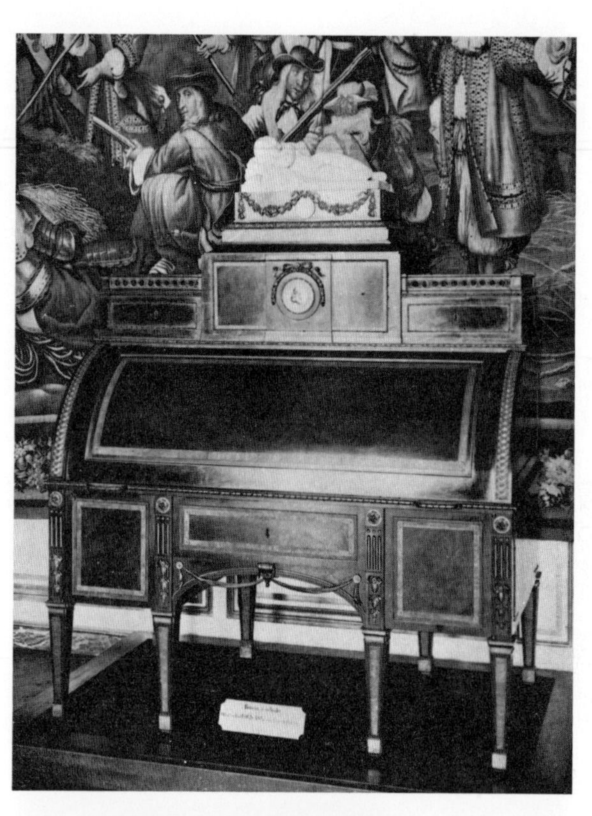

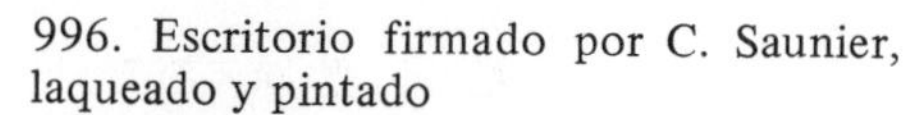

996. Escritorio firmado por C. Saunier, laqueado y pintado

996. Lacquered and painted writing-desk, signed by C. Saunier

997. Gran buró estilo Luis XVI con bronces dorados, de D. Roentgen. Versalles

997. Large bureau in the Louis XVI style, with gilt bronze mounts, by D. Roentgen, Versalles

998. Bureau Luis XVI con tapa de cilindro, por J. F. Oeben. El bronce calado de la parte superior es un elemento característico. Museo Nissim de Camondó. París

998. Louis XVI bureau with cylinder top, by J. F. Oeben. The bronze gallery is a characteristic feature. Musée Nissin de Camondó. Paris

999. Buró de cilindro, por Saunier, estilo Luis XVI. Museo Nissin de Camondó. París

999. Roll-top writing-desk in the Louis XVI style, by Saunier. Musée Nissin de Camondó. Paris

1000. Buró-cómoda con los dos primeros cajones abatibles; con marquetería y bronces, por J.F. Oeben. Colección Penard y Fernández. París

1000. Bureau-commode, the first two drawers can be let down; marquetry with bronze mounts, by J. F. Oeben. Penard & Fernández Collection. Paris

1001. Cómoda de transición, por J. F. Oeben, hacia 1761. Colección Bensimon. París

1001. Commode, transition period, by J. F. Oeben, c. 1761. Bensimon Collection. Paris

1002. Cómoda firmada por Joseph Stockel, Luis XVI con hojas de raíz de olmo. Museo de Artes Decorativas. París

1002. Louis XVI commode, signed by Joseph Stockel, with elm root veneer. Museum of Decorative Arts. Paris

1003. Cómoda chapada de caoba y ébano, por Guillaume Benneman y Joseph Stockel. Museo del Louvre. París

1003. Commode, with mahogany and ebony veneers, by Guillaume Benneman and Joseph Stockel. Louvre. Paris

1004. Cómoda por J. F. Riesener, de caoba y bronces dorados y cincelados. Palacio de Versalles

1004. Commode, by J. F. Riesener, in mahogany with chiselled gilt bronze mounts. Palais de Versailles

1005. Cómoda de J. F. Leleu en marquetería y bronces cincelados. Museo del Louvre. París

1005. Commode, by J. F. Leleu, with marquetry and chiselled bronze decoration. Louvre. Paris

1006. Armario normando Luis XVI, de nogal

1006. Louis XVI Norman wardrobe in walnut

1007. Armario normando Luis XVI

1007. Louis XVI Norman wardrobe

1008. Cama Luis XVI con baldaquino. Castillo Borely. Marsella

1008. Louis XVI bed with canopy. Château Borely. Marseille

1009. Cama, por J. B. Boulard en el Petit Trianon. Versalles

1009. Bed, by J. B. Boulard. Petit Trianon. Versailles

1010. Cama Luis XVI con baldaquino. Museo del Louvre. París

1010. Louis XVI bed with canopy. Louvre. Paris

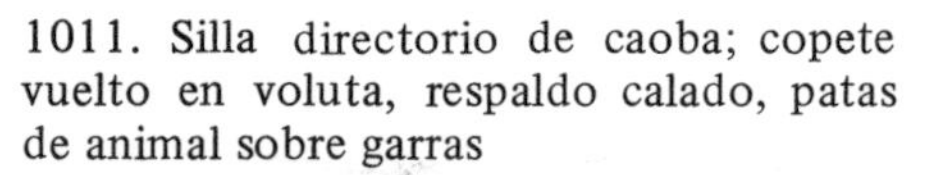

1011. Silla directorio de caoba; copete vuelto en voluta, respaldo calado, patas de animal sobre garras

1011. Directoire chair in mahogany; curved cresting with scroll, fretcut back, legs of animal form terminating in claw feet

1012. Silla directorio de inspiración etrusca, de caoba con aplicaciones de bronce

1012. Directoire chair, with Etruscan influence, in mahogany with bronze appliquéss,

1013. Sillón del tocador de los emperadores. Caoba tallada. Palacio de Compiègne

1013. Armchair of the Emperor's dressing-room, in carved mahogany. Palais de Compiègne

1014. Sillón "a la etrusca", por G. Jacob. Palacio de Versalles

1014. Etruscan style armchair, by G. Jacob. Palais de Versailles

1015. Silla "a la antigua" de caoba, influencia etrusca y romana. Colección particular

1015. Antique style mahogany chair, with Etruscan and Roman influence. Private Collection

1016. Sillón imperio de caoba con tallas y bronces, brazo sobre ménsula en esfinge. Museo de Artes Decorativas. París

1016. Empire style armchair in mahogany with carving and bronze decoration, arms of sphinx form brackets

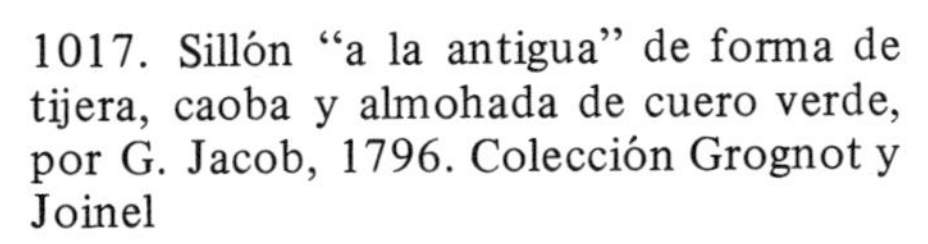

1017. Sillón "a la antigua" de forma de tijera, caoba y almohada de cuero verde, por G. Jacob, 1796. Colección Grognot y Joinel

1017. Antique style X-shaped armchair in mahogany with green leather cushion, by G. Jacob , 1796. Grognot & Joinel Collection

1018. Sillón imperio con tallas de volutas y palmetas, pintado y dorado. Palacio de Fontainebleau

1018. Armchair in the Empire style, scroll and palmette decoration, painted and gilded. Palais de Fontainebleau

1019. Mesa de despacho, por P. A. Bellange; sillón por George Jacob

1019. Study table by P.A. Bellange; armchair by George Jacob

1020. Despacho imperio. Colección particular

1020. Empire study. Private Collection

1021. Sillón de Napoleón en la sala del trono de Fontainebleau

1021. Napoleon's armchair in the Throne Room at Fontainebleau

1022. Sillón con esfinges que indican el paso hacia el estilo imperio, por G. Jacob. Colección Fabius Frères

1022. Armchair with sphinxes indicating the transition to the Empire style, by G. Jacob. Fabius Frères Collection

1023. Dibujo de sillón de Percier y Fontaine

1023. Drawing of armchair by Percier & Fontaine

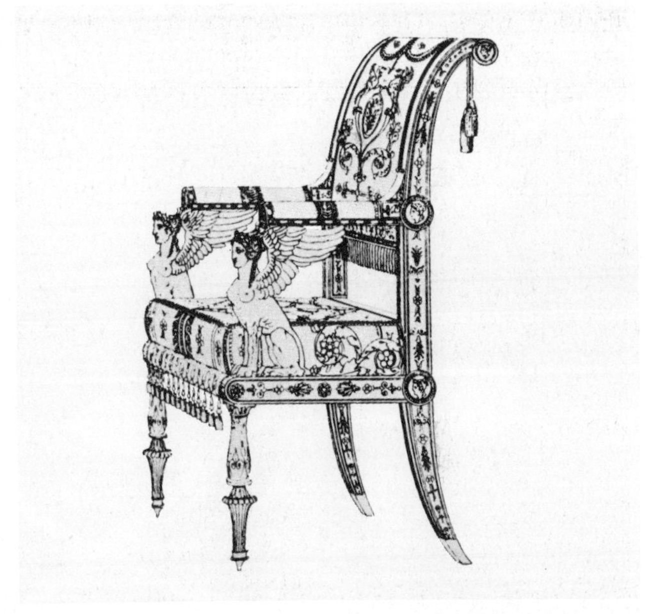

1024. Canapé o "Méridienne" en el despacho del emperador. Compiègne

1024. "Meridienne" or couch in the Emperor's study. Compiègne

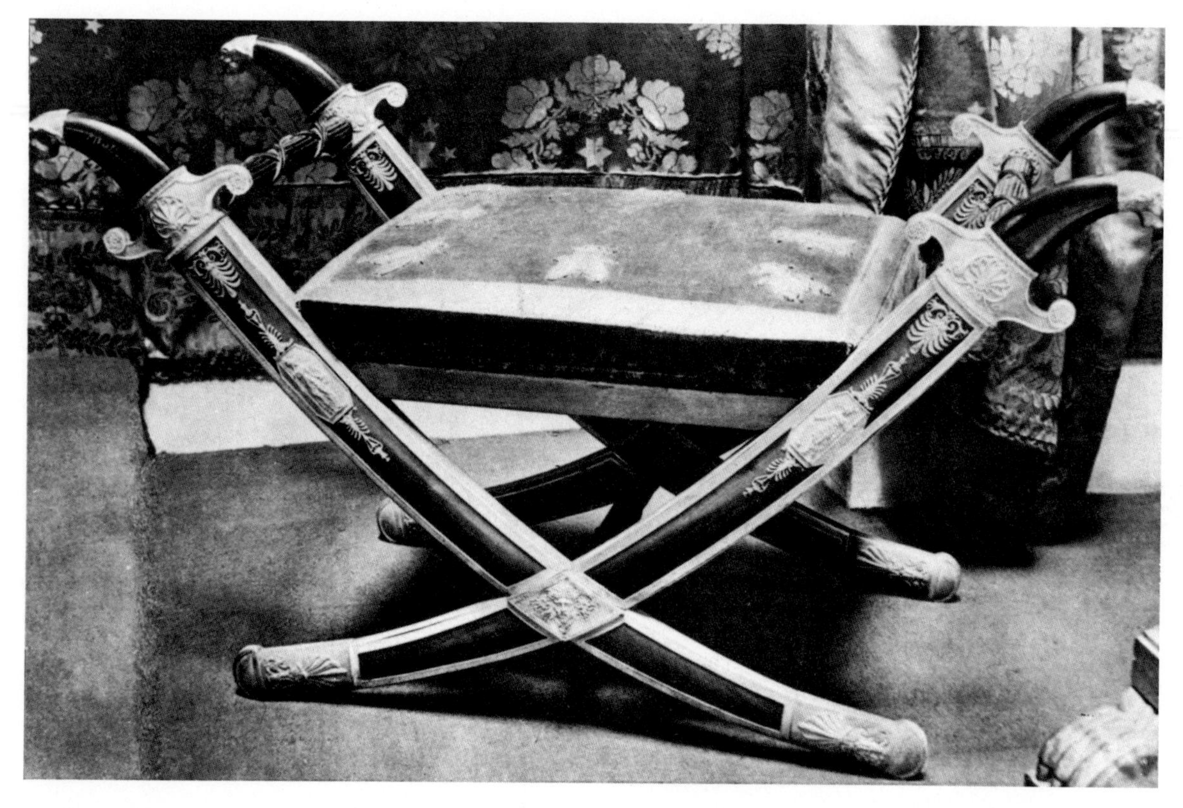

1025. Taburete o banqueta en forma de tijera de caoba y bronces dorados. Colección Vibraye.

1025. X-shaped stool in mahogany with gilt bronze decoration, Vibraye Collection

1026. Espejo "Psique". Dibujo de Percier y Fontaine

1026. "Psyche" mirror. Drawing by Percier and Fontaine

1027. Cuna del rey de Roma, por Prudhan

1027. The cradle of the king of Rome, by Prudhan

1028. Cama con baldaquino, por Percier y Fontaine. Dibujo de su obra *Recueil des décorations intérieures* 1812

1028. Bed with canopy by Percier & Fontaine. Drawing in their Recueil des décorations intérieures, 1812

1029. Dormitorio imperio en caoba y raíz de olmo ofrecido por Napoleón a uno de sus mariscales

1029. Empire style bedroom, in mahogany and elm root, a gift from Napoleon to one of his marshals

1030. Cama de Napoleón. Caoba y bronces cincelados. Gran Trianon. Versalles

1030. Napoleon's bed, in mahogany and chiselled bronzework. Grand Trianon. Versailles

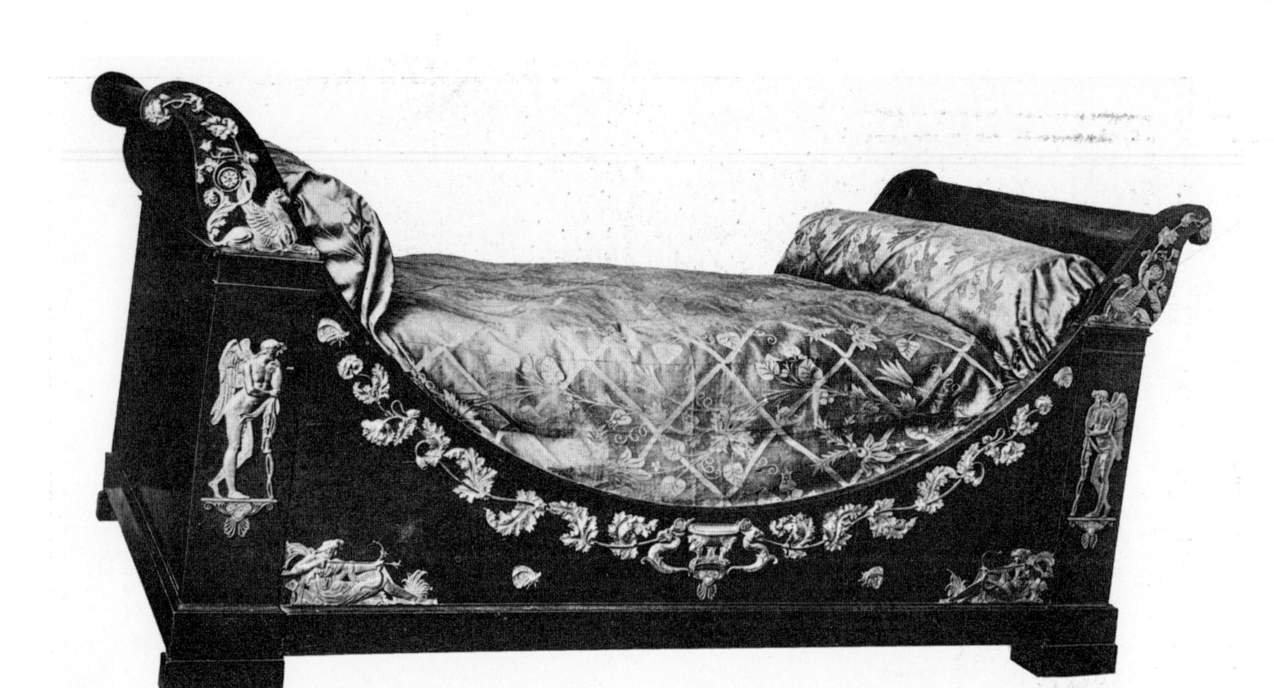

1031. Cama en forma de góndola con bronces cincelados, estilo imperio. Museo de Artes Decorativas. París

1031. Empire style bed in gondola form with chiselled bronze decoration. Museum of Decorative Arts. Paris

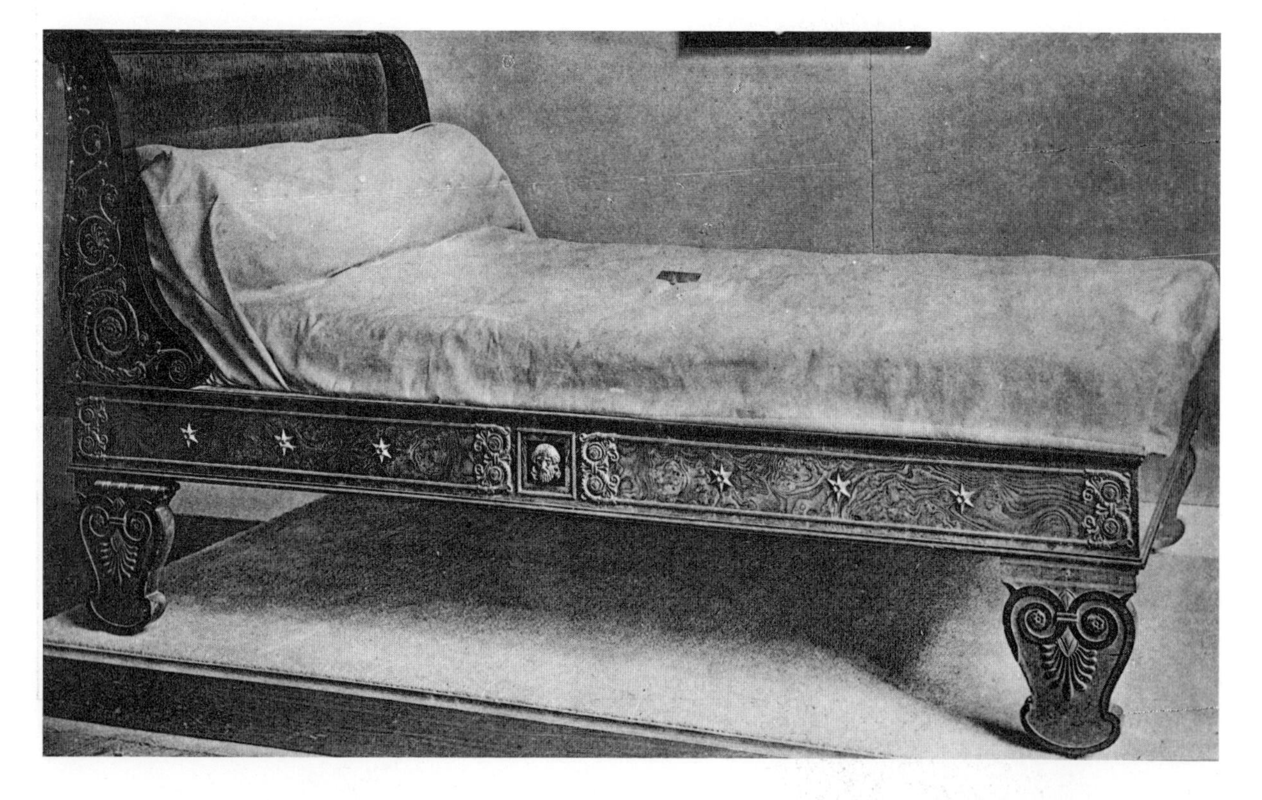

1032. Cama "a la etrusca" estilo imperio de caoba tallada. Museo de Artes Decorativas. París

1032. Empire period bed in the Struscan style, in corved mahagany. Museum of Decorative Arts. Paris

1033. Armario-joyero, regalo de la Villa de París a María Antonieta en 1787, en caoba con paneles pintados por Degault, porcelanas de Sèvres, incrustaciones y bronces de Thomire; realizado por F. Schwerdfeger, y diseñado por Bonnefoy-Duplan

1033. Jewel cabinet, a gift to Marie Antoinette from the Town of Paris in 1787, in mahogany with painted panels by Degault, Sèvres porcelain, incrustations and bronzework by F. Thomire; executed by F. Schwerdfeger and designed by Bonnefoy-Duplan

1034. Dormitorio del emperador en el palacio de la Malmaison

1034. The Emperor's bedroom at the Château de Malmaison

1035. Tocador de caoba y bronce cincelado, estilo imperio, patas en lira. Palacio de Compiègne

1035. Empire style dressing-table in mahogany with chiselled bronze mounts and lyre-shaped legs. Palais de Compiègne

1036. Silloncito de caoba, estilo Adam, 1780. Colección del Duque de Hamilton

1036. Small mahogany armchair in the Adam style, 1780. Duke of Hamilton Collection

1037. Sillón de caoba, estilo Adam, 1770. Hedingham Castle

1037. Mahogany armchair in the Adam style, 1770. Hedingham Castle

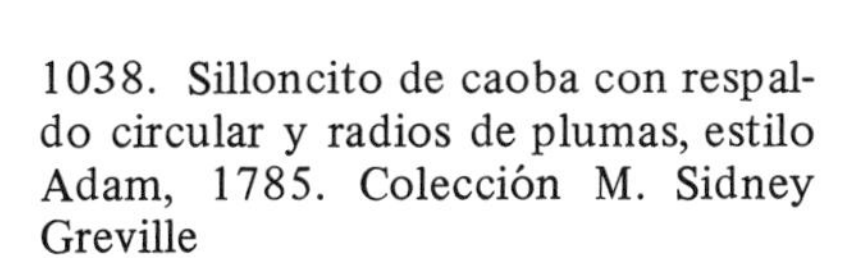

1038. Silloncito de caoba con respaldo circular y radios de plumas, estilo Adam, 1785. Colección M. Sidney Greville

1038. Mahogany armchair with hoop back and feather radius in the Adam style, 1785. Mr. Sidney Greville Collection

1039. Silloncito de respaldo circular con decoración oriental, fin del siglo XVIII. Colección Lady Assheton-Smith

1039. Armchair with hoop back of radial design, late 18th century. Lady Assheton-Smith Collection

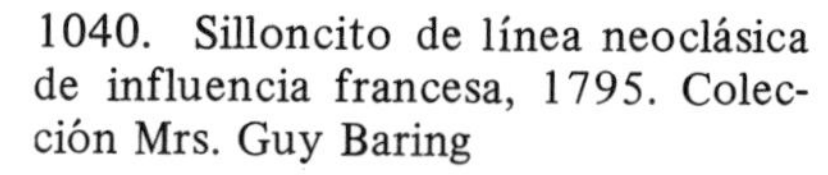

1040. Silloncito de línea neoclásica de influencia francesa, 1795. Colección Mrs. Guy Baring

1040. Armchair of neo-classical lines with French influence, 1795. Mrs. Guy Baring Collection

1041. Sillón de caoba con respaldo tipo lira, hacia 1775. Colección Brocket Hall

1041. Mahogany armchair with lyre--shaped splat, c. 1775. Brocket Hall Collection

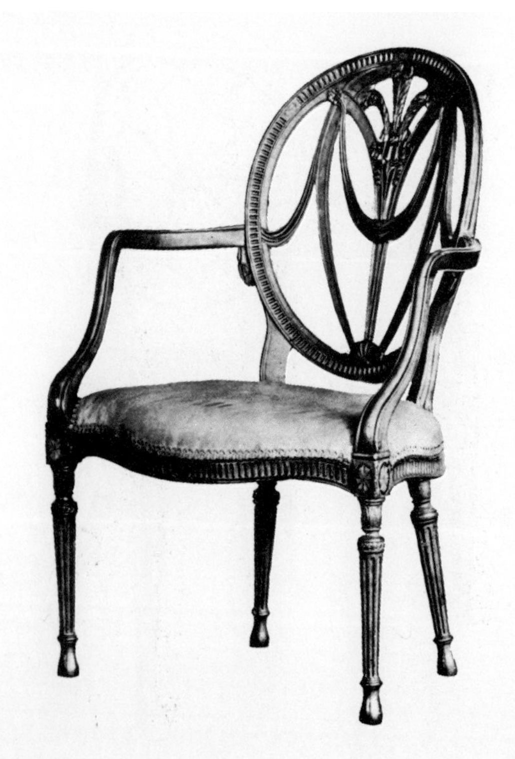

1042. Silloncito de caoba de respaldo ovalado, con las plumas del príncipe de Gales, hacia 1780. Victoria and Albert Museum. Londres

1042. Mahogany armchair with oval back and Prince of Wales's feathers, c. 1780. Victoria and Albert Museum

1043. Silloncito en limoncillo y filetes de ébano de T. Chippendale (hijo), 1802

1043. Small armchair in satinwood with ebony fillets, by T. Chippendale, Jr., 1802

1044. Dibujo de una sala imperio por Thomas Hope

1044. Drawing of an Empire room by Thomas Hope

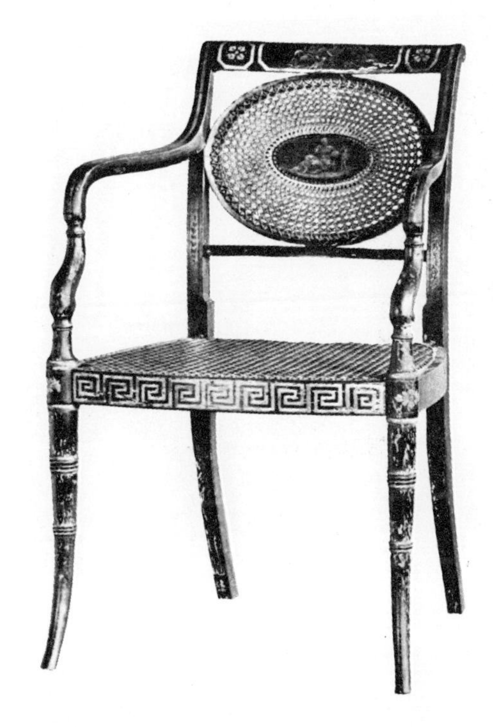

1045. Silloncito estilo imperio pintado con rejillas, 1800. Victoria and Albert Museum. Londres

1045. Small painted armchair in the Empire style, with cane work, 1800. Victoria and Albert Museum

1046. Silloncito pintado estilo imperio con respaldo y asiento con rejilla, 1815

1046. Small painted armchair in the Empire style, with cane back and seat, 1815

1047. Dibujo de silla por Sheraton, publicado en su libro *Drawing Book* 1700

1047. Drawing of chair by Sheraton published in his Drawing Book *1700*

1048. Silla de caoba, fin del siglo XVIII. Colección Arundel Castle

1048. Late 18th-century mahogany chair. Arundel Castle Collection

1049. Silla de caoba de influencia Sheraton, fin del siglo XVIII. Metropolitan Museum, Nueva York

1049. Mahogany chair with Sheraton influence, late 18th century. Metropolitan Museum, New York

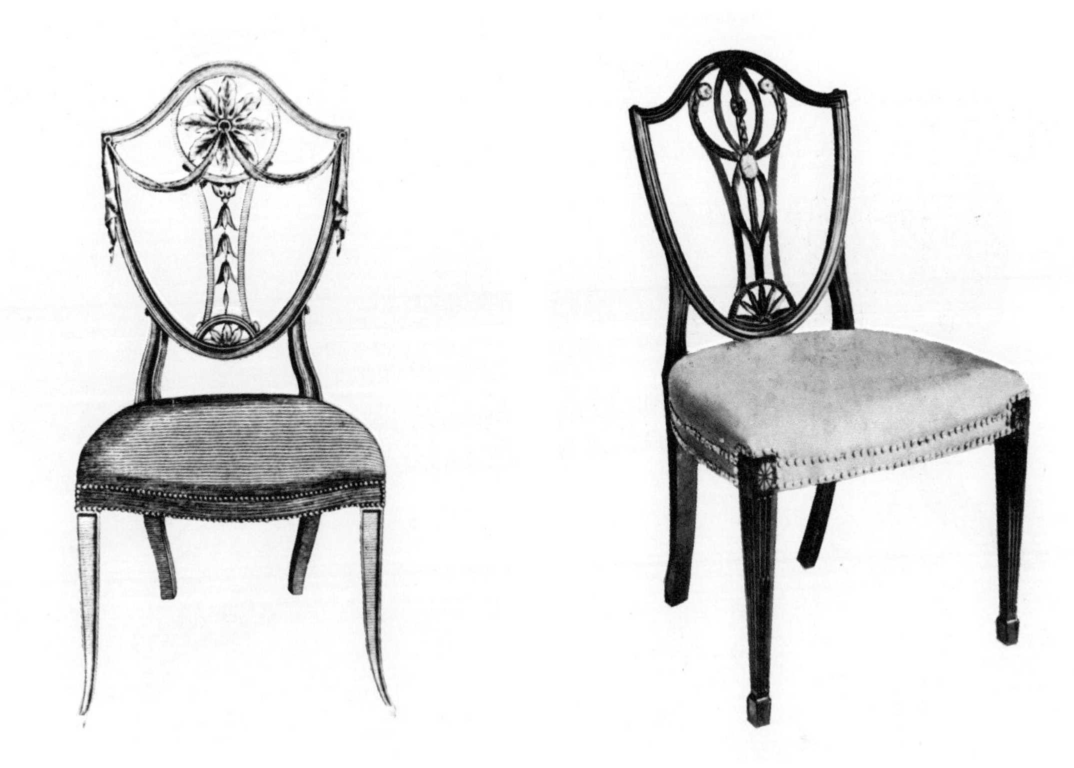

1050. Dibujo de silla por Hepplewhite. En su *Cabinet Maker's Guide* 1788

1050. Drawing of chair by Hepplewhite in his Cabinet Maker's Guide *1788*

1051. Silla de caoba con respaldo tipo Hepplewhite, 1775. Colección Fred Skull

1051. Hepplewhite shield-back mahogany chair, 1775. Mr. Fred Skull Collection

1052. Canapé-sofá con 4 respaldos de silla estilo Hepplewhite, 1781. Colección Denston Hall. Suffolk

1052. Settee with 4 seat backs in the Hepplewhite style, 1781. Denston Hall. Suffolk

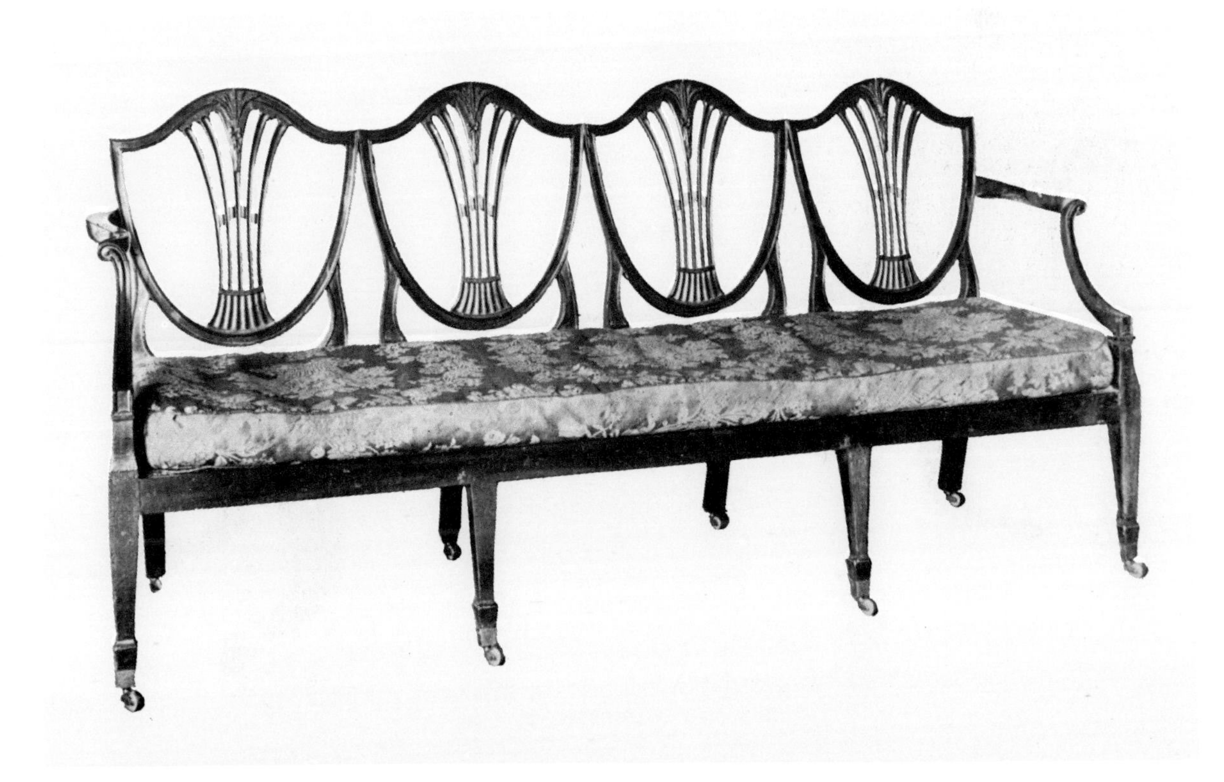

1053. Sofá "chaise-longue" en madera de palo rosa y marquetería. Colección Lenygon and Morant

1053. Chaise-longue in tulip wood with marquetry decoration. Lenygon and Morant Collection

1054. Sofá-cama, hojas de caoba con marquetería y bronce, 1810. Colección Lenygon and Morant

1054. Mahogany veneered couch, with marquetry and bronze decoration, 1810. Lenygon and Morant Collection

1055. Buró-cabinet decorado por Angelica Kauffmann, 1775. Colección Mr. Harris

1055. Bureau-cabinet, decorated by Angelica Kauffmann, 1775. Mr. Harris Collection

1056. Copa-urna sobre pedestal dibujado por R. Adam, 1780. Colección Saltram

1056. Drawing of urn on pedestal by Robert Adam, 1780. Saltram Collection

1057. Copa y pedestal de aparador en caoba con aplicaciones de bronce dorado "ormolu", 1775. Normanton Park. Condado de Rutland

1057. Urn and pedestal of sideboard in mahogany with ormolu appliqués, 1775. Normanton Park. Rutland

1058. Vaso o copa para cuchillos; marquetería de nogal y sicomoro, 1780. Victoria and Albert Museum. Londres

1058. Urn for knives, marquetry of walnut and sycamore, 1780. Victoria and Albert Museum

1059. Caja de cubiertos de caoba. Centro de marquetería, fin del siglo XVIII

1059. Mahogany box for cutlery. Centre with marquetry decoration. Late 18th century

1060. Velador con frentes en palo rosa con mármol y bronces dorados, 1810. Colección Castle Ashby

1060. Occasional table with tulip wood fronts and marble and gilt bronze decoration, 1810. Castle Ashby Collection

1061. Vitrina de caoba y marquetería, hacia 1780. Colección Brace

1061. China cabinet in mahogany with marquetry decoration, c. 1780. Mr. Brace Collection

1062. Mesa consola de caoba cubierta con hojas de maderas finas coloreadas, 1780. Colección Donalson

1062. Mahogany console table with coloured wood veneers, 1780. Donalson Collection

1063. Mesa con tablas abatibles, de George Oakley, 1810. Colección Stileman

1063. Table with drop flaps, by George Oakley, 1810. Mr. Stileman Collection

1064. Mesa de caoba; estilo neoclásico de transición al imperio, hacia 1800. Colección Sackville

1064. Mahogany table in neo-classical style, transition to the Empire period, c. 1800. Sackville Collection

1065. Mesa de caoba para comedor, patas muy elegantes, 1795. Colección Ragley Hall

1065. Mahogany dining-table, with very elegant legs, 1795. Ragley Hall Collection

1066. Mesa de comedor de caoba, columnas torneadas sobre dos trípodes de patas de curva cabriolé 1800. Colección Anthony White

1066. Mahogany dining-table, turned shafts on two tripods with cabriolet legs, 1800. Anthony White Collection

1067. Mesa de nogal tallado, con cajones en el faldón, 1815. Colección Napier Miles

1067. Carved walnut table with drawers in the apron piece, 1815. Mr. Napier Miles Collection

1068. Mesa dibujada por George Smith en su libro *Household Furniture* 1808

1068. Table, drawn by George Smith in his Household Furniture *1808*

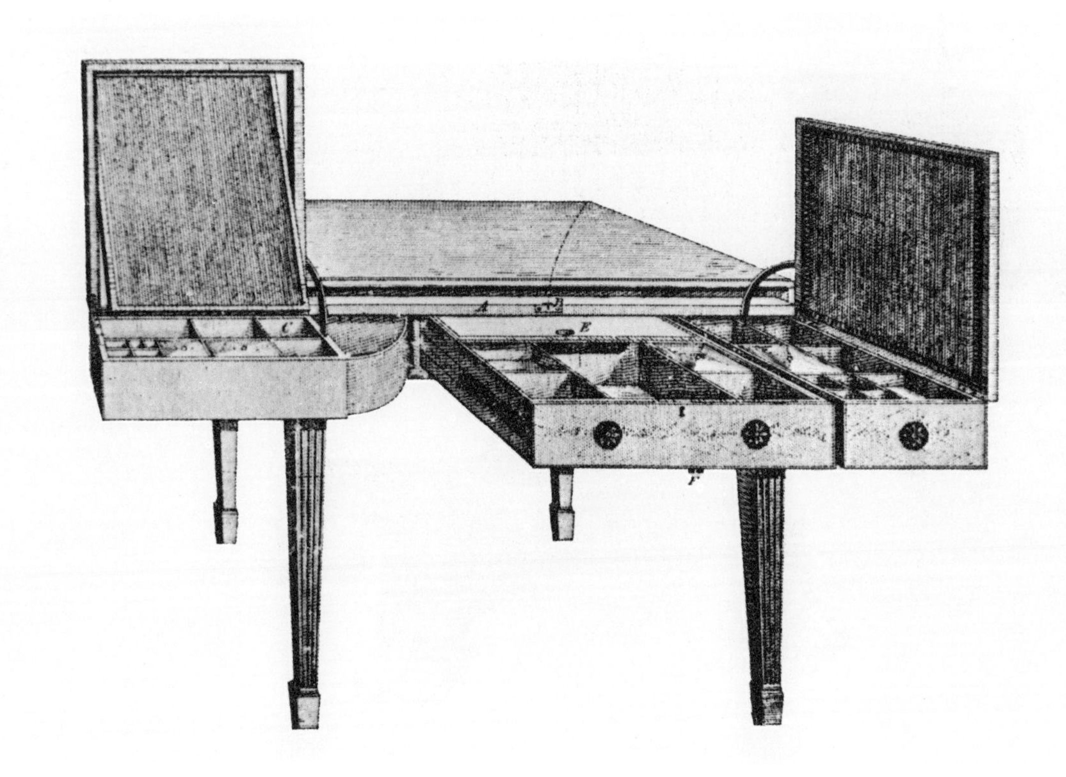

1069. Mesa dibujada por Helpplewhite en su *Cabinet Maker's Guide* 1788

1069. Drawing of table by Hepplewhite in his Cabinet Maker's Guide *1788*

1070. Mesa-librería de caoba, 1800. Colección Devonshire House

1070. Bookcase-table in mahogany, 1800. Devonshire House Collection

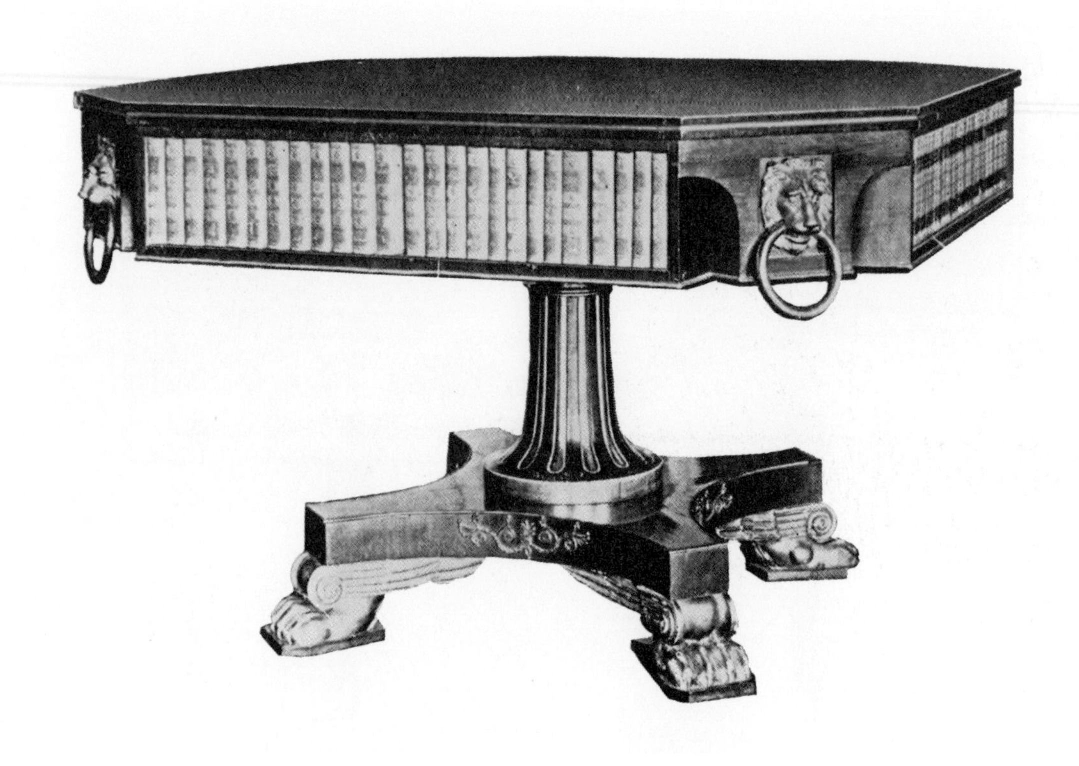

1071. Mesa-librería en madera palo rosa y con aplicaciones de metal, 1810. Colección Normanton Park

1071. Bookcase-table in tulip wood with metal appliqués, 1810. Normanton Park Collection

1072. Librería de caoba dibujada por R. Adam para Sir Watkin Wynne, proporciones muy delicadas, 1770

1072. Drawing of mahogany bookcase by Robert Adam for Sir Watkin Wynne; very fine proportions, 1770

1073. Aparador de caoba y chapas de limoncillo con pedestales para cubiertas por Sheraton, 1786. Colección de Mrs. Letts

1073. Mahogany sideboard with satinwood veneers and pedestals for table-ware, by Sheraton, 1785. Mrs. Letts Collection

1074. Aparador dibujado por Sheraton en su *Drawing Bool* 1791

1074. Drawing of sideboard by Sheraton in his Drawing Book *1791*

1075. Aparador *sideboard* de caoba con palo violeta, 1785. Colección T. Seed

1075. Mahogany and violet wood sideboard, 1785. Mr T. Seed Collection

1076. Cómoda-aparador con aplicaciones de bronce y marquetería, 1775. Colección Syon House. Middlesex

1076. Commode-sideboard with bronze mounts and marquetry, 1755. Syon House Collection. Middlesex

1077. Cómoda con marquetería, patas todavía cabriolé, más suaves, hacia 1770. Colección F. Harper

1077. Commode with marquetry decoration, legs still in the cabriolet style but more delicate, c. 1770. Mr. F. Harper Collection

1078. Cómoda de panza y silueta curva de marquetería, 1770. Colección del Vizconde de Leverhulme

1078. Bombé commode with serpentine profile; with marquetry decoration, 1770. Viscount Leverhulme Collection

1079. Cómoda de planta semicircular, con decoración Adam, marqueteada, 1785. Colección Stourhead

1079. Semicircular commode with marquetry decoration in the Adam style, 1785. Stourhead Collection

1080. Cómoda de planta semicircular en limoncillo y marquetería, estilo Adam, 1785. Colección M. Harris

1080. Semicircular commode in satinwood with marquetry in the Adam style, 1785. Mr. M. Harris Collection

1081. Cómoda de caoba con tiradores de bronce, 1800. Colección Benston Hall

1081. Mahogany commode with bronze handles, 1800. Benston Hall Collection

1082. Espejo de limoncillo, marqueteado, 1750. Colección Percy Macquoid

1082. Mirror in satinwood, with marquetry, 1750. Percy Macquoid Collection

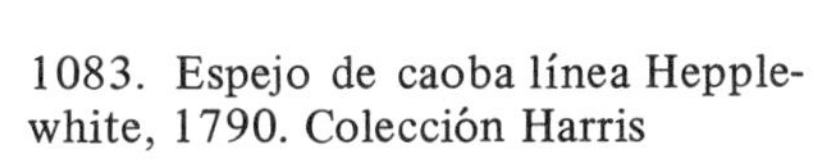

1083. Espejo de caoba línea Hepplewhite, 1790. Colección Harris

1083. Mahogany mirror in the Hepplewhite style. 1790. Mr. Harris Collection

1084. Espejo de tocador de forma circular, de madera tallada, pintada y dorada. Victoria and Albert Museum. Londres

1084. Circular toilet mirror of carved wood, painted and gilt. Victoria and Albert Museum

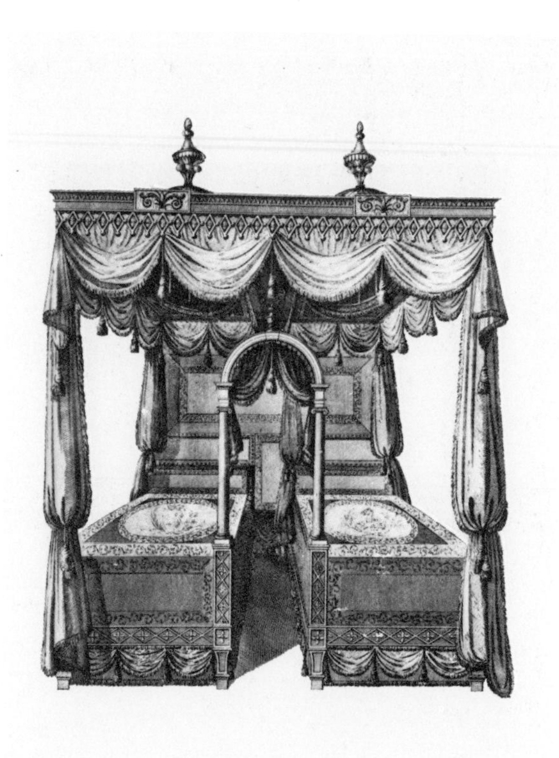

1085. Cama de estilo Sheraton. 1795. Castillo de Hedingham. Essex

1085. Bed in the Sheraton style, 1795. Hedingham Castle. Essex

1086. Dibujo de dos camas en la edición de Sheraton *Drawing Book* de 1791

1086. Drawing of two beds in Sheraton's Drawing Book *1791*

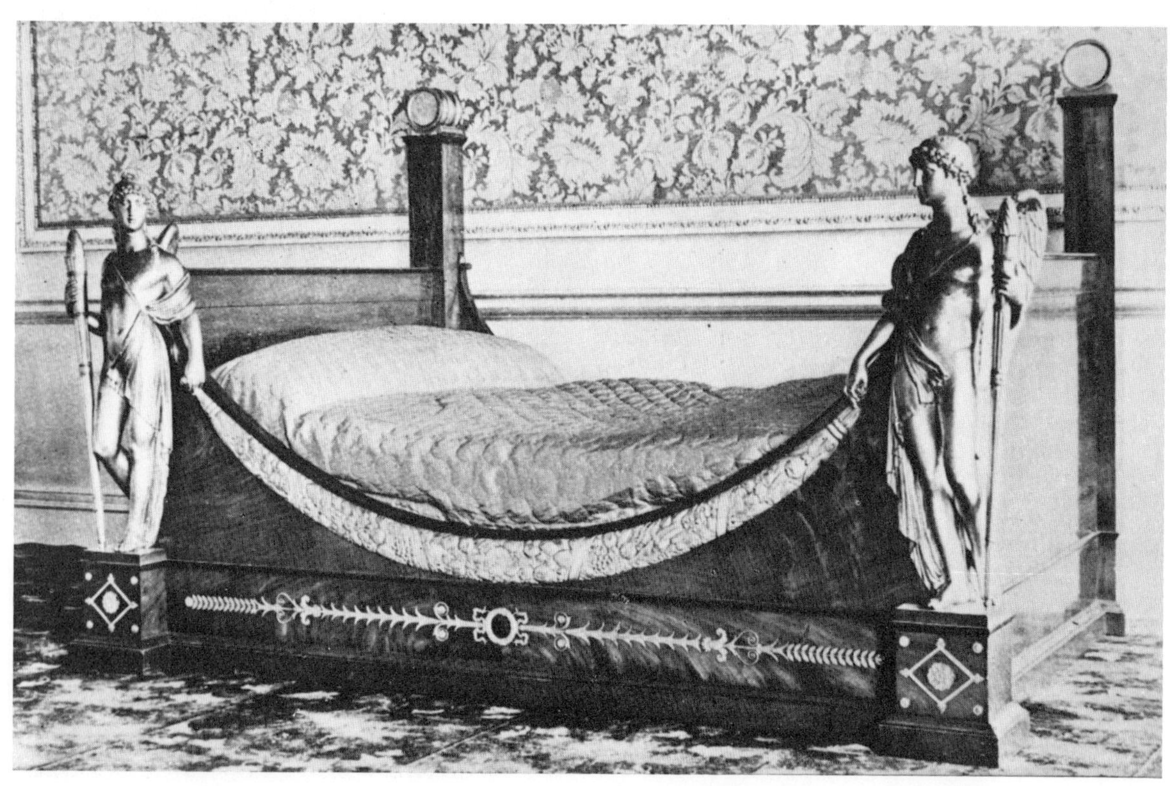

1087. Cama de caoba y bronces dorados estilo imperio, 1810. Colección Hamilton Palace

1087. Mahogany bed with gilt bronze decoration in the Empire style, 1810

1088. Interior del castillo de Mellerstain en Escocia. Decoración de R. Adam, 1770

1088. Interior of Mellerstain Castle in Scotland. Decoration By Robert Adam, 1770

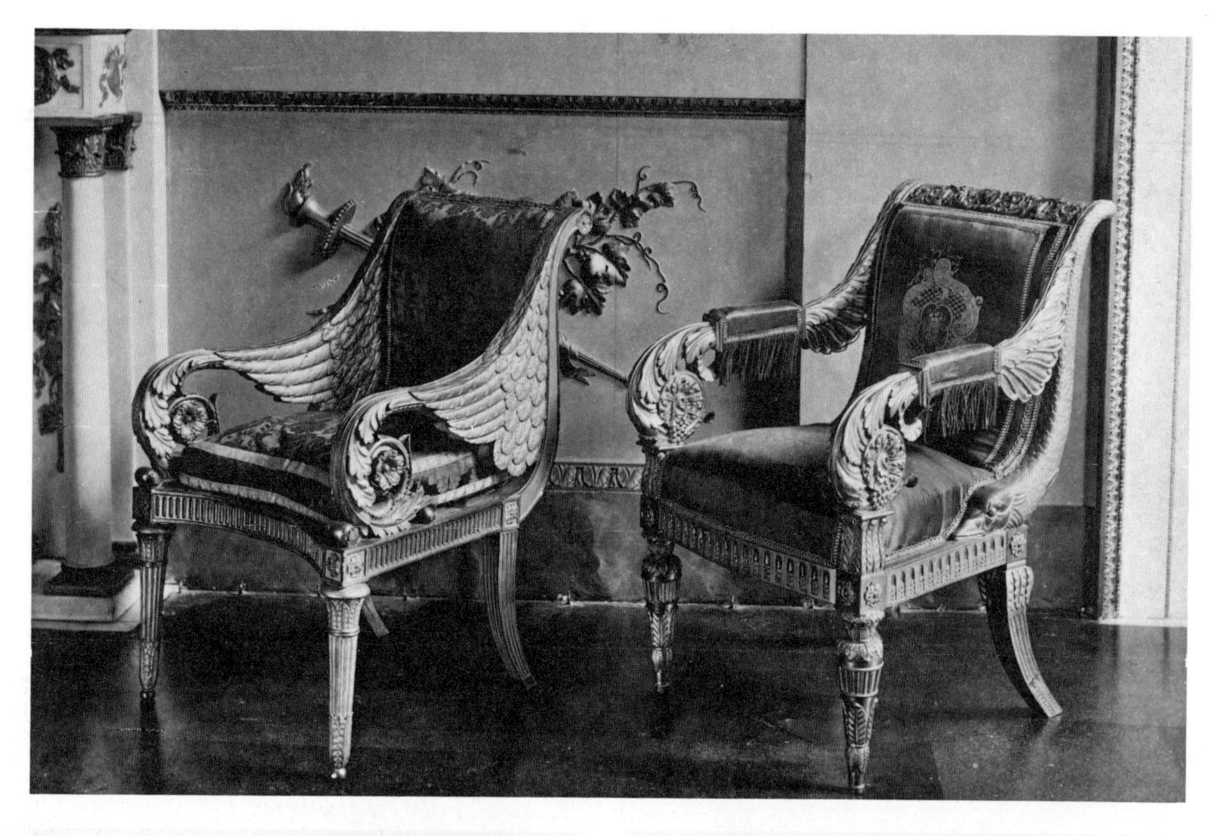

1089. Sillones tallados y dorados. Interpretación del estilo imperio. Palacio Pitti. Florencia

1089. Carved and gilded chairs in the Empire taste. Palazzo Pitti. Florence

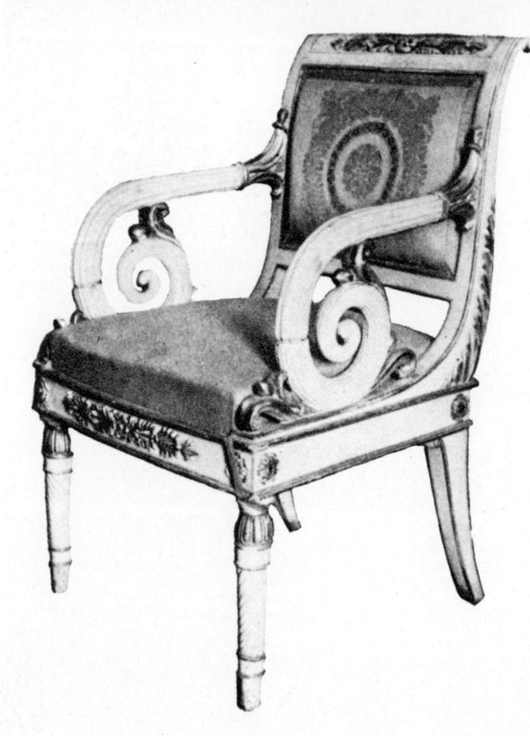

1090. Silloncito pintado y dorado estilo imperio

1090. Small painted and gilded armchair in the Empire style

1091. Sillón "curul" en madera trabajada como bronce. Colección Brunelli. Milán

1091. Curule type armchair with woodwork imitating bronze, Brunelli Collection, Milán

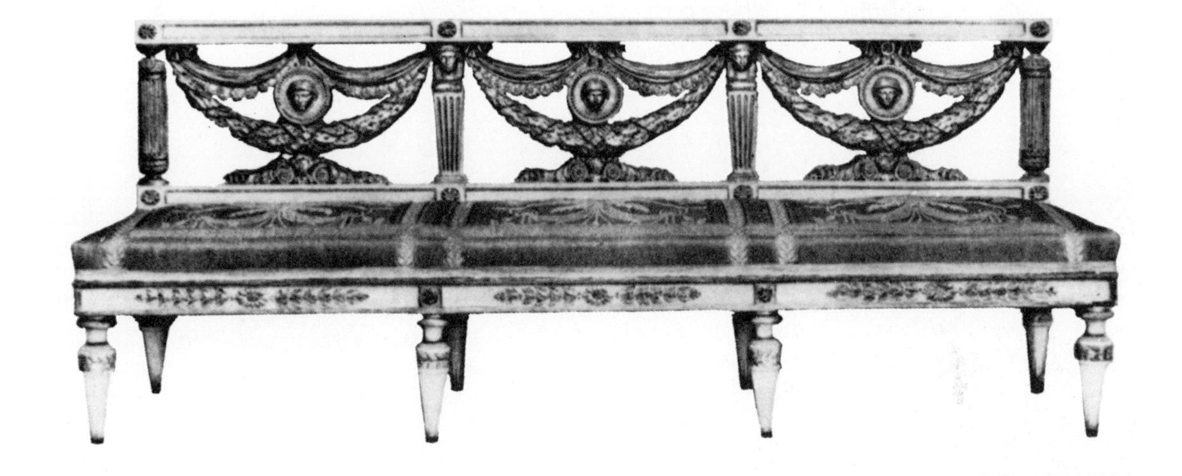

1092. Sofá o canapé de tres plazas tallado, pintado y dorado, con temas Imperio

1092. Carved settee of three seat form, painted and gilded with Empire motifs

1093. Sala de recepción. Palacio Real. Nápoles

1093. Reception Room. Royal Palace. Naples

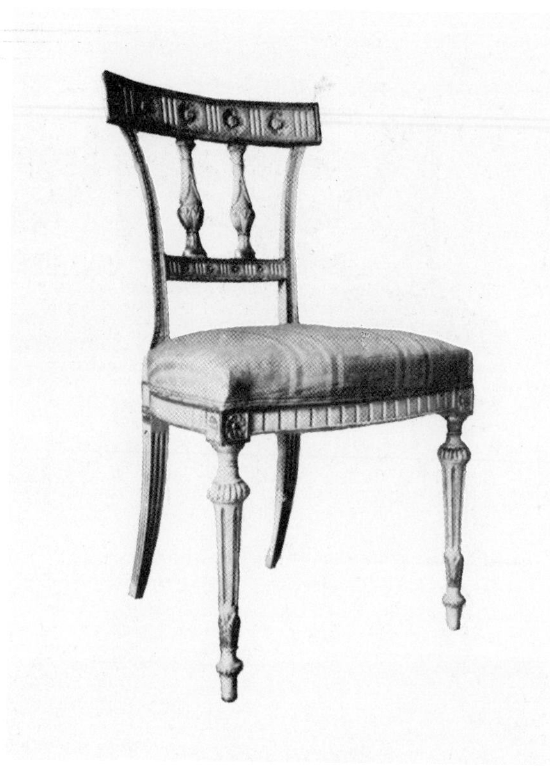

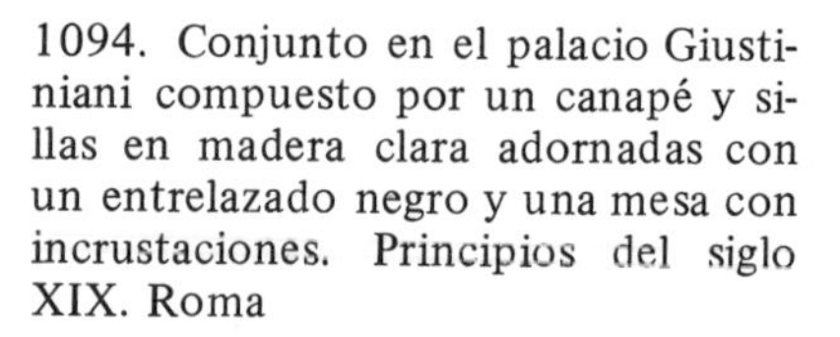

1094. Conjunto en el palacio Giustiniani compuesto por un canapé y sillas en madera clara adornadas con un entrelazado negro y una mesa con incrustaciones. Principios del siglo XIX. Roma

1094. Ensemble at the Palace of Giustiniani comprising a settee and chairs in light-coloured wood with black briding decoration and a table with incrustations. Early 19th century. Rome

1095. Silla de nogal tallado y laqueado en blanco y oro. Arte lombardo, 1790. Palacio Real. Milán

1095. Carved walnut chair, lacquered in white and gold. Lombard art, 1790. Royal Palace. Milan

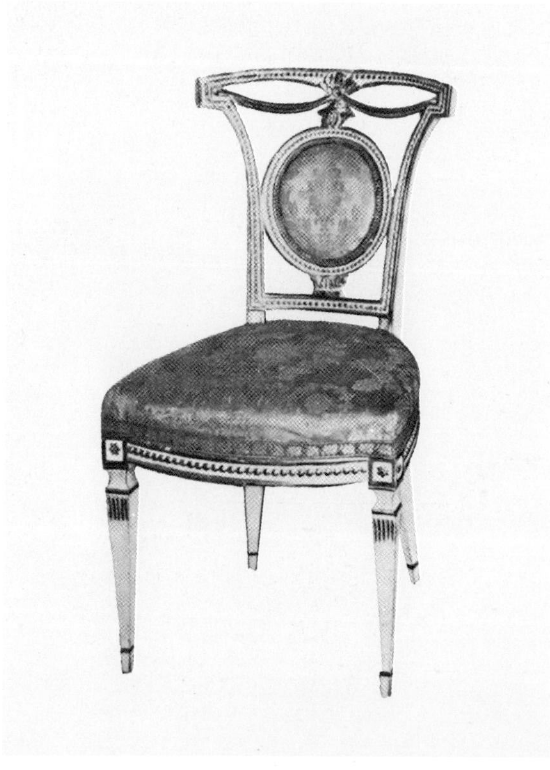

1096. Silla de estilo imperio tallada, pintada y dorada

1096. Empire style chair, carved, painted and gilded

1097. Silla de nogal esculpido, tallado y laqueado en blanco y oro, 1790. Florencia

1097. Walnut chair, carved and lacquered in white and gold, 1790. Florence

1098. Cómoda y sillas de caoba con palmas de caoba con aplicaciones de bronce dorado. Palacio Pitti. Florencia

1098. Commode and chairs with mahogany panels and gilt bronze mounts. Palazzo Pitti. Florence

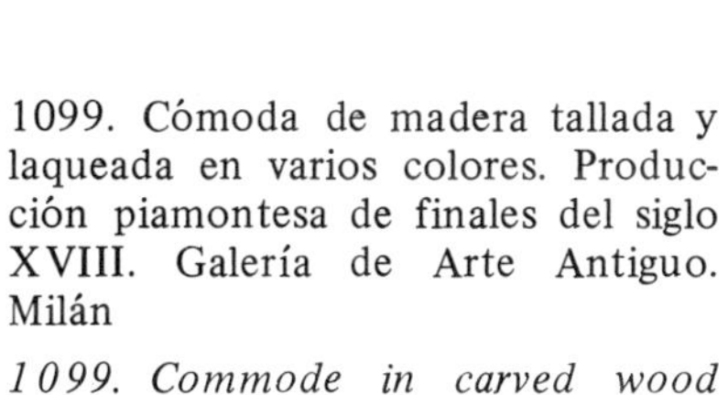

1099. Cómoda de madera tallada y laqueada en varios colores. Producción piamontesa de finales del siglo XVIII. Galería de Arte Antiguo. Milán

1099. Commode in carved wood lacquered in several colours. Piedmont production of the late 18th century. Gallery of Antique Art. Milan

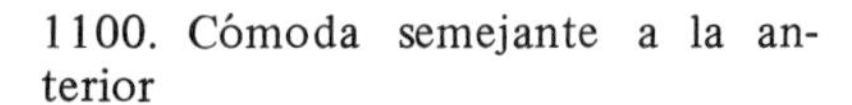

1100. Cómoda semejante a la anterior

1100. Commode, similar to the preceding piece

1101. Escritorio con una puerta abatible de caoba con adornos de bronce dorado y cincelado, 1810. Palacio Real. Milán

1101. Escritoire with drop flap; in mahogany with chiselled gilt bronze appliqués, 1810. Royal Palace. Milan

1102. Secreter cubierto con palmas de caoba y aplicaciones de bronce cincelado. Palacio Pitti. Florencia

1102. Secretaire with mahogany panels and chiselled bronze appliqués. Palazzo Pitti. Florence

1103. Interior con secreter romántico que deriva del imperio; sillas de principio de siglo con respaldo de influencia inglesa y consola muy simple de línea neoclásica

1103. Interior with romantic secretaire stemming from the Empire style; early century chairs with backs in the English taste, console table of very simple neo-classical lines

1104. Consola semicircular en nogal esculpido, laqueado en celeste con relieves dorados. Milán

1104. Semicircular console table in sculptured walnut; celeste lacquered with reliefs. Milan

1105. Mesa tallada y dorada, estilo pompeyano. Palacio Real. Nápoles

1105. Carved and gilded table in the Pompeian style. Royal Palace. Naples

1106. Mesa auxiliar y banqueta de caoba y bronces dorados y cincelados. Ejemplar típico del imperio. Palacio Pitti. Florencia

1106. Occasional table and stool in mahogany with chiselled gilt bronze decoration. A typical example of the Empire period. Palazzo Pitti. Florence

1107. Cama de nogal tallado de línea francesa, alrededor de 1780. Colección Bossi. Génova

1107. Carved walnut bed, with French influence, c. 1780. Bossi Collection. Genoa

1108. Silla de 1800 inspirada en las griegas y romanas, de haya dorada. Dinamarca

1108. Gilt beech chair of 1800, with Greek and Roman influence

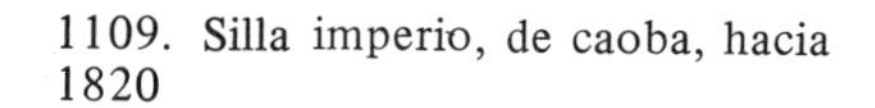

1109. Silla imperio, de caoba, hacia 1820

1109. Empire chair in mahogany, c. 1820

1110. Silla imperio, de caoba, hacia 1820

1110. Empire chair in mahogany, c. 1820

1111. Silla inspirada en las etruscas. Dibujo de N. Abilgaard, 1840. Dinamarca

1111. Chair with Etruscan influence. Drawing by N. Abilgaard, 1840. Denmark

1112. Silla de caoba, diseñada por M. C. Bindesboll, 1845-50

1112. Mahogany chair, designed by M.C. Bindesboll, 1845-50

1113. Silla de madera pintada y dorada por G. Bindesboll. Siglo XVIII. Dinamarca

1113. Wooden chair painted and gilded by G. Bindesboll, 18th century. Denmark

1114. Silla de la sala de los Pavos Reales, 1790. Potsdam

1114. Chair in the Peacock Room, 1790. Potsdam

1115. Mesa y sofá. Castillo-residencia, Wurzburg

1115. Sofa and table. Castle-residence, Wurzburg

1116. Sofá del palacio de mármol. Potsdam

1116. Sofa of the Marble Palace, Potsdam

1117. Sofá imperio, hacia 1840. Dinamarca

1117. Empire sofa, c. 1840. Denmark

1118. Sofá de caoba diseñado por M. G. Bindesboll, 1850

1118. Mahoganny settee, designed by M. C. Bindesboll, 1850

1119. Sofá-canapé de influencia inglesa, 1790

1119. Settee, with English influence, 1790

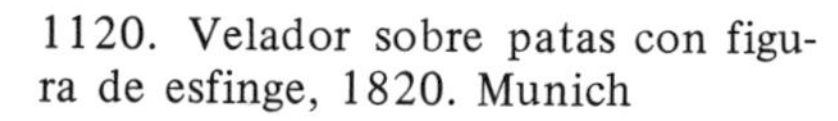

1120. Velador sobre patas con figura de esfinge, 1820. Munich

1120. Round table on legs with sphinx figures, 1820. Munich

1121. Velador imperio, de caoba con bronces cincelados

1121. Mahogany round table in the Empire style, with chiselled bronze decoration

1122. Velador circular, 1830. Potsdam

1122. Round table, 1830. Potsdam

1123. Mesa-velador con copa central, 1830. Worlitz

1123. Round table with central column, 1830. Worlitz

1124. Mesa de despacho, 1820. Viena

1124. Study desk, 1820. Vienna

1125. Mesa escritorio de la escuela de D. Roentgen, 1790. Palacio de Mármol. Potsdam

1125. Writing-table of the D. Roentgen school, 1790. Marble Palace. Potsdam

1126. Escritorio vertical por David Roentgen, 1770. Berlín

1126. Vertical secreter by D. Roentgen, 1770. Berlin

1127. Bureau por David Roentgen, 1780. Berlín

1127. Bureau by David Roentgen, 1780. Berlin

1128. Despacho de Goethe, Francfort

1128. Goeth's study in Francfort

1129. Bureau por David Roentgen, 1790. Colección particular

1129. Bureau by David Roentgen, 1790. Private Collection

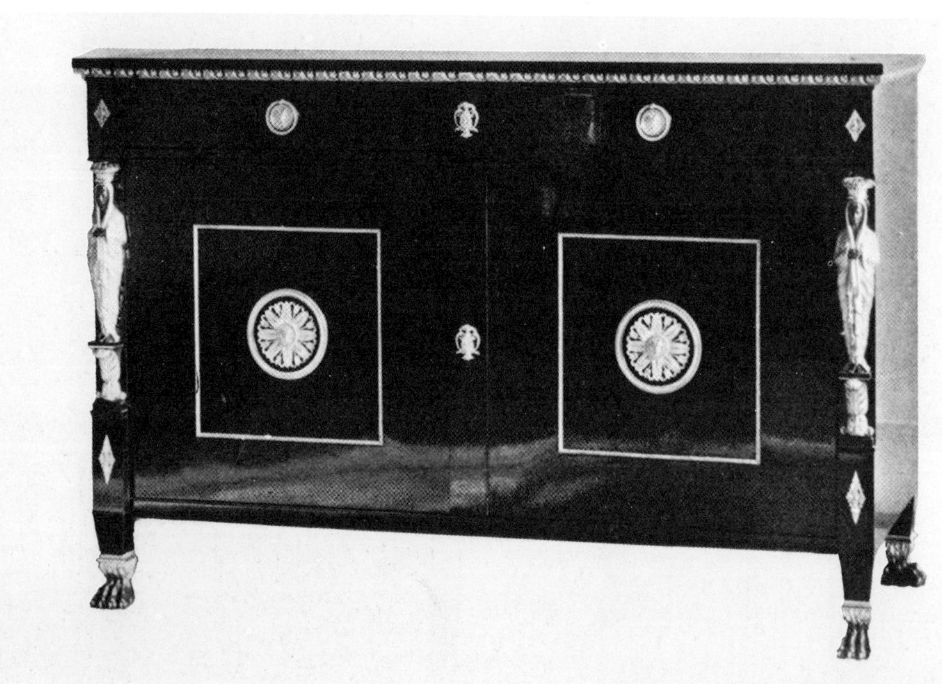

1130. Cómoda, caoba y bronce, 1800. Viena

1130. Mahogany commode with bronze decoration, 1800. Vienna

1131. Cama imperio, 1790. Potsdam

1131. Empire bed, 1790. Potsdam

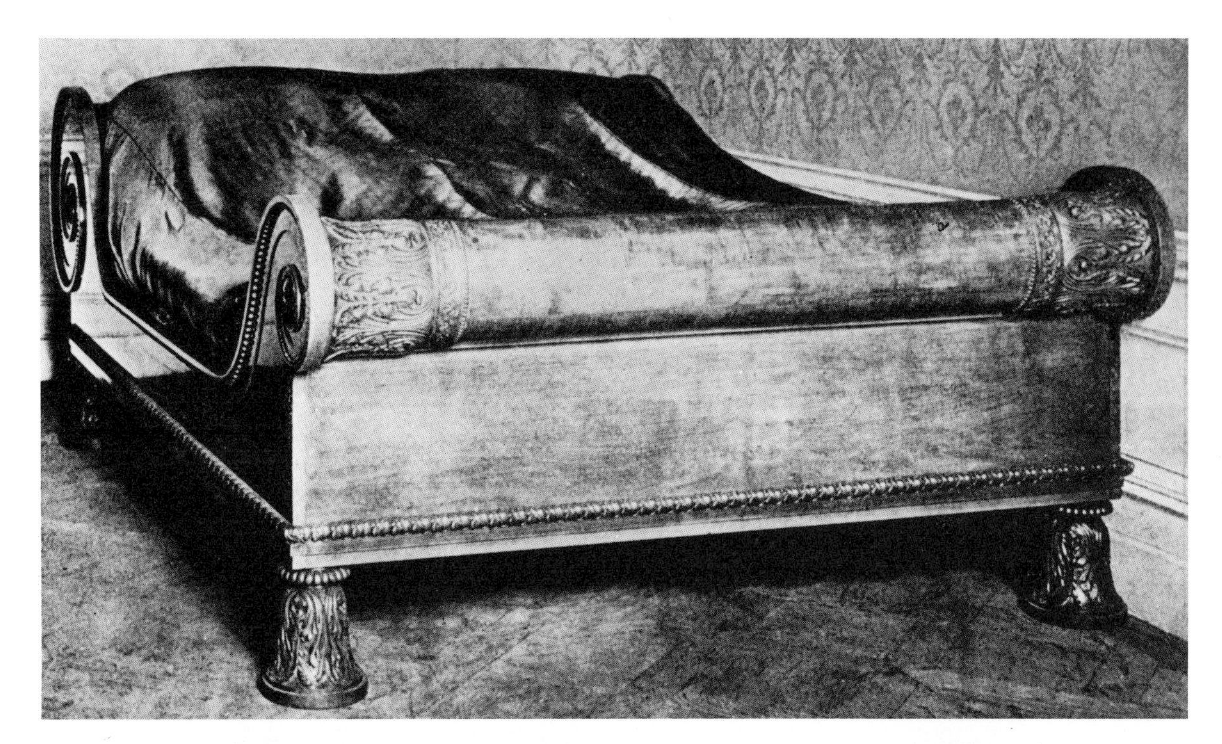

1132., Dormitorio imperio de la duquesa de Módena. Munich

1132. Empire bedroom of the Duchess of Modena. Munich

1133. Cama con dosel imperio. Castillo de Wurzburg

1133. Empire bed with canopy. Castle of Wurzburg

1134. Silloncito de madera de caoba y marquetería; respaldo de peineta. Palacio Nacional. Madrid

1134. Small mahogany armchair with marquetry and comb back. National Palace. Madrid

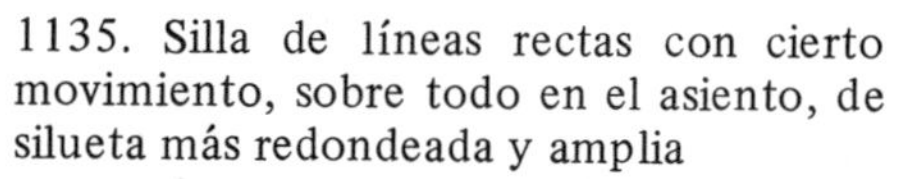

1135. Silla de líneas rectas con cierto movimiento, sobre todo en el asiento, de silueta más redondeada y amplia

1135. This chair has straight lines but with a certain movement especially in the seat, which is rounder and wider than the rest

1136. Interpretación española del sillón Luis XVI, con respaldo "à chapeaux" y dos cuartos de círculo rematando el copete; apoyos en forma de copa y los demás elementos, estriados

1136. A Spanish version of the Louis XVI armchair, with "à chapeaux" back and two quarter circles at the top. Cup-shaped arm rest supports. Other parts are striated

1137. En este sillón Carlos IV, ricamente taraceado, es de destacar el respaldo cuadrado, decorado por una serie de láminas de madera taraceada que lo cubren totalmente. Palacio de Bendinat. Mallorca

1137. Notice of the square back of this richly inlaid Charles IV armchair. It is decorated with a series of inlaid wooden engravings that completely cover it. Bendinat Palace, Majorca

1138. Silloncito de caoba de línea muy pura, patas delanteras ya de estilo imperio. Comedor del palacio del Escorial

1138. Small mahogany armchair of very pure lines, the front legs are already in the Empire style. Dining-room of the Palace of the Escorial

1139. Sofá proyectado por el arquitecto Ventura Rodríguez; bella composición en la que puede estudiarse la unión de los brazos con las patas y la continuidad del respaldo con los brazos. Duques de Sueca. Madrid

1139. Sofa designed by architect Ventura Rodríguez. A beautiful composition in witch the continuity of arms and legs and back and arms can be appreciated. Duke of Sueca. Madrid

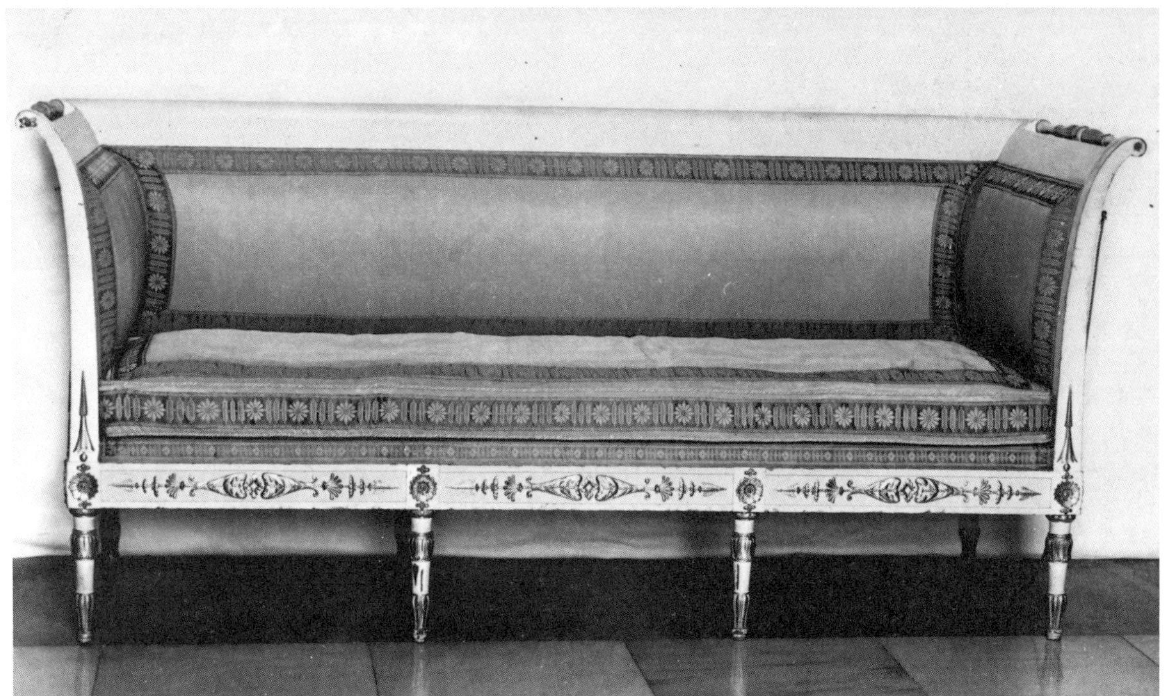

1140. Canapé de brazos abiertos, pintado y dorado, estilo Carlos IV. Palacio del Escorial

1140. Settee with open arms, painted and gilded, in the Charles IV style. Palace of the Escorial

1141. Silla, modelo muy puro del siglo XVI, interpretación española; tapicería de seda bordada. Patrimonio Nacional. Madrid

1141. Chair with very pure 16th-century influence, Spanish execution and upholstered in embroidered silk. National Patrimony. Madrid

1142. Silla Carlos IV pintada y dorada, tapicería bordada. Casita del Príncipe. El Pardo

1142. Charles IV chair, painted and gilt. Embroidered upholstery. "House of the Prince". El Pardo

1143. Silla Carlos IV completamente taraceada y con aplicaciones de bronce cincelado; respaldo ovalado y ligeramente cóncavo. Palacio de los Borbones. El Escorial

1143. Charles IV chair, completely inlaid, has engraved bronze appliqués. The back is oval and slightly concave. Palace of the Bourbons. El Escorial

1144. Silla con asiento de rejilla; composición original de los Talleres Reales. Palacio Real. Madrid

1144. Chair with cane seat. An original creation of the Royal Workshops. Royal Palace. Madrid

1145. Salón Carlos IV. Palacio del Escorial

1145. Charles IV salon. Palace of the Escorial

1146. Consola Carlos IV, tallada y dorada con chambranas. Detalle de la ilustración anterior. Palacio del Escorial

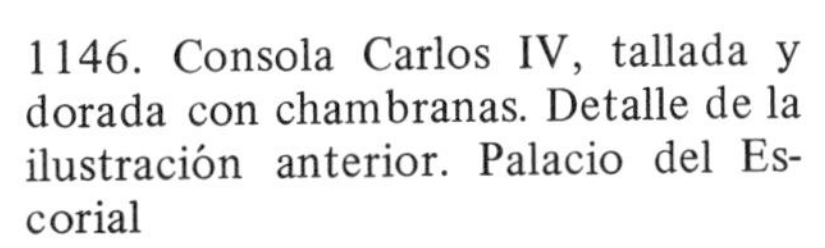

1146. Charles IV console table, carved and gilded, with stretchers. Detail of the preceding illustration. Palace of the Escorial

1147. Consola y silla Carlos IV. Casita del Príncipe. El Pardo

1147. Charles IV console table and chair. "House of the Prince". El Pardo

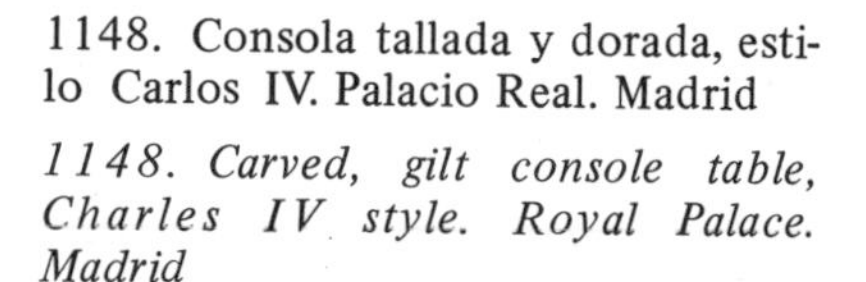

1148. Consola tallada y dorada, estilo Carlos IV. Palacio Real. Madrid

1148. Carved, gilt console table, Charles IV style. Royal Palace. Madrid

1149. Mesa consola con las estrías de las patas torsas y hojas de laurel en el pseudo capitel. Salón pompeyano. El Escorial

1149. Console table with spiral striated legs and laurel leaves on the false capitals. Pompeyan Room, El Escorial

1150. Consola tallada y dorada, por A. Maeso. Palacio del Escorial

1150. Carved and gilded console table, by A. Maeso. Palace of the Escorial

1151. Consola marqueteada por A. Maeso. Palacio del Escorial

1151. Console table withh marquetry decoration, by A. Maeso. Palace of the Escorial

1152. Consola tallada de caoba en color natural, de planta semicircular

1152. Semicircular carved mahogany console table in the natural colour of the wood

1153. Original mesa consola taraceada y con elementos tallados y dorados. Curiosa solución de voluta cuadrada, por Angel Maeso. Palacio de los Borbones. El Escorial

1153. An original console table with inlays and gilt carvings. Interesting square scrolls by Angel Maeso. Palace of the Boubons. El Escorial

1154. Angulo de un salón en la casa de los duques de Sueca. Consola y sofá proyectados por Ventura Rodríguez con influencias de los Luises

1154. Corner of a room in the Duke of Sueca's house. Console table and sofa designed by Ventura Rodríguez with influence of the Louis

1155. Salón Carlos IV. Palacio de Aranjuez

1155. Charles IV salon. Aranjuez Palace

1156. Despacho del palacete de la Moncloa en estilo Imperio (desaparecido)

1156. Study in the Empire style (now disppeared). Palacete de la Moncloa

1157. Mesa de despacho Carlos IV, totalmente taraceada y con aplicaciones de bronce de la época de Fernando VII. El Escorial

1157. Charles IV study table completely inlaid and with bronze appliqués of Fernando VII period. El Escorial

1158. Despacho de las habitaciones de maderas finas. El Escorial

1158. Study interior. Rooms of fine woods. El Escorial

1159. Comedor de la Casita del príncipe. El Escorial

1159. Dining-room. House of the Prince. El Escorial

1160. Secreter de tapa abatible en palo rosa y aplicaciones de bronce. Transición del Luis XVI al imperio. Palacio Real. Madrid

1160. Secretaire with drop flap in tulip wood with bronze appliqués. Transition from Louis XVI to the Empire period. Royal Palace. Madrid

1161. Escritorio o buró alto con tapa superior abatible de estilo Carlos IV; con taraceas sobre temas musicales. Colección Rumeu de Armas. Madrid

1161. Desk or high bureau of Charles IV style. The upper lid opens down. Inlays on musical themes. Rumeu de Armas Collection. Madrid

1162. Librería vitrina sobre un cuerpo inferior en forma de cómoda; decorada en taraceas neoclásicas italianizantes sobre temas de ciudades; estilo Carlos IV

1162. Glass bookcase on a commode, decorated with italianized Neo-classical inlays depicting city themes. Charles IV style.

1163. Papelera neoclásica. Composición muy simple sobre mesa con patas en estípite. Museo Arqueológico. Madrid

1163. Neo-classical cabinet of very simple composition standing on a table with tapering legs. Archaeological Museum. Madrid

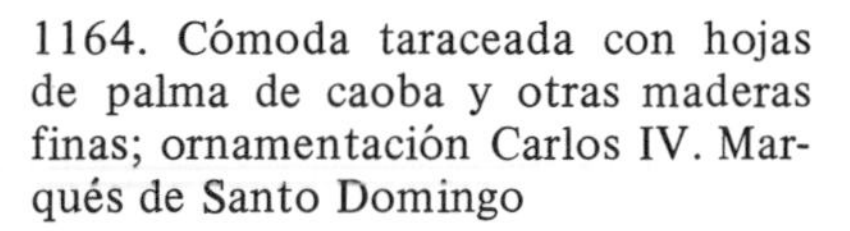

1164. Cómoda taraceada con hojas de palma de caoba y otras maderas finas; ornamentación Carlos IV. Marqués de Santo Domingo

1164. Inlaid commode finished in mahogany and other fine woods. Charles IV style decoration. Marquis of Santo Domingo

1165. Tocador completamente taraceado sobre un fondo de chapas de sicomoro; composición Carlos IV de líneas muy rectas y sencillas. Palacio-castillo de Bendinat. Mallorca

1165. Dressing table completely inlaid in paneles of sycamore. Charles IV style in very straight, simple lines. Palace-castle of Bendinat. Majorca

1166. Cama neoclásica de alto cabecero, pintada y dorada. Modelo muy popular. Olot

1166. Neo-classical bed with high headboard painted and gilt. A very popular type. Olot

1167., Cama pintada y dorada; línea derivada del Luis XVI con el copete "à chapeaux". Palacio de los Marqueses de Viana. Córdoba

1167. Bed painted and gilt. Lines derived from Louis XVI with "à chapeaux" top. Palace of the Marquis of Viana. Cordova

1168. Cama estilo Carlos IV, con tallas doradas y elementos neoclásicos

1168. Charles IV style bed with gilt carving and neo-classical members

1169. Dormitorio de Carlos IV. Cama imperio con aplicaciones de bronce cincelado. El Escorial

1169. Charles IV's bedroom in the Empire style, with chiselled bronze appliqués. El Escorial

1170. Sillón fernandino de caoba con tallas doradas. Palacio del Pardo

1170. Fernandine armchair in mahogany with gilt carvings. Pardo Palace

1171. Sillón fernandino de caoba y bronces, respaldo de góndola calado y copete de peineta, patas de tijera. Palacio del Pardo

1171. "Fernandino" armchair in mahogany with bronze decoration, pierced gondola back, comb cresting and X-shaped legs. Pardo Palace

1172. Sillón fernandino, copete de peineta, las patas delanteras con la característica decoración tallada y dorada fernandina. Palacio de la Granja

1172. "Fernandino" armchair with "comb" top, front legs characteristic Fernandine carved and gilt decoration. Palace of La Granja

1173. Sillón fernandino. Despacho de Alfonso XIII. Palacio Real. Madrid

1173. "Fernandino" armchair. Study of Alfonso XIII. Royal Palace. Madrid

1174. Sillón fernandino, maderas doradas vistas y brazos de volutas, con tallas

1174. "Fernandino" armchair, gilt wood facing and scrolled arms, with carving

1175. Banqueta de tijera, de bronce cincelado, atribuida a Percier y Fontaine. Casita del Labrador. Aranjuez

1175. Sewing stool made of engraved bronze, attributed to Percier and Fontaine. "House of the Farmer". Aranjuez

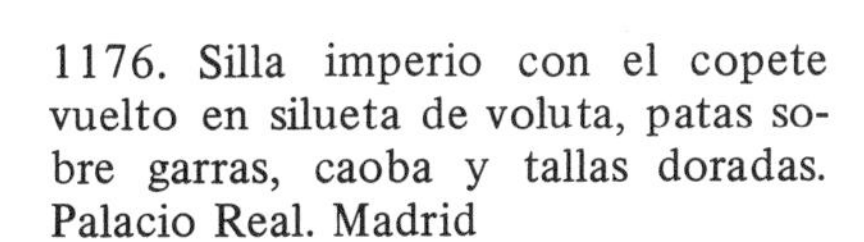

1176. Silla imperio con el copete vuelto en silueta de voluta, patas sobre garras, caoba y tallas doradas. Palacio Real. Madrid

1176. Empire chair in mahogany, with curved scroll profile cresting, legs on claws, with gilt carving. Royal Palace. Madrid

1177. Característico perfil de silla fernandina, con copete de peineta y patas delanteras torneadas. Taracea elemental de filetes metálicos. Colección particular

1177. Characteristic profile of a Fernandine chair with "comb" top and turned front legs. Simple inlays of metal fillet. Private collection

1178. Sofá muy característico del Fernandino, con los brazos abiertos, patas ligeramente curvas y respaldo de lira

1178. Typical Fernandine sofa, with open arms, slightly curved legs and lyre back

1179., Sillería de las flechas, estilo imperio; caoba y tallas doradas. Palacio del Escorial

1179. Arrow chairs, Imperial style, made of mahogany with gilt carvings. El Escorial Palace

1180. Sofá de góndola con tallas doradas sobre esfinges imperio, talladas y doradas. Palacio del Pardo

1180. Gondola sofa with gilt carving on sphinx supports in the Empire style. El Pardo Palace

1181. Sofá fernandino de tres plazas tallas doradas

1181. "Fernandino" sofa of triple seat form; gilt carving

1182., Interpretación fernandina de un sofá; marquetería de boj, brazos muy abiertos y almohadones cilíndricos

1182. "Fernandino" sofa. Boxwood marquetry, arms very open and cylindrical cushions

1183. Velador de caoba y bronces imperio. Palacio Real. Madrid

1183. Study table in the Empire style, with gilt carving. Royal Palace. Madrid

1184. Cómoda isabelina característica, de madera de pino, pero chapeada con hojas de caoba, líneas muy estilizadas derivadas del imperio

1184. Commode characteristic of the "isabelino" period, in pine with mahogany veneer and stylized lines in the Empire taste

1185. Composición del despacho de Napoleón en Chamartín, estilo imperio. Madrid

1185. Composition of Napoleón's study at Chamartin; Empire style. Madrid

1186. Mesa fernandina de despacho, de caoba y tallas doradas; despacho de Alfonso XIII. Palacio Real. Madrid

1186. "Fernandino" study table in mahogany with gilt carving; study of Alfonso XIII. Royal Palace. Madrid

1187. Mesa de despacho, estilo imperio, con tallas doradas. Palacio Real. Madrid

1187. Study table in the Empire style, with gilt carving. Royal Palace. Madrid

1188. Mesita costurero; patas de forma de lira con cuerdas metálicas. Palacio de Perelada. Gerona

1188. Sewing table. Legs in the sape of lyres with metal strings. Perelada Palace. Gerona

1189. Tocador laqueado con tallas de cisnes y leones tallados y dorados. Casa Solá. Olot

1189. Lacquered dressing table with carved swans and gilt carved lions. Solá House. Olot

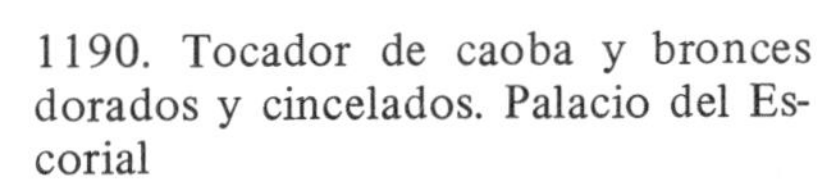

1190. Tocador de caoba y bronces dorados y cincelados. Palacio del Escorial

1190. Dressing-table in mahogany with chiselled gilt bronzework. Palace of the Escorial

1191. Tocador de composición arquitectónica; la parte inferior es una consola con patas en forma de voluta; sobre ella el espejo va también entre dos columnas. Palacio de la marquesa de Benamejí. Santillana del Mar

1191. Dressing of architectural composition. The lower part is a console table with scroll shapes legs. The mirror is also held between two columns. Palace of the Marqués of Benamejí. Santillana del Mar

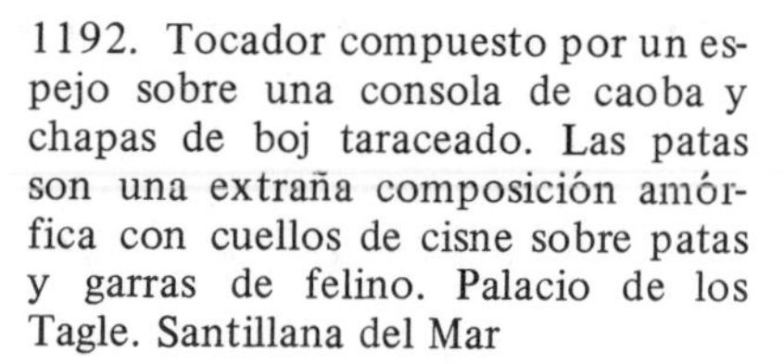

1192. Tocador compuesto por un espejo sobre una consola de caoba y chapas de boj taraceado. Las patas son una extraña composición amórfica con cuellos de cisne sobre patas y garras de felino. Palacio de los Tagle. Santillana del Mar

1192. Dressing table composed of a mirror on a console table of Mahogany and inlaid boxwood leaves. The legs are a strange, amorphous combination of swans'necks on top of feline legs and claws. Palace of the Tagles. Santillana del Mar

1193. "Psiche" de caoba; el gran espejo va compuesto con todos los elementos imperio, como el frontón, las esfinges- cariátides, las garras. Castillo Palacio de Bendinat. Mallorca

1193. Mahogany "Psyche". This great mirror is composed of all the Imperial elements, such as the gable, caryatid sphinxes and claws. Castle-palace of Bendinat, Majorca

1194. Cómoda de caoba; composición muy simple; cajonería entre dos estípites con cabezas de esfinges clásicas de bronce dorado.

1194. Mahogany commode of very simple composition. The drawers are between pedestals with classical gilt bronze sphinx heads

1195. Cama imperio llamada de S'Adriá, por Adrián Ferrant. Palacio de Morell. Palma de Mallorca

1195. Empire style bed, known as S'Adriá, in the Morell Palace, by Adrian Ferrant. Palma, Majorca

1196. Caja en forma de góndola con marquetería de boj y patas zoomórficas talladas y doradas. La mesita de noche, cilíndrica, y el tocador también son fernandinos. Palacio de Pedralbes. Barcelona

1196. Gondola shaped bed with boxwood marquetry and gilt carved zoomorphic legs. The cylindrical night stand and dressing table are also Fernandine. Pedralbes Palace. Barcelona

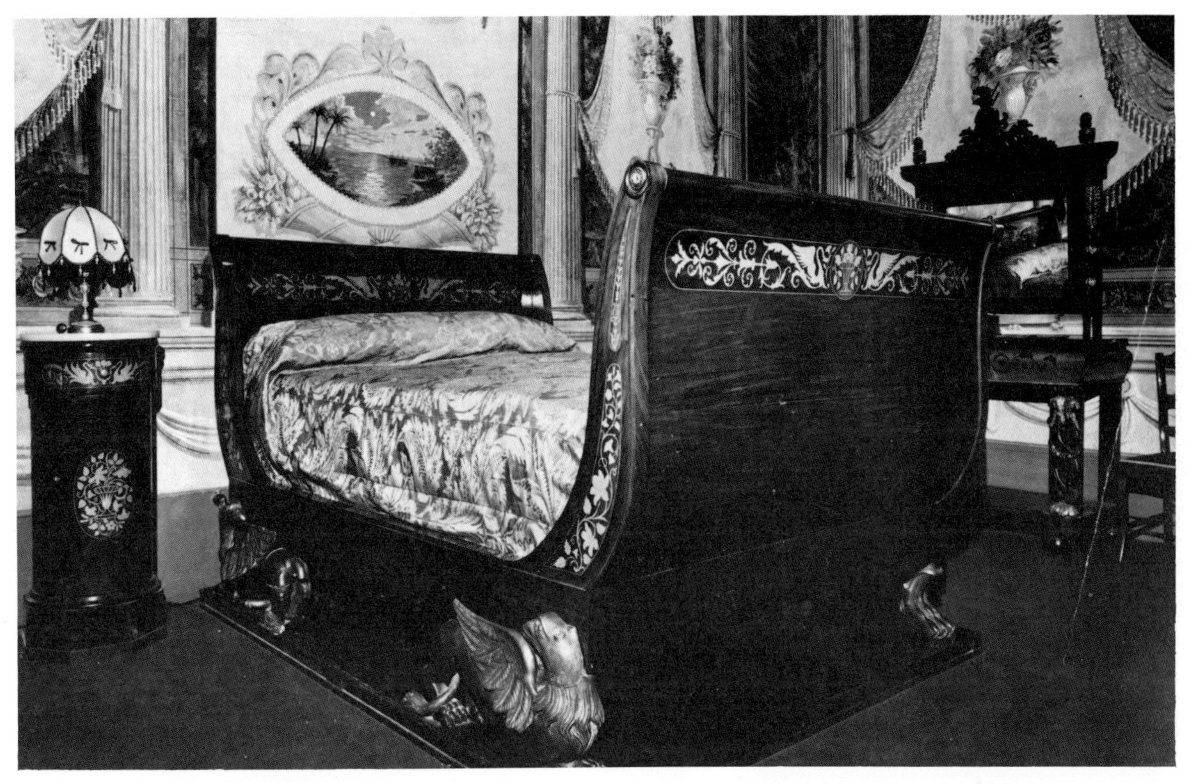

1197. Cama imperio de la región catalana; las patas inician formas de góndola decoradas, con taraceas de boj; los cabeceros llevan unos elementos de formas caprichosas y convencionales con tallas doradas y filetes de boj

1197. Imperial bed from the Catalan region. The legs are gondola shaped and decorated with boxwood inlays. The head and foot have both caprichous and conventional elements with gilt carvings and boxwood fillets

1198.Cama de l'Adrià, decorada con taraceas de boj, patas talladas en forma de cuellos de cisne con una graciosa curva que recoge las colgaduras. Palacio de los marqueses de Campo Franco. Palma de Mallorca

1198. L'Adrià bed, decorated with boxwood inlays. The legs are carved in the shape of swans' necks with a graceful curve to catch the hangings. Palace of Campo Franco. Palma de Majorca

1199. Cuna de estilo imperio de caoba; tallas y aplicaciones en bronce dorado y cincelado. Palacio de Benamejí. Santillana del Mar

1199. Imperial style mahogany cradle. Carvings and gilt engraved bronze appliqués. Benamejí Palace. Santillana del Mar

1200. Ejemplar excepcional de cuna, obra de l'Adrià; de forma ovoide o de góndola y va sobre un pie de línea muy caprichosa con animales fabulosos tallados y en parte dorados. Palacio de los Marqueses de Campo Franco. Palma de Mallorca

1200. Unusual example of a cradle by l'Adrià. Oval or gondola shaped, it rests on a curious base with fabulous carved and partly gilt animals. Palace of the Marquis of Campo Franco. Palma de Majorca

1201. Habitaciones de platino en la Casita del Labrador. Aranjuez

1201. Platinum rooms. "House of the Farmer". Aranjuez

1202. Sillón típico isabelino, derivado del Luis XV, profusamente tallado y dorado. Museo de Artes Decorativas. Madrid

1202. Typical "isabelino" armchair stemming from the Louis XV period, richly carved and gilded. Museum of Decorative Arts. Madrid

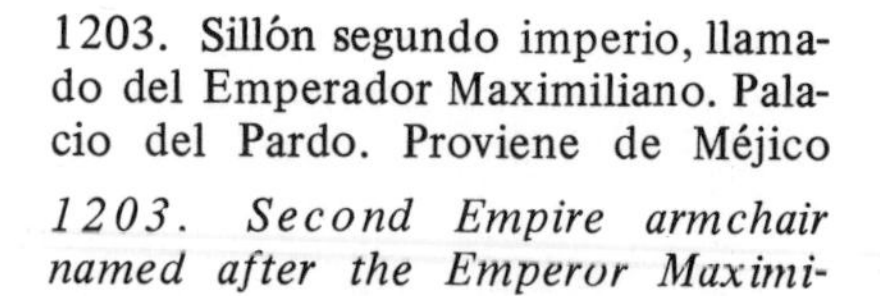

1203. Sillón segundo imperio, llamado del Emperador Maximiliano. Palacio del Pardo. Proviene de Méjico

1203. Second Empire armchair named after the Emperor Maximilian. From Mexico. Pardo Palace

1204. Sillón de caoba típico isabelino; tallas y líneas características de Luis XV, tapizado en terciopelo de seda

1204. Typical "isabelino" type mahogany armchair. Carving and lines are characteristic of the Louis XV period; upholstered in silk velvet

1205. Sillón isabelino de caoba, derivado del Luis XV, respaldo oval "a la reina". Brazos, ménsulas y patas derivadas del estilo; forma muy popular. Museo Romántico. Madrid

1205. "Isabelino" mahogany armchair stemming from the Louis XV period; oval back, arms, brackets and legs derived from the style; a very popular form. Romantic Museum. Madrid

1206. Sillón que señala el paso del fernandino a un isabelino aburguesado; líneas muy populares y estilizadas del estilo anterior; caoba y rejilla. Museo Papiol. Villanueva y Geltrú

1206. Armchair which marks the transition from Fernandine to bourgeois Isabeline. Popular and stylized lines derived from the former style. Mahogany and cane. Papiol Museum. Villanueva y Geltrú

1207. Sillón de caoba (la tapicería es de época posterior) de estilo romántico, derivado del neoclásico e imperio, respaldo vuelto con lira central; talla popular

1207. Mahogany armchair (the upholstery is of the posterior period) in the romantic style stemming from the neoclassical and Empire periods, with curved back and lyre-shaped spalt; popular carving

1208. Sillón de caoba con celosía característica en el respaldo, patas en estípite, respaldo vuelto, estilización del fernandino. Mediados del siglo XIX

1208. Mahogany armchair with characteristic latticework back, tapered legs and curved cresting with "Fernandine" influence. Mid 19th century

1209. Sofá romántico de caoba derivado del imperio. Los brazos semejan popas de navío, tapicería de damasco rojo. Museo de Pontevedra

1209. "Romantic" sofa derived from the Empire style. The arms are of ship's bows form; in mahogany with red damask upholstery. Pontevedra Museum

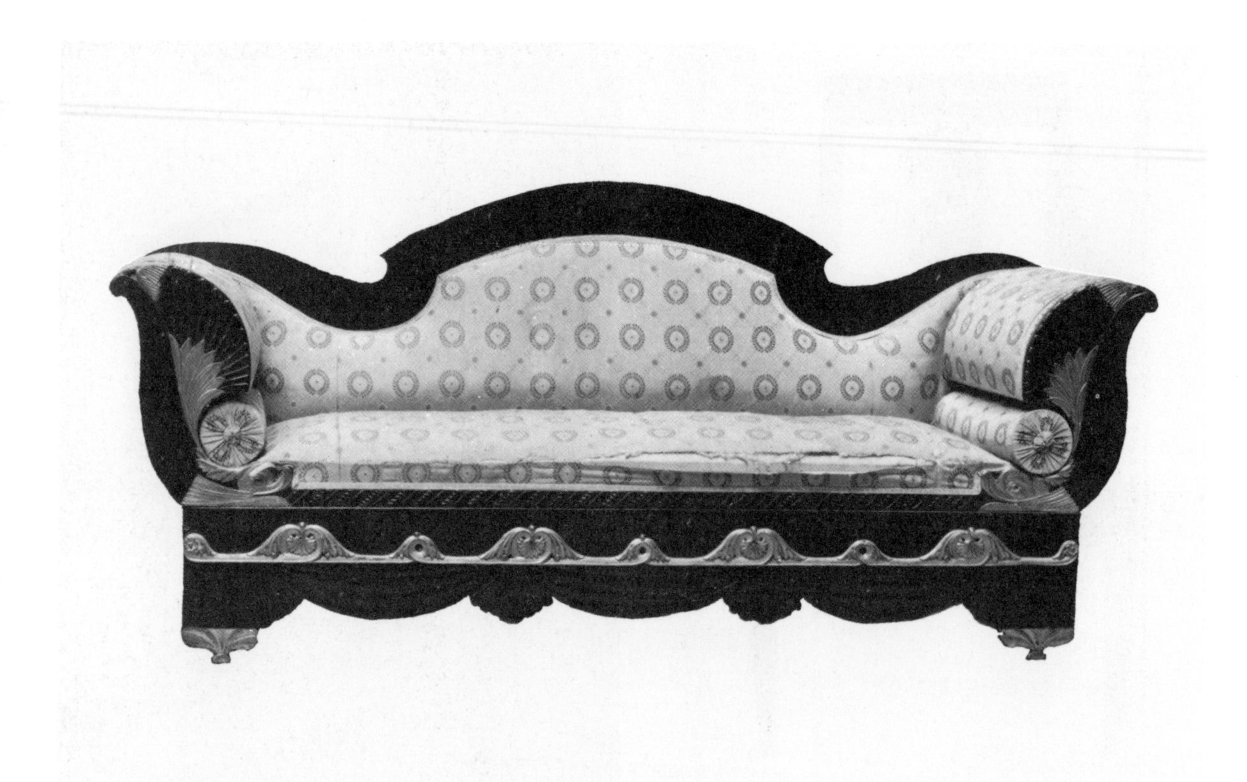

1210. Sofá popular derivado del imperio, madera de pino, chapeado y tallas de madera dorada. Faldón imitando drapeados de tela. Colección particular

1210. Popular sofa in the Empire taste, in pine, veneered and with gilt wood carving; the apron piece imitating drapery. Private Collection

1211. Sofá isabelino capitoné. Museo Romántico. Madrid

1211. "Capitoné" Isabeline sofa. Romantic Museum of Madrid

1212. Salón del palacio de los Borbones; curiosa sillería de estilo gótico, probable obra de Angel Maeso al finalizar el fernandino

1212. Drawing room of the Palace of the Bourbons. Old chairs of Gothic style, probably the work of Angel Maeso at the end of the Fernandine period

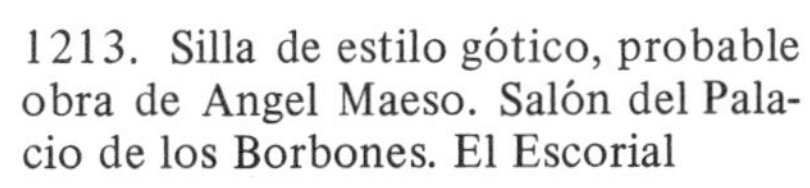

1213. Silla de estilo gótico, probable obra de Angel Maeso. Salón del Palacio de los Borbones. El Escorial

1213. Gothic style chair, probably the work of Angel Maeso. Drawing room of the Palace of the Bourbons. El Escorial

1214. Silla de caoba con celosía característica en el respaldo, patas en estípite

1214. Mahogany chair with characteristic latticework back, tapered legs

1215. Silla segundo imperio, en madera dorada, imitando bambú, influencia oriental. Asiento tapizado o de rejilla. Museo de Cerralbo. Madrid

1215. Gilt wood chair imitating bamboo, in the Second Empire style with oriental influence; upholstered or cane seat. Cerralbo Museum. Madrid

1216. Silla popular de línea neoclásica, con asiento de anea y elementos torneados

1216. A popular chair of the Neoclassical line with rush seat and turned elements

1217. Silla popular derivada de tipos imperio con elementos torneados y asiento de anea. Copete de peineta y lira con copa neoclásica

1217. Popular chair derived from the Empire type, with turned members and rush seat, comb cresting and neo-classical urn splat

1218. Silla isabelina de tipo popular con asiento de anea

1218. Isabeline chair of a popular sort with rush seat

1219. Silla volante de la última época del isabelino, contemporánea del segundo imperio en Francia. La madera lleva aplicaciones de nácar

1219. Late "isabelino" period chair, contemporary with the Second Empire period in France. The wood carries mother-of-pearl appliqués

1220. Velador de nogal y hojas de caoba con taraceas, inspirado en temas imperio. Museo Romántico. Madrid

1220. Walnut table, mahogany veneer with inlay, inspired by Empire motifs. Romantic Museum. Madrid

1221. Mesa-velador y silla románticos de caoba y tallas derivadas del neoclásico e imperio. Museo Romántico. Madrid

1221. "Romantic" tripod table and chair in mahogany with carving in the neo-classical and Empire styles. Romantic Museum. Madrid

1222. Mesa-velador de doce lados sobre copa central y tres pies de ménsula. Caoba y chapas con taraceas en boj y limoncillo, derivados del imperio. Museo Romántico. Madrid

1222. Twelve-side table with central shaft and three bracket feet, in mahogany and veneers with boxwood and satinwood inlay in the Empire taste. Romantic Museum. Madrid

1223. Consola con los temas isabelinos de cisnes y garras, patas de arillos circulares. Casa de Bolós. Olot

1223. Console table with the Isabeline themes of swans and claws, circular legs. Bolós House. Olot

1224. Comedor del Museo Romántico. Madrid

1224. Dining-room. Romantic Museum. Madrid

1225. Interior de la casa "Els Vayrada", con una sillería isabelina de respaldos ovalados "a la reina", patas y ménsulas cabriolé. Olot

1225. Interior of "Els Vayrada" House with oval backed "a la reina" Isabeline chairs. Cabriolet legs and elbow rests

1226. Interior romántico. Museo Papiol. Villanueva y Geltrú

1226. Romantic Interior of the Papiol Museum. Villanueva y Geltrú

1227. Ambiente característico del siglo XIX. Tapicería capitoné, sillas "vis a vis" doradas

1227. Characteristic environment of the 19th century. Button upholstery and gilt sociable chairs

1228. Despacho en el antiguo Senado. Muebles tapizados capitoné, la silueta es la de las butacas isabelinas Luis XV, las patas van ocultas con flecos

1228. Office in the Old Senate, Madrid. Button upholstered furniture, the chairs are similar to Isabeline Louis XV chairs in shape. The legs are hidden under fringes

1229. Buró con librería alta; algunos elementos imperio como las cabezas de bronce en las patas, taracea muy fina de filetes metálicos

1229. Bureau with high bookcase. Some Imperial elements such as the bronze heads on the legs, very fine inlays of metal fillet

1230. Sala de billar con la mesa marqueteada. Casa Museo Papiol. Villanueva y Geltrú

1230. Billiard room with marqueted table. Papiol Museum. Villanueva y Geltrú

1231. Tocador compuesto por un espejo sobre consola de línea muy simplificada derivada del fernandino; ejemplar laqueado en negro con temas dorados y pintados. Palacio del marqués de Viana. Córdoba

1231. Dressing table composed of a mirror on a console table very simplified lines derived from the Fernandine period. Lacquered in black with gilt and painted trim. Palace of the Marquis of Viana. Cordova

1232. Cama metálica con varales que soportan un baldaquino de tela de influencia oriental; época plenamente romántica. Casa Cabanyes. Villanueva y Geltrú

1232. Metal bed with long poles supporting a cloth canopy of oriental derivation. From the Romantic period. Cabanyes House. Villanueva y Geltrú

1233. Cama segundo imperio laqueada en negro y decorada con pinturas y placas de nácar, con alto baldaquino

1233. Second Empire bed lacquered in black, decorated with paintings and mother-of-pearl, with a high canopy

1234. Dormitorio de Isabel II en Aranjuez

1234. Isabel II's bedroom in Aranjuez

1235. Biblioteca del antiguo palacio del Senado; de hierro y en estilo neogótico influenciado por la arquitectura inglesa de aquellos años. Compuesta por el arquitecto E. R. Ayuso en 1882

1235. Library of the old Palace of the Senate. It is made of iron in the Neo-gothic style influenced by the English architecture of that time. Designed by the architect E. R. Ayuso in 1882

EL MUEBLE CONTEMPORANEO

CONTEMPORARY FURNITURE

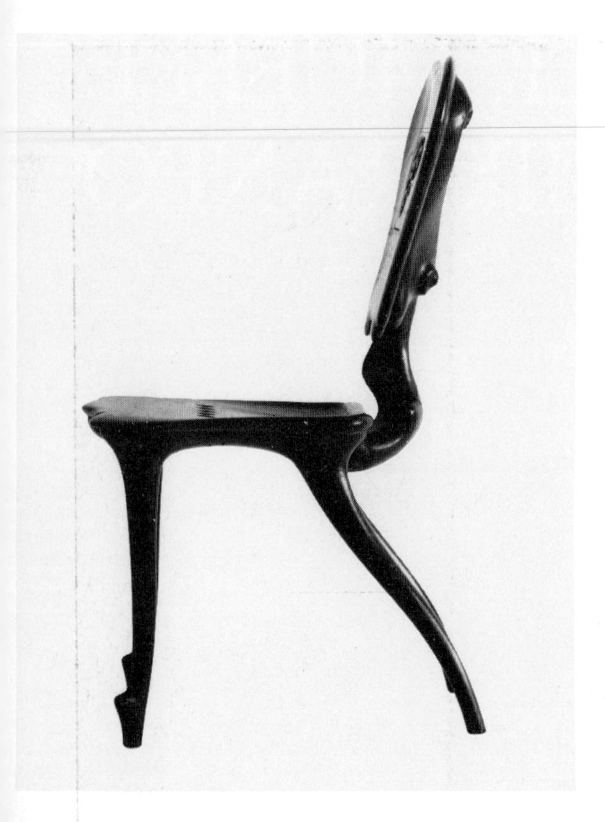

1236.. 1240. Dos realizaciones de Gaudí. Cuidadoso estudio anatómico para la adaptación de la silla; planta y frente de un asiento bipersonal; formas cóncavas en respaldo y asiento, en madera maciza. En el perfil de la silla se aprecia la forma del respaldo con la pieza sustentante, que hoy suele ser metálica y flexible

1236. 1240. Two works by Gaudí. Careful anatomical study in construction of the chair. Chair for two has concave backs and seats in solid wood. The back support seen in profile of the chair is usually made of flexible metal today

1237. Banco de dos plazas con tallas naturalistas excavadas en la madera del asiento y del respaldo; formas muy estudiadas morfológica y constructivamente, reduciendo al máximo los espesores. Casa Calvet. Barcelona

1237. Bench for two with naturalistic carvings in the wooden seat and back. The forms are carefully studied morphologically and constructively to reduce thickness as much as possible. Calvet House. Barcelona

1238. La célebre "chaise-longue", proyectada con una gran originalidad, deriva de los modelos del segundo imperio francés. Son muy importantes las soluciones de apoyos en hierro forjado, artesanía tan querida por Gaudí

1238. This famous "chaise-longue", designed with great originality, derives from Second Empire and French models. The supports are made of forged iron, craftsmanship much employed by Gaudí

1239. Sala de espera del piso principal con hogar chimenea y puerta de entrada al salón, por Antonio Gaudí. Casa Batlló. Barcelona

1239. Waiting room on ground floor with fireplace and door into the drawing room by Antonio. Gaudí. Batlló House. Barcelona

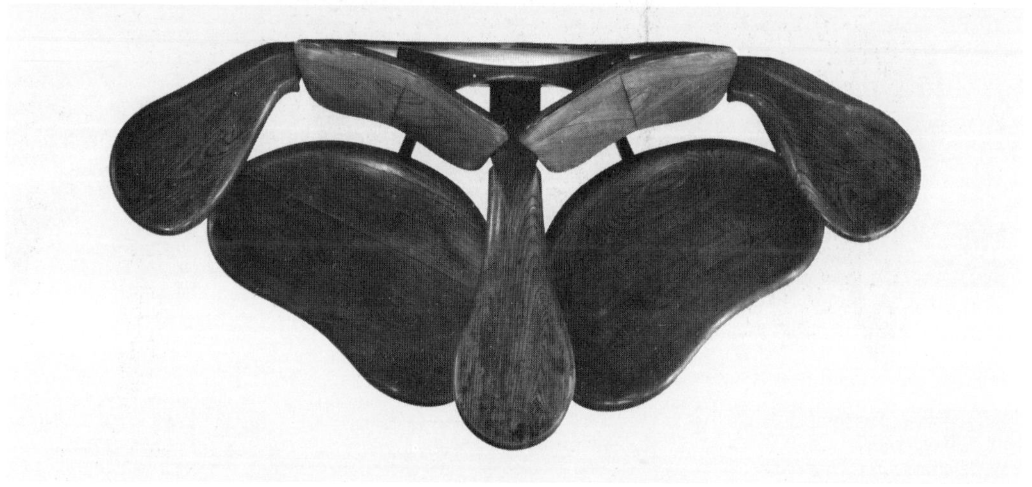

1917 – Gerrit Rietveld (1888-1964)
Holanda – *Netherlands*
Silla azul y roja – *Red Blue chair*

1925 – Marcel Breuer (1902-)
Alemania – *Germany*
Silla Vassily – *Vassily chair*

1926 – Mart Stam (1889-)
Alemania – *Germany*
Silla S 33 – *Chair S 33*

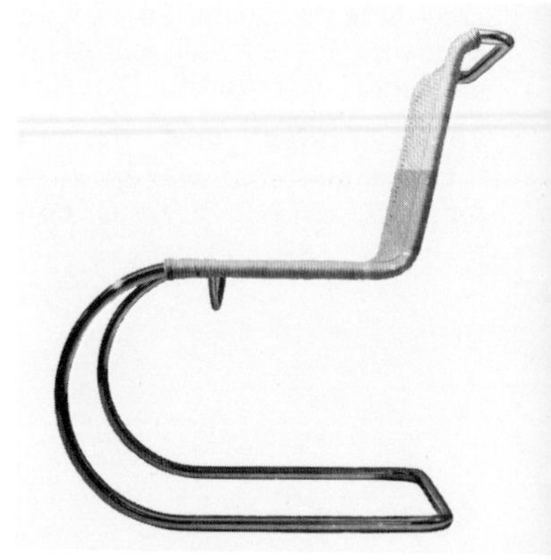

1926 – Mies van der Rohe (1886-1969)
Alemania – *Germany*
Silla MR – *MR chair*

1945 – Charles Eames (1907-)
E.E.U.U. – *U.S.A.*
Silla LCM – *LCM chair*

1949 – Charles Eames
Silla DAR – *DAR chair*

1949 – Finn Juhl (1912-)
Dinamarca – *Denmark*
Sillón en teca – *Armchair, teak frame*

1952 – Hans Wegner (1914-)
Dinamarca – *Denmark*
Silla en teca – *Chair, teak frame*

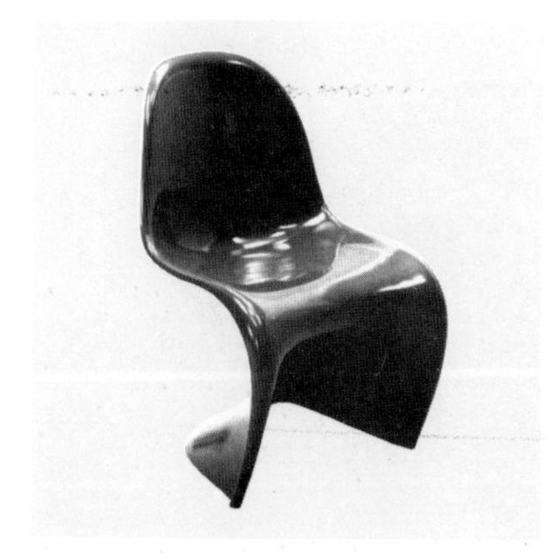

1960 – Verner Panton (1926-)
Suiza - *Switzerland*
Silla Stacking - *Stacking chair*

1961 – Bodo Rasch (1903-)
Alemania- *Germany*
Silla Two-shell - *Two-shell chair*

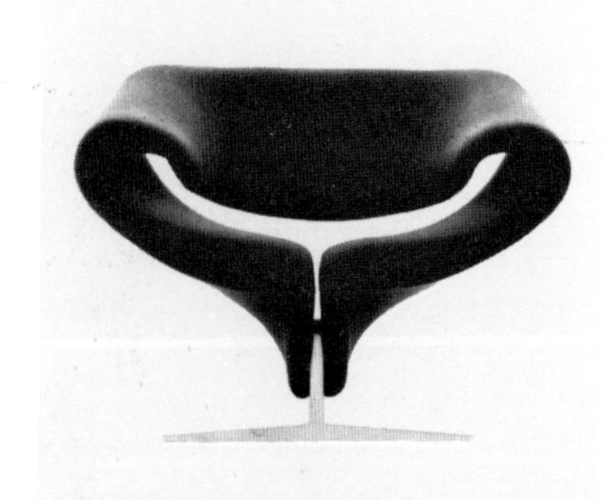

1965 – Pierre Paulin (1927-)
Francia - *France*
Silla 582 - *Chair 582*

1967 – A. Rosselli (1921-)
Italia - *Italy*
Silla "Jumbo" - *Jumbo chair*

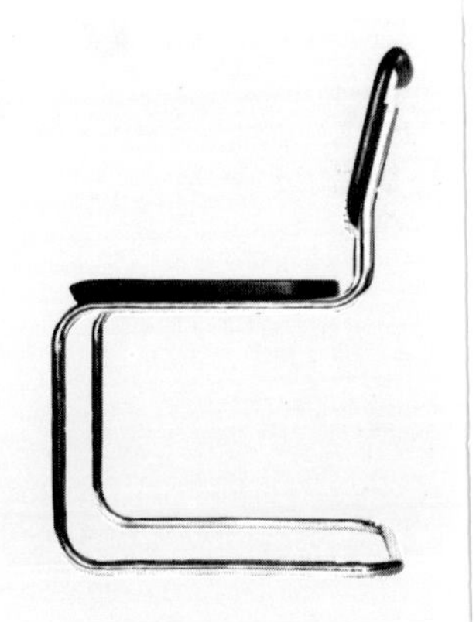

1928 – Marcel Breuer
Silla de rejilla – *Cantilever chair*

1933 – Alvar Aalto
Silla 31 – *Chair 31*

1934 – Gerrit Rietveld
Silla zig-zag – *Zig-zag chair*

1938 – J.F. Hardoy, A. Bonet
Argentina – *Argentine*

1952 – H. Bertoia (1915-) U.S.A.
Silla metálica
Chair welded lattice wire shell

1958 – A. Jacobsen
Silla Swan - *Swan chair*

1958 – Ch. Eames
Sillón 682 - *Chair 682*

1960 – A. Nurmesniemi (1927-)
Finlandia - *Finland*
Silla Trienal - *Triennale chair*

1967 – Jφrn Utzon (1918-)
Dinamarca - *Denmark*
Sillón "Floating Dock" -
"Flocting Dock" chair

1968 – Motomi Kawakami (1940-)
Japón - *Japan*
Silla Fiorenza - *Fiorenza chair*

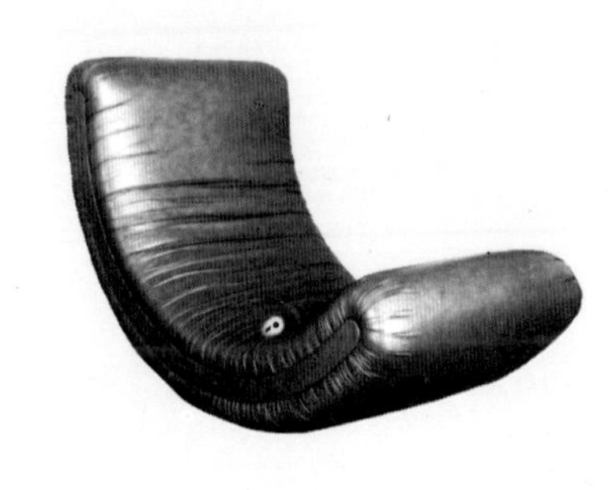

1969 – J. Lafuente (1928-)
España - *Spain*
Tumbona basculante - *Chaise-longue*

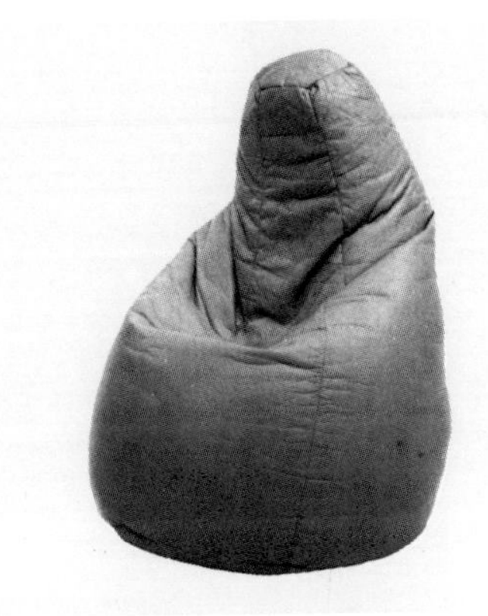

1969 – Gatti, Paolini, Teodoro
Italia - *Italy*
El Saco - *The Sacco*

APPENDICES

SYNOPSIS OF STYLES
LEGS IN DIFFERENT STYLES
COMMON TERMS IN FURNITURE MAKING

	ENGLAND GOTHIC	RENAISSANCE	E
FRANCE	BEGINNINGS 1150 HEIGHT SAINT LOUIS 1270 FLAMBOYANT 15th CENTURY	FRANCIS I* HENRY II* LOCAL SCHOOLS LE DE FRANCE BURGUNDY MIDIE LYON BRITTANY NORMANDY PICARDY LOUIS XIII* TRANSITION	(B
ENGLAND	BEGINNING 13th CENTURY TUDOR HENRY VIII 1509 TRANSITION 1547	ELIZABETHAN JAMES I (JACOBEAN) 1603–1625 CHARLES 1 1625–1649 CROMWELL (REPUBLIC) 1649–1660 CHARLES II 1685 TRANSITION	W
SPAIN	GOTHIC 12th–15th CENTURIES MUDEJAR 11th–15th CENTURIES ISABELINE (CATHOLIC MONARCHS) 1490 TRANSITION	PLATERESQUE MUDEJAR CHARLES V 1515 PHILIP II 1556–1598 CHARLES II 1665 MANUELINE (PORTUGUESE) 1495–1521	
ITALY GERMANY LOW COUNTRIES	PRE-RENAISSANCE 13th CENTURY (ITALY) NATIONAL GOTHIC (ALPS AND TIROL) GOTHIC  	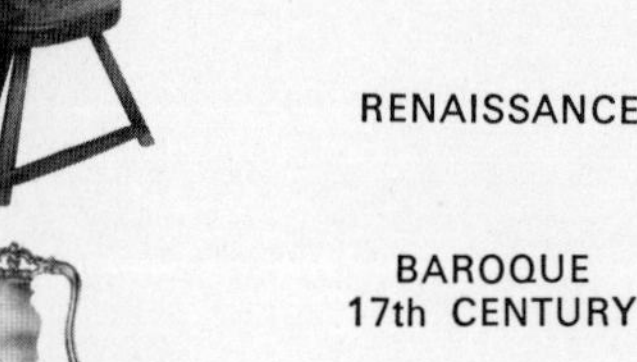 RENAISSANCE BAROQUE 17th CENTURY 	

* 1515 - 1547 1547 - 1559 **1614 - 1643**

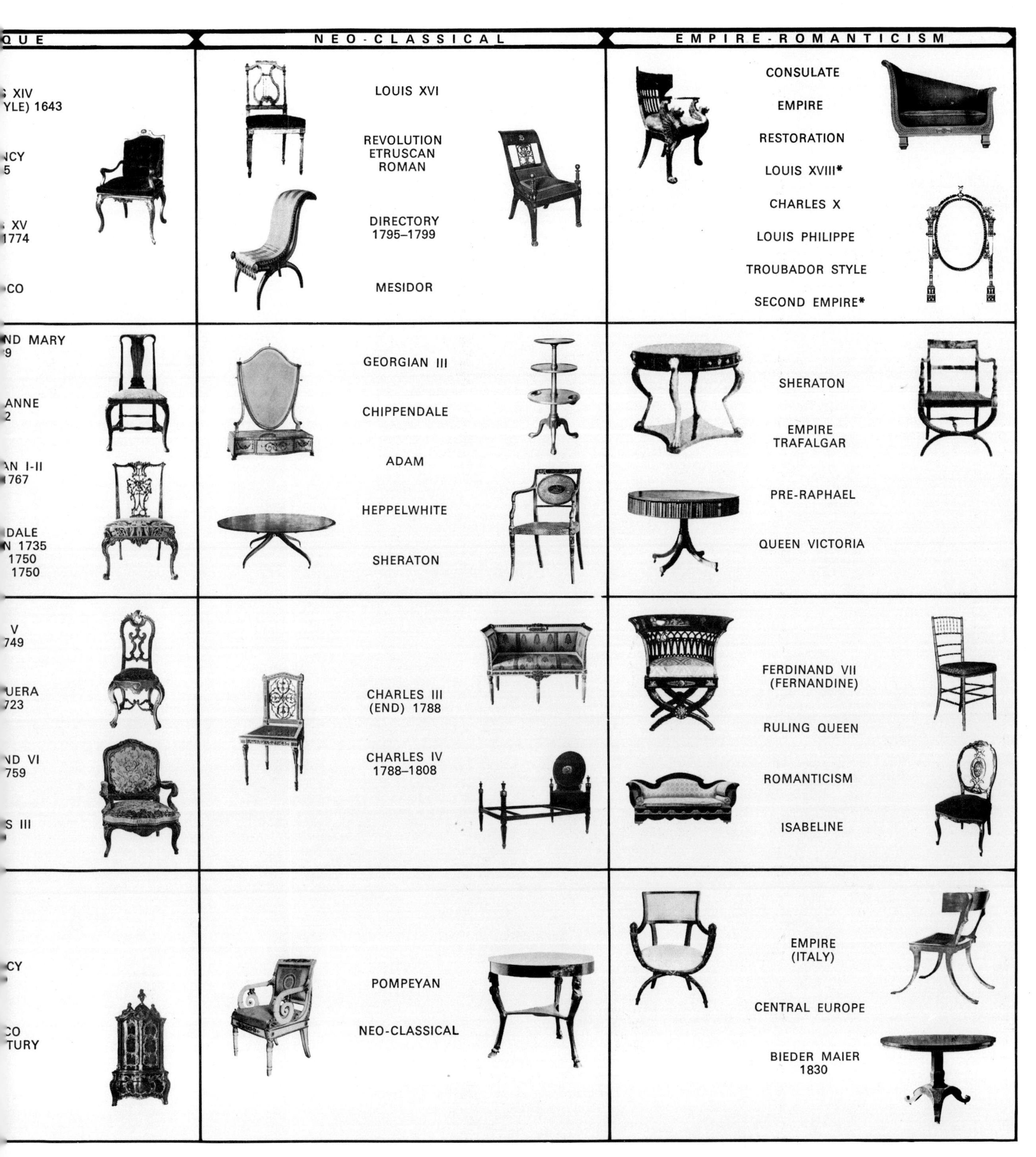
NEO-CLASSICAL
EMPIRE-ROMANTICISM
LOUIS XVI
REVOLUTION
ETRUSCAN
ROMAN
DIRECTORY
1795–1799
MESIDOR
CONSULATE
EMPIRE
RESTORATION
LOUIS XVIII*
CHARLES X
LOUIS PHILIPPE
TROUBADOR STYLE
SECOND EMPIRE*
GEORGIAN III
CHIPPENDALE
ADAM
HEPPELWHITE
SHERATON
SHERATON
EMPIRE
TRAFALGAR
PRE-RAPHAEL
QUEEN VICTORIA
CHARLES III
(END) 1788
CHARLES IV
1788–1808
FERDINAND VII
(FERNANDINE)
RULING QUEEN
ROMANTICISM
ISABELINE
POMPEYAN
NEO-CLASSICAL
EMPIRE
(ITALY)
CENTRAL EUROPE
BIEDER MAIER
1830

* 1799 - 1804 **1804 - 1815** 1815 - 1824 **1830 - 1848**
1850 **1825 - 1870**

LEGS IN DIFFERENT STYLES

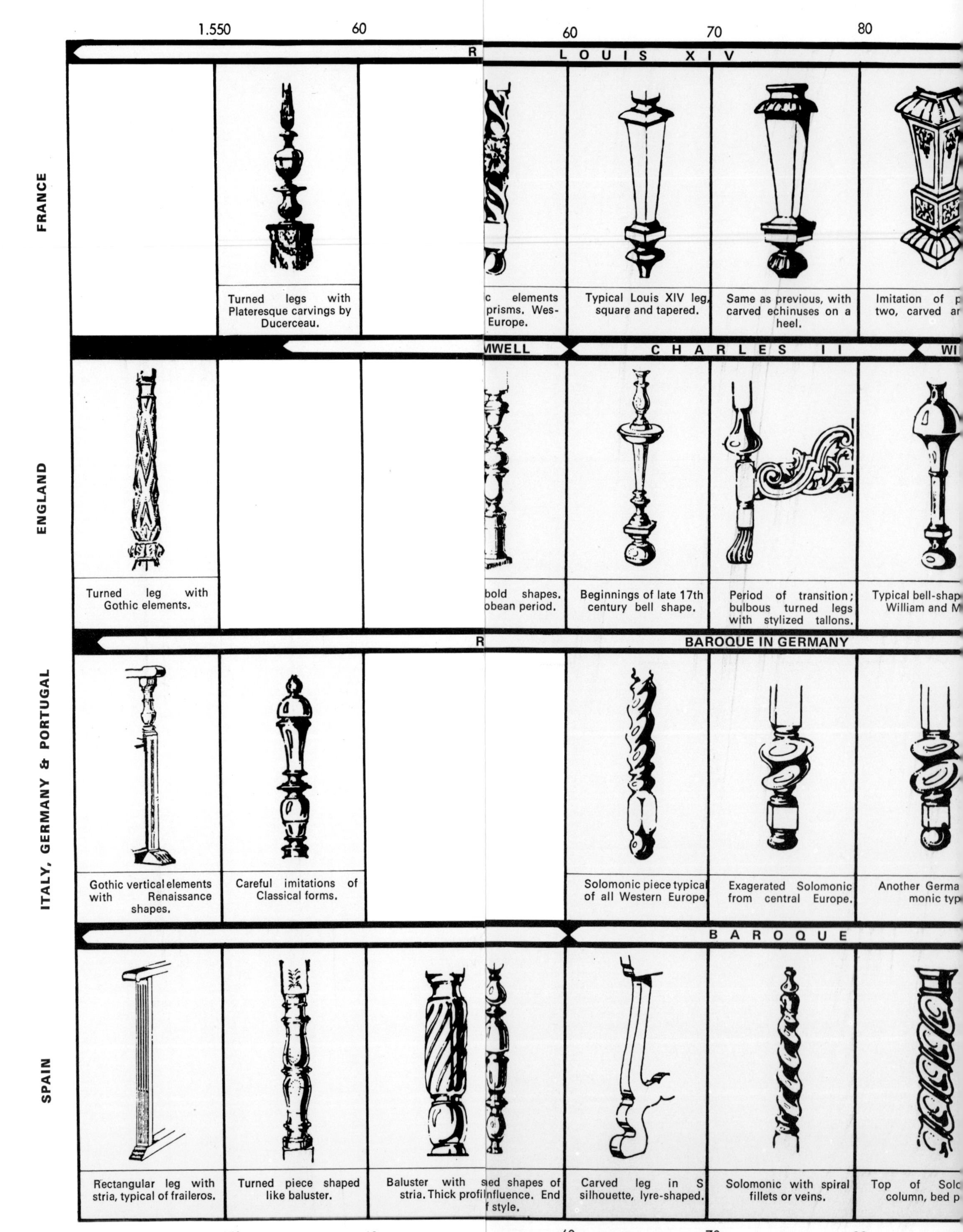

1.550
60
60
70
80
FRANCE
R
L O U I S X I V
Turned legs with Plateresque carvings by Ducerceau.
c elements prisms. Wes- Europe.
Typical Louis XIV leg, square and tapered.
Same as previous, with carved echinuses on a heel.
Imitation of p two, carved ar
ENGLAND
MWELL
C H A R L E S I I
WI
Turned leg with Gothic elements.
bold shapes. obean period.
Beginnings of late 17th century bell shape.
Period of transition; bulbous turned legs with stylized tallons.
Typical bell-shap William and M
ITALY, GERMANY & PORTUGAL
R
BAROQUE IN GERMANY
Gothic vertical elements with Renaissance shapes.
Careful imitations of Classical forms.
Solomonic piece typical of all Western Europe.
Exagerated Solomonic from central Europe.
Another Germa monic typ
SPAIN
B A R O Q U E
Rectangular leg with stria, typical of fraileros.
Turned piece shaped like baluster.
Baluster with stria. Thick profi
sed shapes of Influence. End f style.
Carved leg in S silhouette, lyre-shaped.
Solomonic with spiral fillets or veins.
Top of Solo column, bed p
1.550
60
60
70
80

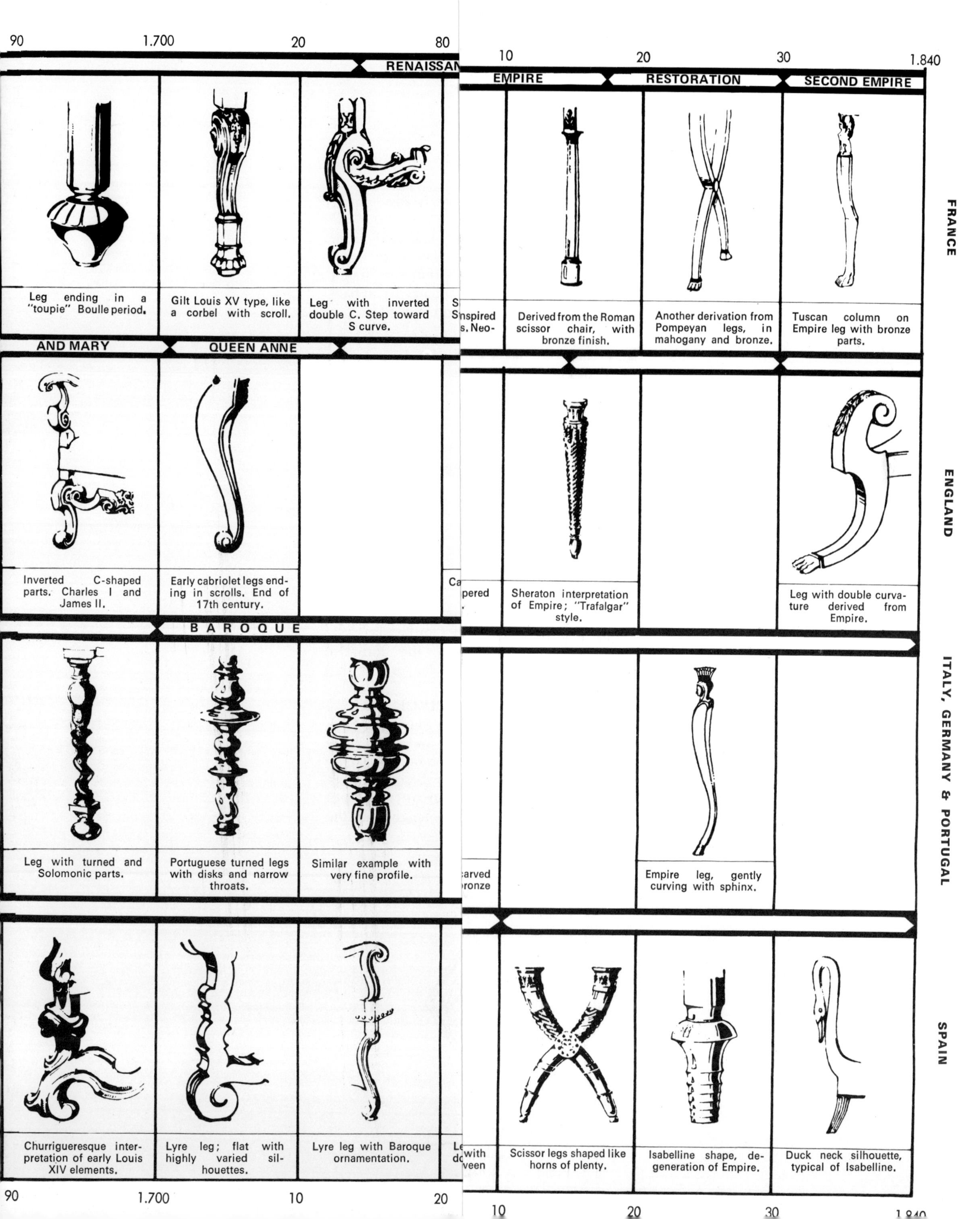

90
1.700
20
80
RENAISSAN
10
20
30
1.840
EMPIRE
RESTORATION
SECOND EMPIRE
Leg ending in a "toupie" Boulle period.
Gilt Louis XV type, like a corbel with scroll.
Leg with inverted double C. Step toward S curve.
S
Inspired
s. Neo-
Derived from the Roman scissor chair, with bronze finish.
Another derivation from Pompeyan legs, in mahogany and bronze.
Tuscan column on Empire leg with bronze parts.
FRANCE
AND MARY
QUEEN ANNE
Inverted C-shaped parts. Charles I and James II.
Early cabriolet legs ending in scrolls. End of 17th century.
Ca
pered
Sheraton interpretation of Empire; "Trafalgar" style.
Leg with double curvature derived from Empire.
ENGLAND
B A R O Q U E
Leg with turned and Solomonic parts.
Portuguese turned legs with disks and narrow throats.
Similar example with very fine profile.
arved
ronze
Empire leg, gently curving with sphinx.
ITALY, GERMANY & PORTUGAL
Churrigueresque interpretation of early Louis XIV elements.
Lyre leg; flat with highly varied silhouettes.
Lyre leg with Baroque ornamentation.
Le
do
with
veen
Scissor legs shaped like horns of plenty.
Isabelline shape, degeneration of Empire.
Duck neck silhouette, typical of Isabelline.
SPAIN
90
1.700
10
20
10
20
30
1.840

A

Abacus A slab forming the uppermost member or division of the capital of a column, supporting the ARCHITRAVE.

Acanthus A prickly, curly leaf stylized and used in the capital of the Corinthian column by the Greeks and Romans. It was also adapted to the Gothic, Renaissance, Baroque, and Empire styles.

Acanthus

Acofr Arabic brass or latten work (from the Arab word for an alloy of copper and zinc).

Acroterion Ornament on the pediment or facade of a Greek temple.

Acroterion

Almocarbec Ornamental interlacing pattern used by the Arabs.

Angareeb Egyptian bed or day-bed. The former had large pillows or bolsters. The latter was a sort of chaise-longue so high that one had to stand on a stool to get into it. It had special back-boards to hold the cushions and rugs.

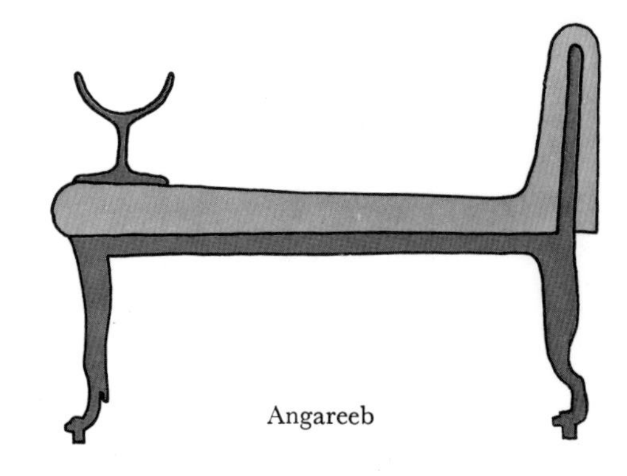

Angareeb

Antefix Ornament at the eaves of a classical building, usually in the form of anthemia.

Anthemion Ornamentation in the form of honeysuckle, palm, or acanthus leaves in a flat, radial pattern.

Apron piece See SKIRTING PIECE.

Arabesque Ornamental designs found on Arab buildings. The frieze, borders, and socle were covered with geometric patterns or interlacing plant motifs. Renaissance arabesques were inspired in nature and display great richness of detail and originality. Raphael's loggians in the Vatican are a good example.

Arabesque

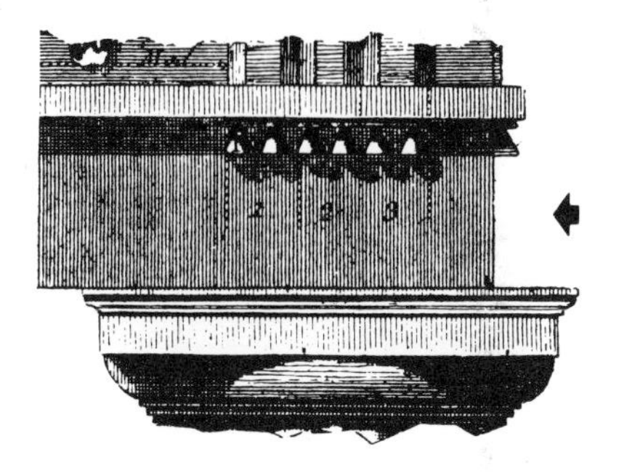

Architrave

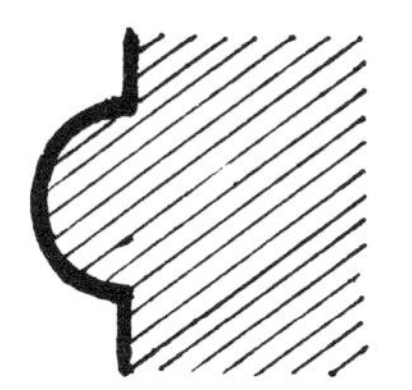
Astragal

Atlante

Arcade The use of a series of arches as a decorative feature.

Arch Curved structure resting on two supports and bridging the space between them. The main types of arches are: round or semicircular, pointed or lancet, segmental, ogee and elliptical, Tudor, horse-shoe, cusped or multifoil, and stilted.

Architrave In architecture, the lowest of the three parts of the classical entablature resting on the capitals. Also, the molding or frame around a door or window.

Archivolt The inside (or underside) of an arch from impost to impost.

Ark Old name for a large chest or coffer, especially one fitted with a special lock or spring, made by an "arkwright".

Assembly The putting together of the various parts of a piece of furniture once they have been made. See JOINT.

Astragal Originally, the half-round convex molding used as a necking (q.v.) ornament on classical columns. Now applied to a similar molding on the edge of a door or to the glazing bars on the door of a cabinet or bookcase.

Atlante A male figure used as a support instead of a column or bracket.

Aubusson A region in central France famous for the manufacture of tapestry and furniture upholstery. The factory was declared a "Fabrique Royale" in 1665.

B

Bahut French name for a chest or coffer.

Baluster Vertical element like a column, usually turned, in a great variety of shapes and forms. It may be quadrangular or polygonal in section, but is similar in profile to a turned baluster (see THURMING).

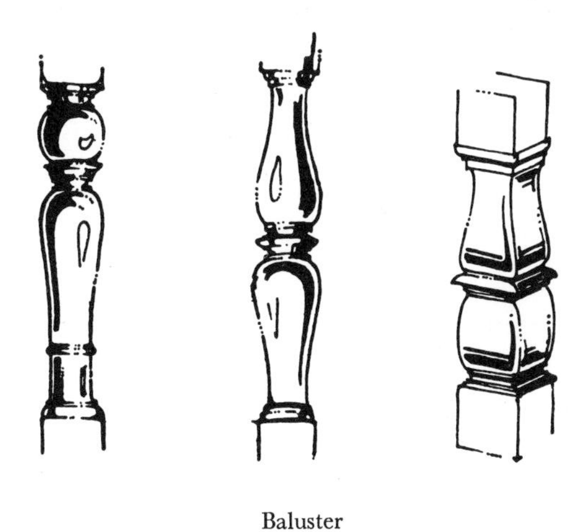
Baluster

Base The part of a column on which the shaft rests. The solid bottom part of a bookcase or cupboard, generally wider than the framework, on which it stands if it has no legs or feet.

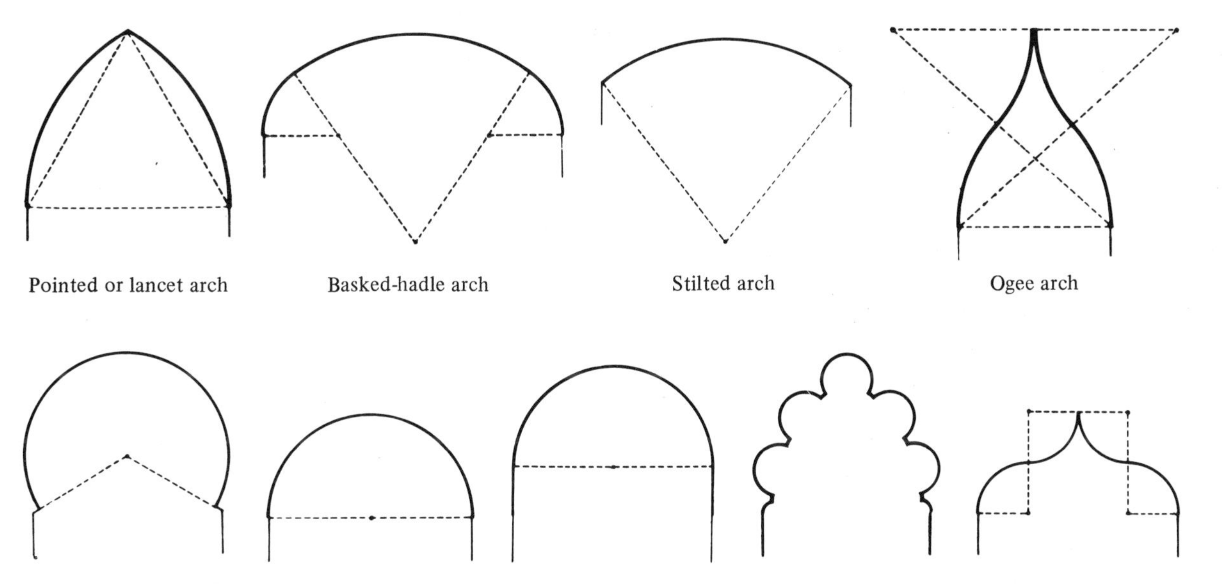
Pointed or lancet arch — Basked-hadle arch — Stilted arch — Ogee arch

Horse-shoe arch — Round semicirculos arch — Surmounted arch — Multifor or cusped arch — Tudor arch

Baseboard The skirting board around the lowest part of the walls of a room.

Battening Strips of wood fastened to the back of a board or boards to strengthen them or prevent them from warping.

Bead-flush Panel with bead set into the edges of a frame so that the faces of the panel, beading, and frame are flush.

Beading Convex cylindrical molding, from a quarter to three quarters of a circle but usually semicircular or "half-round" (see ASTRAGAL). When raised above the adjacent surface it is called COCK-BEAD, when sunk below the surface and separated by a QUIRK it is called a QUIRK-BEAD, and when placed on an edge or corner, a STAFF-BEAD. It is sometimes discontinuous, alternating with some other molding (e.g. BEAD-AND-REEL q.v.). When less than semicircular it is called QUARTER-ROUND or OVOLO.

Bergere An armchair with upholstered arms joined to a concave back and with a loose flat cushion on the seat. Popular in France in the 18th century.

Bevel To cut away a corner or arris at an oblique angle (usually 45°). The edge or surface thus cut away. Also a joiner's tool for making angles.

Bird's mouth Angle or notch cut in a piece of wood to receive the end of another piece.

Bisellium Roman chair of honor for two persons.

Block foot A foot shaped like a cube or rectangular block fastened to the end of a carved leg so that its ornamental molding will not wear off by rubbing on the floor. Other forms serving the same purpose are the BALL FOOT (spherical), BALL AND TALON, and SPADE FOOT (q.v.).

Boiseries French name for wood facing on the interior walls of a room (see WAINSCOT).

Bombe Term applied to French furniture (especially commodes) with a front bulging out in the middle. Also applied to English furniture with the same shape.

Bonheur-du-jour A small lady's writing table of the Louis XV and Louis XVI periods.

Bracket Support for an arch, statue, or shelf projecting out from or fastened to a wall or other vertical surface. A small platform or shelf resting on a vertical element (usually a single piece but sometimes separate and movable) extending upward and outward from the wall or other surface.

Bracket foot A low rectangular support projecting out from the corner of a chest of drawers, bureau, cabinet, or other piece of furniture facing both ways from the corner like a double bracket.

Bridle joint A joint composed of a "bridle" (like the top or bottom half of the letter H) formed by cutting a rectangular groove in the middle of the end of a board one third of its thickness in width to receive a corresponding tongue or tenon left projecting out from the end of another board by cutting away the outer two thirds. If the tongue is inserted sideways into the bridle it forms a "corner bridle". If the second board is joined across the end of the first, a "waist" is cut in the middle of it instead of a tongue. It fits into the bridle in the same way, the two boards thus forming a T. This is called a "T-bridle".

Brocade Interwoven fabric with a raised pattern of gold and silver.

Brocatelle A stiff decorating fabric with patterns in high relief.

Broché Brocaded damask or velvet.

Bulb A turned element roughly in the shape of a melon, typical of Elizabethan and Jacobean furniture.

Bulb

Bulrush *Typha latifolia*. A kind of rush popularly known as cattail. Leaves are used for making chair seats, etc.

Burlap Coarse, heavy fabric used for webbing (q.v.) under the upholstered seat of a chair or sofa.

Butt The flat end of a piece of wood meeting another. To meet another surface abruptly as in the case of a molding.

Butt joint The joining of two pieces of wood end-to-end at right angles to their length.

C

Cabling A molding or decoration resembling a twisted cable or two ropes intertwined.

Cabriolet leg A furniture leg characteristic of the 18th century. It is of oriental origin and came to Europe at the beginning of the century, passing from the Netherlands to England. It is shaped like an elongated S ending in a disc, block foot, scroll, or claw-and-ball.

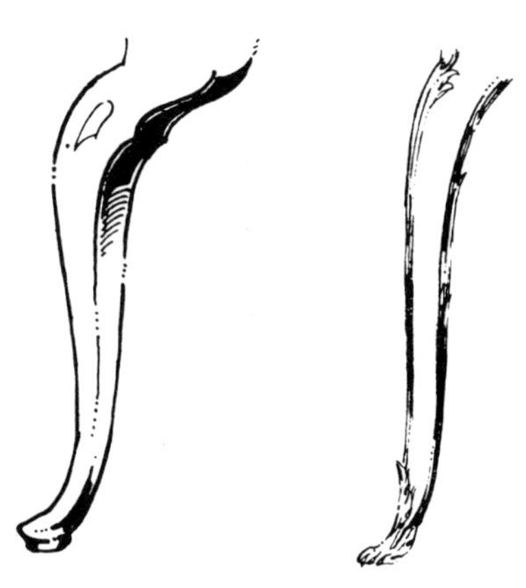

Cabriolet leg

Caduceus Molding, ornament, or emblem shaped like a rod with one or two serpents entwined around it. It was originally the emblem of Mercury, now symbolizes commerce. It is sometimes incorrectly called Aaron's Rod, which is rod with budding leaves or flowers.

Caisson Sunken panel in a coffered ceiling (see COFFERING).

Canapé Seat or sofa with a back large enough to accommodate two or three persons. French term for CHAIR-BACK SETTEE (q.v.).

Canapé-à-confidents Canapé with ends curving slightly inwards in an inviting fashion.

Canterano Catalan name for a combined chest of drawers and bureau with sloping top.

Capital The headpiece of a column often with ornamentation or molding characteristic of the order to which it belongs.

Capital

Caqueteuse Typical chair of the French Renaissance commonly found in the Lyonais. It had a high, narrow back and a broad fronted seat well suited to gossip, whence its English name "conversation chair".

Carcass The skeleton or framework of a box-like piece of furniture.

Cartibulum Marble table used by the Romans, with two legs or feet shaped like mythical animals called trapezophora. Examples found in the house of Cornelius Rufus in Pompei are particularly well known.

Cartouche Carved scroll or rolled up parchment bearing an inscription or used simply as a decorative motif.

Caryatid Female figure used as a support instead of a column. Those in the temple of Erechtheus in Athens are especially famous.

Cassapanca Italian name for a wooden bench with back and arms, origin of the 18th century sofa.

Cassone Italian pre-Renaissance, Renaissance, or Baroque chest or coffer. There are fine examples painted by such great Quattrocento and Cinquecento artists as Fra Angelico, Lippi, Benozzo, Gozzoli, Paolo, Ucello, Signorelli, Dello, etc.

Cavetto Quarter-round concave molding.

Certosina A style of marquetry named after the Charterhouse of Pavia, where many examples of this type of work were made.

Chair-back settee A settee with a continuous seat and back made up of two or three parts like chair backs joined together.

Chamfer To bevel symmetrically. To cut two pieces of arris or molding at 45° to form a right angle between them. Also, the resulting angle.

Chapeau French word used to describe the tops or finials of beds or chairs typical of the Louis XVI style. They were straight in the middle, gently curving along the sides, and joined to the legs by two quarter circles forming a broken line.

Chapeau

Cheval glass See PSYCHE.

Chevron Ornamental motif on a molding in the shape of a raised zig-zig typical of the Romantic period.

Chiffonier A high, narrow chest of drawers typical of the late 18th and 19th centuries.

Chisel To carve, cut, or shape wood, stone, or metal with a steel-edged tool. A tool used for chiseling. Some are used only for smoothing or finishing.

Churrigueresque A common name for the Spanish 18th century Baroque style, from the architects of the Churriguera family of Salamanca.

Clamp Instrument consisting of two pieces of metal connected with a screw and fastened to a carpenter's bench to hold a piece of wood while it is being worked on.

Claw-and-ball foot Foot of English origin found in 18th century furniture. It is shaped like the claw of a lion, eagle, etc. clutching a ball. In some cases, such as certain Spanish cabinets and writing desks of the late 18th century, the body of the piece of furniture rests directly upon the claw-and-ball foot.

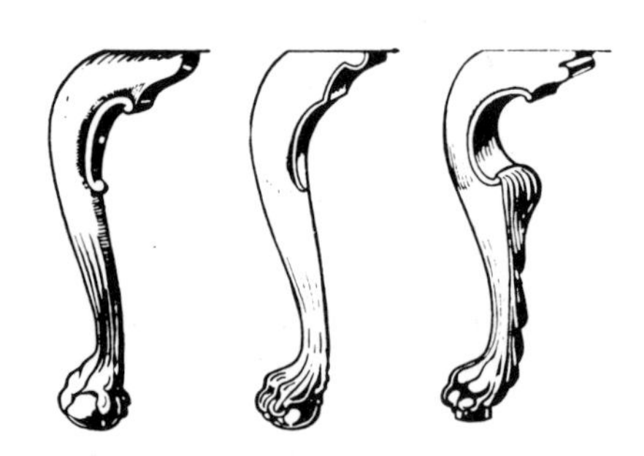

Claw-and-ball foot

Club foot A foot roughly resembling the head of a golf club usually with a disk about half an inch thick underneath, often found on the end of cabriolet legs (q.v.).

Cock-bead A molding of rounded beads projecting from an edge (see BEADING).

Coffer A large chest, especially for keeping valuables. Also one of the sunken panels in a coffered ceiling.

Coffering Ceiling made of sunken panels, usually square though sometimes polygonal, carved or molded between the joists. The centers of the panels are often decorated with floral or other designs. The panels are also called CAISSONS especially in similar vaulted roofs or stone ceilings. In Spain there are many fine examples of this kind of work called "artesonado".

Column Vertical support, usually cylindrical, consisting of capital, shaft, and base. It is usually characteristic of the style of the building or piece of furniture in which it is used, especially in the case of the classical orders, Tuscan, Doric, Ionic, Corinthian, Composite, and Attic. Other descriptions of columns are: engaged (partly or apparently embedded in a wall) and free-standing, fluted and wreathed (see FLUTING, WREATHED).

Comb-back chair Refering to certain types of chairs with a high back and top shaped something like the combs once used by women to keep their hair in place. It was used in Europe in the Neo-classical period and had its origin in the Greek klismos.

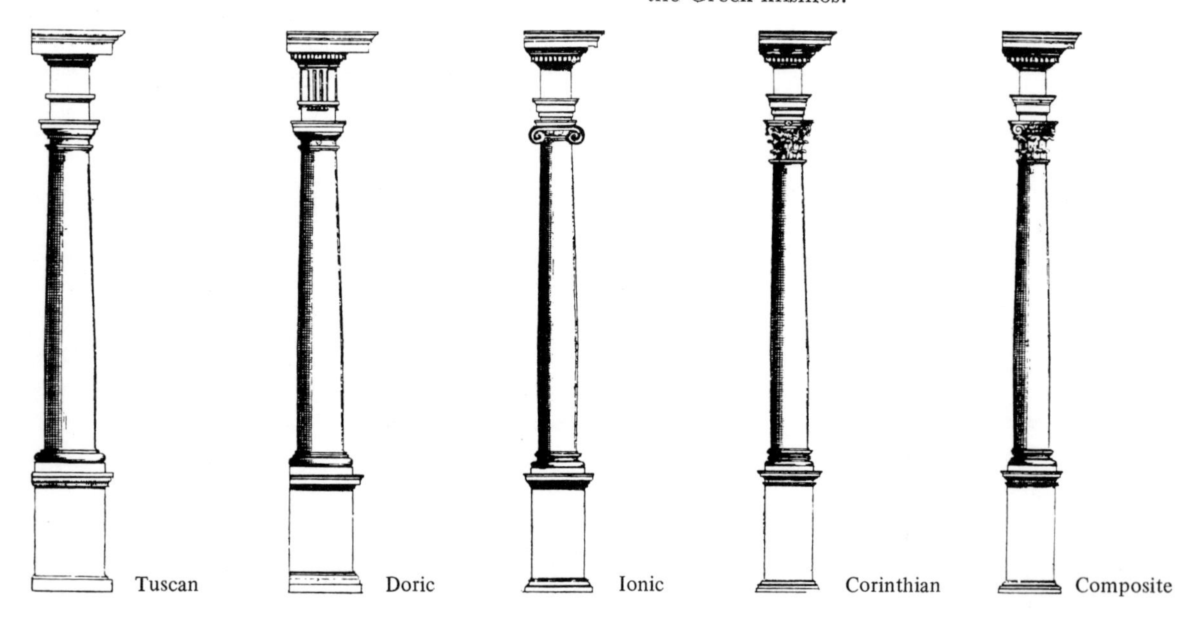

Commode The more ornate predecessor, especially of French design, of the modern chest-of-drawers.

Compo Abbreviation for "composition", a mixture of whitening, resin, and glue molded and applied to furniture instead of carving. The 18th century architect and decorator Robert Adam used this type of stucco, similar to "carton-pierre" and he alone knew its secret "composition". It was used for fine Neo-classical ornamentation consisting of palmettes, paterae, foliage, etc. and was easily applied to the molded or plain surfaces of furniture mirrors, mantelpieces, etc.

Confidente An upholstered settee with seats outside the arms at either end.

Console An ornamental bracket, usually scroll shaped.

Console table A table shaped like a bracket, the back of which is fastened to a wall. The front is supported by one or two scroll-shaped or figure-shaped legs.

Coque A bow or loop of ribbon used especialy as a decorative motif on a Jacobean friese or other molding.

Corbel A projection of stone or timber jutting out from a wall to support a weight.

Cornucopia Horn of Plenty. An ornament shaped like a vase or horn with an abundance of fruit and corn pouring out of it. It is so typical of the Spanish Baroque style that it was even used as a synonym for Churrigueresque (q.v.). It is also used to refer to a small mirror with a gilt frame profusely carved and decorated with scrolls, horns, and floral designs. Sofas with backs and scroll-work resembling cornucopias were made in the early 19th century.

Cornucopia

Cordovan Tanned goatskin or oxhide worked into various ornamental or polychrome patterns. It was made chiefly in Cordova, whence the name, and also in a town in North Africa from which the alternative name GUADAMECI or GUADAMECIL (q.v.) is derived. It was developed by the Arabs who had an important factory at this site. It was used for upholstering furniture such as the so-called "friar's stools" and Portuguese chairs of the late 17th century, and also for lining coffers and chests and even walls and floors.

Core The basic material over which more delicate exterior material is laid and which gives it greater strength or "body". In plywood and veneer the core is usually of coarser wood such as pine, covered with a thin layer of finer wood.

Corner block or **brace** A triangular piece of wood or other material fitted into the corner of a seat frame to reinforce it.

Cornice A horizontal molding at the top of a building or piece of furniture, particularly the uppermost member of the entablature around a top of the walls of a room.

Coromandel A kind of wood from the Coromandel coast much used in cabinet-making, also called "Bombay ebony". A kind of lacquer from the interior of China shipped to Europe from Coromandel. Designs were carved on a colored background and filled with black lacquer. This technique reached its apogee in the 18th century.

Countersink To widen the top part of a hole made in a piece of wood so that the head of a screw fits into the depression and does not project above the surface. To set a screw in this way.

Cradle, cradling A supporting framework used to reinforce a piece of work under construction or while it is being shaped. It looks something like a child's cradle. The bottom part of a mold used for making the curved front of a "bombé" out of ordinary wood which would later be covered with thin strips of finer wood or veneer, all having the same form or curvature as the inside of the cradle (see MOLD).

Cramping When two pieces of wood are glued together, it is frequently necessary to hold them together with screws or by "cramping" them with a clamp, press, or similar apparatus.

Cresting A carved ornament on top of the back of a chair or any other piece of furniture. Crestings in the shape of a crown with cherubs or other elaborate motifs were common in Restoration chairs.
Crimping A wavy appearance given to material by folding or GOFFERING (q.v.).
Crocket An ornament deriving from Gothic architecture shaped like a curled leaf or something similar. It extended from the sloping edge of a pinacle or gable to accentuate the slope of the roof.

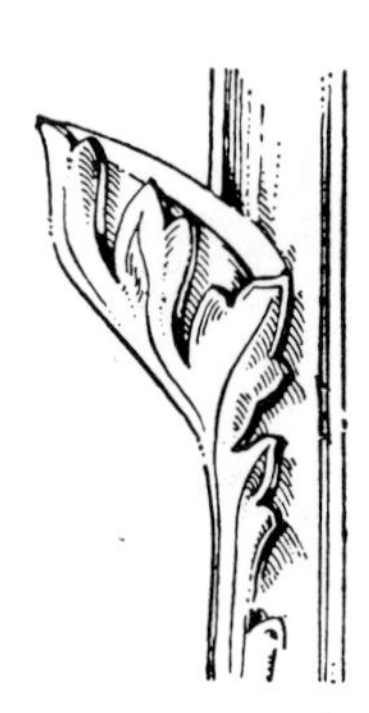
Crocket

Cross-banding Framing of a panel with strips of VENEER (q.v.) of contrasting grain and color.
Cross rail Horizontal bar connecting and strengthening the uprights of a chair back.

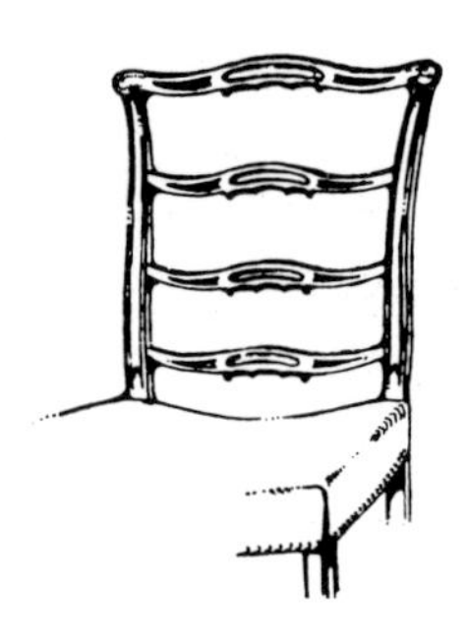
Cross rail

C-scroll Ornamental motif in the shape of a C, typical of Regency and Louis XV styles in France, used also in England.
Cuarterones Spanish word for the PANELS of a door, especially the Moorish paneled doors of the 16th, 17th, and 18th centuries. The Arabs avoided large, plain surfaces which they subdivided into smaller structural or decorative units with polygonal or geomentric patterns.
Cul-de-lampe See DROP ORNAMENT.
Curb A wooden or metal strip around the edge of a circular structure such as the APRON or SKIRTING PIECE or a round table top.
Curule chair Roman chair, usually X-shaped, with rings on the sides that bars could be passed through so it could be carried by slaves.
Cusp Projecting point between the small arches in Gothic tracery or in a MULTIFOIL, or CUSPED, ARCH.
Cyma A molding in the shape of an S (CYMA RECTA), concave above and convex below, or the reverse (CYMA REVERSA), i.e. convex above and concave below (see OGEE).

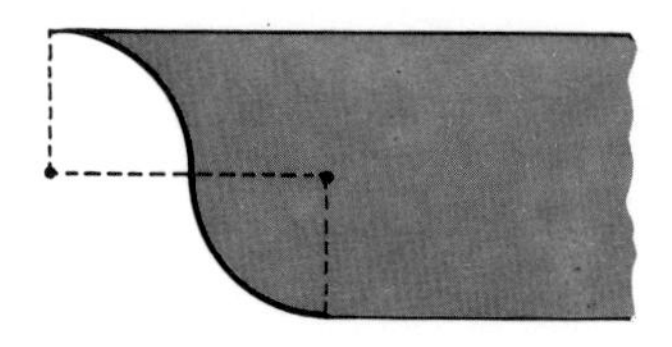
Cyma

Cymatium The top of a CORNICE (q.v.) usually in the shape of a CYMA RECTA or REVERSA.

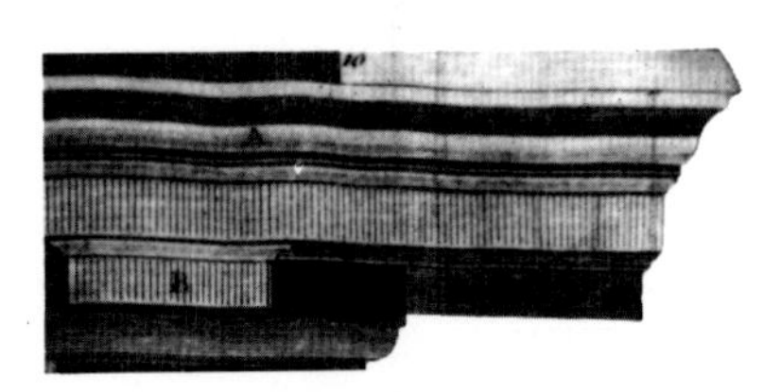
Cymatium

D

Dado Lower few feet of the wall of a room when covered with wood or otherwise ornamented differently from the rest of the room.

Also, the lower part of pedestal without decoration. If the pedestal is an independent unit (e.g. the pedestal of a statue) it usually has a cornice and a base. See PEDESTAL.
Damascene, damaskeen Metal ornamentation with inlaid gold and silver used in the East, in the Italian Renaissance, and in Spain.

Damask Figured woven material, usually silk. Table linen with woven designs reflecting light differently according to the angle at which it is seen. Damascus steel (or imitation) with a wavy pattern produced by a special welding of iron and steel together.

Décapée French term for the chemical treatment of wood, especially mahogany and lignite, giving it a much lighter color, sometimes almost white, e.g. "white mahogany".

Deflection Deformation of wood or other material due to overloading or strain usually appearing as a bulge. See also SAG and WINDING.

Denticulated Decorated with dentils like a frieze of the Ionic order.

Denticulated

Dentil A small tooth-like projection shaped like an oblong block alternating with spaces of the same shape in a denticulated frieze.

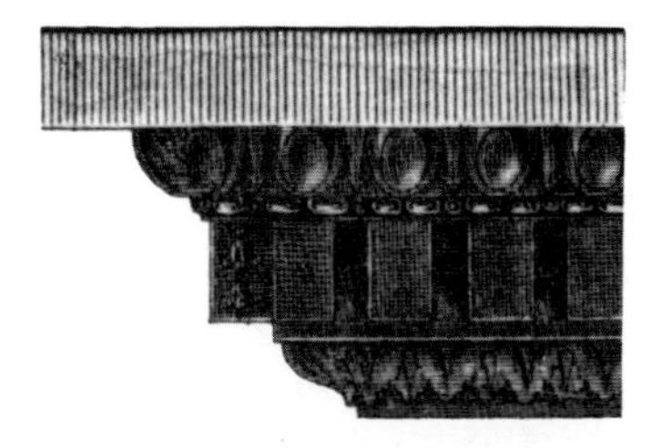

Dentil

Diapering Decorative diamond pattern for walls or panels or fabric with the same pattern. Also a style of decorating or carving with small flowers, leaves, arabesques, or geometric patterns in repetition. In this sense GUILLOCHE (q.v.) may be considered a special form of diapering.

Diapering

Double chest One chest of drawers on top of another making a single piece of furniture. See TALL-BOY.

Die Another word for DADO (q.v.) in its second sense.

Diophros Ancient Greek chair or stool more or less rectilinear. The folding X-shaped type (usually with talon feet) was known as OKLADIAS (camp-stool).

Dovetail A tongue of wood shaped like a trapezoid with the wider part projecting out (like the tail of a dove) to fit into a cut in another piece of wood. This type of joint is widely used for important parts of box-like structures because of its resistance to forces tending to pull pieces apart. To join with this type of joint.

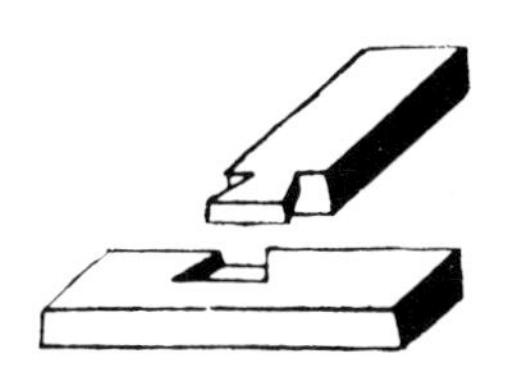

Dovetail

Dowel, dowel pin A cylindrical or slightly conical piece of wood or metal fitting into a hole, used instead of an ordinary nail. To fasten with a dowel.

Draught chair A chair with a high back and lateral pieces called wings. It was first made of wood but later upholstered, including the "wings" and arms. A well-known Spanish example is "Father Sotomayor's confessional" in Churrigueresque style. The French Louis XV type is also well known.

Drop ornament An ornament hanging from the under-frame of a piece of furniture.

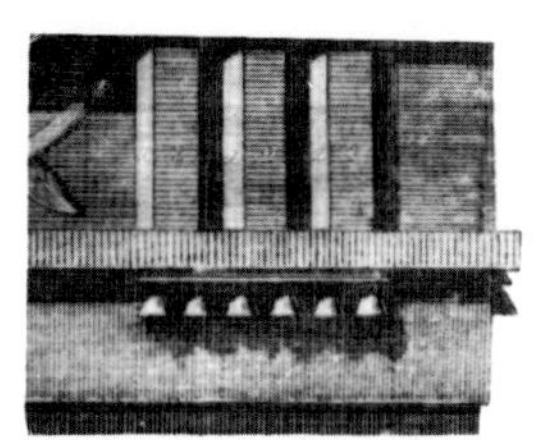

Drop ornament

Duchesse A French term describing a combination of Bergère and chaise-longue, i.e. a sofa or settee with a concave gondola back at one end. Sheraton and Hepplewhite used the term for a double "Péché mortel", two bergère chairs with a stool between them. It is now usually used to refer to a dressing table with a pivoting glass or to a type of satin.

E

Echinus The convex, quarter-elliptical or OVOLO (q.v.) molding around the capital of a Doric column. Often used in English synonymously with, or including, EGG-AND-DART (q.v.).

Ecusson Cartouche (q.v.) with a heraldic device or inscription.

Ecusson

Egg-and-dart molding From the 16th century on, an embellishment of the ECHINUS or OVOLO molding on a classical capital or piece of furniture consisting of half or quarter-eggs alternating with a narrower shape like a small dart or javelin with the head pointing up. Also called Egg-and-Anchor or Egg-and-Tongue according to the shape of the narrower part.

Emboss To carve or mold in relief, to make figures or designs stand out from a surface. When this is done by hammering from the back side it is known as REPOUSSE (q.v.).

Encoignure French name for a small piece of furniture made to fit in a corner.

Encorado Spanish name for a chest or coffer lined with leather. There are notable examples of GUADAMECIL (q.v.) work on old Spanish chests.

Enrichment Ornamental designs and carvings on a piece of furniture for purpose of decoration, applied to enhance the aesthetic effect of the whole rather than for any functional purpose.

Ensayalado Spanish name for a chest or coffer lined or covered with fabrics like velvet, damask, etc. and trimmed with braid or galloon. There are excellent Castilian and Majorcan examples in Renaissance and Baroque styles.

Entablature Horizontal structure on top of a building (or furniture imitating a building) resting on the columns and including cornice, frieze, and architrave.

Entablement A platform above the DADO (q.v.) for supporting a statue.

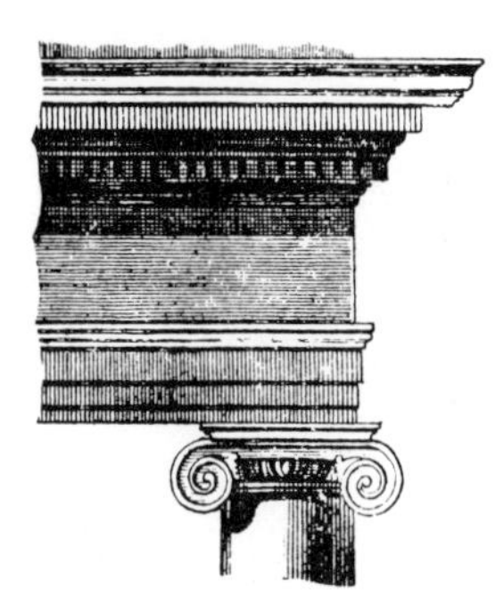

Entablement

Entasis Slight convexity of a column shaft to correct the visual appearance of concavity produced by perfectly straight columns.

Escutcheon A heraldic shield bearing a coat of arms. Also the metal plate around a keyhole.

Espagnolette The long bolt fitted to a French door or window operated by turning a handle in the middle.

Also a bronze figure, usually a female bust, used for a cresting ornament on Regency and Louis XV furniture.

Escutcheon

Espagnolette

Estofado A technique used in Spanish Gothic, Renaissance, and Baroque decoration consisting of covering burnished gold and several coats of paint which is scraped to uncover the background of gold in various designs or patterns. It has extraardinary richness and variety.

Etagère French name for a shelf or piece of furniture like a WHATNOT (q.v.).

F

Faldstool An X-shaped chair of honor generally used by bishops and dignitaries. (From the Latinized form "faldistolium" of the Old High German "faldstuol", meaning a folding chair or stool).

Farthingale chair An armless chair with a broad seat to accomodate a farthingale, i.e. an Elizabethan or Jacobean hooped petticoat. (From the French "verdugale" meaning "rodded" or hooped, derived from the old Spanish word "verdugado".)

Fauteuil French word for an armchair, especially of French design, usually with open arms and upholstered seat and back and of comfortable proportions.

Feather A tongue made in the end of a board to fit into a groove in another board forming a flush joint. To joint with a feather.

Feather-edging Two bands of veneer or marquetry with their grains laid at an angle to suggest a feather pattern. Also called HERRING BONE.

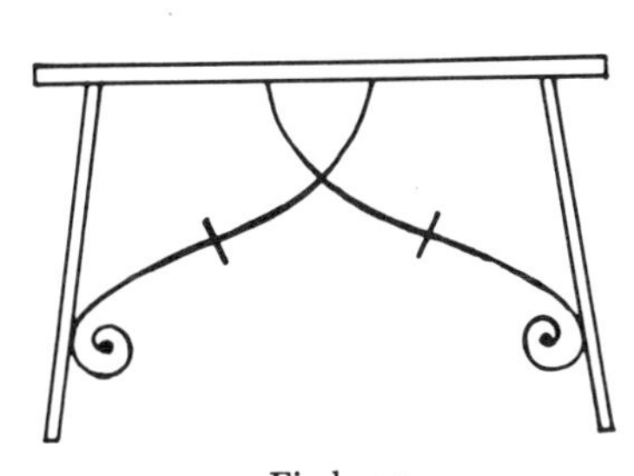

Fiadores

Fiadores S-shaped STRETCHERS made of iron with scrolled ends that replaced simpler forms in 17th and 18th century Spanish "lyre" tables. They connected to the legs in pairs and crossed in the middle. There were single, double, and "hairpin" fiadores, the latter belonging to early Baroque. See also SALTIRE.

Figure Designs found in woods used for veneering and plywood obtained by cutting across irregular fibers like knots and roots. Roots provided the most interesting and original figures.

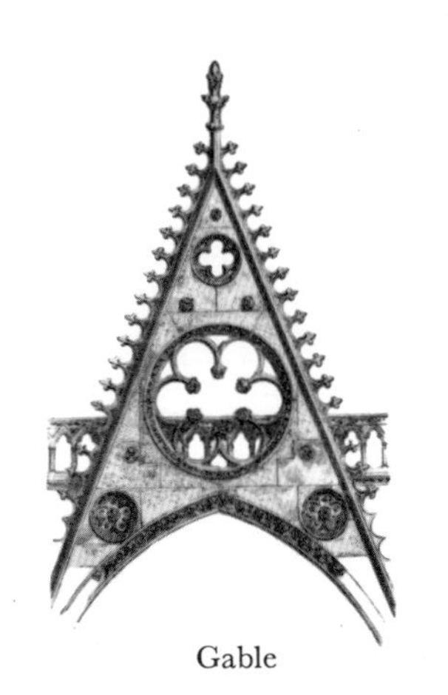

Gable

Fillet A thin, narrow strip of any material. Fillets of zinc or pasteboard are sometimes used for cramping up pieces of wood glued together. Thev are heated to keep the glue from cooling. Small pieces of wood are sometimes rabbeted to hold a fillet in making end joints (FILLET JOINT). Also a narrow, rectangular, flat molding sometimes between other moldings, or a ridge between FLUTES (q.v.).

Filling, filling batten A small, narrow piece of wood inserted in gaps or interstices in carpentry and cabinet work, also called "fill" or "filling batten".

Part of a finishing process for furniture made of oak or other deep-grained woods to fill the pores. See WHITE POLISHING.

Finial An ornament at the top of an arch or gable, in architecture often floral or foliated. In furniture it includes bulbs, knobs, animals, acorns, etc. carved on the ends or tops of various parts such as bed posts, chair backs, and cornices of cabinets.

Flute, fluting A vertical groove on a column shaft for decoration.

Foil Arc between CUSPS (q.v.) in a trefoil, quatrefoil, cinquefoil, or MULTIFOIL arch (q.v.) found especially in Moorish architecture and Gothic tracery.

Footstool In Elizabethan and Jacobean times footstools were normal accessories to chairs (which were something of a luxury in themselves) but were later regarded as an unnecessary refinement.

Fret saw A small narrow saw stretched on a frame for delicate work with thin wood, or FRETWORK.

Fretwork Ornamental work of small pierced designs done with a FRET SAW and used as an openwork decorative motif or laid over a solid background.

Frieze An ornamented part of the entablature between the ARCHITRAVE and the CORNICE (q.v.) in classical buildings. A similar part of a piece of furniture or a band around the top of the walls of a room.

G

Gable The triangular part of a wall under a double sloping roof. In Gothic buildings the eaves or gable ends were often adorned with finials or CROCKETS (q.v.). There is a similarity between a gable and the PEDIMENT (q.v.) of a classical building.

Gadroon Decoration found on silverware and plates as well as furniture. It is either concave or convex (LOBING) and consists of almond-shaped projections or elongated oval elements or shapes like orange sections.

Gain A groove along the edge of a piece of wood in which the edge of another is inserted.

Gain

Galloon Tightly woven braid of gold, silver, silk, etc. used as an edging on upholstered furniture. Threads are sometimes left loose along one edge to form a fringe.

Gauge An instrument used by carpenters and cabinet-makers for drawing parallel lines. It has a small board with an arm ending in a steel point. The board is run along the edge which is to be reproduced and the point at the end of the arm, which can be adjusted, marks a line parallel to the edge.

Goffering To crimp or flute material with a heated goffer, also called a crimping or pleating iron (see CRIMPING).

Gondola chair Chair with a hollow semi-circular back joined to the arms, so called because of its resemblance to boats used on Venetian canals.

Gouge Round chisel used for carving out grooves in wood.

Grandfather chair A winged, upholstered chair developed in the Queen Anne period from the oak winged chair of earlier date.

Greek fret Repeated lines or bars drawn at right angles to form an oriental MEANDER (q.v.) along a border or frieze.

Greek fret

Groove-and-tongue joint If this kind of joint is not glued or covered, the TONGUE (q.v.) can be taken out of the groove in the second board. The two boards can thus be taken apart and put back together quite easily.

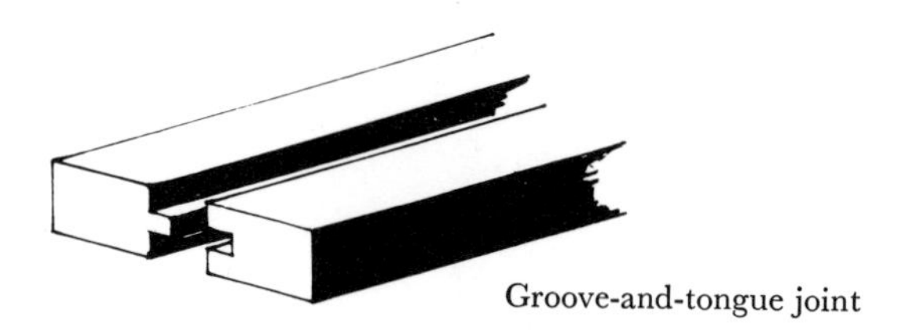

Groove-and-tongue joint

Grotesque Decoration composed of fantastic animals, CARYATIDS (q.v.), vases, interwoven with foliage and leaf scrolls inspired from Roman mural decoration, particularly those found in the grottos of Titus's palace from which Raphael's paintings in the loggias of the Vatican were inspired.

Guadameci; guadamecil; guadamacilla Decorative leather work named after the town of Gadames in North Africa where it was first developed. See CORDOVAN.

Guardainfantes Spanish word for the frame-work of wires or hoops of a crinoline or FARTHINGALE (q.v.) or the skirt itself, and for the kind of chair with very short or no arms made to accomödate it. The word means "child guard", since this type of dress was suitable for expectant mothers, though the English and French words (FARTHINGALE and VERTUGADIN, q.v.) come from another Spanish word for the same thing.

Gueridon A small, round table or stand with a single foot in the middle modeled after the Roman MONOPODIUM. It was usually very ornate and sometimes used a figure support. It was used in the 17th and 18th centuries as "torchères" (for candelabra) or for vases, games, etc.

Gueridon

Grotesque

Guilloche

Guilloche Ornamental pattern of interlaced bands forming circular outlines and suggesting braided ribbons used by the Frenchman Guillot from whom it takes its name.

H

Half-round Semicircular convex molding. See BEADING.

Halving and lapping

Halving and lapping To join two boards by making a REBATE (q.v.) in each equal to half its thickness. The boards are fitted together so that the two halves overlap.

Handle Furniture handles were usually drop handles or knobs or a combination of both ("bail handle"). Wrought iron rings were used on doors and drawers in Jacobean furniture. Brass was first used under William and Mary. Metal back plates and later round and oval handles to match them were introduced at the time of Queen Anne. Handles shaped like rings hanging from a lion's mouth were used by Sheraton.

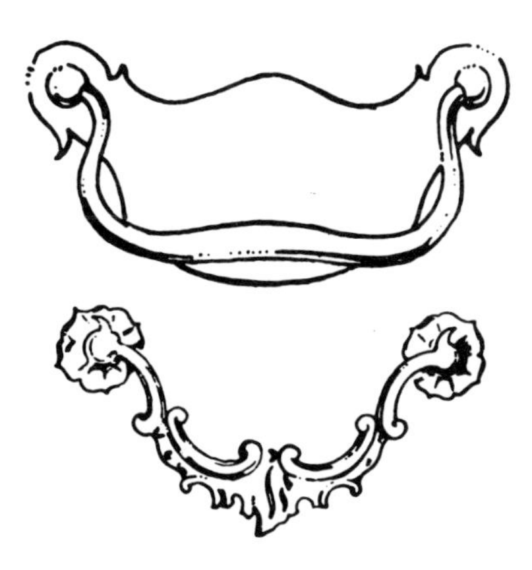
Handle

Haricot

Haricot French word for a C-SCROLL (q.v.) because of its resemblance to a kidney bean when the center is partly filled in.

Highlight Part of a picture or carved design made more prominent by contrast with adjacent shaded parts. To bring out a part in this way.

Hinge The hinge in its simples form is a very ancient device. Many varieties of 15th, 16th, and 17th century wrought iron surface hinges survive in various forms, from butterfly to "strap", "cock's head", and H hinges, all shaped more or less like what the name indicates. Other metals came into use after this period (see MOUNTS) and less attention was paid to shape. Generally speaking, the best hinges are those that are neither seen nor heard.

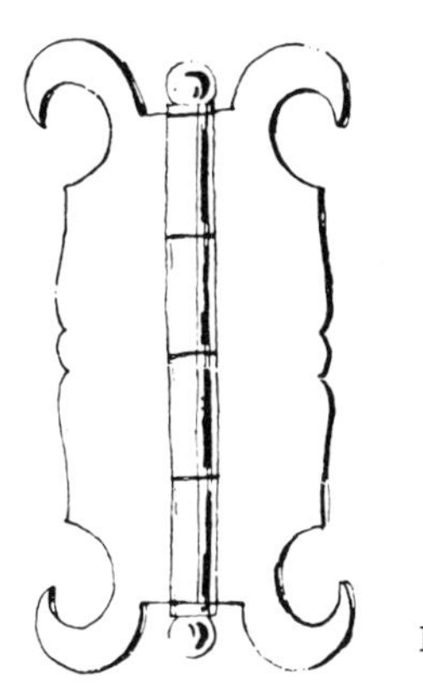
Hinge

H-stretcher Rungs connecting the front and back legs of a chair or table and a crosspiece connecting them, forming an H.

Huche French chest or coffer from the 13th century.

Huchier French word for arkwright (see ARK) dating from the 13th century.

I

Imbrication An often purely ornamental arrangement of leaves or scales one on top of another so that they overlap like the tiles of a slate roof.

Imbrication

Impost The upper course of pilars or the structure supporting an arch.

Inlay To insert pieces of wood or other materials in a background of a different material or color to obtain a decorative design or pattern. An important means of embellishing furniture. The inlaid material, or even the background, may be ivory or metal, though some restrict this term to light wood set in darker wood. In the wider sense there are many different forms of inlay including DAMASCENE, CERTOSINA, INTARSIA, MARQUETRY, TARACEA, TARSIA, and STRINGING.

Intarsia Italian form of MARQUETRY (q.v.) in which the inlaid design comprises a variety of pictorial or architectural motifs covering a large part of the background. Dutch and French marquetry is generally floral or pastoral. The works of 15th and 16th century Italian "intarsiatori" are particularly well known.

Interlacery Any design consisting of interlaced elements, best represented by the arabesques covering large parts of Moorish façades, borders, etc.

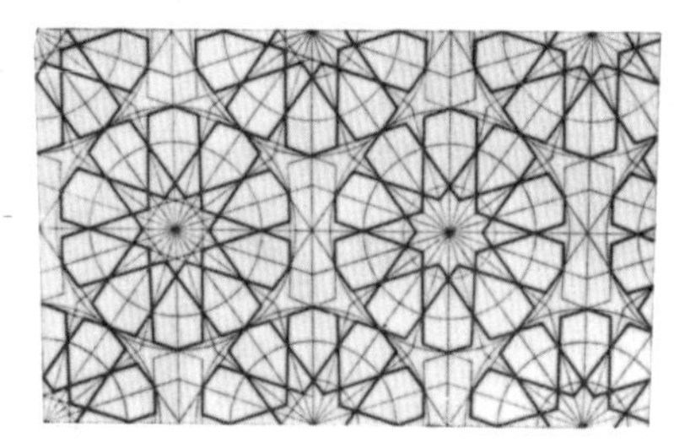

Interlacery

Intrados The lower or interior curve of an arch (see ARCHIVOLT), the upper curve being the EXTRADOS.

J

Jack plane A long plane with a handle for work not requiring fine planing.

Jalousie Blind or shutter with parallel slats sloping upward to partly exclude light and to prevent people from looking in, but allowing for ventilation.

Jamb The side post of a door or window or other similar opening.

Joint One of various ways of joining two pieces of wood together either end-to-end, side-to-side, or at an angle. Some of the various kinds of joints include BRIDLE, BUTT, DOVETAIL, HALVING AND LAPPING, MORTISE, MORTISE-AND-TENON, TONGUE-AND-GROOVE, MITER, and SCRIBED.

Jointer plane A plane used specially for joining or planing the edge or a board to be joined to another.

Jut A ledge or step projecting out from a piece of furniture.

K

Key border Kind of GREEK FRET (q.v.) resembling a twisted ribbon.

Keystone The central stone at the highest point of an arch holding the whole thing together.

L

Lacquer An Oriental varnish composed of sand, fine clay, plant fibers, and gums made of the sap of *Rhus vermicifera*. It is allowed to harden after being applied and then colored or polished. Lacquered cabinets were imported into England in the 17th century and lacquer is used extensively in the West today.

Lacunaria A COFFERED ceiling (q.v.) composed of LAMBRIS (q.v.) rather than structural divisions. The individual coffers or recesses.

Lag screw Screw for securing MOUNTS (q.v.) on furniture.

Lambrequin A PELMET (q.v.) serving as part of the drapery around or behind the head of an 18th-century bed, usually decorated with ACANTHUS leaves (q.v.). Any short piece of drapery hung over the top of a door or window or from a mantelpiece.

Lambrequin

Lambris Decorative covering of walls and ceilings of either painted or gilt wood or stucco.

Lap To overlay or project over; to lie overtop; the part of something thus lying over or on another part, as drawers or doors overlying the RAILS or STILES (q.v.). See also HALVING AND LAPPING

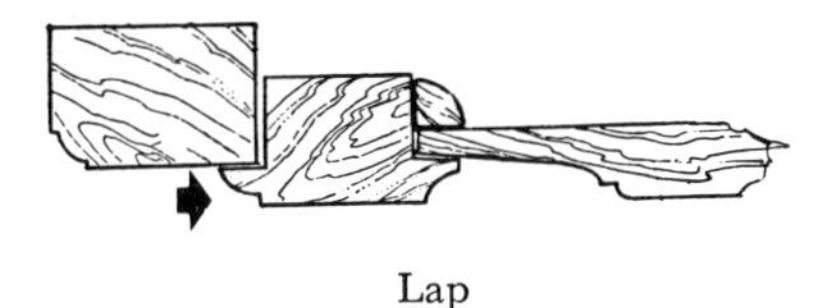

Lap

Lararium The characteristic piece of furniture of architectural form found in the "atrium" of a Roman house; a shrine dedicated to the household gods.

Lattice A structure of crossed laths with interstices serving as a screen, door, etc.

Lathe A machine used for turning and shaping wood or other materials by rotating it on a revolving shaft or disk and working it with a tool to give it the desired shape. See also ROUTER and TURNING.

Linenfold A Gothic type of carved decoration like a folded or pleated parchment with loose folds running vertically and overlapping. Used throughout Europe, mostly for paneling on doors, etc.

Lintel Horizontal timber or stone over a door or window, resting on the JAMBS (q.v.).

Lobing Convex type of GADROON (q.v.) used for edging.

Low-boy A dressing table with draws. When used to support a chest of drawers the whole arrangement is called a HIGH-BOY (q.v.). Both terms are used mostly in America.

Lozenge Diamond shape decoration used especially in Louis XVI MARQUETRY (q.v.) and in a smaller form in the Directory and Empire periods.

M

Magot Grotesque figure found on Chinese porcelain and used in French furniture and paneled surfaces.

Marquetry A form of INLAY (q.v.) consisting of a decorative design in different colored woods set in a dark VENEER (q.v.) and glued to the carcass which was usually of oak. Other forms of marquetry are described under CERTOSINA, INTARSIA, TARSIA, and TARACEA.

Marquetry

Match-board A board with a tongue along one side and a groove along the other to fit into other boards.

Matching To fit together two adjacent but reversed sections of figured veneer to form a "complete face" such as a diamond pattern or feather shapes seen on cupboard doors or large panels. There are other symmetrical patterns or complete faces formed by matching veneers.

Meander An oriental motif frequently used in all periods. The word comes from the River Meander in Asia Minor which has a very winding course. It denotes a winding pattern repeated indefinitely such as a GREEK FRET or KEY BORDER (q.v.).

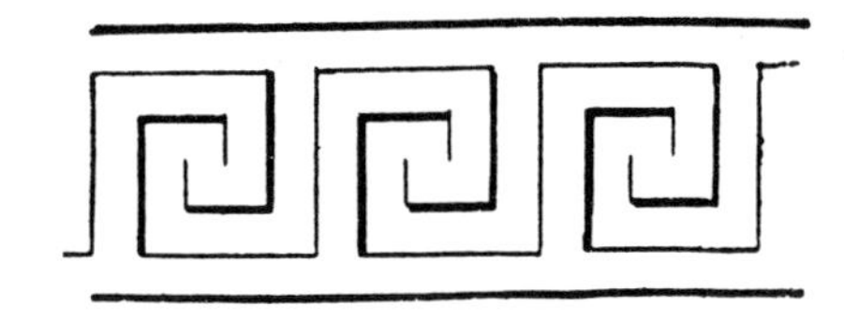

Meander

Medullary ray Markings radiating outward from the heart of a log forming a "SUNBURST" (q.v.). Oak rays are particularly visible. When it is QUARTER-CUT (q.v.) it produces a very striking effect sometimes called SPLASH or SILVERGRAIN, giving it a special value in cabinet-making.

Meridianne A type of sofa with curved arms of different heights in French Empire style.

Metope Rectangular and usually decorated space between the TRIGLYPHS (q.v.) of a FRIEZE, typical of the Doric order.

Milled Marked with very small vertical ridges like the edge of a coin.

Miter joint A corner joint made by cutting two pieces of wood at a 45° angle. It is common in picture or window frames. It was first introduced in Renaissance furniture.

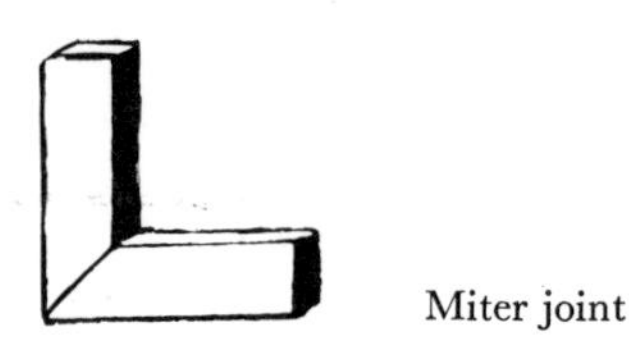

Miter joint

Modillion Projecting support in the form of a BRACKET or CORBEL (q.v.) under a CORNICE.

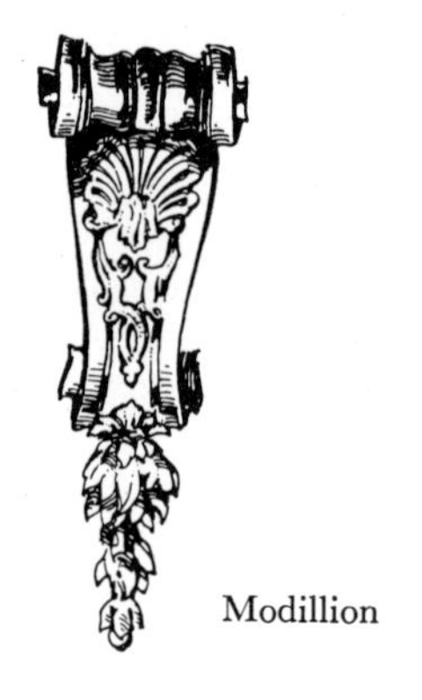

Modillion

Mold A pattern or TEMPLATE (q.v.) used for shaping. In some cases it may consist of two parts, the lower part being the CRADLE (q.v.) with the upper part fitting into it, such as a mold for shaping the curved piece of a "bombé" commode.

Monopodium One legged circular or polygonal Roman torch stand (see GUERIDON and TORCHERE).

Mortise A hole or cavity in a framework or piece of wood to receive the end of another part or a TENON (q.v.). To make such a hole or cut with a machine or mortise chisel.

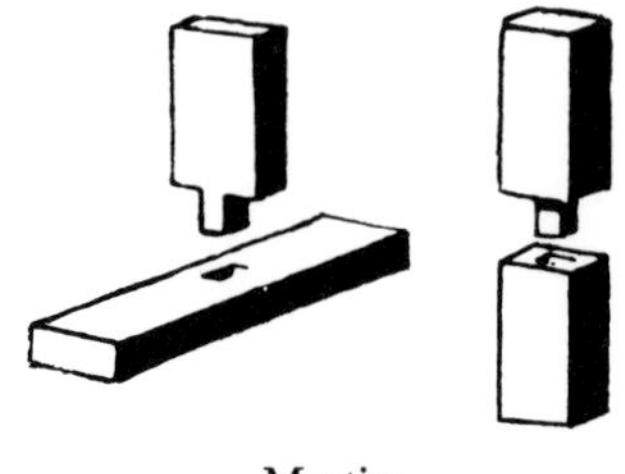

Mortise

Molding A projection either curved or rectangular running along the surface or edge of a building or piece of furniture. There is a variety of shapes depending on the style of the building or furniture and the imagination of the architect or designer.

Various classical and current moldings include:
Concave: CAVETTO (quarter-round), FLUTE (vertical), SCOTIA.
Convex: BEAD, ECHINUS, LOBING, OVOLO, TORUS, ASTRAGAL, REED.
Others: CYMA, EGG-AND-DART, FILLET (plain), GADROON, NULLING, OGEE.

There are various other combinations such as bead-and-reel (a disk viewed from its edge, sometimes double, alternating with a bead) which are more difficult to classify.

Mounts Metal fittings on a piece of furniture both functional and decorative, including handles, keyholes, ESCUTCHEONS (q.v.), etc. Some are merely ornamental reminders of pieces originally used to reinforce the frame.

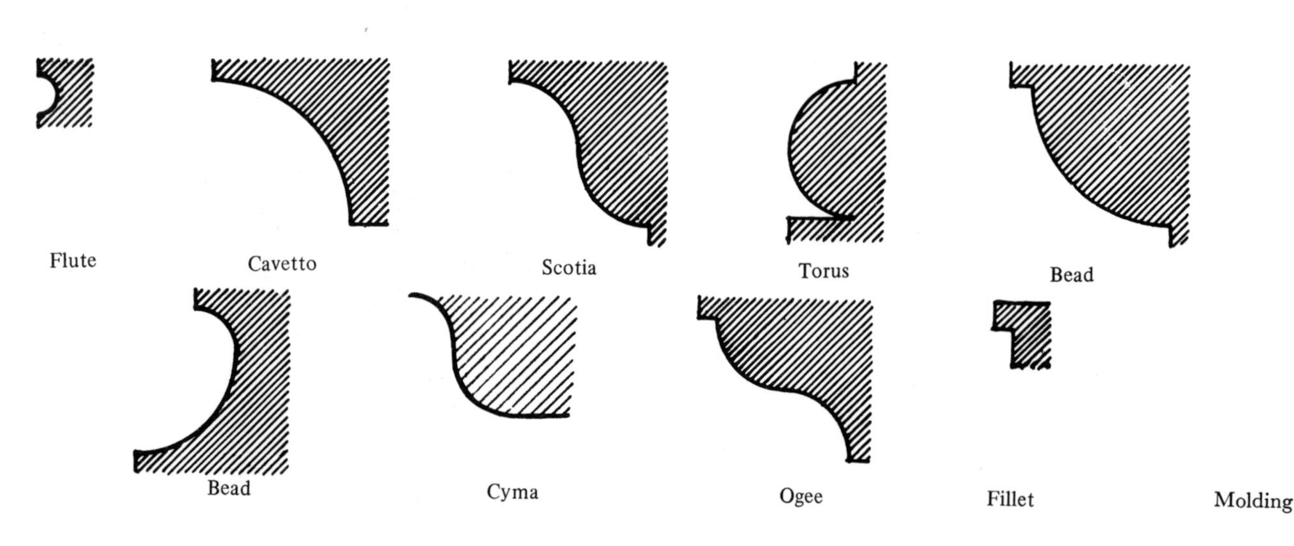

Molding

Mudejar From an Arabic word Meaning "subject", originally referring to a Moorish subject of the Spanish crown after reconquest, later to the type of work done by them. Gothic and Renaissance elements can be found mixed with such Moorish forms as arabesque geometric patterns, stellated polygons, TARACEAS (q.v.), horseshoe arches, "artesonado" (see COFFERING), and the decorative blue glazed tiling typical of Moorish buildings.

Mullion Vertical bar separating the panes of a window.

Multifoil An arch having more than five FOILS (q.v.). If it has three, four, or five it is called trefoil, quatrefoil, or cinquefoil, respectively.

Muntin A vertical member dividing the panels and RAILS (q.v.) of a door. It does not include the outside (left or right) upright members. See STILE.

Mutule Wide MODILLION (q.v.) belonging to a cornice of the Doric order, usually unadorned.

N

Necking Narrowing of a column shaft at the top underneath the capital.

Niello A method of decorating precious metals by engraving designs and filling the lines with black (silver sulphide) or occasionally other colors to produce the effect of an intaglio design.

Nulling A small projection or recession carved along a wooden surface, usually in the form of a succession of beads or bosses. When carved along the edge of a flat surface it is called GADROON (q.v.).

O

Ogee A gentle S-curve inclined slightly forward; a CYMA RECTA or, less correctly, a CYMA REVERSA (see CYMA).

Ogive The diagonal groin or rib of a vault. A pointed or Gothic arch.

Onion foot A plain or molded, often lobed, foot shaped like a slightly flattened sphere sometimes with a claw on top (see CLAW and BALL). It was used little after the William and Mary period.

Onion foot

Order The treatment of different architectural styles with established proportions between parts. The five classical orders were Doric, Ionic, Corinthian, Composite, and Tuscan. The last two were Roman developments of the earlier Greek orders.

Ormolu Ground gold or gold alloy specially prepared for gilding bronze mounts or ornaments on furniture, used for 17th and 18th century French furniture. It also refers to other gold colored alloys such as copper and zinc and to articles made of or decorated with these materials.

Overlap See LAP.

Ovolo Quarter-round convex molding, sometimes refering to quarter-elliptical molding properly called ECHINUS (q.v.).

P

Palmette Stylized palm leaf used as a decorative motif by the Egyptians and Greeks and in later times almost universally. A symbol of victory in classical art, usally called PALMA.

Palmette

Panel, paneling A distinct division made up of RAILS, STILES, and MUNTINS (q.v.) of a door, wainscoting, or other large surface so divided for tectonic or aesthetic reasons. Wooden surfaces so treated.

Patera A small round, oval, or elliptical ornament resembling a shallow dish made of wood or metal or inlaid, often delicately carved with foliage, geometrical, or fan-like designs. It was used in classical and Neo-classical styles especially by Adam in the late 18th century.

Patera

Patina Dark color or bloom on wood produced by age, atmospheric conditions, polishing, wear, etc., or artificially applied to furniture to improve its appearance or make it look old.

Péché mortel An upholstered couch the ends of which resemble a fauteuil, either single with one end, or double with two. When taken apart it forms a chair or chairs with a stool at one end or in the middle.

Pedestal A support under a column, statue, or anything that has to be raised above the level of the ground or floor. In classical form it consists of a base, dado, and cornice (q.v.).

Pediment The triangular part of a Grecian style building especially over a portico. A similar decorative feature above the cornice of a bookcase or cabinet. Among the many varieties are: plain triangular pediments, swan's neck and scroll pediments, and broken pediments with the middle part missing and generally filled in with some ornamental piece such as a vase.

Pelmet A valance or short hanging border especially over a window or door covering the curtain rods.

Pendant See DROP ORNAMENT.

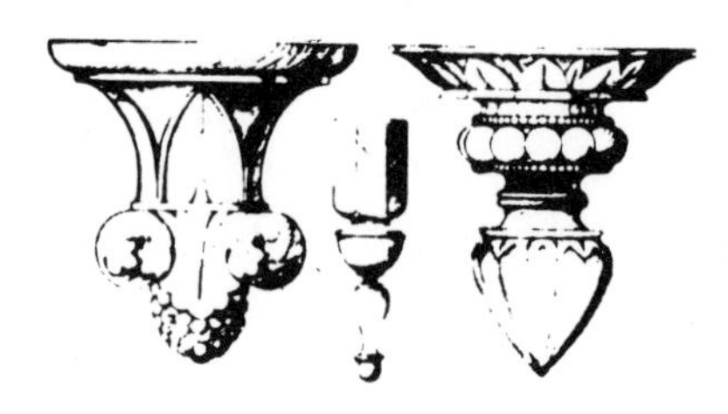

Pendant

Perpendicular Late 15th century architecture, so-called because of the prevailing vertical elements such as small columns and mullions dividing pointed arches and windows. The arches gradually became less pointed and eventually gave way to the Tudor arch in the time of Henry VIII.

Perroquet Folding X-shaped chair with one pair of legs extended to form the back like a medieval cross-stick chair. It was upholstered in red and green leather like the bright colors of a parrot and was used at the time of Louis XIII and XVI when dining room chairs also had to serve as drawing room chairs.

Petit-point Cross-stitch embroidery with wool on canvas.

Pilaster A rectangular column, especially one engaged in a wall or in the front of a piece of furniture.

Pinnacle A small ornamental turret, usually ending in a pyramid, urn, or cone on a rooftop, or used as CRESTING (q.v.) ornament on a piece of furniture.

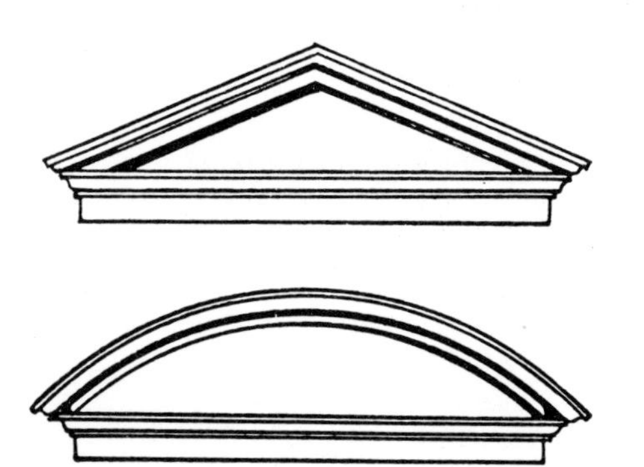

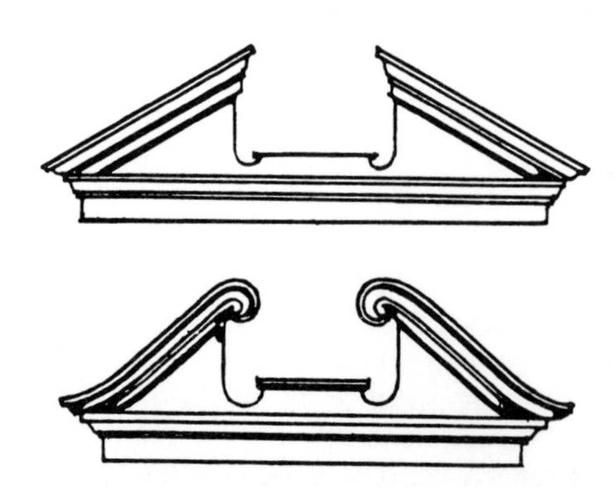

Pediment

Pinyonet Catalan word for pine seed, applied to a variety of MARQUETRY (q.v.) something like WHEAT-GRAIN (q.v.) originating in Granada, but common throughout Catalonia. It consists of small grain-like ornamentations of bone in walnut, especially typical of chests in Gerona.

Plain sawn The usual way of sawing a log or trunk, namely at right angles to the MEDULLARY RAYS (q.v.) and roughly parallel to the annual rings.

Plane Carpenter's tool for smoothing the surface of wood by paring shavings from it. It consists of a wooden or metal stock with a steel blade projecting from the smooth underside.

Plinth The lowest member of a column, quadrangular in section resting on the ground or pedestal. Also a similar rectangular projection at the bottom of any vertical surface (e.g. a wall or the front of a piece of furniture).

Plinth

Plumb A piece of lead on the end of a plumb-line used to test for verticality by gravity. Perfectly vertical.

Plywood A board, usually not more than an inch thick, consisting of "plies" or thin sheets of softwood one sixteenth to one eighth inch thick glued together over a core of hardwood with the grains crossed. Plywood has the advantages of not being easily warped, cracked or split and the effects of contraction and expansion due to atmospheric conditions being eliminated or reduced to a minimum.

Pointe-de-diamant Panels shaped like flattened pyramids such as in 17th century French and 16th and 17th century English and Dutch furniture.

Polishing bag A small bag filled with cotton, wool, or some other soft material dipped in alcohol, lacquer, etc. and used for polishing or varnishing furniture by rubbing gently over the surface in wide circles. Also called "polishing rubber" or "varnishing bag".

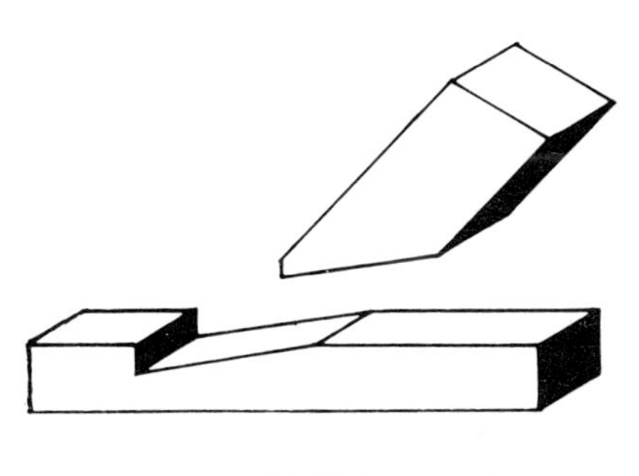

Rabbet

Prie-dieu A kneeling desk, often with upholstered knee-rest and armrest.

Psyché A large mirror supported between two uprights so as to swing forward or backward on a low frame standing on the floor, also called a cheval glass. The first belonged to the Louis XVI period and were very fashionable in the Empire period. They were replaced in the 19th century by looking-glass wardrobes in the heavy style of that period.

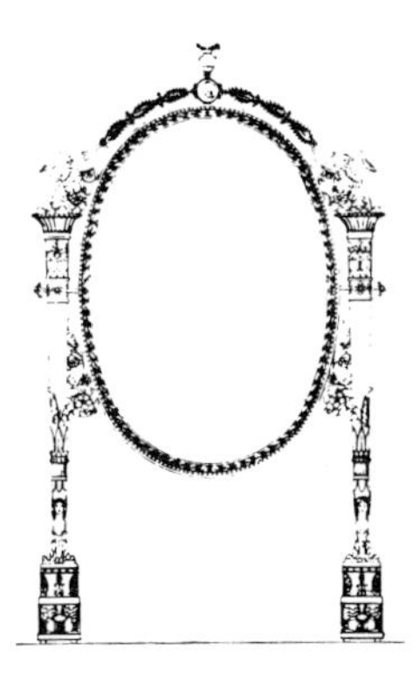

Psyché

Q

Quarter-cut Wood sawn along the MEDULLARY RAYS (q.v.), that is, length-wise through the center of the log. Quarter-sawn hardwoods, especially oak and mahogany, have a better FIGURE (q.v.) than PLAIN SAWN (q.v.), though softwoods produce a better figure when plain sawn. See SILVERGRAIN.

Quarter-round Molding (especially convex) which is a quarter of a circle in section.

Quilting Decorative treatment of leather, velvet, or silk, padded with soft material like cotton, wool, bird down, or horse hair and back-stitched to form a geometrical pattern in relief.

Quirk A deep cut in a molding separating the convex part (usually a bead) from an adjoining member (especially a FILLET q.v.).

R

Rabbet A groove cut along the edge or face of a piece of wood usually to receive the edge or tongue of another piece.

Rabbet plane A narrow plane with the blade reaching clear to the edges for making rabbets and small moldings.

Rail The horizontal member at the top or bottom of a door or panel. See STILE.

Rake The slope or inclination from the perpendicular (of a chair back, for example).

Rance A crosspiece between the legs of a chair.

Rebate See RABBET.

Reed, reeding A small convex half-round or nearly half-round molding. When a surface is decorated with a series of reeds side by side it is called REEDING.

Reed plane A plane with a special blade shaped for round moldings instead of a straight one.

Reel A very narrow half-round convex molding like a vertical half disk, usually alternating with a bead.

Rendering To cover a wall or other surface with single coat of plaster.

Repoussé Ornamental metal work hammered into relief from the reverse side.

Riband back, ribband, ribbon A term used to describe Chippendale chairs with SPLATS representing interlaced ribbon. Other variations such as contemporary French designs used a ribbon with more or fewer folds, especially Louis XV and XVI.

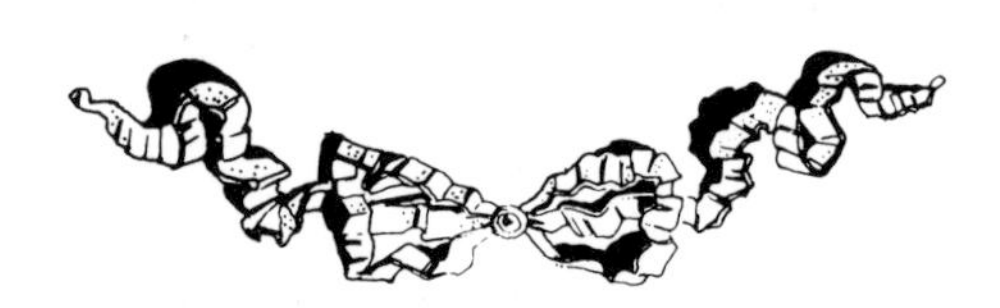

Riband back, ribband, ribbon

Rise The height of an arch from SPRING-LINE to SOFFIT (q.v.).

Rocaille An ornamental style typical of the Louis XV period consisting of artificial rockeries with shells, water, etc., made up of rough stones. A ROCOCO scroll ornament.

Rocaille

Rococo From ROCAILLE, an 18th century decorative style with rock and shell forms, foliage, flowers, C-SCROLLS, flame-like motifs, etc. in assymetrical harmony. Sometimes used to mean extravagant in style or antiquated.

Rosace A rose window or rose-shaped ornament or design, circular with SCALLOPED edges.

Rosette A stylized rose as ornamental motif, especially in a ROSACE.

Rosette

Router Machine with a rapidly revolving vertical spindle and cutter for milling out the surface of wood or metal. A kind of SPOKESHAVE.

Runic knot Ornamental motif of interlaced runes (letters of ancient Scandinavian and Anglo-Saxon alphabets).

S

Sag Curvature of wood caused by its own weight and insufficient props.

Saltire The heraldic name for a St. Andrew's cross, used to describe X-STRETCHERS (q.v.)

Scallop Bi-valved sea mollusk with a fan-shaped shell divided into alternating grooves and ridges radiating out from the center. This shape used as an ornamental motif particularly as an emblem of pilgrims to St. James of Compostella.

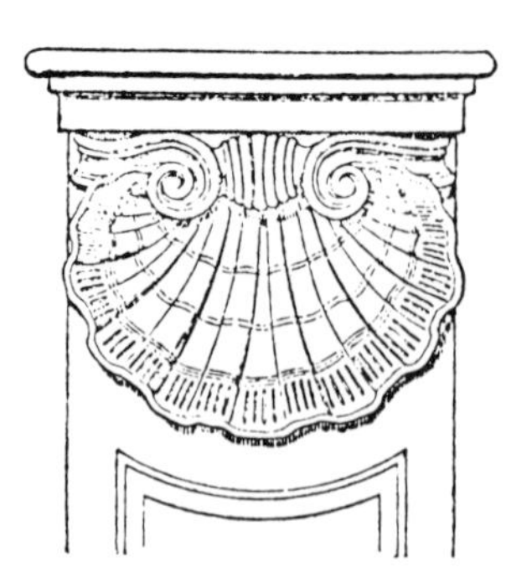

Scallop

Scarf To join the ends of pieces of wood by bevelling or notching them so that they overlap without increasing the thickness. A joint so made.

Scotia A concave molding of any shape found in Greek architecture. Often applied to the most typical form, namely quarter-elliptical whether concave or convex.

Scribe To mark parallel lines with a marking GAUGE (q.v.) or similar tool.

To join two pieces of wood by prolonging the top of one into a tongue which overlaps the end of the other, instead of by mortise-and-tenon. The resulting joint looks like a MITER JOINT (q.v.), but the pieces are only held together by the two overlapping tongues or tails.

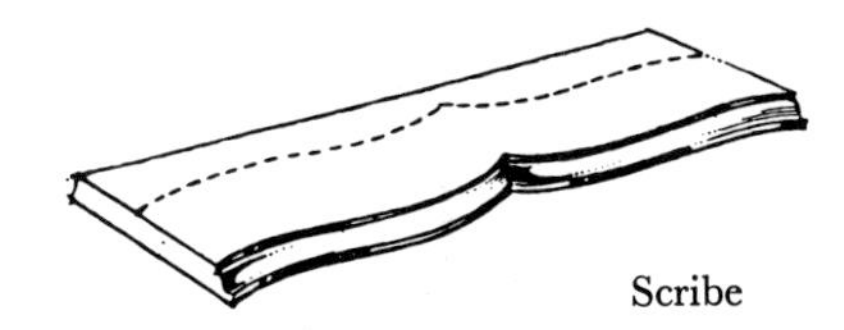

Scribe

Scutcheon ESCUTCHEON (q.v.). Gothic and Renaissance scutcheons around keyholes were usually made of iron, Baroque and Neo-classical of bronze.

Serpentine An undulating curve like the windings of a snake, especially as adapted to the front of a piece of furniture, giving it a large bulge or outward curve in the center and a smaller one at each end.

Settee A long low seat with upholstered back and arms.

Settle A long wooden seat with an arm at each end and a high back.

Scroll An ornament resembling a spiral of loosely coiled parchment or a curled leaf.

Sgraffito A color design made by covering a surface with one or two coats of paint and scratching off the surface coat to reveal the pattern in the underlying color.

Shaft The main body of a column between the base and the capital.

Shellac A resinous substance dissolved in alcohol to make LACQUER (q.v.), secreted by an insect as a protective covering and deposited on plants. Both shellac and Rhus vermicifera gum produce a particularly hard and brilliant variety of varnish (originally developed in the Orient) which protects furniture from the effects of dust, damp, knocks, etc.

Silvergrain The beautiful FIGURE or "splash" of QUARTER-SAWN (q.v.) oak resembling the sheen of mother-of-pearl or watered silk, produced by the MEDULLARY RAYS (q.v.).

Skirting Piece A piece of wood, also called APRON, fitted below the frame of a chair seat or table top or to the base of a cabinet between the legs like a wooden VALANCE.

Slat A cross-rail between the uprights of a chair back.

Smoothing plane A plane used for finishing off and smoothing surfaces already planed with a JACK PLANE (q.v.).

Socle A plain, low, rectangular block serving as a support for a statue or pedestal and for ornamental pieces such as vases and urns.

Soffit A rectangular foot like a truncated, inverted pyramid with four sides, each like a spade, used especially with 18th century square tapered legs.

Span The horizontal distance from one end of an arch or bridge to the other.

Spandrel The roughly triangular space between each of the four corners of a square and the circumference of a circle inscribed within it.

Spindle A bar or rail tapered at both ends.

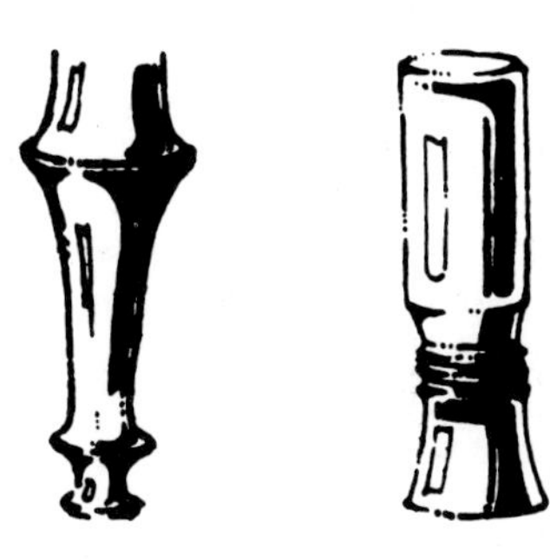

Spindle

Splat A vertical piece in a chair back connecting the back-rail with the top-rail. Plain splats were used at first but openwork ornamental forms became increasingly more common during the Queen Anne period, particularly in Chippendale chairs. The more ornate forms passed from England to the Continent and were imitated in great variety. They include vases, lyres, and other objects and purely ornamental patterns. (See RIBAND BACK).

Spokeshave A small transverse plane with end-handles used for shaping spokes or similar round pieces where an ordinary plane cannot be used.

Springer, spring-line The lowest stone in an arch or the point where the curve begins. The spring-line is the line between and including the two springers. Springer is also the lowest stone of a coping or gable and the rib dividing a groined or vaulted roof.

Staff bead See BEADING.

Stile A vertical member forming the side of a panel or door frame. See MUNTIN.

Stilted Describing an arch with pieces of upright masonry under the SPRINGERS or in which the line of the VOUSSOIRS (q.v.) is continued below the SPRING-LINE.

Stretcher A horizontal bar or rail between the legs of a chair or table. There are various arrangements; some old chairs had only one serving as a foot rest between the front legs. Usually there are two, one on either side, or four running all the way around. Other arrangements are described under FIADORES, H-STRETCHERS, SALTIRE, and X-STRETCHER.

Stringing The fine inlaid lines of lighter wood often used in cabinet work.

Stucco See COMPO.

Stuff-over The wooden framework of upholstered furniture is often left uncovered even in the case of sofas or arm-chairs (e.g. Louis XV and XVI FAUTEUILS) but sometimes the covering material of the upholstery is pulled down over the edges and fronts of the seat rails and secured along the bottom edges. This is called "stuff-over".

Stumps Supports for chair arms when not a continuation of the front legs.

Style Less correct spelling of STILE (q.v.). Also the general tectonic and decorative characteristics of a building or piece of furniture typical of a particular architect, designer, period, or region.

Sunburst The figure produced by the MEDULLARY RAYS (q.v.) when a log is cut crosswise. The sunburst of quarter-cut oak gives the especially decorative SILVERGRAIN (q.v.).

T

Therm leg A tapering square leg ending in a SPADE-FOOT (q.v.).

Therming, Thurming A process for creating moldings on table legs, etc. which are quadrangular in section but with curved sides.

Thistle leaves A decorative motif used especially in Gothic ornamentation.

Thyrsus Rod of Bacchus wreathed in vines and bay leaves and crowned with a pine cone or similar ornament used in the ancient Bacchanalia.

Toile de jouy Fabric with a lively pattern of brightly colored branches and flowers widely used in France in the 18th and 19th centuries. It was manufactured principally at Jouy in the "arrondissement" of Versailles under the direction of Oberjampf (1760-1815).

Tongue A TENON (q.v.) projecting from the end of a piece of wood to fit into the corresponding groove in another piece.

Tongue

Tongue-and-groove joint See GROOVE-AND-TONGUE JOINT.

Tongue-and-groove joint

Torchère A tall ornamental candlestick distinguishable from other forms of GUERIDON (q.v.) by a small gallery rail around the top.

Torus A large half-round convex molding sometimes prolonged at the bottom something like a convex SCOTIA (q.v.).

Tracery Decorative stone openwork especially in the top of a Gothic window, or a similar ornamental pattern.

Transom A horizontal wooden or stone bar (see MULLION) across a window or over the top of a door. A window over a door.

Trapezophrum Ornamental support for a Roman table consisting of a human or animal figure or head (usually of an eagle or lion) on a very large talon. Excellent examples of this type of table can still be found.

Triglyph Ornamental division of a Doric frieze, alternating with a METOPE (q.v.).

Trumeau The portion of a wall between two windows or other openings or its ornamentation (e.g. a column dividing a double doorway). An ornamental mirror occupying such a space or above a mantelpiece on a projecting piece of wall.

Thyrsus

Trapezophrum

Turnery The art of shaping pieces with circular section on a LATHE (q.v.). The pieces are turned on their longitudinal axis and shaped into any curvilinear form from plain round to the more complicated shapes used in the Baroque and more modern styles.

Tympanum The triangular space forming the field of a PEDIMENT (q.v.) or over a door between the lintel and the arch or other shape over the door.

U

Upholstery All the soft parts of an armchair, sofa, or other piece of furniture including the padding, springs, and WEBBING (q.v.) and the covering material. This often leaves the framework uncovered and visible on the bottom but sometimes it is pulled over the rails, arm-rests, etc. to hide them, being secured with nails on the bottom (see STUFF-OVER). Sometimes the covering material hides the entire framework including the legs with a fringe hanging down in front (see GALLOON).

Uol Ancient Egyptian head rest. It allowed the user to sleep comfortably without perspiring about the head and neck in the hot Egyptian nights and without spoiling the elaborate coiffures worn at that time. The finest specimens are made of ivory and delicately carved, inlaid, and gilt exotic woods. There are simpler types made of native wood, stone, or clay, indicating that they were used by common folk just as they are today among some tribes in Africa and Oceania.

Urn A vase with a foot and usually with a rounded body, especially as used in ancient times for keeping the ashes of the dead. In the 18th century it was used as an ornament standing on a pedestal at each side of a table. Some typical Adam urns of the latter type in classical style are well known.

V

Valance A kind of damask used for upholstering furniture. A short curtain around the frame of a canopy or bedstead.

Varnish Resinous substances dissolved in alcohol and sometimes mixed with other materials for application to furniture to give it a glossy finish and to preserve it from injury from damp, dust, etc. (See LACQUER, SHELLAC).

Veneer Thin sheets of usually exotic wood sawn or sliced from various parts of the tree to give a FIGURE (q.v.) and used for covering a CORE (q.v.) of a more solid coarser wood forming the CARCASS of a piece of furniture. Good veneers are also obtained from certain parts of native woods such as a burr (overgrown knot), a crotch (where branches meet or join the trunk), a bough or sapling cut transversely, etc.

Vernis Martin A type of varnish used by the Martin brothers, cabinet makers of the Louis XV period, over painted scenes typical of that period on grey, gold, or ocher background, showing the influence of Chinese lacquer work.

Verre eglomise A form of decoration consisting of a painting of mythological or "genre" scenes covered with glass. It was used on the doors and drawers of 18th century French cabinets or as a border for a wall mirror between the mirror plate and the frame following its contours. It was used in this way particularly in the Queen Anne and William and Mary periods employing arabesque motifs or similar patterns.

Vertugadin See FARTHINGALE and GUARDAINFANTES.

Volute Spiral scroll characteristic of Ionic, Corinthian, and Composite capitals and perhaps the commonest ornamental motif, in one form or another, in all subsequent periods.

Voussoir Any of the wedge-shaped stones forming an arch, narrower on the underside than on top.

W

Wainscot The wooden paneling or boarding on the walls of a room in many Dutch or English Renaissance style houses and not uncommon in later periods.

Wave molding Any wavy or S-shaped molding such as a CYMA (q.v.) and sometimes applied to any undulating form given to a surface such as the front of a commode (more correctly SERPENTINE). On a smaller scale, resembling rippled water on the door of a cabinet or similar furniture.

Webbing The network of crossed bands of BURLAP (q.v.) or other material from two to four inches wide, tacked to the underside of the framework of a piece of furniture to support the padding and keep it in place.

What-not A piece of furniture with shelves used for displaying ornaments.

Wheat-grain A form of MARQUETRY using small pieces of boxwood or bone inlaid in walnut, especially Mudejar work of this kind with a geometric pattern called "wheat grain" (grano de trigo) in Spanish.

White polishing A finishing process applied to certain types of wood, especially long and coarse-grained woods with large pores which are first "filled" with a whitening substance (sometimes whale oil). The effect is to give the wood the opposite appearance to that of the normal PATINA (q.v.) so that the pores are lighter in color instead of darker than the rest of the wood. See FILLING.

Winding Excessive curvature of a piece of wood or its surface caused by warping, bad planing, or some other defect

Wings The lateral pieces projecting out from the back of a GRANDFATHER CHAIR (q.v.) or similar kind of armchair.

Wood screw A screw used for fixing metal pieces such as hinges, locks, etc. onto wood.

Wreathed Column shaft molded or fluted diagonally like a spiral instead of vertically like an ordinary fluted column.

X

X-shape chair The oldest form of chair with crossed legs on either side. It was first used by the Egyptians and later by the Greeks and Romans. It was made on the same principle as the modern folding chair. There is a bronze-gilt specimen by Dagobert from the 17th century in the Louvre and several 14th century Italian examples in Winchester Cathedral and York Minister. It was adopted after the 15th century for ecclesiastical furniture (see FALDSTOOL and CURULE CHAIR).

X-stretchers Diagonal rails joining chair or table legs and crossing under the top or seat.

BIBLIOGRAPHY

Adams, L., *Décorations Interieures et Meubles des Epoques Louis XIII et XIV.*

Adeline, J., *Vocabulario de términos de Arte,* trans. of José Ramón Mélida. Madrid, 1888.

Aronson, J., *Book of Furniture and Decoration.* Ancien and Modern. 1936

Aronson, J., *Enciclopedia Gráfica del Mueble y la Decoración.* Ediciones Centurión, Buenos Aires, 1945.

Association Technique Internationale des Bois Tropicaux, *Momenclature des Bois Tropicaux (Afrique).* Etablie par la Commission des publications présidée par André Thiébault, 1961.

Asúa, M., *El Mueble en la Historia.*

Badauc, Dr. A., *Le mobilier dans l'Ancien Egypte.*

Bajot, E., *Encyclopédie Du Meuble.* 1900.

Ballat, Mlle. J., *Charles Cressent, sculpteur ébéniste, collectioneur.* Paris, 1919.

Bayard, Emile, *L'Style Louis XVII.* Garnier Frères, Paris.

Bayard, Emile, *L'Style Louis XVI.* Garnier Frères, Paris.

Bayard, Emile, *L'Style Empire.* Garnier Frères, Paris.

Bell and Hayden, *The Furniture of George Hepplewhite.*

Berain, *Oeuvre Complète.*

Bergós, Juan, *Maderas de Construcción, Decoración y Artesanía,* Gustavo Gili, Barcelona, 1951.

Blake and Reveirs-Hopkins, *Little Books About Old Furniture.* 4 vols. 1911-13.

Bode, W. von, *Italian Renaissance Furniture.* 1921.

Boulanger, Gisèle, *L'art de reconnaitre les styles.* Hachette. Paris, 1960.

Byne, A. and Stapley, *Spanish interiors and furniture.*

Camps Cazorla, Emilio, *Sillas del Coro de Santa Clara, de Astudillo.*

Capella Martínez, Manuel, *La Industria en Madrid.* 2 tomos. Datos sobre ebanistas. Siglos XII al XVIII. (Cap. IX; T. 1; Cap. VII. T. II). Cámara Oficial de la Industria de Artes Gráficas y Ediciones.

Catalogue de la collection Isaac de Comando, Musée National du Louvre. Paris, 1914.

Cescinsky, H. and Grible. E.R., *Early English Furniture and Woodwork.* 1922.

Claret Rubira, J., *Muebles de estilo inglés.* Gustavo Gili, Barcelona, 1946.

Clouzot, Henri, *L'Ameublement français sous Louis XV.* Paris. Vincennes. 1913.

Colección *Il Mobile nei Secoli.* Fratelli Fabri Editore. Milán, 1969.

Comité Nacional de Maderas Tropicales. *Maderas Tropicales,* Aegor. Bilbao, 1951.

Champeaux, Alfred de, *Le Meuble.* A. Quantin, Editeur. Paris, 1885.

Champier, Victor, *Le Mobilier Flamand. Massin y Cia,* Editeurs. Paris.

Chippendale, Thomas, *Gentlemann and Cabinet Maker's Director.* 1954.

De Felice, Roger, *Le Meuble Français sous Louis XV.* Hachette, Paris and London, 1922.

De Felice, Roger, *Le Meuble Français du Moyen Age à Louis XIII.* Hachette, Paris and London, 1922.

De Felice, Roger, *Le Meuble Français sous Louis XIV et la Régence.* Hachette, Paris and London, 1922.

De Felice, R., *Little Books and old French Furniture,* 1923.

Desathairs, Leon, *Le Chateau de Barcy. Architecture et Décoration, fin du règne de Louis XIV.* Paris, 1911.

Dilke, Lady, *French Furniture and decoration in the XVIIIth. Century.* London. 1901.

Domenech, Rafael y Pérez Bueno, Luis, *Muebles antiguos españoles.* Librería de Arte. Casa Cuetos, Barcelona.

Dornier Gilbert, *L'Ebanisterie.*– Editions de la Tourelle. Paris, 1948.

Downs, J., *American Chippendale furniture. A Picture Book.* The Metropolitan Museum of Art. New York, 1946.

Drepperd, Car. W., *The Primer of American Antiques.* New York, 1945.

Dreyfus Carie, *Le Mobilier Français.* Editions Albert Norancé, 1921.

Dumonthier, E., *Les Sieges Louis XV.*

Dumonthier, E., *Les Sièges Louis XVI.*

Eberlein, H.D. y Mc Clure, E. Abbott. *Practical Book of Period Furniture.* Philadephia, 1914.

Eberlein, H.D., *Spanish Interiors, Furniture and Details.* New York, 1925.

Eberlein, H.D., *Interiors Fireplaces and Furniture of the Italıan, Renaissance Reprint,* 1927.

Eberlein, H.D., y Ramsdell, R.W., *The Practical Book of Italian, Spanish and Portuguese Furniture,* 1915.

Edwards, Ralph., *English Chairs. Victoria and Albert Museum. His Majesty's stationery Office.*

Edwards, Ralph., *Georgian Furniture.* Victoria and Albert Museum. London, 1947.

Edwards, Ralph., *English Chairs.* Victoria and Albert Museum. 1950.

Elliwood, G.M., *Mobel und Raumkunst in England. 1680-1800.*

Enríquez, María Dolores., *El mueble Español en los siglos XV, XVI, y XVII.* Afrodisio Aguado, Madrid, 1951.

Eriksen, Svend, *Waddesdon Manor.* 1965.

Eyne y Stapley, *Spanish interiors and Furniture,* 1928.

Falgas y Sacs, *Arte y Decoración en España,*

Feduchi, Luis, *Antología de la silla española,* Afrodisio Aguado, Madrid, 1957.

Feduchi, Luis, *Los Museos Arqueológicos y Valencia de Don Juan.* Afrodisio Aguado, Madrid, 1950.

Feduchi, Luis, *Historia del Mueble.* Afrodisio Aguado, Madrid, 1946.

Feduchi, Luis, *El Palacio Nacional.* Tomos I y II. Afrodisio Aguado, Madrid, 1957.

Feduchi, Luis, *El Hospital de Afuera.* Afrodisio Aguado, Madrid, 1950.

Feduchi, Luis, *El Mueble Español.* Ediciones Polígrafa, Barcelona, 1969.

Feduchi, Luis, *Estilos del Mueble Español.* Editorial Abantos, Madrid, 1969.

Feduchi, Luis, *El Mueble. Colecciones Reales de España. Patrimonio Nacional.* Madrid, 1965.

Ferrari, G., *Il Legno e la Mobilia nell'Arte italiana.* Ulrico Hoepli, Milán.

Foley, Edwin, *The Book of Decorative Furniture.* London.

Fouche, Maurice, *Percier y Fontaine.* Librairie Renovard, Henry Laurens, éditeur.

Giner de los Ríos, *Artes Industriales.*

Gradmann, E., *Styles des Meubles.* Payot, Lausanne.

Gregorietti, Guido, *Il Mobile italiano dal XV al XIX secolo.* Instituto Geográfico de Agostini. Novara, 1962.

Gregory, E.W., *The Furniture Collector 1916.*

Gregory, E.W., *Old English Furniture of the XVII and XVIII Centuries.* 1919.

Guerrero Lovillo, José, *Estudio arqueológico de las Miniaturas de las Cantigas.* Consejo Superior de Investigaciones Científicas. Madrid, 1949.

Hauglid, Roar, *Norge Flokekunst.* Oslo, 1956.

Havard, Henry, *Dictionaire de l'ameublement. 1887-90.*

Havard, Henry, *L'Art dans la Maison.* Ed. Rouveyre et G. Blond. 1884.

Heinonen, Jorma, *Soumalaisia Kansanhuonekaluja Old Finnish Furniture.* Helsinki, 1969.

Herman Schitz, *Deutsche Möble des Barok und Rokoko.*

Ince and Mayhew, *Universal System of Household Furniture.* 1762.

Instituto Eduardo Torroja. *Léxico de la Construcción.* Talleres Gráficos Juan Torroja.

Iñiguez Almech, Francisco, *El arte en la Carpintería.* Madrid, 1942.

Jarry, Madeleine, *Le Siège en France.* Paul Hartman, éditeur. Paris, 1948.

Jonge, M., *English Decoration and Furniture during the Tudor. Elizabethan and Jacobean periods* (1500-1660). 1924.

Jurdain, M., *English Decoration and Furniture of the Early Renaissance (1500-1650),* 1924.

Jurdain, M., *English Decoration and Furniture of the later XVIII century (1760-1820),* 1922.

Krüger, Fritz, *El Mobiliario Popular en los Países Románticos.* "La cuña", Mendoza, 1959 Argentina.

Lafuente Ferrari, Enrique, *Las Artes de la Madera en España.* Madrid. 1941.

Lassen, Erik, *Dansche Möbel der Klasische Periode.* Kunst I Damark Gyldendal. 1958.

Lehnert, Georg, *Las Artes Industriales.* Labor, Barcelona-Buenos Aires, 1930-33.

Lessing, J., *Italienische Moebel, XVI Jahrhundert.* Berlin, 1893.

Lessing, J., *Gothische Moebel.* Berlin, 1889.

Lightfield, F., *History of Furniture.* 1907.

Lightfield, F., *How, to collet old Furniture.*

Loskomski, G., *Mobilier et Decoration des Anciens Palais Imperiaux Russes.* Paris.

Luthmer and Smidt., *Empire und Biedermaier Möbel.* 1922.

Mac Quoid, Percy Edwars, Ralph, *The Dictionary of English Furniture.* 3 vol. The Offices of "Country Life". London and New York, 1924-27.

Mac Quoid, P., *A History of English Furniture.* 4 vol. 1904-1908.

Maillard, E., *Les Styles Françaises.*

Manwaring, R., *The Cabinet and Chair Maker's Real Friends-Chair Maker's Guide.* 1766.

Marangoni, G., *Enciclopedia delle Moderne Arte Decorative Italiane,* Milán, 1925.

Martin, H., *La Grammaire des Styles.* 3 vol. Libraire d'Art. R. Ducher. Paris, 1926.

Marx and Taylor, *Measured Drawings of English Furniture* (Oak Period), 1931.

Maspero, *L'Egypte.*

Mayer, F.S., *Manual de Ornamentación.* Gustavo Gili, Barcelona, 1929.

Meister, W., Peter y Jedding Hermann., *Das Schöne Möbel in Lauf Jahrhunderte.* Keyserche Verlagsbuchhandlung. Heidelberg, 1958.

Melani, A., *L'Arte di distinguire gli stili.* Editorial Hoepli, Milán, 1919.

Menard y Sauvage, *La vie des anciens.*

Migeon, Gaston et Dreyfus, Carle, *La collection Isaac de Comando.* Paris, 1921.

Moliner, Emile, *Musée du Louvre. Le Mobilier française du XVII et du XVIII siècles.* Paris, 1901.

Nogueira de Brito y Alberto Sousa. *O Nosso Mobiliario.* Livraria Lello.

Orduña, *El arte de la talla.*

Otto von Falke, *Deutsche Möbel des Mittelalter un der Renaissance.*

Pardo Roinsa, Francisco, Prólogo a *El Mueble en América del Sur.* Ediciones Centurión, Buenos Aires.

Pedrini, Augusto, *Il Mobilio, Gli Ambienti e le Decorazione del Rinascimento in Italia. Secoli XV a XVI.* Libraria Editoriale Fiorentina, 1948.

Pérez Bueno, Luis, *El Tesoro Artístico de España.* Barcelona.

Pérez Bueno Luis, *El Mueble Español.*

Pignati, Terisio, *Lo Stile dei Mobile.* Arnold Mondadori, editor, 1955.

Pinto, Piero, *Il Mobile italiano dal XV al XIX secolo.* Instituto Geográfico de Agostini. Novara, 1962.

Poulsen, Frederik, *Artes Decorativas en la Antigüedad.* Labor, Barcelona-Buenos Aires, 1927.

Reveirs-Koplins, A.E., *Le Meuble Anglais. Periode Sheraton.* Librairie Hachette. Paris and London 1924.

Reveirs-Koplins. *Chippendale.*

Reveirs-Koplins. *Periode de la reine Anne.*

Reveirs-Koplins. *Sheraton Period Little Books of Furniture.*

Riaño, *Artes Industriales.*

Ricci, Seymour de, *Louis XVI Furniture,* 1913.

Richter, Gisela. M.A., *The Furniture of the Greeks Etruscans and Romans.* Phaidon Press, London 1966.

Rig, Joseph-Marie, *Bayern Möbel Bibliographie des Institut A.G.,* Leipzig, 1939.

Robinson, F.S., *English Furniture.* 1905.

Roche, Denis., *Le Mobilier française en Russie. Meubles des XVII et XVIII siècles et du commencement du XIX siècle conservés dans les palais et musées impériaux et dans les collections privées.* Paris, 1912 et suiv. 2 vol. in. fol. 100 pl.

Rodríguez de Rivas, Mariano, *El Museo Romantico.* Afrodisio Aguado, Madrid, 1950.

Roe, Fred, *Ancient Coffers and Cupboards.* 1902.

Roe, Fred, *Old Oak Furniture.* 1905.

Rogers, J.C., *English Furniture.* 1923.

Rosa, Gilda, *I Mobili Nelle Civiche Raccolte Artistiche de Milano.* Editorre Aldo Martelli, 1963.

Salomosky, V.C., *Masterpieces of Furniture Design.* Grand Rapids, 1931.

Sanchez-Mesa, Domingo, *L'arredamento spagnolo.* Fratelli Fabri, Editori, 1966.

Sauerland, M., *Norddeustsch Barol Moebel.* 1922.

Schmitz, *Historia del Mueble.*

Schottmuller, Frida, *Möbel der italienischen Renaissance.*

Shearer, T., *The Cabinet Maker and Upholsterer's.* Drawing Book. London, 1791-3.

Sheraton, Thomas, *The Cabinet Maker and Upholsterer's.* Drawing Book, London, 1791-3.

Singleton, E., *Dutch and Flemish Furniture of the Middle Ages and Renaissance,* 1908.

Smith, G., *A Collection of* Designs *for Hausehold Furniture and Interior Decoration* (Regency), London, 1808.

Symonds, R.W., *English Furniture from Charles II to George II.* 1929.

Verlet, Pierre, *Le Mobilier Royal Français Meubles de la Couronne conservés en France.* Tomo I. Paris, 1944. 1 vol. in-8. 64 pl.

Vial H.Marcel et Girodie, A., *Les Artistes decorateurs du Bois. Répertoire alphabétique des Ebénistes, Menuisiers, Sculpteurs, Doreurs sur bois, etc., ayant travaillé en France aux XVIII et XVIII siècles.* Tome I.

Victoria and Albert Museum, *Fifty Masterpieces of Wood Work.* London, 1955.

Victoria and Albert Museum, *A History of English Furniture.* London, 1955.

Viollet le Duc, *Dictionaire du Meuble au Moyen-Age.*

Wright, Lawrence, *Historia de la Cama.* Editorial Noguer, Barcelona, 1964.

INDEX

A

B

C

F

G

J

K

L

M

N

O

P

Q

R

S

T

U

V

W

Y

Z

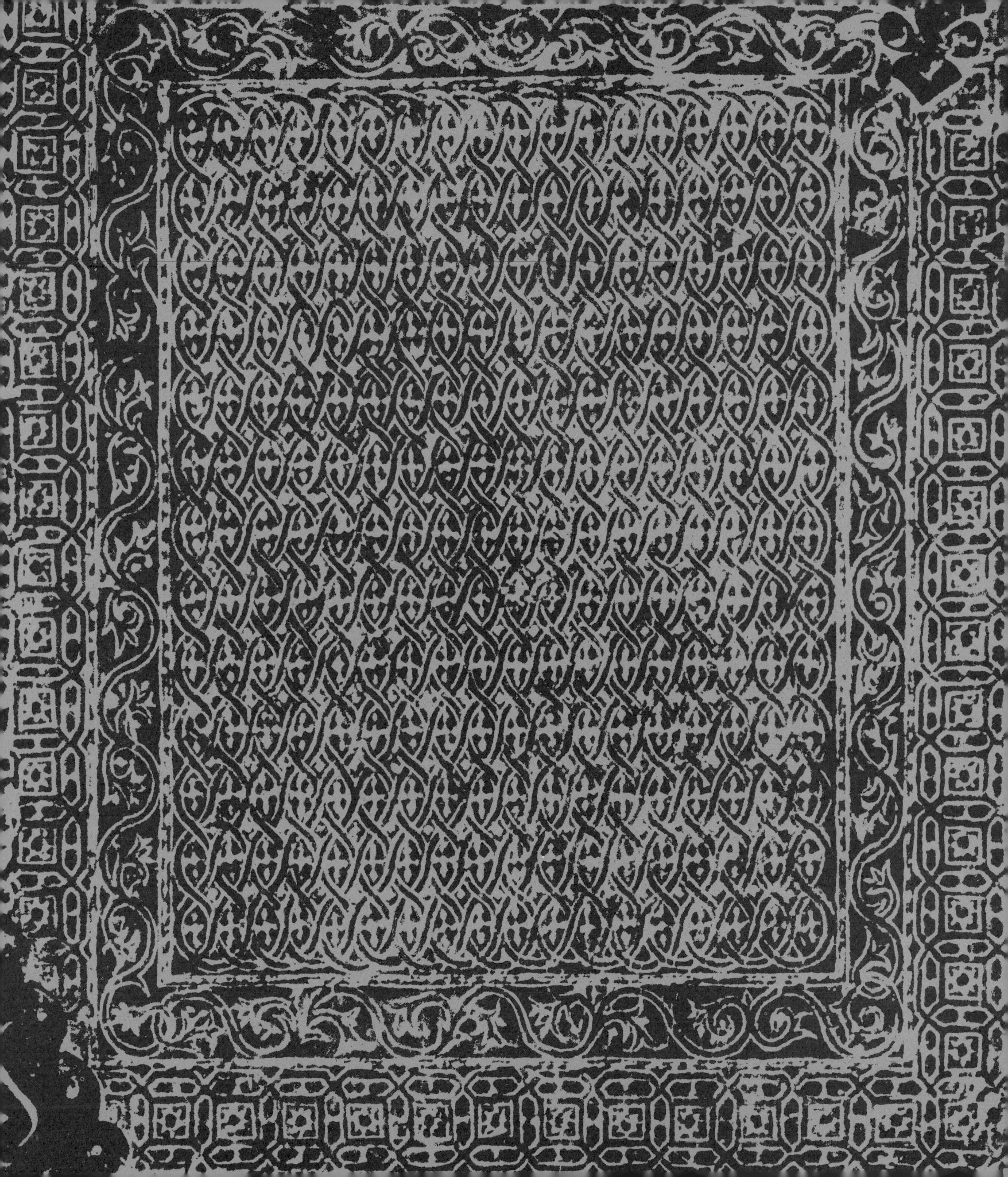